Understanding
PSYCHOLOGY

Third Edition

Understanding
PSYCHOLOGY
Third Edition

RANDOM HOUSE / NEW YORK

Third Edition
987654321
Copyright © 1974, 1977, 1980 by Random House, Inc.

All rights reserved under International and Pan-American
Copyright Conventions. No part of this book may be reproduced in any form or by any means, electronic or mechanical,
including photocopying, without permission in writing from
the publisher. All inquiries should be addressed to Random
House, Inc., 201 East 50th Street, New York, N.Y. 10022. Published in the United States by Random House, Inc., and simultaneously in Canada by Random House of Canada Limited,
Toronto.

Library of Congress Cataloging in Publication Data
Main entry under title:
Understanding psychology.
    Bibliography: p.
    Includes index.
    1. Psychology.
BF121.U52 1980 150 79–19647
ISBN 0-394-32289-4

Text design by Leon Bolognese

Cover design by Jurek Wajdowicz © 1980

Photo Research for Third Edition by Flavia Rando
Photo Editor, R. Lynn Goldberg

Cover art: *Variation within a Sphere, No. 10: The Sun* by Richard Lippold. The Metropolitain Museum of Art, Fletcher Fund,
1956.

Manufactured in the United States of America

Preface

Revising a successful textbook is always a risky project, as change does not necessarily bring improvement. Earlier editions of *Understanding Psychology* have been successful because of several main strengths:

- Clear, straightforward writing style that students find both comprehensible and interesting

- Attractive and informative graphics

- Concise, yet broad coverage of the field of psychology

- Up-to-date coverage of this quickly changing field

In this third edition of *Understanding Psychology*, we tried to build on these strengths to make a good book even better. Here is a brief sketch of the most important changes and additions in this revision:

- Psychologists are becoming more interested in applying theoretical advances to everyday problems, and students invariably appreciate this type of practical orientation. Hence, one of the major changes in the third edition is the increased attention we have devoted to this material. As a means of dramatically highlighting the juxtaposition of concepts and applications, we have included specific sections on applications at pertinent points in the chapters. These sections, entitled "Using Psychology," are shaded in color to distinguish them from the regular text narrative. We have integrated the applications to avoid the implication that somehow this material is a separate topic. For Example,

  - In Chapter 3, Memory and Thought, we describe recent research on eyewitness testimony.

  - In Chapter 5, Body and Behavior, we present an analysis of psychosurgery.

  - In Chapter 14, Psychological Testing, we discuss the controversy over jobs, tests, and discrimination.

- As another way of showing the applicability of psychology to everday concerns, we have added a series of boxed inserts on topical issues. Each box is long enough to convey a point, but short enough to avoid distracting students from the text narrative. For instance,

  - Photographic Memory (Chapter 3)

- Losing Weight (Chapter 6)
- Imaginary Playmates (Chapter 8)
- Are You Type A? (Chapter 10)

• Brevity, lucid prose, accuracy, and comprehensive coverage are often conflicting virtues. The third edition represents a major effort to bring these features into harmony. For this revision we commissioned six specialists (listed opposite the title page) to consult with us in their particular areas of expertise. In addition to being scholars of note, each is a superb teacher very sensitive to the needs of students. These people worked very carefully with us not only to insure the accuracy of the text, but also to make certain that every chapter contained the essential concepts and information that beginning students need to know. Based on the reaction of many users of the second edition and on the advice of our consultants, we have also given the text a slightly stronger research orientation. We selected new research studies that were of general importance in the field and of intrinsic interest to students. Thus, we have added discussions of current research in such areas as

- Taste Aversions (Chapter 2)
- Sociobiology (Chapter 5)
- Meditation (Chapter 7)
- Biofeedback (Chapter 7)
- Middle Age (Chapter 10)
- Psychiatric Diagnosis (Chapter 15)

• A great many parts of the book were reorganized and rewritten. Some of the more general changes include:

- Chapter 1, Introduction, includes new sections on "How Psychologists Find the Answers" and "A Brief History of Psychology" to give students a more concrete feel for the subject.

- Chapter 5, Body and Behavior, includes a completely rewritten section on "Heredity and Environment".

- Chapter 10, Adjustment and Society, includes a new section on "Sexuality" and has been substantially rewritten to describe basic research.

- The three chapters devoted to social psychology in the second edition have been collapsed into two chapters for the revision.

- Chapter 13, Personality Theories, is now clearly organized around major theoretical schools (Psychoanalytic, Behavioral, Humanist, Trait).

But we also wanted to keep *Understanding Psychology* faithful to the principles that made its first and second editions so successful. To present information as clearly and as usefully as possible, we updated the teaching features from previous editions:

1. *Organization.* The book is divided into sixteen chapters, which are grouped into five units. Each unit roughly corresponds to a major field of psychology. The unit openings give an overview of what each section and chapter contains.

2. *Text and Illustrations.* The text, captions, and illustrations work well together to present the research, theories, and ideas central to psychology. Chapters are divided by numerous subheadings that describe the subject of each section, and key terms and concepts are italicized when they are first introduced to draw them to the student's attention. The illustrations and captions are designed to clarify important ideas, to add interesting information, and to provoke thought.

3. *Outlines and Summaries.* Brief outlines at the beginning of each chapter prepare each person for what he or she is about to read. Summaries at the end of the chapters help locate and review the important points.

4. *Glossaries.* Definitions of key terms follow every chapter summary. These lists will help review important ideas.

5. *Activities.* The activities that follow each chapter are intended to help relate the ideas in the chapter to personal experience.

6. *Suggested Readings.* Each chapter contains a description of several interesting and readable books and magazine articles related to the topics presented in the chapter.

7. *References.* After each chapter there is a list of books and articles that provide in-depth coverage of some of the subjects explored in the chapters. These sources are useful for pursuing an interest in a particular topic.

All of this adds up to a very fine revision that provides you with a first-rate teaching tool. I would also highly recommend the student study guide, prepared by Martin Schulman, as an excellent supplement to the text. When used in conjunction with the text, the study guide will ensure that students have mastered essential information and isolated the key concepts covered in each chapter.

The publication of any textbook is a team project, but this is particularly true of a text like *Understanding Psychology.* Random House senior editor Jan Carr was our team's coach and general manager. Like others who work behind the scenes, he rarely got the credit he deserved when things went right. Two excellent project editors solved all the day-to-day problems: Cele Gardner got things off to a smooth start, and Jeannine Ciliotta kept the wheels rolling through the long months that followed. Fred Burns supervised the mysterious process that turns typed pages into a bound book, and art director Dana Kasarsky and designer Leon Bolognese made it all look good. Many others at Random House contributed to the revision in significant ways, including Deborah Slade, Jim Kwalwasser, Mary Schieck, Suzanne Thibodeau, Holly English, June Smith, Barry Fetterolf, Sylvia Shepard, and Mary Falcon. We are especially indebted to the instructors on our editorial review board for providing guidance through the development of the revision. Researcher David Meikle was always one step ahead of me, and Caroline Mebert somehow typed the entire manuscript without a single error. Game show hosts Bob Barker and Chuck Barris kept me entertained at times when the muse slept. And in the final stages of the project, when I just couldn't take it any more, Judy Block came along to write some of the boxes.

But most of all I must thank my wife Pat. Here words fail me. She makes me happy.

James Hassett
September 1979

Contents

Understanding
PSYCHOLOGY

Third Edition

1 Introducing Psychology

Psychology is one of the most popular courses in college for a very simple reason: what could possibly be more interesting than me? Everyone wants to understand himself or herself, and everyone wants to know "what makes other people tick." Although you have probably heard a great deal about psychologists who study unusual, bizarre, or "crazy" behavior, most psychologists are concerned with everyday activities and feelings.

Everyone learns, remembers, and solves problems. Everyone develops intellectually and socially, from infancy to adulthood. Everyone perceives environmental stimuli (sounds, sights, smells, and the like) and interprets this information from his or her senses. Everyone's behavior depends on physiological functions—on signals being transmitted to and from the central nervous system. We all feel emotions and engage in motivated behavior. Everyone has a personality, and most of us are curious about how it develops. And everyone's behavior is affected by the many formal and informal groups to which he or she belongs. Not everyone is psychologically disturbed or in need of therapy, but many people have a friend or relative who is. These everyday things are the focus of psychology.

We can make two promises in this book: first, to answer some of the questions readers have about themselves and other people; and second, to show that everyday behavior is far more complex—and interesting—than most people imagine.

PSYCHOLOGY AND EVERYDAY LIFE

What is it that fascinates psychologists about ordinary behavior? What exactly do they study? One way to answer this question is to look at a slice of life through a psychologist's eyes.

Figure 1.1
Studying psychology can help you gain a perspective on your own behavior.

Figure 1.2
Where we might see two people sitting and talking, a psychologist might see a sequence of complex behaviors.

Ruth, a college student, decides to have lunch at the school cafeteria. She walks to the cafeteria, gets on line, chooses chicken croquettes with mashed potatoes, and pays for it. Ruth then looks around for someone to sit with. She doesn't see any close friends, so she goes to a table by herself, sits down, and begins to eat.

A few minutes later, Gary, a young man in Ruth's English class, comes over to join her. When Ruth looks up at him, she no longer feels like eating. She thinks Gary is better looking than John Travolta or Robert Redford, but he never speaks to Ruth unless he's missed a class and wants to borrow her notes. She greets him coolly, but Gary sits down anyway and begins to tell a long, rambling story about *A Visit from the Little Green Slimy People,* the horror movie on TV he stayed up to watch last night. Meanwhile, Ruth remembers that Gary missed this morning's English class and catches him eyeing her notebook.

Ruth fantasizes dumping her chicken croquettes on Gary's neatly groomed hair, but instead she gets up to leave. Gary attempts a casual smile and asks to borrow her notes. Now Ruth is more than annoyed. Although her English notebook is in plain sight, she tells him curtly that she is sorry but she has left her notes in the library—to which, as a matter of fact, she must return right away. As she leaves the cafeteria, she glances back and sees Gary still sitting at the table, nervously smoking a cigarette. He looks depressed. Suddenly, she feels a bit depressed herself.

This is a simple story, but from a psychologist's point of view, the behavior we witnessed was complex. First of all, Ruth decided to have lunch because of her *physiological state* (she was hungry). She may also have been motivated by *cognitive* elements (she knew she should eat now because she had classes scheduled for the next few hours). When she entered the cafeteria, she *perceived* sensory stimuli different from those outside. But she paid little attention to the new sights, sounds, and smells, except to note that the food smelled good and the line was mercifully short. She went through the line and paid for her food—*learned behavior* not too different from that of a hungry rat that runs a maze for a food reward.

Ruth looked for a *social group* to join, but found none to which she belonged. She sat alone until Gary joined her. He felt free to do so because in most schools there is an informal rule, or *norm*, that students who have a class together may approach each other socially. (This rule usually does not hold for members of a looser group, such as commuters who ride the same bus.) Ruth *remembered* how Gary had behaved toward her in the past and realized that he seemed to be embarking on the same note-borrowing course. This triggered the *emotional* reaction of anger. However, she did not dump her food on his head as a two year old might, but acted in a way that was more appropriate to her stage of *development*. We can assume that her response was characteristic of her *personality:* she told the young man that she didn't have the notes (even though he had seen them) and left.

In the example above, if such situations occurred often, and if they were always followed by depression, either student's behavior could indicate psychological *disturbance*. If Gary always relied on others for help and manipulated people to get his way, his behavior might be a sign of disorder. So might Ruth's, since she interprets simple requests as demands but finds herself unable either to meet or refuse the request in a direct way. However, in this context, neither student's behavior seems *abnormal*.

Viewed in this way, an apparently simple event raises numerous questions about why people behave and feel as they do. How is behavior influenced by physiological states? What motivates people to choose one action instead of another? Nearly all the topics covered in this book appear in this brief story.

WHY STUDY PSYCHOLOGY?

As the example above suggests, one advantage of learning about psychology is that it offers a new framework for viewing daily events: many things we take for granted will be seen in a new way. There are other advantages as well.

Insight

Understanding psychology can provide useful insights into your own and other people's behavior. Suppose, for example, that a student is convinced he is hopelessly shy and doomed forever to feel uncomfortable in groups. Then he learns from social psychology that different kinds of groups tend to have different effects on their members. He thinks about this for a while and notes that although he is miserable at parties, he feels fine at meetings of the school newspaper staff and with the group he works with in the

The more psychology you study, the more respect you gain for the complexity and diversity of human behavior.

biology laboratory. (In technical terms, he is much more uncomfortable in unstructured social groups than in structured, task-oriented groups.) Realizing that he is only uncomfortable in some groups brings a flood of relief. He isn't paralyzingly shy; he just doesn't like unstructured groups. And he is not alone in his feelings. There is something about each of us in this book. You, too, may find that because of one chapter or another, you see yourself in a new way.

Of course, you must be careful in applying your new insights. Few people are more obnoxious than the student who has had one psychology course and proceeds to terrorize family, friends, and strangers with an analysis of every action. Not to mention all the neurotic puppies and goldfish that have been created by psychology students trying out new training methods on their pets.

"A little knowledge is a dangerous thing," according to the old cliché, and the more psychology you study, the more respect you will gain for the complexity and the diversity of human behavior. An introductory psychology course is just one investment in a lifelong process of education about yourself and others.

Practical Information

Some of the chapters in this book include material that has practical application to everyday life. You will read, in concrete and detailed form, how to carry out a number of useful procedures psychologists have developed.

For example, Chapter 3 includes a description of several *mnemonic devices*, or memory aids, that will help you to learn information by rote. The rhyme beginning "Thirty days has September," which helps many people to remember the number of days in each month, is an example. With mnemonic devices you usually associate each item on a list with some sort of mental picture. Although this may require time and effort (especially the first time) memory experts have shown that it is worth the trouble. The techniques described may help you to memorize almost any list of words or numbers—the names of the presidents of the United States and their dates in office (for a history course), the authors and titles of books (for an English course), telephone numbers, shopping lists, and so on.

Chapter 2 describes the systematic way of dispensing rewards and punishments that psychologists call *shaping* (Figure 1.3). You will definitely find this useful if you ever have to train a puppy, and you may find yourself wondering how you shape the behavior of people around you. Perhaps you have a friend who is always happy to join you for coffee or a movie but who never brings any money along. You've loaned him money many times, and just as many times he's failed to pay you back. You know he can afford to pay his share, and you have told him so repeatedly. But he's a good friend, so you end up paying his way again and again. In doing so you are rewarding or reinforcing an undesirable behavior pattern. Is that what you really want to do?

In the chapter on child development you will recognize some of the experiences you had in your own childhood. The chapter on disturbance and breakdown may help you understand the more difficult periods in

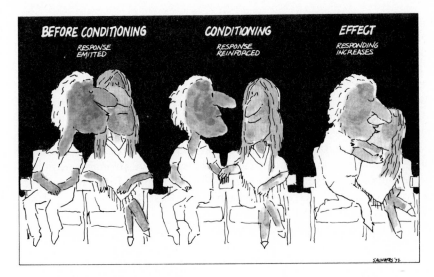

Figure 1.3
Kissing is a response that is subject to shaping. Here the response is emitted tentatively and would probably be repeated only after a considerable time if it produced no result. The kiss is reinforced, however, and immediately the response increases in frequency and in vigor.

your own life and in the lives of those around you. And Chapter 16 will tell you about the different kinds of therapy available to people who are experiencing severe or chronic difficulties. Of course, you should not jump to conclusions on the basis of this introduction to psychology. It takes a trained professional to diagnose and treat developmental and psychological problems (as Chapter 16 explains).

Testing Your Intuitions

After reading this book, you will be able to check some of your assumptions about human behavior and feelings. Psychologists have put common

Figure 1.4
Some of the beliefs about human behavior that psychologists have investigated.

1. The behavior of most lower animals—insects, reptiles and amphibians, most rodents, and birds—is instinctive and unaffected by learning.
2. For the first week of life, a baby sees nothing but a gray blur regardless of what he or she "looks at."
3. A child learns to talk more quickly if the adults around the child habitually repeat the word he or she is trying to say, using proper pronunciation.
4. The best way to get a chronically noisy schoolchild to settle down and pay attention is to punish him or her.
5. Slow learners remember more of what they learn than fast learners.
6. Highly intelligent people—"geniuses"—tend to be physically frail and socially isolated.
7. On the average, you cannot predict from a person's grades at school and college whether he or she will do well in a career.
8. Most national and ethnic stereotypes are completely false.
9. In small amounts, alcohol is a stimulant.
10. LSD causes chromosome damage.
11. The largest drug problem in the United States, in terms of the number of people affected, is marijuana.
12. Psychiatry is a subdivision of psychology.
13. Most mentally retarded people are also mentally ill.
14. A third or more of the people suffering from severe mental disorder are potentially dangerous.
15. Electroshock therapy is an outmoded technique rarely used in today's mental hospitals.
16. The more severe the disorder, the more intensive the therapy required to cure it; for example, schizophrenics usually respond best to psychoanalysis.
17. Quite a few psychological characteristics of men and women appear to be inborn; in all cultures, for example, women are more emotional and sexually less aggressive than men.
18. No reputable psychologist "believes in" such irrational phenomena as ESP, hypnosis, or the bizarre mental and physical achievements of Eastern yogis.

sense to the test to find out whether things many of us take for granted are true or false. The statements about behavior printed in Figure 1.4 represent a small fraction of the beliefs psychologists have examined. Which of these statements do you think are true?

Before telling you the answers, we ask you to consider the implications of these opinions. An employer who believes that retarded people are mentally ill (item 13) and that most mentally ill people are dangerous (item 14) will undoubtedly refuse to hire a retarded person even though he or she may be perfectly suited for the job. Parents who believe that extremely bright people are usually "social failures" (item 6) wil probably suppress signs of unusual intelligence in their child—perhaps turning down a request for a chemistry set or the complete works of Shakespeare. Both reactions would be unfortunate, for psychologists have found that all the statements in this list are false.

HOW PSYCHOLOGISTS FIND THE ANSWERS

Asking the Right Questions

You're sitting in the cafeteria with a group of people, waiting for your next class. Someone across the table says that she thinks psychotherapy is a waste of time and money. You think of a friend who has been seeing a therapist for some time and, in your opinion, is as mixed up now as he was when he started. Before you can say anything, a third person breaks in. He says that his brother has really changed since he entered therapy—he's stopped fighting with their parents, gotten a job, and so on. The person next to you comments that he just needed time to grow up. Someone tells *him* that he's against therapy because he's afraid his girl friend will leave him if she enters therapy as she's planning to do. "She wouldn't need a therapist if she would move away from her crazy family," the person next to you replies somewhat angrily. Another person begins talking about how much he thinks therapy has helped him. The time for class rolls around, and you leave feeling more confused about this topic than you were before. Does therapy work or doesn't it?

How would a psychologist go about answering this question? The answer is that a researcher would not tackle such a broad and ill-defined question. The term "psychotherapy" covers everything from psychoanalysis to token economies, as indicated in Chapter 16. To answer this question you would have to investigate *all* the different kinds of therapy—an enormous task. You might concentrate on one form, leaving the investigation of other methods to other researchers. But even then you would have problems.

Some people see a therapist once a week for a year, some five days a week for six or eight years. Some begin therapy because they want to grow; some because losing their job, getting divorced, or some other crisis has left them confused and unhappy; some because they are hospitalized and cannot function. Some start therapy as children, some in middle age. Some see a therapist of the same sex, some a therapist of the opposite sex. All these factors could make a difference. Whom would you study?

Then there is the question of what you mean by therapy "working." Do you accept the person's statement that he feels better about himself and his life, or do you measure success in terms of observable changes in behavior? Suppose the people you question or observe do change during therapy. How do you know the change is due to therapy and not to other events in their lives? That they wouldn't have changed without therapy? That some other form of treatment wouldn't have been more effective? The more you think about this topic, the more questions you ask.

To do research on the effectiveness of psychotherapy, a psychologist has to take all these factors into account. And this is why researchers focus on limited, well-defined questions. A psychologist might conduct research on whether people with similar problems and in similar life situations benefit from a specific kind of therapy. But a researcher would not attempt to answer the whole question "Does therapy work?" The answers to big questions are arrived at by many psychologists researching limited questions in different ways and examining one another's work with respectful skepticism.

The first step, then, in all psychological research is to ask a precise question about a limited topic. In most cases, the researchers also formulate a *hypothesis*—an educated guess about the relationship between two factors or variables. In a hypothesis researchers state what they expect to find, expressed in such a way that it can be proved or disproved. An example would be: hospitalized schizophrenics who participate in a token economy program begin to make intelligible statements to other people sooner than hospitalized schizophrenics who do not participate in such a program. The research project is designed to test this hypothesis. The hypothesis may prove to be wrong—the researcher may find no difference between the two groups.

Thus, psychology is an empirical science—one in which precise statements are tested to see whether they are true or false. There are many kinds of tests—surveys, experiments, naturalistic observations, and so on—and they are described in detail in the appendix on "How Psychologists Do Research." But answers to general questions are arrived at only by general agreement on the part of experts after years of research on many different aspects of a problem.

Psychologists Disagree

Agreement takes time, and the experts in a given area often disagree. Sometimes this disagreement is very specific and concrete. For example, researcher Lee Salk suspected that unborn babies associate their mother's heartbeat with the security and comfort of the womb. If this is true, Salk reasoned, newborn infants should find the sound of a heartbeat soothing. He tested this idea by placing infants in two separate nurseries and playing the sound of an amplified heartbeat in one. It turned out that the babies in this nursery slept more, cried less, and gained weight faster than babies in the quiet nursery. Salk concluded that his original idea was correct (1962).

Yvonne Brackbill and several of her colleagues were not entirely convinced, however (1966). In a preliminary study they found that two dif-

Figure 1.5
This engraving depicts a forest scene, doesn't it? If you answer yes, it may be because you looked only at the "framed area." If we had said, "Look at the muddy road," you would have seen that the forest is simply a reflection in a puddle. The same thing happens in psychology. Attending to one theoretical view prevents a researcher from seeing others.

ferent rhythmic sounds—a metronome and a lullaby—were just as effective in quieting babies as the heartbeat. Thus it appeared that infants were responding to the constant, monotonous rhythm, not to the heartbeat itself. Brackbill went on to test whether newborn infants responded favorably to other monotonous sensations—constant light, increased heat, and snug swaddling. She found that *all* of these seemed to comfort babies (1971). Thus Salk's conclusions weren't entirely wrong, but neither were they entirely right. He had simply been too specific. Newborn babies seem to find a wide variety of monotonous, constant sensations reassuring.

Similar challenges occur all the time. One researcher reports an interesting finding, and another comes along to study the study and question some aspect of it. With variations on the same theme, the second researcher clarifies, corrects, and extends the results obtained by the first researcher.

But sometimes there are more fundamental disagreements between psychologists. As we will see in our discussion of psychology's history, the followers of B. F. Skinner and Sigmund Freud have very different views of the nature of human beings. Because these researchers start out approaching human behavior from different angles, they often end up with different interpretations (Figure 1.5). It's like the old story of the three blind men and the elephant. Each man groped his way toward the elephant and encountered a different part of the animal's anatomy. "It's like a rope," announced the man who touched the elephant's tail. "No, it's like a wall," said the second man, who walked into the animal's side. "You're both wrong," said the third man, who discovered the trunk. "This is obviously a snake."

As a psychology student, you will not be asked to resolve these differences of opinion, but you should be aware that they exist. Disagreement is the sign of a healthy, growing science.

Basic and Applied Psychology

People often describe psychology as a "basic science." **Basic science** is the pursuit of knowledge for its own sake in order to satisfy curiosity about the nature of things. The immediate "usefulness" of the knowledge is not an issue. **Applied science,** on the other hand, involves using a basic science to accomplish practical goals. Biologists and physicists nearly always practice basic science; physicians and engineers practice applied science.

Psychologists may practice both. A developmental psychologist who is studying the ability of infants to perceive visual patterns is doing basic research. He is not concerned with the implications his findings may have on the design of a crib. A psychologist involved with applied science, perhaps as a consultant to a toy manufacturer, would be. Similarly, a social psychologist who is studying friendship in an office—who likes whom, how much, and why—is doing basic science. If she discovers that one individual has no friends in the office and another has so many he hardly has time to work, she will try to understand and explain the situation. But she will not try to correct it. This is a job for applied scientists, such as clinical or industrial psychologists.

Why is this distinction so important? Because transferring findings from basic to applied science is a tricky business. For example, psychologists doing basic research have found that babies raised in sterile institutional environments are seriously retarded in their physical, intellectual, and emotional development. Wayne Dennis (1960), among others, traces this to the fact that these babies have nothing to look at but a blank white ceiling and white crib cushions, and are only handled when they need to be fed or changed. However, we have to be very careful not to apply this finding too broadly. Because children who lack stimulation tend to develop poorly, we can't jump to the conclusion that by providing a child with maximum stimulation—by playing with him continually, having music piped into his room, surrounding him with fancy toys—we can guarantee that he will grow up emotionally sound and intellectually brilliant. On the contrary, it appears that most babies do best with a medium level of stimulation (White, 1969).

In short, in basic science we are provided with specific findings: what happened in one study conducted at one time and in one place. To generalize these specific findings into a list of general rules is dangerous.

Like almost every other introductory text, in *Understanding Psychology* we focus on basic psychology since these findings provide the foundations on which applications are built. However, we will try to give you some idea of the range of applications in psychology by including many sections called "Using Psychology."

A BRIEF HISTORY OF PSYCHOLOGY

We can trace the roots of the scientific study of human behavior back to the Greeks, but most historians agree that modern psychology began when the German scholar Wilhelm Wundt established the first psychology labo-

Figure 1.6
Sigmund Freud in his Vienna office, 1938.

ratory in 1879. Although Wundt's experiments on analyzing human sensations were very important from a historical point of view, his work has little relevance to modern research. Three of the most important historical trends in psychology's first hundred years involve the study of unconscious processes, individual differences, and observable behavior.

Psychology as the Study of Unconscious Processes

For Sigmund Freud, a physician who practiced in Vienna until 1938, conscious experiences were only the tip of the iceberg. Beneath the surface, he believed, are primitive biological urges that are in conflict with the requirements of society and morality. According to Freud, these unconscious motivations and conflicts are responsible for much human behavior, including many of the medically unexplainable physical symptoms that troubled his patients.

Freud used a new method for indirectly studying unconscious processes. In this technique, known as free association, a patient said everything that came to mind—no matter how absurd or irrelevant it sounded—without attempting to produce logical, meaningful statements. The person would do no editing or censoring, no thinking about the thoughts. Freud's role, that of psychoanalyst, was meant to be objective; he merely sat and listened, then interpreted the associations (Figure 1.6). Free associations, Freud believed, reveal the operation of unconscious processes. Freud also believed that dreams are expressions of the most primitive unconscious urges. To learn more about these urges, he developed dream analysis—basically an extension of free association—whereby the patient free-associated to his or her dreams (Freud, 1940).

While working out his ideas, Freud took careful, extensive notes on all his patients and treatment sessions. He used these records, or case studies, to develop and illustrate a comprehensive theory of personality—that is, of the total, functioning person (Hall and Lindzey, 1978). Freud's theory of personality will be discussed in Chapter 13.

In many areas of psychology today, Freud's view of unconscious motivation remains a powerful and controversial influence. Modern psychologists may support, alter, or attempt to disprove it, but most have a strong opinion about it. The technique of free association is still used by psychoanalysts, and the method of intensive case study still serves as a major tool for investigating behavior.

Psychology as the Study of Individual Differences

Sir Francis Galton, a nineteenth-century English mathematician and scientist, wanted to understand the way in which biology decides how one person's abilities, character, and behavior differ from those of other people (Figure 1.7). Galton (1869) traced the ancestry of various eminent people and found that greatness runs in families. (This was appropriate, since Galton himself was considered a genius and his family included at least one towering intellectual figure, a cousin named Charles Darwin.) He therefore concluded that genius or eminence is a hereditary trait. Of course, this conclusion was premature. Galton did not consider the obvious possibility that the tendency of genius to run in eminent families might be a result of the exceptional environments and numerous socioeconomic advantages that also tend to "run" in such families.

The data Galton used were based on his study of biographies. However, not content to limit his inquiry to indirect accounts, he went on to invent procedures for directly testing the abilities and characteristics of a wide range of people. These tests were the primitive ancestors of the modern personality and intelligence tests that virtually everyone who reads this book has taken at some time. Galton also devised statistical techniques, notably the correlation coefficient, that are still in use today.

Although Galton began his work shortly before psychology emerged as an independent discipline, his theories and techniques quickly became central aspects of the new science. In 1883 he published a book, *Inquiries into Human Faculty and Its Development*, that is regarded as having defined the beginnings of individual psychology. Galton's writings raised the issue of whether behavior is determined by heredity or environment—a subject that has become the focus of controversy, especially in recent years. Galton's influence can also be seen in the current widespread use of psychological tests, in the continuing argument over their use, and in the statistical methods employed to evaluate their findings (all discussed in Chapter 14).

Psychology as the Study of Observable Behavior

The pioneering work of Russian physiologist Ivan Pavlov, who won the Nobel prize in 1904, charted another new course for psychological investi-

Figure 1.7
Sir Francis Galton, who invented procedures for testing abilities and characteristics that are still used in modern personality and intelligence tests.

Figure 1.8
B. F. Skinner at Twin Oaks, the community founded on the principles he outlined in *Walden Two*.

Figure 1.9
(Opposite) Psychologists at work. (a) One to one therapy. (b) An automated instructional system designed by educational psychologists. (c) Administering a standard intelligence test. (d) A therapist working with a mentally disturbed child. (e) Space vehicles designed with the help of psychologists. (f) Doing research on sleep and dreaming. (g) Videotaping a family interaction for later use in family therapy. (h) Brain research: an experiment in chemical stimulation of the brain.

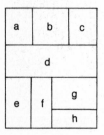

gation. In a now-famous experiment, Pavlov struck a tuning fork each time he gave a dog some meat powder. The dog, of course, would salivate the moment it saw the meat powder. After Pavlov repeated the procedure many times, the dog would salivate when it heard the tuning fork, even if no food appeared.

The concept of the conditioned reflex—a response (salivation) elicited by a stimulus (the tuning fork) other than the one that first produced it (food)—was used by psychologists as a new tool, a means of exploring the development of behavior. Using this tool, they could begin to account for behavior as the product of prior experience. This enabled them to explain that certain acts and certain differences among individuals were the result of learning.

Psychologists who stressed investigating observable behavior became known as *behaviorists*. Their position, as formulated by American psychologist John B. Watson (1924), was that psychology should concern itself *only* with the observable facts of behavior. Watson further maintained that all behavior, even in its apparently instinctive aspects, is the result of conditioning and occurs because the appropriate stimulus is present in the environment.

Though it was Watson who defined and solidified the behaviorist position, it is B. F. Skinner, the contemporary American psychologist, who has refined and popularized it. Skinner has attempted to show how, in principle, his laboratory techniques might be applied to society as a whole. In his classic novel *Walden Two* (1949), he portrays his idea of Utopia—a small town in which conditioning, through rewarding those who display behavior that is considered desirable, rules every conceivable facet of life.

Skinner has exerted great influence on both the general public and the science of psychology. His face is familiar to television audiences, and his book *Beyond Freedom and Dignity* (1971) became a runaway bestseller (Figure 1.8). A number of Walden Two communities have been formed in various parts of the country, and many people toilet-train their children, lose weight, quit smoking, and overcome phobias by using Skinner-inspired methods.

Skinner has been widely criticized, for many people are convinced he seeks to limit personal freedom with his "manipulative" conditioning techniques. He has also been heartily applauded as a social visionary. In any event, his theories and methods have permeated psychology. Behaviorist-inspired techniques compete with more traditional psychotherapy for primacy in the treatment of various psychological disorders. The techniques of *reinforcement*, or controlled reward and punishment, have become increasingly popular in education, and Skinner's teaching machine was the forerunner of modern programmed instruction. Moreover, a vast number of today's psychologists use Skinner's research methodology to obtain precise findings in their laboratory experiments.

PSYCHOLOGY AS A PROFESSION

Psychology today covers an enormous range. There are psychologists working in advertising, education, and criminology; studying death, art,

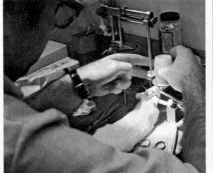

and robots. Psychological themes and terminology have become part of everyday life, and of novels, films, and television programs.

In the process of growing, psychology has become divided into a number of subfields. *Clinical* and *counseling* psychology are the most popular. Specialists in these fields are involved in applied science. Most clinical psychologists are psychotherapists. They work in mental hospitals, prisons, schools, clinics, and private offices, helping people with psychological problems. Some specialize in giving and interpreting personality tests that are designed to determine whether or not a person needs treatment and what kind. Counseling psychologists usually work in schools, industrial firms, and the like, advising and assisting people who would be classified as normal rather than disturbed.

A large number of specialists are also attracted to *personality, social,* and *developmental psychology*. These psychologists usually are involved in basic rather than applied science. Personality psychologists study personality development and traits and devise personality tests. Social psychologists study groups and the way groups influence individual behavior. Some are particularly interested in public opinion and devote much of their time to conducting polls and surveys. Most developmental psychologists focus on children from birth to age fifteen or thereabouts. However, in recent years some have been leaning toward the "life cycle" or "cradle to grave" approach—that is, studying development as something that extends from birth to old age.

Educational psychologists deal with topics related to teaching children and young adults, such as intelligence, memory, problem solving, and motivation. They are concerned with evaluating teaching methods, devising tests, and developing new instructional devices such as films and television. One of their contributions to education is the teaching machine, which allows each student to proceed through a subject at his or her own rate. The machine provides information, asks questions, and tells the student whether his or her answers are right or wrong.

Industrial psychology is another area of specialization. Psychological methods have been used to boost production, improve working conditions, place applicants in the jobs for which they are best suited, devise methods for training people, and reduce accidents. Psychologists have also been involved in improving machines, for example, by making control panels more readable. Industrial psychologists generally work as consultants to private firms or government agencies.

Finally, about a fourth of all psychologists are engaged in *experimental psychology*. These psychologists do everything from testing how electrical stimulation of a rat's brain affects its behavior to studying how disturbed people think and observing how different socioeconomic groups vote in elections. They are basic scientists. Many work in colleges and universities, teaching and writing as well as conducting experiments.

All psychologists have an area of special interest, but most participate in diverse activities. A busy psychologist might divide her or his time between doing research, teaching, administering psychological tests, providing therapy or counseling, writing books and research papers, serving on college committees, figuring departmental budgets, and attending professional conventions.

The working lives of psychologists are not the subject of this book; rather, what psychologists think about, what they know, what experiments they have done, and what their work means to a person who is not a psychologist. **Psychology** is a science dedicated to answering some of the most interesting questions of everyday life:

What happens during sleep?
How can bad habits be broken?
Is there a way to measure intelligence?
Why do crowds sometimes turn into mobs?
What does the world look like to other animals?
Do dreams mean anything?
How does punishment affect a child?
Can memory be improved?
What causes psychological breakdowns?

In trying to answer such questions, psychology ties together all that has been discovered about human behavior and feelings in order to look at the total human being. The picture is far from complete, but much of what is known will be found in the chapters that follow.

SUMMARY

1. The primary focus of psychology is the complexity of everyday behavior.

2. An apparently simple and ordinary meeting in a college cafeteria illustrates the topics psychologists study: physiological states, perception, cognition, motivation, memory, learned behavior, development, social groups, emotions, personality, disturbances, and breakdowns.

3. From this introduction to psychology, you may gain insights, practical information, and an objective test of your beliefs.

4. The first step in psychological research is generating testable ideas. These usually take the form of hypotheses: statements about what a researcher expects to find put in such a way that they can be proved or disproved.

5. Science thrives on debate. The results of a single study should not be mistaken for "the final answer" or for authoritative advice on how to handle everyday situations.

6. Basic science is the pursuit of knowledge for its own sake. Applied science, on the other hand, is the search for ways to put basic science to use in accomplishing practical goals.

7. Sigmund Freud believed that we act the way we do as a result of primitive unconscious urges.

8. Sir Francis Galton was one of the first to study systematically how one individual differs from the next, and today's psychological tests can be traced back to his work.

9. Ivan Pavlov, John Watson, and B. F. Skinner are three key figures in behaviorism, which studies the way learning shapes our observable behavior.

10. Psychology is subdivided in practice as well as in theory. Major areas of specialization in psychology today include clinical and counseling psychology; personality, social, and developmental psychology; educational psychology; industrial psychology; and experimental psychology.

11. In the course of describing in the chapters that follow what psychologists think about and what they have learned, we hope to show what their work means to people who are not psychologists.

GLOSSARY

applied science: Discovering ways to use scientific findings to accomplish practical goals.

basic science: The pursuit of knowledge about natural phenomena for its own sake.

psychology: The study of mental processes and the behavior of organisms.

ACTIVITIES

1. Write your own definition of psychology. How different is your definition from one you would have written before reading the chapter? Put the definition away, and at the end of the course take it out and reread it.

2. How is psychology involved in your life? Considering the information at the end of the chapter regarding the various areas of psychology, make a list of all the ways that psychology affects your life. (Hint: Traffic signs and classroom interiors are often designed by psychologists.)

3. Psychology is generally thought of as being a benevolent science, and it is expected to produce such results as happier people, accident-free and more productive workers, and greater understanding in interpersonal relationships. But well-meaning people throughout history have also applied what they considered to be sound "psychological" techniques that have actually served to increase the torment of or to totally destroy their intended beneficiaries. Can you see any possibilities today that psychological knowledge could be used against the best interests of an individual or society?

4. Much of psychology is in effect an attempt to articulate the nature of human nature. Make a list of characteristics or behavioral tendencies that you think apply to all people. Compare your list to the lists of other students in the class. Do you think there are any characteristics or "laws," comparable to established physical attributes and physical laws in physics, that are universally valid for all of us?

5. Make a list of various professions or occupations. List the ways one or another type of psychologist might contribute to the better functioning within the occupation or profession. What kind of psychologist do you think would be most helpful in performing each job?

SUGGESTED READINGS

A number of magazines include articles on recent developments in the social sciences. Among them are *Psychology Today* and *Scientific American*.

AMERICAN PSYCHOLOGICAL ASSOCIATION. *Careers in Psychology*. Washington, D.C.: American Psychological Association, 1975. This useful booklet provides information on the kinds of careers open to students interested in pursuing their study of psychology, and describes the type of education required for each career.

BAKER, ROBERT A. (ED.). *Psychology in the Wry*. New York: Van Nostrand, 1963 (paper). A collection of amusing, satirical articles in which psychologists make fun of their own pomposity and other shortcomings.

EYSENCK, HANS J. *Fact and Fiction in Psychology*. Baltimore: Penguin, 1965. Eysenck delves into popular notions of psychology and applies the scientific method to come up with some witty and entertaining conclusions. Topics range from criminal personality and the four temperaments to accident proneness. Also of interest are two other books by Eysenck that, together with this one, make up a trilogy: *Uses and Abuses of Psychology* (1953) and *Sense and Nonsense in Psychology* (1957).

GOLDENSON, R. M. *Mysteries of the Mind*. Garden City, N.Y.: Doubleday, 1973. Goldenson has gathered together a wide variety of unusual case studies in human behavior. He discusses such things as child prodigies, voodoo deaths, photographic memory, mass hysteria, and multiple personalities, and tries to find explanations for these fascinating phenomena.

JAMES, WILLIAM. *Psychology (Briefer Course).* New York: Macmillan, 1962 (paper). Published originally in two volumes in 1890 this is the abridgment of James's *Principles of Psychology,* the first major classic in the field of psychology. This book, which remains highly readable and thought-provoking today, attracted many eminent psychologists to the field and has influenced innumerable others in their thinking and research.

MACKAY, CHARLES. *Extraordinary Popular Delusions and the Madness of Crowds.* New York: Farrar, Straus & Giroux, 1932; originally published 1841. A remarkable book describing in vivid detail cases of human folly throughout the ages. Special emphasis is given to mass movements and the psychology of crowds.

SARGENT, D. S., AND STAFFORD, K. R. *Basic Teachings of the Great Psychologists.* New York: Dolphin, 1965 (paper). A good introduction to the major areas of psychology. The authors trace the historical and present-day explorations of such questions as: How can human abilities be measured? What is instinct? How does the nervous system work? What is personality?

SHAPIRO, EVELYN (ED.). *PsychoSources: A Psychology Resource Catalog.* New York: Bantam, 1973 (paper). This large-format paperback is a treasure-house of information about psychology. It contains book and film reviews, access information, and comments and essays about current trends on everything from identity crisis to health care in China.

WILSON, J. *The Mind.* New York: Time-Life Books, 1964. A beautifully illustrated and easy-to-read book about the past, present, and possible future of psychological investigation.

BIBLIOGRAPHY

BRACKBILL, YVONNE. "Cumulative Effects of Continuous Stimulation on Arousal Level in Infants." *Child Development,* 42 (1971): 17–26.

BRACKBILL, YVONNE, ET AL. "Arousal Level in Neonates and Preschool Children Under Continuous Auditory Stimulation." *Journal of Experimental Child Psychology,* 4 (1966): 177–188.

DENNIS, WAYNE. "Causes of Retardation Among Institutional Children: Iran." *Journal of Genetic Psychology,* 96 (1960): 47–59.

FREUD, SIGMUND. *An Outline of Psychoanalysis.* Ed. and trans. by James Strachey. New York: Norton, 1949; originally published 1940.

GALTON, SIR FRANCIS. *Hereditary Genius: An Inquiry into Its Laws and Consequences.* London: Macmillan, 1869.

HALL, CALVIN S., AND LINDZEY, GARDNER. *Theories of Personality.* 3rd ed. New York: Wiley, 1978.

HEBB, D. O. "What Psychology Is About." *American Psychologist,* 29 (1974): 71–79.

SALK, LEE. "Mother's Heartbeat as an Imprinting Stimulus." *Transactions of the New York Academy of Sciences,* 24 (1962): 753–763.

SKINNER, B. F. *Walden Two.* New York: Macmillan, 1968; originally published 1949.

————. *Beyond Freedom and Dignity.* New York: Knopf, 1971.

WATSON, JOHN B. *Behaviorism.* New York: Norton, 1970; originally published 1924.

WHITE, BURTON L. "Child Development Research: An Edifice Without a Foundation." *Merrill-Palmer Quarterly of Behavior and Development,* 15 (1969): 49–79.

WOLMAN, BENJAMIN B. (ED.). *Handbook of General Psychology.* Englewood Cliffs, N.J.: Prentice-Hall, 1973.

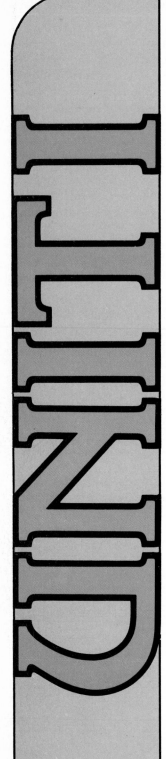

LEARNING AND COGNITIVE PROCESSES

One of the main distinctions between humans and other animals is our dependence on learning. We are not the only species that is capable of learning. Other animals can be taught to work for people, to perform all sorts of tricks, and even (in the case of chimpanzees) to communicate with sign language. Recent experiments suggest that chimpanzees, our nearest relatives in the animal kingdom, are able to think on about the level of a three-year-old child.

But no other species *depends* on learning to the extent that ours does: almost all human behavior is the result of learning.

In this unit we describe what psychologists have discovered about learning, memory, thought, and perception, and how they made these discoveries. In Chapter 2 we focus on what psychologists call "conditioning"—on techniques for changing behavior through the use of rewards and punishments. And in Chapter 3 we discuss the ways in which people acquire, organize, store, and use information to solve problems and to create.

In this unit you will find a number of useful suggestions for improving your memory and study habits, and for changing behavior you do not consider desirable. You may also gain new insight into the way you shape or influence other people's behavior toward you.

Learning: Principles and Applications

Learning is involved in nearly all human behavior. We have to learn to hold ourselves upright, to walk, and to use our hands, as well as to waltz, to play tennis, or to use a can opener. We learn to flip a switch to turn on the lights; to read and memorize information to pass an exam; to get what we want by asking, bargaining, or pouting. We may learn to be afraid of people in positions of authority, of making speeches, or of taking exams—and perhaps how to overcome those fears. We also learn how to learn. **Learning** can be defined as a relatively permanent change in behavior that results from experience.

Thus, if we wish to understand all the things that people do, we must begin with the basic principles of learning. (More complex learning processes will be described in the next chapter on memory and thought.) And the careful application of these principles may help you the next time you want to train your dog—or your roommate. In fact, it may even help you to change your own behavior.

CLASSICAL CONDITIONING

Like many great discoveries, Ivan Pavlov's discovery of the principle of classical conditioning was accidental. This Russian scientist had been studying the process of digestion around the turn of the century. Pavlov wanted to understand how a dog's stomach prepares to digest food when something is placed in the dog's mouth. Then he noticed that the mere sight or smell of food was enough to start a dog salivating. Pavlov became fascinated with these "psychic secretions" that occur before food is actually presented, and decided to investigate how they worked.

Figure 2.1
Skill at a sport is learned behavior, as is almost everything else human beings do.

Figure 2.2
The apparatus Pavlov used to study conditioned salivation in dogs. The harness held the dog steady, while the tube leading from the dog's mouth deposited saliva on an arm connected to the recorder on the left. Drops of saliva moved the pen, making a permanent record of the salivation response to such stimuli as food and sights or sounds associated with food.

Pavlov's Experiment

Pavlov (1927) began his experiments by ringing a tuning fork and then immediately placing some meat powder on the dog's tongue. He chose the tuning fork because it was a **neutral stimulus**—that is, one that had nothing to do with the response (salivation). After only a few times the dog started salivating as soon as it heard the sound, even if food were not placed in its mouth (Figure 2.2). Pavlov went on to demonstrate that any neutral stimulus will elicit an unrelated response (cause it to happen) if it is presented regularly just before the stimulus (here, food) that normally induces that response (salivation).

Pavlov distinguished among the different elements of the experiment as follows. He used the term "unconditioned" to refer to natural stimuli and to automatic, involuntary responses, such as blushing, shivering, being startled, or salivating. In the experiment, food was an **unconditioned stimulus (UCS):** a stimulus that leads to a certain response without previous training. (A dog doesn't have to be taught to salivate when it smells meat.) Food normally causes salivation. This is an **unconditioned response (UCR):** a response that occurs naturally and automatically when the unconditioned stimulus is presented.

Under normal conditions the sound of a tuning fork would not cause salivation. The dog had to be taught or *conditioned* to associate this sound with food. A neutral stimulus that, after training, leads to a response such as salivation is termed a **conditioned stimulus (CS).** The salivation it causes is a **conditioned response (CR).** A conditioned response is learned. A wide variety of stimuli may serve as conditioned stimuli for salivation: the sight of food, an experimenter entering the room, the sound of a tone, a flash of light. Controlling an animal's or a person's responses in this way so that an old response becomes attached to a new stimulus is called **classical conditioning.**

In the same set of experiments, Pavlov also explored the phenomena of generalization and discrimination. **Generalization** occurs when an animal responds to a stimulus that is similar to the original conditioned stimulus. When Pavlov conditioned a dog to salivate at the sight of a circle (the CS), he found that the dog would salivate when it saw an oval shape as well. The dog had generalized its response to a similar stimulus. Pavlov was later able to teach the dog to respond only to the circle by always pairing meat powder with the circle but never pairing it with the oval. He thus taught the dog a **discrimination:** the ability to respond differently to distinct stimuli.

A number of different responses may be conditioned. But for each such response there must be an unconditioned stimulus, one that elicits the response automatically either because it does so innately or because the stimulus is already a strong conditioned stimulus. Most such responses are "reflex" responses—that is, ones that occur automatically whenever the correct unconditioned stimulus occurs. These include responses produced by the glands, such as salivation or weeping, and responses of our internal muscles, such as those of the stomach. In general these responses are controlled by the autonomic nervous system and, as we will see in Chapter 5, "Body and Behavior," are very much involved in our emotions. As you might expect, then, our emotional lives tend to be greatly affected by classical conditioning.

Taste Aversions

Suppose you go out on a date to a fancy restaurant. If you're not paying for the meal, you may decide to try an expensive appetizer you've never had, like snails. But suppose that after dinner you go out to a concert and become violently ill. You will probably develop a taste aversion—you will never be able to look at another snail without becoming at least a little nauseous.

Your reaction to snails was classically conditioned. What makes this situation particularly interesting to learning theorists is the fact that when people or other animals get ill, they seem to decide "It must have been something I ate," even if they ate several hours ago. In the above situation, it is unlikely that the concert hall in which you got sick will be the conditioned stimulus. Nor will other stimuli from the restaurant—the wallpaper pattern or the type of china they use—make you sick in the future. What's more, psychologists can even predict which part of your meal will serve as the conditioned stimulus: you will probably blame a novel food, one that you haven't had before. Thus, if you get sick after a meal of salad, steak, and snails, you will probably learn to hate snails, even if they are really not at fault.

John Garcia and R. A. Koelling (1966) first demonstrated this phenomenon with rats. These animals were placed in a cage with a tube containing flavored water. Whenever a rat took a drink, lights would flash and clicks would sound. Some rats were given an electric shock after they drank, and they showed traditional classical conditioning: the lights and the sounds became conditioned stimuli, and the rats tried to avoid them. But other rats were injected with a drug that made them sick, and they developed an aversion not to the lights or the sounds, but only to the taste of the flavored water.

This special relationship between food and illness was exploited in a controversial study (Gustavson *et al.*, 1974) that tried to make coyotes hate the taste of lamb by giving them a drug to make them sick when they ate sheep. This is an important application because sheep farmers in the western United States would like to eliminate the coyotes that threaten their flocks, while naturalists are opposed to killing the coyotes. These experimenters believe that coyotes could be trained to eat other kinds of meat, and thus learn to peacefully coexist with sheep.

The Case of Little Albert

John B. Watson and Rosalie Rayner (1920) showed how conditioning could work on a human infant. They experimented with a normal eleven-month-old child named Albert. They presented Albert with many objects, including a white rat, a rabbit, blocks, a fur coat, and a hairy Santa Claus mask. Albert showed no fear of any of these objects—they were all neutral stimuli for the fear response.

Watson and Rayner decided that they would attempt to condition Albert to fear rats. They began by placing a rat in front of Albert. Albert would reach out to touch it, and each time he did, one of Watson's assistants would strike a metal bar with a hammer behind Albert's head. The first time the metal bar was struck, Albert fell forward and buried his head in a pillow. The next time that he reached for the rat and the bar was struck, Albert began to whimper. The noise, the unconditioned stimulus,

Figure 2.3
In a classic experiment, Watson and Raynor conditioned an eleven-month-old boy to be afraid of a rat. At first the child enjoyed playing with the animal. Later the presence of the rat was paired with a loud, disturbing noise that caused an instinctive fear reaction in the child. With repeated pairings of the noise and the presence of the rat, the child became more and more afraid of the animal. Finally, the presence of the rat alone was enough to elicit the fear response.

brought about a natural, unconditioned response, fear. After only a few such pairings, the rat became a conditioned stimulus that elicited a conditioned response, crying and cringing (Figure 2.3).

After Watson and Rayner conditioned Albert to fear rats, they presented him with a furry white rabbit. Albert now reacted fearfully to the rabbit. The researchers found that the degree of fear Albert felt toward other neutral stimuli depended upon how much they resembled the furry white rat. His conditioned fear response had generalized to the sight of the rabbit. Other furry white objects, such as a fur coat and a Santa Claus mask, also caused Albert to cry and try to escape whenever Watson and Rayner presented them, although the response was not as great as when the rabbit was presented.

Extinction

Albert learned to respond emotionally to the sight of the rat in the same way that Pavlov's dogs learned to respond with their salivary glands to the sound of a tone. Pavlov discovered, though, that if he stopped presenting food after the sound of the tuning fork, the sound gradually lost its effect on the dogs. After repeatedly striking the tuning fork without giving food, Pavlov found that a previously conditioned dog no longer associated the sound with the arrival of food—the sound of the tuning fork was no longer able to elicit the salivation response. Pavlov called this effect **extinction** because the conditioned response had gradually died out. Similarly, Watson and Rayner could have tried to extinguish fear of rats in Albert by presenting the rats without the jarring sound. Unfortunately, Albert's mother took her son away before such extinction could be accomplished.

This example shows how classical conditioning works with emotional responses. These sorts of responses are not under our voluntary control. But classical conditioning is much less useful in analyzing our "voluntary" responses. When we walk from one class to the next, complain about the high cost of living, or open a box of Rice Krispies, we are engaging in behavior for which there is no obvious UCS. We may speak only in the presence of a certain **stimulus,** namely, other people, but the presence of others does not *elicit* speaking; we may choose to remain silent. Speaking is not a reflex, automatic behavior, as salivation is. Another kind of learning must be responsible for modifying behavior that is not under the control of unconditioned stimuli.

OPERANT CONDITIONING

Suppose a dog is wandering around the neighborhood, sniffing trees, checking garbage cans, looking for a squirrel to chase. A kind person sees the dog and tosses a bone out the kitchen door to it. The next day the dog is likely to stop at her door on its rounds, if not go to her house directly. The kind person produces another bone, and another the next day. The dog becomes a regular visitor.

Figure 2.4
A rat pressing a bar in a Skinner box. The Skinner box is an artificial environment in which lights, sounds, rewards, and punishments can be delivered and controlled and in which some of the animal's behaviors, such as bar pressing, can be recorded by automatic switches.

Behavior that is reinforced tends to be repeated.

Suppose a baby is crawling around a room, vigorously exploring the world as babies will as soon as they are able to crawl. She discovers a large, shiny white box and touches it. The baby pulls back, squealing in alarm. She has touched a hot stove. A short time later she tries again—and gets burned again. From that day forward, she avoids the stove.

Both stories are examples of **operant conditioning**—so named because it occurs when the subject operates on the environment and produces a result that influences whether he or she will operate in the same way in the future. Unlike classical conditioning, operant conditioning involves learning from the consequences of your actions. (Some researchers, however, now question the distinction between operant and classical conditioning.)

In the laboratory, operant conditioning might take the form of allowing an experimental animal to explore a cage at random until it happens to press a bar that releases a food pellet or perhaps one that produces an electric shock (Figure 2.4). In time, the animal will become conditioned to approach or avoid the bar. Operant conditioning constantly occurs in "real life," as the examples above suggest.

Reinforcement

B. F. Skinner (1974) is the psychologist most closely associated with operant conditioning. He and his colleagues believe that most behavior is influenced by one's history of rewards and punishments. Suppose you want to teach a dog to shake hands. One way would be to give the animal a pat on the head or a biscuit every time it reaches up to you with its paw. The biscuit or pat is called a *positive reinforcer.* When such a reinforcer follows some **response,** that response (or one like it) is likely to occur more frequently. In this example, the dog will "get the message" and shake hands to get its reward. Learning from rewards is one kind of operant conditioning. Reinforcement makes the operant behavior more likely to occur again.

On the other hand, if you want to break a dog of the habit of pawing at you and others when it wants attention, you issue a sharp no and perhaps a smack on the rump each time it reaches up with its paw. If you are consistent about this, the dog will eventually stop pawing people. In this example, the consequences of the behavior decrease the likelihood of its occurring again. Negative consequences that have this effect are called **punishers.**

Extinction occurs when the novelty of your dog shaking hands wears off and you stop rewarding it for the trick—you withdraw reinforcement (Figure 2.5). Eventually, the dog will stop reaching up to shake hands. But it takes time. In fact, for a while after you stop rewarding it, the dog will probably become impatient, bark, and paw even more insistently than it did before.

The nature of the consequences, then, influences the organism's tendency to engage in the same behavior in the future. Behavior that is reinforced tends to be repeated; behavior that is not reinforced or is punished tends not to be repeated.

Figure 2.5
This pigeon is showing signs of emotional upset common in extinction of an operantly conditioned response. The bird was trained to obtain food from the square hole by pecking at the key in the round hole. When the experimenter switched off the circuit that made the arrangement work, the bird pecked the key for a while and then, finding no food, began to jump around and flap its wings.

Schedules of Reinforcement

One might suppose that behavior would best be maintained by reinforcing every response. This is called a *continuous schedule* of reinforcement. But one does not get the best results from a continuous schedule. When reinforcement occurs only intermittently, responding is generally more stable and more persistent. Consider, for example, a man who has two cigarette lighters; one lights immediately every time (continuous reinforcement), whereas the other must be flicked four or five times before it lights (intermittent reinforcement). Next, suppose that both lighters stop lighting completely. Which lighter will he give up on first? Most likely, he will discard the first one immediately because it is now functioning differently from his expectations for it. But he will probably not consider it at all unusual for the second lighter to fail for the first four or five attempts (see box).

Although intermittent reinforcement may be arranged in a number of ways, four basic methods, or schedules, have been studied in the laboratory. Schedules of reinforcement may be based either on the number of correct responses that the organism makes between reinforcements (*ratio schedules*) or on the amount of time that elapses before reinforcement is made available (*interval schedules*). In either case, reinforcement may appear on a regular, or fixed, schedule or an irregular, or variable, schedule. The four basic schedules result from the combination of these four possibilities. People respond differently to each type.

In **fixed-ratio schedules,** reinforcement depends on a certain amount of behavior being emitted, for example, rewarding every fourth response. The student who receives a good grade after completing a specified amount of work, the salesperson who is paid a commission for each sale, and the typist who is paid every time he finishes a certain number of pages are all on fixed-ratio schedules. People tend to work hard on fixed-ratio sched-

Baseball Superstitions

Before the start of each inning, baseball pitcher Mark Fidrych gets down on his hands and knees and smooths the dirt on the pitcher's mound; before he throws each pitch, he talks to the baseball. Pitcher Mike Griffin always washes his hair the day before he pitches. During the game, he removes his cap after each pitch, and when the inning is over, he sits in the same spot on the dugout bench. If it sounds like these baseball players are using ritual and magic to help them win games, you're right.

Experiments conducted by B. F. Skinner give us insight into how these rituals get started in the first place. Skinner rewarded pigeons with food pellets every fifteen seconds, no matter what they were doing. He soon found that the pigeons began to associate the onset of the feeding with a particular action—hopping from side to side, for example. Each time the pigeons were rewarded, their response was reinforced and they were more likely to repeat the response again. Even when they were fed irregularly, they did not give up. They still associated their action with the arrival of food, and the irregular feeding kept the connection going.

When a baseball player loads his mouth with a fresh pack of bubble gum before he bats and gets a home run, he may decide that the first event had something to do with the second. If he gets another hit, he is likely to chew bubble gum every time he's up. Since baseball statistics tell us he'll get a hit every fourth turn at bat, his ritualistic behavior will be intermittently reinforced.

For more details, see George Gmelch, "Baseball Magic." *Human Nature* (August 1978), pp. 32–39.

ules, pausing briefly after each reward. However, if the amount of work or number of responses to be completed before the next reward is large, the student, salesperson, or pieceworker is likely to show low morale and few responses at the beginning of each new cycle because there is a long way to go before the next reinforcement.

On **variable-ratio schedules,** the number of required responses varies around some average, rather than being fixed. For example, a door-to-door salesperson may make a sale at the fourth house, the tenth house, and not again until the twentieth house. People on variable-ratio schedules tend to work or respond at a steady high rate. Why? Perhaps because the more the organism produces, the more reinforcement is obtained. Since the next reinforcement may follow the very next response, there is no pausing. The classic example of this is a gambler at a slot machine. The faster he puts money into the machine, the sooner he'll hit the jackpot.

On a **fixed-interval schedule,** reinforcement is available at a predetermined time. Good examples of everyday fixed-interval schedules are hard to find. If your mail comes at the same time every day, the response of a daily trip to your mailbox at 2:30 would be reinforced by picking up your mail (assuming you get mail every day). The likelihood of responding will increase as the end of the fixed interval approaches; thus, you will be more likely to check your mailbox at 2:15 than at noon.

On a **variable-interval schedule,** the time at which a reinforcer will be available varies around some average, rather than being fixed. Dialing your boy friend's telephone number when his line is busy is a good example of a variable-interval schedule. When you finally get through, the sound of his voice will be a reinforcer. Meanwhile, no matter how many times you dial, you cannot increase the likelihood of getting through. Since you don't know when the line will be free, your best bet is to keep dialing at regular intervals. Similarly, a pigeon who is on a variable-interval schedule will tend to distribute his key pecks much more evenly than an animal who is on a fixed-interval schedule.

In general, responses are learned better and are more resistant to extinction when reinforced on a variable-interval or variable-ratio schedule.

Signals

In operant conditioning, stimuli that are associated with getting rewards or punishment become **signals** for particular behaviors. For example, everyone learns to cross a street only when the green light signals safety and to answer the phone only when it rings. These signals simply indicate that if one crosses the street or answers the phone, a reinforcer is likely to follow in the form of safe arrival on the other side of the street or of a voice on the phone.

Just as organisms generalize among and discriminate between conditioned stimuli in classical conditioning, they also generalize among and discriminate between stimuli that serve as signals in operant conditioning. For example, the child who has been rewarded for saying "doggie" every time he or she sees the family's basset hound may generalize and say "doggie" when he or she sees a sheep, a cow, or a horse. These animals are similar enough to the hound for them to become signals that "doggie" will produce a reward. Discrimination results when "doggie" fails to produce a reward in these other cases. The child learns to confine the use of his word to dogs and to respond differently when seeing horses, cattle, or sheep.

Because signals are guides to future rewards and punishers, they often become rewards or punishers in and of themselves. In this case, the signal is called a **conditioned reinforcer,** because without the conditioning process, it would have no positive or negative value to a person. With conditioning, almost any stimulus can acquire almost any value.

One experimenter (Wolfe, 1936) demonstrated this with chimpanzees. Poker chips have no value for chimps—they aren't edible and they aren't very much fun to play with. However, this experimenter used operant conditioning to teach the chimps to value poker chips as much as humans value money. He provided the animals with a "Chimp-O-Mat" that dispensed peanuts or bananas, which are **primary reinforcers,** or natural rewards. (Chimps like these foods.) However, to obtain food the chimps had to first pull down on a heavily weighted bar to obtain poker chips, then insert the chips in a slot in the machine (Figure 2.6). In time, the poker chips became conditioned reinforcers. The value of the poker chips to the

Figure 2.6
Using the Chimp-O-Mat to "buy" peanuts and bananas with poker chips obtained by pulling down on a heavily weighted bar. Through operant conditioning, this chimp had learned to value something that was neither edible nor fun to play with.

chimpanzees was evident from the fact that they would work for them, save them, and sometimes try to steal them from one another.

But we needn't look to animals for examples of this phenomenon. Smiles have little value for a newborn baby, and words of approval have no meaning. However, in time a baby learns that these expressions and sounds mean he or she is about to be picked up, cuddled, perhaps fed (primary reinforcers). They signal the fact that he or she is about to be rewarded. In time, the child begins to value smiles, praise, and other forms of social approval in and of themselves. They become conditioned reinforcers. Social approval is one of the most important conditioned reinforcers for almost all human beings.

Aversive Control

Pleasant consequences are one way of influencing behavior. But unpleasant consequences also occur in life. There are two ways in which unpleasant events, or aversive stimuli, can affect behavior: as punishers and as negative reinforcers. In punishment, an unpleasant consequence *decreases* the frequency of the behavior that produced it. In **negative reinforcement,** the removal of unpleasant consequences *increases* the frequency of the behavior that removed the aversive stimuli (Figure 2.7). Two examples of negatively reinforced behaviors are avoidance and escape. **Escape** involves shutting off the aversive stimulus after it starts. **Avoidance** involves postponing or preventing the recurrence of the stimulus before it starts. A child who feels anxious around strangers may learn to escape this unpleasant feeling by hiding in her room or avoid it by visiting a friend whenever guests are expected.

Anything that brings pain can serve as an aversive stimulus, whether inflicted physically (shocks or blows) or psychologically (isolation or disapproval). A child whose mother becomes angry when he is noisy or messy may learn that if he apologizes he will escape this punishment. He may also become an extremely apologetic, self-effacing person. The child who hides from strangers may grow up to be a loner who avoids social gatherings—if these childhood strategies work. Indeed, the child may be so successful at never meeting strangers that she will never discover the positive reinforcement that may follow. Thus, avoidance behavior may be very long-lasting, even after it has become inappropriate.

As another example, suppose that a child wants to play in the mud. When his parents respond with an emphatic "No!" the child throws a temper tantrum. Exasperated, his parents give in and let him have his way. The parents have positively reinforced the child's tantrums by letting him play in the mud—that is, his tantrum produced the desired event, playing in the mud, and so has been reinforced. At the same time, the child has negatively reinforced the parents' giving in—that is, giving in has escaped the aversive stimulus (the tantrum) and so has been reinforced. (It may help you to understand negative reinforcement if you remember that it *follows* and takes away, or *negates*, an aversive stimulus.) Also, the parents tried to prevent the child from playing in the mud, but he punished their

Figure 2.7
A rat makes the correct choice in a trial on the Lashley jump stand. Learning is rapid in this apparatus because an incorrect choice produces aversive consequences: The rat bumps its nose on the closed door (horizontally striped in this case) and falls into the net below.

Figure 2.8
An analysis of the relationship between the behavior of a child and the behavior of his parents. (from left to right and from top to bottom) The child is about to engage in a positively reinforcing activity (playing in the mud), but his parents are emitting a behavior (forbidding him to play in the mud). He punishes their forbidding behavior with an aversive stimulus (a violent tantrum). Their forbidding behavior decreases in strength and they give in. The parents' giving-in behavior is now negatively reinforced by the removal of the aversive tantrum. The child's tantrum is positively reinforced by playing in the mud. The results of this conditioning process are that tantrums are now more likely, forbidding is less likely, and giving in is more likely. The new behavior may generalize to a new yet similar situation.

efforts with a tantrum. In this way he reduced the likelihood that his parents would attempt to keep him out of mud puddles in the future.

Psychologists have found several disadvantages to using aversive stimuli to change behavior. For one thing, aversive stimuli can produce side effects such as rage, aggression, and fear. For another, the whole situation may become a conditioned aversive stimulus, in the same way that signals for reward situations become conditioned reinforcers. For example, if a parent tries to control a child by punishing her, the child may try to escape and avoid the whole family situation.

Aversive stimuli may achieve the opposite effect of what is desired—the person who is "punished" may actually increase the punished behavior. This occurs when what one person thinks a punisher is actually a reinforcer for the person receiving it. For example, a teacher may find that the more he reprimands a disruptive child, the more the student will misbehave. What such children really want is some sort of attention, and even being yelled at will provide this type of reward. Psychologists thus often recommend to parents and teachers that they try to pay more attention to a child's good behavior than to his or her misbehavior.

FACTORS THAT AFFECT LEARNING

Studies of more complex forms of learning have revealed that several factors can help or hinder the process. Among them are feedback, transfer, and practice.

Feedback

Finding out the results of an action or performance is called **feedback.** Without feedback, you might repeat the same mistakes so many times that you develop a skill incorrectly—you would never learn what you were doing wrong. Even if you were performing correctly, you would not be receiving reinforcement for continuing. If, for example, you always wore earplugs while you practiced the piano, you would never know just how bad your version of "Chopsticks" sounded.

Transfer

Often a skill that you have already learned can help you to learn a new skill. If you have learned to play the saxophone, it will be much easier for you to learn to play the clarinet. You can **transfer** skills you already have such as reading notes and converting them into responses of your lips, tongue, and fingers to the clarinet. When previously learned responses help you learn a new task, it is called *positive* transfer.

When a previously learned task hinders learning, *negative* transfer has occurred. An American may find driving in England to be more difficult than it is for an Englishman who is learning to drive. In England the steering wheel is on the opposite side of the car, and people drive on the opposite side of the road. The learned skill of driving American style makes it difficult to perform the necessary new mental and motor tasks. An American's responses are often the exact opposite of what is needed.

Practice

Practice, the repetition of a task, helps to bind responses together. It is the key element that makes for smooth and fluent movement from response to response.

Because practice takes time, psychologists have been interested in determining how to use that time most efficiently. They have found that whatever type of skill a person is learning, it is usually better to space out practice rather than do it all at once.

It is possible to practice by imagining oneself performing a skill. Athletes imagine themselves making golf swings over and over again or mentally shooting free throws in basketball to improve their performance. Psychologists call such effort *mental practice.* Although it is not as effective as the real thing, it is better than nothing at all.

LEARNING STRATEGIES

It would be difficult to solve problems if people had to relearn the solution process each time a problem occurred. Fortunately, when you learn to solve one problem, some of the problem-solving experiences may transfer to other, similar problems. Once you learn certain strategies for solving problems and learning tasks, you will usually have an easier time on your next attempts. (Such problem-solving strategies are also discussed in Chapter 3.) Strategies are affected by their consequences just as less complex reasons are. If a strategy works, the person or animal is likely to use it again. Many learned principles for dealing with life are valuable; others may actually be handicaps.

Learning to Learn

Harry Harlow (1949) has shown that animals can learn to learn—they can learn to use strategies for solving similar problems and tasks. He gave a monkey the problem of finding a raisin under one of two wooden lids, one red and one green (Figure 2.9). The raisin was always hidden under the green lid. But because the experimenter kept changing the position of the lids, the monkey took a while to realize that color was important, not location.

When the monkey had learned to always pick the green lid, the experimenter changed the problem. Now the monkey had to choose between triangular and circular lids. The raisin was always placed under the circular lid, and the experimenter again changed the location of the lids on each trial. As before, it took several tries for the monkey to learn that the shape of the lid, not its location, indicated where the raisin would be. After doing a number of problems like these, the monkey began to learn that the difference between the two lids always contained the key to the problem. Eventually the monkey could solve any similar two-choice problem with, at most, one error.

The learning of strategies and principles is extremely important in human behavior. In school you practice such skills as reading books, writing essays, and taking tests. In many cases the particular things you have learned will be less important in the long run than what you have learned about learning generally. Learning to extract information from a book, for example, will be helpful whether the book is about physics, grammar, or cooking. Just as Harlow's monkey acquired a general method for quickly solving particular problems, you are acquiring a general strategy for learning particular pieces of information.

Helplessness and Laziness

Psychologists have shown that general learning strategies can affect a person's relationship to the environment. For example, if a person has nu-

Figure 2.9

Harry Harlow presented monkeys with pairs of lids like those shown here and required them to learn strategies for determining which lid in each pair covered a morsel of food. After being presented with a few hundred such problems, the monkeys learned to use the same strategy for dealing with each new pair.

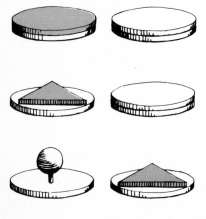

merous experiences in which his actions have no effect on his world, he may learn a general strategy of helplessness or laziness.

Martin Seligman did a number of experiments to show how learned helplessness developed in animals. He strapped dogs into a harness from which they could not escape, and then gave them a series of shocks at irregular intervals. After days of shock treatment, the dogs were unharnessed. Now they could escape the shocks or avoid them entirely simply by jumping over a hurdle into a safe compartment. But more than half the dogs failed to learn to jump. When several dogs that had not been shocked were also tested, almost all of them quickly learned to jump to safety. Apparently, many of the dogs in the first group had learned to stand and endure the shocks, resigned to the fact that any effort to escape would be useless.

Later experiments showed that people reacted in the same way. In the first stage of one study (Hiroto, 1974), some college students were able to turn off an unpleasant loud noise, while others had no control over it. Later, all were placed in a situation in which they merely had to move a lever to stop a similar noise. Only the ones who had control over the noise in the first place learned to turn it off. The others didn't even try.

It is not hard to see how these results can apply to everyday situations. In order to be able to try hard and to be full of energy, people must learn that their actions *do* make a difference. If rewards come without effort, a person never learns to work (learned laziness). If pain comes no matter how hard one tries, a person gives up (learned helplessness).

Seligman believes that learned helplessness is one major cause of depression. He has recently revised his theory (Abramson, Seligman, and Teasdale, 1978) so that it is now somewhat more complicated than the original version (which was based primarily on animal studies). When a person finds that he is helpless, Seligman now says, he asks himself "Why?" The answers the individual comes up with will determine how serious the effects will be. For example, a student who does very poorly on a math test may decide that the problem is specific ("I'm no good at math") or global ("I'm dumb"). Both of these explanations focus on the student himself. Alternately, he may decide that the problem is external ("This was a bad math test"). The person who blames himself and sees it as a global problem is more likely to suffer from a severe depression.

This revision of Seligman's theory is important because it is a good example of several new trends in behaviorism. As learning theorists begin to study people rather than animals, they are finding that some of the old models are too simple. More importantly, they are finding that they cannot focus simply on what people *do*. What people *think* is also important.

Learned helplessness may be a major cause of depression.

LEARNING COMPLICATED SKILLS

When you acquire a skill such as knitting, photography, shooting a basketball, or talking persuasively, you learn more than just a single new stimulus-response relationship. You learn a large number of them, and you learn how to put them together into a large, smooth-flowing unit. Psychologists

Figure 2.10
Psychologists shape behavior by using reinforcement to sculpture new responses out of old ones. In some traditional cultures, new behaviors are taught by literally molding the learner's body.

have devoted considerable attention to how new responses are acquired and to how they are put together in complex skills.

Shaping is a process in which reinforcement is used to sculpt new responses out of old (Figure 2.10). An experimenter can use this method to teach a rat to do something it has never done before and would never do if left to itself. He can shape it, for example, to raise a miniature flag. The rat is physically capable of standing on its hind legs and using its mouth to pull a miniature-flag–raising cord, but at present it does not do so. The rat probably will not perform this unusual action by accident, so the experimenter begins by rewarding the rat for any action similar to the wanted responses, using reinforcement to produce successive, or closer and closer, approximations of the desired behavior.

Imagine the rat roaming around on a table with the flag apparatus in the middle. The rat inspects everything and finally sniffs at the flagpole. The experimenter immediately reinforces this response by giving the rat a food pellet. Now the rat frequently sniffs the flagpole, hoping to get another pellet, but the experimenter waits until the rat lifts a paw before he gives it another reward. This process continues, with the experimenter reinforcing close responses and then waiting for even closer ones. Eventually, he has the rat on its hind legs nibbling at the cord. Suddenly the rat seizes the cord in its teeth and yanks it. Immediately the rat is rewarded, and it begins pulling rapidly on the cord. A new response has been shaped.

Shaping has been used to teach language skills to impaired children. Psychologists at first reward the children for simple sounds, such as "bah." Later the children are only rewarded for complete words, such as "beans," and later for complete sentences, such as "Beans, please." Many such children have successfully learned to use some language by this method (Lovaas *et al.*, 1967).

Combining Responses: Chaining

In order to learn a skill, a person must be able to put various new responses together. Responses that follow one another in a sequence are put together in **response chains.** Each response produces the signal for the next one. For example, to hammer a nail into a board, you would have to put together the following chain of responses: pick up the hammer, pick up the nail, position the nail, swing the hammer, hit the nail, swing the hammer, hit the nail, and so on until the nail is completely sunk in. Each hit of the nail is a signal that you are striking it correctly, and the nail's being flush with the board's surface is a signal that no further responses are required.

In learning, chains of responses are organized into larger *response patterns*. For example, the complex skill of swimming has three major chains that are combined to make up the whole swimming pattern: an arm-stroking chain, a breathing chain, and a leg-kicking chain (Figure 2.11). After much practice, you no longer have to think about the different steps involved. The behavior takes on a rhythm of its own: the chains of responses flow naturally as soon as you dive into the water.

Figure 2.11
In learning a skill, responses that follow one another in sequence are put together in chains, and the chains are then organized into response patterns. The complex skill of swimming has three major parts: arm stroke, breathing, and leg kicking.

It is often necessary to learn simple responses before mastering the complex pattern. If you cannot hit a nail with a hammer, you certainly cannot build a house. Therefore, before a person can learn to perform a particular skill, he or she must learn all the subordinate skills that make the larger skill possible.

MODELING

Up to this point it would seem that there are two types of learning: emotional responding, conditioned by the close association of neutral and unconditioned stimuli; and operant responses, learned either by reward or punishment. But the informal observations you have been making all your life concerning learning probably suggest to you that there is more to learning than this—that, in fact, we most often learn by imitating others. This is especially true of social responses—when we learn how to behave in a new situation by watching how others behave. When you go to a concert for the first time, you may be very hesitant about where to go, when to enter (especially if you are late), when to clap, how to get a better seat after the first intermission, and so on. So you observe others, follow them, and soon you are an "old hand."

We would expect imitation to be responsible for more basic forms of behavior as well, when the proper response is essential to life. Trial-and-error learning is not useful if the punishment for failure to emit the response is to be eaten by a predator. Thus, correct avoidance behavior often must be learned by imitating.

The general term for this kind of learning is *modeling*. It includes three different types of effects. In the simplest case the behavior of others simply increases the chances that we will do the same thing. We clap when others do, look up at a building if everyone else is looking there, and copy the styles and verbal expressions of our peers. But no learning occurs in this case, in the sense of acquiring new responses. We simply perform old responses that we otherwise might be using.

The second type of modeling is usually called observational learning, or simply, imitation. In this sort of learning an observer watches a model perform a behavior and is later able to reproduce it closely, though the observer was unable to do this before observing the model. An example is watching someone use an unfamiliar tool, either live or on film, and afterward being able to handle the tool yourself.

A third type of modeling involves disinhibition. When an observer watches someone else engage in a threatening activity without being punished, the observer may find it easier to engage in that behavior later. For example, someone with a snake phobia may watch another person handling snakes (Figure 2.12). Such observation may help to alleviate the phobia. This procedure is used in clinical work, as we will see in the chapter on therapies.

What happens when an observer learns by watching? Early theorists believed that we have some sort of "instinct" for imitation, and, indeed, it is

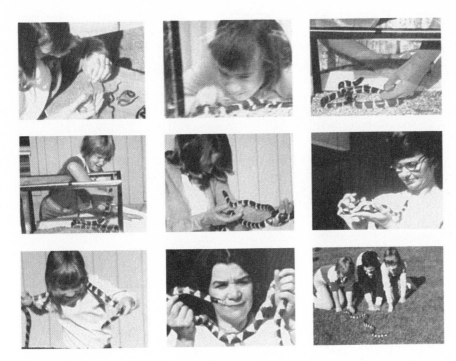

Figure 2.12
Bandura's modeling technique for eliminating snake phobia. In a procedure called live modeling with participation, subjects imitate a model's performance in handling the snake.

probable that some animals do imitate automatically, especially when they are very young and have good models constantly around them: their parents. Operant-conditioning theorists such as Skinner have suggested that imitation itself is a kind of response, one that is often reinforced because it works so well. That is, the behavior of others comes to function as a discriminative stimulus for a sort of matching behavior, which is then reinforced because it works on the environment or because other persons tend to reinforce such matching (as when a mother praises her child for correctly imitating her words).

USING PSYCHOLOGY

Behavior Modification

The term "behavior modification" often appears in magazine articles describing research on changing people's behavior through drugs, "mind control," or even brain surgery. In fact, it is none of these things. **Behavior modification** refers to the systematic application of learning principles to change people's actions and feelings.

When you give your little brother a quarter to leave you alone, that is very much like behavior modification. What distinguishes behavior modification from common-sense approaches is the fact that it involves a careful series of well-defined steps to change behavior. And the success of each step is carefully evaluated to find the best solution for a given situation.

The behavior modifier usually begins by defining a problem very carefully in concrete terms. For example, a mother might complain that her son is messy. If she used behavior modification to reform the child, she would first have to define "messy" in objective terms: he does not make his bed in the morning, he drops his coat on the couch when he comes inside, and so on. She would not worry about where his bad habits come from. Rather she would work out a system of rewards and punishments aimed at getting Johnnie to make his bed, hang up his coat, and so on.

Both operant- and classical-conditioning principles have been used in behavior modification. Classical-conditioning principles are particularly useful in helping people to overcome fears, and we shall discuss them when we consider the problem of treating abnormal behavior (Chapter 16). But, as you will see in the following examples, operant-conditioning principles have also been applied to everyday problems.

The Personalized System of Instruction

The **personalized system of instruction,** or **PSI,** was introduced by Fred Keller at the New University of Brasilia in the 1960s. The Keller Plan, as PSI is sometimes called, is a special system for teaching college courses.

In PSI the course material is broken down into a series of small units consisting of readings, lectures, or labs. Each unit is clearly defined so that students know exactly what skills they have to master and what information they must absorb to complete the unit. Individual students learn the material at their own pace and then come to class for a short quiz whenever they feel they're ready. If they pass the quiz, they go on to the next unit. If they fail the quiz, they either study some more or review the unit with an instructor until they can pass the quiz. A student who completes all the units in the course receives an A, no matter how many tests he or she failed along the way. A student who completes most of the units receives a B, and so on. There are no required lectures in a Keller Plan course.

There are a number of advantages to PSI. First, students receive immediate reinforcement for learning each unit. They do not have to wait for a midterm or final exam to learn how well they are doing. Discussions with instructors also provide immediate reinforcement: students can identify what confuses them, grasp the material, and see that the instructor knows they have grasped it. Second, PSI eliminates some of the aversive aspects of traditional classes. Students do not have a schedule forced on them. They do not have to sit through lectures on material they already know or lectures on material they cannot understand because they haven't read an assignment yet. Indeed, they do not have to attend lectures at all. Finally, students are on a fixed-ratio reinforcement schedule—they know they will get an A if they complete all the units. In addition, the instructor can teach later concepts, knowing that earlier ones have already been mastered.

PSI has proved to be an effective way of teaching and learning. Students who take courses structured in this way generally do better than students in traditional classes. When Arthur Robin (1976) reviewed all the research that compared PSI with traditional courses, he found that PSI students clearly learned more in thirty out of thirty-nine studies. (Traditional students scored better in only one study.) PSI courses were also more popular. They received higher ratings on course-evaluation questionnaires.

One problem with PSI courses, however, is that many students fail to complete them. Robin found a dropout rate of 14 percent in Keller Plan courses versus 10 percent for comparable traditionally run classes. It seems that poor students and procrastinators who put everything off until the last moment are most likely to have problems with this approach.

Token Economies

Psychologists tried an experiment with a group of extremely disenchanted boys in Washington, D.C. In fact, the boys had been labeled "uneducable" and placed in the National Training School. The experimenters used what is known as a **token economy** to motivate the boys. The youngsters received points for good grades on tests. They could "cash" these points in for such rewards as snacks, lounge privileges, or items in a mail-order catalog. In other words, they created a system that worked like the Chimp-O-Mat, discussed earlier. Within a few months, a majority of the students showed a significant increase in IQ scores (an average gain of twelve and a half points). The boys continued to improve in the months that followed, showing that they were, indeed, educable (Cohen and Filipczak, 1971).

In another experiment teachers used a token economy to teach preschoolers in a Head Start program to write, and compared their scores on writing tests with those achieved by children who did not participate in a token economy. The youngsters who received tokens, which they could exchange for food, movies, and other rewards, improved dramatically. Equally important, they seemed to be developing a very positive attitude toward school. The youngsters who did not receive tokens made very little progress (Miller and Schneider, 1970).

Thus, in token economies, people are systematically paid to act appropriately. But in the real world, behaviorists argue, the rewards are just as real; they are simply less systematic. In overcrowded mental hospitals, for example, the only way some patients can get attention is by "acting crazy." Most staff members simply don't have time to bother with people who are not causing trouble. Since attention from the staff is reinforcing for these patients, in effect people are rewarded for undesirable behavior. By systematically rewarding only desirable behavior, token economies have been set up in prisons, mental hospitals, halfway houses, and classrooms. (See also Chapter 16.)

Self-Control

In token economies, a researcher sets up an elaborate system of reinforcers to get people to act the way he wants. One of the most important new trends in behavior modification is a growing emphasis on asking people to set up personal systems of rewards and punishments to shape their own thoughts and actions.

In the past, behaviorists limited their studies to observable behavior (Chapter 1), and made little attempt to observe or change the way people thought. But as more learning researchers began to study humans (instead of focusing exclusively on animals), it became obvious that what people *do* is only part of the story. As we described above, for example, Martin Seligman recently expanded his theory of learned helplessness to try to explain why some people develop long-lasting depressions while others seem to get over them. Part of the difference, Seligman argues, is based on what people *think*—that is, how they interpret their failures.

As in any application of behavior modification, the first step in self-control is to define the problem. A person who smokes too much would be encouraged to actually count how many cigarettes he smoked every hour of the day and note what kinds of situations led him to smoke. (After a meal? When talking to friends? Driving to work?) Similarly, a person who had a very poor opinion of herself would have to define

Breaking a Habit: Smoking

You don't have to be a psychologist to know how difficult it is to quit smoking. Here are some tips from behavior therapists on how to break the habit.

Start by keeping records for a week or so of the times and places you smoke every single cigarette. These records will give you a much clearer picture of your problem and the precise situations that are likely to prove most tempting. Continue to keep these records as you try to cut down or quit to find out what works for you.

You can cut down impulsive smoking by switching the place you carry cigarettes and never carrying matches or a lighter. Searching for the pack each time and having to ask someone for a light will help make you more aware of your habit. You might strike a bargain with yourself— for every day you go without a cigarette, for example, you'll let yourself watch an hour of soap operas or game shows on TV.

Don't think the habit is conquered if you go for a day—or even a month—without a cigarette. Millions of people have stopped smoking, but they never said it was easy.

For more details, see R. L. Williams and J. D. Long, *Toward A Self-Managed Life Style,* 2nd ed. Boston: Houghton Mifflin, 1979.

Figure 2.13
A Smokenders group. This method of learning not to smoke makes use of a variety of techniques to help people break the habit.

the problem more concretely. She might begin by counting the number of self-deprecating remarks she made and thoughts she had. Researchers have found that just keeping track of behavior in this way often leads a person to start changing it.

The next step may be to set up a single behavioral contract. One soda lover who had trouble studying decided that she would only allow herself a Pepsi after she studied for half an hour. Her cola addiction remained strong, but her study time increased dramatically under this system. A behavioral contract simply involves choosing a reinforcer (buying a new shirt, watching a favorite TV program) and making it contingent on some unpleasant but necessary act (getting to work on time, washing the kitchen floor). These contracts are most likely to succeed if you also use successive approximations—starting with an easy task and gradually making it more difficult. For example, you might begin by studying ten minutes before rewarding yourself, and gradually increase it to an hour.

Other more elaborate procedures are sometimes used for self-control. Aversive imagery, or using unpleasant thoughts to control behavior, is one. For example, a young man who eats too much and finds that his waist is going from a 32 to a 44 might try the following technique to help him stick to his diet: every time he is tempted by a chocolate-fudge sundae, he simply imagines his girl friend walking around campus with her arm around another man, giggling about how chubby her former boy friend has gotten.

Behavior modifiers are now developing and testing many other techniques to help people learn to control themselves.

Improving Your Study Habits

One psychologist designed a program to help students improve their study habits and tried it on a group of volunteers. The students were told to set a time when they would go to a small room in the library they had not used before, taking only the materials they wanted to study. They were then to work for as long as they remained interested—and *only* for as long as they were interested. As soon as they found themselves fidgeting, daydreaming, becoming drowsy or bored, they were to make the decision to stop studying. There was only one condition. They had to read one more page, or solve one more simple problem, before they left. But even if this made them want to study longer, they were instructed to hold to their decision to leave the library, go for a cup of coffee, call a friend, or do whatever they wanted to do.

The next day they were asked to repeat the same procedure, adding a second page to the amount they read between the time they decided to leave and the time they actually left the library. The third day they added a third page, and so on. Students who followed this procedure found that in time they were able to study for longer periods than before, that they were studying more effectively, and that they didn't mind studying so much.

Why did this procedure work? Many students force themselves to study. One common technique is to go to the library to avoid distractions. The result may be hours spent staring at a book without really learning anything. Repeated failures to get anything accomplished and sheer discomfort turn studying into a dreaded chore. The library becomes a conditioned aversive stimulus—you hate it because you've spent so many uncomfortable hours there. The procedure was designed to change these feelings.

Requiring students to leave as soon as they felt distracted helped to reduce the negative, punishing emotions associated with studying. The students stopped when these feelings began. Studying in a new place removed the conditioned aversive stimulus. Thus, aversive responses were not conditioned to the subject matter or the room, as they are when students force themselves to work.

Second, the procedure made use of successive approximations. The students began by reading just one page after they became bored, and only gradually increased the assignment. This also reduced the aversive response to studying. The task no longer seemed so difficult.

Finally, when they left their work, the students received two kinds of positive reinforcement. They had the satisfaction of knowing they had followed the procedure and had completed an assignment (namely, one more page). And they were free to do something they enjoyed. Thus they rewarded or reinforced themselves for however much studying they did (Fox, 1966). You might try this procedure.

SUMMARY

1. Learning is a lasting change in behavior that results from experience.

2. Classical conditioning was discovered by Ivan Pavlov. In this form of learning, a previously neu-

tral stimulus comes to elicit a response because it has been paired with a stimulus that already elicited a response. Extinction of a classically conditioned response occurs when the conditioned stimulus is no longer associated with the unconditioned stimulus.

3. Operant conditioning occurs when an organism's activities are either reinforced or punished. Any consequence that increases the likelihood of a response is called a reinforcer. Extinction occurs when a response decreases in frequency because it is no longer reinforced.

4. Different schedules of reinforcement produce different patterns of behavior. When reinforcement depends on number of responses (ratio schedules), the organism tends to respond faster than it does if reinforcement depends on time (interval schedules). When responses are reinforced on a regular basis (fixed schedules), the organism will tend to pause after a reward. If reinforcers appear irregularly (variable schedules), the organism will keep going at a steady rate. Intermittently reinforced responses disappear more slowly during extinction than do continuously reinforced ones. In one sense, then, a response is learned better if it is only reinforced some of the time.

5. Signals are stimuli that come to be associated with getting rewards or punishments. Organisms have the ability to generalize among and discriminate between signals. A signal becomes a conditioned reinforcer when the signal itself serves as a reward or punisher.

6. Aversive control means using unpleasant influ-ences on behavior. In punishment, the unpleasant event comes as a consequence of a response and the response decreases in frequency. In avoidance and escape conditioning, the response has the effect of removing the unpleasant event. In negative reinforcement, the frequency of a response that terminates an unpleasant event increases.

7. Factors that influence learning include feedback, transfer, and practice.

8. Organisms can learn to learn by discovering certain strategies. A strategy for solving problems or learning tasks can be applied to subsequent, similar situations. Organisms learn strategies of laziness or helplessness if they experience situations in which their behavior has no consequences.

9. To learn a complicated skill, a person must acquire and coordinate a number of new responses. The learning of skills may be facilitated by imitation and shaping. To learn a skill, one must put new responses together in chains, which are then organized into response patterns.

10. Modeling is a kind of learning that results from imitation.

11. Behavior modification involves the systematic application of learning principles to change people's actions and feelings. Two examples are the personalized system of instruction and token economies. It is also possible to change one's own habits through reinforcement.

GLOSSARY

aversive control: The process of influencing behavior by means of aversive, or unpleasant, stimuli.

avoidance: A response increases in frequency to postpone or prevent a painful stimulus before it starts.

behavior modification: The systematic application of learning principles to change people's actions and feelings.

classical conditioning: A learning procedure in which a stimulus that normally elicits a given response is repeatedly preceded by a neutral stimulus (one that usually does not elicit the response). Eventually, the neutral stimulus will evoke a similar response when presented by itself.

conditioned reinforcer: A stimulus that increases the frequency of a response because it has become a signal for a stimulus which is reinforcing.

conditioned response (CR): In classical conditioning, the learned response to a conditioned stimulus.

conditioned stimulus (CS): In classical conditioning, a once-neutral stimulus that has come to elicit a given response after a period of training in which it has been paired with an unconditioned stimulus (UCS).

discrimination: The ability to respond differently to similar but distinct stimuli.

escape: Performing a behavior that removes the

organism from a painful stimulus or otherwise terminates the stimulus.

extinction: The gradual disappearance of a conditioned response because the reinforcement is withheld or because the conditioned stimulus is repeatedly presented without the unconditioned stimulus.

feedback: Information received after an action as to its effectiveness or correctness.

fixed-interval schedule: A schedule of reinforcement in which a specific amount of time must elapse before a response will elicit reinforcement.

fixed-ratio schedule: A schedule of reinforcement in which a specific number of correct responses is required before reinforcement can be obtained.

generalization: Responding similarly to a range of similar stimuli.

learning: A lasting change in behavior that results from experience.

negative reinforcement: Increasing the strength of a given response by removing or preventing a painful stimulus when the response occurs.

neutral stimulus: A stimulus that does not initially elicit a response.

operant conditioning: A form of conditioning in which a certain action is reinforced or punished, resulting in corresponding increases or decreases in the likelihood that similar actions will occur again.

personalized systems of instruction (PSI):   Breaking course material down into a number of small units and allowing students to proceed from unit to unit at their own pace.

primary reinforcers: Natural rewards.

punishers: Negative consequences that decrease the likelihood of a behavior occurring again.

reinforcement: Immediately following a particular response with a reward in order to strengthen that response.

response: A unit of behavior.

response chains: Learned responses that follow one another in sequence, each response producing the signal for the next.

shaping: A technique of operant conditioning in which the desired behavior is "molded" by first rewarding any act similar to that behavior and then requiring closer and closer approximations to the desired behavior before giving the reward.

signals: In operant conditioning, behavioral cues (or stimuli) that are associated with reward or punishment.

stimulus: Any environmental event or circumstance to which an organism can respond.

token economy: A form of conditioning in which desirable behavior is reinforced with tokens, which can be accumulated and exchanged for various rewards.

transfer: The effects of past learning on the ability to learn new tasks.

unconditioned response (UCR):   In classical conditioning, an organism's automatic (or natural) reaction to a stimulus.

unconditioned stimulus (UCS):   A stimulus that elicits a certain response without previous training.

variable-interval schedule: A schedule of reinforcement in which varying amounts of time must elapse before a response will obtain reinforcement.

variable-ratio schedule: A schedule of reinforcement in which a variable number of responses are required before reinforcement can be obtained.

ACTIVITIES

1. Try this experiment in classical conditioning: Sit at a table with a lamp you can switch on and off. Place a glass of water and a spoon within easy reach. Have your subject sit across from you so you can observe his or her eyes. First, turn off the lamp to observe how much your subject's eyes dilate under normal conditions. Then switch on the lamp and begin your conditioning trials. Take the

spoon and tap the glass of water, and then immediately turn off the lamp. Let the subject's eyes adjust, then switch the lamp on and repeat the process several times. Be sure to allow time in each case for the eyes to dilate. After several trials, tap the glass but leave the lamp on. What happened to your subject's eyes? Why?

2. Businesses often make use of conditioning techniques in their commercials. They associate the name of their product with pleasant tunes or exciting scenes, so that the name alone will elicit conditioned relaxation or excitement. Think of specific ads that use these techniques. Can you think of selling methods that use operant conditioning?

3. Using the principles outlined in the skill-learning section of the chapter, how would you go about learning to do a simple dance step; to make an omelet; to drive a car; to pitch a baseball?

4. Which of the schedules of reinforcement do your instructors generally use in conducting their classes? How would your classes be different if they used the other schedules? Give examples for your answers and justify your reasoning.

5. Conduct an operant-conditioning experiment of your own to modify the behavior of a member of your family or a friend. Tell him or her as much or as little as you choose, but carefully record everything that you do tell this person. Use positive reinforcement only, and record all results. Using the procedures given in the chapter, write a paper describing your experiment in behavior modification.

6. In the experiment on learned helplessness, the animals who were unable to change their situation for long periods of time seemed unable or unwilling to change when the possibility was opened to them. What implications do such experiments have for humans? Can you think of situations in your life that have had the effect of learned helplessness?

7. Take a real-life situation, such as waiting for an elevator, eating a sandwich, or climbing a tree, and analyze the stimuli, responses, rewards, punishments, and signals in the situation.

8. Select some particular subject of study that you find difficult or unpleasant. Whenever you sit down to study this subject, play one of your favorite records or tapes as you study. In time, the favorable feelings toward this music may become associated with the subject of study, making it easier to learn and remember.

SUGGESTED READINGS

BANDURA, A. (ED.). *Psychological Modeling: Conflicting Theories.* Chicago: Aldine-Atherton, 1971. Discusses the theories behind modeling and observational learning; discusses research on modeling as a therapeutic technique.

CARMAN, ROBERT A., AND ADAMS, W. ROYCE. *Study Skills: A Student's Guide for Survival.* New York: Wiley, 1972. This paperback is in a programmed format. The authors give specific instruction on improving reading abilities, how to approach textbooks, how to take exams, and how to write papers. It is written in a chatty and humorous vein.

MC INTIRE, ROGER. *For Love of Children: Behavioral Psychology for Parents.* Del Mar, Calif.: CRM Books, 1970. As the title suggests, this book is a guide to child rearing based on the principles of operant conditioning. The author's premise is that children (and everyone) behave in ways that have been reinforced. Parents can, therefore, control their child's behavior by making themselves aware of why behavior is occurring and by shaping desired behavior in accordance with conditioning principles.

SELIGMAN, MARTIN E. P. *Helplessness.* San Francisco: W. H. Freeman, 1975. A readable introduction to learned helplessness and its relation to depression.

SKINNER, B. F. *Walden Two.* New York: Macmillan, 1968; originally published in 1949. Skinner's best-known work is a novel of an ideal, behaviorally engineered community. It is readable, interesting, and instructive.

———. *Science and Human Behavior.* New York: Free Press, 1953 (paper). The author, in this widely read book, discusses the relationship between a science of behavior and everyday ways of talking about personality, self, and culture. Skinner begins with an explanation of the scientific principles of behavior and then explains his analysis of "self-control," thinking, social interaction, psychotherapy, economics, and religion.

WHALEY, D. *Contingency Management.* Behaviordelia, P.O. Box 1044, Kalamazoo, Mich. 49001. A 250-page comic book created by Whaley and some of his graduate students. A painless and humorous

introduction to the conditioning approach to learning.

WHALEY, D., AND MALLOT, R. *Elementary Principles of Behavior.* New York: Appleton-Century-Crofts, 1971. One of the most readable introductory texts on Skinnerian behaviorism and the principles of behavior modification. The authors put behavioral techniques to practice by pacing and rewarding the reader throughout the text.

BIBLIOGRAPHY

ABRAMSON, LYN Y., SELIGMAN, MARTIN E. P., AND TEASDALE, JOHN D. "Learned Helplessness in Humans: Critique and Reformulation." *Journal of Abnormal Psychology,* 87 (1978): 49–74.

BANDURA, A. "Analysis of Modeling Processes." In *Psychological Modeling: Conflicting Theories,* ed. by A. Bandura. Chicago: Aldine-Atherton, 1971, pp. 1–62.

COHEN, H., AND FILIPCZAK, J. *A New Learning Environment.* San Francisco: Jossey-Bass, 1971.

FISCHER, K. W. *The Organization of Simple Learning.* Chicago: Markham, 1973.

FOX, L. JUNGBERG. "Effecting the Use of Efficient Study Habits." In *Control of Human Behavior,* ed. by R. Ulrich, T. Stachnik, and J. Mabry. Vol. 1. Glenview, Ill.: Scott, Foresman, 1966.

GARCIA, JOHN, AND KOELLING, R. A. "The Relation of Cue to Consequence in Avoidance Learning." *Psychonomic Science,* 4 (1966): 123–124.

GERST, M. S. "Symbolic Coding Processes in Observational Learning." *Journal of Personality and Social Psychology,* 19 (1971): 9–17.

GUSTAVSON, C. R., ET AL. "Coyote Predation Control by Aversive Conditioning." *Science,* 184 (1974): 581–583.

HARLOW, HARRY F. "The Formation of Learning Sets." *Psychological Review,* 56 (1949): 51–65.

HIROTO, D. S. "Locus of Control and Learned Helplessness." *Journal of Experimental Psychology,* 102 (1974): 187–193.

HONIG, W. H. (ED.). *Operant Behavior: Areas of Research and Application.* New York: Appleton-Century-Crofts, 1966.

LOGUE, ALEXANDRA. "Waiter, There's a Phobia in My Soup." *Psychology Today,* 12 (1978): 36.

LOVAAS, O. I., ET AL. "Establishment of Imitation and Its Use for the Development of Complex Behavior in Schizophrenic Children." *Behavior Research and Therapy,* 5 (August 1967): 171–181.

MIKULAS, WILLIAM L. *Behavior Modification.* New York: Harper & Row, 1978.

MILLER, L. K., AND SCHNEIDER, R. "The Use of a Token System in Project Headstart." *Journal of Applied Behavior Analysis,* 3 (1970): 213–220.

PAVLOV, IVAN P. *Conditioned Reflexes.* Trans. by G. V. Anrep. London: Oxford University Press, 1927.

REYNOLDS, G. S. *A Primer of Operant Conditioning.* Glenview, Ill.: Scott, Foresman, 1968.

ROBIN, ARTHUR L. "Behavioral Instruction in the College Classroom." *Review of Educational Research,* 46 (1976): 313–354.

SAHAKIAN, WILLIAM S. *Psychology of Learning.* Chicago: Markam, 1970.

SKINNER, B. F. *The Behavior of Organisms.* New York: Appleton-Century-Crofts, 1961.

––––––. *About Behaviorism.* New York: Knopf, 1974.

WATSON, DAVID L., AND THARP, RONALD G. *Self-directed Behavior: Self-modification for Personal Adjustment.* Monterey, Calif.: Brooks/Cole, 1972.

WATSON, JOHN B., AND RAYNER, ROSALIE. "Conditioned Emotional Reactions." *Journal of Experimental Psychology,* 3 (1920): 1–14.

WOLFE, JOHN B. "Effectiveness of Token-Rewards for Chimpanzees." *Comparative Psychological Monographs,* 12 (1936): whole no. 5.

Memory and Thought

Is anything more complex than the human mind?

Consider all the material stored in your memory: your social security number, the capital of South Dakota, "The Star Spangled Banner," your first love's phone number, the major generals of the Civil War, the starting lineup for the Boston Red Sox, where you were when Bobby Kennedy was shot, your best friend in the first grade, and so on. What kind of incredible filing system allows you to instantly recover a Beatles' song or your favorite recipe? And how does all that information fit in your head?

Going beyond memory, how do we think? How do we solve problems? How do we create ideas? No mysteries are more fundamental, and researchers are just beginning to investigate human thought. Psychologists refer to all cognitive and mental activities—from memorizing lists of numbers to writing poems and inventing new technologies—as *information processing*. This involves three steps: input, central processing, and output. **Input** is the information people receive from their senses. **Central processing** is the storing (in memory) and sorting (by thought) of this information in the brain. **Output** refers to the ideas and actions that result from processing.

TAKING INFORMATION IN

Information is any event that reduces uncertainty. For example, when a traffic light changes from red to green, it provides you with information—it reduces your uncertainty about whether you should step on the gas. Information is transmitted through the senses in many forms—voices, musical sounds, sweet tastes, pungent odors, colorful images, rough textures, pain-

Figure 3.1
No mysteries are more fundamental than how we think, remember, solve problems, and create ideas.

ful stings. At any given moment a confusing array of sights, sounds, smells, and other sensations compete for your attention. If you accepted all these inputs, you would be completely overwhelmed. Two processes help people to narrow sensory inputs to a manageable number: selective attention and feature extraction.

Selective Attention

The ability to pick and choose among the various available inputs is called **selective attention.** For example, if you are at a large party where the music is turned up and everyone is talking, you can focus on a friend's voice and ignore all other sounds. In a way, selective attention is like tuning in a specific television channel.

Unlike a television dial, however, selective attention does not completely block out the other programs or stimuli. You may be listening attentively to what a friend is saying, but at the same time you are unconsciously monitoring information that is coming in over other channels. If your name is mentioned in a conversation going on three feet away, you will notice it and tune into that input. If someone strolls by dressed in a

Figure 3.2
The "filter model" of how we listen to the input to only one ear at a time during shadowing. (After Broadbent, 1958.)

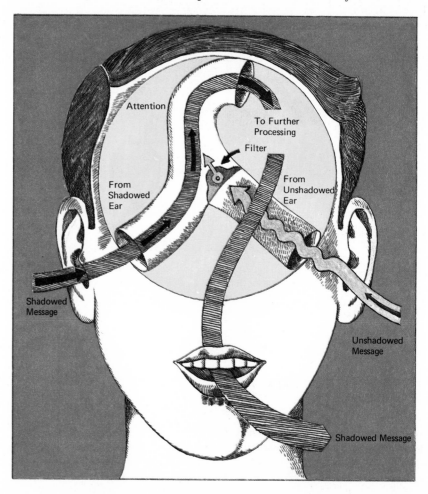

bathing suit, snorkel, and fins, you will notice him. The "cocktail-party phenomenon," as selective attention is sometimes called, allows you to concentrate on one thing without tuning out everything else that is happening.

In laboratory experiments, researchers have shown how selective attention affects the brain (Hernández-Peón, 1961). For example, if people are asked to pay attention to an auditory stimulus, the brain waves that record their response to sound will get larger. While this is happening, the brain waves that record their response to what they see will get smaller because they are not paying close attention to visual stimuli. If the same people are asked to pay attention to visual stimuli, the reverse occurs: visual brain waves increase while auditory brain waves decrease. A similar experiment has shown that a certain kind of brain wave diminishes but does not disappear when people are given a problem to solve or are drawn into conversation. Such experiments seem to indicate that the brain somehow evaluates the importance of the information that comes in over different channels. Top-priority information is allowed to reach the highest brain centers, whereas unimportant information is suppressed (Figure 3.2).

What makes one input more important than another? Information leading to the satisfaction of such needs as hunger and thirst has top priority. (A person who is very hungry, for example, will pay more attention to his dinner than to the dinner-table chitchat.) We also give priority to inputs that are strange and novel, such as an individual who comes to a party dressed for snorkeling. A third director of attention is interest: the more interested you are in something, the more likely you are to notice it. For example, most people "tune in" when they hear their name mentioned; we're all interested in what other people have to say about us. Likewise, if you become interested in chess, you will suddenly begin to notice newspaper articles about chess, chess sets in store windows, and references to chess moves in everyday speech (for example, "stalemate"). These inputs are not new. They were there last year and the year before, but you simply weren't interested enough to notice them.

Feature Extraction

Selective attention is only the first step in narrowing down input. The second step is to decide which aspects of the selected channel you will focus on. This process, called **feature extraction,** involves locating the outstanding characteristics of incoming information (Figure 3.3). If you want to identify the make of a car, you look for certain features—the shape of the fenders, the proportion of height to length, and so on. For the most part, you ignore such features as color, upholstery, and tires, which tell you little about the make of the car. Similarly, when you read, you focus on the important words, skimming over such words as "the," "and," or "for example."

Being able to extract the significant features of an input helps a person to identify it and compare it to other inputs. For example, you are able to distinguish faces from one another and, at the same time, see resemblances. You may notice that all the members of a family have similar

Figure 3.3
Can you spot the hidden faces in this picture? To find them, it is necessary for you to extract those features that define a human face from a large amount of irrelevant and misleading information.

noses, yet you are able to recognize each person on the basis of other features.

Obviously, feature extraction depends to some extent on experience—on knowing what to look for. This is especially true where fine distinctions must be made. It takes considerable expertise to distinguish an original Rembrandt from a skillful forgery. Most of us cannot identify the year of the wine we are drinking or the vineyard from which it came, but a gourmet who knows what to look for can.

Like selective attention, feature extraction is an evaluative process. If you are reading a novel for pleasure, you may look for the "juicy" parts. If you're reading a historical biography to prepare for an exam, you'll probably still look for the juicy parts. When you don't find any, you go ahead and concentrate on the other facts.

STORING INFORMATION

In order to be used, the inputs that reach the brain must be registered, held onto, perhaps "filed" for future reference. We call the storage of inputs **memory.** Psychologists distinguish among three kinds of memory, each of which has a different purpose and time span. **Sensory storage** holds information for only an instant; **short-term memory** keeps it in mind for about twenty seconds; **long-term memory** stores it indefinitely.

Sensory Storage

The senses—sight, hearing, and so on—seem to be able to hold an input for a fraction of a second before it disappears. For example, when you watch a movie, you do not notice the gaps between frames. The actions seem smooth because each frame is held in sensory storage until the next frame arrives.

Sperling (1960) demonstrated this phenomenon in an ingenious experiment. He used a tachistoscope (a device that presents a picture for a very brief time) to present a group of letters to people for a twentieth of a second. Previous studies had shown that if you present a stimulus like this

$$
\begin{array}{ccc}
T & D & R \\
S & R & N \\
F & Z & K
\end{array}
$$

people will usually be able to tell you four or five of the letters. Sperling believed that people took a mental photograph of the letters, and were able to read back only a few before the picture faded. He told the people in his experiment that after he flashed the letters on the tachistoscope screen, he would present a tone. Upon hearing a high tone, the subjects were to tell him the top row, a medium tone the middle row, and a low tone the bottom row. Once people learned this system, they were indeed able to remember any row of letters. Thus, he proved that the subject retains a brief image of the whole picture so that he or she can still read off the items in the correct row *after* the picture has left the screen.

The information held momentarily by the senses has not yet been narrowed down or analyzed. It is like a short-lived but highly detailed photograph or tape recording. However, by the time information gets to the next stage—short-term memory—it has been analyzed, identified, and simplified so that it can be conveniently stored and handled for a longer time.

Short-Term Memory

The things you have in your conscious mind at any one moment are being held in short-term memory. Short-term memory does not necessarily involve paying close attention. You have probably had the experience of listening to someone only partially and then having that person accuse you of not paying attention. You deny it, and, in order to prove your innocence, you repeat to him, word for word, the last words he said. You can do this because you are holding the words in short-term memory. Usually, however, the sense of what he was saying does not register on you until you repeat the words out loud. Repeating the words makes you pay attention to them. This is what psychologists mean by rehearsal.

Rehearsal. To keep information in short-term memory for more than a few seconds, you have to repeat it to yourself, in your mind or out loud. When you look up a telephone number, for example, you can remember the seven digits long enough to dial them *if* you repeat them several times. If you are distracted or make a mistake in dialing, the chances are you will have to look the number up again. It has been lost from short-term memory.

Psychologists have measured short-term memory by seeing how long a subject can retain a piece of information without rehearsal. The experimenter shows the subject a card with three letters on it, such as CPQ. However, at the same time the experimenter makes the subject think about something else in order to prevent her from rehearsing the letters. For example, she might ask the subject to start counting backward by threes from 798 as soon as she flashes the card. If the subject performs this task for only a short time, she will usually remember the letters. But if she is kept from rehearsing for more than eighteen seconds, the information is forgotten. Thus, short-term memory seems to last for less than twenty seconds without rehearsal.

Chunking. Short-term memory is limited not only in its duration, but in its capacity as well. It can hold only about seven unrelated items, If, for example, someone quickly reels off a series of digits to you, you will be able to keep only about seven or eight of them in your immediate memory. Beyond that number, confusion among them will set in. The same would be true if the unrelated items were a random set of words. We may not notice this limit to our capacity because we usually do not have to store so many unrelated items in our immediate memory. Either the items are

Short-term memory can hold only about seven unrelated items.

Figure 3.4
Glance quickly at the left figure in this pair, then look away. How many dots did you see? Now do the same with the right figure. You were probably more sure and more accurate in your answer for the right figure because the organization of the dots into a small number of chunks makes it easier to process the information.

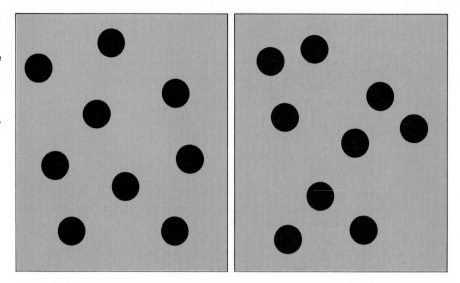

related (as when we listen to someone speak) or they are rehearsed and placed in long-term memory.

The most interesting aspect of this limit, discovered by George Miller (1956), is that it involves about seven items of any kind. Each item may consist of a collection of many other items, but if they are all packaged into one "chunk" then there is still only one item. Thus we can remember about seven unrelated sets of initials, such as COMSAT, DDT, SST, or the initials of our favorite radio stations, even though we could not remember all the letters separately. This occurs because we have connected, or "chunked," them together previously, so that DDT is one item, not three.

One of the tricks of memorizing a lot of information quickly is to chunk together the items as fast as they come in. If we connect items in groups, we have fewer to remember. For example, we remember new phone numbers in two or three chunks (555–6794 or 555–67–94) rather than as a string of seven digits (5–5–5–6–7–9–4). As Figure 3.4 illustrates, we use chunking to remember visual as well as verbal inputs.

Even with chunking, short-term memory is only a temporary device. It contains information labeled "of possible interest." If the information is worth holding onto, it must be transferred to long-term memory.

Long-Term Memory

Long-term memory is where we store information for future use. It can be thought of as a kind of filing cabinet or storage bin for names, dates, words, and faces. When we say someone has a good memory, we usually mean he or she can recall a great deal of this type of information. But long-term memory also contains representations of countless experiences and sensations. You may not have thought about your childhood home for years, but you can probably still visualize it.

Long-term memory involves all the processes we have been describing. Suppose a person goes to see a play. As the actors say their lines, the sounds flow through sensory storage. Selective attention screens out other sounds, and feature extraction turns sounds into words. These words accumulate in short-term memory and form meaningful phrases and sentences.

The viewer attends to the action and changing scenery in much the same way. Together, they form chunks in her memory. An hour or two later, she will have forgotten all but the most striking lines, but she has stored the *meaning* of the lines and actions in long-term memory. The next day, she may be able to give a scene-by-scene description of the play. Throughout this process, the least important information is dropped and only the essentials are retained (Figure 3.5). A month or two later, the woman may remember only a brief outline of the plot and perhaps a few particularly impressive moments. In time she may not remember anything about the play. Other, more recently stored items block access to earlier memories or may even replace them. But if she sees the play again, she will probably recognize the lines of the play and anticipate the actions. Although it has become less accessible, it is still stored in long-term memory.

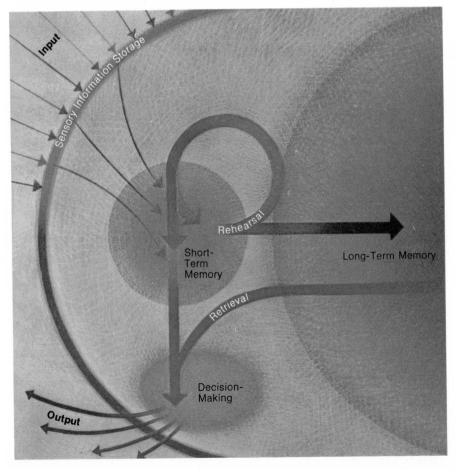

Figure 3.5
The flow of information processing. Input to the senses is stored temporarily, and some of it is passed on into short-term memory. Information may be kept in short-term memory by rehearsal or it may be passed on to long-term memory. Material stored in both short- and long-term memory is used in making decisions. The decision process results in outputs such as talking, writing, or moving.

Memory and the Brain

What happens in the brain when something is stored in long-term memory? This question is highly controversial. Although psychologists agree that some physiological changes must occur in the brain, they do not know what these changes are.

Some researchers believe that memory is due to changes in the form of protein molecules in the brain. In one experiment, a number of mice were trained to run through a maze, avoiding alleys where they would receive an electric shock. Then the mice were injected with a chemical known to disrupt protein production in the brain. Afterward, the mice could no longer remember the safe way out of the maze (Flexner, 1967). Recently, researchers (Flood, Bennett, and Orme, 1975) have been able to control the amount of "amnesia" in mice by injecting varying amounts of the chemical for certain time periods after the training task. The more of the protein-blocking chemical the mice receive, the more forgetful they become. One theory is that senility in the aged may be related to the end of protein production in the brain.

Another theory focuses on chemical-electrical changes in the brain. It may be that memory develops when the characteristics of the synapses change chemically. (As explained in Chapter 5, synapses are the gaps between nerve cells.) When something is learned, some pathways in the brain are facilitated and others inhibited. To date, it is impossible to say which of these theories is closer to the truth.

To complicate matters further, there is some controversy about just where memories are located in the brain. Karl Lashley (1929) argued that no one cell, or group of cells, can be removed to destroy a memory. Indeed, he found that he had to destroy most of the upper part of a rat's brain to erase the memory of a problem it had learned to solve. As a result, many psychologists believe that the same memories may be stored in several parts of the brain, so that destroying one area simply removes one copy. More recently, Richard Thompson (1976) and others have questioned Lashley's view. They believe that more sophisticated physiological techniques may be able to identify specific learning pathways.

All these ideas remain highly speculative. Many psychologists believe, however, that a better understanding of the processes underlying memory will be reached in the near future.

RETRIEVING INFORMATION

Stored information is useless unless it can be retrieved from memory. Once you've forgotten to send a card for your mother's birthday, it's not very consoling to prove that you have the date filed away in your brain. We've all experienced the acute embarrassment of being unable to remember a close friend's name. There are few things in life more frustrating than having a word "on the tip of your tongue," but just not being able to remember it.

The problem of memory is to store many thousands of items in such a way that you can find the one you need when you need it. The solution to **retrieval** is organization. Since human memory is extraordinarily efficient, it must be extremely well organized. Psychologists do not yet know how it is organized, but they are studying the processes involved in retrieval for clues.

Recognition

Human memory is organized in such a way as to make recognition quite easy—people can say with great accuracy whether or not something is familiar to them. If someone asked you the name of your first-grade teacher, for example, you might not remember it. But chances are that you would recognize the name if you heard it. Similarly, a multiple-choice test may bring out knowledge that a student might not be able to show on an essay test. The ability to recognize suggests that much more information is stored in memory than one might think.

The process of **recognition** provides insight into how information is stored in memory. We can recognize the sound of a particular musical instrument (say, the piano) no matter what tune is being played on it. We can also recognize a tune no matter what instrument is playing it. This pattern of recognition indicates that a single item of information may be "indexed" under the several "headings" so that it can be reached in a number of ways. Thus, "the attractive teller at the Five Cents Savings Bank" might be indexed under "Five Cents Savings Bank," "service people," potential friends," "blondes," and possibly under several other headings as well. The more categories an item is filed in, the more easily it can be retrieved.

USING PSYCHOLOGY

Eyewitness Testimony

One of the most dramatic tests of recognition memory involves the account of eyewitnesses to a crime. Few bits of evidence are more impressive than the eyewitness who tells a jury: "He's the one. I saw him do it." Indeed, Elizabeth Loftus (1974) has shown that even after a witness has been discredited (in this study, the defense attorney had proved that the witness's eyesight was too poor to see the face of a robber from where he stood), jurors were still far more likely to convict the defendant.

Lawyers can cite many cases of people who were falsely accused by the eyewitnesses to a crime. For example, in 1972 Frank Doto was arrested after seventeen eyewitnesses identified him as the man who had shot a policeman and robbed three California supermarkets. Fortunately for the innocent

Figure 3.6
Three sketches of the ''Son of Sam'' killer show that eyewitnesses have different memories of his appearance.

Mr. Doto, he was able to prove that he was nowhere near the scenes of these crimes.

Psychologists, too, have provided many demonstrations of eyewitness fallibility. In one study at Brooklyn College, Roger Buckhout (1974) staged a purse snatching in one of his classes. When fifty-two students who had seen the incident looked at two videotaped lineups, all but ten said they recognized the culprit. But thirty-five of these forty-two eyewitnesses picked the wrong man! Interestingly enough, the witnesses who were most sure of themselves were somewhat more likely to accuse an innocent man.

Sam: the latest sketches
Cops' update alters description

Elizabeth Loftus (1974) has done a fascinating series of experiments showing that when people are asked to recall the details of auto accidents, they, too, are likely to distort the facts. After groups of college students saw a filmed accident, she asked some of them, "About how fast were the cars going when they hit each other?" The average estimate was 34 miles per hour. When she substituted the word "smashed" for "hit" in the above question, another group of students remembered the cars as going significantly faster—41 miles per hour.

Lawyers have long been aware of the effects of leading questions, but the courts continue to act as if human memory is a videotape that enables the witness to conjure up an instant replay of a crime. In reality, memory involves an active process of filling in the gaps based on our attitudes and expectations. The eyewitness to a crime or an accident frequently observes a confusing situation under stressful conditions. It is no surprise to psychologists, then, that eyewitnesses are so frequently wrong.

Recall

More remarkable than the ability to recognize information is the ability to recall it. **Recall** is the active reconstruction of information. Just think about the amount of recall involved in a simple conversation. Each person uses hundreds of words involving all kinds of information, even though each word and bit of information must be retrieved separately from the storehouse of memory.

Recall involves more than searching for and finding pieces of information, however. It involves a person's knowledge, attitudes, and expectations. This was demonstrated in the following experiment. The researcher showed a group of young children a bottle of colored water, tilted as shown in Figure 3.7. The children were then asked to draw what they had seen from memory. Most of their drawings did not look at all like the original arrangement. However, six months later, when the same children were asked to draw the bottle they had seen, many did much better (Figure 3.8). Apparently they now had a better idea of what the tilted bottle *should* look like (Inhelder, 1969).

Because of this process of reconstruction, memories may change over time. They may be simplified, enriched, or distorted, depending on the individual's experiences and attitudes. This is why we sometimes make mistakes in memory. One type of mistake is called **confabulation:** a person "remembers" information that was never stored in memory. Confabulation generally occurs when an individual remembers parts of a situation and fills in the gaps by making up the rest. This is precisely what eyewitnesses to a crime often do—they fill in the holes in their memory with reasonable guesses, without even being aware that they are doing it.

Some people do not need to reconstruct information, because they have an **eidetic memory,** usually referred to as a "photographic memory." People with eidetic memories can remember with amazing accuracy all the details of a photograph, or pages of a text, or an experience on the basis of short-term exposure. There is some controversy about just how common

Memories may be simplified, enriched, or distorted over time.

Figure 3.7
Children between the ages of five and seven were shown a bottle half filled with colored water and suspended at an angle, such as is shown in this drawing. After each child had seen this arrangement he was asked to draw it from memory. Some of the results of this experiment are shown in Figure 3.8a, b.

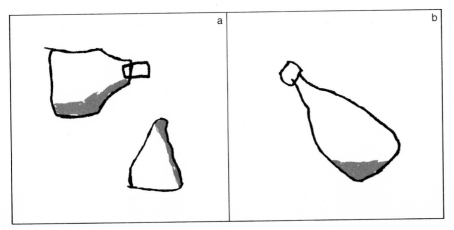

Figure 3.8
Drawings produced by children who had been shown an arrangement like that depicted in Figure 3.7. (a) The five- to seven-year-old children were not too successful in reproducing this arrangement from memory. (b) A drawing done by one of these children six months later. Even though the child had had half a year to forget what he had seen, his reproduction of the arrangement actually improved because he had developed a better idea of what bottles look like and of how water behaves.

photographic memory is. Several researchers have suggested that it is more common in children than in adults.

The Mind of a Mnemonist.   One of the best documented cases of a man with an astounding memory is presented in A. R. Luria's delightful book *The Mind of a Mnemonist* (1968). In the 1920s, a newspaper reporter came to Luria's laboratory to participate in a memory experiment. The Russian psychologist was amazed to learn that S. (as he called the reporter) could easily repeat lists of thirty, fifty, or seventy numbers after he heard them once. He could repeat them backward and forward with equal ease. And when Luria asked him for some of the same lists more than fifteen years later, S. still remembered them.

Perhaps as a result of Dr. Luria's tests, S. began another career as a professional mnemonist: he would repeat complicated lists supplied by people in the audience. How did he do it? Every word or number would conjure up rich visual images which S. easily remembered. For example, in one performance the audience provided him with the following nonsensical formula:

$$N \cdot \sqrt{d^2 \, x \, \frac{85}{vx}} \quad \cdot \quad \sqrt[3]{\frac{276^2 \cdot 86x}{n^2v \cdot 264} \, n^2b} \; = \quad sv \frac{1,624}{32^2} \cdot r^2 \, s.$$

S. was able to repeat this perfectly after studying it for a few minutes. He later told Dr. Luria a story he made up to help remember the formula:

"Neiman *(N)* came out and jabbed at the ground with his cane (.). He looked up at a tall tree which resembled the square root sign ($\sqrt{}$), and thought to himself: 'No wonder the tree has withered and begun to expose its roots. After all, it was here when I built these two houses' *(d²)*" (49). And so on.

But being a professional mnemonist is not all roses. One of S.'s biggest problems was learning to forget. His brain was cluttered with old lists of words, numbers, and letters. Even when he tried to relax, his mind would be flooded with vivid images from the past. S. also had trouble reading: every word brought a sea of images, and he had trouble focusing on the underlying meaning of a passage. Partly because of these problems, Dr. Luria wrote, "S. struck one as a disorganized and rather dull-witted person" (65).

Forgetting

Everyone experiences a loss of memory from time to time. You're sure you've seen that person before but can't quite place her. You have the word on the tip of your tongue, but.... When information that once entered long-term memory cannot be retrieved, it is said to be forgotten. Forgetting may involve decay, interference, or repression.

Some inputs may fade away, or decay, over time. Items quickly decay in sensory storage and short-term memory, as indicated above. It is not

Remembering High School Classmates

Few of us will ever forget our high school days, with all their glory and pain. But how many of us will remember the names and faces of our high school classmates ten, twenty, thirty, and even forty years after graduation? According to a recent study, apparently more of us than you might think.

To find out just how long our long-term memory is, researchers showed nearly 400 high school graduates, ranging in age from seventeen to seventy-four, pictures from their high school yearbooks. Here are some of the surprising results:

- 35 years after graduation, people could identify the faces of 9 out of 10 of their classmates. The size of the high school made no difference in their response.
- 15 years after graduation, subjects could recall 90 percent of their classmates' names.
- Name recall began to fade to between 70 and 80 percent by the time people reached their late thirties.
- Women generally had better memories for names and faces than men.

Researchers explain these amazing results by looking to the way we collect this information in the first place. Our storehouse of names and faces is built over our four-year high school career, and continual repetition helps cement this knowledge in our memories for decades.

So if you're afraid you're going to forget all the classmates you left behind, take heart. They'll probably be part of your memory for a very long time.

For more details, see Harry P. Bahrick, Phyllis O. Bahrick, and Roy P. Wittinger, "Those Unforgettable High School Days," *Psychology Today,* December, 1974.

certain, however, whether long-term memories can ever decay. We know that a blow to the head or electrical stimulation of certain parts of the brain can cause loss of memory. The memories lost are the most recent ones, however; older memories seem to remain (see box). The fact that apparently forgotten information can be recovered through meditation, hypnosis, or brain stimulation suggests that at least some memories never decay. Rather, interference or repression causes people to lose track of them.

Interference refers to a memory being blocked or erased by previous or subsequent memories. This blocking is of two kinds: proactive and retroactive. In **proactive interference** an earlier memory does the blocking. In **retroactive interference** a later memory does the blocking. Suppose you move to a new home. You now have to remember a new address and phone number. At first you may have trouble remembering them because the memory of your old address and phone number gets in the way (proactive interference). Later, you know the new information, but have trouble remembering the old data (retroactive interference).

It may be that interference actually does erase some memories permanently. In other cases the old data have not been lost. The information is in your memory somewhere, if only you could find it. According to Sigmund Freud, sometimes blocking is no accident. A person may subconsciously block memories of an embarrassing or frightening experience. This kind of forgetting is called **repression.** The material still exists in the person's memory, but it has been made inaccessible because it is so disturbing. (We discuss repression further in Chapter 13.)

USING PSYCHOLOGY

Amnesia

In TV soap operas, amnesia victims are usually attractive young adults who cannot even remember their names. In reality, the varieties of memory problems that can result from brain damage are far more complex and interesting.

It is indeed true that a severe blow to the head can cause people to forget events from their past lives. But the period of time that is forgotten is usually measured in minutes or hours rather than months or years. The more severe the injury, the more the patient is likely to forget. No matter how little or how much is forgotten, the loss and later recovery of memory follow a clear pattern.

The memory loss is limited to a specific period of time. You may forget the last six weeks, but everything before that will be clear. Older memories are recovered first: you will remember the fifth and sixth weeks preceding the accident before you remember the day of the accident itself. The last few moments before the accident may never be recovered: the concussion of the brain often seems to erase them from memory entirely. It is believed that this means that events stored in short-term memory at the time of the accident are never transferred to long-term memory.

A case reported by Russell and Nathan (1946) illustrates these general points. A twenty-two-year-old man who was in a motorcycle accident woke up thinking he was fifteen. A week later, he remembered living in Australia from the ages of fifteen to twenty, but the last two years were still a blank. When he returned home, nothing looked familiar. Finally, about ten weeks after the accident, he was able to remember everything but the last few minutes preceding the crash.

Clearly, then, this type of amnesia primarily reflects a problem with retrieval. The memories are still in the patient's head, but he has trouble getting at them.

Another kind of amnesia that seems to affect storage systems is more puzzling for the physician and more confusing for the patient. Korsakoff's syndrome, a brain disease suffered by chronic alcoholics, destroys the ability to remember recent events. This kind of amnesia may also be an undesirable side effect of certain types of brain surgery, or it may be caused by an accident.

Peter Lindsay and Donald Norman (1977: 435) described the problems they had trying to test the memory of one such patient: "N. A. would listen to our explanation of the experiment, nod his head, and say 'Fine, let's go.' Then we would turn around to start the tape recorder.... Just as the first experimental material was to be presented, we would say, 'Are you ready?' Invariably, the reply would be something like, 'Ready for what? Do you want me to do something?' "

Brenda Milner (1965) wrote about another patient who remembered everything from before his brain operation (for severe epilepsy), but nothing afterward. Unfortunately for the patient, his family had moved soon after the operation. He was never able to remember his new address. He also had a habit of reading the same magazine over and over all day long, each time thinking he was reading it for the first time.

It is believed that patients with this type of amnesia can retain information in short-term memory, but have lost the capacity to transfer it to long-term memory.

Improving Memory

Techniques for improving memory are based on efficient organization of the things you learn and on chunking information into easily handled packages. Meaningfulness, association, lack of interference, and degree of original learning all influence your ability to retrieve data from memory.

The more meaningful something is, the easier it will be to remember. For example, you would be more likely to remember the six letters DFIRNE if they were arranged to form the word FRIEND. Similarly, you remember things more vividly if you associate them with things already stored in memory or with a strong emotional experience. As pointed out earlier, the more categories a memory is indexed under, the more accessible it is. If an input is analyzed and indexed under many categories, each association can serve as a trigger for the memory. If you associate the new information with strong sounds, smells, tastes, textures, and so on, any of these stimuli could trigger the memory. The more senses you use when trying to memorize something, the more likely it is that you will be able to retrieve it. This is a key to improving your memory.

For similar reasons, a good way to protect a memory from interference is to *overlearn* it—to keep on rehearsing it even after you think you know it well. Another way to prevent interference while learning new material is to avoid studying similar material together. Instead of studying history right after political science, study biology in between. Still another method is to space out your learning. Trying to absorb large amounts of information at one sitting results in a great deal of interference. It is far more effective to study a little at a time.

Mnemonic Devices. **Mnemonic devices** are techniques for using associations to memorize information. The ancient Greeks memorized speeches by mentally walking around their homes or neighborhoods and "placing" each line of a speech in a different spot. Once they made the associations, they could recall the speech by mentally retracing their steps and "picking up" each line. A more familiar mnemonic device is the rhyme we use to recall the number of days in each month ("Thirty days has September"). Another is the phrase "Every Good Boy Does Fine," in which the first letters of the words are the same as the names of the musical notes on the lines of a staff (E, G, B, D, and F); the notes between the lines spell FACE.

Figure 3.9
A mnemonic device for remembering that Picasso was a Cubist. Often, the sillier the mental picture you form, the better for retrieving the information you have trouble remembering.

Another useful mnemonic device is to form mental pictures containing the information you want to remember—the sillier the better. Suppose you have trouble remembering the authors and titles of books, or which artists belong to which schools of painting. To plant the fact in your mind that John Updike wrote *Rabbit, Run*, you might picture a RABBIT RUNning UP a DIKE. To remember that Picasso was a Cubist, picture someone attacking a giant CUBE with a PICKAX (which sounds like Picasso) (Lorayne and Lucas, 1974: 166–169) (Figure 3.9).

Mnemonic devices are not magical. Indeed, they involve extra work—making up words, stories, and so on. But the very effort of trying to do this may help you to remember things.

CENTRAL PROCESSING OF INFORMATION

If storage and retrieval were the only processes we used to handle information, human beings would be little more than glorified cameras and projectors. But, in fact, we are capable of doing things with information that make the most complex computers seem simple by comparison. These processes—thinking and problem solving—are most impressive when they show originality or creativity.

Thinking

Thinking may be viewed as changing and reorganizing the information stored in memory in order to create new information. By thinking, humans are able to put together any combination of words from memory and create sentences never devised before—such as this one.

Units of Thought. The processes of thought depend on several devices or units of thought: images, symbols, concepts, and rules.

The most primitive unit of thought is an **image,** a mental representation of a specific event or object. The representation is not usually an exact copy; rather, it contains only the highlights of the original. For example, if an adult tries to visualize a grandmother who died when he was seven, he would probably remember only a few details—perhaps the color of her hair or a piece of jewelry that she wore.

A more abstract unit of thought is a **symbol,** a sound or design that represents an object or quality. The most common symbols in thinking are words: every word is a symbol that stands for something other than itself. An image represents a specific sight or sound, but a symbol may have a number of meanings. The fact that symbols differ from the things they represent enables us to think about things that are not present, to range over the past and future, to imagine things and situations that never were or will be. Numbers, letters, and punctuation marks are all familiar symbols of ideas that have no concrete existence.

When a symbol is used as a label for a class of objects or events with certain common attributes, or for the attributes themselves, it is called a

Figure 3.10
This problem was devised by psychologist Edward De Bono, who believes that conventional directed thinking is insufficient for solving new and unusual problems. His approach to problem-solving requires use of nondirected thinking in order to generate new ways of looking at the problem situation. The answer to this problem is provided in Figure 3.15.

An old money-lender offered to cancel a merchant's debt and keep him from going to prison if the merchant would give the money-lender his lovely daughter. Horrified yet desperate, the merchant and his daughter agreed to let Providence decide. The money-lender said he would put a black pebble and a white pebble in a bag and the girl would draw one. The white pebble would cancel the debt and leave her free. The black one would make her the money-lender's, although the debt would be canceled. If she refused to pick, her father would go to prison. From the pebble-strewn path they were standing on, the money-lender picked two pebbles and quickly put them in the bag, but the girl saw he had picked up two black ones. What would you have done if you were the girl?

concept. "Animals," "music," "liquid," and "beautiful people" are examples of concepts based on the common attributes of the objects and experiences belonging to each category. Thus the concept "animal" separates a group of organisms from such things as automobiles, carrots, and Roquefort cheese. Concepts enable us to chunk large amounts of information. We do not have to treat every new piece of information as unique since we already know something about the class of objects or experiences to which the new item belongs.

The fourth and most complex unit of thought is a **rule,** a statement of a relation between concepts. The following are examples of rules: a person cannot be in two places at the same time; mass remains constant despite changes in appearance.

Images, symbols, concepts, and rules are the building blocks of mental activity. They provide an economical and efficient way for people to represent reality, to manipulate and reorganize it, and to devise new ways of acting. A person can think about pursuing several different careers, weigh their pros and cons, and decide which to pursue without having to try them all.

Kinds of Thinking.   People think in two distinct ways. The first, called **directed thinking,** is a systematic and logical attempt to reach a specific goal, such as the solution of a problem. This kind of thinking depends heavily on symbols, concepts, and rules. The other type, called **nondirected thinking,** consists of a free flow of thoughts through the mind, with no particular goal or plan, and depends more on images (Figure 3.10).

Nondirected thinking is usually rich with imagery and feelings. Daydreams, fantasies, and reveries are typical examples. People often engage in nondirected thought when they are relaxing or trying to escape from boredom or worry. This kind of thinking may provide unexpected insights into one's goals and beliefs. Scientists and artists say that some of their best ideas emerge from drifting thoughts that occur when they have set aside a problem for the moment.

In contrast, directed thinking is deliberate and purposeful. It is through directed thinking that we solve problems, formulate and follow rules, and set, work toward, and achieve goals.

Problem Solving

One of the main functions of directed thinking is to solve problems—to bridge the gap, mentally, between a present situation and a desired goal. The gap may be between hunger and food, a column of figures and a total, lack of money and bills to pay, or cancer and a cure. In all these examples, getting from the problem to the solution requires some directed thinking.

Strategies. Problem solving depends on the use of strategies, or specific methods for approaching problems. One strategy is to break down a complex problem into a number of smaller, more easily solved problems. For example, it is the end of the semester and your life is falling apart. You don't even have time to tie your shoelaces. You solve the problem by breaking it down into small pieces: studying for a science exam; finishing that overdue paper; canceling your dinner date; scheduling regular study breaks to maintain what's left of your sanity; and so on.

For some problems, you may work backward from the goal you have set. Mystery writers often use this method: They decide how to end the story ("who did it") and then devise a plot leading to this conclusion.

Another problem may require you to examine various ways of reaching a desired goal. Suppose a woman needs to be in Chicago by 11:00 A.M. on July 7 for a business conference. She checks train departures and arrivals, airline schedules, and car-rental companies. The only train to Chicago that morning arrives at 5:00 A.M. (too early), and the first plane arrives at 11:30 A.M. (too late). So she decides to rent a car and drive.

To determine which strategy to use in a particular situation, most of us analyze the problem to see if it resembles a situation we have experienced in the past. A strategy that worked in the past is likely to work again. The more unusual the problem, the more difficult it is to devise a strategy for dealing with it.

Set. There are times when certain useful strategies become cemented into the problem-solving process. When a particular strategy becomes a habit, it is called a **set**—you are "set" to treat problems in a certain way. For example, a chess player may always attempt to control the four center

Figure 3.11
Given the materials pictured here, how would you go about mounting the candle vertically on a wooden wall in such a way that it can be lit? This problem was formulated by Carl Duncker to test how well people are able to overcome functional fixedness. The solution is presented in Figure 3.15.

squares of the chessboard. Whenever her opponent attacks, she responds by looking for ways to regain control of those four squares. She has a "set" for this strategy. If this set helps her to win, fine. Sometimes, however, a set interferes with problem solving, and then it is called *rigidity*. You probably know the old riddle, "What is black, white, and read all over? A newspaper." When you say the riddle, the word "read" sounds like "red," which is why some people cannot guess the answer. "Read" is heard as part of the black and white set—it is interpreted as being a color. If you asked, "What is read by people every day and is black and white?" the correct answer would be obvious. And boring.

One form of set that can interfere with problem solving is functional fixedness—the inability to imagine new functions for familiar objects. In experiments on functional fixedness, people are asked to solve a problem that requires them to use a familiar object in an unfamiliar way (Duncker, 1945). Because they are set to use the object in the usual way, people tend to pay attention only to the features of the object that relate to its everyday use (see Figure 3.11). They respond in a rigid way.

Another type of rigidity occurs when a person makes a wrong assumption about a problem. In Figure 3.12, for example, the problem is to connect the dots with four straight lines without lifting your pencil. Most people have trouble solving this puzzle because they falsely assume that they must stay within the area of the dots.

People trying to solve the kind of problem shown in Figure 3.13 experience a third kind of rigidity. Most people look for direct methods of solving problems and do not see solutions that require several intermediate steps.

Rigidity can be overcome if the person realizes that his or her strategy is not working and looks for other ways to approach the problem. The more familiar the situation, the more difficult this will be. Rigidity is less likely to occur with unusual problems.

Creativity

Creativity is the ability to use information in such a way that the result is somehow new, original, and meaningful. All problem solving requires

Figure 3.12
Connect these dots with four straight lines without lifting your pencil. The solution appears in Figure 3.15.

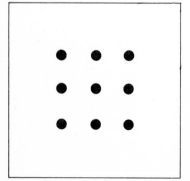

Figure 3.13
How would you go about solving
this problem: Eight soldiers need to
cross a river, but the only way to
cross is in a small boat in which
two children are playing. The boat
can carry at most two children or
one soldier. How do the soldiers
get across? You'll find the answer
in Figure 3.15.

some creativity. Certain ways of solving problems, however, are simply more brilliant or beautiful or efficient than others. Psychologists do not know exactly why some people are able to think more creatively than others, although they have identified some of the characteristics of creative thinking—including flexibility and the ability to recombine elements to achieve insight.

Flexibility. Flexibility is, quite simply, the ability to overcome rigidity. Psychologists have devised a number of ingenious tests to measure flexibility. One test is shown in Figure 3.14. The individual is asked to name a word that the three words in each row have in common. To do this, a person must be able to think of many different aspects of each of these words. Another test of flexibility is to ask people how many uses they can imagine for a single object, such as a brick or a paper clip. The more uses a person can devise, the more flexible he or she is said to be. Whether such tests actually measure creativity is debatable. Nevertheless, it is obvious that inflexible, rigid thinking leads to unoriginal solutions, or no solutions at all.

Recombination. When the elements of a problem are familiar but the required solution is not, it may be achieved by **recombination,** a new mental rearrangement of the elements. In football and basketball, for example, there are no new moves—only recombinations of old ones. Such recombination seems to be a vital part of creativity. Many creative people say that no truly great poem, no original invention, has ever been produced by someone who has not spent years studying his or her subject. The creative person is able to take the information that he or she and others have compiled and put it together in a totally new way. The brilliant philosopher and mathematician Sir Isaac Newton, who discovered the laws of motion, once said, "If I have seen further, it is by standing on the shoulders

Figure 3.14
A test devised to measure flexibility
in thinking. The task is to name a
single word that all three words on
a line have in common. For example, the answer to the first item is
"foot." (The other answers are
given in Figure 3.15.)

1.	stool	powder	ball
2.	blue	cake	cottage
3.	man	wheel	high
4.	motion	poke	down
5.	line	birthday	surprise
6.	wood	liquor	luck
7.	house	village	golf
8.	card	knee	rope
9.	news	doll	tiger
10.	painting	bowl	nail
11.	weight	wave	house
12.	made	cuff	left
13.	key	wall	precious
14.	bull	tired	hot
15.	knife	up	hi
16.	handle	hole	police
17.	plan	show	walker
18.	hop	side	pet
19.	bell	tender	iron
20.	spelling	line	busy

of giants." In other words, he was able to recombine the discoveries of the great scientists who had preceded him to uncover new and more far-reaching truths.

Another result of brilliant recombination is Samuel Taylor Coleridge's unusual poem "Kubla Khan." Scholars have shown that almost every word and phrase came directly from Coleridge's past readings and personal experiences. Coleridge recombined these elements during a period of non-

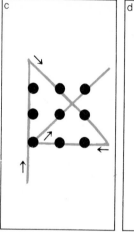

1. foot   11. light
2. cheese 12. hand
3. chair   13. stone
4. slow   14. dog
5. party   15. jack
6. hard   16. man
7. green   17. floor
8. trick   18. car
9. paper   19. bar
10. finger 20. bee

Figure 3.15
Solutions to the problems presented in the chapter. Note that in each case the solution requires breaking certain habits of thought. (a) In the De Bono money-lender problem, it is difficult to imagine that control of the situation can be taken out of the hands of the powerful money-lender. (b) Solving the Duncker candle problem requires one to look at the matchbox and candle box as more than containers to be discarded. The presence of the useless piece of string usually serves to confuse problem solvers. (c) As the text points out, the solution to this problem is blocked if the person avoids going beyond the boundaries of the dots. (d) The answers to the test of flexibility require that the individual ignore common associations and look for unusual ones. (e) The first steps in solution of the river problem. Once the solver discovers the first step in the problem's solution, he or she may become further bogged down if he doesn't realize the lengthy cyclical nature of the process required.

directed thinking—drug-induced sleep. He awoke with the entire poem in his mind, but was only able to commit part of it to paper before he was interrupted by a knock at his door. When Coleridge went back to his poem, it had vanished from his mind.

Insight.   The sudden emergence of a solution by recombination of elements is called **insight**. Insight usually occurs when problems have proved resistant to all problem-solving efforts and strategies. The scientist or artist reaches a point of high frustration and temporarily abandons the task. But the recombination process seems to continue on an unconscious level. When the person is absorbed in some other activity, the answer seems to appear out of nowhere. This sudden insight has appropriately been called the "aha" experience.

Certain animals appear to experience this same cycle of frustration, temporary diversion (during which time the problem "incubates"), and then sudden insight. For example, Wolfgang Köhler (1925) placed a chimpanzee in a cage where a cluster of bananas was hung out of its reach. Also in the cage were a number of wooden boxes. At first the chimpanzee tried various unsuccessful ways of getting at the fruit. Finally it sat down, apparently giving up, and simply stared straight ahead for a while. Then suddenly it jumped up, piled three boxes on top of one another, climbed to the top of the pile, and grabbed the bananas.

SUMMARY

1. Information processing involves three steps: input from the senses, central processing (memory, thought), and output in the form of ideas or behavior.

2. Two processes that help narrow down inputs are selective attention and feature extraction. Selective attention is the ability to pick and choose among various incoming channels, focusing on some and ignoring others. Channels are chosen when they help satisfy needs, are unusual, or relate to one's interests. Feature extraction is the ability to respond to specific characteristics of a given input and to ignore others.

3. The shortest form of memory is sensory storage, which lasts less than a second. Next is short-term memory, which retains information for about twenty seconds. Items stored in short-term memory are quickly forgotten if they are not rehearsed or transferred to long-term memory.

4. Long-term memory contains information that has some significance. There are many theories as to how memories are stored in the brain. One is that memory is due to changes in the form of protein molecules in the brain. Another focuses on chemical-electrical changes in the brain.

5. Retrieval is essential if memory is to be useful. Consequently, memory must be organized. Retrieval takes two forms: recognition and recall. Recall is an active reconstructive process that may give rise to such errors as confabulation, in which memories are reconstructed incorrectly. Recognition simply means deciding whether you've seen or heard something before.

6. Forgetting may be caused by decay, interference, or repression. Decay is the fading away of a memory and, if it occurs at all, is not the main reason for forgetting. Interference occurs when new or old information blocks or erases the mem-

ory of a related piece of information. In repression, access to information has been blocked.

7. Information is stored better and is more easily retrieved when (a) it is organized into meaningful chunks; (b) it has many paths, or associations, leading to it; and (c) it has been overlearned.

8. Thinking is the process of reorganizing and rearranging the information in memory to produce new information or ideas. The units of thought are images, symbols, concepts, and rules.

9. Thinking may be directed or nondirected. Directed thinking is deliberate and purposeful, as in problem solving and decision making. Nondirected thinking is looser and more passive, as in daydreaming and reverie.

10. Problem solving is bridging the gap between a present situation and a desired goal by means of specific strategies. When strategies become habits, they can lead to failure rather than success. This difficulty is called rigidity.

11. Creativity is the ability to manipulate information to produce something new, original, and meaningful. Flexibility and the ability to recombine elements to achieve insight seem to be important aspects of creativity.

GLOSSARY

central processing: The second stage of information processing—storing (in memory) and sorting (by thought) information in the brain.

chunking: The process of grouping pieces of information for easier handling.

concept: A label for a class of objects or events that share common attributes.

confabulation: The act of filling in memory with statements that make sense but that are, in fact, untrue.

creativity: The capacity to use information and/ or abilities in such a way that the results are new, original, and meaningful.

directed thinking: Systematic, logical, goal-directed thought.

eidetic memory: The ability to remember with great accuracy visual information on the basis of short-term exposure; also called "photographic memory."

feature extraction: The identification and analysis of specific features of a sensory input.

image: A rough representation of specific events or objects (the most primitive unit of thought).

input: The first stage of information processing—receiving information through the senses.

insight: The sudden realization of the solution to a problem.

long-term memory: Information storage that has unlimited capacity and lasts indefinitely.

memory: The complex mental function of storage and retrieval of what has been learned or experienced.

mnemonic devices: Methods for remembering items by relating them to information already held in the brain.

nondirected thinking: The free flow of images and ideas, occurring with no particular goal.

output: The final stage of information processing—acting on the basis of information.

proactive interference: The hampering of recall of newly learned material by the recall of previously learned material.

recall: The type of memory retrieval in which a person reconstructs previously learned material.

recognition: The type of memory retrieval in which a person is required to identify an object, idea, or situation as one he or she has or has not experienced before.

recombination: Mentally rearranging the elements of a problem in order to arrive at a novel solution.

repression: The unconscious blocking of memories of frightening or disturbing experiences.

retrieval: The process of obtaining information that has been stored in memory.

retroactive interference: The hampering of recall of learned material by the recall of other material learned more recently.

rule: A statement of the relationship between two or more concepts (the most complex unit of thought).

selective attention: Focusing one's awareness on a limited segment of the total amount of sensory input one is receiving.

sensory storage: The momentary storage of sensory information at the level of the sensory receptors.

set: A habitual strategy or pattern of problem solving.

short-term memory: Memory that is limited in capacity to about seven items and in duration to about twenty seconds.

symbol: An abstract unit of thought that represents an object, event, or quality.

ACTIVITIES

1. Mentally determine where the light switches in your home are located and keep track of them in your head. Do you have to use visual images to count the switches? To keep track of the number? If not, could you do it with images if you wanted to?

2. Present your classmates or other friends with an article or story that presents two perspectives on an issue. Later, test their recall of the article. See if they remember better those facts or arguments that agree with their own.

3. Try this simple learning task on your friends. Give them a list of numbers to memorize: 6, 9, 8, 11, 10, 13, 12, 15, 14, 17, 16, and so on. Tell some of them simply to memorize the material. Tell others that there is an organizational principle behind the number sequence, and to memorize the number with the aid of the principle (which they must discover). In the sequence above, the principle is "plus 3, minus 1."

4. Try to remember what you were doing on your last birthday. As you probe your memory, verbalize the mental steps you are going through. What does this exercise tell you about your thought processes?

5. Suppose you wanted to put together a jigsaw puzzle. What are the problem-solving strategies you might use? Which one do you think would work the best?

6. Solve this problem. A sloppy man has twenty blue socks and twenty brown ones in his drawer. If he reaches for a pair of socks in the dark, how many must he pull out to be sure he has a matched pair? How long did it take you to solve the problem? Can you identify what steps you went through in your mind in order to solve it?

7. In the middle of an ordinary activity, like reading a book, stop for a moment and listen for sounds you normally block out. Jot down the sounds you hear and try to identify them. Why don't you usually hear them? Under what circumstances would you notice them?

8. Relax and engage in nondirected thinking—let your thoughts wander. Things may come into your mind that you thought you had forgotten or that you didn't know you knew. Or reflect on a recent dream you had—where might the various images have come from? You may begin to see the vast amount of information you have stored in your brain.

9. You and your friends can test the way your memories are organized by playing a popular game called Categories. Make a grid with five columns and five rows, and put a category, such as

fruits or furniture, at the top of each column. Now pick five random letters, and assign one to each row. Give yourself five minutes to think of an item starting with each letter for each category and fill in the boxes in the grid. (Example: If your letters are A, G, P, O, and B, your entries under "fruit" might be apple, grape, peach, orange, and banana.)

10. Try the following game to demonstrate the reconstructive aspects of recall. (You will need at least seven or eight people—the more the better.) Before you gather the group together, write or copy a very short (not more than three or four paragraphs) story containing a fair amount of descriptive detail. Memorize, as best you can, the story, and whisper it to one member of the group, making sure the others are out of earshot. Then instruct your listener to whisper the story to another player, and so on until all the players have heard it. When the last person has been told the story, have him or her repeat it aloud to the entire group. Then read the original story from your written copy. Chances are good that the two versions are quite a bit different. Discuss among yourselves how, when, and why the story changed.

SUGGESTED READINGS

DE BONO, EDWARD. *The Mechanism of Mind.* New York: Simon & Schuster, 1969. A nonscientific book about how to use your mind effectively. It is particularly instructive about the nature of memory and models.

FABUN, DON. *Communication: The Transfer of Meaning.* Rev. ed. Beverly Hills, Calif.: Benziger Bruce & Glencoe, 1968 (paper). A graphic and stimulating analysis of how communication between people is affected by selective attention, use of symbols, different meanings of concepts, and the making of inferences.

GARDNER, H. *The Shattered Mind.* New York: Vintage Books, 1974. An overview of the various types of brain damage. Focuses on speech disorders.

GHISELIN, B. (ED.). *The Creative Process.* New York: New American Library, 1952 (paper). An excellent selection of statements by creative people about their own processes of invention.

HALACY, D. S., JR. *Man and Memory.* New York:

Harper & Row, 1970. A clearly written, enjoyable presentation of some of the most important research done on memory. Halacy also covers the various theories of memory, the experiments on memory transfer, and the effects of drugs on memory.

HUNTER, I. M. L. *Memory: Facts and Fallacies.* Baltimore: Penguin, 1964 (paper). An interesting introduction to the study of human memory. Hunter surveys a good deal of experimental literature, dating back to the nineteenth century.

HUTCHINSON, ELIOT D. *How to Think Creatively.* New York: Abington Press, 1949 (paper). This book is deceptively titled. Actually, it is a fascinating account of the role insight has played in the work of famous creative thinkers.

WATSON, JAMES D. *The Double Helix.* New York: Atheneum, 1968 (paper). An intensely personal account of the process of the discovery of the DNA structure by a leading contemporary scientist.

BIBLIOGRAPHY

ADAMS, JACK A. *Human Memory.* New York: McGraw-Hill, 1967.

BRUNER, JEROME S., GOODNOW, JACQUELINE J., AND AUSTIN, GEORGE A. *A Study of Thinking.* New York: Wiley, 1956 (paper).

BUCKHOUT, ROBERT. "Eyewitness Testimony." *Scientific American,* 231, no. 6 (1974): 23–31.

DE BONO, EDWARD. *New Think: The Use of Lateral Thinking in the Generation of New Ideas.* New York: Basic Books, 1968.

DUNCKER, KARL. "On Problem Solving." Trans. by L. S. Lees. *Psychological Monographs*, 58, no. 270 (1945).

————. *The Mechanism of the Mind*. New York: Simon & Schuster, 1969.

FLEXNER, L. "Dissection of Memory in Mice with Antibiotics." *Proceedings of the American Philosophical Society*, 111 (1967): 343–346.

FLOOD, J. F., BENNETT, E. L., AND ORME, A. E. "Relation of Memory Formation for Controlled Amounts of Brain Protein Synthesis." *Physiology and Behavior*, 15 (1975): 97–102.

GHISELIN, B. (ED.). *The Creative Process*. New York: New American Library, 1952 (paper).

HABER, R. N. "How We Remember What We See." *Scientific American*, 222 (1970): 104–112.

HALACY, D. R., JR. *Man and Memory*. New York: Harper & Row, 1970.

HERNÁNDEZ-PEÓN, R. *"Reticular Mechanisms of Sensory Control."* In *Sensory Communication*, ed. by W. A. Rosenblith. New York: Wiley, 1961, pp. 497–520.

INHELDER, BAERBEL. "Memory and Intelligence in the Child." In *Studies in Cognitive Development*, ed. by D. Elkind and J. F. Flavell. New York: Oxford University Press, 1969, pp. 337–364.

KOESTLER, ARTHUR. *The Act of Creation*. New York: Macmillan, 1964.

KÖHLER, WOLFGANG. *The Mentality of Apes*. New York: Harcourt, 1925.

LASHLEY, KARL S. *Brain Mechanisms and Intelligence*. Chicago: University of Chicago Press, 1929.

LINDSAY, PETER, AND NORMAN, DONALD A. *Human Information Processing*. 2nd ed. New York: Academic Press, 1977.

LOFTUS, ELIZABETH. "Reconstructing Memory: The Incredible Eyewitness." *Psychology Today*, 8, no. 7 (1974): 116–119.

LORAYNE, HARRY, AND LUCAS, JERRY. *The Memory Book*. New York: Ballantine, 1974 (paper).

LURIA, A. R. *The Mind of a Mnemonist*. New York: Basic Books, 1968.

MCCONNELL, J. V. "Cannibalism and Memory in Flatworms." *New Scientist*, 21 (1964): 465–468.

MILLER, GEORGE A. "The Magical Number Seven, Plus or Minus Two: Some Limits on Our Capacity for Processing Information." *Psychological Review*, 63 (1956): 81–97.

MILLER, GEORGE A., GALANTER, EUGENE, AND PRIBRAM, KARL H. *Plans and the Structure of Behavior*. New York: Holt, 1960.

MILNER, BRENDA. "Memory Disturbance After Bilateral Hippocampal Lesions." In *Cognitive Processes and the Brain*, ed. by Peter Milner and Stephen Glickman. Princeton, N.J.: Van Nostrand, 1965, pp. 97–111.

NEISSER, ULRIC. *Cognitive Psychology*. New York: Appleton-Century-Crofts, 1967.

PETERSON, LLOYD R., AND PETERSON, MARGARET. "Short-Term Retention of Individual Verbal Items." *Journal of Experimental Psychology*, 58 (1959): 193–198.

RUSSELL, W. RITCHIE, AND NATHAN, P. W. "Traumatic Amnesia." *Brain*, 69 (1946): 280–300.

SPERLING, G. "The Information Available in Brief Visual Presentations." *Psychological Monographs*, 74, no. 11 (1960).

STROMEYER, C. F. "Eidetikers." *Psychology Today*, 4 (1970): 76–80.

THOMPSON, RICHARD F. "The Search for the Engram." *American Psychologist*, 31 (1976): 209–227.

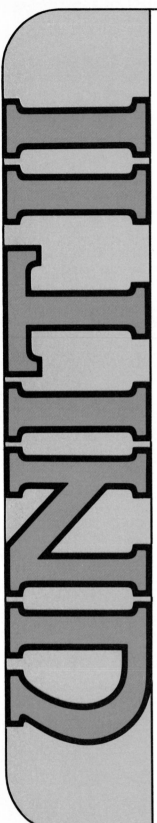

UNIT 2

THE WORKINGS OF MIND AND BODY

Most people think of the mind and body as separate: they imagine the body as something concrete that can be studied in a laboratory and the mind as intangible and beyond the reach of science. Many people assume that we see, hear, and touch with our bodies; plan, dream, decide, and experience moods with our minds. People think that motives and emotions have little in common with vision, hearing, and other bodily phenomena. These cannot, it is thought, be studied in the same way, with the same instruments. Such unusual states of consciousness as hypnotic trances are considered beyond the reach of the scientific method.

This unit is designed to challenge these common assumptions by showing that the line between mental activities and physiological functions is not as clear-cut as you may have imagined. Chapter 4 explains how the nervous and hormonal systems work and how heredity and environment interact and influence behavior. In Chapter 5 we deal with "taking in" information in the first place—how we perceive sights, sounds, and smells. Chapter 6 explores the underlying reasons why we are motivated to act in certain ways, and the importance of emotions. In Chapter 7 we note that, surprisingly, psychologists have found it easier to define and study dreams and hallucinations than to define and study everyday, waking consciousness.

When you complete this section, you will realize that in studying the workings of the mind and body, psychologists have raised nearly as many questions as they have answered. The years ahead will undoubtedly bring new and startling discoveries in this area of research.

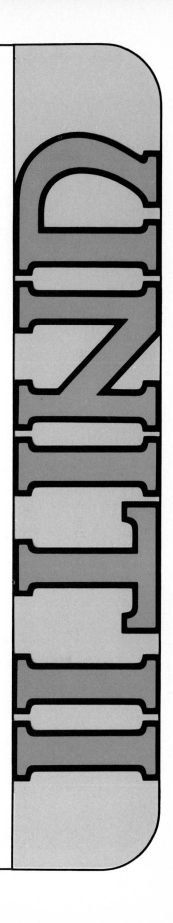

Body and Behavior

You are your brain. Your pleasant personality, your wry sense of humor, and your favorite color are all coded in the thirteen billion nerve cells of your brain. Ordinarily, we pay no attention to our biological nature. But your reliance on the physical properties of the nervous system would become painfully obvious if you were involved in a car accident that damaged your brain: your personality, your memories, and even your sense of humor might be affected.

The Greek physician Hippocrates was the first to notice that head injuries often disturbed thought and behavior. In the twenty-five centuries since his observations, many attempts have been made to explain how this mass of soggy gray tissue could create the theory of relativity, the Sistine Chapel ceiling, and the energy crisis. But the mind remains a mystery to itself.

Some of the most exciting developments in psychology are going on in the brain sciences, and this chapter will help you to understand the newspaper and magazine articles reporting new discoveries that you will probably be reading for the next twenty-five years. In addition to describing the organization of the nervous system, we will discuss studies of lower animals and the possible role of genes in complex human behavior.

THE NERVOUS SYSTEM

In some ways, the nervous system is like the telephone system in a city. Messages are constantly traveling back and forth. As in a telephone system, the messages are basically electrical. They travel along prelaid cables,

Figure 4.1
The control of our bodies rests with our brains. It is the brain and the nervous system that enable us to sit, stand, jump, run—and to think and plan.

linked with one another by relays and switchboards. In the body, the cables are **nerve fibers.** The relays are **synapses,** the gaps that occur between individual nerve cells. The switchboards are special cells that are found along the lines of communication (called *interneurons*) and the networks of nerve cells found in the brain and spinal cord. One major difference is that a telephone system simply conveys messages, while the nervous system actively helps to run the body.

The brain monitors what is happening inside and outside the body by receiving messages from **receptors**—cells whose function is to gather information. The brain sifts through these messages, combines them, and sends out orders to the **effectors**—cells that work the muscles and internal glands and organs. For example, receptors in your eye may send a message to the brain such as "Round object. Size increasing. Distance decreasing rapidly." Your brain instantly connects this image with information from memory to identify this object as a baseball. Almost simultaneously your brain orders the effectors in your arms to position themselves so you don't get beaned in right field.

How the Nervous System Works

Messages to and from the brain travel along the nerves, which are strings of long, thin cells called **neurons** (see Figure 4.2). Chemical-electrical signals travel down the neurons much as flame travels along a firecracker fuse. The main difference is that the neuron can "burn" over and over

Figure 4.2
A few of the billions of neurons in the human body, shown tens of thousands of times bigger than they really are. One (colored blue) has the effect of slowing the firing of the others. The other two have the effect of increasing the firing of any neurons to which they connect. The connections take place at the synapses, where chemical substances cross the gap from one nerve cell to the other.

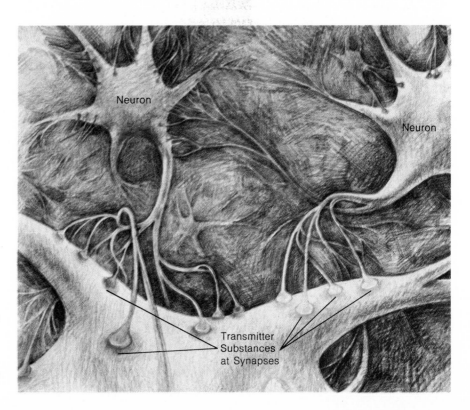

again, hundreds of times a minute. When a neuron transmits one of these chemical-electrical signals, it is said to be **firing.** When the signal reaches the end or ends of a neuron, it releases chemicals called **neurotransmitters** that cross the synapses (gaps) between neurons. These substances make other neurons fire faster or slower. This is how messages travel through the body.

The **central nervous system (CNS)** is a huge mass of neurons clumped together in the brain and spinal cord. You might think of the **spinal cord** as the main cable. It is a bundle of nerves, about as thick as a pencil, running down the length of the back. The spinal cord transmits most of the messages back and forth between the body and the brain.

The spinal cord is well protected by the backbone, just as the brain is protected by the skull. This protection prevents interference with the line of communication between the brain and the rest of the body. Without the spinal cord, messages from the brain would never reach any of our muscles except those in the face. We would be paralyzed from the neck down.

Branching out from the spinal cord and, to a lesser extent, from the brain is a network of nerves called the **peripheral nervous system (PNS)** (see Figure 4.3). These nerves conduct information from the bodily organs to the central nervous system and take information back to the organs. The peripheral nervous system is divided into two parts: somatic and autonomic. The **somatic nervous system** controls voluntary movement of skeletal muscles (such as lifting your hand to turn a page, which involves a number of coordinated movements). The **autonomic nervous system** controls the glands, internal organs, and involuntary muscles (such as the heart). The autonomic nervous system itself has two parts: sympathetic and parasympathetic.

The **sympathetic nervous system** prepares the body for dealing with emergencies or strenuous activities. It speeds up the heart to hasten the supply of oxygen and nutrients to body tissues. It constricts some arteries and relaxes others so that blood flows to the muscles, where it is most needed in emergencies and strenuous activities. It increases the breathing rate and suspends some activities such as digestion. In contrast, the **parasympathetic nervous system** works to conserve energy and to enhance the body's ability to recover from strenuous activity. It reduces the heart rate, slows breathing, and the like.

The Old Brain and the New Brain

Signals from the receptors in the peripheral nervous system travel up the spinal cord and enter the brain. The first part of the brain the messages reach is the **subcortex** (Figure 4.4). Together with the spinal cord, the subcortex controls and coordinates such vital functions as sleeping, heart rate, hunger, and digestion. It also controls many reflex actions—blinking, coughing, tearing, and so on.

The subcortex is sometimes called the "old brain" because it is thought to have evolved millions of years ago in our prehuman ancestors. In fact, it resembles the brain found in frogs, fish, and other lower animals. These animals, like humans, need to sleep, eat, and digest food, so it is not surprising that these areas of the brain are similar in many species.

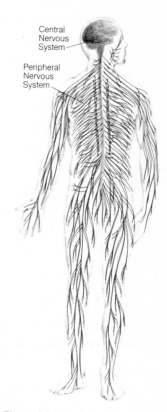

Central
Nervous
System

Peripheral
Nervous
System

Figure 4.3
The central nervous system (CNS) and the peripheral nervous system (PNS) in the human body.

Figure 4.4
A cross section of the human brain, showing the subcortex, or "old brain," and the cerebral cortex, or "new brain."

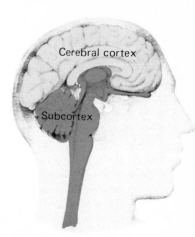

Cerebral cortex

Subcortex

Figure 4.5
The structures of the subcortex. (This illustration shows the brain as it would appear if it were sliced exactly in half from front to back.)

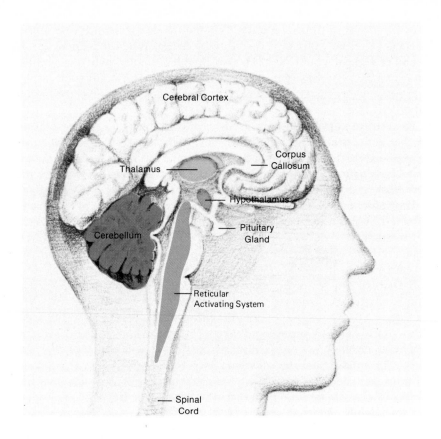

Unlike fish and frogs, people are able to learn to behave in entirely new ways, to think, and to imagine. These powers come from a section of the brain that is minuscule in fish, larger in mammals such as cats and dogs, and huge in humans. This "new brain," the **cerebral cortex,** surrounds the subcortex like a halved peach surrounds the pit (Figure 4.5). Your subcortex guides your biological needs and "animal instincts." Your cerebral cortex enables you, among other things, to read and to solve problems.

The Subcortex.   A portion of the subcortex called the reticular formation controls an activating network of nerves that runs through the whole brain. This network, the **reticular activating system,** may be the brain's waking and attention system. It screens incoming messages, blocking out some signals and letting others pass. During sleep it blocks most inputs, but in response to a loud or unusual sound it sends messages to the rest of the brain, alerting it and raising its activity level to a state of wakefulness.

In the center of the brain is the **thalamus,** the brain's great relaying center. It sorts incoming impulses and directs them to various parts of the brain, and it relays messages from one part of the brain to another.

At the base of the brain, below and to the front of the thalamus, is the **hypothalamus,** a small, closely packed cluster of neurons that is one of the most important parts of the brain. This structure regulates the autonomic nervous system, the system of peripheral nerves that controls internal bodily functioning. The hypothalamus thus regulates such biological functions as digestion, heart rate, and hormone secretion. By sensing the levels of water and sugar in your blood, your hypothalamus can tell when you need food or water and can then cause you to feel hungry or thirsty.

Among its other functions, this portion of the brain regulates body temperature by monitoring the temperature of the blood. If your body is too cold, the hypothalamus causes tiny vibrations in your muscles (shivering) that bring the temperature up to normal. If your body is too hot, the hypothalamus signals your sweat glands to perspire. As perspiration evaporates, your body is cooled. The hypothalamus also plays an important role in determining emotional and sexual responses because it helps regulate the endocrine system, which will be discussed later in this chapter.

At the very back and bottom of the old brain is the **cerebellum**, the brain's "executive secretary." One of the cerebellum's main functions is to control posture and balance as you move about so that you do not fall over or bump into things. It also helps to regulate the details of commands from the cerebral cortex. Without your cerebellum, you might hit a friend in the stomach when you reach out to shake hands.

The Cerebral Cortex.   The cerebral cortex, in which most of the higher brain functions take place, is a great gray mass of ripples and valleys, folded so that its huge surface area can fit inside the skull.

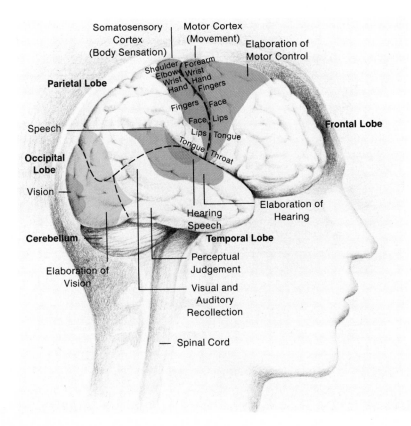

Figure 4.6
An external view of the brain from the side. Most of the areas exposed here are parts of the "new" brain. The functions of the cerebral cortex are not fully understood; areas whose behavioral importance is known are indicated.

Figure 4.7
How the body might appear if the parts were proportional to their representation in the sensory and motor areas of the cortex. (left) The various regions of the body in the order that they are represented in the area of the brain responsible for bodily sensation. (right) A similar arrangement of body regions in the area of the brain that controls muscular movements.

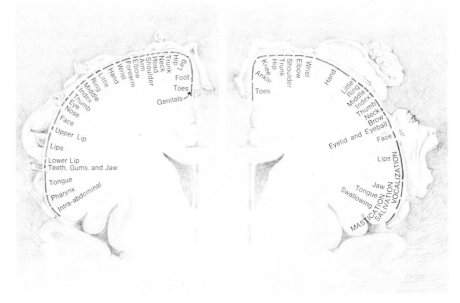

The cerebral cortex is divided into a number of regions, called **lobes** (see Figure 4.6). Some lobes receive specific kinds of information from the senses. Most visual information goes to the **occipital lobes** at the back of the brain. Auditory sensations, or sounds, go primarily to the **temporal lobes** on each side of the brain. The **parietal lobes** integrate visual, auditory, and other sensory input. The **somatosensory cortex,** located at the border of the parietal lobes, at the middle of the brain, receives information from the skin senses (such as touch) and from muscles. As you can see in Figure 4.7, the amount of brain tissue connected to a body part is proportional to that area's sensitivity rather than to its size. For example, the highly developed sense of touch in your hands involves a much larger brain area than your relatively insensitive calves.

The **motor cortex,** which controls body movement, is just in front of the somatosensory cortex, across a deep fold. The motor cortex is part of the **frontal lobes.** Some studies suggest that this area controls creativity and personality: it enables people to be witty, sensitive, or easygoing. For example, in the mid-1800s, a quarryman named Phineas Gage was injured in an explosion. The force of the blast drove an iron stake through Gage's head, damaging the frontal lobes (Figure 4.8). Remarkably, Gage survived and was back at work in a few months. The accident did not impair his bodily functions or his memory or skills. However, Gage's personality changed dramatically. This once trustworthy and dependable man became childish, fitful, impatient, and capricious. Later studies of large numbers of people with similar brain damage suggest that planning future action, emotional control, and the ability to pay attention depend on the frontal lobes.

Figure 4.8
This drawing was adapted from one of the sketches made by the doctor who attended Phineas Gage. It shows the path taken by the iron stake that was propelled through Gage's skull.

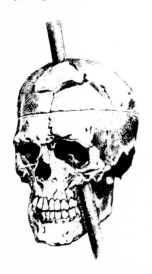

The Hemispheres of the Brain

The cortex is divided into two hemispheres that are roughly mirror images of each other. (Each of the four lobes is present in both hemispheres.) The two hemispheres are connected by a band of nerves called the **corpus callosum,** which carries messages back and forth between the two. Each hemisphere is connected to half of the body in a crisscrossed fashion. The motor cortex of the left hemisphere of the brain controls most of the right side of the body; the right hemisphere motor cortex controls most of the left side of the body. Thus a stroke that causes damage to the right hemisphere will result in numbness or paralysis on the left side of the body. Researchers have also found a number of more subtle differences between the sides of the brain: in right-handed people, the left hemisphere controls language, while the right hemisphere is involved in spatial tasks.

Many psychologists became interested in differences between the cerebral hemispheres when "split brain" operations were tried on epileptics like Harriet Lees. For most of her life Ms. Lees's seizures were mild and could be controlled with drugs. However, at age twenty-five they began to get worse, and by thirty Lees was having as many as a dozen violent seizures a day. An epileptic fit involves massive electrical activity that begins in one hemisphere and spreads to the other. To enable this woman to live a normal life, doctors decided to sever the corpus callosum so that seizures could not spread.

The operation was a success—Lees has not had a seizure since. But psychologists were even more interested in the potential side effects of this dramatic operation. Despite the fact that patients who had this operation now had "two separate brains," they seemed remarkably normal. Researchers went on to develop a number of ingenious techniques to try to detect subtle effects of the operation. To understand the procedures, you need to know a little about brain anatomy. For example, the left half of each eye is connected to the right hemisphere and the right half of each eye is wired to the left hemisphere. To get a message to only one hemisphere at a time, the researchers asked each split-brain patient to stare at a dot while they briefly flashed a word or a picture on one side of the dot. If the word "nut" was flashed to the right of the dot, it went to the left hemisphere. The patient could usually read it quite easily under these circumstances, because the left hemisphere controls language for most right-handed people.

But when the same word was flashed to the right hemisphere (left side of each eye), the patient was not able to repeat it. For an ordinary person, the word "nut" would quickly go from one side of the brain to the other via the corpus callosum. Since this patient's corpus callosum had been cut, however, the message could not get from the nonverbal right hemisphere to the verbal left. Even more amazing was the fact that the patient really did recognize the word: with her left hand (which is also connected to the right hemisphere), she could pick out a nut from a group of objects hidden behind a screen. But even after she correctly picked out the nut and held it in her hand, still she could not remember the word!

In another experiment, a picture of a nude woman was flashed to the right hemisphere (left side of each eye) of another split-brain patient (Figure 4.9). This woman laughed but said she saw nothing. Only her left hemisphere could speak and it did not see the nude; but the right hemisphere, which did see the nude, produced the laugh. When the woman was asked why she laughed, she acted confused and couldn't explain it.

Planning the future, controlling emotions, and paying attention seem to depend on the frontal lobes of the brain.

Figure 4.9
The presentation of a visual stimulus to a single hemisphere of a person who has undergone split-brain surgery. The patient reacts with amusement to the picture of the nude woman flashed on the left side of the screen but is unable to say why.

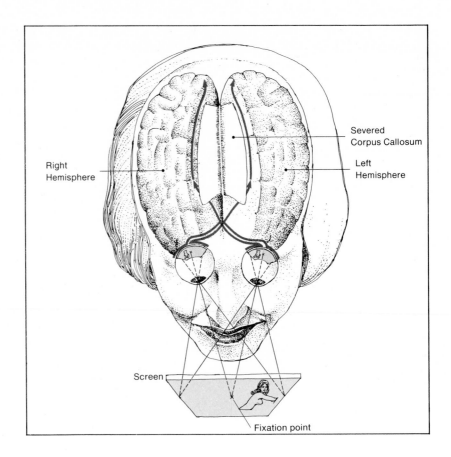

Right Hemisphere

Severed Corpus Callosum

Left Hemisphere

Screen

Fixation point

Right-handed children are genetically predisposed to develop verbal left hemispheres, but the actual specialization develops over the years. If a child suffers damage to the left hemisphere, the right hemisphere will take over the function of speech. The child may learn more slowly than other children, but he or she will learn to speak. However, almost all adults who suffer damage to the left hemisphere have extreme difficulty speaking—if they can speak at all. The effects of right-hemisphere damage are less clear, but they probably include problems with spatial abilities.

Though this specialization of labor is particularly relevant for people with brain damage, it also involves normal people. One group of studies, for example, has looked at the brain waves (or EEG—see below) of right-handed people as they perform verbal and spatial tasks. The EEG shows greater activity in the right hemisphere for spatial tasks like memorizing geometrical designs, remembering faces, or imagining an elephant in a swing. But when the same people were asked to perform verbal tasks—writing a letter in their heads, thinking of words that begin with "t," and listening to boring passages from the *Congressional Record*—their EEG showed relatively greater activity in the left hemisphere (Hassett, 1978). Even more interesting, and far easier to observe, is the fact that normal people tend to move their eyes in a certain way depending on which hemisphere they are using (see box).

Which Way Do the Eyes Move?

Did you know that the direction your eyes move when you think about a question may indicate which side of the brain you are using for the answer?

Ask a friend the following four questions, and secretly watch whether she first looks to the right or the left as she considers each:

1. Make up a sentence using the words "code" and "mathematics."
2. Picture the last automobile accident you saw. In which direction were the cars going?
3. What does the proverb "Easy come, easy go" mean?
4. Picture and describe the last time you cried.

Questions 1 and 3 are verbal, nonemotional questions; a right-handed person should use the left hemisphere to answer and, as a result, tend to look to the right. Questions 2 and 4 are spatial-emotional questions that require the right hemisphere and should, on the average, yield more eye movements to the left than the right.

For more details, see G. E. Schwartz, R. Davidson, and F. Maer, "Right Hemisphere Lateralization for Emotion in the Human Brain: Interactions with Cognition," *Science*, 190 (1975): 286–288.

These clear differences between the hemispheres apply primarily to right-handed people. Some left-handers have the opposite pattern of cerebral dominance—language is found in the right hemisphere. More commonly, lefties have less dramatic differences between the halves of the brain.

One by-product of all the research on cerebral dominance has been to increase interest in the phenomenon of handedness. About nine out of ten people prefer to use their right hand, and this seems to be a distinctly human characteristic with a long history. Even the people pictured in Egyptian tomb paintings usually use their right hand (Figure 4.10). Jeannine Herron (1976) has argued that left-handers are a discriminated-against minority. Teachers often try to get young children to use their right hands. The French word for left is *gauche*, which in English means clumsy or socially inept, as in "left-handed compliment." There is no scientific basis, Herron argues, for believing that right-handed is better.

About nine out of ten people are right-handed.

HOW PSYCHOLOGISTS STUDY THE BRAIN

Mapping the brain's mountains, canyons, and inner recesses has supplied scientists with fascinating information about the role of the brain in behavior. Psychologists who do this kind of research are called physiological

Figure 4.10
An Egyptian tomb painting showing people at work, using their right hands.

psychologists. Among the methods they use to explore the brain are recording, stimulation, and lesioning.

Recording

By inserting wires called **electrodes** into the brain, it is possible to detect the minute electrical changes that occur when neurons fire (Figure 4.11). The wires are connected to electronic equipment that amplifies the tiny voltages produced by the firing neurons. Even single neurons can be monitored. For example, two researchers placed tiny electrodes in the sections of cats' and monkeys' brains that receive visual information. They found that different neurons fired, depending on whether a line, an edge, or an angle was placed before the animal's eyes (Hubel and Wiesel, 1962).

The electrical activity of whole areas of the brain can be recorded with an **electroencephalograph (EEG).** Wires from the EEG machine are taped to the scalp so that millions upon millions of neurons can be monitored at the same time (Figure 4.12). Psychologists have observed that the overall electrical activity of the brain rises and falls rhythmically and that the

Figure 4.11
This rat has an electrode implanted in an area of its ''old'' brain. Each time the animal presses the lever, a tiny pulse is delivered to its brain. The extremely high rates of lever-pressing performed by animals with such implants indicate that a ''pleasure center'' is probably being stimulated by the electricity.

pattern of the rhythm depends on whether a person is awake, drowsy, or asleep (as illustrated in Chapter 7). These rhythms, or brain waves, occur because the neurons in the brain tend to increase or decrease their amount of activity in unison.

EEGs can be used to monitor the brain disorder that causes epilepsy. When an epileptic seizure occurs, abnormal electrical activity begins in a small piece of damaged brain tissue. It then spreads to neighboring areas of the brain until much of the brain is showing abnormally large brain waves on the EEG. By monitoring these brain waves, psychologists can locate the site at which the seizure begins and can follow its spread through the brain. This helps doctors to determine what kind of surgical procedure (if any) would reduce violent seizures.

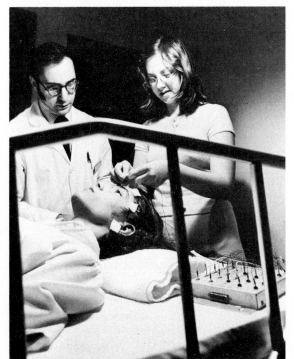

Figure 4.12
Measuring brain waves using an electroencephalograph (EEG) machine.

Stimulation

Electrodes may be used to set off the firing of neurons as well as to record it. Brain surgeon Wilder Penfield stimulated the brains of his patients during surgery to determine what functions the various parts of the brain perform. In this way he could localize the malfunctioning part for which surgery was required, for example, for epilepsy. When Penfield applied a tiny electric current to points on the temporal lobe of the brain, he could trigger whole memory sequences. During surgery, one woman heard a familiar song so clearly that she thought a record was being played in the operating room (Penfield and Rasmussen, 1950).

Using the stimulation technique, other researchers have shown that there are "pleasure" and "punishment" centers in the brain. One research team implanted electrodes in certain areas of the "old brain" of a rat, then placed the rat in a box equipped with a lever that the rat could press. Each time the rat pressed the lever, a mild electrical current was delivered to its brain. When the electrode was placed in the rat's "pleasure" center, it would push the lever several thousand times per hour (Olds and Olds, 1965) (see Figure 4.11).

Scientists have used chemicals as well as electricity to stimulate the brain. In this method, a small tube is implanted in an animal's brain so that the end touches the area to be stimulated (Figure 4.13). Chemicals can then be delivered through the tube to the area of the brain being studied. Such experiments have shown that different chemicals in the hypothalamus can affect hunger and thirst in an animal.

Stimulation techniques have aroused great medical interest. They have been used with terminal cancer patients to relieve them of intolerable pain without using drugs. A current delivered through electrodes implanted in certain areas of the brain seems to provide a sudden temporary relief (Delgado, 1969). Furthermore, some psychiatrists have experimented with similar methods to control violent emotional behavior in otherwise uncontrollable patients.

Figure 4.13
The technique for stimulating the inside of a rat's brain with chemicals. (a) The rat is prepared for brain surgery. (b) A small funnel at the top of a tiny tube is permanently implanted in the rat's skull. The other end of the tube is deep inside the brain. (c) A small amount of some chemical that affects the nervous system is passed into the tube in a solution of water.

a
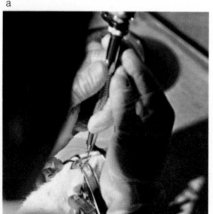

b
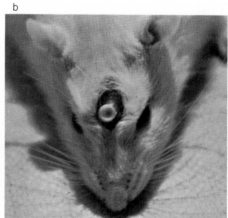

c
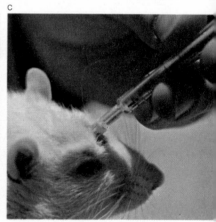

The Courts and Psychosurgery

In 1973, a Michigan court made an important decision which limited psychosurgery.

L.S., a criminal who had been charged with first-degree murder and rape, had been confined to a Michigan mental hospital for eighteen years when he agreed to have brain surgery to try to make him less violent. Legal services lawyer Gabe Kaimowitz brought suit to prevent the operation.

Both L.S. and his parents had given written consent for the operation. But it became clear in court that neither completely understood the implications of the procedure. Furthermore, L.S. suspected that he might be released earlier if he went along with the operation.

The court ruled that the operation should not be done even though L.S. had said he wanted it. Involuntarily confined patients, the court said, simply cannot give legally adequate consent to experimental high-risk procedures like psychosurgery. Thus, the legal status of certain types of psychosurgery is now in doubt.

For more details, see Carol Wade Offir, "The Movement to Pull Out the Electrodes," *Psychology Today,* 7 (May 1974): 69–70.

Lesions

Scientists sometimes create lesions by cutting or destroying part of an animal's brain. If the animal behaves differently after the operation, they assume that the destroyed brain area is involved with that type of behavior. For example, in one classic lesion study, two researchers removed a certain area of the subcortex (or "old brain") from rhesus monkeys. Normally, these animals are aggressive and vicious. After the operation they became less fearful and at the same time less violent (Kluver and Bucy, 1937). The implication was that this area of the brain controlled aggression. Subsequent researchers have learned that the relations revealed by this type of research are far more subtle and complex than people first believed.

USING PSYCHOLOGY

Psychosurgery

We have already discussed the use of lesions in treating violent epileptic seizures (by severing the corpus callosum). Experiments with animals suggested to some researchers that it might be possible to treat certain behavioral problems with similar operations. Brain surgery aimed at changing people's thoughts and actions is called **psychosurgery.**

The first great wave of psychosurgery was from about 1935 to 1955. A number of studies had showed that monkeys were less upset by frustration after portions of the frontal lobe of their brains were destroyed. A similar operation, called a prefrontal lobotomy, was tried on about 50,000 mental patients in the United States and Great Britain. These operations often seemed to help people who had serious mental problems. But they also had some undesirable side effects.

After the frontal lobes were destroyed, many patients lost the ability to deal with new information or pursue goals. For example, a woman who was a very innovative cook before her operation had trouble with new recipes afterward. Even more distressing was the fact that when she went out food shopping, she would sometimes get distracted and would forget why she had left the house (Valenstein, 1973: 298). But it is hard to draw a firm conclusion about the overall effects of frontal lobotomies. After reviewing all the available evidence, Elliot Valenstein wrote: "There is certainly no grounds for either the position that all psychosurgery necessarily reduces people to a 'vegetable status' or that it has a high probability of producing miraculous cures. The truth, even if somewhat wishy-washy, lies in between these extreme positions. There is little doubt, however, that many abuses existed" (Valenstein, 1973: 315). But the matter became academic in the mid-1950s because new drugs were introduced that became the treatment of choice in mental hospitals.

Within the last fifteen years, however, new operations have been introduced, and people have become interested in psychosurgery once again. Instead of destroying large portions of the frontal lobes, these operations used sophisticated techniques to destroy very small areas of tissue deep inside the brain. These operations quickly became controversial, particularly when they were used to change people who had a history of violent behavior. (Michael Crichton's best-selling novel *The Terminal Man* gave a fictional account of one such operation that went wrong.) In recent years, psychosurgeons have operated on about 400 people per year in the United States.

Public attention brought psychosurgery into the courts and the political arena. In 1974, Congress appointed the eleven-member National Commission for the Protection of Human Subjects of Biomedical and Behavioral Research to study several controversial areas. In October 1976, they released their report on psychosurgery. At this time, public and scientific opinion was generally opposed to psychosurgery. The commission's conclusions were, in the words of one reporter

(Culliton, 1976), "surprisingly favorable." They did not approve the older technique of frontal lobotomy, but they did say that some of the newer operations seemed to work. For example, an operation called a cingulotomy (destruction of a major subcortical structure) seems to be very helpful for some people who suffer from pain and severe depression.

The complexity of these operations on the brain and the philosophical issues raised by the idea of changing the way people act by changing their brains guarantees that psychosurgery will remain controversial for some time to come.

THE ENDOCRINE SYSTEM

The nervous system is one of two communication systems for sending information to the brain and returning messages to the body's billions of cells. The second is the endocrine, or hormone, system.

The **edocrine system** is a chemical system. Its messages are chemical substances called **hormones,** which are produced by the endocrine glands and distributed by the blood and other body fluids. (The names and locations of these glands are shown in Figure 4.14.) In many ways the endocrine system resembles a postal system. Hormones, or chemical messages, circulate throughout the bloodstream, but are only delivered to a specific address—the particular organs of the body that they influence.

The pituitary and thyroid glands illustrate how hormones work. Together with the brain, the **pituitary gland** is the center of control of the endocrine system—the "master gland." The pituitary gland secretes a large number of hormones, many of which control the output of hormones by other endocrine glands. The brain controls the pituitary gland and so indirectly controls the activity of the others. It also monitors the amount of hormones in the blood and sends out messages to correct imbalances. In return, certain hormones affect the functioning of the brain. For example, in one study the hormone ACTH improved memory in rats and mice (Rigter *et al.,* 1974). When injected into humans, ACTH reduced anxiety and improved performance on tasks requiring visual attention.

The **thyroid gland** produces the hormone thyroxin. Thyroxin stimulates certain chemical reactions that are important for all tissues of the body. Too little thyroxin makes people feel lazy and lethargic; too much makes them overactive. But the activity of the thyroid gland is itself controlled by a hormone released by the pituitary gland. High levels of thyroxin in the blood reduce the output of the thyroxin-stimulating hormone by the pituitary gland; low levels of thyroxin cause the pituitary gland to produce greater levels of this hormone. The pituitary and thyroid glands thus regulate each other, and the combination regulates general bodily activity.

Through the combined action of the nervous and endocrine systems,

Figure 4.14
The endocrine glands.

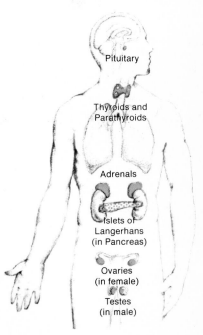

Pituitary

Thyroids and
Parathyroids

Adrenals

Islets of
Langerhans
(in Pancreas)

Ovaries
(in female)

Testes
(in male)

the brain monitors and controls most human behavior. In the next chapter we will see how the endocrine system influences behavior we normally attribute to psychological causes—emotion and motivation.

THE RELATIONSHIP BETWEEN HUMANS AND ANIMALS

Much of the research described in this chapter has been done primarily with lower animals. Researchers often study animals because they cannot perform a risky operation on a human being without a better reason than scientific inquiry. The research that has been done on humans has either occurred as a part of some necessary medical operation or has involved observing people who have suffered an injury by accident.

It is now commonly accepted that the study of animals can help in the study of human beings, even though direct experiments on humans would be even more useful if they could be done. Animal studies are especially valuable in medicine and physiology. Drugs, vaccines, and new forms of surgery are regularly tested on animal subjects. The reason such research is considered useful is that human beings are believed to have evolved from more primitive animal origins, and their bodies are therefore similar to the bodies of other animals.

The Evolution of Behavior

What many people often do not realize is that evolution applies not only to anatomy and physiology but also to behavior. Charles Darwin, the biologist who in 1859 published his theory of evolution, believed that all animal

Figure 4.15
Humans are not totally different from all other animals: our behavior as well as our anatomy can be compared with that of other species.

species are related to one another. Consequently, the structure of their bodies and their behavior patterns can be distinguished and compared just as one may compare a child's nose or his temper to that of his father. The bones in a bird's wing are different but comparable to the bones in a human arm; the way birds flock together can be compared to the way humans gather in groups (Figure 4.15). And just as the parts of a chimpanzee's brain can be compared to a human's, so can a chimpanzee's ability to solve problems be compared to human thinking ability.

Darwin's theory does not mean that humans do not possess unique qualities, but it does make it possible to think of humans as members of a particularly complex, interesting species instead of as totally different from other animals.

Ethology

One of the major outgrowths of Darwin's theory of evolution is **ethology,** the study of the natural behavior patterns of all species of animals from a biological point of view. They attempt to understand how these patterns have evolved and changed, and how they are expressed in humans. Ethologists call these natural patterns **species-specific behaviors,** behaviors that are characteristic of a particular animal species. By observing animals in their natural environment, ethologists hope to discover the links between a species' surroundings and its behaviors.

Ethologists have found that the behavior and experience of more primitive animals (such as insects or fish) are less flexible, or more stereotyped, than the behavior of higher animals, such as apes or humans. Stereotyped behaviors consist of patterns of responses that cannot change readily in response to changes in the environment. They work well only if the environment stays as it was when the behavior pattern evolved.

For example, when a horse is confronted with danger and requires a quiet escape, it is impossible for it to tiptoe away. Its escape behavior consists of only three patterns: walking, trotting, and galloping. Each pattern is a distinct series of movements that vary little from one horse to another, and all normal horses display these patterns. These are called **fixed action patterns** because they are inflexible—an animal can react to certain situations only in these ways.

Fixed action patterns are one kind of **instinct**—a behavior pattern that is inborn rather than learned. People often misuse the word "instinct" to refer to behaviors that become automatic after long practice. A professional baseball player may be described as "instinctively" making the right play, for example. But ethologists use the term "instinct" to refer only to those abilities that seem to be inherited.

Ethologists have found that animals are born with special sensitivities to certain cues in the environment (as well as with special ways of behaving). These cues are called sign stimuli. For example, Niko Tinbergen showed that the male stickleback, a small fish, will attack a model of another stickleback if it has a red belly. Even if the model is distorted, as in Figure 4.16, the male will still attack. Yet if it sees a very lifelike model of a stickleback without a red belly, the male will leave it alone. In this case, the

Figure 4.16
The bright red belly of the male stickleback is a sign stimulus for attack from other sticklebacks. They will attack red-bellied models like the ones below before they will respond to a realistic model of a stickleback that does not have a red belly.

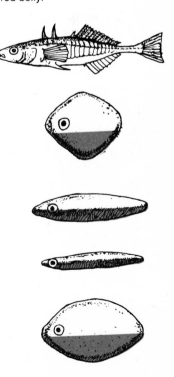

sign stimulus that triggers attack is the color red. In other species other sign stimuli can trigger certain behaviors.

Do sign stimuli occur in humans? Although instincts are less common and less powerful in human behavior, there is evidence that some stereotyped behaviors exist. For example, Konrad Lorenz found that a "parental instinct" seems to be aroused by the appearance of the human baby. When he compared human infants to other young animals, he noticed that they all seem to display a similar set of sign stimuli which appear to stir up parental feelings. Short faces, prominent foreheads, round eyes, and plump cheeks all seem to arouse the parental response.

Sociobiology

Closely related to ethology is another new discipline that studies the hereditary basis of social behavior in animals and humans to determine whether these behaviors are inherited from remote ancestors. This science, known as **sociobiology,** draws on the findings of biology, anthropology, and psychology. It has attracted a great deal of attention, and an even greater amount of controversy. In 1975, Harvard zoologist Edward O. Wilson published *Sociobiology: A New Synthesis*, in which he defined the new discipline as "the systematic study of the biological basis of all social behavior" (1975a: 595). Wilson surveyed the social behavior of all known primates and suggested that certain traits humans share with almost all other primates—prolonged maternal care of offspring, for instance, and male dominance over females—may have been passed along to us in our genes.

Sociobiologists regard their discipline as the last phase of the revolution begun by Charles Darwin. It tries to fill a major gap in Darwin's theory of natural selection: nature's goal is individual survival and reproduction, yet several traits of humans and other animals seem to work directly against this goal. Soldier ants will fight to the death, thus contributing to saving their group from invaders. A bird will often call out a warning to other birds that a predator is nearby, though the warning call itself alerts the enemy to that particular bird's whereabouts and risks the bird's life. Dolphins have been known to band together and support a stricken companion on the surface of the water where it can breathe (Wilson, 1975b). And, of course, among humans, parents die rescuing their children from fires, and soldiers throw themselves suicidally on grenades to save their buddies.

Sociobiologists fit all these acts of self-sacrifice into nature's economy. They explain that altruism itself favors genetic gain: the individual risks itself, but the result of this behavior is that other individuals who share its genes may survive (Figure 4.17). The soldier ant, which is sterile, protects its queen, which then lives to produce more of the soldier ant's kind. The bird who calls a warning in effect also protects its kind, and this increases the chance that its genes will survive, as does the behavior of the mother who saves her baby. The battlefield hero dies confident that the nation will keep his family safe to reproduce—and thus to perpetuate his own genes. The noted British biologist J. B. S. Haldane once joked that he would give his life for his two brothers, each of whom shares about half his genes, or for eight cousins (cited in *Time*, August 1, 1977, 56).

Figure 4.17
Sociobiologists explain firefighters risking their lives to save others as yet another aspect of natural selection: the individual risks itself, but the species survives.

Sociobiology seeks to explain other social behaviors, even aggression, in terms of genetic advantage. The bully who kicks sand in the ninety-seven-pound weakling's face is actually sending a message to the weakling's girl friend: "I have good genes. You ought to mate with me."

The idea that genes determine human social behavior has been so controversial that Wilson has been picketed and even had water thrown in his face at the otherwise sedate 1978 meeting of the American Association for the Advancement of Science. Some critics, notably Richard Lewontin, Stephen Gould, and other members of the Harvard-based Sociobiology Study Group, have expressed fear that sociobiology can be used to support the political, economic, and legal status quo. According to the logic of sociobiology, these must have been determined by our genes (reported in Wade, 1976).

Other critics point out that there is no hard evidence that specific genes exist for altruism, aggression, or other social behaviors, but only theories and guesswork (Washburn, 1978). They also point out that animals may behave very selfishly indeed. Among the lions of the Serengeti plain in East Africa, lionesses have been observed driving their own cubs away from food if the catch was small; many of these cubs have died of starvation. Of

Figure 4.18 A baboon troop in the wild. Although many people believe that primate males dominate females, relations between the sexes are actually quite complicated.

1,400 herring gull chicks studied during one period, 23 percent were killed by attacks from adults of their own species as they strayed from the nest (Marler, 1976).

Along the same lines, anthropologists have repeatedly contested the popular belief that human males are innately aggressive and dominant over females. The supporters of this argument often cite studies of baboons that document male aggression and dominance over females. Opponents point out that the baboons observed in these studies were in a game park, an abnormal environment that exposed them to a heavy concentration of predators (especially human ones) and to a high level of tension. Among baboon troops that live undisturbed in the forest, however, it is female baboons who determine the troop's movements. Males exhibit very little aggression and little dominance (Pilbeam, 1972).

If baboon behavior can vary so widely in different environments, it is even more likely that human behavior will do so. Genes may very well be an important component of human social behavior, but they cannot entirely determine it. If the children of two great athletes are never permitted to exercise, their genes will never make them athletes. Indeed, the flexibility of human social behavior, the extreme differences in various cultures and in different contexts, is almost uniquely human (Pilbeam, 1972). Only human beings construct cultures, passing on large and growing accumulations of learning from generation to generation and thereby to a certain extent overcoming the slow process of genetic evolution. Only human beings exhibit a wide variety of culturally determined behaviors, such as wearing black to funerals in some countries and white in others.

The question of the extent to which heredity does determine human social behavior is far from settled. But Wilson and some other sociobiologists believe that humankind is flexible and must be so, and that genetic inclinations need not always be obeyed and sometimes should not be. Evolution takes place so slowly that we may still be inheriting behavior patterns that were adaptive in prehistoric times but that are no longer useful in our radically different world. In the Stone Age it may well have been important to raise as many healthy children as possible; on today's crowded planet it is not. When humans lived in hunter-gatherer societies, it might have been necessary to wage war against all foreigners in order to survive; now war could mean the end of humankind (Wilson, 1975b). The major contribution of sociobiology has been to remind us that genes do count, but that human beings have the capacity to learn a wide range of behaviors and to unlearn those that cease to be adaptive.

HEREDITY AND ENVIRONMENT

People often argue about whether human behavior is instinctive (due to heredity) or learned (due to environment). Do people learn to be good athletes, or are they born that way? Do people learn to do well in school, or are they born good at it? Do people learn to be homosexual, or are they born that way? The reason for the intensity of the argument may be that many people assume that something learned can probably be changed, whereas something inborn will be difficult or impossible to change. This is wrong. Whenever psychologists investigate a particular case, they find that the issue is not that simple. Inherited factors and environmental conditions always act together in complicated ways. Asking whether heredity or environment is responsible for something turns out to be like asking "What makes a cake rise, baking powder or heat?" Obviously, an interaction of the two is responsible.

> **Inherited factors and environment always act together in complicated ways.**

The argument over the nature-nurture question has been going on for centuries. Sir Francis Galton, a cousin of Charles Darwin, was one of the first to preach the importance of nature in the modern era. In 1869 he published *Hereditary Genius*, a book in which he analyzed the families of over 1,000 eminent politicians, religious leaders, artists, and scholars. He found that success ran in the families and concluded that heredity was the cause.

But most psychologists have emphasized the importance of the environment. The tone was set by John Watson, the father of behaviorism, who wrote in 1930: "Give me a dozen healthy infants, well-formed, and my own specified world to bring them up in and I'll guarantee to take any one at random and train him to become any type of specialist I might select— doctor, lawyer, artist, merchant-chief, and, yes, even beggarman and thief, regardless of his talents, penchants, tendencies, abilities, vocations, and race of his ancestors" (Watson, 1930: 104).

Watson's view now seems a bit extreme. Recent studies that directly looked for evidence of genetic influence on human traits have focused on three general areas: cognitive abilities (like IQ), mental illness, and personality. The argument over IQ (see Chapter 14) has been particularly loud and long, but each of the other areas is also controversial.

One way to find out whether a trait is inherited is to study twins. Identical twins develop from a single fertilized egg (thus, they are called monozygotic) and share the same genes. Fraternal twins develop from two fertilized eggs (thus, dizygotic), and their genes are no more similar than those of brothers or sisters.

Figure 4.19
Because identical twins share the same genes as well as the same environment, studying them is one way to find out whether a trait is inherited or learned.

Obviously, twins growing up in the same house share the same general environment. But identical twins who grow up together also share the same genes. So, if identical twins prove to be more alike on a specific trait than fraternal twins do, it probably means that genes are important for that trait.

For example, many twin studies have been done on the inheritance of mental disease. Schizophrenia is the most common form of serious mental illness and affects about 1 percent of the world population (see Chapter 15). Studies have shown that if one twin becomes schizophrenic, the other twin is three to six times more likely to become schizophrenic if he is an identical twin rather than a fraternal twin (Rosenthal, 1970). Thus, schizophrenia is at least partly genetic. However, it is also clear that in many cases, one identical twin develops schizophrenia and the other does not. Thus, environmental factors are also important.

There are several other ways of studying the nature-nurture problem in humans. In a few cases, identical twins have been separated at birth by adoption agencies or whatever. These twins show the effects of the same genes in different environments. Although such cases are relatively rare, they are extremely important from a scientific point of view. It is also possible to see whether adopted children more closely resemble their biological parents (thus suggesting the importance of genes) or their adoptive parents (emphasizing the influence of environment). Although many such studies are going on, the nature-nurture question will probably continue to be controversial, at least until people gain a more sophisticated understanding of how heredity and environment interact to produce behavior.

Ultimately, understanding the genetic basis of a problem may help to solve it. For example, since the mid-1960s, delivery-room attendants have pricked the heels of more than 10 million American babies shortly after birth and have taken a few drops of blood for analysis (Figure 4.20). This procedure has saved 1,000 babies from severe mental retardation caused by the genetic disorder called phenylketonuria, or PKU.

PKU is caused by a defect in the gene involved with the body's use of phenylalanine, a protein present in milk and many other foods. The defective gene results in the lack of a body chemical needed to convert phenylalanine into another protein. The unconverted phenylalanine builds up and changes to a poison that attacks the cells of the nervous system and causes progressive mental retardation. Children with PKU appear normal at birth, but their intelligence stops developing during the first year. Without treatment, one-third never learn to walk, and two-thirds never learn to talk. Children with PKU have lighter pigmentation of skin and hair, shorter stature, and greater irritability than normal children. The disorder afflicts approximately 1 in 20,000 whites, and is extremely rare among blacks.

With PKU, scientists have been able to break the tragic chain of events that would otherwise begin with the defective gene. The drops of blood taken from the newborn baby's heel are analyzed for the presence of phenylalanine. An abnormally high level indicates the presence of the defective gene, and the baby is immediately started on a diet low in phenylalanine. Simply by adjusting one minor aspect of the infant's internal environment—the level of phenylalanine in the body—doctors can prevent the devastating effects of the faulty gene. Thus, although PKU is inherited, its effects can be changed by controlling the environment.

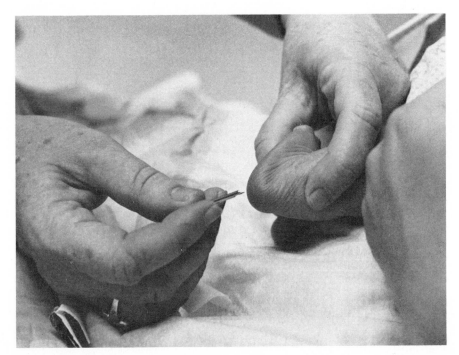

Figure 4.20
The test for PKU, a simple prick on the heel, is now given automatically to all newborns, since early detection can prevent the ravages of this congenital disease.

SUMMARY

1. Messages are constantly traveling back and forth in the body through the nervous system to the brain. The spinal cord, a part of the nervous system, transmits most of the messages back and forth between the body and the brain. The messages to and from the brain are communicated by chemical-electrical signals traveling down long, thin cells called neurons.

2. The autonomic nervous system plays a key role in the physiology of emotion. One of its components, the sympathetic nervous system, prepares the body for dealing with emergencies or strenuous activities. The parasympathetic nervous system, the other part of the autonomic nervous system, works to conserve energy and to enhance the body's ability to recover from strenuous activity.

3. The brain monitors what is happening inside and outside of the body through the use of receptors and effectors. The brain is composed of the cerebral cortex and the subcortex. The subcortex guides a person's biological needs and animal instincts. The cerebral cortex enables a person to read and solve problems.

4. The cortex is divided into two hemispheres, each containing four lobes. For right-handed people, the left hemisphere is more involved with ver-

bal thoughts while the right hemisphere is involved with spatial relations.

5. Recording, stimulation, and lesions are three techniques psychologists use to study the brain. Psychosurgery is brain surgery aimed at changing a person's thoughts or actions.

6. The endocrine or hormone system is a chemical system of communication between the body and the brain. Through the combined action of the nervous and endocrine systems, the brain monitors and controls human behavior.

7. Studies of animal behavior have revealed that many species respond to their environments in terms of fixed action patterns—that is, they can react to certain situations only in set ways. Such automatic responses play a minor role in human behavior.

8. Sociobiologists look for the biological basis of social behavior. For example, they believe that altruism is based on an animal's desire to insure that its genes are passed on to the next generation.

9. All human behavior is based on the interaction of heredity and environment. The comparison of identical and fraternal twins can help discover the influence of genes on a specific trait.

GLOSSARY

autonomic nervous system: Part of the peripheral nervous system that controls internal biological functions such as heart rate and digestion.

central nervous system (CNS): The brain and spinal cord.

cerebellum: A lower portion of the brain which controls posture and balance and regulates the details of motor commands from the cerebral cortex.

cerebral cortex: The gray mass surrounding the subcortex, which controls most of the higher brain functions, such as reading and problem solving.

corpus callosum: A band of nerves that connects the two hemispheres of the cortex and carries messages back and forth between them.

effectors: The cells that work the muscles, internal glands, and organs.

electrode: A type of wire used by scientists to detect the minute electrical changes that occur when neurons fire.

electroencephalograph (EEG): A machine used to record the electrical activity of large portions of the brain.

endocrine system: A chemical communication system, using hormones, by which messages are sent through the bloodstream to particular organs of the body.

ethology: The study of animal behavior in its natural environment.

firing: The transmitting, by a neuron, of a chemical-electrical signal across the synapse to another neuron.

fixed action patterns: Patterns of behavior that are inflexible. Such responses are common to many animal species, but not to humans.

frontal lobes: The lobes located in the front of the brain, which control intellect and personality.

hormones: Chemical substances that carry messages through the body in the blood.

hypothalamus: A small area deep inside the brain that regulates the autonomic nervous system and other body functions.

instinct: A behavior pattern that is inborn rather than learned.

lobes: The different regions into which the cerebral cortex is divided.

motor cortex: The portion of the brain located in the front of the somatosensory cortex, which controls body movement.

nerve fibers: The slender threadlike pieces of nerve cells through which messages are sent to and from the brain.

neurons: The long, thin cells that constitute the structural and functional unit of nerve tissue, along which messages travel to and from the brain.

neurotransmitters: The chemicals released by neurons which determine the rate at which other neurons fire.

occipital lobes: The lobes located at the back of the brain, which receive visual information for the body.

parasympathetic nervous system: The system that works to conserve energy and enhance the body's ability to recuperate after strenuous activity.

parietal lobes: The lobes located in the middle of the brain, which contain the somatosensory cortex.

peripheral nervous system (PNS): A network of nerves branching out from the spinal cord that conducts information from the bodily organs to the central nervous system and takes information back to the organs.

pituitary gland: The center of control of the endocrine system which secretes a large number of hormones.

psychosurgery: Brain surgery aimed at changing a person's thoughts or actions.

receptors: Cells whose function it is to gather information and send messages to the brain.

reticular activating system: The system in the brain that screens oncoming messages, blocking out some signals and letting others pass.

sociobiology: The study of the biological basis of social behavior.

somatic nervous system: The half of the peripheral nervous system that controls voluntary movement of skeletal muscles.

somatosensory cortex: An area of the brain, within the cerebral cortex, that receives information from the skin and muscles.

species-specific behavior: Behavior that is characteristic of a particular animal species.

spinal cord: The bundle of nerves that run down the length of the back and transmit most messages back and forth between the body and the brain.

subcortex: The part of the brain where all messages are first received and that, together with the spinal cord, controls and coordinates vital functions and reflex actions. It is sometimes called the "old brain."

sympathetic nervous system: The system that prepares the body for dealing with emergencies or strenuous activities.

synapses: The gaps that occur between individual nerve cells.

temporal lobes: The lobes on each side of the brain, which receive auditory information.

thalamus: The portion of the brain that sorts incoming impulses and directs them to various parts of the brain. It also relays messages from one part of the brain to another.

thyroid gland: The gland in the endocrine system that produces several hormones, including thyroxin.

ACTIVITIES

1. Can you observe species-specific behaviors in cats, dogs, or any other animals you see regularly? If you have an animal that you can observe carefully, try to identify fixed action patterns that are common to the animal's species. Do they exist in any form in yourself?

2. What aspects of your personality, your way of acting, and your appearance are most obviously the result of heredity? Which seem to be more related to your environmental upbringing? What factors make it difficult to decide whether hereditary or environmental factors are of greatest influence?

3. Ask several of your friends (individually) to perform some mental task, such as multiplying 31 by 24 in their heads, or counting the number of letters in a simple phrase (such as "early to bed"). Observe which way their eyes shift as they begin to think about the problem. If their eyes shift to the right, they are doing the counting in the left hemisphere of the cortex, and vice versa. For more information about the significance of this simple observation, see the Bakan article mentioned in the Suggested Readings.

SUGGESTED READINGS

BAKAN, P. "The Eyes Have It." *Psychology Today* (April 1971): 64–67, 96. Bakan describes his observation that the direction people look in when they think is related to the part of their cortex involved with thinking. He relates this to split-brain research.

CRICHTON, MICHAEL. *The Terminal Man.* New York: Knopf, 1972. An engrossing novel about a man who is turned into a machine, with forty microscopic wires buried in his head. At the end of the novel is a five-page annotated scientific appendix on mind control.

FRENCH, GILBERT M. *Cortical Functioning in Behavior: Research and Commentary.* Glenview, Ill.: Scott, Foresman, 1973. Up-to-date readings and commentary dealing with current views on localization of function within the cortex.

KIMBLE, DANIEL P. *Psychology as a Biological Science.* Pacific Palisades, Calif.: Goodyear, 1973. A readable elementary introduction to physiological psychology.

LAWICK-GOODALL, JANE VAN. *In the Shadow of Man.* Boston: Houghton Mifflin, 1971. For ten years Jane Lawick-Goodall lived in the midst of wild chimpanzees, and in this book she writes about their social structure, their behavior, and their personalities somewhat as if they comprised an interesting and intimate circle of friends. The narrative style of the book reads much like a good novel—it is difficult to put down.

LORENZ, KONRAD Z. *King Solomon's Ring.* New York: Crowell, 1952. A classic study of nature by one of the world's outstanding scientists. An absorbing and beautiful book of essays; light and easy to read.

LUCE, GAY G. *Body Time: Physiological Rhythms and Social Stress.* New York: Pantheon, 1971. Survey of data and theories on how biological rhythms affect behavior and mental life.

MC GAUGH, J., WEINBERGER, N. M., AND WHALEN, R. L. (EDS.). *Psychobiology*. San Francisco: Freeman, 1967. A volume of readings from *Scientific American* on the biological basis of behavior. Research in numerous disciplines is included in this comprehensive book.

VALENSTEIN, ELLIOT. *Brain Control: A Critical Examination of Brain Stimulation and Psychosurgery*. New York: Wiley, 1973. The best introduction to this controversial area.

BIBLIOGRAPHY

CHOROVER, S. L. "Big Brother and Psychotechnology II: The Pacification of the Brain." *Psychology Today*, 7 (May 1974): 59–69.

CULLITON, B. J. *"Psychosurgery: National Commission Issues Surprisingly Favorable Report."Science*, 194 (1976): 299–301.

DELGADO, J. M. R. *Physical Control of the Mind*. New York: Harper & Row, 1969.

GAZZANIGA, MICHAEL S. "The Split Brain in Man." *Scientific American*, 217 (August 1967): 24–29.

HASSETT, J. *A Primer of Psychophysiology*. San Francisco: Freeman, 1978.

HERRON, JEANNINE. "Southpaws: How Different Are They?" *Psychology Today* (March 1976): 50–56.

HUBEL, DAVID H., AND WIESEL, TORSLEN N. "Receptive Fields, Binocular Interaction, and Functional Architecture in the Cat's Visual Cortex." *Journal of Physiology*, 160 (1962): 106–154.

KLÜVER, H., AND BUCY, P. C., "Psychic Blindness and Other Symptoms Following Bilateral Temporal Lobectomy in Rhesus Monkeys." *American Journal of Physiology*, 119 (1937): 532–535.

MARLER, PETER. "On Animal Aggression: The Roles of Strangeness and Familiarity." *American Psychologist*, 31, no. 3 (March 1976): 239–246.

OLDS, J., AND OLDS, M. E. "Drives, Rewards and the Brain." In *New Directions in Psychology II*, ed. by F. Barron *et al.* New York: Holt, Rinehart and Winston, 1965.

ORNSTEIN, R. E. *The Psychology of Consciousness*. 2nd ed. New York.: Harcourt Brace Jovanovich, 1977.

PENFIELD, WILDER, AND RASMUSSEN, THEODORE. *The Cerebral Cortex of Man*. New York: Macmillan, 1950.

PILBEAM, DAVID. "An Idea We Could Live Without—The Naked Ape." *Discovery*, 7, no. 2 (Spring 1972): 63–70.

RIGTER, H., VAN RIEZE, H., AND WIED, D. D. "The Effects of ACTH and Vasopressin Analogues on CO_2-induced Retrograde Amnesia in Rats." *Physiology and Behavior*, 13 (1974): 381–388.

ROSENTHAL, D. *Genetic Theory and Abnormal Behavior*. New York: McGraw-Hill, 1970.

SCHWARTZ, G. E., DAVIDSON, R., AND MAER, F. "Right Hemisphere Lateralization for Emotion in the Human Brain: Interactions with Cognition." *Science*, 190 (1975): 286–288.

VALENSTEIN, ELLIOT. *Brain Control: A Critical Examination of Brain Stimulation and Psychosurgery*. New York: Wiley, 1973.

WADE, NICHOLAS. "Sociobiology: Troubled Birth for a New Discipline." *Science*, 191 (March 19, 1976): 1151–1155.

WASHBURN, S. L. "Human Behavior and the Behavior of Other Animals." *American Psychologist*, 33 (May 1978): 405–418.

WATSON, JOHN B. *Behaviorism*. New York: Norton, 1930.

WILSON, EDWARD O. *Sociobiology: A New Synthesis*. Cambridge, Mass.: Harvard University Press, 1975a.

————. "Human Decency Is Animal." *The New York Times Magazine* (October 12, 1975b), 38–49.

5 Sensation and Perception

In the next few seconds, something peculiar will start hap pening to the material youa rereading. Iti soft ennotre alized howcom plext heproces sofrea ding is. Afe w sim plerear range mentscan ha veyoucomp lete lycon fused!

As you can see, your success in gathering information from your environment, interpreting this information, and acting on it depends considerably on its being organized in ways you expect.

Your knowledge of the external world—and of your internal state as well—comes entirely from chemical and electrical processes occurring in the nervous system, particularly in the brain. Physical change in the external or internal environment triggers chemical, electrical, and mechanical activity in sense receptors. After complex processing in the nervous system, a pattern of activity is produced in certain areas of the brain. You experience this electrical activity as a **sensation**—awareness of colors, forms, sounds, smells, tastes, and so on. Usually you experience some meaningful whole—you see Groucho Marx, hear Paul McCartney's voice, smell an old, dirty sock—rather than a collection of sensations. The organization of sensory information into meaningful wholes is known as **perception.**

This process can be seen in the act of eating. When someone puts two hamburgers in front of you, receptors in your eyes send a message to the brain: the all-beef patties are stacked together in the sesame seed bun, along with some lettuce. Receptors in your nose may tell you there's ketchup and cheese inside, while other receptors in your mouth send messages about pickles and some mysterious sauce. As you grasp this gourmet delight in your hands, receptors in your fingers tell you that the roll is soft and warm. And the brain combines all these inputs into one unified perception: it's a Big Mac.

Figure 5.1
We "take in" information through our senses. Through sight, sound, touch, and smell we perceive the world around us.

In this chapter we will look at each of these steps more closely, focusing on how each organ converts physical changes into chemical-electrical signals to the brain and how perceptions are built from this information. In the last section we will discuss the possibility of gaining information without the known senses—through the process of extrasensory perception.

SENSATION

The world is filled with physical changes—an alarm clock sounds; the flip of a switch fills a room with light; you stumble against a door; steam from a hot tub billows out into the bathroom, changing the temperature and clouding the mirror. All these changes result in sensations—of loudness, brightness, pain in the elbow you bump, heat, tastes, smells, and so on. Any aspect of or change in the environment to which an organism responds is called a **stimulus.** An alarm, an electric light, and an aching muscle are all stimuli for human beings.

A stimulus can be measured in some physical way—by its size, its duration, its intensity, its wavelength, and so on. A sensory experience can also be measured (at least, indirectly). But a sensory experience and a stimulus are not the same. For example, the same English muffin (stimulus) might taste (sensory experience) one way if you had just eaten and quite a different way if you hadn't eaten anything for a week. On the other hand, the same sensory experience (flashing lights, for example) might be produced by different stimuli (a blow to the head or a fireworks display).

Psychologists are interested in the relationship between physical stimuli and sensory experiences. In vision, for example, the sensation of color corresponds to the wavelength of the light, whereas brightness corresponds to the intensity of this stimulus.

What is the relationship between color and wavelength? How does changing a light's intensity affect one's sensation of its brightness? The psychological study of such questions is called **psychophysics.** The goal of psychophysics is to develop a quantified relationship between stimuli from the world (such as frequency and intensity) and the sensory experiences (such as pitch and loudness) produced by them.

Threshold

In order to establish laws about how people sense the external world, psychologists first try to determine how much of a stimulus is necessary for a person to sense it at all. How much energy is required for someone to hear a sound or to see a light? How much of a scent must be in the room before one can smell it? How much pressure must be applied to the skin before a person will feel it?

To answer such questions, a psychologist might set up the following experiment. First, a person (the subject) is placed in a dark room and is instructed to look at the wall. He is asked to say "I see it" when he is able to detect a light. The psychologist then uses an extremely precise machine that can project a low-intensity beam of light against the wall. The experimenter turns on the machine to its lowest light projection. The subject says nothing. The experimenter increases the light until finally the subject responds, "I see it." Then the experimenter begins another test in the opposite direction. He starts with a clearly visible light and decreases its intensity until the light seems to disappear. Many trials are completed and averaged. The **absolute threshold**—the smallest amount of energy that will produce a sensation—is defined as the amount of energy that a subject can see about half the time.

Interestingly enough, thresholds determined in this way are not as absolute as psychologists first believed. The point at which the person says "I see it" may vary with the instructions he is given ("Say you see it only if you're absolutely certain" versus "If there's any doubt, say you see it") or even the order in which the stimuli are presented.

Under ideal conditions, the senses have very low absolute thresholds. That is, sensations will be experienced with very small amounts of stimulation. For example, the eardrum registers a sound if it moves as little as 1 percent of the diameter of a hydrogen molecule. If the ear were any more sensitive, you might hear the sound of air molecules bumping into each other (Geldard, 1972). Similarly, the eye is about as sensitive as it could possibly be.

If the ear were any more sensitive, you might hear the sound of air molecules bumping into each other.

USING PSYCHOLOGY

Subliminal Advertising

On September 12, 1957, an advertising executive held a press conference to announce a revolutionary breakthrough in marketing techniques: **subliminal advertising.** The word "subliminal" comes from the Latin: *sub* ("below") and *limen* ("threshold"). The words "Eat Popcorn" and "Coca-Cola" had been flashed on a movie screen in a New Jersey theater on alternate nights for six weeks, according to the executive. Although the flashes were so brief (1/3,000 of a second, once every five seconds) that none of the moviegoers even seemed to notice them, popcorn sales rose 18.1 percent and Coca-Cola sales went up 57.7 percent.

The public response to this announcement was long, loud, and hysterical. In a TV interview, Aldous Huxley predicted that it would be possible to manipulate people politically with this technique "by about 1964" (quoted in Brown, 1963: 184). Congressmen called for FCC regulations, while several state legislatures passed laws banning subliminal ads.

Meanwhile, more test results began to appear. When the man who made the original claims staged another test for the FCC a few months later, the results were equivocal. Later, WTWO-TV in Bangor, Maine, flashed the words "If you have seen this message, write WTWO" on the screen for 1/60 of a second every day for a week. Nobody wrote. A Seattle radio station experimented with auditory subliminal ads. During regular programming, a very low whisper in the background repeated "TV's a bore" and "Isn't TV dull?" (These experimenters had planned to add the message "TV causes eye cancer," but decided they'd better not risk it.) There is no reason to believe that these ads had any effect.

British television got into the act by flashing the message "Pirie breaks world record" during a ballet program. At the end of the show, an announcer asked the 4.5 million viewers to write to the station if they had noticed anything unusual. Four hundred thirty replies were received; 20 of them repeated the message verbatim and another 134 were close to being right.

This study, and others like it, have proved beyond doubt that very brief messages are indeed noticed by some people. That does not mean that they will be listened to any more than reading the words "Drink Coke" in a magazine ad forces you to run to the kitchen for a tall, frosty one.

In fact, the idea for subliminal ads came from a long series of controversial studies on subliminal perception—noticing stimuli that were believed to affect only the unconscious mind. But most psychologists remained skeptical about the claims for subliminal ads. After all, the original New Jersey study was done by the "Subliminal Projection Company," and was never described in sufficient detail to be evaluated by scientists.

Now, more than twenty years later, the furor has died down. As far as we know, Lyndon Johnson beat Barry Goldwater in 1964 without the help of subliminal ads. Every so often, the idea resurfaces in a magazine article or a TV show. Researchers continue to study the controversial area of subliminal perception. Lloyd Silverman (1976) and his colleagues, for example, have done many studies of how sexual and aggressive subliminal stimuli influence depressed patients and schizophrenics. But whenever it has been tried under controlled conditions, subliminal advertising has been a colossal failure.

Sensory Differences and Ratios

Another type of threshold is the **difference threshold** or just noticeable difference. This refers to the smallest change in a stimulus that will produce a change in sensation. So to return to our example of the person tested in a dark room, a psychologist would test for the difference threshold by gradually increasing the intensity of a visible light beam until the person says, "Yes, this is brighter than the light I just saw." With this technique, it is possible to identify the smallest increase in light intensity that will be noticeable to the human eye.

Psychologists also have found that a particular sensory experience depends more on *changes* in the stimulus than on the absolute size or amount of the stimulus. For example, if you put a three-pound package of food into an empty backpack, the sensation of weight will be greatly increased. But if you add the same amount to a hundred-pound backpack, the sensation will hardly increase at all. This is because the sensation produced by the added weight reflects a proportional change—and three pounds does not provide much change in a one-hundred-pound load.

In psychophysics, this idea is known as **Weber's law:** the larger or stronger a stimulus, the larger the change required for an observer to notice that anything has happened to it (to experience a just noticeable difference) (Weber, 1834).

The amount of stimulus change necessary to produce some increase in sensory experience is different for different cases, but it is almost always proportional. Suppose, for example, that you have a glass of unsweetened lemonade. In order to make it sweet, you add two spoonfuls of sugar. Now to make the lemonade taste "twice as sweet," you must add six spoonfuls—three times the original amount of sugar. Then you discover that in order to make the lemonade "four times as sweet," you must add a total of eighteen spoonfuls (Figure 5.2). Each time the sweetness doubles, the amount of sugar triples (see Stevens, 1962).

Figure 5.2
A change in sensory experience is proportional to the amount of physical change. In this case, each time the amount of sugar triples, the sweetness of the lemonade doubles.

Phantom Limb Pain

Every night Andy woke covered in a cold, soaking sweat. The pain that filled his left hand was more than he could bear. It felt like a razor-sharp scalpel was being jabbed deeper and deeper into the palm of his hand. No one had prepared him for this pain—not even the doctors who had amputated his left hand two years before.

The *phantom limb pain* we've just described is one of the most bizarre phenomenons in medicine. It may take the form of tingling feelings, warmth, coldness, heaviness, or intense pain in a limb that is no longer there.

About one-third of all amputees report phantom limb pain, which in most cases continues for about a year. But as doctors and some unfortunate amputees know, pain may last for decades.

Evidence suggests that phantom limb pain has no single cause. Irritation of the stump, abnormal sympathetic nervous system activity, and emotional disturbance may all play a role. But no one is sure exactly how these factors contribute to the pain or how to rid an amputee of the agony he feels in a limb that is no longer there.

For more details, see Ronald Melzack, *The Puzzle of Pain;* New York: Basic Books, 1973.

By experimenting in this way with variations in sounds, temperatures, pressures, colors, tastes, and smells, psychologists are learning more about how each sense responds to stimulation. Some senses produce huge increases in sensation in response to small increases in energy. For example, the pain of an electric shock can be increased more than eight times by doubling the voltage. On the other hand, the intensity of a light must be increased many times to double its brightness.

Sensory Adaptation

Psychologists have focused on people's responses to changes in stimuli because they have found that the senses are tuned to change: they are most responsive to increases and decreases, to new events rather than to ongoing, unchanging stimulation. This is because our senses have a general ability to **adapt,** or adjust themselves, to a constant level of stimulation. They get used to a new level and respond only to changes away from it.

A good example of this process of adaptation is the increase in visual sensitivity that you experience after a short time in a darkened movie theater. At first you see only blackness, but after a while your eyes adapt to the new level, and you can see seats, faces, and so on. Adaptation occurs for the other senses as well. Receptors in your skin adapt to the cold water when you go for a swim; disagreeable odors in a lab seem to disappear after a while; street noises cease to bother you after you've lived in a city for a time. Without sensory adaptation, you would feel the constant pressure of the clothes on your body, and other stimuli would seem to be bombarding all your senses at the same time.

Motivation and Signal-Detection Theory

Sensory experience does not depend on stimulus alone, however. A person's ability to detect a stimulus also depends on motivation. The individual does not simply receive a signal passively. Rather, the individual's perceptual system makes a decision as to its presence, though the decision-making process is usually entirely unconscious.

Thus the nervous new radar operator may see blips on his screen when there are none while the overrelaxed veteran may not notice the unexpected. To use a more complex example, if you've been thinking a lot about your old boy friend, you may think you see him walking down the street when it's really somebody else. On the other hand, you probably won't expect to meet your gynecologist in a singles' bar, and you might not notice him if he showed up there. Thus feelings, expectations, and motivation influence whether or not you experience a sensation.

Signal-detection theory studies the mathematical relations between motivation, sensitivity, and sensation (Green and Swets, 1966). Detection thresholds involve recognizing some stimulus against a background of noise. A radar operator must be able to detect an airplane on a radar screen even when the plane's blip is faint and difficult to distinguish from blips

Figure 5.3
Air controllers must be able to detect an airplane on the radar screen even when the plane's blip is faint and difficult to distinguish from blips caused by natural phenomena such as flocks of birds or bad weather.

caused by flocks of birds or bad weather, which can produce images that are like visual "noise" (Figure 5.3). Consider radar operators watching a screen in wartime during a storm. How do they decide whether a blip on the screen is an enemy plane or a patch of noise? If they were to call out massive armed forces for every blip, they would create chaos. But if one bomber was mistakenly identified as noise, the results could be disastrous. The radar operator's judgment will be influenced by many factors, and different operators appear to have different sensitivities to blips. Moreover, a specific individual's apparent sensitivity seems to fluctuate, depending on the situation. For example, being watched by a superior will probably affect the operator's performance, as will fatigue or other distractions.

In studying the difficulties faced by radar operators, psychologists have reformulated the concept of absolute threshold to take into account the many factors that affect detection of minimal stimuli. As a result, the signal-detection theory abandons the idea that there is a single true absolute threshold for a stimulus. Instead it adopts the notion that the stimulus, here called a signal, must be detected in the face of noise, which can interfere with detection of the signal. Thus signal detection is similar to standing in a noisy bus terminal, listening for the announcement of your bus departure time over the loudspeaker. Although the volume of the loudspeaker remains constant, you will have more or less difficulty in detecting your "signal," depending on the amount of noise in the bus terminal.

THE SENSES

Although traditionally people are thought to have five senses, there are actually more. In addition to vision, hearing, taste, and smell, there are several skin senses and two "internal" senses: vestibular and kinesthetic.

Each type of sensory receptor takes some sort of external stimulus—light, chemical molecules, sound waves, pressure—and converts it into a chemical-electrical message that can be understood by the brain. So far we know most about these processes in vision and hearing. The other senses have received less attention and are more mysterious in their functioning.

Figure 5.4
The process of vision. (a) A cross-section of the human eye, showing the passage of light. Note that the retina receives an inverted image of the external world, although people are never aware of this inversion. The place where the optic nerve leaves the eye is called the blind spot because it is the only spot on the retina where no sensation takes place. (b) The cell structure of the retina. Note that the light-sensitive cells (the rods and cones) are those furthest from the light, not the closest as one might expect. Light arriving at the retina must pass through various other cells before striking the rods and cones, which convert it into nervous impulses. The impulses then pass through these other cells to be coded and organized before traveling over the optic nerve to the brain.

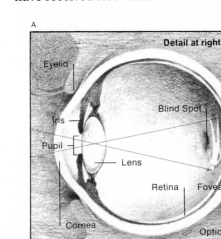
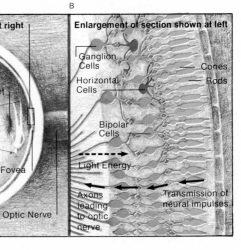

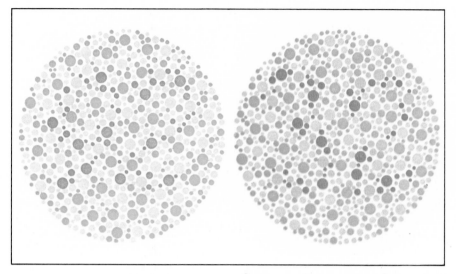

Figure 5.5
A test for color blindness. You should be able to see numerals in the dot patterns that make up these two figures. If you cannot distinguish the numerals in the circle on the left, you may be yellow-blue color-blind. If you cannot see those on the right, you may be red-green color-blind. Color-blind people use brightness differences to distinguish objects that most other people distinguish by color. In this test the dots are carefully equated for brightness, so the only way to see the numerals is to see the color differences. Due to the limitations of color printing, the illustration here may not pick up all cases of color blindness. (The Dvorine Pseudo-Isochromatic Plates.)

Vision

Vision is the most studied of all the senses, reflecting the high importance we place on our sense of sight. Vision provides a great deal of information about one's environment and the objects in it—the sizes, shapes, and locations of things, and their textures, colors, and distances.

How does vision occur? Light enters the eye through the **pupil** (see Figure 5.4a) and reaches the **lens,** a flexible structure that focuses light on the **retina**. The retina contains two types of light-sensitive receptor cells: **rods** and **cones** (see Figure 5.4b). These cells are responsible for changing light energy into chemical and electrical impulses, which then travel over the **optic nerve** to the brain.

Cones require more light than rods before they begin to respond; they work best in daylight. Rods are sensitive to much lower levels of light than cones and are particularly useful in night vision. There are many more rods (75 to 150 million) than there are cones (6 to 7 million), but only cones are sensitive to color. Rods and cones can be compared to black-and-white and color film. Color film takes more light and thus works best in daylight; sensitive black-and-white film works not only in bright light but in shadows, dim light, and other poor lighting conditions.

Color Blindness. When some or all of a person's cones do not function properly, he or she is said to be **color-blind.** There are several kinds of color blindness; most color-blind people do see *some* colors (Figure 5.5). For example, some people have trouble distinguishing between red and green. Other people are able to see red and green but cannot distinguish between yellow and blue. A very few people are totally color-blind. They depend on their rods, so to them the world looks something like black-and-white television programs—nothing but blacks and whites and shades of gray.

Color blindness affects about 8 percent of American men and less than 1 percent of American women. It is believed to result from a hereditary defect in the cones. This defect is carried in the genes of women whose vision is usually normal. These women pass the color-blindness genes on to their sons, who are born color-blind (see Wald, 1964).

Figure 5.6
To experience stereoscopic depth perception, take a tall, thin piece of cardboard and place it perpendicular to the page on the line that marks the separation of the two pictures. Then, with the edge of the cardboard resting between your eyes (as shown in the drawing), look at the left photo with your left eye and the right photo with your right eye and try to let the two images come together as one. (It helps to concentrate on the white dot.) If you are successful in fusing the images, the scene will suddenly jump out in depth. This process of binocular fusion contributes continuously to your ability to perceive depth.

Binocular Fusion and Stereopsis. Because we have two eyes, located about 2.5 inches apart, the visual system receives two images. But instead of seeing double, we see a single image, probably a composite of the views of two eyes. The combination of the two images into one is called **binocular vision.**

Not only does the visual system receive two images, but there is a difference between the images on the retinas. This difference is called **retinal disparity.** You can easily observe retinal disparity by bringing an object such as an eraser close to your eyes. Without moving it, look at the eraser first with one eye, then with the other. You will see a difference in the two images because of the different viewpoint each eye has. When you open both eyes you will no longer see the difference, but will instead see the object as solid and three-dimensional, if you have good binocular vision. **Stereopsis** refers to the phenomenon of seeing depth as a result of retinal disparity (Figure 5.6).

Figure 5.7
The hearing process. Sound vibrations in the air strike the eardrum and set a chain of three tiny bones into motion. These bones are attached to another drum, the oval window, which sets up vibrations in the fluid of the inner ear. The vibrations travel through the cochlea, a long coiled tube with a skinlike membrane running down the center of it. (The dotted line in the diagram represents the end of the cochlea that attaches to the oval window.) Stimulation of the hair cells on this membrane causes them to convert the vibrations into electrical impulses, which are relayed by the auditory nerve to the brain.

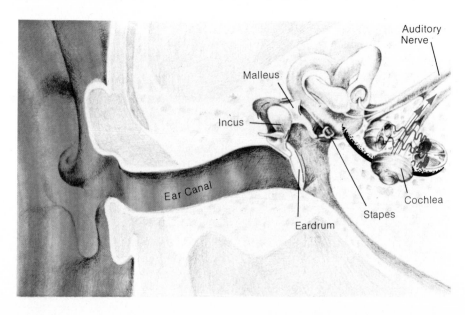

Hearing

Hearing depends on vibrations of the air, called sound waves. Sound waves from the air pass through various bones and fluids (shown in Figure 5.7) until they reach the inner ear, which contains tiny hairlike cells that move back and forth (much like a field of wheat waving in the wind). These hair cells change sound vibrations into chemical-electrical signals that travel through the **auditory nerve** to the brain.

The sensation of loudness depends on the strength of the vibrations in the air. This strength, or energy, is measured in **decibels.** The sounds we hear range upward from zero decibels, the softest sound the human ear can detect, to about 140 decibels, which is roughly as loud as a jet plane taking off. Any sound over 110 decibels can damage hearing, and any sound that is painful when you first hear it *will* damage your hearing if you hear it often enough. Figure 5.8 lists the decibel levels of some common sounds.

Pitch depends on sound frequency, or the rate of the vibration of the medium through which the sound is transmitted. Frequencies range from low to high: low frequencies produce deep bass sounds; high frequencies produce shrill squeaks. If you hear a sound composed of a combination of different frequencies, you can hear the separate pitches even though they occur simultaneously. For example, if you strike two keys of a piano at the same time, your ear can detect two distinct pitches.

Sounds are located through the interaction of the two ears. When a noise occurs on your right, for example, the sound comes to both ears, but it reaches your right ear a fraction of a second before it reaches the left. It is also slightly louder in the right ear. These differences often tell you which direction it is coming from.

Smell and Taste

Smell and taste are known as the chemical senses because their receptors are sensitive to chemical molecules rather than to light energy or sound waves. For you to smell something, the smell receptors in your nose must come into contact with the appropriate molecules. These molecules enter your nose in vapors, which reach a special membrane in the nasal passages on which the smell receptors are located. These receptors send messages about smells over the **olfactory nerve** to the brain.

For you to taste something, appropriate chemicals must stimulate receptors in the taste buds on your tongue. Taste information is relayed to the brain along with data about the texture and temperature of the substance you have put in your mouth.

Some scientists have proposed that all smells are made up of six qualities: flowery, fruity, spicy, resinous, putrid, and burned (Henning, 1916). Other scientists have come up with a similar scheme for taste, which they say is composed of four primary qualities, shown in Figure 5.9: sour, salty, bitter, and sweet (Beebe-Center, 1949).

Much of what is referred to as taste is actually produced by the sense of smell, however. You have undoubtedly noticed that when your nose is blocked by a cold, foods usually taste bland.

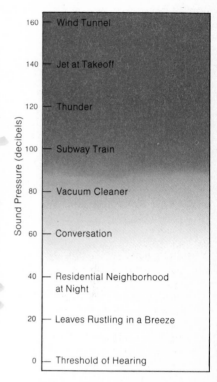

Figure 5.8
The decibel ratings for various common sounds. Sound actually becomes painful at about 130 decibels. Decibels represent ratios: A 20-decibel difference between two sounds indicates that one sound is ten times more intense than the other. Thus a vacuum cleaner puts ten times as much pressure on your eardrums as conversation does.

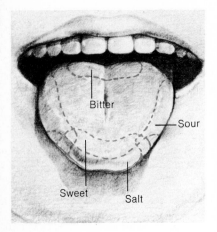

Figure 5.9
A map of the human tongue, indicating the areas that seem more sensitive to one kind of stimulation than to others. Interestingly, it is possible to be taste-blind as well as color-blind: A chemical called phenylthiocarbamide (PTC) tastes extremely bitter to some people and is quite tasteless to others.

Sex and Smell

Many animals communicate by means of odors, as any dog owner whose pet has gone into heat knows. Is it possible that people too communicate by scents? No one knows for sure, but there have been some fascinating studies suggesting that this may be the case.

Martha McClintock tested the "old wives' tale" that women's menstrual cycles synchronize when they live together. She found that the menstrual cycles of college roommates and friends did indeed become more similar as the school year progressed. She believed that pheromones—scented chemical messengers—were the cause.

Richard Michael has shown that female rhesus monkeys secrete certain substances that seem to make them more sexually attractive. In 1974, he reported that human females secrete the same chemical. But so far, no one has been able to prove that the odor increases human sexual desire.

For more details, see James Hassett, "Sex and Smell," *Psychology Today,* 11 (March 1978), pp. 40–45.

Sensations of warmth, cold, and pressure also affect taste. Try to imagine eating cold chicken soup or drinking a hot Pepsi, and you will realize how important temperature is to the sense of taste. Now imagine the textural differences between a spoonful of pudding and a crunchy chocolate bar, and you will see how the texture of food also influences taste.

The chemical senses seem to play a relatively unimportant role in human life when compared to their functions in lower animals. Insects, for example, often depend on smell to communicate with one another, especially in mating. In humans, smell and taste have become more a matter of esthetics than of survival (see box).

The Skin Senses

Receptors in the skin are responsible for providing the brain with at least four kinds of information about the environment: pressure, warmth, cold, and pain.

Sensitivity to pressure varies from place to place in the skin. Some spots, such as your fingertips, are densely populated with receptors and are, therefore, highly sensitive. Other spots, such as the middle of your back, contain relatively few receptors. Pressure sensations can serve as protection. For example, feeling the light pressure of an insect landing on your arm warns you of the danger of being stung.

Some skin receptors are particularly sensitive to hot or cold stimuli. In order to create a hot or cold sensation, a stimulus must have a temperature greater or less than the temperature of the skin. If you plunge your arm into a sink of warm water on a hot day, you will experience little or no sensation of its heat. If you put your arm in the same water on a cold day, however, the water will feel quite warm.

Many kinds of stimuli—scratches, punctures, severe pressure, heat, and cold—can produce pain. Their common property is real or potential injury to bodily tissues. Pain makes it possible for you to prevent damage to your body—it is an emergency system that demands immediate action.

Because pain acts as a warning system for your body, it does not easily adapt to stimulation—you rarely get "used to" pain. Pain tells you to avoid a stimulation that is harmful to you. Without this mechanism, you might "adapt" to a fire when you stand next to it. After a few minutes you would literally begin to cook, and your tissues would die.

Balance

The body's sense of balance is regulated by the **vestibular system** inside the inner ear. Its prominent feature is the three semicircular canals, as shown in Figure 5.10. When your head starts turning, the movement causes the liquid in the canals to move, bending the endings of receptor hair cells. The cells connect with the vestibular nerve, which joins the auditory nerve with the brain.

The stimuli for vestibular responses include movements such as spinning, falling, and tilting the body or head. Overstimulation of the vestibular sense by such movements can result in dizziness and "motion sickness," as you probably have experienced by going on amusement-park rides or by spinning around on a swivel stool. Although you are seldom directly aware of your sense of balance, without it you would be unable to stand or walk without falling or stumbling.

Body Sensations

Kinesthesis is the sense of movement and body position. It cooperates with the vestibular and visual senses to maintain posture and balance. The sensation of kinesthesis comes from receptors in and near the muscles, tendons, and joints. When any movement occurs, these receptors immediately send messages to the brain.

Without kinesthetic sensations, your movements would be jerky and uncoordinated. You would not know what your hand was doing if it were behind your back, and you could not walk without looking at your feet. Furthermore, complex physical activities, such as surgery, piano playing, and acrobatics, would be impossible.

Another type of bodily sensation comes from receptors that monitor internal body conditions. These receptors are sensitive to pressure, temperature, pain, and chemicals inside the body. For example, a full stomach stretching these internal receptors informs the brain that the stomach has ingested too much.

Little is known about pain from the interior of the body except that it seems to be deep, dull, and much more unpleasant than the sharply localized pain from the skin. In some cases, internal pain receptors may send inaccurate messages. They may indicate, for example, that a pain is located in the shoulder when in reality the source of irritation is in the lower stomach. Such sensation of pain in an area away from the actual source is called **referred pain.**

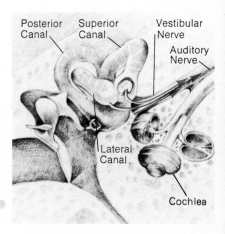

Figure 5.10
The vestibular system. The organs of balance consist of three semicircular canals at right angles to one another, filled with a freely moving fluid. Continuous motion in a straight line produces no response in this system, but starting, stopping, turning, speeding up, or slowing down makes the fluid in at least one of the canals move, stimulating the hair cells attached to the canal walls. These hair cells convert the movement into electrical impulses that are sent to the brain via the auditory nerve.

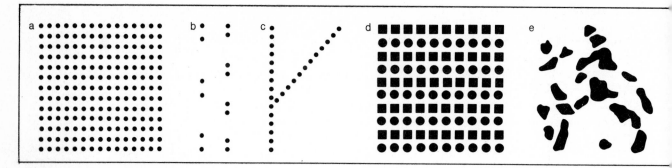

Figure 5.11
Principles of perceptual organization. Human beings see patterns and groupings in their environments rather than disorganized arrays of bits and pieces. For example, it is impossible to look at the array of dots in (a) without seeing shifting patterns of squares and lines. In (b), elements that are close to one another seem to belong together. However, as (c) shows, continuity can be more important: Although the bottom dot in the inclined series is closer to the vertical series, it is not seen as belonging to the vertical row. It is seen as a continuation of the inclined row and therefore as part of it. (d) Similar elements seem to belong to one another and therefore one sees the array as a set of horizontal rows rather than vertical columns, as one might if all the elements were the same. In (e) a principle known as closure is demonstrated. The breaks are ignored; what is seen is a "whole."

PERCEPTION

People do not usually experience a mass of colors, noises, warmths, and pressures. Rather we see cars and buildings, hear voices and music, and feel pencils, desks, and close friends. We do not merely have sensory experiences; we perceive objects. The brain receives information from the senses and organizes and interprets it into meaningful experiences—unconsciously. This process is called perception.

Principles of Perceptual Organization

Through the process of perception, the brain is always trying to build "wholes" out of the confusion of stimuli that bombards the senses. The "whole" experience that comes from organizing bits and pieces of information into meaningful objects and patterns is called a **Gestalt.** Here, the whole is greater than the sum of the parts. ("Gestalt" is a German word meaning pattern or configuration.)

Gestalt psychologists have tried to identify the principles the brain uses in constructing perceptions (Koffka, 1963). Some of the principles they have discovered are demonstrated in Figure 5.11. For example, they have found that people tend to see dots in patterns and groups. Thus when you look at Figure 5.11a, you see shifting patterns of lines and rectangles, not just an array of dots. Two principles that people use in organizing such patterns are proximity and similarity. If the elements of the pattern are close to one another or are similar in appearance, they tend to be perceived as belonging to one another. These principles are demonstrated in Figures 5.11b, c, and d.

The Gestalt principles of organization help to explain how people group their sensations and fill in gaps in order to make sense of the world. In music, for instance, you tend to group notes on the basis of their closeness to one another in time—you hear melodies, not single notes. Similarity and continuity are also important. They allow you to follow the sound of a particular voice or instrument even when many other sounds are occurring. For example, you can follow the sound of a bass guitar through a song.

Figure and Ground

One form of perceptual organization is the division of experience into **figure** and **ground.** Look at Figure 5.12. What do you see? Sometimes the figure looks like a white vase against a black background. At other times it appears to be two black faces against a white background.

When you look at a three-dimensional object against the sky or some other unstructured background, you have no trouble deciding which areas represent objects and which represent spaces between objects. It is when something is two-dimensional, as in Figure 5.12, that you may have trouble telling the figure from the ground. Nevertheless, such figure-ground problems give clues as to the active nature of perception. The fact that a single pattern can be perceived in more than one way demonstrates that we are not passive receivers of stimuli.

Figure and ground are important in hearing as well as in vision. When you follow one person's voice at a noisy meeting, that voice is a figure and all other sounds become ground. Similarly, when you listen to a piece of music, a familiar theme may "leap out" at you: the melody becomes the figure, and the rest of the music merely background.

Perceptual Inference

Often we have perceptions that are not based entirely on current sensory information. When you hear barking as you approach your house, you assume it is your dog—not a cat or a rhinoceros or even another dog. When you take a seat in a dark theater, you assume it is solid and will hold your weight even though you cannot see what supports the seat. When you are driving in a car and see in the distance that the road climbs up a steep hill, then disappears over the top, you assume the road will continue over and down the hill, not come to an abrupt halt (Figure 5.13).

This phenomenon of filling in the gaps in what our senses tell us is known as **perceptual inference** (Gregory, 1970). Perceptual inference is

Figure 5.12
What did you see the first time you looked at this famous illustration? Whatever you saw, you saw because of your past experiences and current expectations. People invariably organize their experience into figure and ground. Whatever appears as figure receives the attention, is likely to be remembered, and has a distinctness of form that is lacking in the vague, formless ground. But, as this figure shows, what is meaningless ground one minute may become the all-important figure the next.

Figure 5.13
Perceptual inference: Even though you cannot see it, you assume that the road will continue beyond the slight rise—not stop abruptly at the limits of your vision from the car.

largely automatic and unconscious. We need only a few cues to inform us that a noise is our dog barking or that a seat is solid. Why? Because we have encountered these stimuli and objects in the past and know what to expect from them in the present. Perceptual inference thus sometimes depends on experience. On the other hand, we are probably born with some of our ability to make perceptual inferences. For example, experimenters have shown that infants just barely able to crawl will avoid falling over what appears to be a steep cliff—thus proving that they perceive depth (Gibson and Walk, 1960). (See Figure 5.14.)

Learning to Perceive

In large part, perceiving is something that people *learn* to do. For example, infants under one month will smile at a nodding object the size of a human face, whether or not it has eyes, a nose, or other human features. At about

Figure 5.14
The visual cliff apparatus. A human infant of crawling age (about six months) will usually refuse to cross the glass surface over the "deep" side even if his mother is on the other side and is urging the child to join her. The infant is perfectly willing to cross the "shallow" side to reach his mother, however. Even though the child can feel the hard solid glass surface beneath him, he refuses to venture out over an edge that appears to be a sudden drop.

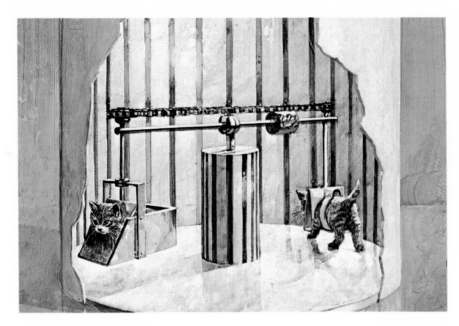

Figure 5.15
A cut-away view of the apparatus used to show that active involvement is necessary for perceptual learning. Both kittens are receiving roughly the same visual input as they move in relation to the vertical stripes painted on the walls of the cylinder, but one kitten is producing the changes in what it sees by its own muscular movements. The other kitten sees similar changes because of the way it is harnessed to the first kitten, but what it sees has nothing to do with its own movements. This second kitten was found not to have developed the ability to see depth in this situation, while the active kitten developed depth perception normally.

twenty weeks, however, a blank oval will not make most babies smile, but a drawing of a face or a mask will. The baby has learned to distinguish something that looks like a person from other objects. Babies twenty-eight weeks and older are more likely to smile at a female than a male face. By thirty weeks most smile more readily when they see a familiar face than when they see someone they do not know. But it takes seven or eight months for babies to learn to recognize different people (Ahrens, 1954).

Experiments show that people and animals must be actively involved in their environments to develop perception. An experiment with newborn kittens demonstrates this. A number of kittens were raised in the dark until they were ten weeks old. Then they were divided into two groups: actives and passives.

For three hours a day an active kitten and a passive kitten were linked together, as shown in Figure 5.15. The kittens were harnessed in such a way that every action of the active kitten moved the passive kitten an equal distance, forward, backward, up, down, and from side to side. The visual stimulation for the two kittens was approximately the same, but the active animal produced its *own* changes in stimulation (by walking, for example). The other kitten was merely a passive receiver of stimulation. When the kittens were tested later, the passive one was not able to discriminate depth—to judge how close or far away various objects were. But the active kitten developed this ability normally. Not until the passive kitten had been allowed to live normally for two days—to move around in a visual environment of its own—did it develop normal depth perception (Held and Hein, 1963).

Experiments with human beings have also shown that active involvement in one's environment is important for accurate perception. People who have been blind from birth and who have had their sight restored by an operation (which is possible in only a few cases) have visual sensations, but initially they cannot tell the difference between a square and a circle or see that a red cube is like a blue cube (Valvo, 1971). In fact some had difficulty making such simple distinctions six months after their vision was restored.

Not all such cases end happily. Gregory (1978) tells the story of S. B., a man who had his sight restored at the age of fifty-two. Before the operation this man had lived an active and productive life. He liked making things in a shed in his garden, and sometimes rode a bicycle with a friend holding his shoulder to guide him. Immediately after the cornea transplant, he could only see a blur, but his sight improved rapidly. He had some trouble judging distance—for example, he thought his hospital window was about 6 feet from the ground when it was really about 60. But he recognized objects by sight that he had learned by touch. He had little trouble learning to tell time—for years he had used a watch with large raised numerals.

But S. B. never learned to completely trust his new sense. When he was blind, he would blithely cross the busiest streets with only his cane to guide him. Later, he was terrified by traffic and never felt comfortable crossing the street. After the initial thrill wore off, S. B. gradually became rather depressed by how drab the world was. Flaking paint and blemishes on things disturbed him. His depressions gradually became deeper and more general, and he died a few years after the operation.

Depth Perception

Depth perception develops in infancy.

Depth perception—the ability to recognize distances and three-dimensionality—develops in infancy. If you place a baby on a large table, he or she will not crawl over the edge. The baby is able to perceive that it is a long distance to the floor. Psychologists test depth perception in infants with a device called the visual cliff, shown in Figure 5.14 (Gibson and Walk, 1960).

People use many cues to perceive depth. One is the information provided by retinal disparity, as discussed earlier in the chapter. Another is **motion parallax**—the apparent movement of objects that occurs when you move your head from side to side or when you walk around. You can demonstrate motion parallax by looking toward two objects in the same line of vision, one near you and the other some distance away. If you move your head back and forth, the near object will seem to move more than the far object. In this way, motion parallax gives you clues as to which objects are closer than others.

You are probably familiar with many other cues to distance. Nearby objects sometimes obscure parts of objects that are farther away. The more distant an object is, the smaller its image. Continuous objects such as railroad tracks, roads, rows of trees, and the walls of a room form converging lines, another cue to distance.

Constancy

When we have learned to perceive certain objects in our environment, we tend to see them in the same way, regardless of changing conditions. You probably judge the whiteness of the various portions of these pages to be fairly constant, even though you may have read the book under a wide range of lighting conditions. The light, angle of vision, distance, and, therefore, the image on the retina all change, but your perception of the object does not. Thus despite changing physical conditions, people are able to perceive objects as the same by the processes of size, shape, and brightness **constancy** (Figure 5.16).

An example of size constancy will illustrate how we have an automatic system for perceiving an object as being the same size whether it is far or near. A friend walking toward you does not seem to change into a giant even though the images inside your eyes become larger and larger as she approaches. To you, her appearance stays the same size because even though the size of your visual image is increasing, you are perceiving an additional piece of information: distance is decreasing. The enlarging eye image and the distance information combine to produce a perception of an approaching object that stays the same size.

Distance information compensates for the enlarging eye image to produce size constancy. If information about distance is eliminated, your perception of the size of the object begins to correspond to the actual size of the eye image. For example, it is difficult for most people to estimate the size of an airplane in the sky because they have little experience judging such huge sizes and distances. Pilots, however, can determine whether a flying plane is large and far away or small and close because they are experienced in estimating the sizes and distances of planes.

Illusions

Illusions are perceptions that are misrepresentations of reality. For example, look at the lines in Figure 5.17. Which lines are longer? Measure the

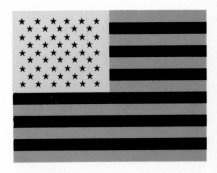

Figure 5.16
This figure can be used to demonstrate two striking features of vision. Stare steadily at the lowest right-hand star for about forty-five seconds, or until the colors start to shimmer. Then stare at a blank piece of paper. After a second or two you should see a *negative afterimage* of this figure in which the flag shows the normal colors. This occurs because the receptors for green, black, and yellow become fatigued, allowing the complementary colors of each to predominate when you stare at the white paper. Since these complements are, respectively, red, white, and blue, you see a normal American flag. Now shift your glance to a blank wall some distance away. Suddenly the flag will appear huge. This happens because of the principle of constancy—the brain interprets the same image as large when it is far away (apparently on the wall) and small when it is close (apparently on a piece of paper in your hand).

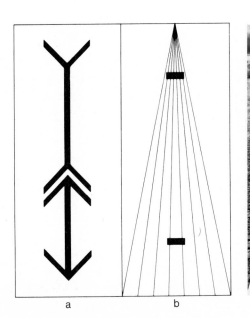 

a   b   c

Figure 5.17
The Muller-Lyer illusion (a) and the Ponzo illusion (b) are two of the most famous illusions in psychology. The lines between the arrow heads in (a) are exactly the same length, as are the heavy black lines in (b). Some psychologists believe that the reason these lines appear to be different in length is that the brain interprets the diagrams in (a) and (b) as though they are scenes such as that in (c).

Figure 5.18
These two women appear to be a
giant and a midget in an ordinary
room. In fact, they are ordinary-
sized women in a very peculiar
room. This room, the true design of
which is shown in the accompanying diagram, was constructed by
psychologist Adelbert Ames. Again,
the illusion is produced by tricking
the brain into accepting an unusual
situation as usual.

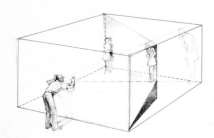

lengths of the pairs of lines with a ruler, then look again. Do the lines *look*
as long now that you *know* they are the same? For most people, the answer
is no.

A possible explanation of this type of illusion is that even though the
patterns are two-dimensional, your brain treats them as three-dimensional.
These illusions have features that usually indicate distance in three-
dimensional space. The top line in Figure 5.17a, for example, can be
thought of as the far corner of a room; the bottom line is like the near
corner of the building. In Figure 5.17b and c the converging lines create the
illusion of distance so that the lower bar looks nearer and shorter than the
upper bar. This "perceptual compensation" seems to be unconscious and
automatic.

Figure 5.18 shows two women in a room. The sizes of the women look
dramatically different because you perceive the room as rectangular. In
fact, the ceiling and walls are slanted so that the back wall is both shorter
and closer on the right than on the left. But even when you know how this
illusion was achieved, you still accept the peculiar difference in the
women's sizes because the windows, walls, and ceiling appear rectangular.
Your experience with rectangular rooms overrides your knowledge of how
this trick is done.

EXTRASENSORY PERCEPTION

In this chapter, we have discussed the perception of tangible and measur-
able aspects of our environment. But humans are rarely content with un-

Figure 5.19
Dr. J. B. Rhine of Duke University administering an ESP test to two subjects using a special deck of cards.

derstanding only what can be seen and directly measured. We are fascinated by things that can't be seen, easily explained, or often even verified—flying saucers, atoms, genes, and extrasensory perception.

Extrasensory perception (ESP)—receiving information about the world through channels other than the normal senses—is a hotly debated topic. Many people are convinced that ESP exists because of an intense personal experience that can never be scientifically validated. For instance, we all have some fears before traveling, and we imagine the worst: our plane will crash, our train will be derailed, or we will have an automobile accident. These events almost never happen, and we easily forget about our frightening premonitions. However, if the improbable should actually take place, our premonitions turn into compelling evidence for the existence of precognition. Such coincidences sometimes become widely publicized evidence supporting paranormal phenomena, and we may quickly forget all the occasions when our premonitions were completely wrong. However, if we are truly interested in validating the existence of ESP, we must keep track of the frequency of its failures as well as its successes.

Scientists have been investigating ESP since the turn of the century. Probably the most famous **parapsychologist** (as these researchers into the supernatural are called) is J. B. Rhine. Around 1930, Rhine began a series of precise statistical tests of ESP. In tests of telepathy, for example, a "sender" focuses one at a time on each of twenty-five cards in a special deck. (The deck includes five cards for each of five different symbols.) A "receiver" locked in a distant room states which card he thinks the sender is focusing on. With luck alone, the receiver will guess about five cards correctly, sometimes a few more, sometimes a few less. Yet thousands of tests have shown that some people consistently respond above the average.

Some ESP researchers have concluded that these people are receiving information through senses or other channels we do not know about.

The results found in these studies are indeed statistically unlikely, but in other ways they are not nearly as impressive. For example, in one recent study (described in Chance, 1976), Charles Tart screened 1,500 college students and found 25 who seemed to have ESP. The students were shown a machine that randomly turned on one of four lights. They had to guess which light would come on next. They guessed nearly 7,500 times, and were right 26.8 percent of the time. Since one would expect people without ESP to be right only 25 percent of the time (one out of four), and since they guessed so many times, the result was statistically significant: the odds were more than 2,500 to 1 against this performance occurring by chance. These are impressive odds, but they are not particularly impressive results. This minimal ESP would not be particularly useful for playing the stock market or a football pool.

And there is one more problem with Tart's experiment. Unsupervised undergraduates collected the data. Many studies have shown that experimenters who believe in ESP tend to make errors supporting their belief, just as skeptics make errors showing that it does not exist. Another problem is that of intentional fraud. It would not be the first time a student falsified data to please his professor or get a good grade. And there have been several rather spectacular cases of fraud in ESP research.

Another reason many scientists do not accept the results of experiments supporting ESP is that the findings are highly unstable. One of the basic principles of scientific research is that one scientist should be able to replicate another scientist's results. Not only do different ESP experiments yield contradictory findings, but the same individual seems to show ESP on one day but not on the next. Proponents of ESP argue that this type of research cannot be consistently replicated because the special abilities are stifled in a laboratory situation. They say that ESP responses are best generated in highly emotional or relevant situations. Laboratory experiments that test people's ability to sense which symbols appear on cards are irrelevant to most people's lives and far from being highly emotional, and are usually a boring way to spend an afternoon. According to this viewpoint, it is remarkable that ESP has been reported to appear in the laboratory setting at all.

Although ESP may indeed be a very fragile phenomenon, the inability to replicate results and the difficulty of verifying ESP events are crucial problems. Many will remain skeptical about the existence of ESP until these problems are solved. However, such skepticism has often been overcome in the past. For example, just a century or so ago, the suggestion that many diseases were caused by invisible organisms was greeted with disbelief. Only after the work of Pasteur and other researchers proved that a clear relationship existed between these organisms and illness, was the "germ theory" of disease accepted. Perhaps the development of appropriate techniques for testing ESP could similarly lead to establishing the existence of paranormal phenomena—and perhaps they won't.

SUMMARY

1. Our information about the outside world comes in through our senses. The sense organs convert stimuli in the environment into chemical-electrical activity that travels to the brain. This process results in sensation.

2. Psychophysics is the study of the relationship between physical stimuli and the sensory experiences they produce. The smallest amount of energy that will produce a sensation is called an absolute threshold. The smallest change in a stimulus that produces a change in sensation is called the difference threshold.

3. Experiencing a sensation depends more on changes in the stimulus than on the absolute size or amount of the stimulus. Sensory adaptation occurs when a stimulus continues without changing. Motivation can influence whether or not certain stimuli will be detected.

4. The chief stimulus in vision is light. The rods and cones in the retina of the eye convert light energy to chemical impulses that travel over the optic nerve to the brain. Cones respond to color and work best in daylight. Rods are more sensitive to brightness but do not detect color. Color blindness results when cones are absent or malfunctioning. Binocular fusion, the combination of images from both eyes, is accompanied by stereopsis, the three-dimensional interpretation of the world. This is made possible by retinal disparity, which is the difference between the images in the two eyes.

5. The stimuli for hearing are sound waves, which are converted to chemical-electrical impulses by hair cells in the inner ear. These messages reach the brain via the auditory nerve.

6. Smell and taste are chemical senses. Receptors in the nose and on the tongue respond to contact with molecules. Most taste sensations involve the sense of smell to some extent.

7. Skin receptors respond to pressure, warmth, cold, and pain. These sensations play an important role in warning the brain of possible external dangers.

8. Internal bodily sensations include balance, kinesthesis, and internal sensitivity to pressure, temperature, pain, and chemicals.

9. Perception is the process of creating meaningful wholes out of information from the senses. Perceptual wholes are called Gestalts. Psychologists study such phenomena as figure-ground relationships, perceptual inference, perceptual development, depth perception, constancy, and illusions to determine how perception works.

10. There has been a great deal of research on extrasensory perception, but the topic is still controversial.

GLOSSARY

absolute threshold: The lowest level of physical energy that will produce a sensation in half the trials.

adaptation: In sensation, an adjustment of the sensitivity of sensory receptors of the brain in response to prolonged stimulation.

auditory nerve: The nerve that carries impulses from the inner ear to the brain, resulting in the sensation of sound.

binocular fusion: The process of combining the images received from the two eyes into a single, fused image.

color blindness: Complete or partial inability to distinguish colors, resulting from malfunction in the cones.

cones: Receptor cells in the retina sensitive to color. Because they require more light than rods to function, they are most useful in daytime vision.

constancy: The tendency to perceive certain objects in the same way, regardless of changing angle, distance, or lighting.

decibel: A measure of the physical intensity of sound, which is lawfully related to the sensation of loudness.

difference threshold: The smallest change in a physical stimulus that produces a change in sensation in half the trials.

extrasensory perception (ESP): An ability to gain information by some means other than the ordinary senses (such as taste, hearing, vision, and so on).

figure-ground: The division of the visual field into two distinct parts, one being the object or objects, the other the background or space between objects.

Gestalt: In perception, the experience that comes from organizing bits and pieces of information into meaningful wholes.

illusions: Perceptions that misrepresent physical stimuli.

kinesthesis: The sense of movement and body position, acquired through receptors located in and near the muscles, tendons, and joints.

lens: A flexible, transparent structure in the eye that, by changing its shape, focuses light on the retina.

motion parallax: The apparent movement of stationary objects relative to one another that occurs when the observer changes position. Near objects seem to move greater distances than far objects.

olfactory nerve: The nerve that carries smell impulses from the nose to the brain.

optic nerve: The nerve that carries impulses from the retina to the brain.

parapsychology: The systematic study of ESP and other unusual phenomena.

perception: The organization of sensory information into meaningful experiences.

perceptual inference: The process of assuming, from past experience, that certain objects remain the same and will behave as they have in the past.

pitch: The sensation associated with a sound's frequency; the "highness" or "lowness" of a sound.

psychophysics: The study of the relationships between sensory experiences and the physical stimuli that cause them.

pupil: The opening in the iris that regulates the amount of light entering the eye.

referred pain: The sensation of pain in an area away from the actual source; most commonly experienced with internal pain.

retina: The innermost coating of the back of the eye, containing the light-sensitive receptor cells.

retinal disparity: The differences between the images on the two retinas.

rods: Receptor cells in the retina that are sensitive to light, but not to color. Rods are particularly useful in night vision.

sensation: The result of converting physical stimulation of the sense organs into sensory experience.

signal-detection theory: The study of mathematical relationships between motivation, sensitivity, and sensation.

stereopsis: The use by the visual system of retinal disparity to give depth information—providing a three-dimensional appearance to the world.

stimulus: Any change in the environment to which an organism responds.

subliminal advertising: The unsuccessful attempt to influence people with messages that are below normal thresholds of detection.

vestibular system: Three semicircular canals located in the inner ear and connected to the brain by the vestibular nerve. They regulate the sense of balance.

Weber's law: The principle that the larger or stronger a stimulus, the larger the change required for an observer to notice a difference.

ACTIVITIES

1. Hold a pencil about twelve inches in front of your face. Look at it with your left eye closed, then with your right eye closed. Notice how the pencil seems to jump around. What happens when you look at the pencil with both eyes? What principle does this experiment demonstrate?

2. Fill three bowls with water—hot water in one, cold in another, and lukewarm in the third. Put one hand in the cold water and the other in the hot water and leave them there for thirty seconds. Now put both hands in the lukewarm water at the same time. What do you feel? How does this demonstrate the principle of sensory adaptation?

3. Get a fresh potato and peel it. Do the same with an apple. Now have a friend close his eyes and smell a fresh onion while he takes a bite of each one. Can he tell which food is which without his sense of smell? Try this experiment with various people, using different foods that have similar textures.

4. If sensation consists entirely of electrical signals in the brain that are subject to interpretation by perception, does everyone experience the world differently? Animals have different sensory apparatus than humans—do they live in a different perceptual world?

5. Have a friend stand with her back to you. Touch various parts of her back with one pencil or with two pencils held close together. Each time you touch her back, ask her how many points she felt. Now touch the points to her hand and arm, again asking how many points she feels. What are your results? What accounts for the results?

6. To demonstrate the information shown in Figure 5.9, prepare solutions of salt water (salt), lemon juice (sour), baking soda (bitter), and sugar water (sweet). Dab each solution on various points on your tongue, and see if you can verify which area of the tongue is predominately sensitive to each of these major tastes.

7. Perform the following experiment to test one kind of sensory adaptation. Write a sentence while looking at your writing in a mirror. Do this until it begins to feel natural. Then write the sentence normally. Does normal writing now feel strange?

8. Try the following experiment to demonstrate an illusion of the sense of touch. Stretch a foot-square piece of chicken wire tautly over a frame. Blindfold your subject(s) and ask him or her to hold the thumb and forefinger of his or her hand to lightly touch each side of the chicken wire. Slide the wire rapidly back and forth between his or her fingers. Ask your subject to report the sensation he or she feels. Most people report feeling a continuous slippery or oily surface. This illusion will probably be stronger if the subject does not know in advance the actual nature of the material he or she is feeling.

9. Station yourself behind a window or glass door (to eliminate sounds and smells that you might give off) and stare intently at someone who has his or her back toward you. Pick someone who is within a ten-yard range and who is not engaged in any particular activity at the moment. Does the person turn around and look at you? If so, how long does it take him or her to "sense" your presence? How can you explain this phenomenon? Can you develop a "control" procedure to see how long it takes someone to turn around when you're not looking at his or her back?

SUGGESTED READINGS

ARNHEIM, RUDOLF. *Art and Visual Perception: A Psychology of the Creative Eye*. Berkeley: University of California Press, 1974. A revision of a classic book by a prolific writer on visual perception. Arnheim relates the Gestalt laws of organization to visual perception in general and to the perception and structure of artistic works in particular.

GREGORY, R. L. *Eye and Brain*. 3rd ed. New York: McGraw-Hill, 1978. One of the most popular and best-written introductions to the "psychology of seeing." Includes many illustrations.

HANSEL, C. E. M. *ESP: A Scientific Evaluation*. New York: Scribner's, 1966. Probably the best critical introduction to the history of ESP research.

HELD, RICHARD, AND RICHARDS, WHITMAN (EDS.). *Perception: Mechanisms and Models*. San Francisco: Freeman, 1972. This book of readings from *Scientific American* provides accounts of some of the most famous research on perceptual processes in animals, including the visual cliff and the active and passive kittens.

KAUFMAN, LLOYD. *Sight and Mind: An Introduction to Visual Perception*. New York: Oxford University Press, 1974. Besides covering such topics as depth perception, attention, and color perception, Kauf-

man reviews and critiques many of the perceptual principles discussed in this chapter. This book provides a challenging, comprehensive, and well-written text on the nature of visual perception.

MUELLER, C. G., AND RUDOLPH, M. *Light and Vision*. New York: Time-Life Books, 1966. This beautifully illustrated book is an excellent introduction to eye function as well as to the nature of light.

STEVENS, S. S., AND WARSHOVSKY, F. *Sound and Hearing*. New York: Time-Life Books, 1967. A highly readable and well-illustrated exploration of the nature of sound, the structure of the ear, and the phenomenon of hearing.

WOLMAN, BENJAMIN B. (ED.). *Handbook of Parapsychology*. New York: Van Nostrand Reinhold, 1977. A definitive portrait of the current status of ESP research. Includes thirty-four articles by the leading experts in the field.

BIBLIOGRAPHY

AHRENS, R. "Beitrag zur Entwicklung des Physiognomie- und Mimikerkennens." *Z. exp. angew. Psychol.*, 2 (1954): 412–454.

ARNHEIM, RUDOLPH. *Art and Visual Perception: A Psychology of the Creative Eye*. Berkeley: University of California Press, 1974.

BEEBE-CENTER, J. G. "Standards for the Use of Gust Scale." *Journal of Psychology*, 28 (1949): 411–419.

BREAN, HERBERT. "Hidden Sell Technique Almost Here." *Life* (March 31, 1958): 102–114.

BROWN, J. A. C. *Techniques of Persuasion*. Baltimore: Penguin, 1963.

CHANCE, PAUL. "Telepathy Could Be Real." *Psychology Today*, 9 (February 1976): 40–44, 65.

DIXON, N. F. *Subliminal Perception: The Nature of a Controversy*. London: McGraw-Hill, 1971.

GELDARD, FRANK A. *The Human Senses*. 2nd ed. New York: Wiley, 1972.

GIBSON, E. J., AND WALK, R. D. "The Visual Cliff." *Scientific American*, 202 (1960): 64–71.

GREEN, DAVID M., AND SWETS, JOHN A. *Signal Detection Theory and Psychophysics*. New York: Wiley, 1966.

GREGORY, R. L. *The Intelligent Eye*. New York: McGraw-Hill, 1970 (paper).

_____. *Eye and Brain*. 3rd ed. New York: McGraw-Hill, 1978.

HELD, R., AND HEIN, A. "A Movement-produced Stimulation in the Development of Visually Guided Behavior." *Journal of Comparative Physiology and Psychology*, 56 (1963): 606–613.

HENNING, HANS. "Die Qualitätenreihe des Geschmacks." *Zeitschrift für Psychologie*, 74 (1916): 203–219.

HOCHBERG, JULIAN. *Perception*. Englewood Cliffs, N.J.: Prentice-Hall, 1964 (paper).

KOFFKA, K. *Principles of Gestalt Psychology*. New York: Harcourt Brace Jovanovich, 1963.

RHINE, JOSEPH B. *Extra-Sensory Perception*. Boston: Branden, 1964.

RHINE, LOUISA E. *Hidden Channels of the Mind.* New York: Apollo, 1961 (paper).

SCIENTIFIC AMERICAN. "Psychokinetic Fraud." *Scientific American,* 238 (September 1974): 68, 72.

SILVERMAN, LLOYD H. "Psychoanalytic Theory." *American Psychologist,* 31 (1976): 621–637.

STEVENS, S. S. "The Surprising Simplicity of Sensory Metrics." *American Psychologist,* 17 (1962): 29–39.

VALVO, ALBERTO. *Sight Restoration After Long-Term Blindness: The Problems and Behavior Patterns of Visual Rehabilitation.* New York: American Foundation for the Blind, 1971.

WALD, G. "The Receptors of Color Vision." *Science,* 145 (1964): 1007–1016.

WEBER, ERNST H. *De Pulse, Resorptione, Audito et Tactu.* Leipzig: Kohler, 1834.

6 Motivation and Emotion

Why do people climb Mount Everest and cross the Atlantic in a balloon? Why do some people spend every waking moment memorizing batting averages while others don't know the difference between the New York Red Sox and the Boston Yankees? And, as the song asks, why do fools fall in love?

Although all psychology is concerned with what people do and how they do it, research on motivation and emotion focuses on the underlying why of behavior.

BIOLOGICAL MOTIVES

We see Ruth studying all weekend while the rest of us hang out, and since we know she wants to go to law school, we conclude that she is "motivated" by her desire to get good grades. We see Harold working after classes at a job he doesn't like, and since we know he wants to buy a car, we conclude that he is "motivated" to earn money for the car. Conceptions of motivation in psychology are in many ways similar to those expressed in everyday language; since motivation cannot be observed directly, psychologists, like the rest of us, infer motivation from goal-directed behavior.

Some behavior is determined by the physiological state of the organism. Like other animals, human beings have certain survival needs. The nervous system is constructed in such a way that dramatic variations in blood sugar, water, oxygen, salt, or essential vitamins lead to changes in

Figure 6.1
Motivation—why we do things—cannot be observed directly; it can only be inferred from goal-directed behavior.

behavior designed to return the body to a condition of chemical balance. The first part of this section discusses the role of such physiological factors in motivating behavior.

But many human motives, such as Ruth's desire to get into law school or Harold's desire to buy a car, do not have a simple physiological basis. Although not all psychologists would be able to agree on an explanation of these behaviors, none would say that they were the result of physiological deficits. The rest of this section discusses some approaches to analyzing the motivational bases of these kinds of human activities.

The Physiology of Motivation

All organisms, including humans, have built-in regulating systems that work like thermostats to maintain body temperature, the level of sugar in the blood, the production of hormones, and so on. As we saw in Chapter 5, when the level of thyroxin in the bloodstream is low, the pituitary gland secretes a thyroxin-stimulating hormone. When the thyroxin level is high, the pituitary gland stops producing this hormone. Similarly, when your body temperature drops below a certain point, you start to shiver, your blood vessels constrict, and you put on more clothes. All these activities reduce heat loss and bring body temperature back to the correct level. If your body heat rises above a certain point, you start to sweat, your blood vessels dilate, and you remove clothes. These processes cool you.

The tendency of all organisms to correct imbalances and deviations from their normal state is known as **homeostasis.** Several of the drives that motivate behavior are homeostatic—hunger, for example.

Hunger.   What motivates people to seek food? Often you eat because the sight and smell of, say, pizza tempts you into a store. Other times you eat out of habit (you always have lunch at 12:30) or to be sociable (a friend invites you out for a snack). But suppose you are working frantically to finish a term paper. You don't have any food in your room, so you ignore the fact that it is dinner time and you keep working. But at some point your body will start to demand food. You'll feel an aching sensation in your stomach. What produces this sensation? What makes you feel hungry?

Your body requires food to function. When you miss a meal, your liver releases stored sugar into your bloodstream to keep you going. After a time, however, this supply runs out and the hypothalamus begins to act.

The hypothalamus, as indicated above, is a structure at the base of the brain that regulates food intake. It not only tells us when we need to eat, it also tells us when to stop eating. How does it work? The hypothalamus is laced with blood vessels that make it extremely sensitive to levels of sugar in the blood. It also has numerous connections to the brain that are capable of raising or lowering the level of certain chemicals in the brain (Ahlskog and Hoebel, 1973). Experiments have shown that this is what makes us crave food or feel too full to eat more.

If the portion of the hypothalamus called the **lateral hypothalamus (LH)** is stimulated with electrodes, a laboratory animal will begin eating, even if it has just finished a large meal. Conversely, if the LH is removed

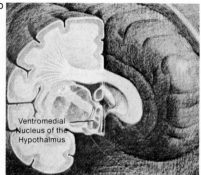

Ventromedial Nucleus of the Hypothalamus

Figure 6.2
(left) The fat rat. (right) A drawing showing the part of the human brain that corresponds to the part lesioned in the rat. The view is from the front of the brain, with one half shown in cross section.

surgically, an animal will stop eating and eventually die of starvation if it is not fed artificially. Thus the LH provides the "go" signals: it tells you to eat.

If a different portion of the hypothalamus called the **ventromedial hypothalamus (VMH)** is stimulated, an animal will slow down or stop eating altogether, even if it has been kept from food for a long period. However, if the VMH is removed, the animal will eat everything in sight until it becomes so obese it can hardly move (Figure 6.2). This indicates that the VMH provides the "stop" signals: it tells you when you have had enough food.

The level of sugar in the blood is not the only thing that causes the hypothalamus to act. If your stomach is empty, the muscles in the stomach walls contract periodically (producing hunger pangs). These contractions activate the LH, which sends "go" or "eat" signals to other areas of your brain. When your stomach is full, the VMH sends "stop" signals, even though the energy from the food you have just eaten has not yet reached your bloodstream (digestion takes time). In addition, the hypothalamus responds to temperature. The LH, or "go" signal, is more active in cold temperatures; the VMH, or "stop" signal, more active in warm temperatures (presumably because people and other animals need to eat more in cold weather).

In summary, the hypothalamus "interprets" at least three kinds of information: the level of sugar in the blood, the amount of food in the stomach, and body temperature. These determine whether the hypothalamus will tell you (via chemical changes in the brain) to eat or stop eating.

Obesity.   Like the rats whose VMHs are destroyed, many people have trouble keeping their hips from looking like the Goodyear blimp. Stanley Schachter (1971) and his colleagues at Columbia University have done a number of ingenious studies which show that obese people respond to external cues—they eat not because they are hungry, but because they see something good to eat or their watches tell them it's time.

Obese people eat not because they are hungry, but because they see something tempting or their watches say it's time.

To prove this, Schachter first set up a bogus taste test in which people were asked to rate five kinds of crackers. He was really not interested in how these people rated the crackers on his elaborate questionnaires. Schachter simply wanted to see how many crackers normal and overweight people would eat. Each person was asked to skip lunch, so they all came to the test hungry. Some were told that the taste test required a full stomach; they were given as many roast beef sandwiches as they wanted. The rest stayed hungry. Schachter's theory predicted that normal people eat because they're hungry while obese people eat whether they are hungry or not. This was true. People of normal weight ate more crackers than overweight people did when both groups were hungry, and fewer crackers after they had eaten the roast beef.

In another study, Schachter put out a bowl of peanuts which people could eat while they sat in a waiting room. Sometimes the nuts were still in their shells, and sometimes they weren't. Fat people ate the nuts only when they didn't have to bother taking the shells off. Thus, again, they ate simply because food was there. People of normal weight were equally likely to try a few nuts whether they were shelled or not. In still another study, Schachter found that fat college freshmen were more likely to cancel dormitory food contracts than normal freshmen. Why? The overweight were more concerned with the taste of their food, and they simply couldn't stand the institutional fishcakes and spaghetti.

In summary, Schachter argues that overweight people respond to external cues (for example, the smell of cookies hot from the oven) while normal people respond to internal cues (the stomach contractions of hunger). His work shows that, for people, even physiological needs like hunger are influenced by complex factors.

Drive Reduction Theory

Drive reduction theory, which dominated psychological thinking in the 1940s and early 1950s, emerged from the work of experimental psychologist Clark Hull and his associates (1943). Hull traced motivation back to basic physiological needs. According to Hull, when an organism is deprived of something it needs (such as food, water, or sex) it becomes tense and agitated. To relieve this tension it engages in more or less random activity. Thus biological needs *drive* an organism to act.

If one of these random behaviors reduces the drive, the organism will begin to acquire a habit; that is, when the drive is again felt, the organism will first try the same response again. Habits channel drives in certain directions. In short, **drive reduction theory** states that physiological needs drive an organism to act in either random or habitual ways until its needs are satisfied.

Hull and his colleagues suggested that all human motives—from the desire to acquire property to striving for excellence and seeking affection or amusement—are extensions of basic biological needs. For example, people develop the need for social approval because as infants they were fed and cared for by a smiling mother or father. Gradually, through generalization and conditioning, the need for approval becomes important in itself. Approval becomes a learned drive.

Losing Weight

If you want to lose weight, begin by keeping detailed records of everything you eat for a week or two. Get a good book on nutrition and analyze your eating habits, particularly the number of calories you consume on an average day. Forget about miracle diets that promise you can have as many cheesecakes as you want. The only people who benefit from miracle diets are the writers who get rich from books about them.

Once you figure out what you are eating and what you should be eating, all that's left is the hard part—doing something about it. Set up a system of rewards for sticking to your diet and punishments for sneaking off for hot fudge sundaes. Continue to monitor what and when you eat and chart your progress.

Some therapists believe you should not start a major weight-reduction program when the rest of your life is a mess. Of course, if your life is always a mess, this may be one place to start.

For more details, see R. L. Williams and J. D. Long, *Toward a Self-Managed Life Style,* 2nd ed. Boston: Houghton Mifflin, 1979.

Drive reduction theory dominated psychologists' thinking for over a decade. However, the results of experiments conducted in the late 1950s suggested that Hull and his colleagues had overlooked some of the more important factors in human—and animal—motivation.

Figure 6.3
Diana Vreeland of Vogue Magazine: a classic study of the hard-driving executive. Researchers have suggested a variety of motives for the drive to excel.

Figure 6.4
The monkeys in Harlow's classic experiment on the determinants of mother love spent most of their time with the terrycloth mother even though they fed from the wire mother. The terrycloth mother was also a security base when they were frightened.

Figure 6.5
This monkey worked hard for the privilege of watching an electric train, but it would be difficult to say what drive is reduced as a result.

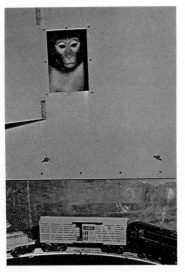

According to drive reduction theory, infants become attached to their mothers because mothers usually relieve such drives as hunger and thirst. Harry Harlow (among others) doubted that this was the only or even the main source of an infant's love for its mother. Harlow decided to challenge drive reduction theory with an experiment. He took infant monkeys away from their mothers and put them alone in cages with two surrogate "mothers" made of wire (Figure 6.4). One of the wire mothers was equipped with a bottle. If drive reduction theory were correct, the monkeys would become attached to this figure, because it was their only source of food. The other wire mother was covered with soft cloth but could not provide food and relief from hunger. In test after test, the small monkeys preferred to cling to the cloth mother, particularly when strange, frightening objects were put into their cages (Harlow and Zimmerman, 1959).

Thus one of the factors that many drive theorists overlooked is that some experiences (such as hugging something or someone soft) are inherently pleasurable. Although they do not seem to reduce biological drives, these experiences serve as incentives or goals for behavior. Another factor that drive theorists overlooked was the pleasure humans and related animals derive from stimulation or arousal (Figure 6.5). Just think about how dogs love to be petted or how children love horror movies and rides at amusement parks that are designed to terrify them. In the end, then, a drive *for* stimulation looked as plausible as a drive to *reduce* stimulation.

Many psychologists concluded that there could be no general theory of motivation of the type Hull suggested. Instead of a drive reduction theory, we are left with a list of unlearned, innate drives that include hunger and thirst, but also curiosity, contact with soft things, and many others.

What Motivates People To Take Unnecessary Risks?

Fifty . . . forty-nine . . . forty-eight . . . forty-seven. . . . The skydiver counted the seconds till it would all be over. There was no chance he would get out of this fall alive . . . no chance his chute would open. As he pulled the cord and felt the chute snap open above his head, only one thought ran through his mind: he would live to try it again.

What motivates skydivers and others to take such risks? Psychologists Richard Solomon and John Corbit believe the answer lies in the emotional responses the risk-taker experiences before, during, and after the feat:

1. The skydiver is terrified the first time he jumps. When he lands, his terror is quickly replaced by a stunned feeling that lasts only a few minutes. This in turn is replaced by normal composure.
2. After several jumps, the skydiver is no longer terrified; instead he feels anxious before the jump. But the main change is in the way he feels afterward. The exhilaration lasts for many hours.
3. This "afterglow" motivates the skydiver to jump again.

According to Solomon and Corbit, another response pattern may also be working at the same time. They propose that the central nervous system automatically opposes highly emotional responses in order to reduce the intensity of these feelings. Thus, after we've taken part in a risky activity for a while, we do not experience the extreme highs and lows we did at first. And we are more willing to take risks we found nearly impossible to take in the beginning.

For more details, see Richard L. Solomon and John D. Corbit, "An Opponent-Process Theory of Motivation," *Psychological Review,* 81 (1974): 119–145.

Figure 6.6
Needs identified by Henry Murray in his formulation of a theory of human personality. Note that Murray distinguishes between a class of primarily physical needs and a—much larger—class of psychological needs.

n Acquisition
(to gain possessions and property)

n Conservance
(to collect, repair, clean, and preserve things)

n Order
(to arrange, organize, put away objects)

n Construction
(to organize and build)

n Achievement
(to overcome obstacles, to exercise power, to strive to do something difficult as well and as quickly as possible)

n Recognition
(to excite praise and commendation)

n Defendance
(to defend oneself against blame or belittlement)

n Dominance
(to influence or control others)

n Autonomy
(to resist influence or coercion)

n Aggression
(to assault or injure)

n Affiliation
(to form friendships and associations)

n Rejection
(to snub, ignore, or exclude)

n Nurturance
(to nourish, aid, or protect)

n Succorance
(to seek aid, protection, or sympathy)

n Play
(to relax, amuse oneself, seek diversion and entertainment)

n Cognizance
(to explore)

SOCIAL MOTIVES

Many psychologists have concentrated their research on social motives rather than on the unlearned, biological motives we have been discussing. Social motives are learned from our interactions with other people.

In Chapter 13 we will discuss the theories of several psychologists who sought to explain the development of personality. One such psychologist was Henry Murray, whose theory of personality identifies sixteen basic needs (see Figure 6.6). Note that most of these are social motives rather than biological needs (see Murray *et al.,* 1934). Lists such as these are sometimes forgotten shortly after they appear in print, because in itself such a list is not very useful. Murray's list has not been forgotten, however. In fact, hundreds of studies have been performed on just one of these needs, the need for achievement.

McClelland and the Need for Achievement

One reason the achievement motive has been so well researched is that David McClelland became interested in finding some quantitative way of measuring social motives (McClelland *et al.*, 1953). Once he did this, he believed he could search for a technique of changing motivation, because he could then have a method of measuring whether a change had occurred. McClelland concentrated his research on the need for achievement because he felt that techniques for increasing this motive might be very useful in improving the lives of millions of people.

McClelland's main tool for measuring achievement motivation was the Thematic Apperception Test (TAT). This test consists of a series of pictures. Subjects are told to make up a story that explains each picture. Tests of this sort are called projective tests, and we will describe them in detail in Chapter 14. At this point, it is only important to know that there are no right

Figure 6.7
A picture of the sort that might be used in the measurement of the need for achievement. Examples of stories that would be scored from fairly high to low are shown beside the picture. The portions of the stories printed in italics are the kinds of themes considered to reflect need for achievement.

This guy is just getting off work. These are all working guys and they don't like their work too much either. The younger guy over on the right knows the guy with the jacket.

Something bad happened today at work—*a nasty accident that shouldn't have happened.* These two guys don't trust each other *but they are going to talk* about it. *They mean to put things to rights. No one else much cares,* it seems.

The guy with the jacket is *worried.* He feels that *something has to be done. He wouldn't ordinarily talk to the younger man but now he feels he must.* The young guy is ready. He's *concerned* too but doesn't know what to expect.

They'll both realize after talking that you never know where your friends are. *They'll both feel better* afterward because they'll feel they have someone they can rely on next time there's trouble.

Harry O'Silverfish has been working on the Ford assembly line for thirteen years. Every morning he gets up, eats a doughnut and cup of coffee, takes his lunch pail, gets in the car, and drives to the plant. It is during this morning drive that his mind gets filled with *fantasies of what he'd like to be doing with his life.* Then, about the same time that he parks his car and turns off his ignition, he also *turns off his mind*—and it remains turned off during the whole working day. In the evenings, he is *too tired and discouraged to do* much more than drink a few beers and watch TV.

But this morning Harry's mind didn't turn off with the car. He had witnessed a car accident on the road—in which two people were killed—soon after leaving home. Just as he reaches the plant gate, Harry suddenly turns. Surprised, he discovers that he has made *a firm decision* never to enter that plant again. He knows that *he must try another way* to live before he dies.

These are hard-hats. It's the end of the shift. There is a demonstration outside the plant and the men coming out are looking at it. Everyone is just walking by. They are not much interested. One person is *angry* and *wants to go on strike,* but this does not make sense to anyone else. He is out of place. Actually he is not really angry, he is just bored. He looks as though he might do a little dance to amuse himself, which is more than the rest of them do. *Nothing will happen* at this time *till more people join* this one man in his needs.

or wrong answers. Since the test questions are ambiguous, the answers a person gives are believed to reflect his or her unconscious desires. Each story is "coded" by looking for certain kinds of themes and scoring these themes according to their relevance to various types of needs, such as achievement. Coding has by now been refined to the point where trained coders agree about 90 percent of the time.

McClelland noted first that hungry subjects tended to include more stories about getting food than subjects who were not hungry. Next he performed an analogous test for the need for achievement: he created a group of subjects who were "deprived" of achievement. He did this by giving them a series of tests designed so that they did poorly and knew it. They were allowed to try again and still did poorly. Then he administered the TAT, saying that it was being used to look for creative, intelligent group leaders. As a control, he gave the TAT to another group with a "relaxed" set of instructions, encouraging them to write stories that pleased them. Then he analyzed the stories to see how they differed. In addition, the TAT stories of all kinds of known successful achievers were studied and compared to those of control groups. (Figure 6.7 shows an example of how need for achievement might be measured.)

Based on these tests, McClelland developed a scoring system for the TAT. For example, a story would be scored high in achievement imagery if the main character was concerned with standards of excellence and a high level of performance, with unique accomplishments (such as inventions and awards), or with the pursuit of a long-term career or goal.

In later studies, people who scored high and low in achievement on the TAT were compared in a variety of situations. For example, it was found that high achievers were able to solve anagrams (unscrambling and rearranging letters into meaningful words) faster than those less interested in achievement (Kolb, 1973). More significantly, McClelland followed up the careers of some students at Wesleyan University who had been tested with the TAT in 1947. He wanted to see which students had chosen entrepreneurial work—that is, work in which they had to initiate projects on their own. He found that eleven years after graduation, 83 percent of the entrepreneurs (business managers, insurance salesmen, real estate investors, consultants, and so on) had scored high in achievement, but only 21 percent of the nonentrepreneurs had scored that high (McClelland, 1965).

Next, McClelland checked to see whether the achievement motive had any real effects on society (1961). He and his associates studied the children's literature of England, Spain, and ancient Athens, scoring it for achievement in the same manner as he would a TAT story. They found that in general, high levels of achievement motivation appeared fifty to one-hundred years before improvements in the economic situation of each country.

Encouraged by this finding, McClelland and others then set about devising a training course in achievement motivation. The trainees in this course learned to score their own TAT stories and to recognize achievement themes in them. They also rewrote their stories again and again, attempting to include more achievement themes in them. Then they discussed everyday life situations and case histories with other members of the group, focusing on achievement themes. Group members also played a business game designed to give them quick feedback for decision making and problem solving.

Success with this program has been reported after applying it in such diverse places as Spain, Mexico, Italy, India, and poverty areas of Kentucky (McClelland and Winter, 1969). For example, a group of seventy-six men running small businesses in Indian villages was given the training and was later compared to a similar group not given the training. The trained groups showed significant and large increases in entrepreneurial activity (such as starting new businesses or gaining large increases in salary), while the untrained group did not change.

McClelland does not believe we should all train ourselves as high achievers. In fact, he has said that such persons are not always the most interesting, and they are usually not artistically sensitive (McClelland and Harris, 1971). They would also be less likely to value intimacy in a relationship. Studies have shown that high achievers prefer to be associated with experts who will help them achieve instead of with more friendly people.

There are many other motives besides achievement, all of which may be equally important to having a highly developed culture. But in a competitive world where some nations are affluent and some extremely deprived, a nation or culture that lacks a sufficient number of high achievers may find it quite difficult to prosper economically.

Fear of Success.   McClelland's work has inspired a wide variety of research on other aspects of motivation. Matina Horner (1970, 1972) asked eighty-nine men to write a story beginning with the line, "After first term finals, John finds himself at the top of his medical school class." Substituting the name Anne for John in the opening line, she also asked ninety women to write a story. Ninety percent of the men wrote success stories. However, over sixty-five percent of the women predicted doom for Anne.

Some of the women feared for Anne's social life. They described her as undatable or unmarriageable, and suggested that she would be socially isolated if she excelled in her studies and career. Some wrote about the guilt and despair she would experience if she continued to succeed. And some refused to believe the opening line. It was impossible for Anne to be first in her class; there must be some mistake.

On the basis of this study Horner identified another dimension of achievement motivation, the *motive to avoid success.* Females in our society are (or were) raised with the idea that being successful in all but a few careers is odd and unfeminine. Thus a woman who is a success in medicine, law, and other traditionally male occupations must be a failure as a woman. It might have been all right for Anne to pass her exams, but the fact that she did better than all the men in her class made the female subjects anxious.

Horner discovered that bright women, who had a very real chance of achieving in their chosen fields, exhibited a stronger fear of success than did women who were average or slightly above average. (Expecting success made them more likely to avoid it, despite the obvious advantages of a

Being a mother might be quite satisfying for one woman, but not for another.

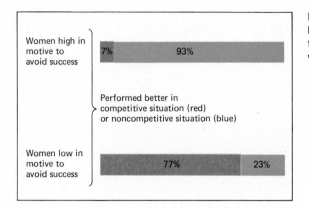

rewarding career.) This seemed to confirm Horner's belief that success involves deep conflicts for women (see Figure 6.8).

Many other researchers then set out to verify Horner's findings. They quickly found that the picture was more complicated than Horner's study seemed to suggest. For one thing, it's very hard to define success. Being a mother might be quite satisfying for one woman, but a sign of failure for someone who would have preferred a career. Also, it is often hard to tell whether a person who doesn't try something is more afraid of success or failure.

Although there is still considerable controversy in this area, many later studies did not support the idea that fear of success was more of a problem for women than men (Tresemer, 1976a, 1976b). Many researchers believe that the story of Anne's achievements in medical school told us a great deal about American stereotypes of women, but relatively little about the actual career choices specific women make (Shaver, 1976). In any case, many different tests of people's attitudes toward success have been invented as a result of Horner's work, and psychologists are beginning to understand the many issues involved in getting ahead in our society. Tresemer (1976b: 215) wrote that researchers are now asking: "When does a person avoid success, and, by the way, what do you mean by success?"

Maslow's Hierarchy of Needs

Abraham Maslow, one of the pioneers of humanistic psychology, believes that *all* human beings need to feel competent, to win approval and recognition, and to sense that they have achieved something. He places achievement motivation in the context of a hierarchy of needs all people share.

Maslow's scheme, shown in Figure 6.9, incorporates all the factors we have discussed so far in this chapter, and goes a step further. He begins with biological drives, including the need for physical safety and security. In order to live, people have to satisfy these **fundamental needs.** If people are hungry, most of their activities will be motivated by the drive to acquire food, and they will not be able to function on a higher level.

Figure 6.9
Maslow's hierarchy of needs. According to Maslow, it is only after satisfying the lower levels of needs that a person is free to progress to the ultimate need of self-actualization.

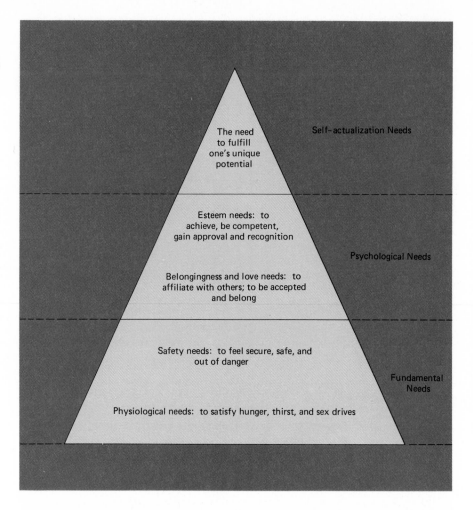

The second level in Maslow's hierarchy consists of **psychological needs:** the need to belong and to give and receive love, and the need to acquire esteem through competence and achievement. Maslow suggests that these needs function in much the same way that biological needs do, and that they can be filled only by an outside source. A lack of love or esteem makes people anxious and tense. There is a driven quality to their behavior. They may engage in random, desperate, and sometimes neurotic or maladaptive activities to ease their tensions. Unless these needs are satisfied, a person will be unable to move on. Most of his or her behavior will be motivated by unfulfilled psychological needs. Thus an unusually intelligent woman who does not feel loved may avoid success in the hope of being accepted as one of the crowd.

Self-actualization needs are at the top of Maslow's hierarchy. These may include the pursuit of knowledge and beauty, or whatever else is required for the realization of one's unique potential. Maslow believes that although relatively few people reach this level, we all have these needs. To be creative in the way we conduct our lives and use our talents, we must first satisfy our fundamental and psychological needs. The satisfaction of these needs motivates us to seek self-actualization.

Maslow thus adds to motivation theory the idea that some needs take precedence over others and the suggestion that achieving one level of satisfaction releases new needs and motivations. (We discuss Maslow's theory in more detail in Chapter 13.)

EMOTION

It is difficult to draw a clear line between motives and emotions. We saw that when a person needs food, the stomach contracts, the level of sugar in the blood drops, neural and endocrine systems are thrown slightly off balance, and taste buds become more sensitive. We saw that when a person is frightened, heart and breathing rates quicken, energy level rises, the senses mobilize, and blood rushes away from the stomach into the brain, heart, and other muscles. Of course, a poet might diagnose a pounding heart, loss of appetite, and heightened awareness of the moonlight and scented breezes as love. Why, if all three involve identifiable physiological changes, do we call hunger a biological drive, and fear and love emotions?

It depends on whether we are describing the source of our behavior or the feelings associated with our behavior. When we want to emphasize the needs, desires, and mental calculations that lead to goal-directed behavior, we use the word "drive" or "motivation." When we want to stress the feelings associated with these decisions and activities, we use the word "emotion" or "affect."

Clearly, the two are intertwined. We frequently explain our motives in terms of emotions. Why did you walk out of the meeting? I was angry. Why do you go to so many parties? I enjoy meeting new people and love to dance. Why did you lend your notes to someone you don't particularly like? I felt guilty about talking behind her back. Why did you apply for a summer job overseas? The idea of flying to Saudi Arabia excites me—and so on.

As these examples demonstrate, emotions push and pull us in different directions. Sometimes emotions function like biological drives: our feelings energize us and make us pursue a goal. Which goal we pursue may be determined by our social learning experiences. Other times we do things because we think they will make us feel good: anticipated emotions are the incentive for our actions. The consequences of striving for one goal or another also evoke emotions.

Expressing Emotions: Innate and Learned Behavior

In *The Expression of the Emotions in Man and Animals* (1872), Charles Darwin argued that all people express certain basic feelings in the same ways. Without knowing a person's language, you can tell whether he or she is amused or infuriated just by looking at that person's face.

Recent studies indicate that Darwin was right. One group of re-

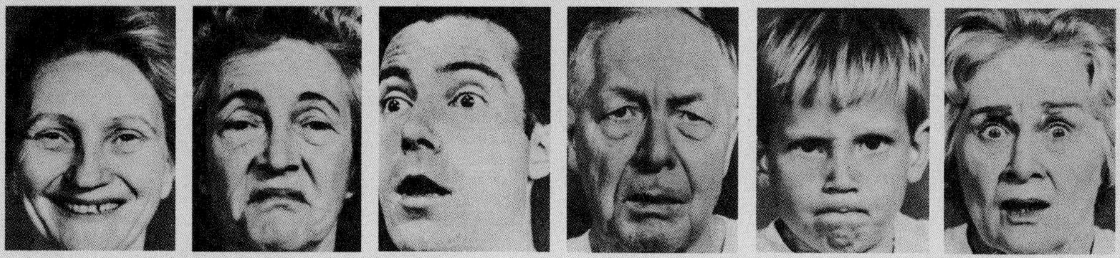

Photograph Judged						
Judgment	Happiness	Disgust	Surprise	Sadness	Anger	Fear
Culture			**Percent Who Agreed with Judgment**			
99 Americans	97	92	95	84	67	85
40 Brazilians	95	97	87	59	90	67
119 Chileans	95	92	93	88	94	68
168 Argentinians	98	92	95	78	90	54
29 Japanese	100	90	100	62	90	66

Figure 6.10

The data in this table show that there is substantial agreement among the members of different cultures about the meaning of various facial expressions. The muscular movements that produce these expressions are probably innate human responses. (After Ekman, Friesen, and Ellsworth, 1972)

searchers selected a group of photographs they thought depicted surprise, anger, sadness, and happiness. Then they showed the photographs to people from five different cultures and asked them to say what the person in each photograph was feeling. The results of this experiment are shown in Figure 6.10. The overwhelming majority of the subjects identified the emotions as the researchers expected they would. Was this simply because they had met Americans, or at least seen American television shows and movies, and so learned how to "read" our facial expressions? Apparently not. A second study was conducted in a remote part of New Guinea, with people who had had relatively little contact with outsiders and virtually no exposure to mass media. They too were able to identify the emotions being expressed (Ekman, Friesen, and Ellsworth, 1972).

These studies imply that certain basic facial expressions are **innate**—that is, part of our biological inheritance. Observations of children who were born blind and deaf lend support to this view. These youngsters could not have learned how to communicate feelings by observing other people. Still, they laugh like other children when they're happy, pout and frown to express resentment, clench their fists and teeth in anger (see Goodenough, 1932).

But even the most basic emotions can be changed by learning. We saw in Chapter 2 how Watson used classical conditioning to teach a child to fear white, furry objects. And we will see in Chapter 16 how psychothera-pists use the same techniques in reverse to help people "unlearn" or rid themselves of irrational fears. Although parents may not consciously apply classical conditioning, they (and others) modify their children's emotions by responding angrily to some outbursts, sympathetically to others, and on occasion ignoring their youngsters. In this way, children are taught which emotions are considered appropriate in different situations and which emotions they are expected to control. For example, in our society, girls are allowed—even expected—to cry, but boys beyond a certain age are not.

Learning explains the differences we find among cultures once we go beyond such basic expressions as laughing or crying. For example, in Vic-torian English novels, women closed their eyes, opened their mouths with a gasp, and fainted when they were frightened or shocked. In Chinese novels, men fainted when they became enraged. Medical records from the period indicate that Chinese men did indeed faint from anger (Klineberg, 1938). What these findings suggest is that all of us are born with the capac-ity for emotion and with certain basic forms of expression, but that when, where, and how we express different feelings depend in large part on learning.

Analyzing facial expressions helps us to describe emotions. But it does not tell us where emotions come from. Over the years, psychologists have proposed several answers to these questions. Some believe emotions derive from physical changes; others, that emotions result from mental processes.

Physiological Theories

In *Principles of Psychology,* a classic work published in 1890, William James attempted to summarize the best available literature on human behavior, motivations, and feelings. When it came to drawing up a catalogue of human emotions, James gave up; he felt there were too many subtle varia-tions, too many personal differences. But he was struck by the fact that nearly every description of emotions he read emphasized bodily changes. James's observations of his own and other people's emotions confirmed this point. We associate feelings with sudden increases or decreases in energy, muscle tension and relaxation, and sensations in the pit of our stomach.

The James-Lange Theory.   After much thought James concluded that we use the word "emotion" to describe our visceral or "gut" reactions to the things that take place around us. In other words, James (1890) believed that emotions are the perception of certain internal bodily changes.

My theory . . . is that *the bodily changes follow directly the perception of the exciting fact, and that our feeling of the same changes as they occur IS the emotion.* Commonsense says, we lose our fortune, are sorry and weep; we meet a bear, are frightened and run; we are insulted by a rival, are angry and strike. . . . [T]he more rational statement is that we feel sorry because we cry, angry because we strike, afraid because we tremble. . . . Without the bodily states following on the perception, the latter would be . . . pale, colorless, destitute of emotional warmth.

In a sense, James was putting the cart before the horse. Other psychologists had assumed that emotions trigger bodily changes; James argued that the reverse is true. Because Carl Lange came to the same conclusion about the same time, this position is known as the **James-Lange theory** (Lange and James, 1922).

The Cannon-Bard Theory.   Techniques for studying bodily changes improved over the next three decades, and evidence that contradicted the James-Lange theory began to grow. For example, the physiological changes that occur during emotional states also occur when people are not feeling angry or sad—or anything. In fact, injecting a drug that produces physiological arousal of the body does not necessarily produce changes in emotions. (If James and Lange had been correct, such physiological changes would always produce emotions.) Also the internal state of the body changes only slowly. "Gut" reactions could not produce the rushes of emotion we all experience from time to time. Indeed, if bodily changes were the seat of emotion, we would all be rather sluggish and dull.

In 1929, Walter B. Cannon published a summary of the evidence against the James-Lange theory. Cannon argued that the thalamus (part of the lower brain) is the seat of emotion—an idea Philip Bard (1934) expanded and refined. According to the **Cannon-Bard theory,** certain experiences activate the thalamus, and the thalamus sends messages to the cortex (or

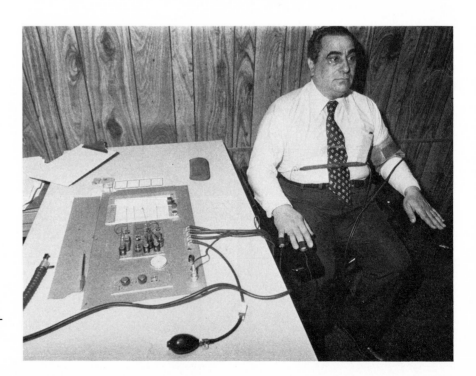

Figure 6.11
Taking a lie detector test: the polygraph measures sweating of the skin, breathing, blood pressure, and heart rate.

Fooling a Lie Detector

Outwitting a lie detection test is not particularly easy, but it can be done.

Since the polygraph simply records the arousal of emotional responses, the trick is to respond emotionally at the wrong time. When you're asked for your name or address, before you respond simply picture yourself in bed with a member of your favorite sex. You can also produce a physiological response by crossing your eyes or tensing the muscles in your leg. Pain also produces arousal; one old trick involves hiding a thumbtack in your shoe and pressing your toe on it whenever the examiner asks a question.

All these strategies work the same way—a polygraph test compares your relaxed physiological state to the response to an emotionally charged question. By confusing the issue when you're supposed to be relaxed, you may be able to make the test inconclusive. Of course, if you get caught, it's not going to look good.

For more details, see G. H. Barland and D. C. Raskin, "The Detection of Deception," in W. F. Prokasy and D. C. Raskin (eds.), *Electrodermal Activity in Psychological Research.* New York: Academic Press, 1973.

higher brain) and to the body organs. (More sophisticated experiments showed that the thalamus is not involved in emotional experience, but the hypothalamus is.) Thus, when we use the word "emotion," we are referring to the *simultaneous* burst of activity in the brain and "gut" reactions. In Cannon's words, "The peculiar quality of emotion is added to simple sensation when the thalamic processes are aroused" (1929).

Cannon also emphasized the importance of physiological arousal in many different emotions. He was the first to describe the "fight or flight" reaction of the sympathetic nervous system that prepares us for an emergency by increasing heart rate and blood pressure, releasing sugar into the bloodstream, and so on. Some of these signs of physiological arousal are measured in one of the most famous applications of psychological knowledge: lie detection.

USING PSYCHOLOGY

Lie Detection

Most of us associate lie detection with shifty-eyed criminals accused of murdering their grandmothers. But in reality, American industry uses the lie detector far more often than the police do. No one knows exactly how many polygraph tests (**polygraph** is another name for a lie detector) are given each year, but one psychologist (Lykken, 1974) places the number at several million. Companies use these tests for everything from finding out whether a job applicant has ever been in trouble to seeing who's got his or her hand in the till at the local hamburger stand.

The first modern "lie detector" was invented by Leonarde Keeler, a member of the Berkeley, California, police force in the 1920s. As you can see in Figure 6.11, a polygraph includes electrodes for measuring the electrical resistance of the skin (often called the GSR, this is a measure of sweating), a tube that is tied around the chest to measure breathing, and an inflatable cuff that measures blood pressure and heart rate. There is no single physiological change that always goes along with a lie. Rather, the lie-detection expert looks for general signs of the activation of the sympathetic nervous system: an irregular breathing pattern, high heart rate and blood pressure, and increased sweating (indicated by decreases in the electrical resistance of the skin). Lie detection is an art rather than a science, so the technique is only as good as the man who uses it (Hassett, 1978).

Surprisingly, almost all of the people who become lie-detection experts have backgrounds not in psychology but in law enforcement. The way they cross-question a person is at least as important as the machine itself. To illustrate this point, polygraphers sometimes tell an old tale about a medieval prince who wanted to find out which of his servants had stolen some food. He called all his servants together and announced that he had a sacred donkey in the next room. The donkey would bray only when the guilty man pulled his tail. One by one, the servants went by themselves into a dark room with the donkey, pulled his tail, and returned to the prince. Finally, the last man returned and still the ass had not made a sound. The prince then told the servants to hold out their hands. He had covered the donkey's tail with soot. Only the guilty man had been afraid to pull the tail, and so only his hands were clean (Sternbach, Gustafson, and Colier, 1962). Similarly, some experts say that if a person believes in the lie detector, it can be used to make him or her tell the truth. Indeed, many people confess during an hour-long interview that usually takes place before the machine is even plugged in.

The polygrapher tries to develop three different kinds of questions for the actual tests. Some are nonemotional (for example "Is your name Richard Nixon?"); some are emotional but not relevant to the investigation ("Have you ever cheated on your lover?"); a few are related specifically to the investigation. The theory is that everyone will react emotionally to the last two categories, but only the guilty party will respond *more* to questions about the crime. It is important that the questions be as specific as possible. A polygrapher would not ask "Did you ever steal anything?" but rather "Did you ever steal more than one hundred dollars from the E-Z Credit Furniture Store?"

How effective are lie detectors? It's hard to say. Like all good businesspeople, polygraph experts advertise their successes and forget about their failures. In one review of many criminal cases (Orlansky, 1965), the lie detector was proved wrong about 2 percent of the time. But this figure is misleading. If a lie detector test says a suspect is innocent, the police often won't bother to look for more evidence. So it's very hard to know when it's wrong. And even if the figure were as low as 2 percent, that's not going to help you if you're one of the people the lie detector lies about.

Overall, the ability of polygraphs to detect the arousal often associated with lying is quite impressive. But lie detectors do make mistakes (see box). For this reason, the results of polygraph tests are not ordinarily allowed as evidence in a court of law. When, if ever, they should be used in industry is a political question rather than one that psychologists are specially qualified to answer.

Cognitive Theories

Cognitive theorists believe that bodily changes and thinking *work together* to produce emotions. Physiological arousal is only half of the story. What you feel depends on how you interpret your symptoms. And this, in turn, depends on what is going on in your mind and in your environment.

The Schachter-Singer Experiment. Stanley Schachter and Jerome Singer designed an experiment to explore this (1962). They told all their subjects they were testing the effects of vitamin C on eyesight. In reality, most received an adrenalin injection. One group was told that the "vitamin" injection would make their hearts race and their bodies tremble (which was true). Another group was deliberately misinformed: the injection would make them numb. A third group was not told anything about how their bodies would react to the shot. And a fourth group received a neutral injection that did not produce any symptoms. Like the third group, these subjects were not given any information about possible side effects.

After the injection, each subject was taken to a reception room to wait for the "vision test." There they found another person who was actually part of the experiment. The subjects thought the stooge had had the same injection as theirs. With some subjects, the stooge acted wild and crazy—dancing around, laughing, making paper airplanes with the questionnaire they'd been asked to fill out. Other subjects had to fill out a long and

Cognitive theorists believe bodily changes and thinking work together to produce emotions.

offensive questionnaire that asked, for example: "With how many men (other than your father) has your mother had extramarital relationships? 4 and under ____; 5–9 ____; 10 and over ____." The stooge for this group acted quite angry.

Subjects from the first group, who had been told how the injection would affect them, watched the stooge with mild amusement. So did subjects who had received the neutral injection. However, those from the second and third groups, who either had no idea or an incorrect idea about the side effects, joined in with the stooge (Figure 6.12). If the stooge was euphoric, so were they; if he was angry, they became angry.

What does this experiment demonstrate? That internal components of emotion (such as those adrenalin produces) affect a person differently, depending on his or her interpretation or perception of the social situation. When people cannot explain their physical reactions, they take cues from their environment. The stooge provided cues. But when people knew that their hearts were beating faster because of the adrenalin shot, they did not feel particularly happy or angry. The experiment also shows that internal changes are important—otherwise the subjects from the neutral group would have acted in the same way as those from the misinformed groups. Perception and arousal *interact* to create emotions.

Arnold's Theory.   According to Magda Arnold, everyday emotions can be analyzed into a series of stages (Figure 6.13). In the first, you *perceive* a person, object, or event. It may take place in your imagination, as when you think about something you expect to happen in the future or replay a scene from your past.

The next stage is *appraisal*. You decide whether what is happening will

Figure 6.12
Two of the conditions in Schachter and Singer's experiment on emotion. (a) A subject is misled about the effects he should expect from an adrenalin injection. Placed with a stooge who joyfully flies airplanes around the room, he attributes his state of arousal to a similar mood in himself and joins in. (b) A subject is told exactly what to expect from the injection. Although placed in the same situation as the first subject, he recognizes his physical sensations as the product of the injection and is not affected by the actions of the stooge.

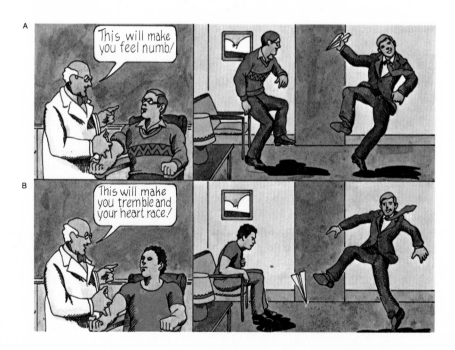

1. Observation: "There are fighter planes coming up."
2. Appraisal: "There is danger; they may catch up with me and hit the plane."
3. Fear (not attended to because the pilot is fully occupied evading the fighter planes).
4. Physiological changes: increase in heart rate; tremor; and fatigue, which becomes cumulative until the mission is finished.
5. Awareness of these changes (will be delayed until the necessity for action is past and attention is free to notice the physiological state).
6. Secondary estimate: "I am chronically tired, trembling, irritable--I must be ill."
7. Secondary emotion: fear of illness, heart disease, and so on.
8. Physiological changes: reinforcement of fatigue, tremor, and so on, increasing the malaise.

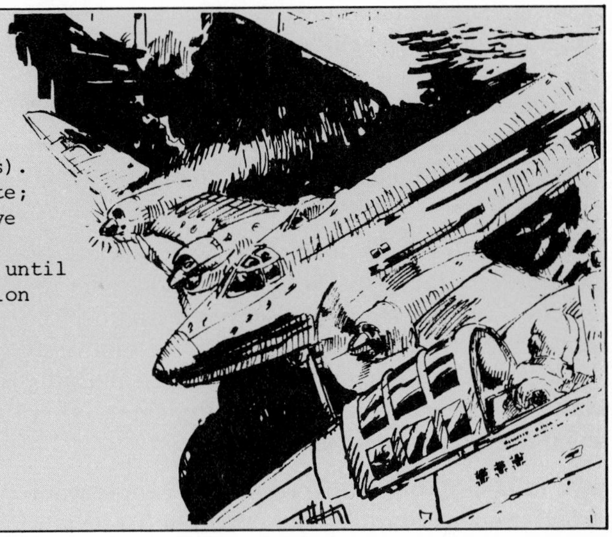

Figure 6.13

Magda Arnold's theory of emotion describes a continuous process of reaction and appraisal. This figure shows how a person may respond immediately and effectively in a dangerous situation and later misinterpret the aftereffects.

help you, hurt you, or have no effect on you. Suppose you see one of your instructors walking toward you. If you have nothing special to gain and nothing to fear from her, you do not react emotionally. You say hello, chat for a moment, and walk on.

However, if you have been cutting class and suspect that the instructor is going to ask for an explanation, or if you know that she was impressed with a term paper you wrote and will probably compliment you, you will react—physiologically and emotionally. Your heart begins to beat a little faster, and you feel nervous or excited (depending on whether you cut classes or wrote an excellent paper). These are the third and fourth stages: *bodily change* and *emotion*.

In most cases, emotion and bodily change occur at the same time. However, in some situations you skip from stage three (bodily changes) to stage five, which is *action*. You see a car rushing toward you, adrenalin pours into your system, and you jump back without stopping to think. Only after you've leaped to safety do you sense your heart pounding and experience the emotion of fright (Arnold, 1960, 1970). (See also the discussion of stress in Chapter 10.)

Emotions and physical changes are interwined. It will probably be many years before we understand all the complex ways in which the two interact in human behavior.

SUMMARY

1. Several of the physiological drives that motivate behavior are homeostatic. That is, they represent a need to correct deviations from the normal state.

2. Drive reduction theory states that physiological needs drive an organism to act in either random or habitual ways until its needs are satisfied. But drive reduction theory overlooks the fact that some experiences are inherently pleasurable, and that even though they do not reduce biological drives, they still provide incentives or goals for behavior.

3. Social needs also motivate behavior. One of these, the need for achievement, has been intensively studied by David McClelland. He and his associates devised a method for measuring achievement motivation. They also developed achievement training programs that have been successful cross-culturally.

4. McClelland's work inspired a wide variety of research on other aspects of motivation. One researcher, Matina Horner, discovered another dimension of achievement motivation: the motive to avoid success. Although Horner believed that this was more of a problem for women than men, other researchers have questioned this.

5. Abraham Maslow believed that all people want to feel competent, to win approval and recognition, and to sense they have achieved something. According to his theory, there is a hierarchy of needs: fundamental needs, psychological needs, and self-actualization needs. Some needs take precedence over others, and the achievement of one level of satisfaction releases new needs and motivations.

6. Emotions and motivations are intertwined.

7. All of us are born with the same basic capacity for emotion. When and where we express different feelings depend in large part on learning.

8. Investigation of where emotions come from brought cognitive theorists to the conclusion that bodily changes and thinking *work together* to produce emotions.

9. Internal sensations affect each person differently, depending on mental interpretation and the social situation.

10. According to Magda Arnold, there are four stages in the development of emotion: perception, appraisal, bodily change, and emotion. The stage following this is action.

GLOSSARY

Cannon-Bard theory: A theory introduced by psychologists Cannon and Bard that attributed emotion to the simultaneous activity of the brain and "gut" reactions.

drive reduction theory: A theory formulated by psychologist Clark Hull that states that physiological needs drive an organism to act in random or habitual ways until its needs are satisfied.

fundamental needs: In Maslow's hierarchy-of-needs theory, these are the biological drives that must be satisfied in order to maintain life.

homeostasis: The tendency of all organisms to correct imbalances and deviations from their normal state.

innate behavior: Behavior that is part of one's biological inheritance.

James-Lange theory: A theory formulated by psychologists James and Lange that suggests that emotions are the perception of bodily changes.

lateral hypothalamus (LH): The part of the hypothalamus that produces hunger signals.

motivation: Inducement to direct one's energies toward achieving a goal that has acquired meaning.

polygraph: A machine used to measure physiological changes, particularly in lie detection.

psychological needs: In Maslow's hierarchy-of-needs theory, these include the need to belong and to give and receive love, and the need to acquire esteem through competence and achievement. If these needs are frustrated, it will be difficult for the person to strive for fulfillment of the next level in the hierarchy—*self-actualization needs.*

self-actualization needs: The top of Maslow's hierarchy of needs. These include the pursuit of knowledge and beauty, or whatever else is required for the realization of one's unique potential. Before these needs can be satisfied, people must first meet their *fundamental* and *psychological needs.*

ventromedial hypothalamus (VMH): The part of the hypothalamus that produces feelings of fullness as opposed to hunger, and causes one to stop eating.

ACTIVITIES

1. Try going without bread in your meals for several days a week. Do you find that you are beginning to think about bread more often, even dream about it? Are you becoming more aware of advertisements for bread? Compare your experience with the description of drive reduction behavior in this chapter.

2. Write down several activities or behaviors you do when your time is your own. In which level of Maslow's hierarchy of needs would you place each of these activities or behaviors; that is, what really motivates you to engage in each of them? Perhaps you will discover a different kind of motive, one that doesn't seem to fit in with Maslow's set. Check the chapter on personality and the Maslow readings to see whether or not it might fit. If none of the activities on your list seems to be motivated by self-actualization, can you imagine activities that would be, and that you might enjoy doing?

3. With a partner or as a group, select ten emotions to express. Then play a variation of charades, with one person attempting to convey each of these emotions by facial expression alone. Are some emotions harder to convey than others? Are there consistent differences in interpretation between individuals? How important do you think context (the social situation in which the facial expression occurs) is in perceiving other people's emotions?

4. Recall the four stages of development of an emotion, described in this chapter. Then observe them in yourself, at a time when you are entering an emotional state. If possible you should take notes, at least "mental notes," to enable you to view yourself with some objectivity even while you are having the emotion. To induce the emotion you might go to a movie that you know will be scary or sad. Or you might attend a religious service or mystical ritual of some sort if that affects you.

5. If you are interested in the achievement motive, you might try the story-writing techniques described in this chapter. Try writing stories with and without achievement themes. Supposedly, those who deliberately attempt to include themes related to the three aspects of achievement motivation will increase their own ability to achieve; at least, such an exercise makes a person more aware of achievement.

6. Collect the fantasies of people in your class. Each person should write several stories or fantasies, possibly around a set of ambiguous pictures. Names should not be placed on fantasies (so as to insure privacy), but each person should mark male or female on the fantasy. Then compare the fantasies of men and women for the achievement motive. Are there differences? Do you think there have been changes in this factor in the last few years?

7. To gain a clearer understanding of the range of emotional reactions you experience, keep an "emotion diary" for one day. Try to jot down what you felt, how you interpreted your feelings, and what brought on your reaction. At the end of the day, analyze your diary to determine the differences in physiological reactions that you experienced in response to each situation. What conclusions can you draw about your emotional responses on that day?

SUGGESTED READINGS

ARNOLD, MAGDA (ED). *Feelings and Emotions.* New York: Academic Press, 1970. A collection of recent symposium papers by many of the theorists mentioned in this chapter and by several others who could not be mentioned because of limited space. An excellent cross section of the field as it exists today.

COFER, CHARLES N. *Motivation and Emotion.* Glenview, Ill.: Scott, Foresman, 1972. A short, comprehensive paperback textbook covering drive and incentive theories, biological aspects of motivation, the need for stimulation, and cognitive consistency theories.

EKMAN, PAUL. "Face Muscles Talk Every Language." *Psychology Today*, 8 (September 1975): 35–39. Does evolution or culture determine the way in which our faces express emotion? This author discusses his research showing that at least some emotions produce the same facial expressions in fifteen different cultures.

GREENE, D., AND LEPPER, M. R. "Intrinsic Motivation: How to Turn Play into Work." *Psychology Today*, 7 (September 1974): 49–54. Suggests that rewarding children (or anyone) for something they like to do may turn enjoyment into drudgery. In the words of the authors, "a person's intrinsic interest in an activity may be decreased by inducing him to engage in that activity as a means to some ... goal."

MC CLELLAND, DAVID. *The Achieving Society*. New York: Van Nostrand Reinhold, 1961. This book addresses the question of the social origins and consequences for society of achievement motivation.

MC CLELLAND, DAVID, AND HARRIS, T. G. "To Know Why Men Do What They Do: A Conversation with David C. McClelland." *Psychology Today*, 4 (January 1971): 35–39. McClelland talks about how he began studying achievement and other motives, and about some of the ways his research could be used to improve our lives.

MASLOW, A. H. *The Farther Reaches of Human Nature*. New York: Viking Press, 1971. Maslow elaborates his concept of self-actualization and other aspects of human potential.

Sex Roles: A Journal of Research, 2, no. 3 (September 1976). This special issue of a scholarly journal is devoted to ten articles describing research on fear of success.

WINTER, D. G. *The Power Motive*. New York: Free Press, 1973. Winter discusses research on this motive, which can be analyzed by means of the TAT, in the same manner as McClelland did for the achievement motive. As Winter makes clear, the two kinds of motives are quite different.

BIBLIOGRAPHY

AHLSKOG, J. ERIC, AND HOEBEL, BARTLEY G. "Overeating and Obesity from Damage to a Noradrenergic System in the Brain." *Science*, 182 (1973): 166–169.

ARNOLD, MAGDA B. *Emotion and Personality*. New York: Columbia University Press, 1960.

———— (ED.). *Feelings and Emotions: The Loyola Symposium*. New York: Academic Press, 1970.

ATKINSON, JOHN W. (ED.). *Motives in Fantasy, Action, and Society*. New York: Van Nostrand Reinhold, 1958.

ATKINSON, JOHN W., AND FEATHER, NORMAN T. *A Theory of Achievement Motivation*. New York: Wiley, 1966.

BARD, PHILIP. "On Emotional Expression After Decortication with Some Remarks of Certain Theoretical Views: Part I." *Psychological Review*, 41 (1934), 309–329, "Part II," 41 (1934), 424–449.

CANNON, WALTER B. *Bodily Changes in Pain, Hunger, Fear and Rage*. New York: Appleton-Century-Crofts, 1929.

COFER, C. N. *Motivation and Emotions*. Glenview, Ill.: Scott, Foresman, 1972.

DARWIN, CHARLES. *The Expression of Emotions in Man and Animals*. Chicago: University of Chicago Press, 1967; originally published in 1872.

EKMAN, PAUL, FRIESEN, WALLACE V., AND ELLSWORTH, PHOEBE. *Emotion in the Human Face: Guidelines for Research and an Integration of Findings*. Elmsford, N.Y.: Pergamon, 1972.

GOODENOUGH, FLORENCE L. "Expression of the Emotions in a Blind-Deaf Child." *Journal of Abnormal and Social Psychology*, 27 (1932): 328–333.

HARLOW, HARRY F., AND ZIMMERMAN, ROBERT F. "Affectual Responses in the Infant Monkey." *Science*, 120 (1959): 421–432.

HASSETT, JAMES. *A Primer of Psychophysiology.* San Francisco: Freeman, 1978.

HORNER, MATINA S. "Femininity and Successful Achievement: A Basic Inconsistency." In *Feminine Personality and Conflict,* ed. by J. Bardwick, E. M. Douvan, M. S. Horner, and D. Gutman. Belmont, Calif.: Brooks/Cole, 1970.

_____. "Toward an Understanding of Achievement-related Conflicts in Women." *Journal of Social Issues,* 28 (1972): 157–175.

HULL, CLARK. *Principles of Behavior: An Introduction to Behavior Theory.* New York: Appleton-Century-Crofts, 1943.

JAMES, WILLIAM. *The Principles of Psychology.* Vol. 2. New York: Holt, 1890.

KLINEBERG, OTTO. "Emotional Expression in Chinese Literature." *Journal of Abnormal and Social Psychology,* 33 (1938): 517–520.

KOLB, D. A. "Changing Achievement Motivation." In *Behavior Change,* ed. by R. Schwitzgabel and D. A. Kolb. New York: McGraw-Hill, 1973.

LANGE, CARL G., AND JAMES, WILLIAM. *The Emotions.* Ed. by Knight Dunlap, trans. by I. A. Haupt. Baltimore: Wilkins & Wilkins, 1922.

LYKKEN, DAVID T. "Psychology and the Lie Detector Industry." *American Psychologist,* 29 (1974): 725–739.

MC CLELLAND, D. C. *The Achieving Society.* Princeton: Van Nostrand, 1961.

_____. "Need Achievement and Entrepreneurship: A Longitudinal Study." *Journal of Personality and Social Psychology,* 1 (1965): 389–392.

MC CLELLAND, D. C., AND HARRIS, T. G. "To Know Why Men Do What They Do: A Conversation with David C. McClelland." *Psychology Today,* 4 (January 1971): 35–39.

MC CLELLAND, D. C., AND WINTER, D. G. *Motivating Economic Achievement.* New York: Free Press, 1969.

MC CLELLAND, D. C., ET AL. *The Achievement Motive.* New York: Appleton-Century-Crofts, 1953.

MARANON, GREGORIO. "Contribution à l étude de l'action émotive de l'adrenaline." *Revue Français d'Endocrinologie,* 2 (1952): 141–147.

MURRAY, HENRY A., ET AL. *Exploration in Personality.* New York: Oxford University Press, 1934.

ORLANSKY, J. "An Assessment of Lie Detection Capability." In *Use of Polygraphs and "Lie Detectors" by the Federal Government.* House Report No. 198, Eighty-ninth Congress, First Session. Washington, D.C.: U.S. Government Printing Office, 1965.

SCHACHTER, STANLEY. *Emotion, Obesity, and Crime.* New York: Academic Press, 1971.

SCHACHTER, STANLEY, AND SINGER, JEROME. "Cognitive, Social, and Physiological Determinants of Emotional State." *Psychological Review,* 69 (1962): 379–399.

SHAVER, PHILLIP. "Questions Concerning Fear of Success and Its Conceptual Relatives." *Sex Roles,* 2 (1976): 305–320.

STERNBACH, R. A., GUSTAFSON, L. A., AND COLIER, R. L. "Don't Trust the Lie Detector." *Harvard Business Review,* 40 (1962): 127–134.

TRESEMER, DAVID. "The Cumulative Record of Research on 'Fear of Success.' " *Sex Roles,* 2 (1976a): 217–236.

_____. "Current Trends in Research on 'Fear of Success.' " *Sex Roles,* 2 (1976b): 211–216.

WHITE, ROBERT W. "Motivation Reconsidered: The Concept of Competence." *Psychological Review,* 66 (1959): 297–333.

7 Altered States of Consciousness

As you read this sentence you are conscious of the words on this page. Or maybe your awareness is drifting to that attractive classmate sitting across from you in the library. In either case, everything you think and feel is part of your conscious experience.

You might expect, then, that normal states of **consciousness** would be one of the most active areas of research in psychology. But this is not the case. Although some of the earliest researchers defined psychology as the study of conscious experience, consciousness proved to be a difficult topic to analyze scientifically. Behaviorism—with its emphasis on studying only what people do, not what they think or feel—became popular partly because studying consciousness had proved to be so difficult. Even today, psychobiologist Roger Sperry (1976: 9) has called consciousness "one of the most truly mystifying unknowns remaining in the whole of science."

But a related area that *has* been the subject of a great deal of research in recent years is the study of altered states of consciousness. An altered state of consciousness involves a change in mental processes, not just a quantitative shift (such as feeling more or less alert). Sensations, perceptions, and thought patterns actually change. The most obvious and familiar example is sleep. People spend about a third of their lives in this altered state of consciousness. Other examples include daydreams, hallucinations, delirium, hypnotic states, being drunk or "high" on drugs, and the heightened awareness people experience during various forms of meditation (Tart, 1972).

In the past twenty years, psychologists have begun to examine altered states of consciousness by having people sleep, undergo hypnosis, or take drugs during laboratory experiments. In the laboratory, researchers can observe changes in behavior and measure changes in breathing, pulse rate, body temperature, and brain activity. (Brain activity, or "waves," can be recorded with a device known as an electroencephalograph, or EEG.) The

Sleep and Dreams
Stages of Sleep
Dream Interpretation

Hypnosis

Hallucinations

Sensory Deprivation

Drug States
Marijuana
Hallucinogens

Biofeedback

Meditation
Using Psychology:
Lowering Blood Pressure

Figure 7.1
An altered state of consciousness like meditation involves a change in mental processes. Sensations, perceptions, and thought patterns actually change.

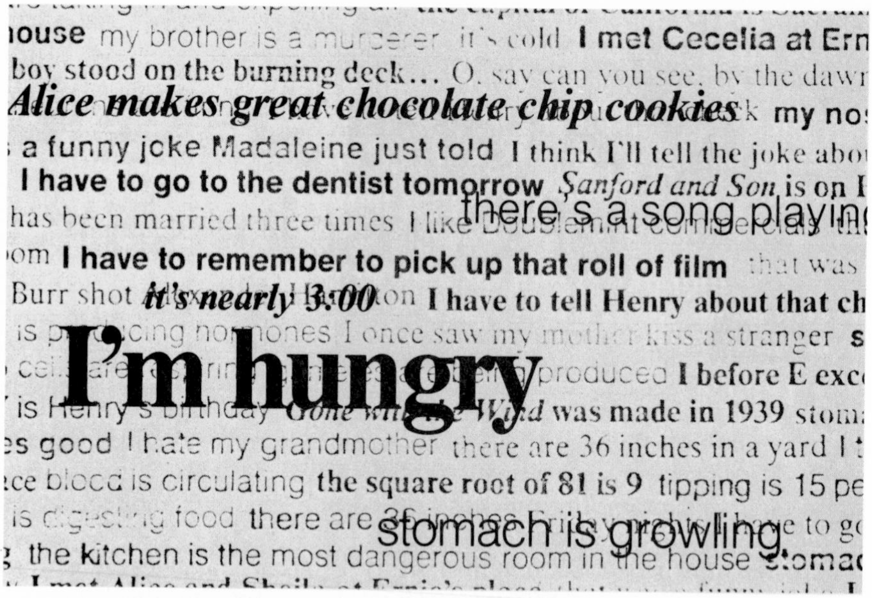

Figure 7.2
Consciousness has proved to be
one of the most difficult areas of
psychological research: everything
we think and feel is part of conscious experience, though we may
be more or less aware of certain
experiences simultaneously.

Figure 7.3
Doing a yoga exercise. One of the
purposes of controlling breathing
in yoga is to achieve an altered
state of consciousness.

subjects' own reports of how they feel or what they remember supplement these data. What have psychologists learned about these phenomena? We begin with sleep.

SLEEP AND DREAMS

Most people think of sleep as a state of unconsciousness, punctuated by brief periods of dreaming. This is only partially correct. Sleep is a state of *altered* consciousness, characterized by certain patterns of brain activity.

Stages of Sleep

As you begin to fall asleep, your body temperature declines, your pulse rate drops, and your breathing grows slow and even. Gradually your eyes close and your brain briefly emits alpha waves, as observed on the EEG, which are associated with the absence of concentrated thought and with relaxation (Figure 7.4). Your body may twitch, your eyes roll, and brief visual images flash across your mind (although your eyelids are shut) as you enter Stage I sleep.

In Stage I sleep your muscles relax and your pulse slows a bit more, but

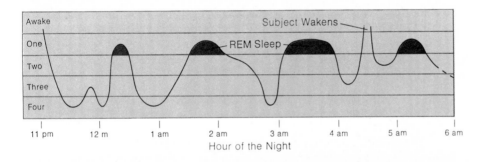

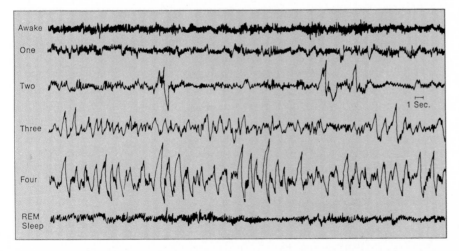

Figure 7.4
(top) A diagram showing the passage of a sleeper through the various stages of sleep over a seven-hour period. (bottom) The patterns of electrical activity (EEGs) in the brain that correspond to the various stages of sleep. The EEG pattern shown for being awake is one that occurs when the person is resting quietly with eyes closed.

Insomnia

Everyone has had a sleepless night at one time or other—a night where nothing you do brings the calm, soothing peace you want. Some people have sleep problems like this all the time, and they rarely get more than an hour or two of uninterrupted sleep a night. To help these insomniacs, psychologists Richard R. Bootzin and Perry M. Nicassio have developed a behavior modification program to strengthen the bed as a cue for sleep and weaken it as a cue for sleep-interfering activities.

They suggest that insomniacs follow these instructions:

1. Lie down to sleep only when you feel sleepy.
2. Don't use the bed for any activity other than sleep. That means no eating, reading, watching television, listening to the radio, or worrying in bed. The only exception is sexual activity.
3. If after you're in bed for about ten minutes you find that you can't sleep, get up and go into another room. This will help you associate your bed with falling asleep quickly and dissociate it with tossing and turning. Return to your bed when you feel sleep coming on.
4. Repeat step 3 if you still can't sleep. Get out of bed as many times as necessary during the night.
5. Get up at the same time every morning no matter how little sleep you had the night before. This will help you develop a consistent sleep pattern.
6. Don't nap during the day.

Laboratory studies have shown the effectiveness of these techniques in helping insomniacs fall asleep and stay asleep. If you have a problem, they may work for you.

For more details, see Richard R. Bootzin, *Behavior Modification and Therapy: An Introduction.* Cambridge, Mass.: Winthrop, 1975.

your breathing becomes uneven and your brain waves grow irregular. This lasts for about ten minutes. At this point your brain waves begin to fluctuate between high and low voltages—a pattern that indicates you have entered Stage II sleep. Your eyes roll slowly from side to side. Some thirty minutes later you drift down into Stage III sleep, and low-voltage waves begin to sweep your brain every second or so.

Stage IV is deep sleep. Large, regular delta waves indicate you are in a state of oblivion. If you are awakened by a loud noise or sudden movement, you will not remember anything and may feel disoriented. Talking out loud, sleepwalking, and bed wetting—all of which may occur in this stage—leave no trace on memory. Deep sleep is important to your physical and psychological well-being. Perhaps this is why people who, for one reason or another, are only able to sleep a few hours at a time descend rapidly into Stage IV and remain there for most of their nap.

However, on an average night, Stage IV sleep lasts only for an hour or an hour and a half. You then climb back through Stages III and II to Stage I. At this point, something curious happens. Although your muscles are even more relaxed than before, your eyes begin to move rapidly. You have

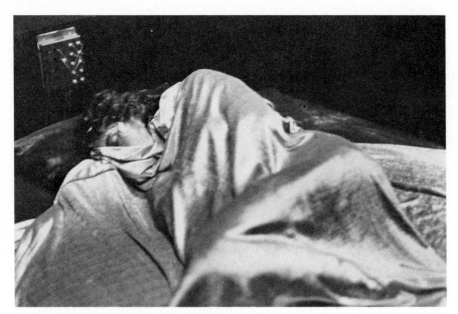

entered rapid-eye-movement, or **REM, sleep.** Your pulse rate and breathing become irregular, and the levels of adrenal and sexual hormones in your blood rise—as if you were in the midst of an intensely emotional or physically demanding activity. Your brain sends out waves that closely resemble those of a person who is fully awake. It is during this stage that almost all dreaming takes place, although sleepwalking and sleeptalking rarely occur during this phase.

REM sleep lasts for about ten minutes, after which you retrace the descent to Stage IV. You go through this cycle every ninety minutes or so. Each time the period of Stage IV sleep decreases and the length of REM sleep increases—until you eventually wake up. But at no point does your brain become inactive.

We call the mental activity that takes place during sleep dreaming. Everybody dreams, although most people are only able to recall a few if any of their dreams. Sleep researchers sometimes make a point of waking subjects at regular intervals during the night to ask them about their dreams. The first few dreams are usually composed of vague thoughts left over from the day's activities. A subject may report that she was watching television, for example. As the night wears on, dreams become longer and more vivid and dramatic, especially dreams that take place during REM sleep. These are the dreams people are most likely to remember when they wake up.

When people are awakened randomly during REM sleep and asked what they had just been dreaming, the reports generally are commonplace, even dull (Hall and Van de Castle, 1966). The dreams we remember and talk about "are more coherent, sexier, and generally more interesting" than those collected in systematic research (Webb, 1975: 140).

Researchers who have recorded the contents of thousands of dreams

Everybody dreams, but most people can recall very few of their dreams.

Figure 7.6
Freud on dreams.

Dreams are not meaningless, they are not absurd. . . . On the contrary, they are psychical phenomena of complete validity—fulfillments of wishes. . . .

If I eat anchovies or olives in the evening . . . I develop thirst during the night which wakes me up. But my waking is preceded by a dream . . . That I am drinking.

Dreams which can only be understood as fulfillments of wishes and which bear their meaning upon their faces without disguise are to be found under the most frequent and various conditions. They are mostly short and simple dreams. . . .

But in cases where the wish-fulfillment is unrecognizable, where it has been disguised, there must have existed some inclination to put up a defense against the wish; and owing to this defence the wish was unable to express itself except in a distorted shape. . . .

A young physician had sent in his income tax return, which he had filled in perfectly honestly, since he had very little to declare. He then had a dream that *an acquaintance of his came to him from a meeting of the tax commissioners and informed him* *that, while no objection had been raised to any of the other tax returns, general suspicion had been aroused by his and a heavy fine had been imposed on him.* The dream was a poorly disguised fulfilment of his wish to be known as a doctor with a large income. . . .

Strikingly innocent dreams may embody crudely erotic wishes. . . .

She was putting a candle into a candlestick; but the candle broke so that it wouldn't stand up properly. The girls at her school said she was clumsy; but the mistress said it was not her fault.

The occasion for the dream was a real event. The day before she had actually put a candle into a candlestick, though it did not break. Some transparent symbolism was being used in this dream. A candle is an object which can excite the female genitals; and, if it is broken, so that it cannot stand up properly, it means that the man is impotent. ("It was not her fault.")

From Sigmund Freud, *The Interpretation of Dreams.* Translated from the German and edited by James Strachey. Third English edition. New York: Avon Books, 1965, pp. 155, 156, 160, 175, 190, 432, 219–220.

have found that most—even the late-night REM adventures—occur in such commonplace settings as living rooms, cars, and streets. Most dreams involve either strenuous recreational activities or passive events such as sitting and watching, not work or study. A large percentage of the emotions experienced in dreams are negative or unpleasant—anxiety, anger, sadness, and so on. Contrary to popular belief, dreams do not occur in a "split second"; they correspond to a realistic time scale.

Dream Interpretation

Although dreams may contain elements of ordinary, waking reality, these elements are often jumbled in fantastic ways. The dreamer may see people in places they would never go, wander through strange houses with endless doors, find her- or himself transported backward in time. The dreamer may be unable to speak—or able to fly. What do these distortions mean?

Dream interpretations have been discovered dating back to 5,000 years before Christ. Sigmund Freud was the first in the modern era to argue that dreams are an important part of our emotional lives (see Figure 7.6).

Freud believed that no matter how simple or mundane, dreams may contain clues to thoughts and desires the dreamer is afraid to acknowledge or express in his or her waking hours. Indeed, he maintained that dreams are full of hidden meanings and disguises.

Freud believed that the symbolism of dreams is a private language that each individual has invented for himself or herself. These symbols vary greatly from person to person. Suppose that a dreamer sees herself standing naked among fully clothed strangers. For one person, this dream may symbolize a desire to show her true self to people, without pretense. For another person, the dream may symbolize a fear of having her inadequacies exposed in public. In his work with patients, Freud tried to break through the disguise of dream imagery and discover the true desires and wishes of the dreamer.

However, some social scientists are skeptical of dream interpretations. Nathaniel Kleitman, one of the pioneers who discovered REM sleep, wrote in 1960: "Dreaming may serve no function whatsoever." According to this view, the experience of a dream is simply an unimportant by-product of stimulating certain brain cells during sleep. McCarley (1978), for example, argues that the common experience of feeling paralyzed in a dream simply means that brain cells that inhibit muscle activity were randomly stimulated.

HYPNOSIS

Hypnosis is a form of altered consciousness in which a person becomes highly suggestible and does not use his critical thinking ability. By allowing the hypnotist to guide and direct him, a person can be made conscious of things he is usually unaware of and unaware of things he usually notices. (The subject may recall in vivid detail an incident he had forgotten, or feel no pain when his hand is pricked with a needle.)

Hypnosis does not put the subject to sleep, as many people believe. A hypnotic trance is quite different from sleep. In fact, the subject becomes highly receptive and responsive to certain internal and external stimuli. He is able to focus his attention on one tiny aspect of reality and ignore all other inputs. The hypnotist induces a trance by slowly persuading the subject to relax and to lose interest in external distractions. Whether this takes a few minutes or much longer depends on the purpose of the hypnosis and the method of induction.

Figure 7.7
A hypnotist, drawn by Daumier, a famous nineteenth-century French painter and caricaturist.

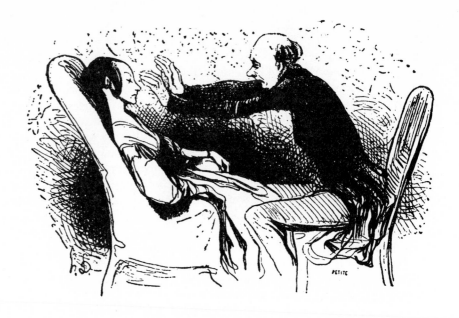

A subject must cooperate in order to be hypnotized; he or she is not under the hypnotist's "power."

Psychologists who use hypnosis stress that the relationship between the hypnotist and subject involves cooperation, not domination. The subject is not under the hypnotist's "power" and cannot be forced to do things against his will. Rather, the person is simply cooperating with the hypnotist by becoming particularly responsive to the hypnotist's suggestions. *Together* they try to solve a problem or to learn more about how the subject's mind works. Anyone can resist hypnosis by simply refusing to open his or her mind to the hypnotist, and people under hypnosis cannot be induced to do things they would not do when "awake" unless they want to.

Hypnotists can also suggest things for their subjects to remember when the trance is over, a phenomenon known as **posthypnotic suggestion**. For example, the hypnotist might suggest that after the person is awakened she will be unable to hear the word "psychology." When she comes out of the trance, the subject may report that some people around her are speaking strangely. They seem to leave out some words occasionally, especially when they are talking about topics involving the taboo word "psychology." The subject is not aware that part of her consciousness has been instructed to block out that word. Posthypnotic suggestion has been found to be particularly helpful in changing unwanted behaviors, such as smoking or overeating.

Psychologists do not agree about the nature of hypnosis. Some, like Theodore Barber (1965), argue that hypnosis is not a special state of consciousness. If people are simply given instructions and told to try their hardest, they will be able to do anything that hypnotized people can do. Barber has shown that unhypnotized people can hold a heavy weight at arm's length for several minutes; they can lie stiff as a board with only one chair under their shoulders and another under their feet to support them; they can even stick needles through their hands.

Others, like Ernest Hilgard (1977), believe that there is something special about the hypnotic state. People who are hypnotized are very suggestible; they go along with the hypnotist and do not initiate activities themselves; and they can more easily imagine and remember things. Hilgard believes that consciousness includes many different aspects that may become separated, or dissociated, during hypnosis. This view is called neo-dissociation theory.

In some experiments, Hilgard has shown that consciousness can be broken down into a number of parts. For example, a person who is hypnotized may be told that her left arm is unable to feel pain, but that her right arm will act as a "hidden observer"—noting how painful the situation is, but not consciously feeling any pain. With appropriate hypnotic instructions, Hilgard later asks the "hidden observer" what the subject felt and is told that the right arm really did notice pain, even though the hypnotized person earlier said that she didn't feel anything at all.

Whether hypnosis is a special state of consciousness or not, it does reveal that people often have potential abilities that they don't use. Continued study may help us to understand where these abilities come from and how to use them better.

HALLUCINATIONS

Hallucinations are sensations or perceptions that have no direct external cause—seeing, hearing, smelling, tasting, or feeling things that do not exist.

Hypnosis, meditation, certain drugs, withdrawal from a drug to which one has become addicted, and psychological breakdown may produce hallucinations. (We discuss the hallucinations associated with drug withdrawal and mental breakdowns in Chapter 15.) But they also occur under "normal" conditions. People hallucinate when they are dreaming and when they are deprived of the opportunity to sleep. Periods of high emotion, concentration, or fatigue may also produce false sensations and perceptions. For example, truck drivers on long hauls have been known to swerve suddenly to avoid stalled cars that do not exist. Even daydreams involve mild hallucinations.

Interestingly enough, it seems that hallucinations are very much alike from one person to the next. Soon after taking a drug that causes hallucinations, for example, people often see many geometric forms in a tunnellike perspective. These forms float through the field of vision, combining with each other and duplicating themselves. While normal imagery is often in black and white, hallucinations are more likely to involve color.

When Seigel (1977) traveled to Mexico's Sierra Madre to study the reactions of Huichol Indians who take peyote, he found that their hallucinations were much like those of American college students who took similar drugs. Seigel believes that these reactions are similar because of the way such drugs affect the brain: portions of the brain that respond to incoming stimuli become disorganized while the entire central nervous system is aroused.

SENSORY DEPRIVATION

In 1951, Donald Hebb began a series of experiments on the effects of boredom. As one of the researchers (Heron, 1957: 52) later described it: "The aim of this project was to obtain basic information on how human beings would react in situations where nothing at all was happening."

Male college students were paid to lie all day on a comfortable bed—they would get up only for meals and to go to the bathroom. Plastic visors over their eyes kept them from seeing anything but diffuse light; U-shaped foam-rubber pillows around their heads and the hum of a small air conditioner kept out any sounds; and cotton gloves and long cardboard cuffs restricted the sense of touch (see Figure 7.8). In short, the subjects could not see, hear, or touch anything—they were in a state of sensory deprivation.

Most people had signed up for the experiment hoping to catch up on their work—planning term papers, lectures, and so on. But under these conditions they quickly became irritable and found that they had trouble concentrating. After a while, some of them even began to hallucinate.

Many other studies of sensory deprivation have been performed since (Zubeck, 1969). They have used a variety of techniques for restricting sensory input, including lying in a tub of warm water for several days and submerging completely in a pool heated to body temperature while wearing nothing but a diving helmet to supply oxygen. Not all techniques and conditions had the same effects. Hallucinations were generally not as common in later experiments, but sensory deprivation consistently did lead to irritability, restlessness, and emotional upset.

DRUG STATES

The drugs of interest for the study of consciousness are those that interact with the central nervous system to alter a person's mood, perception, and behavior. Such drugs range from the caffeine in coffee and in cola drinks to powerful consciousness-altering substances like marijuana, alcohol, amphetamines, and LSD (see Table 7.1).

Marijuana

Marijuana has been used as an intoxicant among Eastern cultures for centuries. In some societies it is legally and morally acceptable whereas alcohol is not. Before 1960, marijuana use in the United States was common only among members of certain subcultures, such as jazz musicians and artists in big cities. By 1960, however, college students had discovered marijuana, and since then its rate of use has increased by a factor of perhaps ten thousand. According to government figures, about one out of every seven Americans over the age of fifteen uses marijuana in any given week.

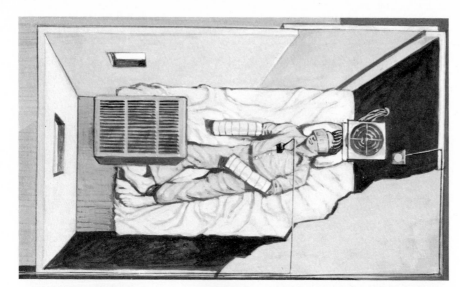

Figure 7.8
Experimenting on the effects of boredom. Gloves and cotton cuffs prevented input to the hands and fingers; a plastic visor diffused the light coming into the eyes; a foam pillow and the continuous hum of the air conditioner and fan made input to the ears low and monotonous. Except for eating and using the bathroom, the subjects did nothing but lie on the bed. (After "The Pathology of Boredom," by Woodburn Heron. © 1957 by Scientific American, Inc. All rights reserved.)

Figure 7.9
Smoking marijuana. The effects of the drug vary from person to person and also with the setting in which it is taken.

Table 7.1 / Major Consciousness-Altering Substances

Name of Drug or Chemical	Duration of Action (hours)	Method of Taking	Potential for Psychological Dependence (habituation)
Depressants			
Sedatives	4	Swallowing pills or capsules	High
Barbiturates			
Amytal			
Nembutal			
Seconal			
Phenobarbital			
Tuinal			
Doriden (glutethimide)			
Chloral hydrate			
Miltown, Equanil (meprobamate)			
Methaqualone	6	Swallowing	
Quaalude, Sopor			
Alcohol	2–4	Swallowing liquid	High
Whiskey, gin, beer, wine			
Narcotics (opiates, analgesics)			
Opium	4	Smoking (inhalation) Injecting in muscle or vein	High
Heroin			
Dilaudid			
Morphine			
Codeine			
Percodan			
Demerol			
Methadone			
Cough syrup (Cheracol, Hycodan, Robitussin AC, etc.)		Swallowing	
Stimulants			
Amphetamines	4	Swallowing pills or capsules or injecting in veins	High
Benzedrine			
Methedrine			
Dexedrine			
Methamphetamine		Swallowing, injecting, or snorting	
Desoxyn			
Biphetamine			
Cocaine		Sniffing or injecting	
Caffeine	2–4		Moderate
Coffee, tea, Coca-Cola		Swallowing liquid	
No-Doz, APC		Swallowing pills	

Source: Table used by permission of Joel Fort, M.D., the National Center for Solving Special Social and Health Problems (FORT HELP), San Francisco. Adapted and revised from Joel Fort, *The Pleasure Seekers: The Drug Crisis, Youth and Society* (New York: Grove, 1970).

Tolerance Potential	Potential for Physical Dependence (addiction)	Usual Short-Term Effects (psychological, pharmacological, social)	Usual Long-Term Effects (psychological, pharmacological social)
Yes	Yes	CNS depressants; sleep induction; relaxation (sedation); sometimes euphoria; drowsiness; impaired judgment, reaction time, coordination, and emotional control; relief of anxiety-tension; muscle relaxation	Irritability, weight loss, addiction with severe withdrawal illness (like DTs); habituation, addiction
Yes	Yes	CNS depressant; relaxation (sedation); sometimes euphoria; drowsiness; impaired judgment, reaction time, coordination, and emotional control; frequent aggressive behavior	Diversion of energy and money from more creative and productive pursuits; habituation; possible obesity with chronic excessive use; irreversible damage to brain and liver, addiction with severe withdrawal illness (DTs), possible death
Yes	Yes	CNS depressants; sedation, euphoria, relief of pain, impaired intellectual functioning and coordination	Constipation, loss of appetite and weight, temporary impotency or sterility; habituation, addiction with unpleasant and painful withdrawal illness
Yes	No	CNS stimulants; increased alertness, reduction of fatigue, loss of appetite, insomnia, often euphoria	Restlessness, irritability, weight loss, toxic psychosis (mainly paranoid); habituation
Yes	No	CNS stimulant; increased alertness; reduction of fatigue	Sometimes insomnia, restlessness, or gastric irritation; habituation

The active ingredient in marijuana is a complex molecule called tetra-hydrocannabinol (THC), which occurs naturally in the common weed *Cannabis sativa*, or Indian hemp. Marijuana is made by drying the plant; hashish is a gummy powder made from the resin exuded by the flowering tops of the female plant. Both marijuana and hashish are usually smoked, but they can also be cooked with food and eaten.

The effects of the drug vary somewhat from person to person and also seem to depend on the setting in which it is taken. But, in general, most sensory experiences seem greatly enhanced or augmented—music sounds fuller, colors are brighter, smells are richer, foods taste better, and sexual and other sensations are more intense. Users become elated, the world seems somehow more meaningful, and even the most ordinary events may take on an extraordinary profundity. A person who is stoned may, for example, suddenly become aware of the mystical implications of door-knobs. The sense of time is greatly distorted. A short sequence of events may seem to last for hours. Users may become so entranced with an object that they sit and stare at it for many minutes. A musical phrase of a few seconds' duration may seem to stretch out in time until it becomes isolated from the rest of the composition, and the hearer perceives it as never before.

As many users of marijuana have discovered, however, the drug can heighten unpleasant as well as pleasant experiences. If a person is in a frightened, unhappy, or depressed mood to begin with, the chances are excellent that taking the drug will blow the negative feelings out of pro-portion, so that the user's world, temporarily at least, becomes very upset-ting. Cases have been reported in which marijuana appears to have helped bring on psychological disturbances in people who were already unstable before they used it.

Despite the obvious need for careful research on marijuana, the first well-controlled scientific studies of its effects on human beings did not appear until the late 1960s. One of the first of these studies used college students as subjects, some of whom had smoked dope before and some of whom had not. All the experienced users got "high." But only one of the people who had not tried the drug before reported the typical euphoria. In tests of both intellectual and motor skills, all the inexperienced subjects displayed impairment, while the experienced users did not (Weil, Zinberg, and Nelsen, 1968).

Hallucinogens

Hallucinogens—so-called because their main effect is to produce halluci-nations—are found in plants that grow throughout the world, and have been used for their effects on consciousness since earliest human history (Schultes, 1976). These drugs are also called "psychedelic" ("mind-mani-festing") because they are seen as demonstrating the ways in which the mind has the potential to function.

Among the more common hallucinogenic plants are belladonna, hen-bane, mandrake, datura (jimson weed), one species of morning-glory, pey-ote, many kinds of mushrooms, and also cannabis. While we still do not

Figure 7.10
South American Indians in a drug state during a mourning ritual. In these cultures, hallucinogens are used to heighten religious and ritual experiences.

know the exact chemical effects of hallucinogens on the brain, some contain chemical compounds that seem to mimic the activity of certain neurotransmitters, the chemical messengers that regulate brain-cell activity.

LDS (lysergic acid diethylamide), the best-known and most extensively studied of the hallucinogens, is also the most potent; in fact, it is one of the most powerful drugs known. LSD, which is a synthetic substance, is 100 times stronger than psilocybin, which comes from certain mushrooms, and 4,000 times stronger than mescaline, which comes from the peyote. A dose of a few millionths of a gram has a noticeable effect; an average dose of 100 to 300 micrograms produces a "trip" that lasts from six to fourteen hours.

During an LSD trip a person can experience any number of mood states, often quite intense and rapidly changing. The person's "set"—expectations, mood, beliefs—and the circumstances under which he or she takes LSD can affect the experience, making it euphoric or terrifying. Perceptual hallucinations are very common with LSD. A typical hallucinatory progression begins with simple geometric forms, progresses to complex images, and then to dreamlike scenes (Seigel, 1977). The user may encounter such distortions in form that familiar objects become almost unrecognizable. A wall, for example, may seem to pulsate or breathe. One's senses, too, seem to intermingle; sounds may be "seen" and visual stimuli may be "heard." A person may experience a dissociation of the self into one being who observes and another who feels. Distortions of time, either an acceleration or a slowing down, are also common. A single stimulus may become the focus of attention for hours, perceived as ever-changing or newly beautiful and fascinating.

As measured by the ability to perform simple tasks, LSD impairs thinking, even though the user may feel that he or she is thinking more clearly and logically than ever before. Life-long problems may suddenly seem resolved, or the need to solve them may seem absurd. The person often experiences the "great truth" phenomenon—that is, he or she feels that previously hidden and ultimate inner truths have been revealed. When the trip is over, the magnitude of these discoveries shrinks, and the solutions reached may turn out to be trivial. After three to five hours the experience begins to become less intense; after six hours or so the hallucinations and illusions disappear—if no complications occur.

Panic reactions are the most common of LSD's unpleasant side effects, and they may be terrifying. Those who experience panic and later describe it often say that they felt trapped in the experience of panic and were afraid that they would never get out or that they would go mad. Panic usually arises when a person tries to ignore, change, or otherwise get rid of the effects of the drug (rather than yielding to the sensations it generates), then realizes he or she cannot. The best treatment, if the panic is not too severe, seems to be the comfort offered by friends and the security of pleasant, familiar settings. Medical attention is sometimes necessary for very intense reactions.

LSD is proving valuable in the study of certain biochemical and physiological functions of the brain. Serotonin, a substance that may help transmit nerve impulses in the brain and that may play an important role in the regulation of sleep and emotion, is chemically similar to part of the LSD molecule. Apparently, LSD blocks the effects of serotonin on brain tissue, which may account for some of its effects on human behavior. But the exact mechanism by which LSD works has yet to be discovered.

BIOFEEDBACK

Biofeedback involves learning to control your internal physiological processes with the help of feedback from these physiological states. For example, you can be hooked up to a biofeedback machine so that a light goes on every time your heart rate goes over 80 (Figure 7.11). You could then learn to keep your heart rate below 80 by trying to keep the light off. How would you do it? When researcher David Shapiro (1973) asked a participant in one of his experiments how he changed his heart rate, the subject asked in return, "How do you move your arm?"

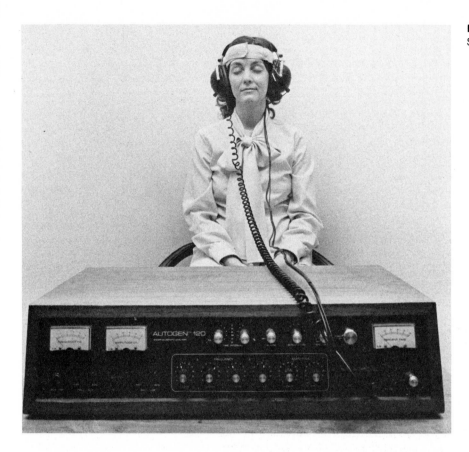

Figure 7.11
Subject practicing biofeedback.

However people do it, biofeedback has been used to teach people to control a wide variety of physiological responses, including brain waves (EEG), heart rate, blood pressure, skin temperature, and sweat-gland activity (Hassett, 1978a). The basic principle of biofeedback is simple: feedback makes learning possible. Imagine trying to learn to play the saxophone if you were deaf. If you couldn't hear all the squeals and honks you made by mistake, your version of "The Star-Spangled Banner" would probably cause all your neighbors to move. It is only through the feedback of hearing your errors that your playing improves.

But our bodies are not designed to provide subtle feedback about internal physiological states. I have no idea whether my heart rate is now 60, 80, or 100 unless I take my pulse. Biofeedback involves using machines to tell people about very subtle, moment-to-moment changes in the body. People can then experiment with different thoughts and feelings while they watch how each affects their bodies. In time, most people can learn to change their physiological processes.

One of the most widely publicized uses of biofeedback was "alpha training." Alpha refers to a certain type of brain-wave activity, typically seen in the EEG when a person relaxes. Alpha has also been observed in the brain waves of some people when they meditate. As a result, a few years ago alpha biofeedback was widely advertised as a quick and easy way to achieve an altered state of consciousness—a sort of instant medita-

Biofeedback has more potential for treating physical disease than for spiritual well-being.

tion. Most researchers are very skeptical of such claims. These days, most people feel that biofeedback has more potential for treating physical disease than for spiritual well-being.

Before biofeedback, scientists believed that responses like heart rate and sweat-gland activity were involuntary, that people could not consciously control them. When researchers in the 1960s began to find that people could, there was a great deal of excitement about these newly discovered potentials of the nervous system. Many began experimenting with biofeedback to cure medical and stress-related conditions like high blood pressure, migraine headaches, and tension headaches. At first, many biofeedback cures were reported in the press. But psychologists were suspicious that these miraculous cases had more to do with the power of suggestion than with biofeedback itself. (Doctors are very familiar with the fact that patients often improve when they believe in a treatment, even if it's only a sugar pill.)

Therefore, more careful studies were started to see what medical conditions could be helped by biofeedback. Some of the best-documented biofeedback cures involve special training in muscular control. Tension headaches often seem to result from constriction of the frontalis muscle in the forehead. Thomas Budzynski and others (1973) used biofeedback to teach people to relax this specific muscle. The practice went on for several weeks while other people were given similar treatments without biofeedback. Only the biofeedback group improved significantly.

Migraine headaches have been successfully treated by a more controversial process—biofeedback for hand warming. People watch a meter that gives a very precise reading of the temperature of their fingers and gradually learn to warm up their hands slightly. Some researchers believe that this works because it changes the pattern of blood flow in the body, decreasing circulation to arteries in the forehead. Others think that the technique simply relaxes people. A third group continues to wonder whether the power of suggestion isn't the most important element in this particular cure.

Using biofeedback to treat conditions from partial paralysis to epilepsy is a very active area of research; but it will take at least several years to discover the problems for which biofeedback is the best solution medical science can offer.

MEDITATION

In the 1960s, psychologists began to study **meditation,** focusing attention on an image or thought with the goal of clearing one's mind and producing an "inner peace." In one of the first experiments, people were simply asked to concentrate on a blue vase.

The participants soon reported that the color of the vase became very vivid and that time passed quickly. The people could not be distracted as easily as they normally might. Some people felt themselves merging with the vase. Others reported that their surroundings became unusually beautiful, filled with light and movement. All the meditators found the experience pleasant. After twelve sessions they all felt a strong attachment to the vase and missed it when it was not present during the next session (Deikman, 1963).

Other researchers went on to show that when people meditated, their physiological state changed. The most famous of these studies was done by Robert Keith Wallace at UCLA (1970). He measured the brain waves (EEG), heart rate, oxygen consumption, and sweat-gland activity of fifteen people as they practiced Transcendental Meditation. (Transcendental Meditation is a Westernized version of yoga meditation techniques that was developed by the Maharishi Mahesh Yogi.) For two twenty-minute periods each day, meditators sit in a comfortable position and repeat a special word—called a *mantra*—over and over again. Wallace found that when people did this, electrical measurements of their bodies proved that they were deeply relaxed.

Further studies suggested that the regular practice of meditation was not only physically relaxing (Woolfolk, 1975), but also led to changes in behavior such as decreased drug use (Benson and Wallace, 1972). Dr. Leon Otis recently warned that a few people who meditate develop anxiety, depression, and other problems (Hassett, 1978c). But researchers generally agree that most people can benefit from the sort of systematic relaxation that meditation provides.

There is some controversy over how meditation techniques differ and what their specific effects are. In his best-selling book *The Relaxation Response*, Herbert Benson (1975) argues that most forms of meditation produce the same result, which he called the "relaxation response." Benson believes that all through recorded history, people have been using various techniques to elicit the relaxation response. He cites many examples, including the contemplative practices of St. Augustine and Martin Luther's instructions for prayer.

Figure 7.12
The *mandala* is a symbol of the universe used as an aid to meditation. This one is Tibetan and is now in the Newark Museum.

How to Meditate

Want to try meditation? Here are the instructions researcher Herbert Benson gives his patients:

Sit quietly in a comfortable position. Close your eyes. Deeply relax all your muscles, beginning at your feet and progressing up to your face. Keep them deeply relaxed.

Breathe through your nose. Become aware of your breathing. As you breathe out, say the word "one" silently to yourself. Continue for 20 minutes. You may open your eyes to check the time, but do not use an alarm. When you have finished, sit quietly for several minutes, at first with closed eyes and later with opened eyes.

Do not worry about whether you are successful in achieving a deep level of relaxation. Maintain a passive attitude and permit relaxation to occur at its own pace. Expect distracting thoughts. When these distracting thoughts occur, ignore them and continue repeating "one."

Practice the technique once or twice daily, but not within two hours after a meal, since the digestive processes seem to interfere with elicitation of anticipated changes.

For further details, see Herbert Benson, "Systemic Hypertension and the Relaxation Response," *New England Journal of Medicine,* 296 (May 19, 1977): 1152–1156.

The opposite of Walter Cannon's famous "fight or flight" response, the relaxation response is said to be physiologically distinct from more casual states of relaxation or sleep. Four basic elements are required to elicit the relaxation response: a quiet environment, a comfortable position, a "mental device" (such as a word that is repeated over and over again, or a physical object that the meditator concentrates on), and a passive attitude. Although not all psychologists agree that the relaxation response is entirely different from sleep or that all relaxation yields the same physical pattern, most do believe that Benson's technique can be helpful for many people. It is described in detail in his book. (See box for a short form of the instructions Benson gives his own patients.)

USING PSYCHOLOGY

Lowering Blood Pressure

One out of every three American adults has high blood pressure. More than 90 percent of these cases are diagnosed as essential **hypertension**—a euphemism that means nobody really knows what is causing it. Traditionally, physicians have treated this problem with pills. But now doctors are shifting their emphasis from pills to people. Patients with high blood pressure are being taught to relax, often with the help of meditation and biofeedback (Hassett, 1978b).

Blood pressure is the force of the blood moving away from the heart, pushing against the artery walls. It changes from instant to instant, peaking as the heart beats and blood spurts through the arteries, and gradually decreasing to a minimum just before the next beat. Blood pressure is expressed as two numbers: systolic pressure (the maximum value when the heart beats) over diastolic pressure (the minimum pressure between beats). It is measured in millimeters of mercury (abbreviated mmHg), a standard unit of force. Normal blood pressure is somewhere around 120/80 mmHg.

Blood pressure varies constantly and increases under stress. Visiting the dentist, taking an examination, thinking about trying out skydiving with the new friend you're trying to impress, even drinking a cup of coffee (a mild stimulant) will increase your blood pressure temporarily. Strong emotions, particularly suppressed anger, will also raise blood pressure.

When blood pressure goes up and stays up, the medical condition is called hypertension. Definite hypertension refers to a blood pressure greater than 160/95. Hypertension is called the silent killer because it usually produces no pain, no other symptoms or warnings before causing severe damage to the cardiovascular system or other organs. But a killer it is. It is a primary cause of stroke (blood-vessel damage in the brain) and, like smoking and high cholesterol levels, increases the risk of suffering heart attacks and coronary-artery disease.

After researchers discovered that normal people could raise and lower blood pressure with the help of biofeedback, it was but a small step to the idea that hypertensives could be taught to lower their blood pressure. In 1971, Harvard researchers Herbert Benson, David Shapiro, Bernard Tursky, and Gary Schwartz reported in *Science* that they had done just that. Five essential hypertensives had learned to lower their systolic pressure over the course of several weeks of training. Since then, others have found that biofeedback can be used to reduce both systolic and diastolic blood pressure.

Even in the first study, however, there were hints that biofeedback's effects don't always last after the subject leaves the laboratory. Gary Schwartz, for example, noticed that one man had a puzzling pattern of successes and failures. Five days a week, this hypertensive man faithfully attended training sessions, collecting $35 every Friday for his success in lowering his systolic pressure. When he returned each Monday morning, however, he again had high blood pressure. After several weeks of this, Schwartz took the patient aside and asked for an explanation. It seemed that Saturday nights the man took his biofeedback earnings to the race track, gambled, and lost both his money and his controlled level of blood pressure.

So it was clear from the start that biofeedback was not a magical cure, only part of the answer. Since blood-pressure biofeedback requires complex and expensive equipment, it wasn't practical to use it with large numbers of patients. Other researchers therefore experimented with teaching hypertensives to relax their muscles, using a simpler form of biofeedback. This too led to lower blood pressure, at least temporarily.

Herbert Benson has experimented with meditation as a partial treatment for high blood pressure, and again it has been successful. Finally, one group of researchers (Surwit, Shapiro, and Good, 1978) directly compared the effects of blood-pressure biofeedback, muscle-tension biofeedback, and meditation. All three reduced blood pressure, and there were no significant differences among the groups. Since biofeedback requires elaborate instruments and meditation does not, it seems likely that the latter will be more widely used (Hassett, 1978).

SUMMARY

1. The most common altered state of consciousness is dreaming. People are mentally active throughout the night, although the degree of activity varies with each stage in the sleep cycle.

2. The stage of sleep in which vivid dreams occur is called REM sleep. Dreams may symbolically depict significant emotional problems and disturbances that are part of a person's daily experiences.

3. Hypnosis may be an altered state of consciousness in which a subject becomes highly receptive to the suggestions of another person. He or she does so willingly and cannot be made to do anything he or she would not normally do while awake.

4. Hallucinations—sensations or perceptions that have no direct external cause—may occur during drug states, after sleep deprivation, or under sensory deprivation.

5. Marijuana and LSD are the two most common hallucinogens—drugs that alter awareness and produce hallucinations.

6. Biofeedback involves learning to control your physiological state with the help of machines that give you feedback about bodily processes.

7. Meditation is a state of consciousness involving high levels of concentration—a drug-free "high" for many people. Experienced meditators are able to achieve a high state of relaxation with greatly reduced anxiety.

GLOSSARY

biofeedback: The process of learning to control bodily states with the help of machines that provide information about physiological processes.

hallucination: A sensation or perception that has no direct external cause.

hallucinogens: Drugs that often produce hallucinations.

hypertension: Unhealthy levels of high blood pressure.

hypnosis: An altered state of consciousness resulting from a narrowed focus of attention and characterized by heightened suggestibility.

LSD: An extremely potent psychedelic drug that produces hallucinations and distortions of perception and thought.

marijuana: The dried leaves and flowers of Indian hemp (*Cannabis sativa*) that produce an altered state of consciousness when smoked or ingested.

meditation: Focusing of attention on an image, thought, bodily process, or external object with the goal of clearing one's mind and producing an "inner peace."

posthypnotic suggestion: A suggestion made during a hypnotic trance that influences the subject's behavior after the trance is ended.

REM sleep: The period of sleep during which the eyes dart back and forth (rapid eye movement) and dreaming usually occurs.

ACTIVITIES

1. What behaviors do you perform automatically? Pick one of your automatic behaviors and pay close attention to how you perform it. What are the individual parts that make up the behavior? How does consciously thinking about the behavior affect your performance of it?

2. Keep track of your dreams for at least a week. Dreams are difficult to remember, so keep a paper and pencil by your bed. When you wake up after a dream, keep your eyes closed and try to remember it in your mind. Then write it down, including as much detail as you can. Also write down any ideas you may have about what the dream means and any feelings you may have about the dream. After you have kept track of your dreams for several days, ask yourself: Am I able to consciously control my dreams in any way? Am I better able to understand myself by examining my dreams?

3. One way of becoming aware of your consciousness is through meditation. Meditation is not concentration in the normal sense of the word. It is opening up one's awareness to the world at the present. Try the following for ten to fifteen minutes a day. Find a quiet spot without distractions. Listen quietly without making any generalizations on what you hear. Listen for the sounds without naming them. After each period, write down your observations. Which sounds did you "hear" for the first time? In this simple form of meditation, do not be surprised if you actually hear yourself talk to yourself.

4. Hypnosis is a form of suggestibility. You may discover which of your friends is susceptible to hypnosis by doing the following test in hypnosis. Have your subjects place a coin in their open palm. Repeatedly suggest to them that they feel the palm slowly turning over, until the coin falls out of the palm. You may be surprised at the results.

5. Pick any word and say it one hundred times. What happens?

6. Have you ever hallucinated a sight or sound—perhaps when you were very tired or upset? What did you experience? Why do you suppose you created this particular hallucination?

SUGGESTED READINGS

BENSON, HERBERT. *The Relaxation Response*. New York: Avon, 1975. A former best seller, this book describes Benson's meditation procedure.

BORING, E. G. *The Physical Dimensions of Consciousness*. New York: Dover, 1963. In describing and analyzing the diverse aspects of our conscious experience, Professor Boring changed the whole philosophical basis of psychology in 1933, when this book first appeared. His observations are just as fresh and relevant today, especially in relation to the so-called altered states of consciousness.

CASTANEDA, CARLOS. *A Separate Reality*. New York: Simon & Schuster, 1971 (paper). In this sequel to his first book, *The Teachings of Don Juan: A Yaqui Way of Knowledge*, Castaneda describes his continuing efforts to learn to think in a new way, to move outside old patterns of thought learned in his own culture.

DEMENT, WILLIAM C. *Some Must Watch While Some Must Sleep*. San Francisco: Freeman, 1974. One of the pioneers in modern dream research presents a brief, readable, up-to-date account of what is known about sleep and dreaming. Gives special attention to the relationship between sleep and psychological disorders, including insomnia and mental illness.

HASSETT, JAMES. *A Primer of Psychophysiology*. San Francisco: Freeman, 1978. An introduction to the physiological-measures studies in biofeedback, meditation, and other topics.

NARAJANO, C., AND ORNSTEIN, R. *On the Psychology of Meditation*. New York: Viking, 1971. A comparative discussion on the wide range of meditative techniques and their relations to the control of internal body and brain states.

ORNSTEIN, ROBERT. *The Psychology of Consciousness*. 2nd ed. Harcourt Brace Jovanovich, 1977. Ornstein explores the idea that humans have two modes of consciousness, one in each brain hemisphere. Among the phenomena he discusses are meditation and biofeedback.

RAY, OAKLEY. *Drugs, Society, and Human Behavior*. St. Louis: Mosby, 1978. A lucid, lively, and thorough presentation of drug research and the impact of "recreational" drugs on society. Includes a section on psychotherapeutic drugs.

SMITH, ADAM. *Powers of Mind*. New York: Random House, 1975. A witty and readable introduction to many different techniques for altering consciousness.

TART, C. T. (ED). *Altered States of Consciousness*. 2nd ed. New York: Wiley, 1972. A collection of fascinating readings on a wide range of topics, including dreaming, hypnosis, drugs, and meditation. Also included is a "fact sheet" on marijuana and many useful papers that are difficult to obtain elsewhere.

WEIL, ANDREW. *The Natural Mind*. Boston: Houghton Mifflin, 1972. Weil examines alternatives to ordinary consciousness. He is particularly interested in what he calls "stoned thinking," a non-drug-induced state.

BIBLIOGRAPHY

AARONSON, BERNARD, AND OSMOND, H. *Psychedelics: The Uses and Implications of Hallucinogenic Drugs*. Garden City, N.Y.: Doubleday, 1970.

BARBER T. X. "Measuring 'Hypnotic-like' Suggestibility With and Without 'Hypnotic Induction': Psychometric Properties, Norms, and Variables Influencing Response to the Barber Suggestibility Scale (BSS)." *Psychological Reports*, 16 (1965): 809–844.

BENSON, HERBERT. *The Relaxation Response*. New York: Avon, 1975.

BENSON, HERBERT, AND WALLACE, ROBERT KEITH. "Decreased Drug Abuse with Transcendental Meditation: A Study of 1862 Subjects." In *Drug Abuse: Proceedings of the International Conference*, ed. by C. J. D. Arafonetis. Philadelphia: Lea & Febiger, 1972.

BUDZYNSKI, T. H., ET AL. "EMG Biofeedback and Tension Headache: A Controlled Outcome Study." *Psychosomatic Medicine*, 35 (1973): 484–496.

DEIKMAN, ARTHUR J. "Experimental Meditation." *Journal of Nervous and Mental Disease*, 136 (1963): 329–373.

ESTABROOKS, G. (ED.). *Hypnosis: Current Problems.* New York: Harper & Row, 1962.

FARADAY, ANN. *The Dream Game.* New York: Harper & Row, 1974.

FOULKES, DAVID. *The Psychology of Sleep.* New York: Scribner's, 1966.

GRINSPOON, LESTER. *Marijuana Reconsidered.* Cambridge, Mass.: Harvard University Press, 1970.

HALL, CALVIN S., AND VAN DE CASTLE, R. L. *The Content Analysis of Dreams.* New York: Appleton-Century-Crofts, 1966.

HASSETT, JAMES. *A Primer of Psychophysiology.* San Francisco: Freeman, 1978a.

————. "Teaching Yourself to Relax." *Psychology Today,* 12 (August 1978b): 28–40.

————. "Caution: Meditation Can Hurt." *Psychology Today,* 12 (November 1978c): 125–126.

HERON, W. "The Pathology of Boredom." *Scientific American,* 196 (January 1957): 57–62.

HILGARD, E. R. *Hypnotic Susceptibility.* New York: Harcourt Brace Jovanovich, 1965.

————. *Divided Consciousness.* New York: Wiley, 1977.

JOUVET, MICHEL. "The Stages of Sleep." *Scientific American,* 216 (1967): 62–72.

KLEITMAN, NATHANIEL. "Patterns of Dreaming." *Scientific American,* 203 (November 1960): 82–88.

————. *Sleep and Wakefulness.* Rev. ed. Chicago: University of Chicago Press, 1963.

LUCE, GAY GAER, AND SEGAL, JULIUS. *Sleep.* New York: Coward, McCann & Geoghegan, 1966.

MC CARLEY, ROBERT W. "Where Dreams Come From: A New Theory." *Psychology Today,* 12 (December 1978): 54–65.

NARAJANO, C., AND ORNSTEIN, R. *On the Psychology of Meditation.* New York: Viking, 1971.

ORNE, MARTIN T. "The Nature of Hypnosis: Artifact and Essence." *Journal of Abnormal and Social Psychology,* 58 (1959): 277–299.

ORNSTEIN, ROBERT. *The Psychology of Consciousness.* 2nd ed. New York: Harcourt Brace Jovanovich, 1977.

PENFIELD, WILDER. "Consciousness, Memory, and Man's Conditioned Reflexes." In *On the Biology of Learning,* ed. by Karl H. Pribram. New York: Harcourt Brace Jovanovich, 1969.

SCHULTES, R. E. *Hallucinogenic Plants.* New York: Golden Press, 1976.

SEIGEL, RONALD K. "Hallucinations." *Scientific American,* 237 (October 1977): 132–140.

SHAPIRO, DAVID. "Preface." In *Biofeedback and Self-Control 1972,* ed. by D. Shapiro *et al.* Chicago: Aldine, 1973.

SHOR, R. E., AND ORNE, M. T. (EDS.). *The Nature of Hypnosis.* New York: Holt, Rinehart & Winston, 1965.

SPERRY, ROGER W. "Changing Concepts of Consciousness and Free Will." *Perspectives in Biology and Medicine,* 20, no. 1 (Autumn 1976): 9–19.

SURWIT, R. S., SHAPIRO D., AND GOOD, M. I. "Comparison of Cardiovascular Feedback, Neuromuscular Feedback, and Meditation in the Treatment of Borderline Essential Hypertension." *Journal of Consulting and Clinical Psychology,* 46 (1978): 252–263.

TART, C. T. (ED.). *Altered States of Consciousness.* 2nd ed. New York: Wiley, 1972.

THOMPSON, RICHARD F. (ED.). *Physiological Psychology.* San Francisco: Freeman, 1971.

WALLACE, ROBERT KEITH. "Physiological Effects of Transcendental Meditation." *Science,* 167 (1970): 1751–1754.

WEBB, WILSE B. *Sleep: The Gentle Tyrant.* Englewood Cliffs, N.J.: Prentice-Hall, 1975.

WEIL, ANDREW. *The Natural Mind.* Boston: Houghton Mifflin, 1972.

WEIL, ANDREW, ZINBERG, N., AND NELSEN, J. M. "Clinical and Psychological Effects of Marijuana in Man." *Science,* 162 (1968): 1234–1242.

WOOLFOLK, ROBERT L. "Psychophysiological Correlates of Meditation." *Archives of General Psychiatry,* 32 (1975): 1326–1333.

ZUBECK, J. P. *Sensory Deprivation: Fifteen Years of Research.* New York: Appleton-Century-Crofts, 1969.

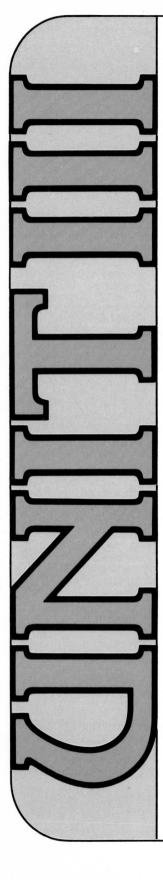

UNIT IID

THE
LIFE SPAN

Human beings have an extended childhood. We are physically immature and dependent on others for much longer than any other animal. During this period, we learn to use our bodies and our minds. We develop a distinctive personality and an understanding of the social rules that govern the people among whom we live, and acquire language and the ability to think in more complex ways than any other creatures on earth.

Development does not stop with full physical and mental growth, however. Our bodies continue to change. As we grow older, society makes new demands on us, and we demand new kinds of satisfaction from society. We learn to adjust to—and perhaps enjoy—young adulthood, middle age, and old age.

This unit surveys the entire life cycle, from birth to death. Chapter 8 details the intellectual, social, and psychological developments of childhood, with special emphasis on how a child develops into a unique individual and member of society. Chapter 9 examines the different ways people respond to the opportunities and problems of adolescence, adulthood, and old age. Chapter 10 describes the lifelong process of adjustment—how "normal" people cope with stress and deal with issues like love and marriage, college, and work.

There was a time when Western peoples considered children miniature adults. Maturing was thought to be a simple matter of growing bigger and learning more. However, psychologists have shown that human development involves qualitative as well as quantitative changes—transformations in the way we think and feel as well as in growth.

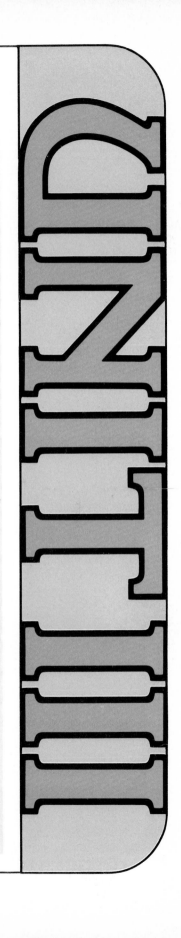

8 Infancy and Childhood

The young child lives in a strange world of wonders and delights. A doorknob or the leg of a table is a mysterious object that an infant will fondle and taste for hours. Mommy and Daddy are the source of all life's great pleasures, and many of its pains. Each day there is something new to be learned.

It is hard to believe that twenty or forty years ago we were only two feet tall and were taking our first step. And that just a year or two after that, we spent our days intently playing house, cops and robbers, and doctor. Most of the events from our early lives are long forgotten, but we changed faster and learned more in childhood than we ever will again.

Developmental psychology is the study of the changes that occur as people grow up and grow old. It covers the entire life cycle, from conception to death. What are we born with? How do we learn to walk and talk, to think, to love and hate? What makes each human being become a unique individual? How do people change over the years? These are the questions developmental psychologists attempt to answer.

In this chapter we describe the many different psychological processes we experience from infancy through childhood. In the next chapter we will look at adolescence, adulthood, and old age.

THE BEGINNING OF LIFE

Development begins long before an infant is born. Expectant mothers can feel strong kicking and sometimes hiccuping inside them during the later stages of pregnancy, and it is common for a fetus (an unborn child) to suck its thumb, even though it has never suckled at its mother's breast or had a bottle.

Figure 8.1
Childhood is a time of rapid learning. We change faster and learn more in these years than we ever will again.

Figure 8.2
(a) The strength of the grasping reflex is demonstrated in a baby only a few days old. (b) This infant is responding to a touch on the cheek by opening his mouth and turning his head. The response is called the rooting reflex.

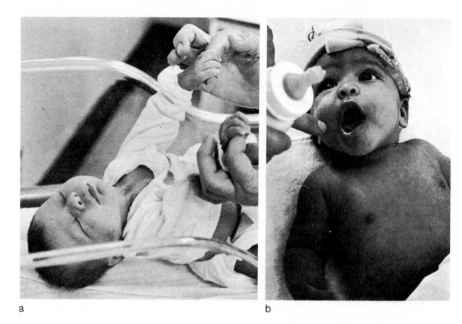

a   b

Birth puts staggering new demands on a baby's capacity to adapt and survive. He goes from an environment in which he is totally protected from the world to one in which he is assaulted by lights, sounds, touches, and extremes of temperature. The newborn is capable of certain coordinated movement patterns, called reflexes, that can be triggered by the right stimulus (Figure 8.2). The **grasping reflex,** for example, is a response to a touch on the palm of the hand. Infants can grasp an object, such as a finger, so strongly that they can be lifted into the air. We suspect this reflex is left over from an earlier stage in human evolution, when babies had to cling to their apelike mothers' coats while their mothers were climbing or searching for food.

Also vital is the **rooting reflex.** If an alert newborn is touched anywhere around the mouth, he will move his head and mouth toward the source of the touch. In this way the touch of his mother's breast on his cheek guides the baby's mouth toward her nipple. The sucking that follows contact with the nipple is one of the baby's most complex reflexes. The baby is able to suck, breathe air, and swallow milk twice a second without getting confused. This is at least as difficult as learning to walk and chew gum at the same time.

Besides grasping and sucking, the newborn spends a lot of time just looking. From birth, unless he is sleeping, feeding, or crying, the baby is watching with curiosity, directing his gaze toward bright patterns and tracing the outlines of those patterns with his eyes.

How do newborn infants, lying in a hospital nursery, perceive the world? Do they see a roomful of stable objects and hear distinct sounds? Or is the sensory world of newborns an ever-changing chaos of meaningless shapes and noises—as William James put it, "one great booming, buzzing confusion"?

These are difficult questions to answer. How does one measure the capabilities of newborn infants who cannot speak or understand the questions of curious psychologists? One reasonable approach is to take advantage of the things babies *can* do. And what they can do is suck, turn their heads, look at things, cry, smile, and show signs of surprise or fright. The vigor of a baby's sucking, the patterns of eye movements, and expressions of pleasure and displeasure are all closely tied to how the baby is being stimulated. By measuring these behaviors while stimulating the baby in different ways, it is possible to infer how the infant perceives the world. For example, infants spend less time looking at out-of-focus movies than they do looking at the same movies in focus. Moreover, infants quickly learn to suck vigorously on a pacifier attached to the focusing mechanism of a movie projector in order to cause an out-of-focus picture to become more sharply defined (Figure 8.3). This suggests that babies are attuned to distinct edges; if the visual world were a blurry confusion for infants, they would not care that a movie was slightly blurry (Kalmis and Bruner, 1973). Studies like this have refuted the notion that the world is essentially disorganized and chaotic to a baby.

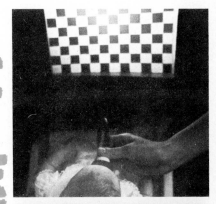

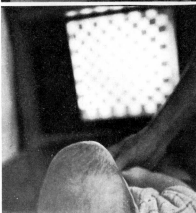

Figure 8.3
Inferring how an infant perceives the world: the four-month-old baby sucks on the pacifier to keep the pattern in focus.

HOW DO BABIES GROW?

In the space of two years this grasping, rooting, searching infant will develop into a child who can walk, talk, and feed herself or himself. This transformation is the result of both maturation and learning.

Maturation

To some extent a baby is like a plant that shoots up and unfolds according to a built-in plan. Unless something is wrong with an infant, she will begin to lift her head at about three months, smile at four months, and grasp objects at five to six months. Crawling appears at eight to ten months. By this time the baby may be able to pull herself into a standing position, although she will fall if she lets go. Three or four months later she will begin to walk, tentatively at first, but gradually acquiring a sense of balance.

Psychologists call internally programmed growth **maturation.** Maturation is as important as learning or experience, especially in the first years. Unless a child is persistently underfed, severely restricted in her movements, or deprived of human contact and things to look at, she will develop more or less according to this schedule. Conversely, no amount of coaching will push a child to walk or speak before she is physiologically ready.

This was demonstrated in an experiment with identical twins (Gesell and Thompson, 1929). One twin, but not the other, was given special training in climbing stairs, building with blocks, and the like. This child did acquire some skill in these areas. But in a short time the second child learned to climb and build just as well as his twin—and with much less practice. Why? Because he had matured to the point where he could coordinate his legs and hands more easily.

Ethnic Differences in Infants

It probably won't surprise you to learn that different breeds of puppies show striking differences in temperament and behavior. Young beagles, for example, are irrepressibly friendly; wire-haired terriers are tough and aggressive. But it probably will raise both your eyebrows to discover that newborn infants belonging to different ethnic groups start out life with different sets of responses that seem to relate more to their genes than to their individual personalities.

To learn just how important ethnic differences are in the way we respond, psychologist Daniel G. Freedman studied the responses of newborn Chinese and Caucasian babies. His results show that in many ways Chinese and Caucasian babies behave like two different breeds.

Here are some examples of the differences Dr. Freedman found. The Chinese babies were far more adaptable than the Caucasians. They cried less easily and were easier to console. In addition, they seemed comfortable in almost any position they were placed while the Caucasian infants tossed and turned until they were satisfied. When a cloth was briefly placed against the babies' noses, the Caucasian infants responded with a fight; they immediately turned their faces or swiped at the cloth with their hands. The Chinese babies adapted to the cloth's presence in the simplest possible way—by breathing through their mouths. As Dr. Freedman points out, "It was as if the old stereotypes of the calm, inscrutable Chinese and the excitable, emotionally changeable Caucasian were appearing spontaneously in the first 48 hours of life."

For more details, see Daniel G. Freedman, "Ethnic Differences in Babies," *Human Nature,* January 1979.

No two babies are exactly alike, and no two mature according to the same schedule.

The process of maturation becomes obvious when you think about walking. An infant lacks the physical control walking requires. However, by the end of the first year the nerves connected to the child's muscles have grown. He or she is ready to walk.

By recording the ages at which thousands of infants first began to smile, to sit upright, to crawl, and to try a few steps, psychologists have been able to draw up an approximate timetable for maturation (Figure 8.4). This schedule helps doctors and other professionals to spot problems and abnormalities. If a child has not begun to talk by the age of two and a half, a doctor will recommend tests to determine if something is wrong.

However, one of the facts to emerge from this effort is that the maturational plan inside each child is unique. On the average, babies start walking at twelve to thirteen months. However, some are ready at nine months, and others delay walking until eighteen months. And each baby has his or her own temperament. Some infants are extremely active from birth and some quiet. Some are cuddly and some stiff. Some cry a great deal while others hardly ever whimper. No two babies are exactly alike, and no two mature according to the same timetable.

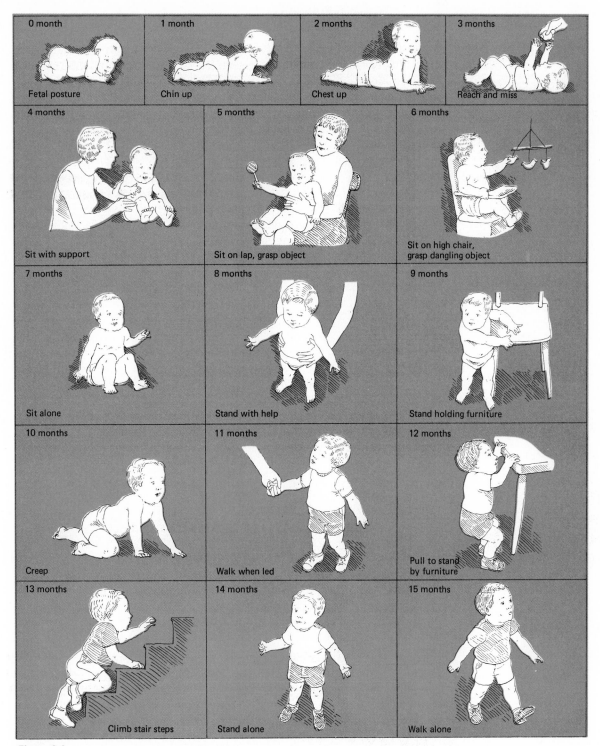

Figure 8.4
The sequence of motor development. The age given for the appearance of each skill is approximate; there is a wide range of individual differences. (Adapted from Shirley, 1933)

Learning

Maturation is only part of the process of growing up. Infants and small children are exceptionally responsive. Each experience changes the child, teaches him something, pushes him in some direction. The child learns to make associations, to expect certain events—such as mother and food—to come together. Children learn to do things that produce rewards and to avoid doing things that produce punishments. They also learn by imitating other people.

Recent experiments indicate that infants too are able to learn new behaviors. Even newborn babies change their behavior in response to the environment—which, as you will recall from Chapter 2, is the basic definition of "learning." One team of psychologists taught two- and three-day-old infants to turn their heads at the sound of a buzzer by rewarding them with a bottle each time they did so.

Another researcher built a small theater for four- to five-week-old babies. The infants were placed in a well-padded seat opposite a blank wall that served as a movie screen, and were given pacifiers. The pacifiers were connected to the projector. As we described earlier, the infants had to suck on the pacifiers to focus the picture. Soon the babies had learned the trick and sucked hard, pausing for only a few seconds to catch their breath. When the researcher reversed the procedure, so that sucking blurred the picture, they quickly learned to lengthen the pause to eight seconds (Pines, 1970). We can assume that infants are just as responsive to everyday events as they are to experiments.

Clearly, then, learning is an important part of the process of growing up. In the pages that follow we will show how inner plans and outside influences—maturation and learning—work together in the development of intellect, language, love, and morality.

INTELLECTUAL DEVELOPMENT

If you have a younger brother or sister, you may remember times when your parents insisted that you let the little one play with you and your friends. No matter how often you explained hide-and-seek to your four-year-old brother, he spoiled the game. Why couldn't he understand that he had to keep quiet or he'd be found right away?

This is a question Swiss psychologist Jean Piaget set out to answer more than fifty years ago. Of the several theories of intellectual development, Piaget's is the most comprehensive and influential. Common sense told him that intelligence, or the ability to understand, develops gradually, as the child grows. The sharpest, most inquisitive four year old simply cannot understand things a seven year old grasps easily. What accounts for the dramatic changes between the ages of four and seven?

Piaget spent years observing, questioning, and playing games with babies and young children—including his own. He concluded that younger children aren't "dumb" in the sense of lacking a given *amount of informa-*

tion. Rather they think in a different *way* than older children and adults; they use a different kind of logic. A seven year old is completely capable of answering the question "Who was born first, you or your mother?" but a four year old isn't (Chukovsky, 1963). Intellectual development involves quantitative changes (growth in the *amount* of information) as well as qualitative changes (differences in the *manner* of thinking).

In time Piaget was able to detail the ways in which a child's thinking changes, month by month, year by year. Although the rate at which different children develop varies, every child passes through the same predictable stages. Each stage builds on the last, increasing the child's ability to solve more complex problems.

How Knowing Changes

Understanding the world involves the construction of *schemes,* or plans for knowing. Each of us is an architect and engineer in this respect, constructing intellectual schemes, applying them, and changing them as necessary. When we put a scheme into action, we are trying to understand something. In this process, we **assimilate**—we try to fit the world into our scheme. We also **accommodate**—we change our scheme to fit the characteristics of the world.

According to Piaget, a baby begins with two schemes, grasping and sucking. In other words, the baby understands things by grasping or sucking them—whether they be breasts, bottles, fingers, rattles, or wooden blocks (Figure 8.5). Consider what happens when a baby grasps a block. He assimilates the block to his grasping scheme. But he cannot do so without also accommodating—fitting his grasp to the particular block.

Assimilation and accommodation work together to produce intellectual

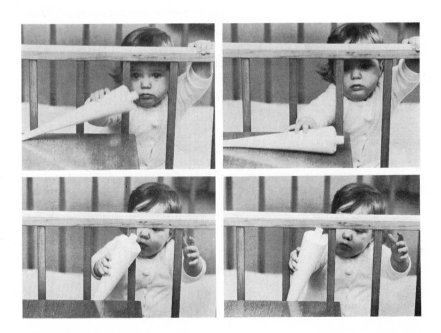

Figure 8.5
(from left to right and top to bottom) This child possesses a scheme for grasping objects and pulling them to her that does not adequately match the features of the environment she is now trying to assimilate. Her scheme will not get the toy through the bars of the playpen. An accommodation—the addition of turning to grasping and pulling—achieves a state of equilibrium.

Figure 8.6
This infant of about six months cannot yet understand that objects have an existence of their own, away from her presence. (a) The infant gazes intently at a toy elephant. (b) When the elephant is blocked from view, she gives no indication that she understands the toy still exists. This thinking pattern changes by age two, as shown in Figure 8.7.

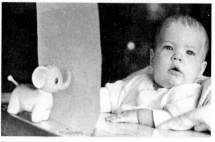

a   b

growth. When events do not fit into existing schemes, new and grander schemes have to be created. The child begins to see and understand things in a new light. Progressive changes in the way a baby conceives objects illustrate this.

Object Permanence.   A baby's understanding of things lies totally in the here and now. The sight of a toy, the way it feels in her hands, the sensation it produces in her mouth are all she knows. She does not imagine it, picture it, think of it, remember it, or even forget it. How do we know this?

When a infant's toy is hidden from her, she acts as if it had ceased to exist (Figure 8.6). She doesn't look for it; she grabs whatever else she can find and plays with that. Or she may simply start crying. At ten to twelve months, however, this pattern begins to change. When you take the baby's toy and hide it under a blanket—while she is watching—she will search for it under the blanket. However, if you change tactics and put her toy behind your back, she will continue to look for it under the blanket—even if she was watching you the whole time.

You can't fool a twelve- to eighteen-month-old baby quite so easily. A child this age watches closely and searches for the toy in the last place she saw you put it. But suppose you take the toy, put it under the blanket, conceal it in your hands, and then put it behind your back. A twelve month old will act surprised when she doesn't find the toy under the blanket—and keep searching there. An eighteen or twenty-four month old will guess what you've done and walk behind you to look (Figure 8.7). She knows the toy must be somewhere (Ginsburg and Opper, 1969: 50–56).

This is a giant step in intellectual development. The child has progressed from a stage where she apparently believed that her own actions created the world, to a stage where she realizes that people and objects are independent of her actions. This new scheme, **object permanence,** might be expressed: "Things continue to exist even though I cannot see or touch them." The child now conceives of a world of which she is only a part.

Representational Thought.   The achievement of object permanence suggests that a child has begun to engage in what Piaget calls **representational thought.** The child's intelligence is no longer one of action only. Now, children can picture (or represent) things in their minds. At fourteen months of age, Piaget's daughter demonstrated this. When she was out visiting another family, she happened to witness a child throwing a temper tantrum. She had never had a tantrum herself, but the next day she did—screaming, shaking her playpen, and stamping her feet as the other child had. She had formed so clear an image of the tantrum in her mind that she was able to create an excellent imitation a day later (Ginsburg and Opper, 1969: 65). To Piaget, this meant that his daughter was using symbols. Soon she would learn to use a much more complex system of symbols—spoken language. Where the infant is limited to solving problems with his or her actions, the older child can mentally represent the problem and use language to think it through. Thinking with actions, in other words, comes before thinking with language.

The Principle of Conservation. More complex intellectual abilities emerge as the infant grows into childhood. Somewhere between the ages of five and seven, most children begin to understand what Piaget calls **conservation,** the principle that a given quality does not change when its appearance is changed. For example, if you have two identical short, wide jars filled with water and you pour the contents of one of these jars into a tall, thin jar, a child under five will say that the tall jar contains more water than the short one. If you pour the water back into the short jar to show the amount has not changed, the child will still maintain that there was more water in the tall container. Children under five do not seem to be able to think about two dimensions (height and width) at the same time. That is,

Figure 8.7
By the age of two, a child realizes that the disappearance of an object does not mean that it no longer exists. In fact, if an object is concealed, a child will search for it because he or she knows it still exists somewhere.

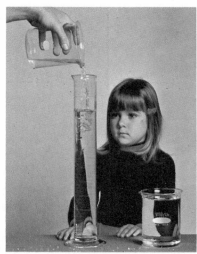

Figure 8.8
The girl taking part in this demonstration thinks there is more water in the tall beaker; she has not yet acquired conservation. Although she has seen the liquid poured from one beaker to another, she bases her decision on the height of the column of water and ignores its diameter.

they do not understand that a change in width is made up for by a change in the height of the tall glass (Figure 8.8).

Within two years, the same child will tell you that the second jar contains the same amount of water as the first. If you ask why, he may say because the short jar is fatter than the tall jar—indicating that he is able to coordinate his perceptions of height and width. Or he may point out that if you poured the water back into the short jar, it would be the same—indicating that he is able to think in reverse, to retrace the steps of the experiment. Younger children generally cannot do this.

Another type of conservation experiment begins when a child is shown two identical balls of clay. Then, the child watches the experimenter flatten one ball and roll it into the shape of a sausage. Again, the young child believes that the amount of clay has changed. The older child conserves. That is, she recognizes that the amount of clay is unaffected by the change in appearance.

Many such cognitive advances take place between the years of five and twelve. This is the stage when children develop a working knowledge of the world. They develop skills in the trial-and-error approach to problem solving. But in general, their thinking is extremely concrete. They need to try solutions out; they cannot work through problems in their heads, and have difficulty thinking about hypothetical situations or abstract concepts.

Some Implications of Intellectual Development

A clear picture of the development of cognitive abilities sheds light on some of the other areas of child behavior. For example, at about ten or twelve months, many children go through a period of **separation anxiety.** They become extremely upset when their mothers take them to a friend's or relative's house and leave without them. A five-month-old baby does not react this way. Why does a one year old?

Perhaps the answer is that the older child is more confused by Mom's

Table 8.1 / Piaget's Stages of Cognitive Development

SENSORIMOTOR STAGE (birth to two years): Thinking is displayed in action, such as the grasping, sucking, and looking schemes. Child gradually learns to discover the location of hidden objects at about eighteen months, when the concept of object permanence is fully understood.

PREOPERATIONAL STAGE (two to six years): Beginning of symbolic representation. Language first appears; child begins to draw pictures that represent things. Child cannot represent a series of actions in his or her head in order to solve problems.

CONCRETE OPERATIONAL STAGE (six to twelve years): Ability to understand conservation problems. Ability to think of several dimensions or features at same time. Child can now do elementary arithmetic problems, such as judging the quantity of liquid containers and checking addition of numbers by subtraction.

FORMAL OPERATIONAL STAGE (twelve years to adulthood): Thinking becomes more abstract and hypothetical. The individual can consider many alternative solutions to a problem, make deductions, contemplate the future, and formulate personal ideals and values.

disappearance. One study consistent with this view found that infants were not particularly upset when their mothers left a room through a familiar exit, like the nursery door. But when Mom left in a surprising way—for example, by stepping into a closet—the baby became upset. Thus, separation anxiety arose when the mother's disappearance led to uncertainty.

Piaget's theory also helps explain why seven and eight year olds are more conscious of sexual identity than younger children are. If you've worked with children, you will know that four- or five-year-old boys object loudly to playing baseball with girls—and vice versa. Why?

Four-year-old children can tell you whether they are boys or girls, and many are fully informed about anatomical differences. Yet if you question children this age, you'll find that they believe people can change their sex by wearing clothes designed for the opposite sex, changing their haircut, playing games associated with the opposite sex, and the like. In other words, if you pour a boy into a female container, he'll change. Only when they understand conservation do they realize that one's sex is permanent. It is at this point that children become concerned about their own sexual identity.

USING PSYCHOLOGY

"Sesame Street"

TV is this nation's number one "baby sitter." Nearly every American household has a television set, and most sets are turned on for forty to fifty hours a week. Youngsters spend more time watching TV than they spend at any other waking

Figure 8.9
(Opposite) The Cookie Monster
from Sesame Street.

activity—for a total of 15,000 hours by the time they graduate from high school, compared to 12,000 hours in the classroom (Lesser, 1974: 19). And children come away from TV with all sorts of information and misinformation—for example, that eating a particular cereal will turn them into star athletes. Since the mid-1960s there have been several attempts to produce television programs that are both educational and so interesting that children will ask to watch them. "Sesame Street" was the first one to succeed on such a large scale, and it has become a model for many others.

The Children's Television Workshop (CTW) set out to create a television program that would teach preschool skills to children between three and six. Harvard psychologist Gerald S. Lesser organized a panel of advisers that included writers and filmmakers as well as educators to establish general goals for the series. The basic idea was to prepare children for school in two ways. The first and most obvious was to lay the foundation for future learning. The second and perhaps more important was to foster confidence by showing children they could learn the kinds of things that impress parents and teachers—and have fun doing so.

The advisers decided that the best way to present information to young children was to use techniques developed for TV commercials: short, fast-paced segments that would not tax a child's attention span; a mix of live characters, puppets, and cartoons; such attention-getting tricks as speeding the film up or running it backward; catchy rhymes and jingles; music to encourage participation; and a healthy dose of slapstick comedy. They also decided to use a good deal of repetition because studies have found that children are not bored by seeing and hearing the same material over and over, and in fact continue to learn from each repetition.

For example, one goal was to teach children to count backward from 10. (Number sequences were not to go beyond 10: psychologists believed this was as much as a three year old could handle.) How did they make this task both memorable and amusing? By showing a rocket countdown over and over, until the sequence became familiar: 10, 9, 8, 7 . . . To prevent boredom and inattention, the producers varied the ending. One time the rocket took off too early; one time it took the rocket launcher with it, his final "onnne" fading off into space; another time the rocket shot down, underground, instead of up. The idea was to encourage children to start counting in anticipation of the surprise.

The next step in putting "Sesame Street" together was to test programs on children from different socioeconomic

backgrounds and from various parts of the country. In each location psychologist Edward Palmer created an informal setting, and by using a slide projector that changed pictures every eight seconds, he simulated the distractions a child would be likely to encounter at home. A researcher watched each child constantly, recording when the child was watching TV and when he or she looked away. In addition, the children were asked questions about the material being presented before and after the pilot show and again a month later.

As a result of these pretests, a number of segments were revised and some dropped altogether. The researchers discovered that children learn best when a show elicits either physical activity or mental activity, such as having to guess answers or speculate on characters' motives (Lesser, 1974: 161). The writers and producers began to depend on the observations and suggestions of Palmer and his associates.

Evaluation did not stop when "Sesame Street" went on the air in November 1969. Researchers from the Educational Testing Service were hired to test and retest a cross section of 1,300 children. The results were very encouraging. Three year olds who became "Sesame Street" regulars scored higher than "nonregular" five year olds, suggesting that small children can learn skills educators have traditionally held back until kindergarten or first grade (Bogatz and Ball, 1971). Other investigators found that both "Sesame Street" and a related show, "Mr. Rogers' Neighborhood," tend to make children more outgoing (Coates, Pusser, and Goodman, 1976). And white children who saw nonwhites on these shows began to seek out nonwhite playmates in their nursery schools (Gorn, Goldberg, and Kanungo, 1976).

Overall, researchers have found that children whose parents encourage them to watch "Sesame Street" show impressive gains. But the effects for children who watch "Sesame Street" with no feedback or reward from their parents are not as clear (Cook and Conner, 1976). Researchers are now trying to discover just how parental encouragement affects learning in this situation. Meanwhile, the research and planning devoted to "Sesame Street" paid off in numbers as well. By the end of the first season, no fewer than six million preschoolers had switched from commercial programs to education-made-fun. In all of the shows the CTW has created, testing has become an integral part of production. In Edward Palmer's words, these shows are "an endless experiment—a laboratory on public display."

MENTAL RETARDATION

The term "mentally retarded" is applied to people who have since childhood been less able to learn and understand things than most people of the same age. Retarded children have difficulty learning to tie their shoes, find it impossible to keep up in school, and cannot join in the games that other children their age enjoy.

Mental retardation is an intellectual disability rather than an emotional one. But it is possible for retarded people to find the world so unpleasant that they withdraw from it in a neurotic or psychotic manner. Retarded people are often made worse by the way other people treat them. Most retarded people are capable of living relatively normal lives if given the chance. They must, however, be given special attention, affection, and understanding if they are to reach their full potential as human beings.

Unfortunately, retardates are often treated as if they were unseeing, unhearing, uncomprehending "objects." The presence of a retarded child in a household may cause a great deal of friction and resentment among members of the family. This situation does not go unnoticed by the retarded child. Despite his intellectual handicaps, the child is a sensitive human being who understands the meaning of anger and resentment as well as of love and acceptance. Conflict and rejection can rob the child of the supportive environment necessary for his maximum development.

Only about one-fourth of the six million people who are called retarded in the United States actually have something physically wrong with their brains. Their retardation is due to diseases contracted before birth or during early infancy, to brain injuries, to poor nutrition in childhood, or to some other physical factor.

The majority of people who are called retarded are people who seem never to have learned to use their minds. They may have been brought up in lonely, dull, or frightening environments in which there was no opportunity or reward for thinking. This situation occurs most often with children born into poor or unstable families and reared in slums or orphanages. If such children are given the opportunity and the encouragement to use their minds early enough, they are often able to live normal lives.

THE DEVELOPMENT OF LANGUAGE

Language and thought are closely intertwined. Both abilities involve using symbols, as we saw in Chapter 3. We are able to think and talk about objects that are not present and about ideas that are not necessarily true. A child begins to think, to represent things to himself, before he is able to speak. But the acquisition of language propels the child into further intellectual development (see Piaget, 1926). We have been able to learn a good deal about the acquisition of language from our nearest relative in the animal kingdom, the chimpanzee.

Figure 8.10
Washoe at about five years of age.
She is shown here using the
American Sign Language sign for
"hat."

Figure 8.10
Washoe at about five years of age. She is shown here using the American Sign Language sign for "hat."

Can Animals Use Language?

Psychologists believe that chimpanzees must develop at least as far as two-year-old humans because, like two year olds, they will look for a toy or a bit of food that has disappeared. They can represent the existence of that toy or bit of food in their minds. Can they be taught to "talk" about it?

Many psychologists have tried to teach chimpanzees to use language, but only recently have such efforts been successful. One husband-and-wife team, the Gardners, raised a baby chimp named Washoe in their home and taught her to use the American Sign Language for deaf people (Figure 8.10). At three-and-one-half years of age, Washoe knew eighty-seven signs for words like "food," "dog," "toothbrush," "gimmee," "sweet," "more," and "hurry."

Making these signs at the appropriate times would not be enough to be called language, though. A dog or a parrot might make signs that its owner could interpret as demands for a walk or for food. Washoe's remarkable achievement was that some of her signs had abstract meanings and that she could put signs together in new ways to produce new meanings. For example, she learned the sign for "more" (putting her fingertips together over her head) because she loved to be tickled and wanted more. But she was not simply doing something like a dog does when it rolls over to be tickled; she was able to use the same sign later in entirely new circumstances—asking for more food or more hair brushing.

Since the original experiments with Washoe, several chimpanzees have been taught to "talk" in other ways. Lana the chimpanzee was trained on a special typewriter connected to a computer. The machine has fifty keys, each marked with a different symbol which stands for a word in Yerkish, a special monkey language devised just for this study. When Lana presses a key, the symbol appears on the screen in front of her. Lana has learned to type out sentences and thus converse with the experimenters. Sometimes, she types a word out of order, reads the sentence on the screen, and erases it (by pressing the erase key) before she has been corrected. In other cases, Lana has made up phrases to describe objects she's never seen before. For example, the first time Lana saw a ring, she identified it as a "finger bracelet."

The ability to arrange symbols in new combinations to produce new meanings is especially well developed in the human brain. The rules for such organization of symbols are called *grammar*. Grammatical rules are what make the sentence "the rhinoceros roared at the boy" mean the same thing as "the boy was roared at by the rhinoceros." On the surface, these sentences appear different because the word position is changed. But on a deeper level, we know that the first is an active sentence and the second a passive transformation of it. It may be in our ability to use such grammatical rules that we surpass the simpler language of the chimpanzee.

How Children Acquire Language

The example of Washoe shows that there are several steps in learning language. First, one must learn to make the signs; then, one must give them meaning; and finally, one must learn grammar. Each child takes these steps at his or her own rate. During the first year of life, the "average child" makes many sounds. Crying lessens, and the child starts making mostly cooing sounds, which develop into a babble that includes every sound humans can make—Chinese vowels, African clicks, German rolled *r*'s, and English *o*'s.

Late in the first year, the strings of babbles begin to sound more like the language that the child hears. Children imitate the speech of their parents and their older brothers and sisters, and are greeted with approval whenever they say something that sounds like a word. In this way children learn to speak their own language, even though they could just as easily learn any other.

The leap to using sounds as symbols occurs some time in the second year. The first attempts at saying words are primitive, and the sounds are

Figure 8.11
A two-year-old's telegraphic speech: the two-word phrases leave out words but still get the message across.

incomplete: "Ball" usually sounds like "ba," and "cookie" may even sound like "doo-da." The first real words usually refer to things the infant can see or touch. Often they are labels or commands ("dog!" "cookie!").

By the time children are two years old, they have a vocabulary of at least fifty words. Toward the end of the second year, children begin to express themselves more clearly by joining words into two-word phrases (Figure 8.11).

But at age two, a child's grammar is still unlike that of an adult. Children use what psychologists call **telegraphic speech**—for example, "Where my apple?" "Daddy fall down." They leave out words but still get the message across. As psychologists have discovered, two year olds already understand certain rules (Brown, 1973). They keep their words in the same order adults do. Indeed, at one point they overdo this, applying grammatical rules too consistently. For example, the usual rule for forming the past tense of English verbs is to add "ed." But many verbs are irregular: "go"/ "went," "come"/"came," "swim"/"swam," "fall"/"fell." At first children learn the correct form of the verb: "Daddy went yesterday." But once children discover the rule for forming past tenses, they replace the correct form with sentences like "Daddy *goed* yesterday." Although they have never heard adults use this word, they construct it in accordance with the rules of grammar that they have extracted from the speech they hear.

By the age of four or five children have mastered the basics of the language. Their ability to use words will continue to grow with their ability to think about and understand things.

EMOTIONAL DEVELOPMENT

While the child is developing his ability to use his body, to think and to express himself, he is also developing emotionally. He begins to become attached to specific people and to care about what they think and feel. In most cases, the child's first relationship is with his mother.

Experiments with Animals

The early attachment of a child to his mother and the far-reaching effects of this attachment provide a good example of the way in which maturation and learning work together in development. Experiments with baby birds and monkeys have shown that there is a maturationally determined time of readiness for attachment early in life. If the infant is too young or too old, the attachment cannot be formed. But the attachment itself is a kind of learning. If the attachment is not made, or if an unusual attachment is made, the infant will develop in an unusual way as a result.

Imprinting.   Konrad Lorenz, a student of animal behavior, was a pioneer in this field. Lorenz discovered that infant geese become attached to their mothers in a sudden, virtually permanent learning process called **imprint-ing.** A few hours after they struggle out of their shells, goslings are ready to

Figure 8.12
Konrad Lorenz and the baby geese imprinted on him instead of a mother goose.

start waddling after the first thing they see. Whatever it is, they stay with it and treat it as though it were their mother from that time on. Usually, of course, the first thing they see is the mother goose, but Lorenz found that if he substituted himself or some moving object like a green box being dragged along the ground, the goslings would follow that (Figure 8.12). Goslings are especially sensitive just after birth, and whatever they learn during this **critical period** makes a deep impression that resists change. From this early experience with their mother—or mother substitute—the goslings form their idea of what a goose is. If they have been imprinted with a human being instead of a goose, they will prefer the company of human beings to other geese and may even try to mate with humans later in life.

Surrogate Mothers. Lorenz's experiments showed how experience with a mother—whether real or a substitute—can determine an infant bird's entire view of itself and others. An American psychologist, Harry Harlow, went on to study the relationship between mother and child in a species closer to humans, the rhesus monkey. His first question was: What makes the mother so important? He tried to answer this question by taking baby monkeys away from their natural mothers as soon as they were born, as described in Chapter 6. To review: Harlow raised the monkeys with two surrogate, or substitute, mothers. Each monkey could choose between a mother constructed of wood and wire and a mother constructed in the same way but covered with soft, cuddly terry cloth. In some cages, the cloth mother was equipped with a bottle; in others, the wire mother was.

The results were dramatic. The young monkeys became strongly attached to the cloth mother, whether she gave food or not, and for the most part ignored the wire mother (Figure 8.13). If a frightening object was placed in the monkey's cage, the baby monkey would run to the terry-cloth mother for security, not to the wire mother. It was the touching that mattered, not the feeding.

Effects Later in Life. In another set of experiments, Harlow discovered that monkeys raised without real mothers grew up with serious emotional problems. As adults they did not seem to know how to play or defend themselves or even mate, although they tried. In fact, when frightened by a strange human they often attacked their own bodies instead of making threatening signs of aggression as normal monkeys do.

The monkeys who had cloth mothers with bottles grew up more normally than the others, but even they were not well adjusted to normal monkey life. A partially adequate substitute for a mother turned out to be peers—other baby monkeys. Infant monkeys who played with other monkeys like themselves grew up fairly normally even if they never saw their mothers. To grow up completely normally, however, both mother *and* peers were necessary (Figure 8.14). Why were real mothers and other infant monkeys so essential?

One possible answer is that no matter how much contact comfort the cloth mother could provide, "she" could not encourage independence. A normal mother, brother, or sister often becomes annoyed at an infant's

Figure 8.13
An infant rhesus monkey in one of Harry Harlow's experiments.

Figure 8.14
One of Harry Harlow's series of experiments with monkeys showed the importance of early peer contact for normal development.

clinging as he gets older, forcing him to stand on his own two feet. The cloth mother, however, is always available. The encouragement of independence is only one factor. Interactions with mother and peers also allow the baby to see and learn from the behavior of other monkeys. The silent surrogate provided no such opportunities.

Human Babies

Can these findings be applied to human babies? Is there a critical period when infants need to become attached to a mothering person, as Lorenz's experiments suggest? Do children who are temporarily or permanently separated from their mothers or raised in institutions without benefit of a single mothering person develop abnormally, as Harlow's monkeys did?

Some psychologists would answer these questions with a firm "yes." Babies begin to form an attachment to their mothers (or to a surrogate mother) at about six months, when they are able to distinguish one person from another and are beginning to develop object permanence. This attachment seems to be especially strong between the ages of six months and three years. By three years, the child has developed to the stage where he is able to remember and imagine his mother and maintain a relationship with her (in fantasy) even if she is absent.

According to one psychologist, children who are separated from their mothers during this period may never be able to form attachments to other people. Suppose a child is hospitalized for an extended period. At first she will show signs of intense distress, crying and fussing as if she were trying to bring her mother back. When this fails, she will lapse into a state of apathy, which may last for several days. If the separation continues, she will begin to respond to attention and to act cheerfully, but her relations with others take on a superficial quality. She does not become attached to any one person (Bowlby, 1960–1961).

Some psychologists believe that institutionalization causes intellectual as well as psychological damage. Their studies indicate that children who are deprived of a stable mothering person at an early age are retarded in their ability to use words and solve problems. Restless and unable to concentrate, they do poorly in school. Their aggressiveness makes them unpopular with their schoolmates (Spitz and Wolff, 1946).

However, new research suggests that inadequate care and lack of learning opportunities, not mother deprivation, cause these problems. Orphanages and other institutions vary considerably in the care they give children, and so do the children who enter them. One team of psychologists found that although infants in an orphanage were slow to develop, they caught up with children raised at home by the age of four or five. Other researchers were unable to detect any difference in intelligence or emotional development between institutionalized and noninstitutionalized children. Indeed, a few psychologists believe that children raised in well-run orphanages are friendlier, more inquisitive, and in general develop faster than children raised in the average home. It depends on the child and the institution (see Thompson and Grusec, 1970: 606–607).

Imaginary Playmates

There's nothing new about polka dot elves, pink teddy bears, and other imaginary playmates; children have had them since childhood began. But there's a lot new in our understanding of the role these invisible, mysterious friends play in the normal development of children.

When Dr. Jerome L. Singer and Dr. Dorothy G. Singer studied a group of three- and four-year-olds, they found a number of striking differences between children with imaginary playmates and those without. Here are some of their results:

- Imaginary playmates are more common than you might think; more than half the children had them.
- Children with imaginary playmates are less aggressive and more cooperative than other children.
- They are rarely bored and have a rich vocabulary, far advanced for their age.
- They watch fewer hours of television than other children, and the programs they watch have fewer cartoons and violence.
- They have a greater ability to concentrate than other children.

Above all, imaginary playmates are true companions to children. They are always there to listen and talk, to be supportive and forever loyal. They seem to fill a gap in children's lives and are especially important to children who are first-born or who have no brothers or sisters. They are an adaptive mechanism that helps children get through the boring times of life.

Instead of worrying that imaginary playmates are a sign of insecurity and withdrawal, we should all look in wonderment at how creative and adaptive a healthy child can be.

For more details, see Maya Pines, "Invisible Playmates," *Psychology Today*, September 1978.

The debate over this issue is likely to continue for some time. What we do know is that up to six or seven months, most infants are indiscriminate. They respond to strangers as readily as they respond to their mothers and other familiar people; they will coo or whine at just about anyone. At six months, however, they begin to develop a strong attachment to their mother (or whoever is caring for them). In fact, at about eight months many babies rather suddenly develop an intense fear of strangers—crying, hiding against their mothers, and showing other signs of distress when someone they do not know or remember approaches them. Separation anxiety, which appears at ten to twelve months, is further proof of attachment. Children do not remain exclusive for long, however. By eighteen months nearly all babies have developed attachments to their father, siblings, grandparents, or other people who play an active role in their lives (Maccoby and Masters, 1970).

An infant begins to develop a strong attachment to its mother by the age of six months.

Figure 8.15
A year-old infant clings to his mother: at this age, attachment to the mother is strong and exclusive.

SOCIALIZATION

Learning the rules of behavior of the culture in which you are born and grow up is called **socialization.** To live with other people, a child has to learn what is considered acceptable and unacceptable behavior. This is not as easy as it sounds. Some social rules are clear and inflexible. For example, you are not permitted to have sexual relations with members of your immediate family.

But most social rules leave room for individual decisions, so that the "gray area" between right and wrong is vast. Some rules change from situation to situation. Some apply to certain categories of people but not others. For example, the rules for boys in our society are different from the rules for girls. We tend to encourage boys to express aggression but not fear; traditionally, girls have been raised to express emotions but not ambitions. Of course the rules for feminine behavior change over the years. We do not expect adolescent girls to act like little girls, or middle-aged women to act like adolescents. To complicate matters, we require different behavior from single and married women, housewives and career women, female executives and female secretaries.

Learning what the rules are, when to apply and when to bend them, is only part of socialization. Every society has ideas about what is meaningful, valuable, beautiful, and worth striving for. Every society classifies people according to their family, sex, age, skills, personality characteristics, and other criteria. Every culture has notions about what makes individuals behave as they do. In absorbing these notions, a child acquires an identity as a member of a particular society, a member of different social categories (such as male or female), a member of a family—and an identity as an individual. This is a second dimension of socialization.

Finally, socialization involves learning to live with other people and with yourself. Anyone who has seen the shock on a two year old's face when another child his age takes a toy he wants, or the frustration and humiliation a four year old experiences when she discovers she can't hit a baseball on the first try, knows how painful it can be to discover that other people have rights and that you have limitations.

In the pages that follow we examine several theories about how the child becomes socialized. We begin with Freud's theory of psychosexual development, which has been a major influence on our understanding of socialization.

Figure 8.16
Learning social rules: table manners are but one of many rules of behavior children must learn in order to function as members of a particular society.

Freud's Theory of Psychosexual Development

Freud believed that all children are born with powerful sexual and aggressive urges that must be tamed. In learning to control these impulses, children acquire a sense of right and wrong. They become "civilized." The process—and the results—are different for boys and girls.

In the first few years of life boys and girls have similar experiences. Their erotic pleasures are obtained through the mouth, sucking at their mother's breast. Weaning is a period of frustration and conflict—it is the child's first experience with not getting what he wants. Freud called this the **oral stage** of development. Later the anus becomes the source of erotic pleasure, giving rise to what Freud called the **anal stage.** The child enjoys holding in or pushing out his feces until he is required, through toilet training, to curb this freedom.

The major conflict comes between the ages of three and five, when children discover the pleasure they can obtain from their genitals. As a consequence, they become extremely aware of the differences between themselves and members of the opposite sex. In this **phallic stage,** according to Freud, the child becomes a rival for the affections of the parent of the opposite sex. The boy wants to win his mother for himself and finds himself in hostile conflict with his father. The girl wants her father for herself and tries to shut out her mother. These struggles take place on an unconscious level; generally the child and the parents do not have any clear awareness that it is going on.

Freud called this crisis the **Oedipal conflict,** after Oedipus, the king in Greek tragedy who unknowingly killed his father and married his mother. Freud believed that the boy's feelings for his mother create intense conflicts. The boy finds that he hates his father and wishes him gone or dead. But his father is far stronger than he is. The boy fears that his father will see how he feels and punish him, perhaps by castrating him. (A parent telling the child that masturbation is nasty, or perhaps that it will make him sick, merely confirms his fears.) To prevent this horrible punishment, the boy buries his sexual feelings and tries to make himself "good." He tries to become as much like his father as possible so that his father will not want to hurt him. He satisfies himself with becoming *like* the person who possesses mother, instead of trying to possess her himself. In this process, which is called **identification** with the aggressor, the boy takes on all his father's values and moral principles. Thus, at the same time that he learns to behave like a man, he **internalizes** his father's morality. His father's voice becomes a voice inside him, the voice of conscience.

Freud believed that in girls the Oedipal conflict takes a different form. The girl finds herself in the similarly dangerous position of wanting to possess her father and to exclude her mother. To escape punishment and to possess the father vicariously, she begins to identify with her mother. She feels her mother's triumphs and failures as if they were her own, and she internalizes her mother's moral code. At the same time, the girl experiences what Freud called penis envy. Whereas the boy is afraid of being castrated, the girl suspects that her mother has removed the penis she once

Figure 8.17
Learning roles: identifying with the same-sex parent.

had. To make up for this "deficiency," she sets her sights on marrying a man who is like her father and develops the wish to have babies.

Freud believed that at about age five children enter a **latency stage.** Sexual desires are pushed into the background, and children busy themselves with exploring the world and learning new skills. This process of redirecting sexual impulses into learning tasks is called **sublimation.** Although children this age often avoid members of the opposite sex, sexual interest reappears in adolescence. The way in which a person resolves the Oedipal conflict in childhood influences the kind of relationships he or she will form with members of the opposite sex throughout life. Ideally, when one reaches the **genital stage,** one derives as much satisfaction from giving pleasure as from receiving it.

Today relatively few psychologists believe that sexual feelings disappear in childhood, that all young girls experience penis envy, or that all young boys fear castration. Freud was attempting to set off a revolution in our thinking about childhood. Like many revolutionaries, he probably overstated the case. Yet the idea that children have to learn to control powerful sexual and aggressive desires, and the belief that such early childhood experiences can have a long-term effect on adult personality and behavior, would be difficult to deny. (We shall return to Freud in the chapter on personality theories.)

Erikson's Theory of Psychosocial Development

To Erik Erikson, socialization is neither so sudden nor so emotionally violent. Erikson takes a broader view of human development than Freud in

Table 8.2 / Erikson's Stages of Psychosocial Development

Approximate Age	Crisis
0–1	TRUST VS. MISTRUST: If an infant is well cared for, she will develop faith in the future. But if she experiences too much uncertainty about being taken care of, she will come to look at the world with fear and suspicion.
1–2	AUTONOMY VS. DOUBT: Here the child learns self-control and self-assertion. But if he receives too much criticism, he will be ashamed of himself and have doubts about his independence.
2–5	INITIATIVE VS. GUILT: When the child begins to make her own decisions, constant discouragement or punishment could lead to guilt and a loss of initiative.
5–Puberty	INDUSTRY VS. INFERIORITY: The child masters skills and takes pride in his competence. Too much criticism of his work at this stage can lead to long-term feelings of inferiority.
Adolescence	IDENTITY VS. ROLE CONFUSION: The teen-ager tries to develop her own separate identity while "fitting in" with her friends. Failure leads to confusion over who she is.
Early Adulthood	INTIMACY VS. ISOLATION: A person secure in his own identity can proceed to an intimate partnership in which he makes compromises for another. The isolated person may have many affairs or even a long-term relationship, but always avoids true closeness.
Middle Age	GENERATIVITY VS. STAGNATION: A person who becomes stagnated is absorbed in herself and tries to hang onto the past. Generativity involves a productive life which will serve as an example to the next generation.
Later Adulthood	INTEGRITY VS. DESPAIR: Some people look back over life with a sense of satisfaction, and accept both the bad and the good. Others face death with nothing but regrets.

terms of both time and scope. Although he recognizes the child's sexual and aggressive urges, he believes that the need for social approval is just as important (hence his term, psychosocial development). And although he believes that childhood experiences have a lasting impact on the individual, he sees development as a lifelong process.

We all face many "crises" as we grow from infancy to old age, as we mature and people expect more from us. Each of these crises represents an issue that everyone faces. The child—or adolescent or adult—may develop more strongly in one way or another, depending on how other people respond to his or her efforts.

For example, the two year old is delighted with his new-found ability to walk, to get into things, to use words, and to ask questions. The very fact that he has acquired these abilities adds to his self-esteem. He's eager to use them. If the adults around him applaud his efforts and acknowledge his achievements, he begins to develop a sense of autonomy, or independence. However, if they ignore him except to punish him for going too far or being a nuisance, the child may begin to doubt the value of his achievements. He may also feel shame because the people around him act as if his new desire for independence is bad.

This is the second of eight stages in Erikson's theory. Each stage builds on the last. A child who has learned to trust the world is better equipped to seek autonomy than one who is mistrustful; a child who has achieved autonomy takes initiative more readily than one who doubts himself; and so on. The basic question in each stage is whether the individual will find ways to direct his needs, desires, and talents into socially acceptable channels and learn to think well of himself.

Erikson's eight crises are outlined in Table 8.2. We will refer back to this theory as we continue our discussion of the life cycle in the next chapter.

Learning Theories of Development

Both Freud and Erikson stress the emotional dynamics of social development. Their theories suggest that learning social rules is altogether different from learning to ride a bicycle or to speak a foreign language. Many psychologists disagree. They believe children learn the ways of their social world because they are rewarded for conforming and because they copy older children and adults in anticipation of future rewards. In other words, social development is simply a matter of conditioning and imitation.

Conditioning. Adults—especially parents and teachers—have the power to reward and punish. Consciously and unconsciously they use praise, smiles, and hugs to reward a child for behaving in ways they consider good and for expressing attitudes that support their own. They tend to ignore or to be hostile toward the expression of opinions that are contrary to their own and toward behavior of which they disapprove.

Sex-role training provides obvious examples of this. At home and in school, boys are encouraged to engage in athletics and to be assertive. Girls are discouraged from doing these things, but are rewarded for being helpful and nice, looking neat, and acting cute. Even the rewards children receive are usually sex-typed. How many girls receive footballs or tool kits as presents? How many boys get dolls or watercolor sets?

These are some of the ways in which adults use conditioning to shape a child's development. Children gradually learn to behave in the way that leads to the greatest satisfaction, even when no one is watching. To avoid punishment and gain rewards from those around them, they learn to reward and punish themselves. A child may criticize herself for making a mistake that has led to punishment in the past. The mistake may be a moral one—lying, for example. A boy may learn to be hard on himself for showing sensitivity, because in the past his tears and blushes were met with humiliating laughter.

This is not to say that children always do as they are told. Adults also teach youngsters how to get away with misbehavior—for example, by apologizing or by giving a present to someone they have wronged. In this way, some children learn that they may receive praise instead of punishment for bad conduct.

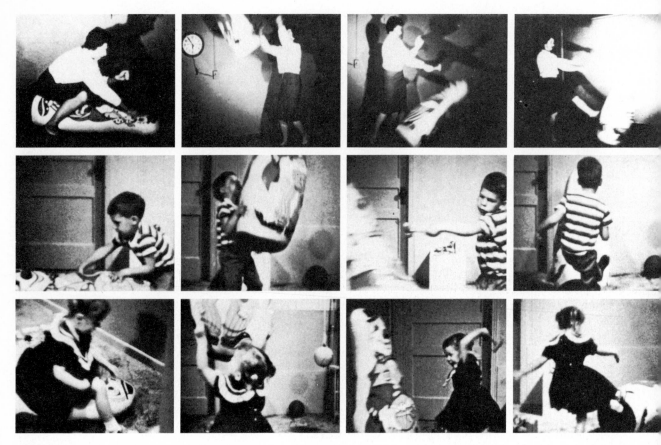

Figure 8.18
Imitation of aggression in children. (top row) Frames from one of the films psychologist Albert Bandura showed to children. (bottom two rows) Behavior of children who watched the film and were given a chance to play with similar objects.

Imitation.   A second way in which children learn social rules is by observing other people. When youngsters see another child or an adult being congratulated for behaving in certain ways or expressing certain attitudes, they are likely to imitate that person in the hope of obtaining rewards themselves.

Albert Bandura's experiments indicate that children are very quick indeed to imitate other people's behavior (Bandura and Walters, 1963). Bandura's basic technique is to show children movies of a person reacting to a situation. He then puts the children in the same situation to see how they behave.

In one experiment Bandura showed a film of a frustrated adult taking out her anger on a "Bobo" doll (Figure 8.18). The woman assaulted the doll—yelling, kicking, and punching it with all her might. After the film, children who had been deliberately frustrated with broken promises and delays were led to a room that contained an identical doll. Taking their cue from the film, they launched furious attacks—imitating the actress's behavior down to the last kick.

Later Bandura added two different endings to the film. In one the actress was praised and given candy and soft drinks after she had attacked the doll. In the other she was severely scolded for her behavior. Most of the children who saw the second version learned from the actress's experience and did not attack the doll so they would not be punished. What this suggests is that conditioning and modeling work together. Children do not imitate everything they see, only the behavior that seems to bring rewards.

The Cognitive-Developmental Approach

Theorists who emphasize the role of cognition or thinking in development view the growing child quite differently. Learning theory implies that the child is essentially passive—a piece of clay to be shaped. The people who administer rewards and punishments and serve as models do the shaping. Cognitive theorists see the *child* as the shaper. Taking their cue from Piaget, they argue that social development is the result of the child's acting on the environment and trying to make sense out of his experiences. The games children play illustrate this.

Play. Children's games are serious business. When left to their own devices, youngsters spend a great deal of time making up rules. This enables them to learn for themselves the importance of agreeing on a structure for group activities. A child can relax and enjoy himself without fear of rejection as long as he does not break the rules. The world of play thus becomes a miniature society, with its own rules and codes.

Another function of most games is to teach children about aspects of adult life in a nonthreatening way. In young children's games, it is the experience of playing, not winning, that counts. Children can learn the

Figure 8.19
Children's games are not just fun: seeing the need for and making rules, trying on adult roles, and learning the dimensions of competition are all part of the developmental process.

dimensions of competition of various kinds, including testing themselves against their outer limits, but they will not be hurt by comparison as they may be in win-or-lose situations.

Much of children's play involves **role taking.** Youngsters try on such adult roles as mother, father, teacher, storekeeper, explorer, and rock star. Role taking allows them to learn about different points of view firsthand. Suppose a child plays a mother opposite another child who plays a whiny, disobedient baby. When she finds herself totally frustrated by the other child's nagging she begins to understand why her mother gets mad. You can't cook even a pretend meal when the baby keeps knocking over the pots and pans.

Moral Development.   Lawrence Kohlberg's studies show just how important being able to see other people's points of view is to social development in general and to moral development in particular. Kohlberg (1968) studied the development of moral reasoning—deciding what is right and what is wrong—by presenting children of different ages with a series of moral dilemmas. For example:

> In Europe, a woman was near death from cancer. One drug might save her, a form of radium that a druggist in the same town had recently discovered. The druggist was charging $2,000, ten times what the drug cost him to make. The sick woman's husband, Heinz, went to everyone he knew to borrow the money, but he could only get together about half of what it cost. He told the druggist that his wife was dying and asked him to sell it cheaper or let him pay later. But the druggist said "No." The husband got desperate and broke into the man's store to steal the drug for his wife. Should the husband have done that? Why?

At every age, some children said that the man should steal, some that he should not. What interested Kohlberg, however, was how the children arrived at a conclusion. He wanted to know what sort of reasoning they used. After questioning about a hundred children, Kohlberg identified six stages of moral development. He then replicated his findings in several different cultures.

In stage one, children are totally egocentric. They do not consider other people's points of view and have no sense of right and wrong. Their main concern is avoiding punishment. A child in this stage will say that the man should steal because people will blame him for his wife's death if he does not, or that he should not steal because he might get caught and go to prison.

Children in stage two have a better idea of how to "work the system" to receive rewards as well as to avoid punishment. Kohlberg calls this the "marketplace orientation." Youngsters at this level interpret the Golden Rule as "help someone if he helps you, and hurt him if he hurts you." They are still egocentric and premoral, evaluating acts in terms of the consequences, not in terms of right and wrong.

In stage three, children become acutely sensitive to what other people want and think. A child in this stage will say that the man in the story should steal because people will think he is cruel if he lets his wife die, or that he should not steal because people will think he is a criminal. In other words, children want social approval in stage three, so they apply the rules other people have decreed literally and rigidly.

In stage four, a child is less concerned with the approval of others. The key issue here is "law and order"—a law is seen as a moral rule and is obeyed because of a strong belief in established authority. Many people remain at the fourth stage of moral development for their whole lives. Moral thinking here, as at stage three, is quite rigid.

In the remaining two stages, people begin to broaden their perspective. The stage-five person is primarily concerned with whether a law is fair or just. He believes that laws must change as the world changes, and they are never absolute. The important question is whether a given law is good for society as a whole. Stage six involves an acceptance of ethical principles that apply to everyone, like the Golden Rule: "Do unto others as you would have them do unto you." Such moral "laws" cannot be broken; they are more important than any written law.

To reach the highest levels of moral development, a child must first be able to see other people's points of view. But this understanding is no guarantee that a person will respect the rights of others. Thus, cognitive abilities influence moral development, but there is far more to morality than simple understanding.

USING PSYCHOLOGY

Implications for Child Rearing

All the theories we have discussed are best treated as different perspectives on the same process. The most complete picture of child development would contain all these points of view, and all have practical implications for child rearing.

First, each child is *unique*. Some babies are active and responsive; some fussy; some passive and withdrawn. Some quickly develop regular schedules for eating and sleeping; some are erratic and resist schedules. Individual differences become more apparent as the months and years go by. Each baby, each growing child, requires a different style of parenting. Each of the theories we presented stresses this view. Psychoanalysts trace the unique way each child experiences various conflicts. Cognitive developmentalists recognize that while each child goes through the stages in the same order, children move at different paces, and teaching should respect the child's current developmental stage. Behaviorists believe that good instruction is individualized.

Second, from Piaget's theory we learn how important it is that the child is *trying to understand the world for himself*. A child who is given the freedom to figure out certain things on his own will begin to structure the world according to his individual needs. Many parents do not realize how important it is that the child develop skills on his own. A mother who tells her young child to color the sky blue instead of orange may not realize that she is inhibiting the child's natural tendency to experiment. Or a mother who finds it more convenient to tie her five year old's shoelaces, instead of teaching him to do it himself, may not realize that she is depriving her child of satisfaction and a sense of accomplishment.

Third, behaviorists teach us the value of having *rules for reward and punishment that are appropriate, clear, and consistent.* A child who grows up with no boundaries has no framework within which to operate. He does not know what is possible and what is not possible. He may also feel that his parents do not really care about him, because they do not seem sufficiently interested to direct his behavior.

Rules must not require more of a child than he is capable of giving. If a two year old is punished for spilling her milk, she will begin to feel responsible for things she cannot control. If parents punish the unintentionally clumsy behaviors of a two year old, the child may eventually come to view herself as worthless—everything she does is bad.

Consistent rules are important because they allow the child to generalize from one situation to the next. If he is punished for hitting his younger brother one day but not punished the next, he cannot know whether the behavior is permissible. He may experience the punishment as cruelty rather than as a consequence of hitting the smaller child. One way to establish consistency is to keep charts and records of misbehavior and the consequences. What times of day do the children fight? Are they quarreling because they have nothing better to do, or to get a parent's attention? How do older members of the family react to their misbehavior? Keeping records enables a parent to see patterns in the children's behavior, gain insight into the children's motives, and to see the effects of his or her reaction. A chart recording good behavior—for example, with the stars teachers often use—will give a child concrete evidence of his progress.

Parents and older brothers and sisters should remember that small children use them as *models.* A child learns to behave as he observes others behaving, whether they want him to or not.

SUMMARY

1. Developmental psychology is the study of the changes that occur as people mature.

2. At birth an infant is capable of certain coordinated movement patterns that can be triggered by the right stimulus. One of these, the grasping reflex, is a response to a touch on the palm. Another, the rooting reflex, involves the movement of the infant's head toward the source of any touch near his or her mouth.

3. As a result of maturation (internally programmed growth) and learning, infants are able to walk, talk, and feed themselves in about two years' time. Learning and maturation work together in the development of intellect, language, love, and morality.

4. Swiss psychologist Jean Piaget has formulated a comprehensive theory of intellectual development. Intellectual growth involves changes in the amount of information we have as well as in the way we think.

5. The child's grasp of object permanence at about eighteen months marks a giant step in his or her intellectual development. Understanding that objects still exist when out of sight means the child can now engage in representational thinking. He or she can picture an object in his or her mind without seeing or touching the object.

6. The best methods psychologists have devised to teach young children through television combine the use of short, fast-paced segments—with music, comedy, and attention-getting film tricks. Pretesting is used to calculate the effectiveness of the presentation of certain programs. Psychologists observe children from different socioeconomic backgrounds as they watch selected shows to see how often and when they are distracted. Afterward, appropriate revisions in the program's style or content can be made.

7. Mental retardation is an intellectual disability rather than an emotional one. It means that the person afflicted is less able to learn and understand things than most people of the same age.

8. In order to acquire language children spend the first year of life practicing sounds, then imitating the speech they hear around them. In the second year they use sounds as symbols, and their first real words usually refer to something they can see or touch. By four or five years of age, children have usually mastered the basics of their native language.

9. While children learn to use their body, to think, and to express themselves, they also develop emotionally. They begin to form attachments to people; their first relationship is usually with their mother. By eighteen months nearly all babies have developed attachments to their father, siblings, grandparents, or anyone else playing an active role in their lives.

10. Socialization involves learning the rules of behavior of the culture in which a child is born and will grow up.

11. The theories of Sigmund Freud and Erik Erikson stress the emotional dynamics of social development. They both believe that children must learn to control the sexual and aggressive urges they are born with, but Erikson would add that the need of children for social approval is just as important to their social development.

12. Learning theorists give much less emphasis to the emotional dynamics of social development. They argue that children learn appropriate social behavior.

13. Cognitive theorists argue that social development is more than just the result of the child being shaped by rewards and punishments. These psychologists see the *child* as the shaper. They argue that social development results from the child acting on the environment, trying to make sense out of his or her experience.

14. Lawrence Kohlberg has observed that the moral development of a child progresses in six stages. Essentially, each stage represents an advance in the child's ability to take the roles of other people. At stage one, the child is egocentric and

has no sense of right or wrong. At each successive stage, the child's awareness of other people and society increases, until at stages five and six he or she is finally able to develop universal ethical principles based on ideals of reciprocity and human equality.

15. The implications for child rearing of the various theories of child development (emotional, behavioral, and cognitive) are numerous. Each child is unique and should be given the freedom to understand the world for herself or himself. A child should have rules for punishment and rewards that are appropriate, clear, and consistent. Parents and older siblings should remember that small children use them as models.

GLOSSARY

accommodation: In Piaget's theory of cognitive development, the adjustment of one's scheme for understanding the world to fit newly observed events and experiences.

anal stage: According to Freud, the stage at which children associate erotic pleasure with the elimination process.

assimilation: In Piaget's theory of cognitive development, the process of fitting objects and experiences into one's scheme for understanding the environment.

conservation: The principle that a given quantity does not change when its appearance is changed. The discovery of this principle between the ages of five and seven is important to the intellectual development of the child.

critical period: A specific time in development when certain skills or abilities are most easily learned.

developmental psychology: The study of changes that occur as individuals mature.

genital stage: According to Freud, the stage during which an individual's sexual satisfaction depends as much on giving sexual pleasure as on receiving it.

grasping reflex: An infant's clinging response to a touch on the palm of his or her hand.

identification: The process by which a child adopts the values and principles of the same-sex parent.

imprinting: A social learning capacity in some species by which attachments are formed to other organisms or to objects very early in life.

internalization: The process of incorporating the values, ideas, and standards of others as a part of oneself.

latency stage: According to Freud, the stage at which sexual desires are pushed into the background and the child becomes involved in exploring the world and learning new skills.

maturation: The internally programmed growth of a child.

object permanence: A child's realization, developed between the ages of one and two, that an object exists even when he or she cannot see or touch it.

Oedipal conflict: According to Freud, a boy's wish to possess his mother sexually, coupled with hostility toward his father. Correspondingly, girls desire their fathers sexually and feel hostile toward their mothers. In order to reduce his or her fear of punishment from the same-sex parent, the child begins to identify with the parent of the same sex.

oral stage: According to Freud, the stage at which infants associate erotic pleasure with the mouth.

phallic stage: According to Freud, the stage at which children associate sexual pleasure with their genitals.

representational thought: The intellectual ability of a child to picture something in his or her mind.

role taking: An important aspect of children's play that involves assuming adult roles, thus enabling the child to experience different points of view firsthand.

rooting reflex: An infant's response toward the source of touching that occurs anywhere around his or her mouth.

separation anxiety: A phase many children experience after twelve months, characterized by fear and anxiety at any prolonged absence of the mother.

socialization: The process of learning the rules of behavior of the culture within which an individual is born and will live.

sublimation: The process of redirecting sexual impulses into learning tasks that begins at about the age of five.

telegraphic speech: The kind of speech used by young children. Words are left out, but the meaning is still clear.

ACTIVITIES

1. Observe an infant under eighteen months of age, keeping a log of the baby's activities. Compare your notes with the developmental descriptions in this chapter. How closely does the baby follow the norm? What differences did you note?

2. Talk with children who are under five years old, paying particular attention to their grammar. What kinds of errors do they make? What kinds of grammatical rules do they already seem to know?

3. Do you and your parents share the same religious beliefs? Political orientation? Feelings about violence? Attitudes toward sex? Goals for living? Opinions about money? Views on drugs? Do you have similar tastes in clothing colors and styles? Music? Pets? Housing? Furniture? Foods? Cars? Entertainment? After asking yourself these questions, determine how well your beliefs, opinions, and tastes agree with those of your parents. How important do you think your early social training was for what you believe, think, and like?

4. What happens when a boy plays with G. I. Joe dolls? How does this behavior fit into the concept of modeling? Is this behavior liberating to boys, or does it feminize their behavior? Explain your answer. What would be the effect of girls playing football? Explain the difference(s) between your answers about boys and girls.

5. How are sex roles communicated to people in American society? Look carefully through magazines and newspapers, watch television commercials, and listen to the radio. What activities, interests, worries, virtues, weaknesses, physical characteristics, and mannerisms are presented as attributes of typical men and women? Are sex roles portrayed differently in different media? Are there various stereotypes within each sex?

6. Write a brief autobiography. What are the events that you feel have been the most significant in your life? What have been the main influences on your social and emotional development?

7. If you have an infant brother or sister, or a pet dog or cat, perform a simple experiment to test for object permanence. Be sure to use several different objects for your test, and be certain that the baby or animal is not afraid of, or uninterested in, the object. Most dogs or cats will probably search for vanished objects.

8. Ask children of different ages the following questions: Where does the sun go at night? Could you become a girl (a boy) if you wanted to? Does your brother (sister) have any brothers (sisters)? What makes leaves fall off trees? If you find some of their theories interesting, it is easy to think of many other questions.

SUGGESTED READINGS

BOWER, T. G. R. *A Primer of Infant Development.* San Francisco: Freeman, 1977. A brief and very readable survey of psychological development during infancy.

FLEMING, J. D. "Field Report on the State of the Apes." *Psychology Today,* 7 (January 1974): 31. A review of all the work across the country in teaching language to chimpanzees.

GINSBURG, HERBERT, AND OPPER, SYLVIA. *Piaget's Theory of Intellectual Development: An Introduction.* Englewood Cliffs, N.J.: Prentice-Hall, 1969 (paper). The clearest, most popular introduction to Piaget's work available.

KAGAN, J. *Understanding Children: Behavior, Motives, and Thought.* New York: Harcourt Brace Jovanovich, 1971. A practical overview of child development, written for teachers.

KOHLBERG, LAWRENCE. "Stage and Sequence: The Cognitive-Developmental Approach to Socialization." In *Handbook of Socialization,* ed. by D. Goslin. Chicago: Rand McNally, 1969, pp. 347–480. An inspired summary of Kohlberg's work on moral development that shows how he developed his six-stage theory.

LESSER, GERALD S. *Children and Television: Lessons from Sesame Street.* New York: Random House, 1974. One of the originators of "Sesame Street," the innovative educational TV program for children based on cognitive-developmental theory, discusses some of the effects it has had on elementary education.

LIEBERT, R. M., NEALE, J. M., AND DAVIDSON, E. S. *The Early Window: Effects of Television on Children and Youth.* New York: Pergamon Press, 1973 (paper). A balanced discussion of the effects of television on children. The book also provides a good introduction to social learning, since most of the research on television's impact has been done from this perspective.

PINES, MAYA. *Revolution in Learning: The Years from Birth to Six.* New York: Harper & Row, 1966 (paper). An exciting, easy-to-read account of what children learn before they start elementary school.

RUGH, R., AND SHETTLES, L. *From Conception to Birth: The Drama of Life's Beginnings.* New York: Harper & Row, 1971. Extraordinary pictures of life as it actually begins and develops in the uterus. Color photographs of the fetus, showing close-ups of its hands, face, and actions.

SPOCK, BENJAMIN. *Baby and Child Care.* New York: Pocket Books, 1971 (paper); originally published 1946. For decades this book has served as a handy and practical guide for parents on almost every conceivable issue of child rearing. In recent editions, Dr. Spock has recommended a less rigid approach to child rearing than he used to advocate.

SUTTON-SMITH, BRIAN, AND SUTTON-SMITH, SHIRLEY. *How to Play with Your Children (and When Not To).* New York: Hawthorn, 1974 (paper). What children play at different ages is presented along with a host of good ideas about how adults can join in and help children develop further. The first author is the leading authority on the psychology of play, the second has taught elementary school for many years, and both are quite playful themselves. The result is a fascinating and very funny book.

BIBLIOGRAPHY

BALDWIN, ALFRED A. *Theories of Child Development.* New York: Wiley, 1967.

BANDURA, A., AND WALTERS, R. H. *Social Learning and Personality Development.* New York: Holt, Rinehart & Winston, 1963.

BELLUGI, U., AND BROWN, R. (EDS.). *The Acquisition of Language.* Chicago: University of Chicago Press, 1970.

BOGATZ, GERRY ANN, AND BALL, SAMUEL. "Some Things You Wanted to Know about 'Sesame Street.'" *American Education,* 7 (1971): 11–15.

BOWLBY, J. "Separation Anxiety: A Critical Review of the Literature." *Journal of Child Psychology and Psychiatry,* 1 (1960–1961): 251–269.

————. *Child Care and Growth of Love.* 2nd ed. Baltimore: Penguin, 1965.

BROWN, ROGER. *A First Language: The Early Stages.* Cambridge, Mass.: Harvard University Press, 1973.

CHUKOVSKY, K. *From Two to Five.* Berkeley: University of California Press, 1963.

COATES, BRIAN, PUSSER, H. ELLISON, AND GOODMAN, IRENE. "The Influence of 'Sesame Street' and 'Mr. Rogers' Neighborhood' on Children's Social Behavior in Preschool." *Child Development,* 47 (1976): 138–144.

COOK, THOMAS D., AND CONNER, ROSS F. "Sesame Street Around the World: The Educational Impact." *Journal of Communication,* 26 (1976): 155–164.

FISCHER, KURT W. *Piaget's Theory of Learning and Cognitive Development.* Chicago: Markham, 1973.

FLAVELL, JOHN H. *The Developmental Theory of Jean Piaget.* New York: Van Nostrand, 1963.

FURTH, HANS. *Piaget and Knowledge.* Englewood Cliffs, N.J.: Prentice-Hall, 1969.

GARDNER, R. A., AND GARDNER, B. T. "Teaching Sign Language to a Chimpanzee." *Science,* 1965 (1969): 644–672.

GESELL, A., AND THOMPSON, HELEN. "Learning and Growth in Identical Twin Infants." *Genetic Psychological Monograph,* 6 (1929): 1–124.

GINSBURG, HERBERT, AND OPPER, SYLVIA. *Piaget's Theory of Intellectual Development: An Introduction.* Englewood Cliffs, N.J.: Prentice-Hall, 1969.

GORN, GERALD J., GOLDBERG, MARVIN E., AND KANUNGO, RABINDRA N. "The Role of Educational Television in Changing Intergroup Attitudes of Children." *Child Development,* 47 (1976): 277–280.

HARLOW, HARRY F. "The Development of Affectional Patterns in Infant Monkeys." In *Determinants of Infant Behavior,* ed. by B. M. Foss. New York: Wiley, 1961, pp. 75–100.

HARLOW, HARRY F., AND ZIMMERMAN, R. R. "Affectional Responses in the Infant Monkey." *Science,* 140 (1959): 421–432.

KALMIS, ILZE V., AND BRUNER, J. S. "The Coordination of Visual Observation and Instrumental Behavior in Early Infancy." *Perception,* 2 (1973): 304–314.

KOHLBERG, LAWRENCE. "The Child as Moral Philosopher." *Psychology Today,* 2 (September 1968): 25–30.

KOHLBERG, LAWRENCE, AND TUNEL, E. *Research in Moral Development: The Cognitive-Developmental Approach.* New York: Holt, Rinehart & Winston, 1971.

LESSER, GERALD S. *Children and Television: Lessons from Sesame Street.* New York: Random House, 1974.

LITTENBERG, R., TULKIN, S., AND KAGAN, J. "Cognitive Components of Separation Anxiety." *Developmental Psychology,* 4 (1971): 387–388.

LORENZ, KONRAD Z. *Studies in Animal and Human Behavior,* trans. by Robert Martin. 2 vols. Cambridge, Mass.: Harvard University Press, 1972.

MACCOBY, ELEANOR, AND MASTERS, JOHN C. "Attachment and Dependency." In *Manual of Child Psychology,* ed. by Paul H. Mussen. Vol. 2. New York: Wiley, 1970, pp. 159–260.

PIAGET, JEAN. *The Language and Thought of the Child.* London: Routledge and Kegan Paul, 1926.

PINES, MAYA. "Infants Are Smarter than Anybody Thinks." *The New York Times Magazine* (November 29, 1970).

RUMBAUGH, DUANE M., GILL, TIMOTHY V., AND VON GLASERSFELD, E. C. "Reading and Sentence Completion by a Chimpanzee." *Science,* 182 (1973): 731–733.

SEARS, ROBERT, MACCOBY, ELEANOR, AND LEVIN, HARRY. *Patterns of Child Rearing.* New York: Harper & Row, 1957.

SPITZ, RENÉ, AND WOLFF, K. M. "Analclitic Depression: An Inquiry into the Genesis of Psychiatric Conditions in Early Childhood, II." In *The Psychoanalytic Study of the Child,* ed. by A. Freud *et al.* Vol. II. New York: International Universities Press, 1946, pp. 313–342.

THOMPSON, WILLIAM R., AND GRUSEC, JOAN. "Studies of Early Experience." In *Manual of Child Psychology,* ed. by Paul H. Mussen. Vol. 2. New York: Wiley, 1970, pp. 565–656.

Adolescence, Adulthood, and Old Age

As you read this, somewhere a thirteen-year-old boy is shuffling his feet, trying to punch like Muhammad Ali. A young woman is staring in horror at the new pimple she just noticed in the mirror; she is thinking that she would rather die than be seen with such an ugly zit. Elsewhere, a young married couple is arguing about money. The newborn bundle of joy they just brought home from the hospital has turned their private love nest into a threesome. And in still another spot, a recently retired couple is sitting together mildly depressed at being forced to rediscover each other; they miss the excitement of having teen-agers around making too much noise.

A list of the variations in adult life styles and adjustments to changing circumstances would fill volumes. But until recently, developmental psychologists paid relatively little attention to the changes that take place after people are grown. As indicated in the preceding chapter, Freud believed that human beings reach the final stage of psychosexual development—the genital stage—in adolescence. Piaget's study of intellectual development led him to a similar conclusion: the adolescent is fully equipped mentally. Indeed, most psychologists have looked at adulthood as variations on themes written in childhood.

Erik Erikson (1950) was one of the first to consider the psychosocial tasks that confront human beings in our culture as they grow older. Following his lead, increasing numbers of psychologists have begun to study the physiological, social, psychological, and intellectual changes that occur from adolescence through old age. In this chapter we shall attempt to summarize their findings, completing the story we began in the preceding chapter.

Adolescence
Physical Changes / Social Development: Family and Friends / The Transition to Adult Thinking

Identity: Self and Society
Sexual Identity / Identity Resolution

Adulthood
Physical Changes / Intellectual Changes / Social and Personality Development

Old Age
Adjusting to Old Age / Dying / Using Psychology: Hospices

Figure 9.1
Human development does not stop at adolescence or adulthood. Growth and change occur at every stage in the life cycle.

Figure 9.2
The last stage of a New Guinea puberty rite, when the boys gather in the hut from which they will emerge as adults of the tribe.

ADOLESCENCE

In most preliterate societies, the village or tribe holds elaborate ceremonies to mark the transition from childhood to adulthood (Figure 9.2). Once a young person has been initiated, he or she is considered ready for courtship and marriage, and is expected to assume adult responsibilities. Choices in life style are limited: the economic, social, and sexual roles of adulthood are clearly defined. As a result, there are few questions about "how far to go" sexually or what to do with one's life—and hence few conflicts (see Mead, 1961). The no man's land between childhood and adulthood that we call "adolescence" simply does not exist.

In 1904, G. Stanley Hall published a book that made "adolescence" a household word in America. Hall pointed out that through most of the nineteenth century, the family was an economic unit in this country. All hands were needed. Youngsters worked alongside their parents in fields and shops and small factories, gradually assuming more and more responsibility. The line between children and adults was not as clearly drawn as it is today.

Industrialization changed this. First, machines made it possible for one person to do the work of many. The economy no longer needed child and teen-age labor. Second, the demand for specialized skills increased, and parents could not teach children these new skills. Moreover, with the decline of family businesses and the rise of wage labor, young people could not know for sure what they would be doing with their lives. The solution to all of these problems was school. School kept unemployed young people off the streets, gave them training, and provided some with career options their parents had not enjoyed.

This combination of events created what we call **adolescence**—a developmental stage between childhood and adulthood. Young people who were physically mature began to remain in training, doing economically nonproductive work, depending on their families for support, and delaying decisions about their future for longer and longer periods. Today, a large number of young Americans remain in school well into their twenties.

Hall believed adolescence to be a period of great "storm and stress"—perhaps the most difficult stage of human development. Being an adolescent is something like being a fully grown animal in a cage, an animal who sees freedom but doesn't know quite when he will be freed or how he will handle it. Society treats the adolescent as a child one minute, as an adult the next. Adolescents are expected to act maturely, but also to do as they are told. They are denied the chance to earn a living (unemployment rates among teen-agers are higher than among any other group), but often are reminded that their parents had to work at their age. They are envied for their youth, but resented for their lack of responsibility.

Because adolescence is often painful and distressing in technological societies, Erikson, for one, believes that many young people need a **psychological moratorium.** By this he means a period during which they can explore and experiment without having to commit themselves to a life style, career, or mate, or to suffer the consequences of mistakes (Erikson, 1968: 125–138). This enables people to learn enough to successfully resolve the crises of adolescence and young adulthood.

Physical Changes

Puberty, or sexual maturation, is the biological event that marks the end of childhood. Hormones trigger a series of internal and external changes. At about ten, girls rather suddenly begin to grow—sometimes as much as two or three inches a year. During this growth spurt, a girl's breasts and hips begin to fill out, and she develops pubic hair. Between ten and seventeen she has her first menstrual period, or **menarche.** Another year or so will pass before her periods become regular and she is capable of conceiving a child. Yet girls in most societies consider menarche the beginning of womanhood.

At about twelve, boys begin to develop pubic hair and larger genitals. Within a year or two they become capable of ejaculation. They too begin to grow rapidly and to fill out, developing the broad shoulders and thicker trunk of an adult man. Their voices gradually deepen. Hair begins to grow on their faces and later on their chests.

Variations in the rate of sexual maturation make it difficult to apply norms or standards to puberty. In general, girls begin to develop earlier than boys and for a year or two may tower over male age-mates.

Reactions to Growth.   In general young people today are better informed about sex than they were two or three generations ago. Most do not find menarche or nighttime ejaculations upsetting. Nevertheless, the rather sudden bodily changes that occur during puberty make all adolescents somewhat self-conscious. This is particularly true if they are early or late to

Figure 9.3
The physiological changes of puberty bring a new kind of self-awareness that did not exist in childhood.

develop. Adolescents desperately want to be accepted by their peers, to conform to ideals of how a male or female their age should act, dress, and look. In one study, over half of the adolescent girls and a third of the boys spontaneously expressed concern about their appearance (Dwyer and Mayer, 1968–1969).

Research indicates that boys who mature early have an advantage. They become heroes in sports, leaders in formal and informal social activities. Other boys look up to them; girls have crushes on them; adults tend to treat them as more mature. As a result they are generally more self-confident and independent than other boys. Late-maturing boys, whose high-pitched voices and less-than-ideal physiques may make them feel inadequate, tend to be withdrawn or rebellious. However, the early advantage soon fades. Indeed, in their mid-thirties, men who were late to mature tend to be more flexible and expressive than early maturers.

With girls the pattern is somewhat different. Girls who mature early may feel embarrassed rather than proud of their height and figure at first. Some begin dating older boys and become bossy with people their own age. Late-maturing girls tend to be less quarrelsome and to get along with their peers more easily. In their late teens, girls who matured early may be more popular and have a more favorable image of themselves than girls who matured slowly. However, the differences between early maturers and late maturers do not seem to be as pronounced among girls as they are among boys (Dwyer and Mayer, 1968–1969).

Sexual Attitudes and Behavior.   Most adolescent girls are less conscious of sexual urges than boys. They are less likely to be aroused by sexual symbols, to have explicitly sexual fantasies, or to reach sexual climax in dreams than are boys their age. They are less concerned about finding sexual release than boys are, and more concerned about affection, trust, sharing, and love. In a word, girls are more romantic. Yet most adolescent girls (more than two-thirds in one survey) believe that women enjoy sex as much as men (Mussen, Conger, and Kagan, 1974: 565).

Recent data indicate that 95 percent of boys have experienced orgasm by the age of fifteen. Although 90 percent of women age thirty-five have had orgasms, only 23 percent report orgasms by age fifteen, 53 percent by age twenty. About 65 percent of men reach their first climax through masturbation, whereas 50 percent of women discover orgasm through petting or sexual intercourse. On the average, sixteen- or seventeen-year-old boys masturbate about three times a week. Girls are much more variable: some never masturbate, some on rare occasions (about twice a year), some as often as ten or twelve times a week. By age nineteen, over 70 percent of males and nearly 60 percent of females have had sexual intercourse—usually with one person with whom they are emotionally involved.

Do these statistics represent a dramatic change in behavior over past generations—a "sexual revolution"? The answer is a qualified no. Middle- and upper-class girls who attend college seem to be more sexually active than college girls were twenty years ago. But sexual behavior in other social categories is about the same today as it was when Kinsey made his famous studies in the late 1940s.

The main change in recent years seems to be in attitudes. The majority of young people believe it is morally acceptable for an engaged couple to have sexual intercourse; the majority of adults do not. This is not to say that the younger generation approves of promiscuity. On the contrary. According to one survey, young people place more emphasis on affection and meaningful relationships than adults do. They consider premarital intercourse between two people who love each other more acceptable than casual petting between two people who are not attached to each other (something adults accept more readily). Some people believe that the most significant change is that most adolescents today believe in being open and honest about sex (Simon and Gagnon, 1970).

Social Development: Family and Friends

One of the principal developmental tasks for adolescents is becoming independent of their families. Unfortunately, the means of achieving this status are not always clear, either to the adolescents or to their parents. First, there are mixed feelings on both sides. Some parents have built their life styles around the family and are reluctant to let the child go. Such parents know they will soon have to find someone else on whom to shift their emotional dependence. Also, parents whose children are old enough to leave home sometimes have to wrestle with their own fears of advancing age. Many parents worry about whether their children are really ready to cope with the harsh realities of life—and so do adolescents. At the same time that young people long to get out on their own and try themselves against the world, they worry a lot about failing there. This internal struggle is often mirrored in the adolescent's unpredictable behavior, which parents may interpret as "adolescent rebellion." Against this background of uncertainty, which is almost universal, there are various family styles of working toward autonomy.

The way in which adolescents seek independence and the ease with which they resolve conflicts about becoming adults depend in large part on the parent-child relationship.

In **authoritarian families** parents are the "bosses." They do not feel that they have to explain their actions or demands. In fact such parents may feel the child has no right to question parental decisions.

In **democratic families** adolescents participate in decisions affecting their lives. There is a great deal of discussion and negotiation in such families. Parents listen to their children's reasons for wanting to go somewhere or do something, and make an effort to explain their rules and expectations. The adolescents make many decisions for themselves, but the parents retain the right to veto plans of which they disapprove.

Figure 9.4
The style of the parent-child relationship—authoritarian, democratic, or permissive—plays a large part in determining how adolescents gain independence and make the transition to adulthood.

Figure 9.5
The adolescent peer group, with which most teenagers spend much of their time, is a source of self-identity. It is also a source of social pressure to conform.

In **permissive** or **laissez-faire** families children have the final say. The parents may attempt to guide the adolescents, but give in when the children insist on having their own way. Or the parents may simply give up their child-rearing responsibilities—setting no rules about behavior, making no demands, voicing no expectations, virtually ignoring the young people in their house.

Numerous studies suggest that adolescents who have grown up in democratic families are more autonomous, in the sense of having more confidence in their own values and goals than other young people do. They are also more independent, in the sense of wanting to make their own decisions (with or without advice). There are several reasons for this.

First, the child is able to assume responsibility gradually. He is not denied the opportunity to exercise his own judgment (as in authoritarian families) or given too much responsibility too soon (as in permissive families). Second, a child is more likely to identify with parents who love and respect him than with parents who treat him as incompetent or who seem indifferent to him. Finally, through their behavior toward the child, democratic parents present a model of responsible, cooperative independence for the growing person to imitate.

Children raised in authoritarian families lack practice in negotiating for their desires and exercising responsibility. They tend to resent all authority, to rebel without cause. Children raised in permissive families tend to feel unwanted and to doubt their own self-worth. They often do not trust themselves or others (Conger, 1973: 208–215).

The people all adolescents can trust not to treat them like children are their peers. Teen-agers spend much of their time with friends—they need and use each other to define themselves.

High schools are important as places for adolescents to get together. And they do get together in fairly predictable ways. Most schools contain easily recognizable and well-defined sets, or crowds. And these sets are arranged in a fairly rigid hierarchy—everyone knows who belongs to what set and what people in that set do with their time. Early in adolescence the sets are usually divided by sex, but later the sexes mix. Sets usually form along class lines. Some school activities bring teen-agers of different social classes together, but it is the exception rather than the rule that middle-class and lower-class adolescents are close friends. Belonging to a **clique** (a group within a set) gives the adolescent status and a means of defining herself or himself; it is a handle the adolescent can hold onto while shaping an identity.

Of course, there are drawbacks to this kind of social organization. One of the greatest is that the fear of being disliked leads to **conformity.** A teen-ager's fear of wearing clothes that might set him or her apart from others is well known. But group pressures to conform often lead young people to do things that run contrary to their better judgment—or to do things they fear. One of the factors that undoubtedly made it possible for the use of drugs to spread so rapidly in many American schools is the social pressure for adolescents to conform to the group. (We will discuss social pressures and conformity again in Chapter 12.)

The Transition to Adult Thinking

During adolescence, the thinking patterns characteristic of adults emerge. From about age eleven or twelve, people are capable of systematic experimentation. Given a problem—in school, under the hood of a car, or in an art studio—the adolescent can consider all possible combinations of events and eliminate all the combinations that are irrelevant to the task until he or she discovers the correct one. One important side effect of this new intellectual skill is the ability to consider hypothetical propositions and to reason from them. Adolescents can, for example, consider what would happen if there were another Civil War or imagine what the world would be like without cars. Such situations would seem absurd to an eight year old because they are so contrary to his or her experience (Inhelder and Piaget, 1964).

With comprehension of the hypothetical comes the ability to understand abstract principles. Not only is this capacity important for studying higher-level science and mathematics, it leads the adolescent to deal with such abstractions in his or her own life as ethics, conformity, and phoniness. It allows for introspection—examining one's own motives and thoughts. One adolescent is quoted as saying, "I found myself thinking about my future, and then I began to think about why I was thinking about my future, and then I began to think about why I was thinking about why I was thinking about my future."

These new intellectual capacities also enable the adolescent to deal with overpowering emotional feelings through **rationalization.** After failing a test, for example, an individual may rationalize that it happened "because I was worried about the date I might be going on next week." An eight year old is too tied to concrete reality to consider systematically all the reasons why he or she might have failed.

Perhaps the main difference between the way adolescents and adults think is that young people are very idealistic. This, too, is related to the fact that, for the first time, they can imagine the hypothetical—how things might be. When they compare this to the way things are, the world seems a sorry place. They often become impatient with what they see as the adult generation's failures. They don't understand why, for example, a person who feels a job compromises his or her principles doesn't just quit. In other words, adolescents tend to be somewht unrealistic about the complexities of life. But at the same time, their idealism can help keep older adults in touch with ways in which the world could be improved.

IDENTITY: SELF AND SOCIETY

A major developmental task in adolescence is building an identity. Children are aware of what other people (adults and peers) think of them. They know the labels others apply to them (good, naughty, silly, talented, brave, pretty, and the like). They are also aware of their biological drives and of their growing physical and cognitive abilities. Children may dream of being this or that person and act these roles out in their play. But they do not brood about who they are or where they are going in life. Children live in the present; adolescents begin to think about the future.

Several factors contribute to what Erikson (1968) has called the adolescent **identity crisis**—worrying about who you are. These include the physiological changes we have described, awakening sexual drives and the possibility of a new kind of intimacy with the opposite sex, and cognitive developments. Adolescents begin to see the future as a reality, not just a game. They know they have to confront the almost infinite and often conflicting possibilities and choices that lie ahead. In the process of reviewing their past and anticipating their future, they begin to think about themselves.

Building an identity involves looking both inward and outward. Looking inward, an adolescent seeks the feeling of **self-sameness:** that she knows how she feels about different issues, situations, and people, and that her thoughts and behavior make sense. Looking outward, she seeks confirmation of this self. Do other people see her as she sees herself? The feeling that nobody really knows or understands you is quite common in adolescence. Another dimension to the problem of identity is developing a sense of **continuity**—a feeling that in an important way you are the same person you were when you were younger and that you will be in the future. Although you have changed in many ways, your basic identity remains the same.

Erikson suggests that the identity crisis stems from the adolescent's

> **Children live in the present; adolescents begin to think about the future.**

Figure 9.6
Totalism, Erikson's term for complete immersion in a group, is another sign of the "identity crisis" of adolescence. Joining a gang, for example, provides the individual with guidelines and rules for every aspect of life, and relieves him or her of the burden of making decisions.

desire to feel unique and distinctive on the one hand, and to "fit in" on the other. Some young people have great difficulty satisfying these contradictory desires. This may be one reason why so many American adolescents are drawn to radical political or religious movements, fraternities and sororities, or gangs. These groups provide a ready-made identity. Strict codes of dress and behavior relieve the individual of the burden of making choices. The adolescent rebels against adult rules by rigidly conforming to peer-group standards. Erikson calls such complete immersion in a group **totalism.** (Obviously, in other cultures, adolescent conflicts and concerns may be very different.)

Adolescents who are comfortable with their maturing bodies, who have a realistic sense of where they want to go in life, and who feel sure of acceptance by the people who matter to them will not experience as severe an identity crisis. But to some degree all adolescents become conformists for a period. Peer groups provide structure when adolescents are ready to be less dependent on their families, but not quite ready to be independent.

Sexual Identity

A significant part of a person's self-definition and self-knowledge is his or her sexual identity. Sexual identity is related not only to one's personal relationships but also to the work one does, the opinions one holds, and the responsibilities one feels. American society appears to be undergoing major changes in its definition of the roles the sexes should play and in the attitudes it holds toward sexual behavior.

In a classic work on adolescents, James Coleman (1961) showed how stereotypes about the way males and females should behave operate in high school. Typically, boys considered having a car one of the most important things in life; girls, having nice clothes. When asked if they wanted to be remembered as the "best scholars," more freshman boys than girls answered yes. The gap increased as students moved toward the senior year. Girls' grades were more consistent over the years, but few excelled. Apparently they operated on the principle "Girls should get good grades—but not too good."

But there is evidence that sex roles in our society are changing. Psychologist Sandra Bem argues that people should accept new **androgynous** roles—that is, roles that involve a flexible combination of male and female characteristics. She began her research by asking college students to say how desirable various characteristics were "for a man" and "for a woman." Not surprisingly, she found that traits like ambition, self-reliance, independence, and assertiveness were part of the male role. Women were expected to be affectionate, gentle, understanding, and sensitive to the needs of others.

These and other traits were then listed in a questionnaire called the Bem Sex Role Inventory. People were asked to rate how each of these traits applied to them on a scale from one ("never or almost never true") to seven ("always or almost always true"). In one early report (Bem, 1975), she described the results for 1,500 Stanford undergraduates: about 50 percent stuck to "appropriate" sex roles (masculine males or feminine females), 15 percent were "cross-sex typed" (women who described themselves in traditionally male terms, or men who checked feminine adjectives), and 35

Figure 9.7
Changing sex roles. (a) An Episcopal priest gives communion. (b) A soldier marches with other members of her unit.

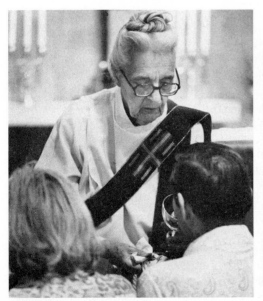

percent were androgynous people who checked off both male and female characteristics when they described themselves.

In later studies, Bem found that the androgynous people were indeed more flexible. They were able to be assertive when it was required (so could traditional males, but traditional females could not). Such people were also able to express warmth, playfulness, and concern (which traditional females could, but traditional males could not). In our complex world, Bem argues, androgyny should be our ideal: there is no room for an artificial split between "woman's work" and "a man's world."

Identity Resolution

Resolution of the identity problem is necessary if the person is to be able to make commitments in adult life. Without a clear sense of who one is, it is impossible to make a mature commitment in love. And without a clear sense of what one's goals are, it is difficult to choose work that will be fulfilling. It may be, since adolescence in America lasts so long, that the identity crisis is not resolved until after the adolescent years. No one wakes up one morning before his or her twentieth birthday and bounds out of bed saying, "Eureka! I know who I am!" A few people do have a good sense of self early in life. For others, it may not come until much later. But of all human psychological processes, the knowledge of who one is—and a commitment to that self—is probably the most important.

ADULTHOOD

In the preface to *The Seasons of a Man's Life* (1978), Yale researcher Daniel Levinson wrote: "Young adults often feel that to pass 30 is to be 'over the hill,' and they are given little beyond hollow clichés to provide a fuller sense of the actual problems and possibilities of adult life at different ages. The middle years, they imagine, will bring triviality and meaningless comfort at best, stagnation and hopelessness at worst. . . . Adults hope that life begins at 40—but the great anxiety is that it ends there. The result of this pervasive dread about middle age is almost complete silence about the experience of being adult. The concrete character of adult life is one of the best-kept secrets in our society."

Until quite recently psychologists knew little about adulthood. One reason is that it is difficult to study the entire life cycle. A cross-sectional study (which compares individuals of different ages at the same point in time) may reflect changes in the way different generations were raised and the challenges they face, not changes that occur as a result of aging. A longitudinal study (which compares the way the same individuals think and act at different points in time) would take years to complete. However, by combining these techniques psychologists have begun to shed new light on the process of growing older. The opportunities and problems individuals face and the nature of their interests do change significantly over the adult years.

Physical Changes

In general, human beings are at their physical peak between the ages of eighteen and twenty-five. This is the period when we are strongest, healthiest, and have the quickest reflexes. One has only to think of the average age of professional athletes or dancers to verify this.

For most adults, the process of physical decline is slow and gradual. Strength and stamina begin to decline in the late twenties. A twenty year old manages to carry four heavy bags of groceries; a forty year old finds it easier to make two trips. In middle age appearance changes. The hair starts to turn gray and perhaps to thin out. The skin becomes somewhat dry and inelastic; wrinkles appear. People may become overweight, or develop hypertension or arthritis, which accelerate the aging process. In old age, muscles and fat built up over the years break down, so that people often lose weight, become shorter, and develop more wrinkles, creases, and loose skin.

With time the senses require more and more stimulation. During their forties most people begin having difficulty seeing distant objects, adjusting to the dark, and focusing on printed pages, even if their eyesight has always been good. Many experience a gradual or sudden loss of hearing in their later years. In addition, reaction time slows. If an experimenter asks a young person and an older person to push a button when they see a light flash on, the older person will take longer to do so. People over sixty-five have a higher rate of accidents on the road and in jobs requiring coordination than middle-aged people—although not as high as the rate for late adolescents (Kimmel, 1974).

Some of the changes we associate with growing older are the result of the natural processes of aging. Others result from diseases and from simple disuse and abuse. A person who eats sensibly, exercises, avoids cigarettes, drugs, and alcohol, and is not subjected to severe emotional stress will look and feel younger than someone who neglects his or her health.

Menopause. Between the ages of forty-five and fifty, a woman's production of sex hormones is sharply reduced. This biological event is called **menopause.** The woman stops ovulating (producing eggs) and menstruating, and therefore cannot have any more children. However, menopause does not cause any reduction in a woman's sexual drive or sexual enjoyment.

Many women experience hot flashes and some degree of discomfort during menopause. However, the headaches, dizzy spells, anxiety attacks, irritability, and severe depression some women experience with "the change of life" appear to have an emotional rather than physical origin. Menopause may occur at a time when a woman is worrying about her children leaving home (and what she will do if she has been a full-time homemaker), is concerned about her own and her husband's health, and is for the first time facing the fact that she is growing old. In addition, some women have heard that menopause is painful and that they will never feel the same again. This combination of worries may produce the symptoms listed above.

Figure 9.8
Sexual interest and activity do not suddenly cease at a certain age: as more and more studies show, those who have partners and remain active, productive people also continue to enjoy active sex lives.

A recent study shows that these negative effects are greatly exaggerated. Half of the women interviewed said they felt better, more confident, calmer, and freer after menopause than they had before. They no longer had to think about their periods or getting pregnant. Their relations with their husbands improved; they enjoyed sex as much as or more than they had before. Many said the worst part of menopause was not knowing what to expect (Neugarten *et al.*, 1963).

Men do not go through any biological change equivalent to menopause. The number of sperm a man's body produces declines gradually over the years, but men have fathered children at an advanced age.

Sexual Behavior. Is there sex after forty? According to one recent study, most college students believe their parents have intercourse no more than once a month, never have oral sex, and never had intercourse before they were married. Many of the midwestern university students who answered this questionnaire were upset by the very idea of the survey. For example, one wrote: "Whoever thinks about their parents' sexual relations, except perverts?" (Pocs *et al.*, 1977). One-fourth of the students believed that their parents had had intercourse only once or not at all in the last year.

Of course, what people believe about their parents' sexual activity may be different from what they believe about that of other people their parents' age. Still, it is interesting to compare this belief with the following statistics and observations: in the Kinsey studies the average reported frequency of sexual intercourse for men sixty-five and older was about four times a month, and their partners were typically their spouses; 25 to 30 percent of the older married men and women in the studies also claimed to supplement intercourse with another sexual outlet, masturbation.

In a more recent study of 800 men over the age of sixty-five selected from *Who's Who in America*, it was found that about 70 percent regularly had sexual intercourse one to four times a month. The oldest subject in this study who enjoyed intercourse regularly was a ninety-two-year-old clergyman (Rubin, 1963).

Other, more recent, studies have found essentially the same thing: that rather than suddenly reaching an age at which sexual interests disappear, most old people for whom a partner is available maintain relatively vigorous sex lives. Those who are most sexually active tend to be those who also were most active in their youth (Newman and Nichols, 1960).

It is true that with aging, hormone production decreases in both sexes, and vaginal lubrication and erectile vigor diminish; but these changes are gradual. Masters and Johnson (1970) emphatically pointed out that for most people who are in good health there is no physiological reason for stopping sexual activity with advancing age. The reasons people do so apparently are related to such factors as lack of a partner, boredom with a partner of long standing, poor physical condition caused by a lack of exercise and excessive eating and use of alcohol, socially defined expectations of a loss of "sex drive" with aging, and illness (such as advanced heart disease) not directly related to sexual physiology and functioning. Perhaps one significant contribution that modern sex research will make to society will be to provide rational arguments against the expectation that sex stops or somehow becomes "improper" after a certain age. This may enable a large segment of our population to continue to enjoy a healthy sex life.

Intellectual Changes

People are better at learning new skills and information, solving problems that require speed and coordination, and shifting from one problem-solving strategy to another in their mid-twenties than they were in adolescence (Baltes and Schaie, 1974). These abilities are considered signs of intelligence; they are the skills intelligence tests measure.

At one time many psychologists thought that intellectual development reached a peak in the mid-twenties and then declined. The reason was that people do not score as high on intelligence tests in middle age as they did when they were younger. Further investigation revealed that some parts of these tests measure speed, not intelligence (Bischof, 1969). As indicated above, a person's reaction time begins to slow in the early thirties. Intelligence tests "penalized" adults for this fact.

Allowing for the decline in speed, we find that people continue to acquire information and to expand their vocabularies as they grow older. The ability to comprehend new material and to think flexibly improves with the years. This is particularly true if a person has had higher education, lives in a stimulating environment, and works in an intellectually demanding career. One researcher studied over seven hundred individuals who were engaged in scholarship, science, or the arts. Although the patterns varied from profession to profession, most of the subjects reached their peaks of creativity and productivity in their forties (Dennis, 1966).

In old age most people slow down dramatically. In addition, many older people tend to be somewhat rigid or conservative in their thinking. They are more likely to agree with clichés; they are reluctant to guess when they do not know the answer to a question. However, memory loss and senility are not part of the natural process of aging. They result from hardening of the arteries and other diseases. Many elderly people continue to be alert, productive, and inventive throughout their lives. Leo Tolstoy, Pablo Picasso, Artur Rubinstein, Eleanor Roosevelt, and Grandma Moses are some of the obvious examples. Howard Wizniak is another, less obvious example. You don't have to be famous to be productive.

Social and Personality Development

A person's style of adapting to situations remains the same throughout life.

All available evidence suggests that an individual's basic character—his or her style of adapting to situations—is relatively stable over the adult years. A number of researchers have given the same attitude and personality tests to individuals in late adolescence and again ten or fifteen years later. Many of the subjects believed that they had changed dramatically. But the tests indicated they had not. The degree of satisfaction they expressed about themselves and about life in general in their middle years was consistent with their earlier views. Confident young people remained confident; self-haters, self-hating; passive individuals, passive—unless something upsetting had happened to them, such as a sudden change in economic status (see Kimmel, 1974).

Erikson's View.   Until recently, Erikson's theory of the eight crises of psychosocial adjustment (see Table 8.2) was the only major description of life-cycle changes in adulthood.

Erikson believes that the major crisis in early adulthood revolves around questions of intimacy versus isolation. The ability to create intimate relationships depends in large part on whether a person has established a sense of identity. Someone who is insecure is likely to avoid closeness—because he fears the other person will see through him, or because

Figure 9.9
Mentor and protégé: the desire to transmit one's knowledge and experience to the next generation is a sign of what Erikson calls the "generativity" resolution of the crisis of middle age. The opposite resolution—stagnation—results in self-absorption, bitterness, and looking backward.

How Babies Train Parents

Pick up any newspaper or women's magazine and you'll find pages of advice to mothers on how to bring up their babies. But no matter how hard you look, you won't find a word to babies on the latest parent-training rules. If this sounds a bit facetious, it's meant to be—but there's some truth in our jest. Even though infants can't read, they *can* train parents to bring them up in a certain way.

No matter how good a mother's child-rearing intentions are before her child is born, she may find herself playing by a different set of rules when she brings her child home. Her approach will depend just as much on her child's temperament as on her skill and dedication to parenting. If she is lucky enough to have a calm, placid baby who seems to take life in stride, caring for her child will be its own reward; her baby's temperament will give her the feedback she needs to do her best. But if her baby is cranky, easily excitable, and prone to sleepless, tearful nights, she is likely to be filled with anger and self-pity at her own misfortune and her misfortunate child.

It should not surprise you, then, that children can turn their own parents on or off through their temperament and behavior. And it should be even less of a surprise that difficult infants may face some difficult parent-child problems as they grow.

For more details, see Julius Segal and Herbert Yahraes, ''Bringing Up Mother,'' *Psychology Today*, November 1978.

he feels uncomfortably dependent on people he is close to. Erikson believes that the failure to achieve intimacy leds to isolation, perhaps disguised by a series of intense but brief affairs or a stable but distant relationship.

Middle age may trigger either a new sense of generativity or a slide into stagnation. By **generativity,** Erikson means the desire to use one's accumulated wisdom to guide future generations—directly, as a parent, or indirectly. **Stagnation** occurs when a person wants to hang onto the past. The most graphic examples of this are women who try to recapture youth with face-lifts, and men who attempt to recapture it by having affairs with young women. Stagnation may take the form of childish self-absorption, preoccupation with one's health, and bitterness about the direction one's life has taken.

Ideally, a middle-aged person feels that the way he sees himself, what he would like to be, and the way others perceive him fit together. He has developed a number of effective strategies for dealing with stress and the complexities of life. He has a new self-assurance born of the feeling that he knows he can handle things. And he wants to share this experience with others.

In middle age, people begin to devote more time and energy to the outside world. Although their interest in family and friends continues, they become more deeply involved in organizations—professional associations, unions, political campaigns, civic committees, and the like. This new out-ward orientation may be most obvious in housewives who now have the time to go back to school or to full-time work, to chair committees or run for political office. But it is also true of working people whose experience and heightened productivity command new respect. Involvement in outside affairs is an extension of generativity beyond the family.

Levinson's Theory of Male Development.   In 1976, Gail Sheehy published the best-selling book *Passages: Predictable Crises of Adult Life*. It was the first major attempt to go beyond Erikson, and it attracted a tremendous amount of public attention. The book was based partly on Sheehy's journalistic interviews with 115 people who described their experiences as adults, and partly on the work of various social scientists.

Daniel Levinson and his colleagues at Yale were one of the major groups Sheehy borrowed from. Their studies were more careful, more systematic, and more scientific than *Passages*. They interviewed four groups of men between the ages of thirty-five and forty-five: ten were executives, ten were hourly workers in industry, ten were novelists, and ten were university biologists.

A life structure was developed for each man based on these interviews. Each life structure was an account of the major periods of the man's life as determined by his activities, his associations, and his relationships. A careful analysis of these life structures revealed a pattern that seemed to apply to almost all the men sampled.

The model of adult development for men that Levinson and his colleagues proposed is shown in Figure 9.10. The three major eras are early adulthood (from about age seventeen to about age forty), middle adulthood (forty to sixty), and late adulthood (beginning at about sixty). Between these eras are important transition periods lasting approximately five years. Levinson's research focused on the early adult era and the mid-life transition. The following discussion concentrates on what he learned about these stages.

Entering the adult world. From about age twenty-two to age twenty-eight, the young man is considered, both by himself and by society, to be a novice in the adult world—not fully established as a man, but no longer an adolescent. During this time he must attempt to resolve the conflict between the need to explore the options of the adult world and the need to establish a stable life structure. He needs to sample different kinds of relationships, to keep choices about career and employment open, to explore the nature of the world now accessible to him as an adult. But he also needs to begin a career and to establish a home and family of his own. The first life structure, then, may have a tentative quality. The young man may select a career or a job but not be committed to it. He may form romantic attachments and may even marry during this period; but the life structure of early adulthood often lacks a full sense of stability or permanence.

The age-thirty crisis. A few years ago the motto of the rebellious, politically oriented young people who sought to change American society was "Never trust anyone over thirty." Levinson's data reveal that the years between twenty-eight and thirty-three are indeed often a major transition

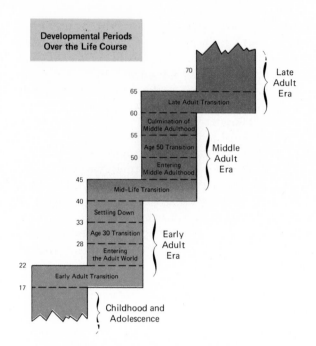

**Developmental Periods
Over the Life Course**

70

65 — Late Adult Transition

60

Culmination of
Middle Adulthood

55

Age 50 Transition

50

Entering
Middle Adulthood

45

Mid-Life Transition

40

Settling Down

33

Age 30 Transition

28

Entering
the Adult World

22

Early Adult Transition

17

Late
Adult
Era

Middle
Adult
Era

Early
Adult
Era

Childhood and
Adolescence

Figure 9.10
A model of the developmental sequence of a man's life proposed by Levinson. The scheme emphasizes that development is an ongoing process that requires continual adjustment.

period. The thirtieth birthday can truly be a turning point; for most men in Levinson's sample, it could be called "the age-thirty crisis." During this transitional period the tentative commitments that were made in the first life structure are reexamined, and many questions about the choices of marriage partner, career, and life goals are reopened, often in a painful way. The man feels that any parts of his life that are unsatisfying or incomplete must be attended to now, because it will soon be too late to make major changes.

Settling down. The questioning and searching that are part of the age-thirty crisis begin to be resolved as the second adult life structure develops. Having probably made some firm choices about his career, family, and relationships, the man now begins actively carving out a niche in society, concentrating on what Levinson calls "making it" in the adult world. The man attempts to move up the ladder of prestige and achievement in his chosen career or profession and to be a full-fledged member of adult society.

Levinson found that near the end of the settling-down period, approximately between the ages of thirty-six and forty, there is a distinctive phase that he has labeled "becoming one's own man." Whereas earlier the young man had looked to an older, more experienced man as a mentor, someone who would share his experience and wisdom, the relationship with the mentor is often fundamentally changed, or even broken off, in the process of becoming one's own man. Now it is time to become fully independent. During this period the man strives to attain the seniority and position in the world that he identified as his ultimate goal at the beginning of the settling-down period.

The mid-life transition. At about age forty the period of early adulthood comes to an end and the mid-life transition begins. From about age forty to age forty-five, the man begins again to ask questions, but now the questions concern the past as well as the future. He may ask: "What have I done with my life?" "What have I accomplished?" "What do I still wish to accomplish?" At age thirty the man had primarily looked ahead toward goals, but at the mid-life transition he is in a position to assess his accomplishments and to determine whether or not they have been satisfying. During this transition he begins to develop yet another life structure that will predominate during the period of middle adulthood.

The mid-life transition has been the most discussed aspect of Levinson's work. About 80 percent of the men in his sample experienced the mid-life transition as a moderate to severe crisis, characterized by the questioning of virtually every aspect of their lives. But it is a period of questioning from which a new life structure must emerge. Often a successful mid-life transition is accompanied by the man's becoming a mentor for a younger man. This event signals the attainment, in Erikson's terms, of generativity rather than stagnation.

Female Development. When he described the nature of his study, Levinson (Levinson *et al.*, 1978: 9) wrote: "Despite my strong desire to include women, I finally decided against it. A study of twenty men and twenty women would do justice to neither group." There are several systematic studies of female life cycles now underway, but, for the moment, less is known about women than men.

Career versus family. Until recently, both men and women in industrial societies felt that women had to make an either-or choice between home and career. However, as Gail Sheehy has pointed out in *Passages*, there are all kinds of options in between, and the decision can be renegotiated again and again. A woman may, for example, "piggyback" her career ambitions by opting at a young age for marriage and children with a man whose career she will enjoy vicariously. Ten years later, with her children no longer demanding so much of her time and attention, she may go back to school or begin her own career. Conversely, the woman who opts for a career may put off marriage and children until her mid-thirties, and only then begin to emphasize the nurturing side of her personality.

Physical attractiveness in mid-life. The selection of a partner for courtship and marriage depends to a great extent on physical attractiveness, which is also an important variable in many other aspects of social interaction. As a woman comes to be considered less attractive with age, she may need to adjust to a different image of herself. It has been shown that physical attractiveness, which eased social adjustment for college women, actually made adjustment more difficult for them twenty years later (David Campbell, as reported in Berscheid and Walster, 1974: 200–201). Perhaps the contrast between their socially active college years and the unexciting routine of family life results in more dissatisfaction than is experienced by their less attractive schoolmates, who were not "spoiled" by previous pleasures nor misled by great expectations.

The "empty nest" syndrome. For the woman who has chosen primarily a family orientation, a crisis occurs as her children grow up and leave home. She finds that her role as mother has diminished. She thinks, "Nobody

Figure 9.11
Many women experience what is called the "empty nest" syndrome when grown children leave home and the twenty-four-hour-a-day job in which they have been absorbed for probably two decades is suddenly over. Some women find new careers; others return to those they gave up when the children were born. For all, however, this is a period of stress and readjustment.

needs me any more." When coupled with the physical changes associated with menopause, the psychological effects of the "empty nest" syndrome are often experienced as intense depression. In order to adjust to the changes in herself and her family, the woman in mid-life may search for satisfying work outside the home, possibly returning to an interrupted career or starting a new one. A warm relationship with her husband can provide important support as the woman adjusts to her changing situation.

More research is needed in this area so that we will better understand how American women develop in middle age. Our current knowledge of the psychology of old age is even more limited.

OLD AGE

According to Erikson, old age and the prospect of dying lead some people either to a heightened sense of ego integrity or to despair. By ego integrity, Erikson means greater self-acceptance. Looking back, the elderly person concludes that if he had his life to live over, he'd like it as it was—with all the bumps, false starts, and disappointments as well as the joys and triumphs. By despair, Erikson means the inability to accept oneself and one's life. Looking back, the old person may see little but lost chances, bad decisions, people who spoiled his plans.

American culture makes it difficult for an old person to maintain a sense of integrity. In other societies (most notably in the Orient), old age is considered an achievement and old people are revered. In contrast, we tend to fear growing old and to be somewhat patronizing toward the elderly.

A number of stereotypes support these attitudes. First, we assume—wrongly—that a person's mind deteriorates as he or she grows old. Loss of memory and senility are not inevitable side effects of aging; they are symptoms of disorders. Second, we tend to believe that old people resist change. In fact, people who have always enjoyed challenges may become increasingly imaginative and flexible in their old age. The people who fight change in their seventies usually fought change in their thirties and forties. Finally, we tend to regard old people as useless. But one-third of this country's senior citizens work at least part time and take an active role in civic affairs (Butler and Lewis, 1973). And others could also work or contribute if there were more opportunities.

Adjusting to Old Age

The elderly face a number of special problems that may be difficult for younger people to understand. The first is often retirement. Whether they want to or not, many workers are forced to retire at age sixty-five. This means loss of an occupational identity, perhaps too much time on one's hands, and often feelings of uselessness. Second is the loss of loved ones. The older a person gets, the more of his friends and relatives die. This

Here are some excerpts from autibiographical essays written by a 44 year old man and a 48 year old woman. They illustrate some of the life cycle changes described above, and also suggest some of the traditional differences between options open to men and women.

A MAN AT MID-LIFE

After I graduated from law school I took the bar examination [and] . . . flunked . . . [and] learned a pretty good lesson regarding ego. Defeats and losses have never had as great an impact upon me.

While studying for the bar for the second round, I obtained employment with an attorney . . . and I spent one of the most fascinating years of my life doing really what amounted to political work, rather than legal work, in helping to prepare defense and testimony for the Committee [for lawyers who had been subpoenaed by the House Committee on Un-American Activities]. . . .

[Shortly afterward] I went into the general practice of law where I struggled for five years building a practice completely on my own . . . but I received no satisfaction from the practice or from the struggle to establish one. I knew few lawyers who would undertake a civil rights case, and I felt that this was what I wanted to do as well as establish my-

self economically. So I formed a partnership with . . . [another lawyer] who felt exactly the same as I. . . . We did build a successful general practice with heavy emphasis on free work and civil liberties.

For the first few years each of us . . . received a great deal of satisfaction what we felt we were accomplishing for ourselves [and] for our community. . . . [But] I slowly began to develop more of a practice in representing injured persons in personal injury cases, and my income increased [and] so did my guilt. . . . [Now] I no longer have any feelings of guilt about the type of legal practice in which I am engaged, but neither do I receive any satisfaction from my work as I did in the earlier years, even though then I had economic problems which I no longer face.

. . . Concerning beliefs and values, . . . I no longer feel I am the idealist I was some twenty years ago. . . . Whereas in the past I would have been the writer of a petition, or the petition circulator, I now might be the petition signer. . . .

My personal life has not been such as I would have anticipated when I was a student. I married shortly after graduation from law school, and can't even now explain why I did. . . . The hardest decision of my life was to leave [my wife], in view of the fact that we had three children . . . [but] I remarried shortly after my divorce and am very happily married now. . . .

. . . I would advise any young man today to do what he feels he wants to do and to make his own

Figure 9.12
(Above) The life cycle: case studies.

Figure 9.13
Many of our society's stereotyped attitudes about the elderly are not valid. Old people do not always become senile; they are not necessarily resistant to change; and they are not useless.

decisions in that regard. . . . It took me quite a while to see the wisdom [of this].

From: Robert W. White, Margaret M. Riggs, and Doris C. Gilbert. *Case Workbook in Personality.* New York: Holt, Rinehart and Winston, 1976. Abridged from pages 56–60.

A WOMAN AT MID-LIFE

20s

I worked for eight years before I married [mostly] in an advertising agency. I liked the field, but my job was menial and not satisfying in any way. . . . I couldn't break out of the secretarial mold. . . . I was confident that if someone could pick me up and put me in an important position I could do it, but I just couldn't seem to get there on my own.

About the age of 27 I began to get depressed—when I would visit married friends with children I would come away with the keen realization that I was not the center of anyone's life—that I was not important to anyone or ones. . . .

About this time I met my husband, Don. . . . We became engaged in three weeks and married within three months. [We] share the same attitudes, interests and intensity of feeling toward these attitudes. . . . Our first marital years were stormy—problems from without and those of our own making . . .

30s

We had three children in the first five years. . . . I guess life would have gone along as usual . . . if something tragic had not occurred to make us stop and think. Our oldest child, Paul, died suddenly at the age of seven. . . . We went through a period of grieving. [It] was the beginning of a turning point in our marital relationship, parental handling of children, outlook and actions as human beings as part of a larger society.

. . . My religious beliefs were challenged. . . . My whole faith began to shatter [but it] was slowly rebuilt, and this time had new strength because I was more mature. . . .

40s

I always knew I would go back to work. . . . I made up my mind that I would do something that was interesting. . . . I realized I would need further education. [I enrolled in] a program in community psychology. This seemed to be the direction I should go in because of my desire to work in the field of social action. I enjoyed being back in the academic atmosphere. . . . I landed a good [job]. I am project director of a senior citizens' volunteer program, and I enjoy this very much. . . .

I believe that I have more confidence in myself now [at 48]. . . . I am much crankier and more argumentative . . . [but] I think I am a happier person now than I was in college.

From: Robert W. White, Margaret M. Riggs, and Doris C. Gilbert. *Case Workbook in Personality.* New York: Holt, Rinehart and Winston, 1976, pp. 90–103.

happens at a time when it is becoming increasingly difficult to get around, visit distant friends, and meet new people. Losing a spouse may be devastating, particularly for those who do not live near other members of their family. Finally, there is the fear of becoming sick, disabled, and physically and financially dependent on others. Maintaining a sense of pride and dignity when one can no longer care for oneself requires a good deal of inner strength.

What are the solutions to these problems? Some psychologists believe that aging is easier if a person gradually and voluntarily disengages himself from such social roles as worker or head of household. Forced disengagement (being told you can no longer participate) or forced engagement (being expected to do things you do not feel capable of performing) can be damaging. According to this view, elderly people want to slow down, withdraw, spend time thinking about themselves and reminiscing. Other psychologists believe that aging is easier if people remain active, get out, find

Are Old People Lonely?

Perhaps more than any other group, old people seem lonely. As their family and friends die off and as their health fails, old people appear to be isolated by their own old age.

That's the myth. Now here's what studies on loneliness tell us about old age. On the average, old people are less lonely than young adults. They are more satisfied with the friends they have, and feel better about themselves and more independent than younger people. They even complain less about such physical and psychological symptoms as headache, depression, and irritability. All this is true in spite of the fact that old people are more likely to live alone than younger people and less likely to see their friends and family on a regular basis.

Old people have once again taught us an invaluable lesson. Living alone is not the reason for our loneliness. Our perception of loneliness—our feelings of being alone—are far more devastating than our physical circumstances.

For more details, see Carin Rubenstein, Philip Shaver, and Letitia Ann Peplau, "Loneliness," *Human Nature,* February 1979.

substitutes for social roles they have given up and loved ones they have lost (see Havighurst, 1972).

Which course a person chooses reflects his or her earlier life. People who always led active lives adapt more easily to old age if they remain as active as they can. People who were always somewhat withdrawn and introspective adapt best to aging through disengagement.

Dying

Elisabeth Kübler-Ross's work (1969) has become a classic in the relatively new field of **thanatology**—the study of death and dying. Kübler-Ross has identified five stages of psychological adjustment to terminal illness, based on interviews with over two hundred patients. The first stage is *denial.* The most common response is "It can't happen to me; there must be a mistake." The second stage is *anger:* "Why me?" The dying person may resent and become hostile toward the people he will leave behind and toward all healthy people. He attempts to *bargain* (perhaps with God) for more time. The next stage is a growing sense of loss, or *depression.* Kübler-Ross suggests that it helps a dying person if loved ones allow him to express his sadness and do not attempt to cover the situation up or force him (by their own denial) to act cheerful. Near the end, when the person is tired and weak, he *accepts* the inevitable. It is almost as if the dying person had said his good-byes, made his peace with himself, and is resting before the final journey.

USING PSYCHOLOGY

Hospices

Death is one of the few taboos left in twentieth-century America. The breakdown of extended families and the rise of modern medicine have insulated most people in our society from death. Many people have no direct experience with death, and, partly as a result, they are afraid to talk about it. In 1900, two-thirds of those who died in the United States were under fifty, and most of them died at home in their own beds. Today, most Americans live until at least sixty-five, and they die in nursing homes and hospitals. Elaborate machines may prolong existence long after a person has stopped living a normal life.

Figure 9.14
Patients at St. Christopher's Hospice in England.

A new movement to restore the dignity of dying revolves around the concept of the hospice—usually a special place where terminally ill people go to die. Doctors in hospices do not try to prolong life, but rather to relieve pain and provide contact with loved ones during the last days of life. The first and most famous facility of this sort was St. Christopher's Hospice in London, England. The 600 patients who died there in 1977 stayed an average of twelve days. The vast majority were cancer patients since hospice care is particularly suited to this disease. The patient in a hospice leads the most normal life he or she is able to, and is taken care of as much as possible by members of his or her own family. If it can be arranged, a patient may choose to die in his or her own home.

The first United States facility devoted exclusively to the care of the dying, Hillman Hospice in Tucson, Arizona, was opened a few years ago. Other hospices are being organized in hospitals and nursing homes. According to one recent count, there are now hospice societies in thirty-three of the fifty states. The success of this movement may signal a change in the American attitude toward death.

SUMMARY

1. Adolescence is the transition period between childhood and adulthood during which people reach the final stage of psychosexual development.

2. Adolescents have a strong need to be accepted by their peers and tend to conform to ideals of how males and females their age should look, act, and dress.

3. One of the principal developmental tasks for adolescents is becoming independent of their families. The way in which an adolescent seeks independence and the ease with which he or she resolves conflicts about becoming a full-fledged adult depend in large part on the parent-child relationship.

4. In adolescence the thinking patterns of adulthood emerge. The main difference between the way adolescents and adults think is that young people are highly idealistic and tend to be unrealistic about the complexities of life.

5. A major developmental task in adolescence is building an identity. This involves looking both inward and outward to discover who one truly is. A significant part of a person's self-identification and self-knowledge is his or her sexual identity. Society is undergoing major changes in its definition of the roles the sexes should play and in the attitudes it holds toward sexual behavior.

6. The popular picture of dramatic physical changes at menopause and decreasing sexual desire in middle age is greatly exaggerated. Intellectual ability also remains fairly constant throughout middle age.

7. According to Erikson, young adults must resolve questions of intimacy versus isolation, while the middle-age crisis concerns generativity versus stagnation.

8. Daniel Levinson has described several stages in the lives of adult males: entering the adult world (ages twenty-two to twenty-eight), the age-thirty crisis, settling down (mid-thirties to forty), and the mid-life transition (ages forty to forty-five). Comparable studies of female development have not yet been completed.

9. Old age and the imminent prospect of dying lead some people to a heightened sense of integrity, others to despair. American culture makes it difficult for an old person to maintain a sense of integrity.

GLOSSARY

adolescence: The developmental stage between childhood and adulthood during which sexual maturation begins, identity is shaped, and life goals are considered.

androgyny: A flexible combination of male and female personality traits.

authoritarian family: A family in which parents are the "bosses" and do not feel they have to explain their actions or demands to their children.

clique: A group within a set or crowd.

conformity: Compliance to group standards.

continuity: A person's sense of the constancy of his or her identity throughout life.

democratic family: A family in which the adolescent participates in decisions affecting his or her life. Parents maintain the ultimate right to veto plans of which they disapprove.

generativity: The desire, in middle age, to use one's accumulated wisdom to guide future generations.

identity crisis: The period in a person's life during which he or she seeks confirmation of self by selecting, among many and often conflicting possibilities, the direction and goals of his or her life.

laissez-faire family: A permissive family in which the children have the final say in decisions concerning themselves.

menarche: The onset of menstruation, considered in most societies to be the beginning of womanhood.

menopause: The period, occurring at approximately forty to fifty years of age, when a woman ceases to ovulate, menstruate, and produce sex hormones.

permissive family: A family in which the children have the final say in decisions concerning themselves; sometimes termed *laissez-faire*.

psychological moratorium: A period during which young people can explore and experiment without having to commit themselves to a life style, career, or mate, or suffer the consequences of mistakes.

puberty: Sexual maturation; the biological event that marks the end of childhood.

rationalization: A process whereby an individual seeks to explain an often unpleasant emotion or behavior in a way that will preserve his or her self-esteem.

self-sameness: An individual's sense of knowing how he or she feels about different issues, situations, and people, and that these opinions make sense.

stagnation: A discontinuation of development and desire to recapture the past, characteristic of some middle-aged people.

thanatology: The study of death and dying.

totalism: Complete immersion in a group or movement.

ACTIVITIES

1. The notion of establishing an identity, though discussed at length in the popular press as well as in psychological literature, remains difficult to pin down in concrete terms. Try to write one or two paragraphs describing your own identity. From these descriptions compare the dimensions which you and your classmates focused on in your written descriptions.

2. Ask your parents how they think they've changed since their youth. Do they perceive their basic personalities as remaining relatively stable or going through marked changes? What are the major factors they think had the most significant effects on their personality development?

3. What provisions does your community make for its retired and elderly adults? How do you think these services could be improved to make the experience of old age a more fruitful and happier time?

4. Do some reading on how the transition from childhood to adulthood was made in a past period of history and in other cultures. Compare the concerns of today's youth with those of yesteryear and in other cultures.

5. Death and dying have only recently become topics that are discussed openly. Given this growing openness, what changes do you see being made to make the adjustment to the prospect of dying less severe? How do you think hospitals and homes for the aged might change in the future along these lines?

6. Try to imagine that you have teen-age children of your own. Your sixteen-year-old daughter demands more freedom and wants to borrow the family helicopter. How do you respond?

7. List several controversial questions, such as, "Do you believe in fighting for your country no matter what the circumstances?" Ask people of different age groups to respond to your questions. Do you notice differences in the levels of reasoning? Use the explanations contained in this chapter to account for the differences.

SUGGESTED READINGS

BEM, SANDRA L. "Androgyny vs. the Little Lives of Fluffy Women and Chesty Men." *Psychology Today*, 8 (September 1975): 59–62. Bem argues, with supporting data, that the most flexible and adaptable male or female is one who possesses both the qualities traditionally associated with men and the qualities traditionally associated with women.

CHOWN, SHEILA M. *Human Aging*. Baltimore: Penguin, 1972. A comprehensive collection of readings on various aspects of aging, including intellectual performance, learning and memory, adaptation to stress, and general personality development during old age.

CONGER, JOHN J. *Adolescence and Youth*. New York: Harper & Row, 1973. An excellent overview of physical, personality, and intellectual development during adolescence. Also includes such topics as alienation and commitment, dropping out and delinquency, sexual attitudes and drug use.

EVANS, R. I. *Dialogue with Erik Erikson*. New York: Dutton, 1967 (paper). A long interview with Erikson, in which he discusses his eight stages of psychosocial development and problems young people have in finding their identity, a satisfying life career, and an intimate relationship with another person.

FRIEDENBERG, EDGAR Z. *The Vanishing Adolescent*. Boston: Beacon, 1959. One of the best-known authorities on adolescence presents his views in an exciting and highly readable fashion. Friedenberg stresses the importance of adolescent conflict as a means of establishing a relationship between the individual and the society.

GORDON, SOL. *Facts About Sex—A Basic Guide*. New York: Day, 1970. The author describes this book as "simple and brief—especially useful if you don't like to read too much and welcome lots of pictures."

KIMMEL, DOUGLAS C. *Adulthood and Aging*. New York: Wiley, 1974. Provides an excellent and highly readable summary of psychological and sociological research and theory on the developmental changes and tasks during adulthood and old age. Includes such topics as identity and intimacy, families and singles, work and retirement, and the physical changes that occur during these years.

KÜBLER-ROSS, ELISABETH. *On Death and Dying*. New York: Macmillan, 1969 (paper). As we read a number of very moving interviews with patients who are terminally ill, the author allows us to share their private pain and final dignity. We see the stages they pass through: from denial, anger, bargaining, and depression to eventual acceptance.

LEVINSON, DANIEL J., ET AL. *The Seasons of a Man's Life*. New York: Knopf, 1978. This is the long-awaited report of Levinson's research on stages of development in adult males. On the basis of intensive interviews with forty men from four different occupational groups, Levinson proposes a model of the stages, crises, and transitions experienced by most men.

SHEEHY, GAIL. *Passages*. New York: Dutton, 1976. A popular account of predictable crises of adulthood. Sheehy is not the systematic theorist that Levinson (above) is, but she has a rich data base in the interviews she personally conducted, and she deals with the life crises of women as well as of men.

BIBLIOGRAPHY

BALTES, P. B., AND SCHAIE, K. W. "Aging and IQ: The Myth of the Twilight Years." *Psychology Today,* 7 (March 1974): 35–40.

BEM, SANDRA. "Androgyny vs. the Little Lives of Fluffy Women and Chesty Men." *Psychology Today,* 8 (September 1975): 59–62.

BERSCHEID, ELLEN, AND WALSTER, ELAINE. "Physical Attractiveness." In *Advances in Experimental Social Psychology,* ed. by Leonard Berkowitz. New York: Academic Press, 1974.

BISCHOF, L. *Adult Psychology.* New York: Harper & Row, 1969.

BUTLER, R. N., AND LEWIS, M. I. *Aging and Mental Health.* St. Louis: Mosby, 1973.

COLEMAN, J. S. *The Adolescent Society.* New York: Free Press, 1961.

CONGER, J. J. *Adolescence and Youth: Psychological Development in a Changing World.* New York: Harper & Row, 1973.

DENNIS, W. "Creative Productivity Between the Ages of Twenty and Eighty Years." *Journal of Gerontology,* 21 (1966): 1–8.

DWYER, JOHANNA, AND MAYER, JEAN. "Psychological Effects of Variations in Physical Appearance During Adolescence." *Adolescence* (1968–1969): 353–368.

ERIKSON, ERIK. *Childhood and Society.* New York: Norton, 1950.

———. *Identity: Youth and Crisis.* New York: Norton, 1968.

HALL, G. STANLEY. "The Moral and Religious Training of Children." *Princeton Review* (January 1882): 26–48.

HAVIGHURST, R. J. *Developmental Tasks and Education.* 3rd ed. New York: McKay, 1972.

INHELDER, B., AND PIAGET, J. *The Early Growth of Logic in the Child.* New York: Harper & Row, 1964.

KIMMEL, DOUGLAS C. *Adulthood and Aging.* New York: Wiley, 1974.

KINSEY, ALFRED C., ET AL. *Sexual Behavior in the Human Female.* Philadelphia: Saunders, 1953.

KINSEY, ALFRED C., POMEROY, W. B., AND MARTIN, C. E. *Sexual Behavior in the Human Male.* Philadelphia: Saunders, 1948.

KÜBLER-ROSS, ELISABETH. *On Death and Dying.* New York: Macmillan, 1969.

LEVINSON, DANIEL J., ET AL. *The Seasons of a Man's Life.* New York: Knopf, 1978.

———. "Living with Dying." *Newsweek* (May 1, 1978): 52–61.

MASTERS, WILLIAM H., AND JOHNSON, VIRGINIA E. *Human Sexual Inadequacy.* Boston: Little, Brown, 1970.

MEAD, MARGARET. *Coming of Age in Samoa.* New York: Morrow, 1961.

MUSSEN, PAUL H., CONGER, JOHN J., AND KAGAN, JEROME. *Child Development and Personality.* 4th ed. New York: Harper & Row, 1974.

NEUGARTEN, BERNICE, ET AL. "Women's Attitudes Towards the Menopause." *Vita Humana,* 6 (1963): 140–151.

NEWMAN, G., AND NICHOLS, C. R. "Sexual Activities and Attitudes in Older Persons." *Journal of the American Medical Association,* 173 (1960): 33–35.

POCS, OLLIE, ET AL. "Is There Sex After 40?" *Psychology Today,* 10 (June 1977): 54–57.

RUBIN, I. "Sex over 65." In *Advances in Sex Research,* ed. by H. G. Beigel. New York: Harper & Row, 1963.

RUBIN, ZICK. "Measurement of Romantic Love." *Journal of Personality and Social Psychology,* 16 (1970): 265–273.

SHEEHY, GAIL. *Passages.* New York: Dutton, 1976.

SIMON, W., AND GAGNON, J. H. (EDS.). *The Sexual Scene.* Chicago: Transaction Books, 1970.

WHITE, ROBERT. *Lives in Progress: A Study of the Natural Growth of Personality.* 2nd ed. New York: Holt, Rinehart & Winston, 1966.

WHITE, ROBERT W., RIGGS, MARGARET M., AND GILBERT, DORIS C. *Case Workbook in Personality.* New York: Holt Rinehart & Winston, 1976.

WILL, GEORGE F. "A Good Death." *Newsweek* (January 9, 1978): 72.

10 Adjustment in Contemporary Society

The McCaslins and their five children live in a rural area of eastern Kentucky. The father is a tall, gangly man who broke his back several years ago while working in a local coal mine. He is not able to perform any kind of physical labor and has been unable to find any other kind of work. The coal company refused to give him a disability pension, and, probably because he is living at home, his family has been denied welfare. Consequently, the family is forced to survive on garden vegetables and what little food they can buy with some assistance from relatives.

In spite of this hard, meager existence, they all work at maintaining a close, loving relationship with each other. The father has strong ideas, talks a lot, and involves himself with his wife and children. The parents do not touch each other very much in front of strangers or their children, but "they give each other long looks of recognition, sympathy, affection, and sometimes anger or worse. They understand each other in that silent, real, lasting way that defies . . . labels," writes psychiatrist Robert Coles (1971).

Psychologists who study **adjustment** attempt to understand how people deal with extreme hardship, as well as how they cope with the more ordinary yet stressful experiences of life, such as college, marriage, divorce, and work. Adjusting to each of these experiences involves unique challenges and difficulties.

We shall begin this chapter by discussing a key issue in any process of adjustment: stress and its effects. Then, we shall look at some of the situations most people experience during their lives and how they adjust to them. By **adjustment,** psychologists mean adapting to as well as actively shaping one's environment. When a psychologist says that a person is well adjusted, she does *not* mean that the individual has managed to avoid problems and conflicts. She means that the person has learned to cope

Figure 10.1
Adjustment is adapting to as well as actively shaping one's environment. It is coping with the ordinary experiences and stresses of life as well as with the moments of extreme hardship.

with frustration, disappointment, and loss, and is making the most of himself and his opportunities. In Chapter 15, we suggest why individuals may become unable to cope with everyday life and, in Chapter 16, how psychotherapists can help them.

STRESS

Emotion—love, anger, joy, frustration—gives texture and meaning to our lives. But severe or prolonged stress can take a harsh toll on the body. And stress is everywhere; it cannot be avoided. Stress is not always undesirable; it can represent the body's response to pleasure as well as to pain. As Hans Selye, the dean of stress researchers, puts it:

> Stress is the body's nonspecific response to *any* demand placed on it, whether that demand is pleasant or not. Sitting in a dentist's chair is stressful, but so is enjoying a passionate kiss with a lover—after all, your pulse races, your breathing quickens, your heart beat soars. And yet who in the world would forego such a pleasurable pastime simply because of the stress involved? Our aim shouldn't be to completely avoid stress, which at any rate would be impossible, but to learn how to recognize our typical response to stress and then to try to modulate our lives in accordance with it (Selye and Cherry, 1978: 60).

As we shall see below, the stresses we long for and the stresses we dread may be equally hard on us: on one scale of common stressful life events that may contribute to disease (the Holmes-Rahe Social Readjustment Rating Scale, Table 10.1), a sexual problem and a big increase in salary have been found to produce almost equal amounts of stress.

Of course, people in similar situations experience different amounts of stress. Giving a public lecture may be a terror to a student, a tonic to a politician, a bore to an ambassador. But under any kind of stress, emotional or physical, all bodies react in the same, predictable manner. These physiological responses are known as the "stress syndrome," the body's response to viruses, starvation, frostbite, and other attacks.

Responses to Stress: Selye's Three Stages

According to Selye (1956), the body reacts to stress in three stages: alarm, resistance, and exhaustion. Whether the stress is the result of prolonged fear or exposure to extreme cold, the body reacts with immediate sympathetic arousal (speeding of the heart and so forth). The endocrine system then acts to sustain this state of arousal. The pituitary gland stimulates the part of the adrenal glands that produces hormones that increase blood sugar, for extra energy. At the same time, the brain sends signals to another part of the adrenal glands that secretes adrenalin. Adrenalin not only causes rapid heart action and breathing, it enables the body to use energy at a faster rate. All of this is designed to prepare a person for self-defense.

However, if stress persists for a long time, the body's resources are used up. The person becomes exhausted and, in extreme cases, dies.

The way that people react to emergencies and disasters can be seen in terms of the same three stages (Selye, 1969). When tragedy hits, people mobilize for "fight or flight." They become exceptionally alert and sensitive to stimuli in the environment. They try to keep a firm grip on their emotions. Selye calls this the alarm stage. An example would be people running from an explosion. They don't think about where they are running to—they just run.

In the second stage, which Selye calls resistance, people intensify their efforts. They deny that the situation is hopeless, much as a dying person at first refuses to accept his condition. Thus people caught in a fire will crowd toward the nearest exit, however narrow. They are in too much of a panic to consider alternatives.

In the third stage, people become exhausted and disoriented. The classic example of this is a mother sitting in the ruins of a bombed-out house rocking a dead or wounded baby as if nothing had happened. But her eyes are glazed. Soldiers have been known to wander about aimlessly or even fall asleep under fire (Toffler, 1970: 344–346). Selye suggests this is because it is easier for the person to give up than to face the situation and look for solutions. An individual may withdraw completely or experience delusions. A period of prolonged stress due to internal or familial conflicts may have the same effects as a sudden disaster. All efforts to adjust fail, and the individual reaches his or her breaking point.

Most people recover their equilibrium and "come back" to reality. This may take time. Studies indicate that people who lose their sight or a limb, their home or their spouse, go through a period of depression and self-pity best described as mourning. But eventually they face their situation, salvage what they can from the past, and begin to restructure their lives (Cholden, 1954; Parkes, 1972).

Stress and Disease

Some people thrive on stress, working hard and racing the clock happily enough. But in most cases, prolonged stress may contribute to disease. One estimate (Schmale, 1972) holds that as much as 80 percent of all disease today may have its origin in stress.

Emotional stress is very clearly related to such illnesses as peptic ulcers, hypertension, certain kinds of arthritis, asthma, and heart disease. Those who work in high-stress occupations may pay a high price. Air-traffic controllers, for example, who spend their days juggling the lives of hundreds of people on air routes where a minor error can mean mass death, are said to suffer from the highest incidence of peptic ulcers of any professional group (Cobb and Rose, 1973).

Recent research suggests that emotional factors are implicated in the onset of many, and conceivably of *all*, diseases, including diabetes and cancer. We are all familiar with the idea of psychosomatic disease, the notion that mind and body are so intimately connected that the body can

a

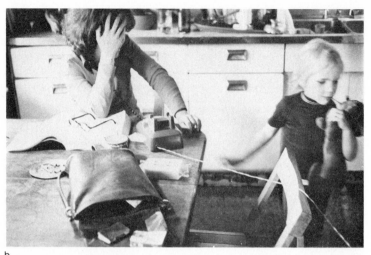

b

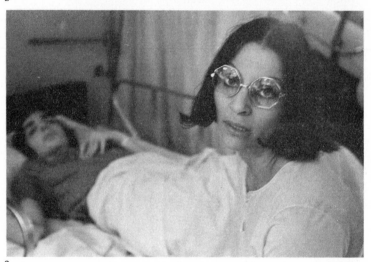

c

Figure 10. 2
Our reactions to the events of life
depend on our own personalities
and attitudes as well as on the severity of the event itself. The student waiting to find out whether or
not he has made it into college (a),
the harried young mother (b), the
woman coping with the illness of a
loved one (c), and the man deso-
lated by the loss of his home (d)
are all experiencing various levels
and degrees of stress.

d

Table 10.1 / Social Readjustment Rating Scale

Rank	Life Event	Mean Value
1	Death of spouse	100
2	Divorce	73
3	Marital separation	65
4	Jail term	63
5	Death of close family member	63
6	Personal injury or illness	53
7	Marriage	50
8	Fired at work	47
9	Marital reconciliation	45
10	Retirement	45
11	Change in health of family member	44
12	Pregnancy	40
13	Sex difficulties	39
14	Gain of new family member	39
15	Business readjustment	39
16	Change in financial state	38
17	Death of close friend	37
18	Change to different line of work	36
19	Change in number of arguments with spouse	35
20	Mortgage over $10,000	31
21	Foreclosure of mortgage or loan	30
22	Change in responsibilities at work	29
23	Son or daughter leaving home	29
24	Trouble with in-laws	29
25	Outstanding personal achievement	28
26	Wife begin or stop work	26
27	Begin or end school	26
28	Change in living conditions	25
29	Revision of personal habits	24
30	Trouble with boss	23
31	Change in work hours or conditions	20
32	Change in residence	20
33	Change in schools	20
34	Change in recreation	19
35	Change in church activities	19
36	Change in social activities	18
37	Mortgage or loan less than $10,000	17
38	Change in sleeping habits	16
39	Change in number of family get-togethers	15
40	Change in eating habits	15
41	Vacation	13
42	Christmas	12
43	Minor violations of the law	11

suffer from the mind's distress. A student may come down with flu on the day before an important exam, or a director may have an asthma attack on the opening night of a play.

Measuring Stress.   Thomas Holmes and Richard Rahe (1967) developed the Social Readjustment Rating Scale to measure the impact of many different sources of stress. Their results are shown in Table 10.1. Each person was asked to rate items on a list of life changes for impact and difficulty of adjusting. As you can see, respondents considered obvious success (outstanding personal achievement) almost as unsettling as financial problems (foreclosure of a mortgage or loan) and trouble with in-laws.

Holmes, Rahe, and other researchers went on to show that people who experienced a great deal of stress were far more likely to become physically ill than those who led more peaceful lives. Some of these correlations—like the one between stress and heart disease (Rahe and Lind, 1971)—were not particularly surprising. But others were. For example, one researcher found that people are more likely to break bones during stressful periods (Tollefson, 1972), and another found that children under stress are more likely to develop leukemia (Wold, 1968).

In some cases, severe stress may even lead to sudden death. Psychiatrist George Engel (1977) collected 275 cases of apparently healthy people who died within minutes or hours of some major event in their lives. For example, the fifty-one-year-old president of CBS died on his way to his father's funeral. A fifty-six-year-old woman, seeing the wreckage of her husband's truck, ran to the scene, collapsed, and died (her husband had escaped uninjured). An elderly man was accidentally locked in a public lavatory and died while struggling to get out. Even joy can be so intense as to be overwhelming: a seventy-five-year-old man collapsed at the race track as he was about to cash in his winning ticket for $1,683 on a $2 bet, and a fifty-six-year-old minister who had been "elated" to talk to President Carter on a radio phone-in show had a fatal heart attack soon after hanging up. Although it is difficult to prove that any of these events definitely caused death, Engel believes stress can be a major factor.

"Type A Behavior" and Heart Attacks.   In some cases, a man's personality may make him more vulnerable to stress. For example, two researchers have recently suggested that persons who exhibit a behavior pattern they call "Type A" are very likely to have coronary artery disease, often followed by heart attacks, in their thirties and forties. Those who do not have this pattern (Type B people) almost never have heart attacks before the age of seventy (Friedman and Rosenman, 1974).

The Type A person's body is in a chronic state of stress, with an almost constant flow of adrenalin into the bloodstream. This adrenalin apparently interacts with cholesterol or other chemical agents to block the coronary arteries, which lead to the heart. (It may be that high levels of adrenalin prevent the normal chemical breakdown of cholesterol in the blood.)

Type A people are always prepared for fight or flight. They have a great deal of "free-floating" hostility—that is, anger that has no real object or focus. They are extremely irritable, and one of the things that irritates Type A people most is delay of any kind. They become impatient waiting in line,

Are You Type A?

Are you high strung, tense, always concerned about time? Then you might have a Type A personality. To find out for sure, ask yourself the following questions. Your answers will tell you whether you're giving your heart a hard time.

- Are you continually aware of time? Type A people live by the clock and measure their day in terms of how much they accomplish each minute.
- Are you always in a rush? Type A people do everything very quickly. They eat, move, walk, and talk at a speeded-up pace.
- Do you lose your patience when things take too long? Type A people get outraged when a salesclerk spends an extra minute ringing up a sale.
- Do you always try to do more than one thing at the same time? Type A people feel that one of the best ways to get more accomplished is to do two or more things at once.
- Do you tend to use nervous gestures to emphasize your point? Type A people express their tension by clenching their fists, pointing their fingers, and banging on the desk.
- Do you evaluate your life in terms of how much you accomplish rather than what you accomplish? Type A people emphasize such quantitative measures as the number of A's they got in school and the number of sales they made during the month.

If you answered yes to most of these questions, it may be time to slow down. Not because slower is better, but because slower is less taxing on your heart.

For more details, see Meyer Friedman and Ray Rosenman, *Type A Behavior and Your Heart.* New York: Knopf, 1974.

always move and eat rapidly, often try to do two or three things at once (such as reading while eating), and feel guilty when they aren't doing *something*. They are also extremely competitive. In short, Type A people are always struggling—with time, other people, or both. Note that we have been describing an extreme version of the Type A personality. Most people respond to the world with Type A behavior at some times, but are not in a constant state of stress. According to Friedman and Rosenman, about half of the American white male population exhibits enough Type A behavior to bring on the high adrenalin and cholesterol levels that precede coronary disease.

Ulcers and Executives.   In a classic experiment on stress, Joseph Brady (1958) linked two monkeys together so that they received an equal number of shocks. The only difference between them was that one of the monkeys could prevent the shocks by pushing a lever. The other monkey could not. One of the monkeys developed ulcers. Which was it? The one that was powerless to protect itself? No. It was the other monkey—later named the

Figure 10.3
The "executive monkey" experiment. The monkey at the left, which could prevent the shocks by pushing a lever, was the one that developed ulcers.

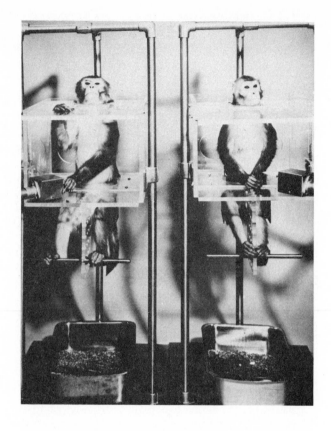

"executive monkey" (Figure 10.3). Brady concluded that constantly worrying about when to press the lever made this monkey sick.

More recent research suggests that people develop ulcers when they have to make a great many responses, but receive no feedback about whether their responses were correct or not (Weiss, 1971). Lack of feedback produces uncertainty, and uncertainty is stressful. According to this view, the "executive monkeys" developed ulcers because they were never sure whether pressing the lever would prevent the shock.

One might extend this reasoning to a group of people known for developing ulcers: human executives. Those who get ulcers may be men and women who never quite know where they stand with their superiors and those who have to wait years to see if the work they are doing is successful.

Stress is an unavoidable part of life. Physiological responses to stress can assist a person in coping with it. But the same responses can ultimately cause bodily harm if the stress continues for too long. Unfortunately, the precise nature of stress is still something of a mystery.

One person who is fired from a job may cheerfully set out to find another. A second person may regard being fired as an opportunity to take a long-postponed European vacation. A third person may begin to experience agonizing migraine headaches. Hans Selye (Selye and Cherry, 1978) now believes that some people thrive on stress. But although questionnaires like the Holmes and Rahe scale are very useful for studying how people in general react to stress, a tremendous amount will have to be learned before we can apply this knowledge to any specific individual.

Many potential problem areas can become sources of stress for the average person. We will begin our discussion of adjustment by considering how widely different people's sexual desires and activities may vary, and what types of problems may result. Then we will go on to discuss love and marriage, college, and work. Each may be tremendously rewarding, and each may sometimes become a source of stress.

SEXUALITY

One major issue that people have to deal with to adjust to society is sexuality. Much of what we now know about sexual behavior can be traced back to the work of one man: Alfred C. Kinsey.

Kinsey was an interesting candidate for his pioneering role in the history of sex studies. A biologist by training, he had spent twenty years collecting data on gall wasps when, in 1930, he was asked to teach a course on sex education at Indiana University. Unable to find reliable information on sexual behavior, Kinsey decided to collect data himself (Pomeroy, 1972). He and his associates spent the next eighteen years talking to people of different ages, backgrounds, and marital status about their sex lives. The results of interviews with 5,300 American men, *Sexual Behavior in the Human Male* (Kinsey, Pomeroy, and Martin, 1948), and with 5,940 women, *Sexual Behavior in the Human Female* (Kinsey *et al.*, 1953), made history—and headlines.

As a scientist, Kinsey's goal was to substitute facts for myths about the sexual behavior of Americans and to gather data on the population as a whole. His method was to collect sexual histories in detailed, confidential interviews, concentrating on Americans' "sexual outlets" (the number and kinds of sexual experiences they had).

Of course, many sex researchers have made important contributions since Kinsey began his surveys more than thirty-five years ago. Masters and Johnson's studies of the physiology of sexual response are particularly well known. But if you want to know "who does what with whom and how often," Kinsey's surveys are still the place to start.

Human sexual behavior is as varied as people are.

The most important conclusion of the Kinsey reports was that human sexual behavior is as varied as people themselves are. Just as some people exercise constantly and others rarely get out of bed, some people seem to have great sexual needs (which can be satisfied in many different ways) while others have more modest desires. Although it is not possible to describe what is "normal," it is possible to say what is "average." Our discussion below summarizes findings for some of the most common sexual activities.

The Varieties of Sexual Experience

Masturbation. Attitudes toward masturbation have changed in the last two decades. Forty or fifty years ago physicians regularly warned youngsters that self-stimulation (or "self-abuse," as masturbation was then called) would cause acne, fever, blindness, even insanity. Today most people with acne and fevers know that this is ridiculous. According to a survey of 2,026 Americans conducted by Morton Hunt in 1974, only about one in six people who are eighteen to thirty-four think that masturbation is wrong, although the figure for older adults (fifty-five and over) is one in three. Apparently the idea lingers that "playing with yourself" is immature behavior, symptomatic of personal inadequacies or of dissatisfaction with one's spouse as a sexual partner.

Nevertheless, surveys indicate that masturbation is common. Ninety-two percent of the men and 62 percent of the women in Kinsey's sample (Kinsey, Pomeroy, and Martin, 1948; Kinsey *et al.*, 1953) masturbated to orgasm at least once. Men reported that they began masturbating at age ten to twelve after reading or hearing about it. Rates of masturbation for the males in Kinsey's survey reached a peak of about twice a week around age twenty, then declined to about once every other week for unmarried men forty-five to fifty and once a month for married men. Most of the women who masturbated said that they discovered this outlet by accident, some as late as their thirties. Rates of masturbation for unmarried females varied from daily to yearly, for an average of once every two or three weeks. Married women masturbated about once a month.

Premarital Sex.   Traditionally, American women and, to a lesser degree, men were expected to "save themselves" for marriage. Intimate sexual activity was supposed to take place only between husband and wife. Do Americans still profess a belief in premarital chastity and postmarital fidelity? Do we practice what we preach? Did we ever?

In Kinsey's day, most Americans claimed that they strongly disapproved of premarital sex. Yet 98 percent of men who had grade-school educations, 85 percent of male high-school graduates, and 68 percent of men with college educations claimed to have had sexual intercourse before getting married. Nearly half the women in Kinsey's sample had also had some premarital sexual experience—a shocking revelation at the time. These women had not treated sex casually, however. Over half had had sex only with their future husbands.

The incidence of premarital sex for men appears to have increased somewhat, particularly among college men. By age seventeen, half the college men in the Hunt sample (1974) were no longer virgins, compared to 23 percent in Kinsey's sample (1948). The biggest change for college men may be in the women they choose as partners. In Kinsey's day most single young men who had sex had it with prostitutes or casual pickups. Today most college men have sex with women they care deeply for and with whom they have a continuing relationship (McCary, 1978: 273). Even so, men's attitudes have not changed as much as one might expect. According to one survey (Pietropinto and Simenauer, 1977), 33 percent of American men still want to marry virgins. Another 25 percent want to marry a woman who has had only one previous sexual partner.

The incidence of premarital sex for women has increased dramatically. Eighty-one percent of the women aged eighteen to twenty-four in the Hunt

Figure 10.4
Young men and women today have more premarital sexual experience than they did a generation ago, although underlying attitudes have not changed all that much: many men still want to marry a virgin or a woman with limited sexual experience, and most women are no more casual about sex than their mothers were.

sample had sexual intercourse before they got married—compared to only 31 percent of the women fifty-five and older. However, the majority of the women in the Hunt survey were no more casual about sex than their mothers had been. Over half had had sex with only one partner. In contrast, the median number of premarital sex partners for men was six.

It seems, then, that the double standard persists—one code of acceptable sexual behavior for men, another for women. Sixty percent of the men and 37 percent of the women in the Hunt sample thought it was all right for men to have sex with someone for whom they felt no strong affection; only 44 percent of the men and 20 percent of the women thought it was all right for women to do so. (Interestingly, the men in this survey granted women more sexual freedom than the women allowed themselves.)

Extramarital Sex. About half the husbands and a quarter of the wives in Kinsey's sample (Kinsey, Pomeroy, and Martin, 1948; Kinsey *et al.*, 1953) had had sexual intercourse with someone other than their spouse while they were married. To judge from the Hunt survey (1974), the percentage of married men who "play around" has not changed much since the 1940s, but the percentage of married women who do —especially young wives— has. Twenty-four percent of the wives under age twenty-five in the Hunt sample claimed to have had extramarital sexual experiences, compared to 8 percent in the Kinsey sample. But again, women are more conservative. Twice as many husbands as wives have had sex with six or more extramarital partners. According to the Hunt survey, it seems that men are more likely than women to seek extramarital sex for sex's sake, without emotional involvement. Women are less likely to separate sexual desire from affection: they tend to embark on affairs only when they are dissatisfied with their marriages (Tavris and Offir, 1977: 70).

Although the proportion of people having affairs is rising, attitudes toward extramarital sex have remained about the same: over 80 percent of the couples in the Hunt survey regarded it as wrong. Open marriages, in which both the man and the woman agree that both will have sex outside the marriage, seem to be rare. Only 4 percent of the men in one survey said that they had had extramarital relations with the knowledge and consent of their wives (Pietropinto and Simenauer, 1977). Thus, most extramarital sex takes the form of "cheating" on one's partner.

Homosexuality. Who is a homosexual? Any person who has ever had *any* sexual contact with a member of the same sex? People who have sex *only* with members of the same sex? What about a man who usually has homosexual lovers but occasionally has sex with a woman? What about a woman who usually has male lovers but occasionally has sex with other women? The tendency in the United States has been to label anyone who has had any homosexual experience, however infrequent, a homosexual.

People who are exclusively homosexual consider themselves, and are considered by others, to be "true" homosexuals. There is considerable variation in how people who have some degree of interest in both sexes classify themselves and in how they are viewed by others. As a rule, however, psychologists consider a homosexual to be a person whose primary source of sexual gratification is members of the same sex.

In line with this definition, Kinsey created for his survey a seven-point scale of sexual behavior. At one extreme (category 0) were people who were exclusively heterosexual; at the other (category 6) were people who were exclusively homosexual. Individuals who were predominantly heterosexual or homosexual but had a passing interest in the other sex were assigned to categories 2 and 4, respectively. Category 3 was for bisexuals, who had about equal interest in members of their own and the opposite sex. In this way Kinsey deliberately avoided classifying all people as *either* completely homosexual or completely heterosexual, but instead represented the range of sexual preferences as a continuum.

According to Kinsey, 37 percent of the men he surveyed and 13 percent of the women had at least one homosexual orgasm by age forty-five. Today's best estimates (Katchadourian and Lunde, 1975) suggest that about 2 percent to 4 percent of all males and ½ percent to 1 percent of all females are exclusively homosexual.

In 1973, the American Psychiatric Association reversed the position it had held for nearly a century and declared that homosexuality itself is not a mental disorder. People who are troubled by their attraction for the same sex are said to suffer from a "sexual orientation disturbance"; those who are content are considered normal.

The best study to date of homosexual life styles was conducted by members of Kinsey's Institute for Sex Research. Alan Bell and Martin

Homosexuality

Sex therapists William Masters and Virginia Johnson, known for their pioneering studies of human sexual response, have broken new ground in an even more controversial area. In their latest book, *Homosexuality in Perspective,* they reveal the results of years of research on homosexual love making. Here are some of their findings:

- Homosexuals in a long-standing relationship have a better understanding of their partners' sexual needs than most heterosexual couples. Looking at the same issue from the heterosexual perspective, Masters and Johnson found that heterosexuals often communicate poorly, misread signals, and hurry sex along. In their preoccupation with achieving orgasm, they often fail to enjoy the entire sexual experience.
- Only three percent of the homosexuals studied failed to reach orgasm—the same percentage found in the heterosexual sample the researchers studied.
- Lesbian lovers spend much more time in sexual foreplay then heterosexual couples.
- Homosexuals commonly experience heterosexual sex fantasies.

Even though homosexual sex in the Masters and Johnson lab may not be the same as it is at home, these research findings shed light on the human sexual response of a group too long ignored.

For more details, see William Masters and Virginia Johnson, *Homosexuality in Perspective.* Boston: Little, Brown, 1979.

Weinberg (1978) studied 1,500 male and female homosexuals who lived in the San Francisco Bay area around 1970. Even in that relatively liberated time and place, most of the volunteers they found were somewhat secretive about their homosexuality, especially with parents and relatives. The greatest lesson of this study is that not all homosexuals are alike: they are just as diverse and hard to generalize about as heterosexuals are.

Bell and Weinberg describe five different homosexual life styles. "Close-coupled" and "open-coupled" homosexuals are analogous to marriages. Couples who live together in a strong, well-adjusted relationship are generally faithful to each other; the "open couples" usually had a less stable and less satisfying relationship. "Functionals" are the homosexual equivalent of swinging singles—they have active sex lives with many partners, and lead active lives with their friends. "Dysfunctionals" come closest to the stereotype of the tormented homosexual; they have problems with their sexuality and with other aspects of their lives as well. Finally, "asexuals" have withdrawn from the world—both socially and sexually.

In conclusion, Bell and Weinberg write (230): "Homosexuality is not necessarily related to pathology. Thus, decisions about homosexual men and women, whether they have to do with employment or child custody or counseling, should never be made on the basis of sexual orientation alone."

LOVE AND MARRIAGE

The idea of love without marriage is no longer shocking. The fact that a couple is developing a close and intimate relationship, or even living together, does not necessarily mean that they are contemplating marriage. Still the idea of marriage without love remains heresy in Western thought. Marrying for convenience, companionship, financial security, or *any* reason that doesn't include love strikes most of us as immoral or at least unfortunate.

And this, according to Zick Rubin (1973), is one of the main reasons why it is difficult for many people to adjust to love and marriage. Exaggerated ideas about love may also help to explain the growing popularity of divorce. Fewer couples who have "fallen out of love" are staying together for the sake of the children or to avoid gossip than did in the past. But let us begin at the beginning, with love.

Love

Figure 10.5

Distinguishing between liking and loving: a portion of Rubin's questionnaire.

Liking

1. *Favorable evaluation.*

   I think that _____ (my boyfriend or girlfriend) is unusually well-adjusted.
   It seems to me that it is very easy for _____ to gain admiration.

2. *Respect and confidence.*

   I have great confidence in _____'s good judgment.
   I would vote for _____ in a class or group election.

3. *Perceived similarity.*

   I think that _____ and I are quite similar to each other.
   When I am with _____, we are almost always in the same mood.

Loving

1. *Attachment.*

   If I could never be with _____, I would feel miserable.
   It would be hard for me to get along without _____.

2. *Caring.*

   If _____ were feeling badly, my first duty would be to cheer him (her) up.
   I would do almost anything for _____.

3. *Intimacy.*

   I feel that I can confide in _____ about almost anything.
   When I am with _____, I spend a good deal of time just looking at him (her).

Some years ago, psychologist Zick Rubin (1973) covered the University of Michigan campus with requests for student volunteers. The top line of his posters—"Only dating couples can do it!"—attracted hundreds of students, so many that he had to turn most away. Those who remained—couples who had been going together for anywhere from a few weeks to six or seven years—filled out questionnaires about their feelings toward their partners and their same-sex friends. Their answers enabled Rubin to distinguish between liking and loving (see Figure 10.5).

Liking is based primarily on respect for another person and the feeling that he or she is similar to you. Loving is rather different. As Rubin writes, "There are probably as many reasons for loving as there are people who love. In each case there is a different constellation of needs to be gratified, a different set of characteristics that are found to be rewarding, a different ideal to be fulfilled" (228–229). However, looking beyond these differences, Rubin identified three major components of romantic love: *need, the desire to give,* and *intimacy.*

People in love feel strong desires to be with the other person, to touch, to be praised and cared for by their lover. Whether men and women look to their partners to fill leftover needs that were never satisfied in childhood, as many psychologists suggest, is debatable. But the fact that love is so often described as a longing, a hunger, a desire to possess, a sickness that only one person can heal suggests the role need plays in romantic love.

Equally central is the desire to give. Love goes beyond the cost-reward level of human interaction. It has been defined as "the active concern for the life and growth of that which we love" (Fromm, 1956: 26), and as "that state in which the happiness of another person is essential to our own" (Heinlein, in Levinger and Snoek, 1972:10). Without caring, need becomes a series of self-centered, desperate demands; without need, caring is charity or kindness. In love, the two are intertwined.

Need and caring are individual experiences. What people in love share is intimacy—a special knowledge of one another derived from uncensored self-disclosure. Exposing your "true self" to another person is always risky. It doesn't hurt so much if a person rejects a role you are trying to play. But it can be devastating if a person rejects the secret longings and fears you ordinarily disguise, or if he or she uses private information to manipulate you. This is one of the reasons why love so often brings out violent emotions—the highs and lows of our lives.

Rubin conducted a number of experiments to test common assumptions about the way people in love feel and act. He found that couples who

Figure 10.6
It is easy to think of love in a narrow context and consider only the sexual relationship that exists between a man and a woman. But this view omits the kinds of love that exist between members of the same sex, between parents and children, between very young or very old people, and between some people and their animals.

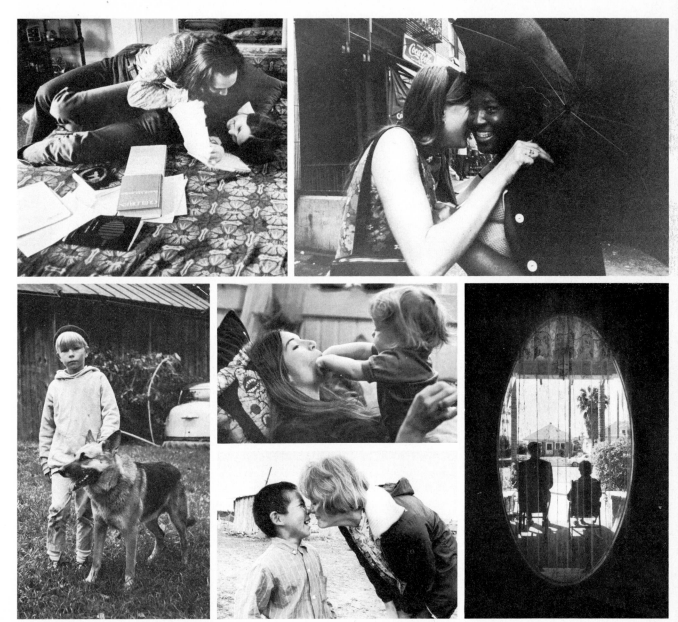

rated high on his "love scale" did, indeed, spend more time gazing into one another's eyes (while waiting for the experimenter) than other couples did. However, he was unable to prove that lovers sacrifice their own comfort for that of their partners.

Perhaps the most interesting discoveries in "love research" concern the differences between men and women. Rubin found that most couples were equal on the love scale: the woman expressed the same degree of love for her partner as he did for her. However, women tended to *like* their boy friends—to respect and identify with them—more than their boy friends liked them. Women also tended to love and share intimacies with their same-sex friends more often than men did with theirs.

This is not surprising. As Rubin suggests, women in our society tend to specialize in the social and emotional dimensions of life. However, the revelation that men are significantly more romantic than women is surprising. Men tended to agree with statements like "As long as they love each other, two people should have no difficulty getting along together in marriage," but disagree with unromantic statements like "One should not marry against the serious advice of one's parents." Women tended to take practical and social considerations more seriously. A full 72 percent of the women in the study were undecided about whether they would marry someone who possessed all the qualities they looked for in a mate but whom they did not love. In contrast, 65 percent of the men answered this question with a flat no.

A follow-up questionnaire, sent a year after Rubin's original study, indicated that when both a man and woman are romantic, the relationship is likely to progress—that is, they become more intimate and committed to each other. The implication of this finding? That love is not something that happens *to* you; it is something you seek and create.

Marriage

A couple decides to make a formal and public commitment to one another. They marry. Will they "live happily ever after"? Their chances are good if they come from similar cultural and economic backgrounds, have about the same level of education, and practice (or fail to practice) the same religion. Their chances are better still if their parents were happily married, they had happy childhoods, and they maintain good relations with their families. All of these are good predictors of marital success. Study after study has shown that marital success tends to run in families, and particularly in families whose members marry "their own kind." This is the principle of homogamy: like marrying like (Arkoff, 1968: 467–474). What the statistics do not tell us is *how* couples who report they are satisfied with their marriages adjust to one another's hopes and demands, moods and quirks.

J. F. Cuber and Peggy Harroff (1965) found a wide range of adjustments in the upper-middle-class community they studied. Cuber and Harroff chose to study affluent families for two reasons: first, because they believed that too many marital studies focus on families in crisis; second, because such families represent the American ideal in many respects.

About one in six of the marriages they studied did in fact live up to the ideal. The couple enjoyed one another's company and spent a good deal of time together. At the same time, both husband and wife had a strong sense of individual identity and participated in separate activities. Cuber and Harroff called this a **vital marriage.** In a smaller number of **total marriages,** the husband and wife were deeply involved in one another's careers and hobbies, spent most of their time together, and seemed to live for each other.

More common were what the researchers labeled devitalized and passive-congenial marriages. **Devitalized marriages** had begun with passionate love affairs and high hopes for a life of marital bliss. Over the years the couple had drifted apart, but they still got along well enough to stay together. The couples who had worked out **passive-congenial marriages** had never been deeply involved with one another. For these individuals, marriage was a convenience. Living together and sharing responsibilities made it easier for both husband and wife to pursue individual interests. They had not been looking for a lifelong honeymoon and were content with their relationship.

Cuber and Harroff used the term **conflict-habituated marriage** to describe husbands and wives who spent most of their time fighting. These couples were always at each other's throats. But they did not see their battles as a reason for divorce. Indeed, the fighting seemed to bind them together.

Mirra Komarovsky's study of blue-collar marriages (1964) provides an interesting contrast. Nearly all the couples Komarovsky studied saw marriage as a utilitarian arrangement and had settled into passive-congenial

Figure 10.7
Healthy adjustment to marriage seems to depend on whether the couple's needs are compatible, on whether their images of themselves coincide with their images of each other, and on whether they agree on what the roles of husband and wife should be.

relationships. In general these couples believed that males and females have different needs and interests. They thought it natural for a woman to feel closer to her female friends and relatives than to her husband; a husband, closer to his male friends and relatives than to his wife. So long as the husband filled his role as breadwinner and the wife her role as home-maker and mother, both felt satisfied. There were some exceptions, some vital marriages, in the group studies. Komarovsky notes that the couples who enjoyed one another's company and shared leisure activities had higher levels of education and higher incomes than the other couples she interviewed (see Skolnick, 1973: 238–246).

Statistics on the reasons why couples file for divorce reveal a similar pattern. Lower-class couples are more likely to complain of lack of finan-cial support, physical cruelty, or drinking; middle-class couples, of mental cruelty or incompatibility (Levinger, 1966).

Marital Problems and Divorce

In general, healthy adjustment to marriage seems to depend on three factors: whether the couple's needs are compatible; whether the hus-band's and wife's images of themselves coincide with their images of each other; and whether they agree on what the husband's and wife's roles in marriage are.

Conflict is likely to develop if the husband or wife has a deep need for achievement but the spouse is content with a leisurely, comfortable, un-distinguished life. If a husband sees himself as sensitive and compassion-ate but the wife considers him crude and unfeeling, they are not likely to get along very well. Problems may erupt when a wife discovers that her husband expects her to quit her job when he finishes school and estab-lishes himself in his career (something they may never have discussed). Similarly, a marriage may founder when a husband finds his wife devoting to their children the attention she once gave to him.

External factors may make it impossible for one or both to live up to their own role expectations. A man who is unemployed cannot be the good provider he wants to be and may take his frustration out on his family, who constantly remind him of this. A woman trying to raise a family in a slum tenement cannot keep the kitchen with a broken sink clean, provide good meals for her family, or keep her children safe. She gives up.

And often couples just grow apart: the husband becomes totally en-grossed in his work or in a hobby; the wife, in her career, children, or community affairs. One day they wake up and realize that they stopped communicating years ago (see Arkoff, 1968: 469–487).

Let us suppose they are unable or unwilling to fill one another's needs and role expectations through accommodation or compromise. Perhaps they cannot face their problems. Many people have a taboo about discuss-ing—much less seeking help for—sexual problems, for example. Perhaps they have sought professional help, talked their difficulties out with each other and with friends, and come to the conclusion that they want more from life than their current marriage allows. For whatever reasons, they decide on divorce. What then?

In many ways, adjusting to divorce is like adjusting to death—the death of a relationship. Almost inevitably, divorce releases a torrent of emotions: anger (even if the person wanted a divorce), resentment, fear, loneliness, anxiety, and above all the feeling of failure. Both individuals are suddenly thrust into a variety of unfamiliar situations. A man may find himself cooking for the first time in years; a woman, fixing her first leaky faucet. Dating for the first time in five or ten years can make a formerly married person feel like an adolescent. Friends may feel they have to choose sides. Some may find the idea of giving up on a marriage or being unattached and free to do whatever you like unsettling. One of the biggest problems may be time—the free time a person desperately wanted but now has no idea what to do with.

All of this adds up to what Mel Krantzler (1973) calls "separation shock." The shock may be greatest for individuals who saw divorce as liberation and did not anticipate difficult times. But whatever the circumstances, most divorced people go through a period of mourning that lasts until the person suddenly realizes that he or she has survived. This is the first step toward adjustment to divorce. Resentment of his or her former spouse and of the opposite sex in general subsides. The pain left over from the past no longer dominates the present. The divorced person begins calling old friends, making new ones, and enjoying the fact that he or she can base decisions on his or her own, personal interests. In effect, the divorcee has begun to construct a new single identity, much as students do after an initial period of "college shock" (Krantzler, 1973: 94–95).

COLLEGE LIFE

College students are freer than they ever have been or may ever be again. This can be a personally liberating and stimulating experience. But it also requires adjustment. The emotional upheaval many freshmen feel has been called "college shock."

Peter Madison (1969) spent close to ten years collecting data on how several hundred students adjusted to college. Each student provided a detailed life history and kept a weekly journal. Madison had classmates write descriptions of some of the students, and tested and retested some at various points in their college career. The results?

Madison found that many students approach college with high, and often unrealistic, aspirations. For example, Trixie wanted to be an astronomer. She liked the idea of being different, and considered astronomy an elite and adventuresome field. But she didn't know how many long, hard, unadventuresome hours she would have spend studying mathematics to fulfill her dream. Sidney planned to become a physician for what he described as "humanitarian" reasons. But he had never thought about working in a hospital or watching people sicken and die.

These two students, like many others, based their goals on fantasy. They didn't have the experience to make realistic choices or the maturity to evaluate their own motives and needs. Their experiences during the first

Many students approach college with unrealistically high expectations.

Figure 10.8
College life makes many demands on students away from home for the first time. Organizing one's time, meeting new people, and confronting ideas that challenge old assumptions all require adjustment.

semesters of college led them to change both their minds and their images of themselves.

Sources of Change

How does going to college stimulate change? First, college may challenge the identity a student has established in high school. A top student who does extremely well on the College Boards is likely to go to a top college. Nearly everyone there is as bright and competitive as she is. Within a matter of weeks the student's identity as a star pupil has evaporated; she may have to struggle to get average grades. Young people who excelled in sports or drama or student politics may have similar experiences. The high-school president discovers two other high-school presidents in his dormitory alone.

Second, whether students come from small towns or big cities, they are likely to encounter greater diversity in college than they ever have before—diversity in religious and ethnic background, family income level, and attitudes. During his first quarter, Bob dated a Catholic woman, a Jewish woman, and an Oriental woman; a history major, a music major, a writer, and a math major. Fred found that the students living in his house ranged from "grinds," who did nothing but study, to "liberals," who were involved in all sorts of causes, from athletes, who cared more about physical than intellectual competition, and business types, who saw college as a place to get vocational training and make contacts for future use, to guys who just wanted to have a good time.

A student who develops a close relationship with another, then discovers that the person holds beliefs or engages in behavior he has always considered immoral, may be extremely shaken. If you come from a strict fundamentalist background, how do you reconcile the fact that a woman you have come to admire drinks heavily on occasion and thinks nothing of sleeping with a man on their first date? You are faced with a choice between abandoning deeply held values and giving up an important friendship. Madison calls close relationships between individuals who force one another to reexamine their basic assumptions **developmental friendships.** He found that developmental friendships in particular and student culture in general have more impact on college students than professors do.

However, if instructors and assigned books clarify thoughts that have been brewing in a student's mind, they can make all the difference. This was true for Sidney. Sidney did extremely well in the courses required for a pre-med student, but found he enjoyed his literature and philosophy classes far more. He began reading avidly. He felt as if each of the authors had deliberately set out to put all his self-doubts into words. In time Sidney realized that his interest in medicine was superficial. He had decided to become a doctor because it was a respected profession that would give him status, security, and a good income—and would guarantee his parents' love. The self-image Sidney had brought to college was completely changed.

Coping with Change

Madison found that students cope with the stress of going to college in several different ways. Some "tighten up" when their goals are threatened by internal or external change. They redouble their efforts to succeed in the field they have chosen and avoid people and situations that might bring their doubts to the surface. Bob, for example, stuck with a chemical-

Figure 10.9
After completing a year or two of college, students may find that the career goals they had as high school seniors no longer suit their interests.

engineering program for three years, despite a growing interest in social science. By the time he realized that this was not the field for him it was too late to change majors. He got his degree, but left college with no idea where he was heading.

Others avoid confronting doubt by frittering away their time, going through the motions of attending college but detaching themselves emotionally.

And some students manage to keep their options open until they have enough information and experience to make a choice. Sidney is an example. In June of his freshman year he wrote in his diary,

> I must decide between philosophy and medicine. If I have enough confidence in the quality of my thought, I shall become a philosopher; if not, a comfortable doctor. (58)

By June of the following year he had decided.

> Sitting on a tennis court I had the very sudden and dramatic realization that my life was my own and not my parents', that I could do what I wanted and did not necessarily have to do what they wanted. I think I correlated this with dropping out of the pre-med program. Material values became less and less important from then on. (58)

Madison calls this third method of coping **resynthesis.** For most students this involves a period of vacillation, doubt, and anxiety. The student tries to combine the new and old, temporarily abandons the original goal, retreats, heads in another direction, retreats again—and finally reorganizes his or her feelings and efforts around an emerging identity. Thus Trixie changed her major to psychology and found she was able to combine her desire to be a scientist with her interest in people.

SUMMARY

1. According to Selye, the reaction to stress includes three stages: alarm, resistance, and exhaustion.

2. Emotional stress can lead to psychosomatic disease (such as ulcers and high blood pressure), physical illness, or even sudden death.

3. Studies of sexuality have shown wide differences between people in their sexual needs and preferences. Although many people say they don't approve of masturbation, it is quite common. The number of people who have had premarital or extramarital sex seems to have gone up in the last thirty years.

4. Kinsey developed a seven-point scale of homosexuality because many people are neither completely homosexual nor completely heterosexual. Psychiatrists now recognize that homosexuals who are satisfied with their sexual preferences are well adjusted.

5. There are three major components of romantic love: need, the desire to give, and intimacy. Love is not something that happens to you; it is something you seek and create.

6. Healthy adjustment in marriage depends on at least three factors: whether the couple's needs are compatible, whether their images of themselves coincide with their images of each other, and whether they agree on what their individual roles should be within the marriage.

7. Students entering college meet people from many different backgrounds and are exposed to new ideas. Many students find that their career aspirations are unrealistic. They may also begin to question their own beliefs and behavior.

8. Some of the ways students cope with the stresses of college life include redoubling their efforts to maintain past choices, avoiding anything or anyone that could foster doubt, detaching themselves emotionally or dropping out, and re-synthesizing their feelings and experiences.

GLOSSARY

adjustment: The process of adapting to and actively shaping one's environment.

conflict-habituated marriage: A marriage in which the partners spend most of their time fighting.

developmental friendship: The type of friendship in which the partners force one another to reexamine their basic assumptions and perhaps adopt new ideas and beliefs.

devitalized marriage: A marriage, originally based on love, in which the partners no longer attempt or expect passion or bliss, but get along well enough to remain together.

passive-congenial marriage: A marriage based on convenience, in which the partners live together and share responsibilities in order to make it easier for each to pursue individual interests.

resynthesis: The process of combining old ideas with new ones and reorganizing feelings in order to renew one's identity.

stress: The tension or strain people feel when they are unable to satisfy their needs and feel their well-being threatened by forces beyond their control.

total marriage: A marriage in which the husband and wife are deeply involved in one another's careers and hobbies, spend most of their time together, and seem to live for one another.

vital marriage: A marriage in which the partners enjoy each other's company and spend a great deal of time together. At the same time, each maintains his or her own sense of individual identity, and they participate in separate activities.

ACTIVITIES

1. A basic theme of this chapter has been the disparity between expectation and reality. Somehow, our dreams often manage to be better than what turns out to happen, whether in love affairs or going to college. Think of an experience you have had where reality turned out more disappointing than you originally thought, and discuss how you adjusted to it.

2. The idea of "romantic love" is fostered in fairy-tales like *Cinderella* and *Sleeping Beauty*, in popular songs, novels, short stories, and TV commercials. Take an example from one or two of these areas and discuss how they express the romantic ideal of falling in love with the perfect stranger.

3. Cuber and Harroff (1965) classify marriages as either vital, total, devitalized, passive-congenial, or conflict-habituated. Think of some of the marriages of people in your family, neighbors, or friends, and discuss why you think they would be classified in one of these five categories.

4. If any of the marriages of people you know ended in divorce, make some notes on why you think this occurred. If some of these people are available, ask them how they adjusted to being divorced and what kind of problems they had.

5. The class could divide into small groups, with females and males in each, to discuss the particular problems of adjustment facing contemporary women. Each group could turn in a list of these problems and then the whole class could discuss them. What did people tend to list most often? What did they leave out? Did groups disagree among themselves on some of these issues?

SUGGESTED READINGS

CSIKSZENTMIHALYI, MIHALY. *Beyond Boredom and Anxiety*. New York: Jossey-Bass, 1976. Maslow studied "healthy" individuals and found many commonly have "peak experiences" of intense enjoyment and happiness. Csikszentmihalyi has now made an in-depth study of these experiences, asking surgeons, rock climbers, chess players, dancers, and basketball players what precedes these moments and how they feel during them. The result is an exciting and inspiring picture of healthy adjustment.

KAPLAN, HELEN SINGER. *The New Sex Therapy: Active Treatment of Sexual Dysfunctions*. New York: Brunner/Mazel, 1974. An excellent presentation of the basis of sexual dysfunction and its treatment. The author combines psychoanalytic and behavioral therapeutic techniques with assigned sexual "tasks" to treat specific sexual problems.

KATCHADOURIAN, HERANT A., AND LUNDE, DONALD T. *Fundamentals of Human Sexuality*. 2nd ed. New York: Holt, Rinehart & Winston, 1975. An outstanding and well-written basic textbook with broad coverage of biological, behavioral, and cultural facets of human sexuality.

KINSEY, ALFRED C., ET AL. *Sexual Behavior in the Human Female*. Philadelphia: Saunders, 1953.

KINSEY, ALFRED C., POMEROY, WARDELL B., AND MARTIN, C. E. *Sexual Behavior in the Human Male*. Philadelphia: Saunders, 1948. The classic "Kinsey studies" of sexual behavior, which provided the first broad survey and comprehensive statistics concerning the sexual behaviors of Americans.

ROGERS, CARL. *Becoming Partners: Marriage and Its Alternatives*. New York: Delta, 1972 (paper). In this thought-provoking discussion of interpersonal relationships, the life styles of many different people are presented in their own words followed by commentaries by the author.

TERKEL, STUDS. *Working*. New York: Avon Books, 1974 (paper). A panorama of viewpoints of what Americans from many different walks of life think about their jobs, by a reporter who seemed to ask just the right questions to elicit the most personal and revealing answers.

WALSTER, ELAINE, AND WALSTER, G. WILLIAM. *Love*. Reading, Mass.: Addison-Wesley, 1978. A review of theories and data concerning the sometimes mysterious topic of love by authors who have contributed significantly to recent research in that area.

BIBLIOGRAPHY

ARKOFF, ABE. *Adjustment and Mental Health*. New York: McGraw-Hill, 1968.

BELL, ALAN P., AND WEINBERG, MARTIN S. *Homosexualities: A Study of Diversity Among Men and Women*. New York: Simon & Schuster, 1978.

BRADY, JOSEPH V. "Ulcers in 'Executive' Monkeys." *Scientific American*, 199 (October 1958): 95–100.

CHOLDEN, L. "Some Psychiatric Problems in the Rehabilitation of the Blind." *Menninger Clinic Bulletin*, 18 (1954): 107–112.

COBB, SIDNEY, AND ROSE, ROBERT. "Hypertension, Peptic Ulcers, and Diabetes in Air Traffic Controllers." *Journal of the American Medical Association*, 224 (1973): 489–492.

COLEMAN, JAMES C., AND HAMMEN, CONSTANCE L. *Contemporary Psychology and Effective Behavior*. Glenview, Ill.: Scott, Foresman, 1974.

COLES, R. "Life in Appalachia: The Case of Hugh McCaslin." *Life at the Bottom*, ed. by G. Armstrong. New York: Bantam, 1971, pp. 26–42.

CUBER, J. F., AND HARROFF, P. *Sex and the Significant American*. Baltimore: Penguin, 1965.

ENGEL, GEORGE. "Emotional Stress and Sudden Death." *Psychology Today*, 11 (November 1977): 114–118, 153–154.

FRIEDMAN, M., AND ROSENMAN, R. H. *Type A Behavior and Your Heart*. New York: Knopf, 1974.

FROMM, ERICH. *The Art of Loving*. New York: Harper & Row, 1956.

HOLMES, T. H., AND RAHE, R. H. "The Social Readjustment Rating Scale." *Journal of Psychosomatic Research*, 11 (1967): 213.

HUNT, MORTON. *Sexual Behavior in the 1970's*. New York: Dell, 1974.

KATCHADOURIAN, H. A. AND LUNDE, D. T. *Fundamentals of Human Sexuality*. 2nd ed. New York: Holt, Rinehart & Winston, 1975.

KENISTON, K. "Alienation in American Youth." In *The Psychology of Adolescence: Essential Readings*, ed. by A. H. Esman. New York: International Universities Press, 1975, pp. 434–450.

KINSEY, ALFRED C., ET AL. *Sexual Behavior in the Human Female*. Philadelphia: Saunders, 1953.

KINSEY, ALFRED C., POMEROY, W. B., AND MARTIN, C. E. *Sexual Behavior in the Human Male*. Philadelphia: Saunders, 1948.

KOMAROVSKY, M. *Blue-Collar Marriage*. New York: Random House, 1964.

KRANTZLER, MEL. *Creative Divorce*. New York: Evans, 1973.

LEVINGER, G. "Sources of Dissatisfaction Among Applicants for Divorce." *American Journal of Orthopsychiatry*, 36 (1966): 803–807.

LEVINGER, GEORGE, AND SNOEK, J. DIDRICK. *Attraction in Relationship: A New Look at Interpersonal Attraction*. Morristown, N.J.: General Learning, 1972.

LOPICCOLO, JOSEPH, AND LOPICCOLO, LESLIE (EDS.). *Handbook of Sex Therapy*. New York: Plenum, 1978.

MCCARY, JAMES LESLIE. *McCary's Human Sexuality*. 3rd ed. New York: Van Nostrand, 1978.

MADISON, PETER. *Personality Development in College*. Reading, Mass.: Addison-Wesley, 1969.

MASTERS, WILLIAM H., AND JOHNSON, VIRGINIA E. *Human Sexual Response*. Boston: Little, Brown, 1966.

———. *Human Sexual Inadequacy*. Boston: Little, Brown, 1970.

PARKES, C. M. "Components of the Reaction to Loss of Limb, Spouse, or Home." *Journal of Psychosomatic Research*, 16 (1972): 343–349.

PIETROPINTO, A., AND SIMENAUER, J. *Beyond the Male Myth*. New York: Quadrangle, 1977.

POMEROY, WARDELL B. *Dr. Kinsey and the Institute for Sex Research*. New York: Harper & Row, 1972.

RAHE, RICHARD H., AND LIND, E. "Psychosocial Factors and Sudden Cardiac Death: A Pilot Study." *Journal of Psychosomatic Research*, 15 (1971): 19–24.

RUBIN, ZICK. *Liking and Loving*. New York: Holt, Rinehart & Winston, 1973.

SCHEIN, E. H. "The First Job Dilemma." *Psychology Today*, 1 (1968): 26–37.

SCHMALE, A. "Giving Up as a Final Common Pathway to Changes in Health." *Advances in Psychosomatic Medicine*, 8 (1972): 20–40.

SELYE, H. "Stress." *Psychology Today*, 3 (1969): 24–26.

———. *The Stress of Life*. New York: McGraw-Hill, 1956.

SELYE, HANS, AND CHERRY, L. "On the Real Benefits of Eustress." *Psychology Today*, 11 (March 1978): 60–70.

SKOLNICK, ARLENE. *The Intimate Environment*. Boston: Little, Brown, 1973.

TAVRIS, CAROL, AND OFFIR, CAROLE. *The Longest War: Sex Differences in Perspective*. New York: Harcourt Brace Jovanovich, 1977.

TERKEL, STUDS. *Working*. New York: Avon, 1974.

TOFFLER, A. *Future Shock*. New York: Bantam, 1970.

TOLLEFSON, D. F. "The Relationship Between the Occurrence of Fractures and Life Crisis Events." Master of Nursing thesis, University of Washington, Seattle, 1972.

WEISS, JAY M. "Effects of Coping Behavior in Different Warning-Signal Conditions on Stress Pathology in Rats." *Journal of Comparative and Physiological Psychology*, 77 (1971): 1–13.

WERNER, ARNOLD. "Sexual Dysfunction in College Men and Women." *American Journal of Psychiatry*, 132 (1975): 164–168.

WOLD, D. A. "The Adjustment of Siblings to Childhood Leukemia." Medical thesis, University of Washington, Seattle, 1968.

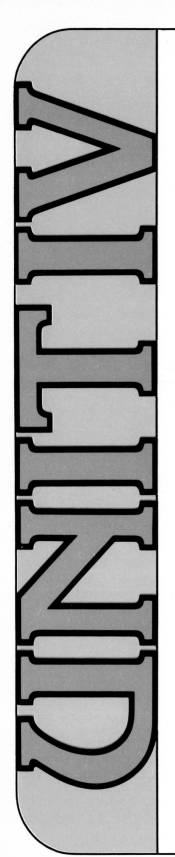

UNIT V

HUMAN RELATIONS

Although we may deny it, all of us are concerned with the impression we make on other people and attempt to "read" their reactions to what we say and do. The way we interact with friends and strangers is governed by a variety of social rules. We may not think about these rules very often, but we become embarrassed when we break them. We relate to other people in terms of the social groups to which they belong (their sex, age, occupation, and the like), as well as in terms of individual characteristics. And we all try to influence other people's attitudes and behavior. These familiar, everyday occurrences are what social psychologists, who specialize in human relations, study.

In this unit we look at several different dimensions of human relations. Chapter 11 deals with interpersonal relationships—the kinds of interactions that occur between two people, and within and between groups, from families to communities to corporations. Chapter 12 explores the roles that people play in influencing one another. Your friends and relatives, television producers, advertising executives, textbook publishers, and lawmakers all affect your thoughts, your feelings, and your actions. This chapter explains how and why they do.

Many people take these social processes for granted. Because they are familiar, we assume we understand them. But the scientific study of human relations has revealed that common-sense ideas about "how things are" are often wrong. The main goal of this unit is to help you achieve a deeper understanding of social interaction. Along the way, you may discover many things that surprise you.

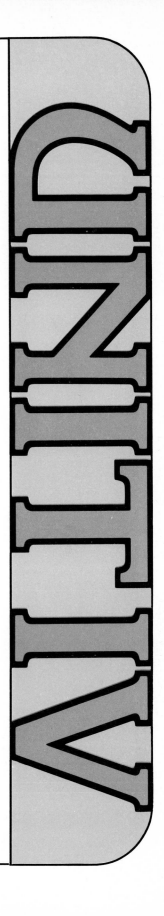

11 Human Interaction

People vary considerably in their need for social contact and in their desire and ability to be alone. You have probably heard tales of hermits and recluses who voluntarily isolate themselves, but most people would not welcome a solitary life. What is so important about being around other people? And what do psychologists know about human interaction?

NEEDING OTHER PEOPLE

From infancy we depend on others to satisfy our basic needs. In this relationship we learn to associate close personal contact with the satisfaction of basic needs. In later life we seek personal contact for the same reason, even though we can now care for ourselves.

Being around other human beings, interacting with others, has become a habit that would be difficult to break. Moreover, we have developed needs for praise, respect, love and affection, the sense of achievement, and other rewarding experiences. And these needs, acquired through social learning, can only be satisfied by other human beings (Bandura and Walters, 1963).

Anxiety and Companionship

Social psychologists are interested in discovering what circumstances intensify our desire for human contact. It seems that we need company most when we are afraid or anxious, and we also need company when we are unsure of ourselves and want to compare our feelings with other people's.

Figure 11.1
How much we need other people varies, but interaction with others is a way of satisfying the needs we all have for praise, respect, love, and affection.

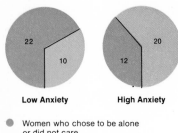

Women who chose to be alone
or did not care

Women who chose to affiliate

Figure 11.2
The results of Schachter's 1959 experiment about the effects of anxiety on affiliation.

Psychologist Stanley Schachter (1959) decided to test the old saying "Misery loves company." His experiment showed that people suffering from a high level of anxiety are more likely to seek out company than those who feel less anxious. He arranged for a number of college women to come to his laboratory. One group of women was greeted by a frightening-looking man in a white coat who identified himself as Dr. Gregor Zilstein of the medical school. Dr. Zilstein told each woman that she would be given electric shocks in order to study the effect of electricity on the body. He told the women, in an ominous tone, that the shocks would be extremely painful. With a devilish smile, he added that the shocks would cause no permanent skin damage. For obvious reasons, this group of women was referred to as the high-anxiety group.

The doctor was friendly to the other group of women, and told them that the shocks would produce only ticklish, tingling sensations, which they might even find pleasant. These women formed the low-anxiety group.

Zilstein told each subject that she would have to leave the laboratory while he set up the equipment. He then asked each woman to indicate on a questionnaire whether she wished to wait alone in a private room or with other subjects in a larger room. Most women in the low-anxiety group chose to wait alone. However, the overwhelming majority of high-anxiety women preferred to wait with others. Thus, the experiment demonstrated that high anxiety produces a need for companionship (Figure 11.2).

Comparing Experiences and Reducing Uncertainty

People also like to get together with one another to reduce their uncertainties about themselves. For example, when you get exams back, you probably ask your friends how they did. You try to understand your own situation by comparing it to other people's. You learn your strengths and weaknesses by asking: Can other people do it, too? Do they do it better or worse? Many individuals use the performance of others as a basis for self-evaluation. According to this theory, one of the reasons why the women in the shock experiment sought company was to find out how they should respond to Dr. Zilstein. Should they feel fear or anger, or should they take the whole thing in stride? One way to get this information was to talk to others.

Schachter conducted another experiment to test this idea. It was essentially the same as the Dr. Zilstein experiment, but this time *all* the women were made anxious. Half of them were then given the choice between waiting alone and waiting with other women about to take part in the same experiment. The other half were given the choice between waiting alone and passing the time in a room where students were waiting to see their academic advisers.

As you might expect, the women who had a chance to be with other women in the same predicament seized the opportunity. These women wanted to compare their dilemma with others. But most of the women in the second group chose to spend the time alone rather than with the unconcerned students. As the experimenter put it, "Misery doesn't love just any kind of company, it loves only miserable company."

Other researchers have shown that the more uncertain a person is, the more likely he or she is to seek out other people. Like Schachter, Harold Gerard and J. M. Rabbie recruited volunteers for an experiment. When the volunteers arrived, some of them were escorted to a booth and attached to a machine that was suppose to measure emotionality. The machine was turned on, and the subjects were able to see not only their own ratings but the ratings of three other participants as well. In each case the dial for the subject registered 82 on a scale of 100; the dials for the other participants registered 79, 80, and 81. (As you've undoubtedly guessed, the machine was rigged.) A second group of subjects was attached to a similar machine and was shown their own ratings but not those of other participants. A third group was not given any information about themselves or other participants in the experiment. When asked whether they wanted to wait alone or with other subjects, most of the people in the first group chose to wait alone. They had seen how they compared to others and felt they were reacting appropriately. However, most of the subjects in the other two groups, who had no basis for evaluating themselves, chose to wait with other people (Gerard and Rabbie, 1961).

Seeking company when you are frightened or uncertain about your feelings seems to work. People who choose to be in a group when they are afraid of an experimental procedure or lack information about how they compare to others are less anxious than those who "tough it out" and wait alone (Wrightsman, 1960).

CHOOSING FRIENDS

Most people feel they have a great deal of latitude in the friends they choose. Easy transportation, telephones, and the spare time available to most Americans would all seem to ease communication among them and, therefore, to permit them a wide range of individuals from whom to choose companions, friends, and lovers. But in fact, we rarely venture beyond the most convenient methods in making contact with others.

Proximity

Would it surprise you to learn that the most important factor in determining whether two people will become friends is **physical proximity**—the distance from one another that people live or work? In general, the closer two individuals are geographically to one another, the more likely they are to become attracted to each other. And it is more than just the opportunity for interaction that makes the difference.

Psychologists have found that even in a small two-story apartment building where each resident was in easy reach of everyone else, people were more likely to become close friends with the person next door than with anyone else (Figure 11.3). Psychologists believe that this is a result of the fears and embarrassments most people have about making contact with strangers. When two people live next door to one another, go to the same class, or work in the same place, they are able to get used to one

The single most important factor in choosing friends is physical proximity.

Figure 11.3
A set of apartments such as this one was used in a study of friendship choice. It was found that the fewer doors there were between people, the more likely they were to become friends.

another and to find reasons to talk to one another without ever having to seriously risk rejection. To make friends with someone whom you do not see routinely is much more difficult. You have to make it clear that you are interested and thus run the risk of making a fool of yourself—either because the other person turns out to be less interesting than he or she seemed at a distance or because that person expresses no interest in you. Of course, it may turn out that both of you are very glad someone spoke up.

Reward Values

Proximity helps people make friends, but it does not ensure lasting friendship. Sometimes people who are forced together in a situation take a dislike to one another that develops into hatred. Furthermore, once people have made friends, physical separation does not necessarily bring an end to their relationship. What are the factors that determine whether people will like each other once they come into contact?

One reward of friendship is stimulation. A friend has **stimulation value** if she is interesting or imaginative or if she can introduce you to new ideas or experiences. A friend who is cooperative and helpful, who seems willing to give his time and resources to help you achieve your goals, has **utility value.** A third type of value in friendship is **ego-support value:** sympathy and encouragement when things go badly, appreciation and approval when things go well. These three kinds of rewards—stimulation, utility, and ego support—are evaluated consciously or unconsciously in every friendship. A man may like another man because the second man is a witty conversationalist (stimulation value) and knows a lot about gardening (utility value). A woman may like a man because he values her opinions (ego-support value) and because she has an exciting time with him (stimulation value).

Who Is Shy?

If you would rather disappear into the wallpaper than go to the class dance, you're shy. If you prefer to spend evenings at home instead of risking the possibility of meeting new people, you're shy too. But contrary to what you probably think, you are not alone. More than 80 percent of people questioned in one survey on shyness said they had been shy at some time in their lives. Out of this number, 40 percent said they felt shy now.

This does not mean that everyone is equally shy: There are degrees of shyness ranging from slight discomfort in some situations to sheer panic in all situations. Only 25 percent of the sample approached the far end of the scale, considering themselves to be chronically shy. An even smaller group—4 percent—said they were shy all the time in all situations.

If you are shy, it may give you some comfort to know that shyness is not a purely American trait. It is found to differing degrees in cultures throughout the world. In fact, right at this moment, 60 percent of Orientals would say they were shy too.

For more details, see Philip G. Zimbardo, *Shyness*. Reading, Mass.: Addison-Wesley, 1977.

By considering the three kinds of rewards that a person may look for in friendship, it is possible to understand other factors that affect liking and loving.

Physical Appearance. A person's physical appearance greatly influences others' impressions of him or her. People feel better about themselves when they associate with people others consider desirable. This is true of same-sex as well as opposite-sex relationships. Physical attractiveness influences our choice of friends as well as lovers.

In one study (Dion, Berscheid, and Walster, 1972), subjects were shown pictures of men and women of varying degrees of physical attractiveness and were asked to rate their personality traits. The physically attractive people were consistently viewed more positively than the less attractive ones. They were seen as more sensitive, kind, interesting, strong, poised, modest, and sociable, as well as more sexually responsive. It seems, therefore, that although we have all heard that "beauty is only skin deep," we act as if it permeates one's entire personality.

Homely people are generally viewed in an unfavorable light. Research has shown that obese adults, who in our culture are considered unattractive, are often discriminated against when they apply for jobs. Even homely children are targets of prejudice (Figure 11.4). An unattractive child is far more likely to be judged "bad" or "cruel" for a particular act of misbehavior than is a more attractive peer (Dion, Berscheid, and Walster, 1972).

Interestingly, psychologists have found that both men and women pay

How to Relate to People

If you're like most people, you want others to like you, but knowing exactly how to make them like you is not always that easy. Most psychologists believe that the principle of *reciprocal reinforcement* has a lot to do with how you get along with others. In simple terms, this principle states that people will like you if your behavior makes them feel good about themselves.

Here are some reinforcement techniques you can use to get a head start on winning and keeping friends:

- When you're talking to another person, try to spend at least 50 percent of the time listening to what the other person says. That may mean cutting down on your chatter, but the results will be well worthwhile.
- Be an active rather than a passive listener. By commenting directly on what the other person says, you will show that you are really interested in his conversation.
- Instead of focusing on your own accomplishments, ask questions about the person you are with. This tells him in no uncertain terms that you care about what he has done. The best time to talk about yourself is when the other person asks.
- Approval is one of the best reinforcers if it is used correctly, but another person is easily turned off if it is not sincere. Be sure to praise only those things the other person considers important and don't use an overlavish or repetitive approach.

For more details, see Robert L. Williams and James D. Long, *Toward a Self-managed Life Style,* 2nd ed. Boston: Houghton Mifflin, 1979.

much less attention to physical appearance when choosing a marriage partner or a close friend than when inviting someone to go to a movie or a party. But neither men nor women necessarily seek out the most attractive member of their social world. Rather, people usually seek out others whom they consider their equals on the scale of physical attractiveness (Levinger and Snoek, 1972).

Approval. Another factor that affects a person's choice of friends is approval. All of us tend to like people who say nice things about us because they make us feel better about ourselves—they provide ego-support value.

The results of one experiment suggest that other people's evaluations of oneself are more meaningful when they are a mixture of praise and criticism than when they are extreme in either direction. No one believes that he or she is all good or all bad. As a result, one can take more seriously a person who sees some good points and some bad points. But when the good points come first, hearing the bad can make one disappointed and angry at the person who made them. When the bad points come first, the effect is opposite. One thinks, "This person is perceptive and honest. At

Figure 11.4
In one experiment, adult women were shown reports about and photographs of children participating in a variety of antisocial behaviors. The adults tended not only to see the behaviors committed by the unattractive children as more generally antisocial, but to attribute a more inherently negative moral character to these children than to the attractive ones. (Adapted from Dion, 1972)

first she was critical but later she saw what I was really like" (Aronson and Linder, 1965).

Similarity.   People tend to choose friends whose backgrounds, attitudes, and interests are similar to their own. Nearly always, husbands and wives have similar economic, religious, and educational backgrounds.

There are several explanations for the power of shared attitudes. First, agreement about what is stimulating, worthwhile, or fun provides the basis for sharing activities. People who have similar interests are likely to do more things together and to get to know one another better.

Figure 11.5
These two men obviously enjoy each other's company. In addition to having stimulation value for each other, they probably provide considerable utility value: they may be able to give each other advice about business problems and opportunities.

Second, most of us feel uneasy around people who are constantly challenging our views, and we translate our uneasiness into hostility or avoidance. We are more comfortable around people who support us. A friend's agreement bolsters your confidence and contributes to your self-esteem. In addition, most of us are self-centered enough to assume that people who share our values are basically decent and intelligent (unlike others we know).

Finally, people who agree about things usually find it easier to communicate with each other. They have fewer arguments and misunderstandings; they are better able to predict one another's behavior and thus feel at ease with each other.

Some social scientists have reported that married couples often have **complementary** needs (Winch, 1958). For example, a dominant person might look for a submissive mate. But most psychologists agree that similarity is a much more important factor. Although the old idea that opposites attract seems reasonable, researchers have not been able to verify it (Berscheid and Walster, 1978: 78–81).

PRESENTING OURSELVES

Nearly everything we say and do in public is part of a performance, tailored for the audience at hand. Like actors, we use our faces, movements, and words to create an effect (Goffman, 1959, 1971).

Creating Impressions

If you think about the different ways you act with different people and in different situations, you will begin to see that, like professional actors, people in everyday life play a number of **roles**—they behave in different ways in different situations (Figure 11.6). You undoubtedly behave one way with your family, another way with friends, and still another way with teachers. In your life you may play many other roles, such as worker, parent, customer, athlete, lover, and so on, and you will undoubtedly create a different impression in each one.

Why do people play different roles? One reason is that other people treat us as *they* see us and cast us into different roles. To a degree, your parents will always see you as a child, even when you approach middle age. One friend may look to you as an older brother or sister and come to you for advice; another may consider you scatter-brained, impractical, and amusing. Each of us has a little bit of the older brother or sister as well as the child in us; each of us, a touch of the clown. So we go along with the roles other people write for us. In time, the friend seeking comfort begins to elicit serious behavior from you, while the other friend makes you feel and act frivolous. You learn to associate different parts of yourself with different people.

A second reason why people perform is to get what they want out of a social interaction. All of us seek praise and other rewards and try to avoid blame and punishment. As a result, all of us are somewhat manipulative. Suppose you are given a promotion and put in charge of a number of workers who are older and more experienced in some ways than you are. You would probably make a big show of feeling self-confident, even when you were confused and afraid, to earn their respect. Otherwise, you might not be able to carry out your new responsibilities. Thus in many cases we try to create certain impressions to achieve our goals—whether that goal be

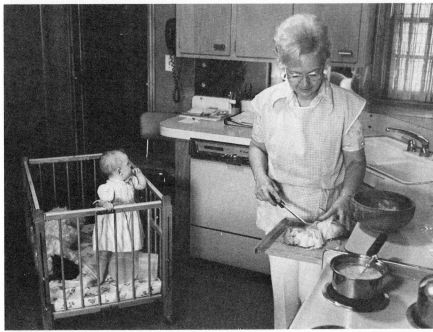

Figure 11.6
One person, two roles: (a) business executive, and (b) grandmother.

inspiring confidence in subordinates or reassuring patients, getting a job or finding a sexual partner.

Perhaps the most interesting thing about role playing is that people do not seem to go through life consciously and deliberately faking. Psychologists who studied people as they went from role to role found that most subjects felt they were presenting true and accurate pictures of themselves from moment to moment (Gergen, 1971: 86).

The situation in which you find yourself may call for a specific kind of behavior or role. You wouldn't act the same way at a football game as you would at a formal tea with the dean, for example—unless you wanted to outrage your "audience."

Apparently, we are capable of wide ranges of behavior depending on the context—you may appear dominant and powerful in one setting and weak and submissive in another. Yet, you will probably *feel* that you are being yourself in both situations.

Nonverbal Communication

Going along with all the things you say to other people and do in company are subtle, indirect communications about yourself and your relationships to others. The patron in a topless bar who circumspectly looks away when his waitress leans over the table (see Goffman, 1971) says through his behavior that he is basically a decent, respectful person. When you laugh at a dull joke you may be saying you do not want to break the circle of politeness and become more intimate with the other person. Laughing politely is a way of maintaining distance. Communication that does not directly depend on words is called **nonverbal communication.**

All of us are conscious of nonverbal communication from time to time. You have probably heard someone say "It doesn't matter" but show, by speaking in a low voice and looking away, that he or she really means "My feelings are hurt." You don't need to be told in so many words that a friend is elated or depressed, angry or pleased, nervous or contented. You sense these things. How do people communicate nonverbally? Through their use of space, body language (their posture and gestures), and, of course, facial expressions (Figure 11.7).

Personal Space.   Anthropologist Edward T. Hall became acutely aware of the importance people attach to space when he found himself backing away from a colleague he particularly liked and respected. The associate was not an American, which led Hall to wonder if people from different cultures have different ideas about the proper distance at which to hold an informal conversation. He decided to pursue the question.

After much observation, Hall concluded that Americans carry a two-foot "bubble" of privacy around them. If another person invades this bubble, we feel slightly threatened, imposed upon, and generally uncomfortable. For Germans, the bubble of privacy is much larger; for Arabs, much smaller. Thus when an Arab is talking to a German he will try to establish his accustomed talking distance. He moves closer. The discomfited German concludes that the Arab is "pushy." When the German moves

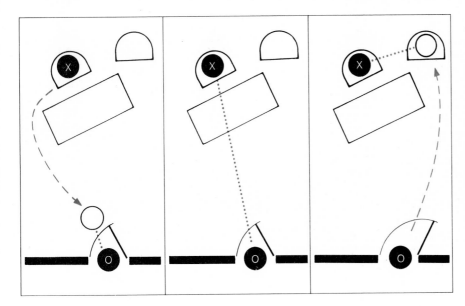

Figure 11.7
These diagrams illustrate how un-written rules about occupational status are subtly communicated by physical position. O comes to visit X. The broken lines indicate move-ment; the dotted lines, conversa-tion. See whether you can tell, be-fore reading further, who has the superior status in each case. (left) X rises and moves to greet O. X's deference indicates that O is senior in rank. (center) O speaks from the doorway while X remains seated. O is deferring this time, suggesting that X is the superior. (right) O walks in and sits down beside X. This interaction indicates that X and O have roughly equal status.

back to what he feels is normal distance, the Arab interprets this as a sign of coldness and concludes that the man is aloof (Hall, 1959).

Hall observed Americans to see how we use space to communicate our feelings about other people and to define relationships. He found that Americans allow only intimates (lovers, close friends, and family members) closer than two feet, a point at which touching is almost inevitable. When we are forced to stand very close to nonintimates, as in a crowded elevator, we try to hold our bodies immobile and avoid eye contact.

When we maintain a distance of four feet or so, we are essentially holding the other person "at arm's length." People who work together generally observe this boundary. When we want to hold people off, con-sciously or unconsciously, we create a four- to seven-foot bubble between us and them. Sometimes we use social distance to show status. An execu-tive of a large corporation may put visitors' chairs nine feet from her desk to create this impression of status, but many executives are aware of this form of communication and will try to counter this impression by placing the chairs closer than four feet.

If you go to an uncrowded beach you will probably settle down be-tween twelve and twenty-five feet from other people (Figure 11.8). If you arrange a room for a speaker, you will probably leave a similar amount of space between the podium and the first row of seats. Hall calls this "public distance" and suggests it provides a sense of safety. At twelve feet an alert person can take defensive action if threatened. At the same time, twelve feet or more does not invite personal communication. To talk, two people would move closer (Hall, 1966). The ways in which people use a space to communicate will become clear if you keep this scheme in mind. When you put your beach towel five feet from another person's when there is plenty of empty space, you are issuing an invitation. If you step back when someone at a party comes within two feet you are discouraging further intimacy. But we are usually not aware of the nonverbal messages we send.

Figure 11.8
"Public distance" at the beach. People place themselves between 12 and 25 feet apart, a signal that no direct personal communication is desired.

Figure 11.9
Body language: The postures we adopt and the gestures we make convey messages. Like all other kinds of behavior, how we use our bodies is governed by social rules.

Body Language.   The way you carry your body also communicates information about you. If you stand tall and erect, you convey the impression of self-assurance. If you sit and talk with your arms folded and legs crossed, you communicate that you are protecting yourself. But when you unfold your arms and stretch out, you may be saying that you are open to people.

One group of researchers found that women who adopt an open body position are better liked and are listened to more closely than women who assume a closed position. A number of students were given a questionnaire that measured their opinions on everything from the legalization of marijuana to the custom of tipping. A few weeks later they were invited back and asked to evaluate one student's responses. Some were shown a slide of this female student sitting in a closed position; others saw a slide of her sitting in a neutral or open position. A high percentge of those who saw the open-looking student indicated they liked her and changed many of their opinions to agree with hers when they filled out a second questionnaire (McGinley, LeFevre, and McGinley, 1975).

Although the use of body language is often unconscious, many of the postures we adopt and gestures we make are governed by **social rules** (Figure 11.9). These rules are very subtle. For example, your boss is much more likely to touch you than you are to touch him—unilateral touching is a prerogative of higher status.

There are cultural differences in body language, just as there are in the use of space. For example, Americans move their heads up and down to show agreement and shake them back and forth to show disagreement. The Semang of Malaya thrust their heads sharply forward to agree and lower their eyes to disagree, while the Dayak of Borneo agree by raising their eyebrows and disagree by bringing them together.

But you don't have to go to Borneo to observe cultural variations in nonverbal communication. In a field study conducted in hospitals, airports, and fast-food restaurants, LaFrance and Mayo (1976) found that American blacks and whites use eye contact in very different ways. Although people of both races looked at each other for the same proportion of time during a conversation, the timing was different. Blacks tend to look at their partner when they are speaking, and to look away while listening; whites do just the opposite. These unconscious differences may sometimes make blacks and whites uncomfortable when they talk to each other.

HOW PEOPLE PERCEIVE ONE ANOTHER

It takes people very little time to make judgments about one another. From one brief conversation, or even by watching a person across a room, you may form an impression of what someone is like. And first impressions influence the future of a relationship. If a person *seems* interesting, he or she becomes a candidate for future interaction. A person who seems to have nothing interesting to say—or much too much to say—does not. We tend to be sympathetic toward someone who seems shy; to expect a lot from someone who impresses us as intelligent; to be wary of a person who strikes us as aggressive.

Forming an impression of a person is not a passive process in which certain characteristics of the individual are the input and a certain impression is the automatic outcome. If impressions varied only when input varied, then everyone meeting a particular stranger would form the same impression of him or her. This, of course, is not what happens. One individual may judge a newcomer to be "quiet," another may judge the same

Intelligent
Warm
Confident
Practical

Figure 11.10
What is your impression of this person? Do you think you would like him? What do you think of the way he is dressed? What sort of expression does he have on his face? When you have formed an impression, turn to the drawing in Figure 11.11 and do the same.

person to be "dull," and still another person may think the person "mysterious." These various impressions lead to different expectations of the newcomer and to different patterns of interaction with him or her.

Implicit Personality Theory

One reason different people tend to develop different impressions of the same stranger is that we each have our own **implicit personality theory**—our own set of assumptions about how people behave and what traits or characteristics go together. When you meet someone who seems unusually intelligent, you may assume she is also active, highly motivated, conscientious, and so on. Another person in the group may have an altogether different "theory" about highly intelligent people—that they are unrealistic, boastful, insensitive, and the like. Whatever the person does provides "evidence" for both theories. You are impressed by how animated she becomes when talking about her work; the other person is impressed by how little attention she pays to other people. Both of you are filling in gaps in what you know about the person, fitting her into a type you carry around in your head.

Experiments indicate that our impressions are strongly influenced by a few traits (Figures 11.10, 11.11). For example, one researcher invited a guest lecturer to a psychology class. Beforehand all the students were given a brief description of the visitor. The descriptions were identical in all traits but one. Half the students were told that the speaker was cold, the other half that he was warm. After the lecture the researcher asked all the students to evaluate the lecturer. Reading their impressions, you would hardly

Intelligent
Cold
Confident
Practical

Figure 11.11
If your impressions of this person are different from your impressions of the person in Figure 11.10, the difference must be due to the change in a single word—the illustrations are otherwise identical.

know that the two groups of students were describing the same person. The students who had been told he was cold saw a humorless, ruthless, self-centered person. The other students saw a relaxed, friendly, concerned person. Changing one word—substituting "warm" for "cold"—had a dramatic impact on the audience's perception of the lecturer. It also affected their behavior. Students in the "warm group" were warm themselves, initiating more conversations with the speaker than did the students in the other group (Kelley, 1950).

Stereotypes.   The line between applying implicit personality theories to people (as the students did) and thinking in stereotypes is a very thin one. A **stereotype** is a set of assumptions about people in a given category. The belief that Jews are clannish or that students who wear suits are not to be trusted are examples. Stereotypes are based on half-truths and nontruths, and tend to blind us to differences among people and to the way individuals actually behave.

Implicit personality theories are useful because they help us to predict with *some* degree of accuracy how people will behave. Without them, we would spend considerable energy observing and testing people to find out what they are like, whether we want to pursue a relationship with them, and so on. Like stereotypes, the assumptions we make about people from our first impressions tend to weaken as we get to know them better.

Personality Versus Circumstance: Attribution Theory

First impressions and the decision to pursue or abandon a relationship depend in large part on the situations in which we observe people. Suppose you walk into a library and find a man pacing back and forth. You sit down. He continues to pace for what seems like hours. The chances are you would want to avoid this man. He seems like an extremely unhappy and nervous person. But suppose the setting is the waiting room for a maternity ward. Your feelings about him would be entirely different (Rubin, 1973: 100–101).

The conclusions we draw about people thus vary according to whether we attribute their actions to personal qualities (such as general nervousness) or to the situation or role in which they find themselves (such as an expectant father). In recent years, many social psychologists have become interested in **attribution theory**—the attempt to understand how we interpret people's actions (Shaver, 1975). One key step involves deciding, as we did in the case of the pacing man, whether behavior is a result of personal qualities or external pressure (Figure 11.12).

Another important issue involves motive and intent: "What did he hope to accomplish by that?" If a new friend, for example, starts off your day by telling you that the sweater you just bought is hideous, you can interpret that as an attempt to be helpful or as an act of hostility. Your opinion of this person will depend on the motive you accept.

Of course, some actions are more revealing than others. Some behavior is so common that it reveals very little about personality. If a bank teller cashes your check without comment and gives you a half smile, you prob-

Figure 11.12
Who attributes what to whom? In this first part of an experiment, actors A and B were talking while observers C and D watched B and A, respectively. Both actors later rated their own behavior in terms of personal characteristics about themselves or characteristics of the situation. Observers C and D similarly rated each of their target actors. The results showed that actors attributed their own behavior more to situational factors than to enduring personality factors. Observers, however, saw the actors' behavior more in terms of personality factors. (Adapted from Storms, 1973)

How we interpret another's behavior depends just as much on how we perceive it as on what it is.

ably will not be able to tell much about her personality. But if she greets you with a warm hello (even though you've never laid eyes on this person in your life) and proceeds to get you in a long discussion of the weather, politics, and football, you might infer a great deal more about her personality. According to one theory (Jones and Davis, 1965), behavior that is unexpected or unusual and that can most plausibly be explained by only one motive provides the most important clues to a person's real nature.

In one study investigating attribution theory, a group of researchers asked subjects to watch three individuals take a test, and to evaluate their intelligence at various points during the test and after it was finished. *All* three individuals answered fifteen of thirty questions correctly. However, one started out well but then did poorly; the second did poorly at first but then improved; the third alternated between right and wrong answers, showing no pattern. Most subjects indicated that they thought the first individual was more intelligent than the others, although they all received the same score (Jones *et al.*, 1968). Why? Because once you have committed yourself to a judgment about a person (as subjects were required to do), changing your evaluation means admitting you made a mistake. Most of us find this somewhat hard to do. The subjects in this experiment clung to their original evaluation rather than admit a mistake.

The point is that we all actively perceive other people's actions. And what we conclude about other people depends not just on what they do, but also on our interpretations. This is true not just when we deal with individuals, but also when we react to groups.

WHAT ARE GROUPS?

What do the Rolling Stones, the St. Stanislaus Parish Bowling Team, the National Association for Retired Midgets, and Argentina have in common?

Each can be classified as a group. In general, the features that distinguish a group from a nongroup are interdependence and shared goals.

Interdependence

All the people in the world who have red hair and freckles make up a category of people, but they are not a group. The people in this collection are not interdependent. Interdependence occurs when any action by one of them will affect or influence the other members or when the same event will influence each one. For instance, in groups of athletes, entertainers, or roommates, each member has a certain responsibility to the rest of the group; if he or she does not fulfill his or her responsibility, the other members will be affected. For the athletes, the consequence may be losing the game; for the entertainers, a bad show; for the roommates, a messy apartment.

In small groups, members usually have a direct influence on one another: one person yells at another, smiles at him, or passes him a note. In larger groups, the influence may be indirect. The interdependence between you and the president of the United States is not a result of personal contact. Nevertheless, one of the things that make the people of the United States a group is the fact that the president's actions affect you and that your actions, together with those of many other Americans, affect him.

Common Goals

Group members become interdependent because they see themselves as sharing certain common goals. Groups are usually created to perform tasks

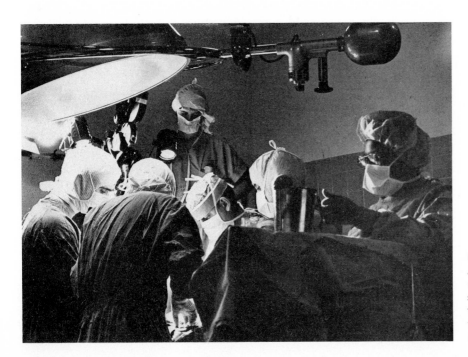

Figure 11.13
A task-oriented group. Whether or not the doctors and nurses in this surgical team are friendly outside the operating room does not matter; their main purpose as a group is to do a certain job.

or to organize activities that no individual could handle alone. Members of a consumer group, for example, share the common goal of working for consumer protection. Members of ethnic and religious groups desire to perpetuate a common heritage or set of beliefs.

The purposes groups serve are of two general kinds: **task functions,** those directed toward getting some job done; and **social functions,** those directed toward filling the emotional needs of members. In most groups, task and social functions are naturally combined and cannot easily be separated.

Political parties, teams of surgeons, and crews of construction workers are all task-oriented groups (Figure 11.13). Although social interactions occur within each of these groups, their main purpose is to complete a project or achieve some change in the environment. Social functions are emphasized in more informal, temporary groups. When people take walks together, attend parties, or participate in conversations, they have formed a group to gain such social rewards as companionship and emotional support. But again, every group involves both task and social functions, at least to some degree.

HOW GROUPS ARE HELD TOGETHER

The factors that work to hold groups together—that increase cohesiveness—include the attitudes and standards they share, and their commitment to them.

Norms

One way in which groups keep their members going in the same direction is by developing group norms. **Norms** are rules for the behavior and attitudes of group members. These rules are not necessarily rigid laws. They may be more like tendencies or habits. But group members are expected to act in accordance with group norms and are punished in some way if they do not. If a college student shaved her hair off, her friends would not hesitate to say something about it. And strangers might point and giggle—simply because she violated the norm that hair should be a certain length and style. Thus, the punishment may take the form of coldness or criticism from other group members. If the norm is very important to the group, a member who violates it may receive a more severe punishment or may be excluded from the group.

Ideology

For a group to be cohesive, members must share the same values. In some cases, people are drawn together because they discover they have common ideas, attitudes, and goals—that is, a common **ideology.** In other instances, people are attracted to a group because its ideology provides them with a new way of looking at themselves and interpreting events, and a new set of goals and means for achieving them. The civil-rights and black-power movements, for example, provided an explanation of black oppression in America and the hope that something could be done to change things. Similarly, the women's movement focused on female discontent. Leaders, heroes and heroines, rallies, books and pamphlets, slogans, and symbols all help to popularize an ideology, win converts, and create feelings of solidarity among group members.

Commitment

Cohesiveness will be high if members are committed to their group. One factor that increases individual commitment is the requirement of personal sacrifice. If a person is willing to pay money, endure hardship, or undergo humiliation to belong to a group, he or she is likely to stick with it. For example, college students who undergo embarrassing initiation rites to join sororities or fraternities tend to develop a loyalty to the group that lasts well beyond their college years.

Another factor that strengthens group commitment is participation. When people actively participate in group decisions and share the rewards of the group's accomplishments, their feeling of membership increases—they feel that they have helped make the group what it is. For example, social psychologists have compared groups of workers who participate in decisions that affect their jobs with other workers who elect representatives to decision-making committees or workers who are simply told what to do. Those who participate have higher morale and accept change more readily than the other workers (Coch and French, 1948).

The processes that hold a group together must work both ways. The individual must be responsive to the norms of the group, subscribe to its ideology, and be prepared to make sacrifices in order to be a part of it. But the group must also respond to the needs of its members. It cannot achieve cohesiveness if its norms are unenforceable, if its ideology is inconsistent with the beliefs of its members, or if the rewards it offers do not outweigh the sacrifices it requires.

INTERACTIONS WITHIN GROUPS

Providing an individual with values and a sense of identity is only one aspect of the group's meaning to him or her. The particular part he or she plays in the group's activities is also important. Each group member has certain unique abilities and interests, and the group has a number of different tasks that need to be performed. The study of the parts various members play in the group, and of how these parts are interrelated, is the study of **group structure.**

There are many different aspects to group structure: the personal relationships between individual members, such as liking relationships and trusting relationships; the rank of each member on a particular dimension, such as power, popularity, status, or amount of resources; and the roles

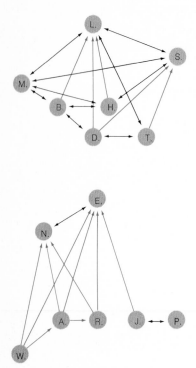

Figure 11.14
Sociograms showing patterns of friendship choices within two groups. The blue arrows indicate liking that is not returned; the black arrows indicate a two-way friendship. The more a person is liked, the higher in the pattern he or she appears. The pattern of the bottom group shows a hierarchical structure, with E and N clearly the leaders. The sociogram of the top group indicates strong group cohesiveness, with even D and T, the two least-liked members, clearly tied in to the group and having friends who like them.

various members play. (A few typical group roles are leader, joker, black sheep, and the silent member.)

Communication Patterns

One technique psychologists use to analyze group structure is the **sociogram.** All members of a group are asked to name those people with whom they would like to interact on a given occasion or for a specific purpose, those they like best, and so on. For example, the members may be asked with whom they would like to go to a party, to discuss politics, to spend a vacation, or to complete an organizational task. Their choices can then be diagramed, as shown in Figure 11.14. Sociograms can help psychologists predict how that individual is likely to communicate with other group members.

Another way to discover the structure of a group is to examine the communication patterns in the group—who says what to whom, and how often.

One experiment on communication patterns was done by Harold Leavitt in 1951. He gave a card with several symbols on it to each person in a group of five. (Leavitt put each person in a separate room or booth and allowed the members to communicate only by written messages.) In this way he was able to create the networks shown in Figure 11.15. Each circle represents a person; the lines represent open channels. Subjects placed in each position could exchange messages only with the persons to whom they were connected by channels.

The most interesting result of this experiment was that the people who were organized into a "circle" were the slowest at solving the problem but the happiest at doing it. In this group everyone sent and received a large number of messages until someone solved the problem and passed the information on. In the "wheel," by contrast, everyone sent a few messages to one center person, who figured out the answer and told the rest what it was. These groups found the solution quickly, but the people on the outside of the wheel did not particularly enjoy the job.

Following the experiment, the members in each group were asked to identify the leader of their group. In the centralized groups (wheel, Y, and chain), the person in the center was usually chosen as the group leader. But in the circle network half the group members said they thought there was no real leader, and those who did say there was a leader disagreed on who that leader was. Thus a centralized organization seems more useful for task-oriented groups, whereas a decentralized network is more useful in socially oriented groups.

Leadership

All groups, whether made up of gangsters, soldiers, workers, or politicians, have leaders. A leader embodies the norms and ideals of the group and represents the group to outsiders. Within the group, a leader initiates action, gives orders, makes decisions, and settles disputes. In short, a leader is one who has a great deal of influence on the other members of the group.

Most of us think of leadership as a personality trait. To an extent this is true. Leaders tend to be better adjusted, more self-confident, more energetic and outgoing, and slightly more intelligent than other members of their group (Gibb, 1969). However, the nature of the group in part determines who will lead. Different circumstances call for different kinds of leaders. A group that is threatened by internal conflict requires a leader who is good at handling people, settling disputes, soothing tempers, and the like. A group that has a complex task to perform needs a leader with special experience to set goals and plan strategies for achieving them (Fiedler, 1969).

Within a group there may be two kinds of leaders, then. They are easy to tell apart by the things they say. One kind, the **social leader,** tends to make encouraging remarks, to break any tension with a joke, to solicit the reactions of others to whatever is going on. The other, the **task leader,** takes over when it is time to convey information, give opinions, or suggest how to do something. This leader is bossier and is not reluctant to disagree and press for a particular idea or course of action even if it creates tension in the group. A task leader usually has special knowledge or skills, and so different people may fill this role, depending on what the group is doing. The social leader is likely to be the same person, whatever the group does, because the need for promoting cohesion is always there. The social leader usually commands the loyalty of the group (Bales, 1958).

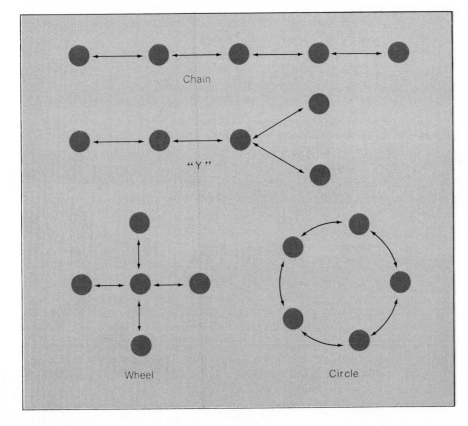

Figure 11.15
Harold Leavitt's communication network.

There are many ways in which a person can acquire enough influence to become the leader of a group. Three of the most common are expertise, charisma, and power.

An expert directs the group's activity because he or she has the knowledge that the group needs to achieve its goals. For example, a ship's captain must know how to run a ship and how to meet an emergency at sea. Many leaders also possess a strong emotional appeal, or **charisma.** President John F. Kennedy was a striking example of a political leader with a charisma that aroused strong feelings among both followers and enemies. Influence can also come from the power to control rewards and punishments. A president of a company can give raises and promotions; he can also fire or demote people. He is a leader not because members like him, but because he owns the most shares in the company or because he has been appointed by those who own shares.

For whatever reason a member becomes a leader, the way he or she leads will affect the structure of his or her group and the roles other members play. A powerful leader may make all the important decisions for the group and assign relatively unimportant tasks to other members. A more democratic leader may try to involve as many members as possible in the decision-making process.

Diffusion of Responsibility

Sometimes, several people are faced with a common problem although they have no leader and may not even see themselves as a group. There have been many famous examples of muggings, rapes, and murders that were committed in public while a large group of people watched without intervening or calling for help.

Psychologists have tried to find out why these people didn't act by studying artificial crises. In one experiment, college students were asked to participate in a discussion of personal problems. They were asked to wait in separate rooms. Some were told that they would be communicating with only one other person; others were given the impression that they would be talking with five other people. All communication, the psychologist told each student, was to take place over microphones so that everyone would remain anonymous and thus would speak more freely. Each person was to talk in turn.

In reality, there were no other people—all the voices the subjects heard were on tape. As the discussion progressed, the subject heard one of the participants go into what sounded like an epileptic fit. The victim began to call for help, making choking sounds. The experimenters found that most of the people who thought they were alone with the victim came out of their room to help him. But of those who believed there were four other people nearby, less than half did anything to help.

The experimenters suggested that this behavior was the result of **diffusion of responsibility.** In other words, because several people were present, each subject assumed someone else would help. The researchers found that in experiments where people could see the other participants, the same pattern emerged. In addition, bystanders reassured one another that it would not be a good idea to interfere. These findings on diffusion of responsibility suggest that the larger the crowd or group of bystanders, the more likely any given individual is to feel that he or she is not responsible for whatever is going on (Darley and Latane, 1968).

Another influence that inhibits action is the tendency to minimize the *need* for any response. To act, you must admit that an emergency exists. But you may not know exactly what is going on when you hear screams or loud thumps upstairs. You are likely to wait before risking the embarrassment of rushing to help where help is not needed or wanted. It is easier to persuade yourself that nothing needs to be done if you look around and see other people behaving calmly. Not only can you see that they think nothing is wrong, but you can see that not doing anything is entirely proper. You are able to minimize the need to act and shift any responsibility to those around you.

USING PSYCHOLOGY

Environmental Psychology

Crime victims who are ignored by passersby are usually found in cities. Some of the other problems of urban areas—crowding, stressors like air and noise pollution, and the design of housing projects—are the focus of research in an exciting new area called **environmental psychology.** In the broadest sense, this can be defined as the study of how people are affected by their physical environments.

Crowding and Behavior: Exposing a Myth

Psychologist Jonathan Freedman (1975) tackled a complex topic—the effects of crowding on human behavior—in a number of separate studies extending over a period of years. At the start, Freedman assumed (as most of us do) that crowding has a negative effect on people. For centuries people have believed that the high rates of crime, mental illness, and other sicknesses found in cities are the direct result of too many people living in too little space.

Research seemed to support this. In a now classic experiment, John B. Calhoun (1962) showed that when rats are overcrowded some become aggressive and bite other rats; some neglect and even kill their young; some withdraw completely. Reading Calhoun's results, you have the feeling you are reading about an overcrowded city slum.

What Freedman discovered, however, was that Calhoun's findings simply do not apply to people. The number of people per square mile, or population density, of a city varies considerably from one neighborhood to the next. So does the amount of space people have in their homes. Freedman selected groups of people who had similar incomes, years of education, and ethnic and religious backgrounds, but who lived in neighborhoods with very different densities. Some might have only five families per acre; others had hundreds. Some had large homes, other had less living space. In short, the groups were matched for many characteristics, but were deliberately *mismatched* for one—the density of their neighborhoods and dwellings. Freedman found that crowding was *not* directly related to rates of crime, or physical and mental illness. The researchers then conducted a number of experiments to determine whether groups of people in larger rooms with plenty of space perform tasks better than similar groups packed into rooms so small they cannot help bumping into one another. They also wondered whether people in each group would act differently toward one another. Again the results were negative. Crowding did not make people nervous, anxious, or aggressive.

Studies of people who are required to spend relatively large amounts of time in cramped quarters—as astronauts do during training and in space—confirmed this. People tend to become friendlier and more cooperative under such conditions.

In the end Freedman concluded that the effects of crowding depend on the situation. If the situation is pleasant, crowding makes people feel better; if the situation is unpleasant, crowding makes them feel worse. In other words,

Figure 11.16
It is not crowding that makes people nervous, aggressive, or anxious, but the situation. If the situation is unpleasant, crowding makes people feel worse.

being packed together *intensifies* people's reactions, but it does not create feelings of pleasantness or unpleasantness, competitiveness or cooperation, anxiety or ease.

In retrospect, this seems obvious. Research on early humans indicates that Neanderthal and Cro-Magnon men and women—who had abundant space—chose to crowd together. Relatively small caves often housed as many as sixty people. (In a sense, these caves were the first "apartment houses.") But we needn't go so far back in time. Riding in a subway car, waiting in line, or taking an exam are basically unpleasant experiences—and crowding makes them more so. On the other hand, what is more depressing than watching a sports event or a rock concert in an almost-empty auditorium, or finding that only a dozen people showed up for a party in a large apartment? Crowding makes these experiences exciting: the more the merrier!

Architecture

At first glance, Freedman's findings seem to have obvious implications for city planning. If crowding does not necessarily cause hostility, it makes sense to build high-density housing and leave open spaces where people can congregate or wander by themselves, rather than spread housing out.

But other research suggests that it's not quite that simple. In an elaborate survey of architecture and crime, Oscar Newman (1972) found that high-rise housing projects have a much higher crime rate than smaller projects. For example, the Pruitt-Igoe Housing Project (thirty-three eleven-story high rises built in downtown St. Louis in the early 1950s) was plagued with so much crime and vandalism that some of the buildings had to be demolished in 1972. The problems were based not on crowding, but on the way the buildings were designed.

Elevator buildings with long corridors tend to isolate neighbors. You can't see very much through your peephole, and your windows look out on distant public space. People don't get to know each other, and they can't see the vandals at work in the building. People who live in smaller buildings with walk-up apartments develop a stronger sense of territoriality—a specific area is defined as "home" and they know who belongs there and who does not. Residents in these smaller buildings watch for outsiders and help prevent vandalism.

Other environmental psychologists have studied the way different types of dormitories encourage different types of behavior. One series of studies (Baum and Valins, 1977) com-

Figure 11.17
The Pruitt-Igoe housing project: curtainless and boarded-up windows give evidence of the link between architecture and a high rate of crime and vandalism.

pared college students who lived in traditional corridor dormitories (in this case, sixteen bedrooms with a central lounge and a bathroom) with those whose dormitories were organized into suites (three bedrooms with a small bathroom and lounge). Despite the fact that the two dorms had almost exactly the same number of square feet per student, corridor residents felt much more crowded. Corridor life was more stressful: people felt that they were forced to deal with people they didn't want to bother with, and as a result they became withdrawn. Later experiments proved that this withdrawal was not limited to the dormitory. Finally, students who lived in the corridor dormitories felt that they had little control over their daily lives, while suite residents felt and acted like masters of their own fate. Overall, there was no doubt that the suite arrangements were superior.

Obviously, the buildings people live in and the nature of their physical environment are important influences on the way they behave. There is every indication that environmental psychologists will learn more about these relationships in the next few years.

GROUP CONFLICT VERSUS COOPERATION

Conflicts between groups are a fact of everyday life: some level of hostility exists between women and men, young and old, workers and bosses, blacks and whites, Catholics and Protestants, students and teachers. Why do these conflicts exist, and why do they persist? In the next chapter, we discuss prejudice, discrimination, and related issues. But first let us consider the findings of a group of psychologists who created a boys' camp in order to study intergroup relations. The camp at Robber's Cave offered all the usual activities, and the boys had no idea that they were part of an experiment.

From the beginning of the experiment, the boys were divided into two separate groups. The boys hiked, swam, and played baseball only with members of their own group, and friendships and group spirit soon developed. After a while the experimenters (working as counselors) brought the groups together for a tournament. The psychologists had hypothesized that when these two groups of boys were placed in competitive situations, where one group could achieve its goals only at the expense of the other, hostility would develop. They were right.

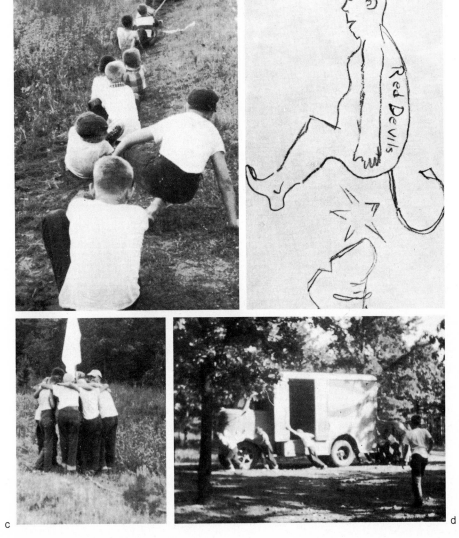

Figure 11.18
Scenes from the Robber's Cave experiment. (a) The boys in competition against one another in such activities as tug-of-war. (b) The considerable hostility that developed between the two groups was expressed in drawings like this one. (c) Hostility was also expressed in fights and in raids on "enemy" cabins. (d) The hostility was eliminated by having the boys perform tasks that needed cooperation, such as pushing a truck that supplied food to the camp.

Although the games began in a spirit of good sportsmanship, tension mounted as the tournament continued. Friendly competition gave way to name calling, fistfights, and raids on enemy cabins. The psychologists had demonstrated the ease with which they could produce unity within the two boys' groups and hatred between them. The experimenters then tried to see what might end the conflict and create harmony between the two groups. They tried to bring the groups together for enjoyable activities, such as a movie and a good meal. This approach failed. The campers shoved and pushed each other, threw food and insults, and generally used the opportunity to continue their attacks.

Next, the psychologists deliberately invented a series of "emergencies" so that the boys would either have to help one another or lose the chance to do or get something they all wanted. For instance, one morning someone reported that the water line to the camp had broken. The boys were told that unless they worked together to find the break and fix it, they would all have to leave camp. By afternoon, they had jointly found and fixed the damage. Gradually, through such cooperative activities, intergroup hostility and tensions lessened. Friendships began to develop between individuals of the opposing groups, and eventually the groups began to seek out occasions to mingle. At the end of the camp period, members of both groups requested that they ride home together on the same bus.

The results of this experiment were striking. A group of boys from identical backgrounds had developed considerable hostility toward each other, simply because they were placed in competition. The crucial factor in eliminating group hostility was cooperation (Sherif *et al.*, 1961).

SUMMARY

1. Social psychologists have found that people need other people most when they are afraid, anxious, unsure of themselves, or want to compare their feelings to the feelings of others in the same situation.

2. The most important factor in determining whether two people will become friends is physical proximity. Psychologists have found that individuals become friends with the people to whom they are close physically.

3. Some of the rewards found in friendships are stimulation, utility, and ego support. These are evaluated consciously or unconsciously in every friendship. Other factors that affect a person's choice of friends are physical appearance, approval, and similarity.

4. People play different roles in everyday life. Yet in all settings people usually feel that they are honest and authentic.

5. Body language—gestures, positions, and movements of the body—communicates information about you. Much of it is unconscious, and many gestures are governed by social rules. Since social rules vary from culture to culture, body language varies as well.

6. In forming impressions of other people, each person has his or her own implicit personality theory—a set of assumptions about how people behave and what traits or characteristics go together. These theories only have some degree of accuracy and tend to weaken as we develop relationships.

7. Attribution theory attempts to understand how we interpret people's actions. For example, the conclusions we draw about people vary according

to whether we attribute their actions to personal qualities or to the situation in which we find them.

8. Groups are aggregates of people who are interdependent—that is, the actions of any one group member will affect or influence other members. Group members become interdependent because they see themselves as sharing common goals.

9. The two primary purposes of groups are to perform task functions and to perform social functions. Most groups serve both functions to some extent.

10. Group interdependence is maintained through the use of group norms that direct the behavior of members. Violation of group norms results in disapproval from other group members.

11. Group structure is the way in which individuals fit together into a whole unit. The way people interact in a group is studied through the use of sociograms and the analysis of communication patterns. An important element in the group's structure is leadership. A leader is the person who exerts the most influence in a group.

12. Diffusion of responsibility is similar to mob action in that people in a crowd seem to feel they are not responsible for whatever is going on. In a crisis, people often refrain from acting because they minimize the emergency, because they expect other people to act, or because they do not want to be "different."

13. Environmental psychology studies how people are affected by their physical environment. For example, researchers have found that crowding is not good or bad in itself, it simply tends to intensify people's reactions.

14. Group conflict can be broken down when members of hostile groups need to cooperate.

GLOSSARY

attribution theory: A theory that tries to understand how we interpret people's behavior.

body language: Nonverbal communication through gestures, positions, and movements of the body.

charisma: A leader's strong emotional appeal that arouses enthusiasm and loyalty.

cohesiveness: The degree to which members of groups are closely attached to one another and committed to the group's goals.

complementarity: The attraction that often develops between opposite types of people because of the ability of one to supply what the other lacks.

diffusion of responsibility: The tendency of the presence of others to lessen an individual's feelings of responsibility for his or her actions or failure to act.

ego-support value: The ability of a person to provide another person with sympathy, encouragement, and approval.

environmental psychology: The study of how people are affected by their physical environments.

group: An aggregate of people characterized by shared goals and a degree of interdependence.

ideology: The set of principles, attitudes, and defined objectives for which a group stands.

implicit personality theory: A set of assumptions each person has about how people behave and what personality traits or characteristics go together.

nonverbal communication: The process of communicating through the use of space, body language, and facial expression.

norms: Shared standards of behavior accepted by and expected from group members.

personal space: The space between two people that communicates their feelings about one another and defines the relationship.

physical proximity: The physical nearness of one person to another person.

reward values: The emotional bonuses obtained from personal interactions with other people that cause people to develop friendships.

social functions: In groups, those functions directed toward satisfying the emotional needs of members.

social leader: The leader within a group who promotes group cohesion and commands group loyalty.

social rule: Any agreement among members of society about how people should act in particular situations; also called a *norm*.

sociogram: A diagram representing relationships within a group.

stereotype: A set of assumptions about people in a given category based on half-truths and non-truths.

stimulation value: The ability of a person or subject to interest or to expose you to new ideas and experiences.

task functions: In groups, those functions directed toward getting a job done.

task leader: The leader within a group who takes over when the group must accomplish something.

utility value: The ability of a person or subject to help another achieve his or her goals.

ACTIVITIES

1. We may think that stereotyping does not influence us. Watch a television program about (a) a detective, (b) a black family, (c) an independent woman. What character traits does each have? Do we laugh at some of these characterizations when they do not fit the stereotypes? Which stereotypes do we not laugh at?

2. Examine the interactions between members of your family, your friends, or even strangers, paying as little attention as possible to verbal interaction and noting instead proximity, posture, gesture, facial expression, eye contact, relative position, and nonlinguistic verbal cues. Are you able to interpret the body language? Does this nonverbal communication conflict with what people communicate verbally? What happens if you reply verbally to nonverbal messages?

3. How do you analyze new instructors at the beginning of a term? On what do you base your impressions? How do your impressions affect how you behave toward each instructor? Have you ever changed your mind after getting the "wrong impression" about someone?

4. Conduct an experiment on personal space by going to the library and sitting at a table with another person. After a few minutes begin to "invade" his or her space by placing your books and papers across the imaginary line that divides the space between the two of you. Describe his or her reactions to your encroachments.

5. Get on an elevator and stand facing the back wall. Have a friend watch the other riders to see how they react to the violation of this simple social norm.

6. Describe several situations in which you either "put on an act" or disguised your true feeling regarding a person or situation. Did your deception occur consciously or unconsciously? How did others react?

7. List in detail the main things you look for when you choose close friends. What are your reasons for rejecting certain people as either close friends or acquaintances?

8. Write down the first ten or fifteen words or phrases that come to mind when you ask yourself "Who am I?" Now, categorize these items as either physical traits, psychological characteristics, or group affiliations. How much of your self-concept is built on your identification with groups?

9. Consider your primary (or most important) group. What do you have to do to belong? What sacrifices would you be willing to make in order to remain in the group? What sacrifices would you be

unwilling to make? For what reason(s), if any, would you be willing to sacrifice your life for this group?

10. Do any of the groups to which you belong have rivals—other groups you compete against (for example, a rival team)? If so, what are the people like in the rival group? What information did you use to arrive at an answer to this question?

11. In the groups to which you belong (clubs, your school, and so on) you have undoubtedly had leaders or people with influence over you. Pick a few such leaders and try to analyze the sources of their influence. Are they experts? Do they have charisma? Are they socially attractive? How much power do they have? How have they obtained it?

12. Ask one male and one female to reverse sex roles and discuss the following contentions. (1) Men need liberation as much as women. (2) Men are at least as vain as women. (3) Women do not mind being dominated as long as they are loved and cared for. (4) Women can never be as competent as men, or men as women in which of the following occupations: scientist; child rearer; politician; construction worker; nurse; airplane pilot?

SUGGESTED READINGS

ARONSON, ELLIOT. *The Social Animal.* 2nd ed. San Francisco: Freeman, 1976. A conversationally written textbook in social psychology. It is excellent reading for the person who wants to go deeper into the ideas presented in this and the next chapter.

BERSCHEID, ELLEN, AND WALSTER, ELAINE. *Interpersonal Attraction.* 2nd ed. Reading, Mass.: Addison-Wesley, 1978. A well-organized and valuable review of research in this area.

CARTWRIGHT, DORWIN, AND ZANDER, ALVIN (EDS.). *Group Dynamics: Research and Theory.* 3rd ed. New York: Harper & Row, 1968. A collection of classic papers accompanied by an excellent integrative introductory chapter written by the editors.

HALL, EDWARD T. *The Silent Language.* Garden City, N.Y.: Doubleday, 1959. Hall suggests that "communication occurs simultaneously on different levels of consciousness, ranging from full awareness to out-of-awareness." An excellent book on nonverbal communication.

_____. *The Hidden Dimension.* Garden City, N.Y.: Doubleday, 1966. A thorough and well-written book that describes the bubbles of privacy people carry about them and the purpose of personal space.

HASTORF, ALBERT H., SCHNEDIER, DAVID J., AND POLEFKA, JUDITH. *Person Perception.* 2nd ed. Reading, Mass.: Addison-Wesley, 1979. This book provides a brief but comprehensive overview of how people perceive one another. The authors pay special attention to attribution theory and implicit personality theory.

HOFFER, ERIC. *The True Believer.* New York: Harper & Row, 1951 (paper). Hoffer identifies and analyzes the characteristics of the "true believer"—the person who identifies so much with a group that he or she has no identity away from it.

LA FRANCE, MARIANNE, AND MAYO, CLARA. *Moving Bodies: Nonverbal Communication in Social Relationships.* Monterey, Calif.: Brooks/Cole Publishing, 1978.

PARKINSON, C. NORTHCOTE. *Parkinson's Law and Other Studies in Administration.* New York: Ballantine, 1957 (paper). A clever analysis of organizations based on Parkinson's experience in the British civil service. Parkinson's law says that work expands to fill the time available for its completion.

SHAW, MARVIN E. *Group Dynamics: The Psychology of Small Group Behavior.* New York: McGraw-Hill, 1976. An excellent text in which the author reviews the field, summarizes what is known, and points to problems for future research.

BIBLIOGRAPHY

ARONSON, E., AND LINDER, D. "Gain and Loss of Esteem as Determinants of Interpersonal Attractiveness." *Journal of Experimental Social Psychology*, 1 (1965): 156–171.

BALES, R. F. "Task Roles and Social Roles in Problem-solving Groups." In *Readings in Social Psychology*, ed. by E. Maccoby, T. M. Newcomb, and E. L. Hartley. 3rd ed. New York: Holt, Rinehart & Winston, 1958, pp. 347–447.

BANDURA, A., AND WALTERS, R. H. *Social Learning and Personality Development*. New York: Holt, Rinehart & Winston, 1963.

BAUM, ANDREW, AND VALINS, STUART. *Architecture and Social Behavior*. Hillsdale, N.J.: Lawrence Erlbaum Associates, 1977.

BERSCHEID, ELLEN, AND WALSTER, ELAINE. *Interpersonal Attraction*. 2nd ed. Reading, Mass.: Addison-Wesley, 1978.

CALHOUN, JOHN B. "Population Density and Social Pathology." *Scientific American*, 206 (1962): 139–148.

COCH, L., AND FRENCH, J. R. P., JR. "Overcoming Resistance to Change." *Human Relations*, 1 (1948): 512–532.

DARLEY J. M., AND LATANE, B. "Bystander Intervention in Emergencies: Diffusion of Responsibility." *Journal of Personality and Social Psychology*, 8 (1968): 377–383.

DION, K. L., BERSCHEID, E., AND WALSTER, E. "What Is Beautiful Is Good." *Journal of Personality and Social Psychology*, 24 (1972): 285–290.

FIEDLER, F. E. "Style or Circumstance: The Leadership Enigma." *Psychology Today*, 2 (1969): 38–43.

FREEDMAN, JONATHAN L. *Crowding and Behavior*. San Francisco: Freeman, 1975.

GERARD, H. B., AND RABBIE, J. M. "Fear and Social Comparison." *Journal of Abnormal and Social Psychology*, 62 (1961): 586–592.

GERGEN, KENNETH J. *The Concept of Self*. New York: Holt, Rinehart & Winston, 1971.

GIBB, C. "Leadership." In *The Handbook of Social Psychology*, ed. by G. Lindsey and E. Aronson. Vol. 4. 2nd ed. Reading, Mass.: Addison-Wesley, 1969.

GOFFMAN, ERVING. *The Presentation of the Self in Everyday Life*. New York: Doubleday, 1959 (paper).

———. *Relations in Public*. New York: Harper & Row, 1971.

HALL, EDWARD T. *The Silent Language*. Garden City, N.Y.: Doubleday, 1959.

———. *The Hidden Dimension*. Garden City, N.Y.: Doubleday, 1966.

HASTORF, ALBERT H., SCHNEIDER, DAVID J., AND POLEFKA, JUDITH. *Person Perception*. 2nd ed. Reading, Mass.: Addison-Wesley, 1979.

IZARD, CARROLL E. *The Face of Emotion*. New York: Appleton-Century-Crofts, 1971.

JONES, EDWARD E., AND DAVIS, KEITH E. "From Acts to Dispositions: The Attribution Process in Person Perception." In *Advances in Experimental Social Psychology*, ed. by Leonard Berkowitz. Vol. 2. New York: Academic Press, 1965, pp. 219–266.

JONES, E. E., ET AL. "Internal States or Emotional Stimuli: Observers' Attitude Judgments and the Dissonance Theory–Self-Presentation Controversy." *Journal of Experimental Social Psychology*, 4 (1968): 247–269.

JOURARD, SIDNEY M. *The Transparent Self*. 2nd ed. New York: Van Nostrand, 1971 (paper).

KELLEY, H. H. "The Warm-Cold Variable in First Impressions of Persons." *Journal of Personality*, 18 (1950): 431–439.

LA FRANCE, MARIANNE, AND MAYO, CLARA. "Racial Differences in Gaze Behavior During Conversations: Two Systematic Observation Studies." *Journal of Personality and Social Psychology*, 33 (1976): 547–552.

LEAVITT, H. J. "Some Effects of Certain Communication Patterns on Group Performance." *Journal of Abnormal Social Psychology*, 46 (1951): 38–50.

LEVINGER, GEORGE, AND SNOEK, J. DIDRICK. *Attraction in Relationship: A New Look at Interpersonal Attraction.* Morristown, N.J.: General Learning Press, 1972.

MACKAY, CHARLES. *Extraordinary Popular Delusions and the Madness of Crowds.* New York: Farrar, Straus & Giroux, 1932.

MC GINLEY, HUGH, LE FEVRE, RICHARD, AND MC GINLEY, PAT. "The Influence of a Communicator's Body Position on Opinion Change in Others." *Journal of Personality and Social Psychology*, 31 (1975): 686–690.

MIDDLEBROOK, PATRICIA NILES. *Social Psychology and Modern Life.* New York: Knopf, 1974.

MILLER, GERALD R., AND FONTES, NORMAN E. "Trial by Videotape." *Psychology Today*, 12 (May 1979): 92–101.

NEWMAN, OSCAR. *Defensible Space.* New York: Macmillan, 1972.

RUBIN, ZICK. *Liking and Loving.* New York: Holt, Rinehart & Winston, 1973.

SCHACHTER, STANLEY. *The Psychology of Affiliation.* Stanford, Calif.: Stanford University Press, 1959.

SCHULMAN, JAY, ET AL. "Recipe for a Jury," *Psychology Today*, 6 (May 1973): 37–44.

SHAVER, KELLY G. *An Introduction to Attribution Processes.* Cambridge, Mass.: Winthrop, 1975.

SHERIF, MUZAFER, ET AL. *Intergroup Conflict and Cooperation: The Robber's Cave Experiment.* Norman, Okla.: Institute of Group Relations, 1961.

SIFFRE, MICHEL. "Six Months Alone in a Cave." *National Geographic*, 147 (March 1975): 426–435.

SUE, S., SMITH, R. E., AND CALDWELL, C. "Effects of Inadmissible Evidence on the Decisions of Simulated Jurors." *Journal of Applied Social Psychology*, 3 (1973): 345–353.

WINCH, R. F. *Mate Selection: A Study of Complementary Needs.* New York: Harper & Row, 1958.

WRIGHTSMAN, L. S. "Effects of Waiting with Others on Changes in Level of Felt Anxiety." *Journal of Abnormal and Social Psychology*, 61 (1960): 216–222.

12 Attitudes and Social Influence

Are you convinced that vitamin C is the best cure for the common cold? Did the oil companies cause the energy crisis? How do you feel about atheism, patriotism, and the Los Angeles Rams? Each of us has a wide variety of opinions, attitudes, and beliefs. Some of them are worth dying for, and others aren't worth the time it takes to explain them.

This chapter is about our attitudes, opinions, and beliefs—where they come from and how they change. It is also about the subtle and complex relationships between what we think, what we say, and what we do.

WHERE ATTITUDES COME FROM

An **attitude** is a predisposition to respond in particular ways toward specific things. It has three main elements: (1) a belief or opinion about something; (2) feelings about that thing; and (3) a tendency to act toward that thing in certain ways. For example, what is your attitude toward the senators from your state? Do you *believe* they are doing a good job? Do you *feel* you trust or distrust them? Would you *act* to vote for them?

We have very definite beliefs, feelings, and responses to things about which we have no firsthand knowledge. Where do these attitudes come from? The culture in which you grew up, the people who raised you, and those with whom you associate—your peers—all shape your attitudes.

Culture. Culture influences everything from our taste in food to our attitudes toward human relationships and our political opinions. For example,

Figure 12.1
Our attitudes, opinions, and beliefs can be strongly reinforced and supported by being with others who share them.

most (if not all) Americans would consider eating grubs, curdled milk spiced with cattle blood, or monkey meat disgusting. Yet in some parts of the world these are considered delicacies. Most Americans believe eating meat is essential for good health. Hindus consider our relish for thick, juicy steaks and hamburgers disgusting.

Almost all Americans would agree that in polygamous societies, where a man is allowed to have more than one wife, women are oppressed. But women in polygamous societies feel nothing but pity for a woman whose husband hasn't acquired other wives to help with the work and to keep her company.

Most of us would also agree that parents who interfere in their children's choice of a marriage partner are behaving outrageously and that a person should be able to marry the person he or she loves. But in India, parents choose husbands for their daughters, and Indian girls are relieved not to have to make such an important choice:

> "We girls don't have to worry at all. We know we'll get married. When we are old enough our parents will find a suitable boy and everything will be arranged. We don't have to go into competition with each other.... Besides how would we be able to judge the character of a boy? ... Our parents are older and wiser, and they aren't deceived as easily as we would be. I'd far rather have my parents choose for me" (Mace and Mace, 1960: 131).

The list of culturally derived attitudes is endless. Indeed, it is only by traveling and reading about other ways of life that we discover how many of the things we take for granted are *attitudes*, not facts.

Parents.   There is abundant evidence that all of us acquire many basic attitudes from our parents. How else would you account for the finding that 80 percent of a national sample of elementary school children favored the same political party as their fathers (Hess and Torney, 1967), and 76 percent of high school seniors in a nationwide sample also preferred the same party as both their parents (Jennings and Niemi, 1968)? Parental influence wanes as children get older, of course. A sample of college students selected the same party as their father only 50 to 60 percent of the time (Goldsen *et al.*, 1960). Despite the decline, this study still suggests significant parental influence even after a person has become an adult.

Peers.   It is not surprising that parental influence declines as children get older and are exposed to many other sources of influence. In a now classic study, Newcomb (1943) questioned and requestioned students at Bennington College about their political attitudes over a period of four years. Most of the young women came from wealthy, staunchly conservative families. In contrast, most Bennington faculty members were outspoken liberals. Newcomb found that many of the students were "converted" to the liberal point of view. In 1936, 54 percent of the juniors and seniors supported Franklin D. Roosevelt and the New Deal—although praising Roosevelt to their families would have produced about the same reactions as praising

Figure 12.2
Scenes from Bennington College at
the time Newcomb was there; Newcomb himself is shown on the left.
The marked change in reference
groups experienced by Bennington students is shown in a remark
by one subject: "Family against
faculty has been my struggle
here."

Karl Marx to Ronald Reagan. Indeed, nearly 30 percent of the students favored Socialist or Communist candidates. Newcomb contacted the subjects of his study twenty-five years after they had graduated, and found that most had maintained the attitudes they had acquired in college. One reason was that they had chosen friends, husbands, and careers that supported liberal values (Newcomb *et al.*, 1967). People tend to adopt the likes and dislikes of groups whose approval and acceptance they seek.

ATTITUDE FORMATION

Having suggested where attitudes come from, we can now look at how they develop. The three main processes involved in forming or changing attitudes are compliance, identification, and internalization (Kelman, 1961).

If you praise a certain film director because everyone else does, you are complying. If you find yourself agreeing with everything a friend you particularly admire says about the director, you are identifying with the friend's attitudes. If you genuinely like the director's work and, regardless of what other people think, regard it as brilliant, you are expressing an internalized attitude.

Compliance

One of the best measures of attitude is behavior. If a man settles back into "his chair" after dinner, launches into a discussion of his support of the women's movement, then shouts to his wife—who is in the kitchen washing the dishes—to bring more coffee, you probably wouldn't believe what he had been saying. His actions speak louder than his words. Yet the same man might hire women for jobs he has always considered "men's work" because the law requires him to do so. And he might finally accept his wife's going to work because he knows that she, their children, and many of their friends would consider him old-fashioned if he didn't.

People often **comply** with the wishes of others in order to avoid discomfort or rejection and to gain support. As one Bennington student who professed to be a liberal explained,

> "It's very simple, I was so anxious to be accepted that I accepted the liberal complexion of the community here. I just couldn't stand out against the crowd . . ." (Newcomb, 1943: 132).

But under such circumstances, attitudes do not really change. Social pressure often results in only temporary compliance. Later in this chapter, however, we shall see that compliance can sometimes affect one's beliefs. We shall also discuss in detail how group pressure can lead to conformity.

Identification

One way in which attitudes may really be formed or changed is through the process of **identification.** Suppose you have a favorite uncle who is everything you hope to be. He is a successful musician, has many famous friends, and seems to know a great deal about everything. In many ways you identify with him and copy his behavior. One night, during an intense conversation, your uncle announces he is an atheist. At first you are confused by this statement. You have had a religious upbringing and have always considered religious beliefs as essential. However, as you listen to your uncle, you find yourself starting to agree with him. If a person as knowledgeable and respectable as your uncle holds such beliefs, perhaps you should, too. Later you find yourself feeling that atheism is acceptable. You have adopted a new attitude because of your identification with your uncle.

Identification occurs when a person wants to define himself or herself in terms of a person or group, and therefore adopts the person's or group's attitudes and ways of behaving. Identification is different from compliance because the individual actually believes the newly adopted views. But because these attitudes are based on emotional attachment to another person or group rather than the person's own assessment of the issues, they are fragile. If the person's attachment to that person or group fades, the attitudes may also weaken. Thus, one Bennington student ultimately rejected the liberal point of view:

> "Family against faculty has been my struggle here. As soon as I felt really secure I decided not to let the college atmosphere affect me too much. Everytime I've tried to rebel against my family I've found how terribly wrong I am, and I've very naturally kept to my parents' attitudes" (Newcomb, 1943: 124).

For this student, identification with the college community was only temporary.

Internalization

Internalization is the wholehearted acceptance of an attitude: it becomes an integral part of the person. Internalization is most likely to occur when an attitude is consistent with a person's basic beliefs and values and supports his or her self-image. The person adopts a new attitude because he or she believes it to be right—not because he or she wants to be like someone else.

Internalization is the most lasting of the three sources of attitude formation or change. Your internalized attitudes will be more resistant to pressure from other people because your reasons for holding these views have nothing to do with other people: They are based on your own evaluation of the merits of the issue. A Bennington student put it this way:

> "I became liberal at first because of its prestige value; I remain so because the problems around which my liberalism centers are important. What I want now is to be effective in solving the problems" (Newcomb, 1943: 136).

As this example suggests, compliance or identification may lead to the internalization of an attitude. Often the three overlap. You may support a political candidate in part because you know your friends will approve, in part because someone you admire speaks highly of the candidate, and in part because you believe his or her ideals are consistent with your own.

PREJUDICE

Prejudice means, literally, prejudgment. It means deciding beforehand what a person will be like instead of withholding judgment until it can be based on his or her individual qualities. To hold stereotypes about a group of people is to be prejudiced about them. Prejudice is not necessarily negative—whites who are prejudiced against blacks are often equally prejudiced in favor of whites, for example.

Stereotypes and Roles

Prejudice is strengthened and maintained by the existence of stereotypes and roles. A stereotype is an oversimplified, hard-to-change way of seeing people who belong to some group or category. Black people, scientists, women, Mexicans, and the rich, for example, are often seen in certain rigid ways, rather than as individuals. A role is an oversimplified, hard-to-change way of acting. Stereotypes and roles can act together in a way that makes them difficult to break down. For example, many whites have a stereotype of blacks. Blacks are believed to be irresponsible, superstitious, unintelligent, lazy, and good dancers. Whites who believe this expect blacks to act out a role that is consistent with a stereotype. Blacks are expected to be submissive, deferential, and respectful toward whites, who act out the role

Figure 12.3
These lines from James Baldwin's novel *Nobody Knows My Name* express the impossible dilemma of being black in a white world and the way it feels to try to break free of the roles and stereotypes which are part of that situation.

of the superior, condescending parent. In the past, both blacks and whites accepted these roles and looked at themselves and each other according to these stereotypes. In recent years many blacks and whites have tried to step out of these roles and drop these stereotypes, and to some extent they are succeeding.

Stereotypes are also preserved in the communications media, which have traditionally portrayed American Indians as villains, Italians as greasy gangsters, Jews as misers, and teen-agers as car-crazy rock fans. Many of these stereotypes are changing now, but new ones have replaced them. For example, doctors on television are usually heroes, housewives are charming idiots, and so on. A critical look at television programs and movies reveals a lot about what is widely believed in American society.

Oppression

Group conflict often involves the oppression of one group by another. It is not hard to see how such domination gives rise to feelings of hostility on the part of the oppressed group. In addition, the powerful group stereotypes the oppressed group because it wants to justify its unfair actions and because it wants to stop the oppressed group from fighting back.

This is called a master-slave relationship, for obvious reasons. The present relationship between blacks and whites in America is a result of the fact that at one time blacks were literally the slaves and whites were literally the masters. The oppression of blacks by whites has lessened only gradually. Psychologists are learning that the master-slave relationship exists between other groups, too. For example, the freedom of women has been restricted by men.

The Authoritarian Personality

The most extreme forms of racial oppression were practiced by European Fascists in the 1930s and 1940s. One group of researchers (Adorno *et al.*, 1969) tried to analyze this phenomenon by studying the kinds of people who are attracted to the ideas of racial superiority. They found that highly prejudiced people share a number of traits which they called the **authoritarian personality.** These people tend to have inflexible ideas about themselves and others. Highly conventional, they view differences with suspicion and hostility, and like the sense of security that comes from a very structured authority. They tend to glorify their own qualities and upbringing, despite the fact that their fathers were inclined to be punitive and exacted obedience and unquestioning loyalty through harsh discipline.

The researchers who originally uncovered the relationships among prejudice, personality traits, and upbringing believed that punitive parents create insecure and hostile children. As adults, these people fear their own aggressiveness and cannot admit their own fears and shortcomings. It is easier to claim that others are inferior than to recognize one's own shortcomings. The authoritarian person falls back on the use of stereotypes about others to keep from facing his or her own inadequacies.

This is not the only interpretation of highly prejudiced people, however. The link may be simpler: authoritarian parents teach their views to their children. Or perhaps prejudice and authoritarianism may actually be characteristics of lower social standing rather than quirks of personality.

Prejudice and Discrimination

We can see, then, that there are many possible causes for prejudice. Psychologists have found that people tend to be prejudiced against those less well-off than themselves—they seem to justify being on top by assuming that anyone of lower status or income must be inferior. People who have suffered economic setbacks also tend to be prejudiced—they blame others for their misfortune.

Prejudice also arises from "guilt by association." People who dislike cities and urban living, for example, tend to distrust people associated with cities, such as Jews and blacks. Also, people tend to be prejudiced *toward* those they see as similar to themselves and *against* those who seem different.

Whatever the original cause, prejudice seems to persist. One reason is that children who grow up in an atmosphere of prejudice conform to the prejudicial norm—at first because their parents do and later with the personal conviction that it is the right way to be. Children are socialized into the prejudicial culture of their parents; that is, they encounter numerous forces that induce them to conform to the thoughts and practices of their parents and other teachers, formal and informal.

Prejudice, which is an attitude, should be distinguished from **discrimi-**

Figure 12.4
After the assassination of Martin Luther King in 1968, a third-grade teacher gave her students a lesson in discrimination. On the basis of eye color the teacher divided the class into two groups and favored one group (the blue-eyed children the first day) with privileges. The next day she reversed the situation, favoring the brown-eyed children. On the day they were favored, the blue-eyed children reportedly "took savage delight" in keeping "inferiors" in their place and said they felt "good inside," "smarter," and "stronger." On that day, one child drew the picture shown on the right. The next day, the same child, now one of the "inferiors," drew the picture on the left. The children who had felt "smart" and "strong" on their favored day became tense, lacked confidence, and did badly at their work on the day they were discriminated against. They said they felt "like dying" and "like quitting school."

nation, the unequal treatment of members of certain groups. It is possible for a prejudiced person not to discriminate. He or she may recognize his or her prejudice and try not to act on it. Similarly, a person may discriminate, not out of prejudice, but in compliance to social pressures. Personal discrimination may take the form of refusing to rent to black people or allowing only men to frequent a particular bar or paying Mexican-Americans substandard wages.

Many social institutions serve to reflect and preserve prejudice and discrimination. For example, many institutions, such as schools and businesses, maintain such discriminatory practices as segregation, unfair hiring, and unequal pay scales. The person who has the job of discriminating in the name of "business as usual" may maintain discrimination in our society even as she tells herself that *she* is not prejudiced: it's just the company policy; she's just following orders.

Integration

Centuries of racial prejudice in the United States and throughout the world seem to indicate that racial hatred poses an extremely complicated problem. One barrier to cooperation between the races is segregation. In one research project, a group of psychologists reasoned that if people of different races had the opportunity to meet as equals, they might come to recognize that their prejudices had no basis. Therefore, they interviewed people who had been placed in integrated and segregated buildings of a housing project just after World War II. The results of the interviews showed clearly that the amount and type of contact between black and white neighbors greatly influenced their opinions toward each other.

In the integrated buildings more than 60 percent of the white housewives reported having "friendly relations" with blacks. In the segregated buildings less than 10 percent reported friendships, and more than 80 percent reported no contact at all. In the integrated buildings, two out of three white women expressed a desire to be friendly with blacks. In the segregated buildings only one in eleven expressed such a desire. Similar effects occurred in the attitudes of black women toward whites.

The integrated housing situation gave the housewives a chance to have contact with one another and to interact informally and casually. The housewives were likely to encounter each other in the elevators, hallways, and laundry room. In this informal climate they did not have to worry that trying to strike up a conversation might be misinterpreted. In contrast, contact in the segregated buildings would have to be more deliberate and might be considered suspicious (Deutsch and Collins, 1951).

Similar changes in attitude were observed in the first army infantry company to be integrated. After living, fighting, and suffering with black soldiers, in 1945 64 percent of the white soldiers said they approved of giving blacks combat assignments. In contrast, over 80 percent of soldiers in all-white companies disapproved of integration (Star, Williams, and Stouffer, 1965).

Contact does not always reduce prejudice, however. Studies of schools that were integrated after the 1954 Supreme Court decision show mixed results. While some students became less prejudiced after a semester in an integrated school, others became *more* prejudiced than they had been before integration (Campbell, 1958). One exception was a community that voluntarily integrated its schools before the 1954 ruling. Children in that community were significantly less prejudiced than children in a similar community with all-white schools (Singer, 1964).

In a more recent study (Aronson *et al.*, 1975), structured classroom activities that fostered cooperation reduced the tensions created by forced busing. In effect, each child in a racially mixed group was responsible for part of the lesson. Like the boys in the camp experiment (Sherif *et al.*, 1961; see Chapter 11), these children liked each other more after they were forced to cooperate.

Why does contact reduce intergroup hostility in some instances but not in others? Several factors seem to be involved. First, the need to cooperate forces people to abandon negative stereotypes. Second, contact between people who occupy the same status is more likely to break down barriers than contact between people who do not perceive themselves as equals. Frequent contact with a white landlord is not likely to change a black person's stereotype of whites; nor is the relationship between an upper-class white housewife and a black maid likely to change the white woman's stereotype of blacks. The housewives in the integrated buildings and the soldiers in the integrated company were social equals: they had about the same incomes, lived under similar conditions, faced the same problems, and so on.

Finally, when social norms support intergroup cooperation, people are likely to turn contacts into friendships. Presumably parents and teachers in the community that voluntarily desegregated its schools wanted to break down racial barriers. In accepting integration, the children were conforming to group norms. So were the young people whose communities integrated their schools only after they were required to do so by law. Those whose families and friends approved of integration were open to interracial friendships; those whose families and friends opposed desegregation kept their distance.

COGNITIVE CONSISTENCY AND CHANGING ATTITUDES

Many social psychologists have theorized that people's attitudes change because they are always trying to get things to fit together logically inside their heads. Holding two opposing attitudes can create great conflict in an individual, throwing him or her off balance. A socialist who inherits ten million dollars, a doctor who smokes, and a parent who is uncomfortable with children all have one thing in common: they are in conflict.

According to Leon Festinger (1957) people in such situations experience cognitive dissonance (Figure 12.5). **Cognitive dissonance** is the uncomfortable feeling that arises when a person experiences contradictory or conflicting thoughts, beliefs, attitudes, or feelings. To reduce dissonance, it is necessary to change one or both of the conflicting attitudes. Our newly rich socialist, for example, believes that wealth should be shared, but he may also be opposed to paying millions in taxes to the government or contributing to traditional charities. (Not to mention the temptation of wine, women, song, and a Rolls Royce.) One solution is for him to give all the money to CARE and forget about his reservations regarding capitalist charities. Another is to decide that a mere ten million dollars can't do much to stamp out poverty anyway, so he might as well hire an expensive tax lawyer and enjoy it.

Some people attempt to evade dissonance by avoiding situations or exposure to information that would create conflict. For example, they may make a point of subscribing to newspapers and magazines that uphold their political attitudes, of surrounding themselves with people who share the same ideas, and of attending only those speeches and lectures that support their views. It is not surprising that such people get quite upset when a piece of conflicting information finally does get through.

The process of dissonance reduction does not always take place consciously, but it is a frequent and powerful occurrence. In fact, remarkably long-lasting changes in attitudes were produced in an experiment in which students were made aware that their emphasis on freedom was inconsistent with their indifference to equality and civil rights. In the initial forty-minute session, students ranked a number of values by importance to themselves—including the key variables "freedom" and "equality." They were also asked to express their attitudes toward civil rights. The students then compared their answers with a table of typical answers, which was interpreted for them by the researchers. The researchers said that the typical tendency to rank freedom high and equality low not only showed

Figure 12.5
An example of cognitive dissonance. Mary has a positive attitude toward Bill and a negative attitude toward certain clothing styles. She can maintain both attitudes until a situation arises in which they are brought into conflict. Then she is faced with a state of dissonance that can be reduced only by a change in attitude. Mary may decide she really does not care so much for Bill; she may decide she really likes the clothes; or she may decide that Bill's "poor taste" is a minor fault.

that students in general are "much more interested in their own freedom than in other people's" but also that such rankings are consistent with a lack of concern for civil rights. Finally, students were asked whether their results left them satisfied or dissatisfied. The control group, who did not receive the researchers' explanation, simply filled out their rankings and went home, oblivious to any inconsistencies in attitude they might have expressed.

Three to five months after the initial test, the researchers sent out a solicitation for donations or memberships on NAACP stationery, to test whether students tested would act on the values they expressed. They received many more replies from students in the experimental group than in the control group. They concluded that the test had somehow made the first group of students more receptive to civil-rights issues. On tests fifteen to seventeen months later, changes in attitude were much more likely in subjects who had been dissatisfied with what they had been told about the results of their original test than in subjects who had not been dissatisfied.

This suggests that cognitive dissonance spurred changes in attitudes toward civil rights.

This is a powerful and lasting impact from a simply forty-minute session and a few follow-up tests. One of the researchers was disturbed by the implications, for "If such socially important values as equality and freedom can be altered to become more important to human subjects, they can surely be altered to also become less important. Who shall decide ..." (Rokeach, 1971: 458).

ATTITUDES AND ACTIONS

Social psychologists have discovered several interesting relationships between attitudes and actions. Obviously, your attitudes affect your actions: if you like Fords, you will buy a Ford. Some of the other relationships are not so obvious.

Doing Is Believing

If you speak and act as if something is true, you yourself may come to believe it.

It turns out, for example, that if you like Fords but buy a Chevrolet for some reason (perhaps you can get a better deal on a Chevy), you will end up liking Fords less. In other words, actions affect attitudes.

In many instances, if you act and speak as though you have certain beliefs and feelings, you may begin to *really* feel and believe this way. For example, people accused of a crime have, under pressure of police interrogation, confessed to crimes they did not commit. They have confessed in order to relieve the pressure; but having said that they did the deed, they begin to believe that they really *are* guilty.

One explanation for this phenomenon comes from the theory of cognitive dissonance. If a person acts one way but thinks another, he or she will experience dissonance. To reduce the dissonance, the person will have to change either the behavior or the attitude. A similar explanation is that people have a need for **self-justification**—a need to justify their behavior.

In an experiment that demonstrated these principles, subjects were paid either one dollar or twenty dollars to tell another person that a boring experiment in which they both had to participate was really a lot of fun. Afterward, the experimenters asked the subjects how they felt about the experiment. They found that the subjects who had been paid twenty dollars to lie about the experiment continued to believe that it had been boring. Those who had been paid one dollar, however, came to believe that the experiment had actually been fairly enjoyable. These people had less reason to tell the lie, so they experienced more dissonance when they did so. To justify their lie, they had to believe that they had actually enjoyed the experiment (Festinger and Carlsmith, 1959).

The phenomenon of self-justification has serious implications. For example, how would you justify to yourself the fact that you had intentionally injured another human being? In another psychological experiment, subjects were led to believe that they had injured or hurt other subjects in some way (Glass, 1964). The aggressors were then asked how they felt about the victims they had just harmed. It was found that the aggressors had convinced themselves that they did not like the victim of their cruelty. In other words, the aggressors talked themselves into believing that their defenseless victims had deserved their injury. The aggressors also considered their victims to be less attractive after the experiment than before—their self-justification for hurting another person was something like, "Oh well, this person doesn't amount to much, anyway."

Self-Fulfilling Prophecy

Another relationship between attitudes and actions is rather subtle—but extremely widespread. It is possible, it seems, for a person to act in such a way as to make his or her attitudes come true. This phenomenon is called **self-fulfilling prophecy.** Suppose, for example, you are convinced that you are a bad cook. Every time you go into the kitchen, you start thinking poorly of yourself. Because you approach the task of baking a cake with great anxiety, you fumble the measurements, pour in too much milk, leave out an ingredient, and so on. As a result, your cake is a flop. You thus confirm that you *are* a bad cook.

Self-fulfilling prophecies can influence all kinds of human activity. Suppose you believe that people are basically friendly and generous. Whenever you approach other people, you are friendly and open. Because of your smile and positive attitude toward yourself and the world, people like you. Thus your attitude that people are friendly produces your friendly behavior, which in turn causes people to respond favorably toward you. But suppose you turn this example around. Imagine that you believe people are selfish and cold. Because of your negative attitude, you tend to avert your eyes from other people, to act gloomy, and to appear rather unfriendly. People think your actions are strange and, consequently, they act coldly toward you. Your attitude has produced the kind of behavior that makes the attitude come true.

Practical Implications

The psychological findings related to self-justification and self-fulfilling prophecy show that there is truth in the saying "Life is what you make it." What you do affects you directly, and it affects the way the world acts toward you. The fact that all people tend to justify their actions by changing their attitudes has several practical consequences. If you give in to pressure and act against your better judgment, you will be undermining your own beliefs. The next time you are in a similar situation, you will find it even harder to stand up for what you believe in because you will have begun to wonder whether you believe it yourself. If you want to strengthen your convictions about something, it is a good idea to speak and act on your beliefs at every opportunity. If you do make a mistake and act against your beliefs, you should admit that you are wrong and not try to justify yourself.

The phenomenon of self-fulfilling prophecy shows that the way the world seems to you may be a result of your own actions. Other people, who act differently, will have different experiences and produce different effects. When you find the world unsatisfactory, remember that to some extent, you are creating it. When you find the world a joyful place, remember, too, that it is making you happy partly because you believe that it can.

PERSUASION

Persuasion is a direct attempt to influence attitudes through the medium of communication. At one time or another everyone engages in persuasion. When a smiling student who is working her way through college by selling magazine subscriptions comes to the door, she attempts to persuade you that reading *Newsweek* or *Sports Illustrated* or *Ms.* will make you better informed and give you lots to talk about at parties. Parents often attempt to persuade a son or daughter to conform to their values about life. And young men try to persuade their dates that sex without love is perfectly natural. In each case the persuader's main hope is that by changing the other person's attitudes he or she can change that person's behavior as well.

The Communication Process

Enormous amounts of time, money, and effort go into campaigns to persuade people to change their attitudes and behavior. Some succeed on a grand scale; others seem to have no effect. One of the most difficult questions social psychologists have tried to answer is: What makes a persuasive communication effective?

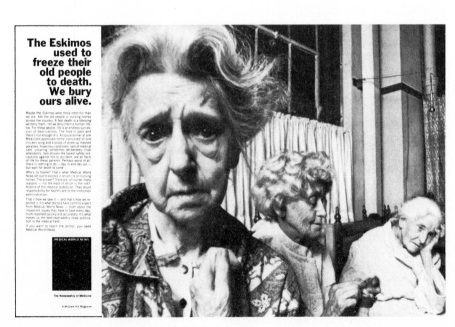

Figure 12.6
Successful advertising. This advertisement presents a powerfully emotional picture and headline to shock readers into attention and arouse their concern. It then gives some hard facts to further involve them in the subject matter.
Readers might have ignored the ad if it had simply said, "Doctors need to know about current issues relevant to the medical profession. Subscribe to *Medical World News.*"

Sex in Advertising

Pick up any newspaper or magazine and you'll see dozens of scantily-clad beauties and rugged, sensual he-men trying to sell products in the best way they know how. As they drape themselves over automobiles and puff provocatively on their cigarettes, they tell consumers that sex and their product are a package deal.

This may sound like a message few of us could resist, but according to recent findings, our will power is stronger than advertisers think. Research has shown that sexy ads get readers' attention, but the wrong audience actually reads the message. More women than men read the ads in which a sexy woman appears, and more men than women read ads showing attractive men.

Researchers have also found that sex does not increase product recall, and may in fact get in the way of remembering a brand name. In one study, subjects were shown some ads containing sexy pictures and some without. One week after seeing the ads, subjects could remember more about the "nonsexy" products than they could about the "sexy" ones.

Results like these are sure to change at least some advertisers' approaches. But it will take a lot more than this to convince others that sex is not the advertiser's best friend.

For more details, see Duane P. Schultz, *Psychology in Use.* New York: Macmillan, 1979.

The communication process can be broken down into four parts. The **message** itself is only one part. It is also important to consider the **source** of the message, the **channel** through which it is delivered, and the **audience** that receives it.

The Source. How a person sees the source, or originator, of a message may be a critical factor in his or her acceptance or rejection of it. The person receiving the message asks himself or herself two basic questions: Is the person giving the message trustworthy and sincere? Does he or she know anything about the subject? If the source seems reliable and knowledgeable, the message is likely to be accepted.

Suppose, for example, that you have written a paper criticizing a poem for your English class. A friend who reads the paper tells you about an article that praises the poem and asks you to reconsider your view. The article was written by Agnes Stearn, a student at a state teachers college. You might change your opinion—and you might not. But suppose your friend tells you the same positive critique was written by T. S. Eliot. The chances are that you would begin to doubt your own judgment. Three psychologists tried this experiment. Not surprisingly, many more students changed their minds about the poem when they thought the criticism was written by T. S. Eliot (Aronson, Turner, and Carlsmith, 1963).

A person receiving the message also asks: Do I like the source? If the communicator is respected and admired, people will tend to go along with

Figure 12.7
Winston Churchill, in a speech to the British House of Commons in 1940. Churchill's long record as a soldier (in India, South Africa, and in World War I) and as a political leader made him a source whose knowledge and trustworthiness were beyond question by the time he was needed to lead the fight against Hitler.

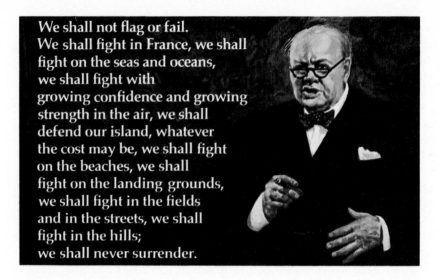

We shall not flag or fail. We shall fight in France, we shall fight on the seas and oceans, we shall fight with growing confidence and growing strength in the air, we shall defend our island, whatever the cost may be, we shall fight on the beaches, we shall fight on the landing grounds, we shall fight in the fields and in the streets, we shall fight in the hills; we shall never surrender.

the message, either because they believe in his or her judgment or because they want to be like him or her. The identification phenomenon explains the frequent use of athletes in advertisements. Football players and Olympic champions are not (in most cases) experts on deodorants, electric razors, or milk. Indeed, when an athlete endorses a particular brand of deodorant on television, we all know he or she is doing it for the money. Nevertheless, the process of identification makes these sales pitches highly effective.

Similarly, people are much more likely to respond favorably to a physically attractive source than to one who does not make a good appearance. In the 1960 presidential campaign Richard Nixon apparently lost many votes as a result of his poor appearance on a televised debate with John F. Kennedy. During the 1968 campaign Nixon was coached on how to present a likable image to the camera. His campaign managers filmed him in informal settings, hired people to applaud and crowd around him, encouraged him to joke and smile more often, and even used make-up to erase the shadows that gave many people the impression that he had "shifty eyes" (McGinniss, 1970). Nixon, of course, won that campaign.

However, attempts to be friendly and personal can backfire. When a group of college students who opposed the war in Southeast Asia visited homes in the surrounding community in the hope of persuading townspeople to support their cause, they succeeded in further alienating residents. Why? Apparently the townspeople perceived the students as radicals and resented the invasion of their privacy (Nesbitt, 1972). When people dislike the individual or group delivering a message, they are likely to respond by taking the opposite point of view. This is known as the **boomerang effect**.

As the students' failure to persuade townspeople of the wrongfulness of the war suggests, people are more apt to agree with those who are *similar* to them (or who resemble what they would like to be) than with those who are not.

The Message.   Suppose two people with opposing viewpoints are trying to persuade you to agree with them. Suppose further that you like and trust both of them. In this situation the message becomes more important than the source. The persuasiveness of a message depends on the way in which it is composed and organized as well as on the actual content.

Should the message arouse emotion? Are people more likely to change their attitudes if they are afraid or angry or pleased? The answer is yes, but the most effective messages combine emotional appeal with factual information and argument. A communication that overemphasizes the emotional side of an issue may boomerang. If the message is too upsetting, it may force people to mobilize their defenses. For example, showing pictures of accident victims to people who have been arrested for drunken driving may convince them not to drive when they've been drinking. But if the film is so bloody that people are frightened or disgusted, they may also stop listening to the message. On the other hand, a communication that includes only logic and information may miss its mark because the audience does not relate the facts to their personal lives.

When presenting an argument, is it more effective to present both sides of an issue or only one side? For the most part, a two-sided communication is more effective because the audience tends to believe that the speaker is objective and fair-minded. A slight hazard of presenting opposing arguments is that they might undercut the message or suggest that the whole issue is too controversial to make a decision about.

People usually respond positively to a message that is structured and delivered in a dynamic way. But a communication that is forceful to the point of being pushy may produce negative results. People generally resent being pressured. If listeners infer from a message that they are being left with no choice but to agree with the speaker's viewpoint, they may reject an opinion for this reason alone.

The Channel.   Where, when, and how a message is presented also influences the audience's response. In general, personal contact is the most effective approach to an audience. For example, in one study in Ann Arbor, Michigan, 75 percent of voters who had been contacted personally voted in favor of a change in the city charter. Only 45 percent of those who had received the message in the mail and 19 percent of those who had only seen ads in the media voted for the change (Eldersveld and Dodge, 1954).

However, as we saw earlier, personal contact may boomerang: people may dislike the communicator or feel that they are being pressured. Besides, you can reach a great many more people through mailings and radio and television broadcasts than you can in person.

There is some evidence that television and films are more effective media of persuasion than printed matter. People tend to believe what they see and hear with their own senses (even if they know the information has been edited before it is broadcast). In one experiment, 51 percent of people who had watched a film could answer factual questions about the issue in question—compared to 29 percent of those who had only seen printed material. And more of the people who had viewed the film altered their viewpoints than did people who had read about the issue (Hovland,

We've got over 300 good, steady jobs.

Jobs in construction, transportation, communications, computers.

Jobs for photographers, printers, truck drivers, teachers, typists, TV cameramen and repairmen. Cooks, electricians, medical aides, meteorologists. Motor and missile maintenance men.

Jobs for young men. And young women.

Jobs in Europe, Hawaii, Panama, Alaska. And just about any place in the States.

We'll train you to do the jobs. Train you well, in good schools, under excellent instructors, with the best equipment obtainable.

And you get full pay while you train.

You also get unusually good fringe benefits, including a chance to continue your education. In many cases at our expense. In all cases with at least 75% of your tuition paid.

And if you qualify we'll give you your choice of training. We'll put it in writing, before you sign up.

Today's Army wants to join you.

Figure 12.8

Audiences change from generation to generation, so the means of persuading them must also change. Attitudes toward the armed services, for example, have changed markedly since World War II, thus requiring army recruiters to alter their approach.

Lumsdaine, and Sheffield, 1949). But the most effective channel also depends in part on the audience.

The Audience.   The audience includes all those people whose attitudes the communicator is trying to change. Being able to persuade people to alter their views depends on knowing who the audience is and why they hold the attitudes they do (Figure 12.8).

Suppose, for example, you are involved in a program to reduce the birth rate in a population that is outgrowing its food supply. The first step would be to inform people of various methods of birth control as well as how and where to obtain them. However, the fact that people know how to limit their families does not mean that they will do so. To persuade them to use available contraceptives, you need to know why they value large families. In some areas of the world, people have as many children as they can because they do not expect most babies to survive early childhood. In this case you might want to tie the family-planning campaign to programs of infant care. In some areas, children begin working at odd jobs at an early age and bring in needed income. In this case, you might want to promote an incentive system for families who limit themselves to two or three children.

If the people are not taking advantage of available means of birth control, you will want to know who is resisting. Perhaps men believe fathering a child is a sign of virility. Perhaps women consider motherhood an essential element of femininity. Perhaps both sexes see parenthood as a symbol of maturity and adulthood (see Coale, 1973). Knowing who your audience is and what motivates them is crucial.

One way to maximize the chances of persuasion is to capitalize on the audience's emotional needs. For example, one advertising researcher was able to help the Red Cross collect blood donations from men by analyzing their fears. He thought that men associated loss of blood with weakness and loss of manliness. He suggested that the Red Cross publish ads telling prospective donors how manly they were and offer donors pins shaped like drops of blood as medals for bravery. The campaign worked: blood donations from men increased sharply (Dichter, 1964).

The Sleeper Effect

Changes in attitudes are not always permanent. In fact, efforts at persuasion usually have their greatest impact immediately and then fade away. However, sometimes people seem to be persuaded by a message after a period of time has elapsed. This curious **sleeper effect** has been explained in several ways.

One explanation of the delayed-action impact depends on the tendency to retain the message but forget the source. As time goes by, a positive source no longer holds power to persuade nor does a negative source undercut the message. When the source is negative and the memory of the source fades, the message then "speaks for itself" and more people may accept it (Kelman and Hovland, 1953).

Perhaps the original message also sensitizes people to subsequent information and events that reinforce the ideas. Repetition is a valuable tool, and the sleeper effect may simply be the result of hearing or reading similar messages from a number of different sources (Middlebrook, 1974).

It may also be that it simply takes time for people to change their minds. As the message "sinks in," attitudes change more. A dramatic example of this was the experiment mentioned earlier in which students who were made aware of inconsistencies in their values concerning civil rights changed their ideas more after fifteen to seventeen months than after three weeks.

The Inoculation Effect

What can you do to resist persuasion? Research has shown that people can be educated to resist attitude change. This technique can be compared to an inoculation (McGuire, 1970). Inoculation against persuasion works in much the same way as inoculation against certain diseases. When a person is vaccinated he is given a weakened or dead form of the disease-causing agent, which stimulates his body to manufacture defenses. Then, if that person is attacked by a more potent form of the agent, his defenses make him or her immune to infection. Similarly, a person who has resisted a mild attack on her beliefs is ready to defend herself against an onslaught that might otherwise have overwhelmed her.

The **inoculation effect** can be explained in two ways: it motivates the person to defend her beliefs more strongly, and it gives her some practice in defending those beliefs. The most vulnerable attitudes you have, therefore, are the ones that you have never had to defend. For example, you

The most vulnerable attitudes are those you have never had to defend.

might find yourself hard put to defend your faith in democracy or in the healthfulness of beefsteak if you have never had these beliefs questioned.

USING PSYCHOLOGY

Promoting Energy Conservation

Americans use—and waste—more energy than any other people on earth. The fuel crisis, ad campaigns on the need to conserve energy, and the steadily rising cost of gasoline, oil, and electricity have hardly made a dent in our rate of energy use. How can Americans be persuaded to conserve energy?

Three psychologists attempted to answer this question with an extremely simple experiment (Kohlenberg, Phillips, and Proctor, 1976). The demand for electricity tends to peak in the morning and again in the late afternoon, when people take showers and use vacuum cleaners, washing machines, and other electrical appliances. Unlike other forms of energy, electricity cannot be stored. Power companies therefore have to maintain generators that are in full use for only a few hours each day. One solution to the growing demand for electricity is to build more generators. The other solution is to change people's habits, cutting back the peak demand.

Kohlenberg and his colleagues tried three techniques for convincing volunteer families to reduce their electricity use during peak periods. The first was to provide information. Researchers explained the problem, asked the families to try to cut back, and suggested how they might do so. Monitors installed in each house indicated that this approach had little or no effect. (Considering that all the families were conservation-minded, this was surprising.)

Next, the researchers tried feedback. A bulb that lit up whenever the family approached peak consumption levels was placed in each house. Immediate and direct evidence of electricity overuse was expected to help the families cut back. Although somewhat more effective than information alone, feedback did not break the families' habits of electricity use.

Finally, the researchers gave the experimental households an incentive. Families would earn twice the amount of their electricity bill if they reduced their peak use 100 percent, the full amount if they cut back 50 percent, and so on. This strategy worked. None of the families reduced their peak use 100 percent, but all did cut back. A follow-up revealed that all returned to the convenience of using appliances during peak hours after the incentive was removed.

What this simple experiment demonstrated was that campaigns to reduce the use of electricity during peak periods are

> largely ineffective. However, if power companies were to provide incentives—say, reduced rates for families that cut back during the peaks—they might save themselves the cost of building and maintaining partially used plants.

SOCIAL INFLUENCE

Brainwashing

The most extreme means of changing attitudes involves a combination of psychological gamesmanship and physical torture, aptly called **brainwashing.** The most extensive studies of brainwashing have been done on Westerners who had been captured by the Chinese during the Korean War and subjected to "thought reform." Psychiatrist Robert Jay Lifton interviewed several dozen prisoners released by the Chinese, and, from their accounts, he outlined the methods used to break down people's convictions and introduce new patterns of belief, feeling, and behavior (1963).

The aim in brainwashing is as much to create a new person as to change attitudes. So the first step is to strip away all identity and subject the person to intense social pressure and physical stress. Prison is a perfect setting for this process. The person is isolated from social support, is a number not a name, is clothed like everyone else, and can be surrounded by people who have had their thoughts "reformed" and are contemptuous of "reactionaries." So long as the prisoner holds out, he is treated with contempt or exhorted to confess by his fellow prisoners. He is interrogated past the point of exhaustion by his captors, and is humiliated and discomfited by being bound hand and foot at all times, even during meals or elimination. Any personal information the prisoner uses to justify himself is turned against him as evidence of his guilt.

At some point, the prisoner realizes that resistance is impossible; the pressures are simply intolerable. Resistance gives way to cooperation, but only as a means of avoiding any more demoralization. The prisoner is rewarded for cooperating. Cooperation involves confessing to crimes against the people in his former way of life.

Throughout the process his cell mates are an integral part of the brainwashing team, berating him at first, then warming to him after his confession. For most of his waking hours, the prisoner is part of a marathon group therapy session built on Marxist ideology. The prisoner is asked not only to interpret his current behavior that way but also to reinterpret his life before capture. Guilt is systematically aroused and defined by Marxist standards. What the prisoner does is to learn a new version of his life, and his confession, provided at first to get some relief from the isolation and pain, becomes more elaborate, coherent, and ideologically based. And with every "improvement" in his attitudes, prison life is made a little more pleasant. Finally, by a combination of threat, peer pressure, systematic rewards, and other psychological means, the prisoner comes to believe his confession. But as one survivor recalled, "it is a special kind of belief . . . you accept it—in order to avoid trouble—because every time you don't agree, trouble starts again" (Lifton, 1963: 31). These techniques appear to succeed only as long as the person remains a prisoner.

It's hard to say just where persuasion ends and brainwashing begins. (Some researchers believe that brainwashing is just a very intense form of persuasion.) Drawing this line has become particularly important to the courts in recent years—from the case of Patty Hearst to lawsuits over deprogramming members of religious cults.

Margaret Thaler Singer (1979) has studied over 300 former members of religious cults. Many had joined during periods of depression and confusion. The cults offered structure and gave life meaning: they provided friends and ready-made decisions about marriage and careers, dating and sex. Being cut off from the outside world and intensive indoctrination into a new ideology often increased the new member's sense of commitment.

When people become dissatisfied and quit, many have trouble readjusting to the world they left behind. Among the problems Singer has observed are depression, loneliness, indecisiveness, passivity, guilt, and

Figure 12.9
Members of the Hare Krishna cult.

blurring of mental activity. The average person takes six to eighteen months to return to normal.

Group Pressure to Conform

Most Americans claim they would never become supporters of Hitler if they had lived in Germany during World War II. Yet a nation of Germans did. Under pressure from others, individuals at least complied with the prevailing attitudes. Everyone conforms to group pressure in many ways. Have you ever come home and surprised your parents by wearing the latest fad in clothing? Possibly the conversation that followed went something like this:

"How can you go around looking like that?"

"But everyone dresses like this."

Psychologist Solomon Asch (1952) designed a famous experiment to test conformity to pressure from one's peers. He found that people may conform to other people's ideas of the truth, even when they disagree. The following is what you would have experienced if you had been a subject in this experiment.

You and seven other students meet in a classroom for an experiment on visual judgment. You are shown a card with one line on it. You are then shown another card containing three lines and are asked to pick the one that is the same length as the first line. One of the three is exactly the same length and is easy to determine. The other two lines are obviously different (Figure 12.13). The experiment begins uneventfully. The subjects announce their answers in the order in which they are seated in the room. You happen to be seventh, and one person follows you. On the first comparison, every person chooses the same matching line. The second set of cards is displayed, and once again the group is unanimous. The discriminations seem easy, and you prepare for what you expect will be a rather boring experiment.

On the third trial, there is an unexpected disturbance. You are quite certain that line 2 is the one that matches the standard. Yet the first person in the group announces confidently that line 1 is the correct match. Then, the second person follows suit and he, too, declares that the answer is line 1. So do the third, fourth, fifth, and sixth subjects. Now it is your turn. You are suddenly faced with two contradictory pieces of information: the evidence of your own senses tells you that one answer is clearly correct, but the unanimous and confident judgments of the six preceding subjects tell you that you are wrong.

The dilemma persists through eighteen trials. On twelve of the trials, the other group members unanimously give an answer that differs from what you clearly perceive to be correct. It is only at the end of the experimental session that you learn the explanation for the confusion. The seven other subjects were all actors, and they had been instructed to give incorrect answers on those twelve trials (Figure 12.11).

How do most subjects react to this situation? Asch found that almost one-third of his fifty subjects conformed at least half the time. These conformers he called the "yielders." Most yielders explained to Asch afterward

Figure 12.10
These two cards were shown to subjects in one trial of Asch's experiment on conformity. The actual discrimination is easy.

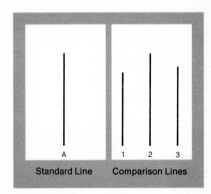

Standard Line   Comparison Lines

Figure 12.11

Photographs taken during Asch's experiment on conformity. Subject 6 is the only real subject; the others are confederates of the experimenter (seen at the right in the first photograph). The subject listens to the others express identical judgments that differ from his own. He is in a dilemma: does he express the judgment he knows to be correct and risk being different from the group, or does he conform to the group's judgment?

that they knew which line was correct but that they yielded to group pressure in order not to appear different from the others. Asch called those who did not conform "independents." They gave the correct answer despite group pressure. Why so much conformity? According to one theory, most children are taught the overriding importance of being liked and of being accepted. Conformity is the standard means of gaining this approval.

One of the most important findings of Asch's experiment was that if even one person failed to conform to the group's judgment, the subject was able to stick to his own perceptions. It seems that it is hardest to stand alone. Later researchers have shown that, under some conditions, a minority view can come to win over the larger group (Moscovici, 1976).

Obedience to Authority

The influence other people have on your attitudes and actions is considerable. Sometimes this influence is indirect and subtle; at other times it is quite direct. People may simply tell you what to believe and what to do. Under what conditions do you obey them?

Everyone in this society has had experiences with various authorities, such as parents, teachers, police officers, managers, judges, clergymen, and military officers. **Obedience** to these authorities can be either useful or destructive. For instance, obeying the orders of a doctor or firefighter in an emergency would be constructive. Psychologists are more interested, however, in the negative aspects of obedience. They know from such cases in history as German Nazism and American atrocities in Vietnam that individuals frequently obey irrational commands. In fact, people often obey authority even when obedience goes against their conscience and their whole system of morality.

The most famous investigation of obedience was conducted in 1963 by social psychologist Stanley Milgram. The experiment was set up as follows. Two subjects appeared for each session. They were told that they would be participating in an experiment to test the effects of punishment on memory. One of the subjects was to be the "teacher" and the other, the "learner." (In reality, the learner was not a volunteer subject; he was Milgram's accomplice.) The teacher was to read a list of words into a microphone for the learner, who would be in a nearby room, to memorize. If the learner failed to recite the list back correctly, the teacher was to administer an electric shock. The alleged purpose of the experiment was to test whether the shock would have any effect on learning. In actuality, however, Milgram wanted to discover how far the teacher would follow his instructions; how much shock would he be willing to give a fellow human being?

As the experiment began, the learner continually gave wrong answers, and the teacher began to administer the prescribed shocks from an impressive-looking shock generator. The generator had a dial that ranged from 15 volts, which was labeled "Slight Shock," to 450 volts, which was labeled "Danger: Severe Shock." After each of the learner's mistakes, the teacher was told to increase the voltage by one level, thus increasing the severity of the shock. The teacher believed that the learner was receiving these shocks because he had seen the learner being strapped into a chair in the other room and had watched electrodes being attached to the learner's hands. In reality, however, the accomplice was receiving no shocks at all from the equipment.

As the experiment progressed, the learner made many mistakes and the teacher had to give increasingly severe shocks. At 300 volts the learner

Figure 12.12
Stanley Milgram's experiment on obedience. (a) The fake "shock generator" used by the "teacher." (b) The "learner" is connected to the shock apparatus. (c) Milgram explains the procedure to the "teacher." (d) This subject refuses to shock the "learner" any further and angrily arises in protest. (e) Milgram explains the truth about the experiment. (© 1965 by Stanley Milgram. From the film *Obedience*. Distributed by New York University Film Library.)

pounded on the wall in protest and refused to provide any further answers. At this point the experimenter instructed the subject to treat the absence of an answer as a wrong answer and to continue the procedure. The experiment ended either when the maximum 450 volts was administered or when the teacher refused to administer any more shocks. If at any point the teacher indicated that he wanted to stop, the experimenter calmly told him to continue: "Whether the learner likes it or not," the experimenter asserted, "you must go on until he has learned all the word pairs correctly. So please go on."

Before Milgram began this study, he had checked with forty psychiatrists in order to get their predictions. These experts thought that most people would not continue beyond the 150-volt level, and that only one in one thousand would actually give the highest shock. Yet in Milgram's experiments more than half of the forty subjects gave the full shock!

These subjects were not sadists. Many of them showed signs of extreme tension and discomfort during the session, and they often told the experimenter that they would like to stop. But in spite of these feelings, they continued to obey the experimenter's commands. They were ordinary men—salesmen, engineers, postal workers—placed in an unusual situation.

What accounts for this surprisingly high level of obedience? A large part of the answer is that the experimenter represents a legitimate authority. People assume that such an authority knows what he is doing, even when his instructions seem to run counter to their own standards of moral behavior.

Milgram's subjects could have walked out at any time—they had already been paid and had nothing to lose by leaving. Nevertheless, social conditioning for obeying legitimate authorities is so strongly ingrained that people often lack the words or the ways to do otherwise. Simply getting up and leaving would have violated powerful unwritten rules of acceptable social behavior.

Subsequent experiments showed that there were three ways in which subjects could be helped to resist authority in this situation. One was the removal of the physical presence of the experimenter. Even more effective was putting the subject face to face with his victim. The third and most effective variation of the experiment was to provide other "teachers" to support the subject's defiance of the experimenter (Milgram, 1964).

SUMMARY

1. An attitude is an enduring set of beliefs, feelings, and tendencies to act toward people or things in predisposed ways. Culture, parents, and peers—as well as personal experience—shape a person's attitudes.

2. The processes involved in attitude formation include compliance (acting as though one has a certain attitude in order to avoid discomfort or rejection and win approval); identification (the adoption of new attitudes as a result of a strong emotional attachment to another person or group); and internalization (the incorporation of attitudes into a person's belief system).

3. Prejudice is judging people on the basis of stereotypes. Prejudice seems to have a number of causes, and it is perpetuated by social institutions.

Discrimination is the unequal treatment of people.

4. People have a need for cognitive consistency—that is, a need to fit their attitudes together into a nonconflicting set of beliefs. People who simultaneously hold two or more opposing attitudes experience cognitive dissonance. In order to reduce dissonance, they change one or more of the attitudes.

5. People's actions affect their attitudes. People often justify actions that go against their beliefs by changing their beliefs. Self-fulfilling prophecy is the phenomenon of acting in such a way as to make one's attitudes come true.

6. Persuasion is a direct attempt to change attitudes and behavior through the process of communication.

7. Four components of the communications process are the source, the message, the channel, and the audience. For attitude change to occur, the source must be trustworthy and sincere, the message should combine fact and emotional arousal, the channel should be appropriate to the message, and the audience must be receptive.

8. The effects of persuasion are usually short-lived. However, a "sleeper effect," in which attitudes change more as time passes, can occur.

9. People can be educated to resist persuasion by hearing a mild attack on their beliefs. This spurs them to defend their attitudes more strongly and gives them practice in their defense. The inoculation effect helps people resist stronger attacks on their beliefs that may follow.

10. The most extreme means of attitude change is called brainwashing. First, identity is destroyed and the will to resist is broken. Then intensive indoctrination is combined with rewards for compliance. New attitudes are drilled into the subject. The effects seem to diminish once the victim returns to his former life.

11. Asch's experiment showed that conformity to pressure from peers may be so strong that people will question or deny their own senses.

12. One of the strongest ways in which social influence is exerted is through authority. Milgram's experiment showed that social conditioning produces such a strong tendency toward obeying legitimate authorities that people may easily be induced to do harm to others against their conscience or better judgment.

GLOSSARY

attitudes: Predispositions to act, think, and feel in particular ways toward particular things.

audience: In the communication process, the person or persons receiving a message.

authoritarian personality: A personality type characterized by rigid thinking; denial and projection of sexual and aggressive drives onto others; respect for and submission to authority; prejudice regarding people unlike himself or herself.

boomerang effect: A change in attitude or behavior opposite to the one desired by the persuader.

brainwashing: The most extreme form of attitude change, accomplished through peer pressure, physical suffering, threats, rewards for compliance, manipulation of guilt, intensive indoctrination, and other psychological means.

channel: In the communication process, the means by which a message is transmitted from the source to the audience.

cognitive dissonance: The uncomfortable feeling that arises when a person experiences contradictory or conflicting thoughts, attitudes, beliefs, or feelings.

compliance: A change of behavior in order to avoid discomfort or rejection and gain approval; a superficial form of attitude change.

discrimination: The unequal treatment of individuals on the basis of their race, ethnic group, class, sex, or membership in another category, rather than on the basis of individual characteristics.

identification: The process of seeing oneself as similar to another person or group, and accepting the attitudes of another person or group as one's own.

inoculation effect: A method of developing resistance to persuasion by exposing a person to arguments that challenge his or her beliefs so that he or she can practice defending them.

internalization: The wholehearted acceptance of an attitude because of its consistency with an individual's basic beliefs, values, and self-image; the most enduring form of attitude change.

message: In the communication process, the actual content transmitted from the source to the audience.

obedience: A change in attitude or behavior brought about by social pressure to comply with people perceived to be authorities.

persuasion: The direct attempt to influence attitudes through the communication process.

prejudice: Preconceived attitudes toward a person or group that have been formed without sufficient evidence and are not easily changed.

self-fulfilling prophecy: A belief, prediction, or expectation that operates to bring about its own fulfillment. (Also discussed in the Appendix.)

self-justification: The need to rationalize one's attitudes and behavior.

sleeper effect: The delayed impact on attitude change of a persuasive communication.

source: In the communication process, the person or group from which a message originates.

ACTIVITIES

1. Collect magazine ads of ten different brands of cigarettes. Using a scale of 0 to 10, have subjects rate the cigarettes as being weak or strong—0 being the weakest and 10 being the strongest. Have different subjects rate the same brands on the same scale for masculinity or femininity—0 being the most feminine and 10 being the most masculine. Now average your scores. What conclusions can you draw from your results? (From Sol Gordon, *Psychology and You*, New York: Oxford Book Company, 1972, p. 452.)

2. Collect samples of advertising that depict various techniques of persuasion—identification, social approval, fear of disaster, and so on. Analyze each ad on the basis of effectiveness and what type of person it might appeal to.

3. Do researchers have the right to fool their subjects, even in the name of science? Consider, for example, the effects on Milgram's subjects of believing they had harmed a fellow subject by obliging the order of a stranger. Do you think this experiment was valuable for allowing the subjects to realize the extent of their conformity? If you answered the first question no, and the second, yes, how would you reconcile these two conflicting attitudes?

4. Choose some issue on which you have a strong opinion. If you were given an unlimited budget, how would you go about persuading people to agree with you? Describe the sources you would employ, the channels you would use, the content of your message, and the audience you would try to reach.

5. To what extent does advertising influence your choice of foods? Find several people who prefer butter to margarine. Ask them why they prefer butter. If they say it tastes better, then ask them to participate in an experiment to test their claims. Get several brands of both butter and margarine and spread them lightly on the same kind of crackers or toast. Blindfold your subjects and provide them with a glass of water to rinse their mouths whenever they wish. Ask them to identify the samples. Run through the series about four times, varying the order of presentation. Try similar experiments with people who prefer certain brands of milk, cola, or coffee.

6. Try this experiment to test the effects of self-fulfilling prophecy. Approach someone you vaguely dislike and whom you generally ignore and ask him or her to eat lunch with you, to go to the library, or to do some other socially oriented

activity. Make a conscientious effort to get to know the person and see if your attitude of dislike is really justified or if the person's behavior was a function of the way you previously responded to him or her.

7. One of the primary objectives of advertising is to get the viewers/listeners to remember the product. To what extent do you think familiarity with brand names influences your choices in the market? How many television commercials do you find obnoxious? Do you find that you remember the products advertised in "obnoxious" commercials better than you remember products that appear in less offensive advertisements? Do you think there is a possibility that some commercials are deliberately offensive?

8. Choose a controversial topic, such as abortion, drug abuse, or women's rights, and devise ten questions to measure people's attitudes toward this issue. Give the questionnaire to a number of different people and see whether your results make sense in terms of what you already know about these people. (Psychologists are greatly concerned with devising questionnaires that really tell something about how people tend to act.)

9. Experiments have shown that enforced integration in housing has resulted in less interracial hostility. What is your opinion of legally enforcing racial integration in housing, employment, and schools?

10. Make a list of ten or more nationalities, religions, races, and occupations. Have friends or family members list five things that come to mind when these groups are mentioned. What are your conclusions?

SUGGESTED READINGS

BEM, DARYL J. *Beliefs, Attitudes and Human Affairs*. Belmont, Calif.: Brooks/Cole, 1970. A well-written and enjoyable book on attitudes and their social implications.

DELLA FEMINA, JERRY. *From Those Wonderful Folks Who Gave You Pearl Harbor*. New York: Simon & Schuster, 1970. A hilarious and insightful look at the world of advertising agencies through the eyes of a creative man with plenty of firsthand experience.

HELLER, JOSEPH. *Catch-22*. New York: Dell, 1961 (paper). One of the saddest and funniest novels ever written about war. But more than that. A commentary about social influence—the factors that lead people into double binds, self-fulfilling prophecies, and unwilling obedience.

LIFTON, ROBERT JAY. *Home from the War*. New York: Simon & Schuster, 1973. An interesting account of how veterans of the Vietnam war have had to use self-justification for their wartime actions. Lifton points out that self-justification leads to new and different political consciousness not felt by the men before their overseas experiences.

MC GINNISS, JOE. *The Selling of the President, 1968*. New York: Pocket Books, 1970 (paper). This book shows how advertising people manufacture, package, and market their most lucrative product: the president of the United States. The book is fascinating, frightening, and essential reading for anyone interested in the psychology of advertising and in the ways the public can be manipulated.

SHIRER, WILLIAM L. *The Rise and Fall of the Third Reich*. New York: Simon & Schuster, 1960 (paper). A fully detailed and documented account of the dynamics that created and destroyed the most evilly totalitarian political regime in modern history: Nazi Germany. A classic study of propaganda, obedience, and conformity.

SINGER, MARGARET T. "Coming Out of the Cults." *Psychology Today*, 12 (January 1979): 72–82. Describes Singer's research on why people join cults, and what happens to them when they quit.

VARELA, JACOBO. *Psychological Solutions to Social Problems*. New York: Academic Press, 1971. This book is practically a manual on how to persuade people. It includes a chapter on how to go about correcting social ills.

ZIMBARDO, P. G., EBBESEN, E. B., AND MASLACH, C. *Influencing Attitudes and Changing Behavior*. 2nd ed. Reading, Mass.: Addison-Wesley, 1977. A short introduction to methodology, experimentation, and theory in the field of attitude change. Designed for readers without extensive background.

BIBLIOGRAPHY

ADORNO, T. W., ET AL. *The Authoritarian Personality*. New York: Norton, 1969 (paper).

ALLPORT, GORDON. *The Nature of Prejudice*. Garden City, N.Y.: Doubleday, 1954 (paper).

ARONSON, E., ET AL. "Busing and Racial Tension: The Jigsaw Route to Learning and Liking." *Psychology Today*, 9 (February 1975): 43–50.

ARONSON, E., TURNER, J., AND CARLSMITH, M. "Communicator Credibility and Communicator Discrepancy as Determinants of Opinion Change." *Journal of Abnormal and Social Psychology*, 67 (1963): 31–36.

ASCH, S. *Social Psychology*. New York: Prentice-Hall, 1952.

————. "Effects of Group Pressure upon the Modification and Distortion of Judgments." In *Basic Studies in Social Psychology*, ed. by J. Proshansky and B. Seidenberg. New York: Holt, Rinehart & Winston, 1965, pp. 393–401.

BEM, DARYL J. *Beliefs, Attitudes and Human Affairs*. Belmont, Calif.: Brooks/Cole, 1970.

CAMPBELL, E. "Some Social Psychological Correlates of Direction in Attitude Change." *Social Forces*, 36 (1958): 335–340.

COALE, A. J. "The Demographic Transition Reconsidered." In *International Population Conference*, Leige, 1973.

COHEN, A. R. *Attitude Change and Social Influence*. New York: Basic Books, 1964.

DEUTSCH, M., AND COLLINS, M. *Interracial Housing: A Psychological Evaluation of a Social Experiment*. Minneapolis: University of Minnesota Press, 1951.

DICHTER, ERNEST. *Handbook of Consumer Motivations*. New York: McGraw-Hill, 1964.

ELDERSVELD, S., AND DODGE, R. "Personal Contact or Mail Propaganda? An Experiment in Voting Turnout and Attitude Change." In *Public Opinion and Propaganda*, ed. by D. Katz *et al*. New York: Dryden Press, 1954, pp. 532–542.

FESTINGER, L. *A Theory of Cognitive Dissonance*. Stanford, Calif.: Stanford University Press, 1957.

FESTINGER, L., AND CARLSMITH, J. M. "Cognitive Consequences of Forced Compliance." *Journal of Abnormal and Social Psychology*, 58 (1959): 203–210.

FLACK, R. "The Liberated Generation: An Exploration of the Roots of Student Protest." *Journal of Social Issues*, 23 (1967): 52–57.

GLASS, D. C. "Changes in Liking as a Means of Reducing Cognitive Discrepancies Between Self-Esteem and Aggression." *Journal of Personality*, 32 (1964): 531–549.

GOLDSEN, R., ET AL. *What College Students Think*. New York: Van Nostrand, 1960.

HESS, R., AND TORNEY, J. *The Development of Political Attitudes in Children*. Chicago: Aldine, 1967.

HOLBORN, HAJO. *A History of Modern Germany 1850–1945*. New York: Knopf, 1969.

HOVLAND, C., LUMSDAINE, A., AND SHEFFIELD, F. *Experiments on Mass Communication*. Princeton, N.J.: Princeton University Press, 1949.

JENNINGS, M., AND NIEMI, R. "The Transmission of Political Values from Parent to Child." *American Political Science Review*, 62 (1968): 169–184.

KELMAN, H. C. "Processes of Opinion Change." *Public Opinion Quarterly*, 21 (1961): 57–78.

KELMAN, H. C., AND HOVLAND, C. I. " 'Reinstatement' of the Communicator in Delayed Measurement of Opinion Change." *Journal of Abnormal and Social Psychology*, 48 (1953): 327–335.

KLAPPER, J. T. *The Effects of Mass Communications*. New York: Free Press, 1960.

KOHLENBERG, ROBERT, PHILLIPS, THOMAS, AND PROCTOR, WILLIAM. "A Behavioral Analysis of Peaking in Residential Electrical Energy Consumers." *Journal of Applied Behavioral Analysis*, 9 (1976): 13–18.

LEE, ALFRED M., AND LEE, ELIZABETH. *The Fine Art of Propaganda*. New York: Farrar, Straus, 1939.

LIFTON, ROBERT JAY. *Thought Reform and the Psychology of Totalism: A Study of "Brainwashing" in China.* New York: Norton, 1963 (paper).

_____. *Home from the War.* New York: Simon & Schuster, 1973.

MC GINNISS, JOE. *The Selling of the President, 1968.* New York: Pocket Books, 1970 (paper).

MC GUIRE, W. J. "A Vaccine for Brainwash." *Psychology Today,* 3 (February 1970): 36–39, 62–64.

MACE, D., AND MACE, V. *Marriage: East and West.* New York: Doubleday, 1960.

MIDDLEBROOK, PATRICIA NILES. *Social Psychology and Modern Life.* New York, Knopf: 1974.

MILGRAM, STANLEY. *Obedience to Authority.* New York: Harper & Row, 1964.

MOSCOVICI, SERGE. *Social Influence and Social Change.* New York: Academic Press, 1976.

NESBITT, P. "The Effectiveness of Student Canvassers," *Journal of Applied Psychology,* 2 (1972): 252–258.

NEWCOMB, T. *Personality and Social Change.* New York: Dryden Press, 1943.

NEWCOMB, T., ET AL. *Persistence and Change: Bennington College and Its Students After 25 Years.* New York: Wiley, 1967.

REISMAN, D., GLAZER, N., AND DENNEY, R. *The Lonely Crowd.* New Haven, Conn.: Yale University Press, 1953 (paper).

ROKEACH, M. "Long-Range Experimental Modification of Values, Attitudes, and Behavior." *American Psychologist,* 26 (1971): 453–459.

SHERIF, MUZAFER, ET AL. *Intergroup Conflict and Cooperation: The Robber's Cave Experiment.* Norman, Okla.: Institute of Group Relations, 1961.

SINGER, D. "The Impact of Interracial Classroom Exposure on the Social Attitudes of Fifth Grade Children." Unpublished study, 1964.

SINGER, MARGARET T. "Coming Out of the Cults." *Psychology Today,* 12 (January 1979): 72–82.

STAR, S., WILLIAMS, R., JR., AND STOUFFER, S. "Negro Infantry Platoons in White Companies." In *Basic Studies in Social Psychology,* ed. by H. Proshansky and B. Seidenberg. New York: Holt, Rinehart & Winston, 1965, pp. 680–685.

ZIMBARDO, P. G., EBBESEN, E. B., AND MASLACH, C. *Influencing Attitudes and Changing Behavior.* 2nd ed. Reading, Mass.: Addison-Wesley, 1977.

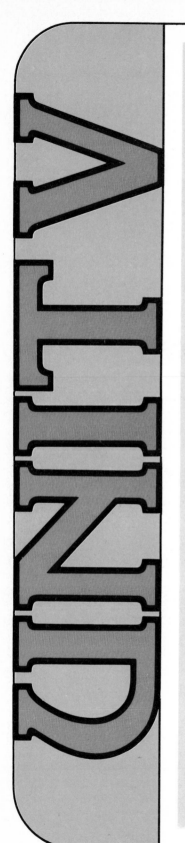

INDIVIDUAL DIFFERENCES AND MENTAL HEALTH

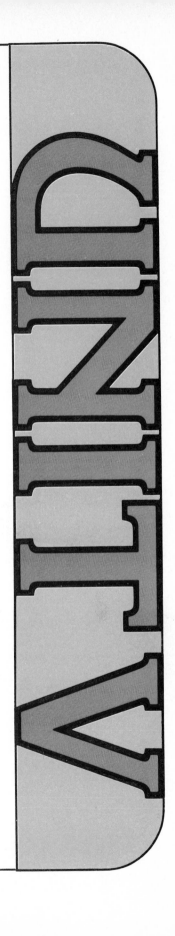

There are billions of people in this world, and each one is unique. Each individual has not only a unique appearance and genetic endowment, but also a personal way of dealing with the world, of viewing other people, and of viewing him- or herself. You may have noticed that the other units in this book have for the most part ignored this individuality in order to explore the ways people are alike—in physiological functioning, in mental processes, in growth and development, and in interacting with one another. This unit, however, focuses on the ways in which people are different—and why.

Chapter 13 presents the theories of several psychologists who have tried to explain why individuals are different from one another. These theorists have addressed such questions as: How is character formed? To what extent can a person know himself or herself? What determines a person's actions? How can a person be happy? Chapter 14 examines the uses and abuses of intelligence, aptitude, and personality tests. Chapter 15 discusses the problem of people who are so different from everyone else that they are considered abnormal. Such people are often painfully unhappy and are sometimes unable to handle the simplest tasks of everyday life. Chapter 16 focuses on the ways in which such people can be helped to achieve better contact with reality, with others, and with themselves.

13 Personality Theory

Nancy and Ruth both failed their midterm examinations in psychology, but they reacted in very different ways. When Nancy saw her grade, she felt sick to her stomach and had to fight back tears. She cut her next class, rushed home, and shut herself up in her room to lie in bed, stare at the ceiling, and feel inadequate. Ruth, on the other hand, was all bluster. She too cut her next class after learning her grade, but she ran to the cafeteria to join her friends and make loud jokes about her stupid psychology professor.

Why did Nancy and Ruth act so differently in similar situations? Speaking loosely, there is something inside people that makes them think, feel, and act differently. And that "something inside" is what we mean by **personality.** It accounts for both the differences among people and for the consistencies in an individual's behavior over time and in different situations.

A theory of personality is an attempt to explain human nature in all its complexity and contradictions. While other psychologists confine their studies to more limited problems (like how the eye works, or why we remember some situations better than others), personality theorists face the most complex problem of all: Why do we do the things we do? The psychologists and psychiatrists whose insights we will be describing based their theories on what they learned from their own lives; from patients whose emotional difficulties they helped to ease; and from literature, philosophy, science, and the theories of other psychologists. Directly and indirectly, these theorists have changed the way we think about ourselves.

Figure 13.1
Psychologists who study personality study whatever it is that makes one person think, feel, and act differently from another—what causes one person to like the spotlight and another to hate it.

WHAT PERSONALITY THEORIES TRY TO DO

You might assume that a theory of personality is little more than one person's philosophy of life and speculations about human nature. In fact, personality theories serve a number of very practical functions.

First, personality theories provide a way of organizing the many facts you know about yourself and other people. You know people may be outgoing or shy, bossy or meek, quick-tempered or calm, witty or dull, fun-loving or gloomy, responsible or lazy.

All these words describe *personality traits,* or general ways of behaving that characterize an individual. Personality theorists try to determine whether certain traits go together and why, why a person has some traits and not others, and why a person might exhibit different traits in different situations. There is a good deal of disagreement among theorists as to which traits are significant, and whether personality traits are stable over time or represent the individual's response to specific circumstances. Nevertheless, all theorists share one common goal: to discover patterns in the ways people behave.

A second purpose of any personality theory is *to explain the differences between individuals.* In so doing, theorists probe beneath the surface. Suppose a man you know is humble to the point of being self-effacing. When the conversation turns to him, he seems embarrassed. He is much happier bustling about, making people comfortable, and asking about their lives than he is talking about himself. A woman you know is just the opposite. She enjoys nothing better than talking about the work she is doing, the people she's met, her plans for the future. When she asks about your life you suspect it's either because she's being polite or because you might be useful to her. You explain their different behaviors in terms of motives: the man's primary goal in life is to please other people; the woman is extremely ambitious. But these explanations are little more than descriptions. How did these two individuals come to have different motives in the first place? Here, too, personality theorists disagree. One might suggest that the man had parents who discouraged any aggressive behavior while the woman's parents encouraged achievement and aggressive behavior. Another might seek less obvious causes—arguing, for example, that the roots of these differences could be traced back to toilet training.

A third goal of personality theory is to explore how people conduct their lives. It is no accident that most personality theorists began as psychotherapists, attempting to help people overcome emotional problems. In working with people who experienced considerable psychological pain and had difficulty coping with the everyday problems of life, they inevitably developed ideas about what it takes to live a relatively happy, untroubled life. Personality theorists try to explain why problems arise, and why they are more difficult for some people to manage than for others.

In addition, personality theorists are concerned with determining how life can be improved. It seems obvious that many people are dissatisfied with themselves, their parents, their husbands or wives and children, their home lives. People resign themselves to unrewarding jobs, and there is a widespread feeling that much is wrong with society and the world. Almost

Instant Personality Analysis and Astrology

Suppose someone handed you an astrological reading and told you it was specially written for you. Would you believe it? According to several studies, you probably would.

Subjects who were shown general personality assessments, which could have been written for almost anyone, readily believed they were prepared just for them. Believers—both men and women alike—rated the accuracy of the description at approximately 4.5 on a scale of 1 to 5, with 5 being the highest rating.

Researchers also found that the more personal facts an individual believes are used to compile a personality description, the greater his or her faith in its accuracy. Thus, an individual who thinks a horoscope is based on the year, month, and day of birth is more likely to believe its description than someone who thinks no personal information was used at all.

Our willingness to accept general descriptions of ourselves as accurate may be due to the universal human failing of being a bit too gullible. This is especially true when the words we hear are filled with praise.

For more details, see C. R. Snyder and Randee Jane Shenkel, "The P. T. Barnum Effect," *Psychology Today,* March 1975.

everyone recognizes that we need to grow and change, individually and collectively. But what are the proper goals of growth and change? How can we cope with the inevitable conflicts of life?

Personality psychologists attempt to answer these questions with systematic theories about human behavior. These theories are used to guide research; and research, in turn, can test parts of a theory to see whether they are right or wrong. Thus, while we all have our pet theories about why people act certain ways, formal personality theories try to make such ideas more scientific by stating them very precisely and then testing them.

Psychology is still a very young science, and these tests have just begun. There are now many conflicting theories of personality, each with its friends and foes. In this chapter, we will describe four major schools of thought among personality theorists.

Psychoanalytic theories, developed by Sigmund Freud and his followers, emphasize the importance of motives hidden deep in the unconscious. B. F. Skinner and the behaviorists study the way rewards and punishments shape our actions. Humanistic theorists, like Abraham Maslow and Carl Rogers, emphasize human potential for growth, creativity, and spontaneity. Finally, trait theorists, like Gordon Allport and Raymond Cattell, stress the importance of understanding basic personality characteristics such as friendliness and aggression.

Each of the theorists we will discuss has a different image of human nature. What they have in common is a concern with understanding the differences among people.

PSYCHOANALYTIC THEORIES

Charming, spacious, homelike 1 rm. apts. Modern kitchenette. Hotel service. Weekly rats available.

—from classified advertisement, *New York Times*

This advertisement was received and typeset by someone at the *Times*. The person who set the ad probably did not leave the "e" out of "rate" deliberately, but was it just an innocent mistake?

Slips like these are common. People usually laugh at them, even if they are meaningful. But sometimes they are disturbing. Everyone has had the experience of making some personal remark that hurt a friend and has later asked himself, "Why did I say that? I didn't mean it." Yet, when he thinks about it, he may realize that he was angry at his friend and wanted to "get back" at him.

Sigmund Freud: Psychosexuality and the Unconscious

It was Sigmund Freud who first suggested that the little slips that people make, the things they mishear, and the odd misunderstandings they have are not really mistakes at all. Freud believed there was something behind these mistakes, even though people claimed they were just accidental and quickly corrected themselves. Similarly, when he listened to people describe their dreams, he believed the dreams had some meaning, even though the people who dreamed them did not know what they meant.

Freud was a physician who practiced in Vienna in the early 1900s. Since he specialized in nervous diseases, a great many people talked to him about their private lives, their conflicts, fears, and desires. At that time most people thought, as many still do, that we are aware of all our motives and feelings. But Freud reasoned that if people can say and dream things without knowing their meaning, they must not know as much about themselves as they think they do. After years of study he concluded that some of the most powerful influences on human personality are things we are *not* conscious of.

Freud was the first modern psychologist to suggest that every personality has a large **unconscious** component. Life includes both pleasurable and painful experiences. For Freud, experiences include feelings and thoughts as well as actual events. Freud believed that many of our experiences, particularly the painful episodes of childhood, are forgotten or buried in the unconscious. But although we may not consciously recall these experiences, they continue to influence our behavior. For example, a child who never fully pleases his demanding mother or father may feel unhappy much of the time and will doubt his abilities to succeed and to be loved. As an adult, the person may suffer from feelings of unworthiness and low self-esteem, despite his very real abilities. Freud believed that unconscious motives and the feelings people experience as children have an enormous impact on adult personality and behavior.

> **Freud concluded that some of the most powerful influences on human personality are things we are not conscious of.**

The Id, Ego, and Superego

Freud tried to explain human personality by saying that it was a kind of energy system—like a steam engine or an electric dynamo. The energy in human personality comes from two kinds of powerful drives, the life drives and the death drives. Freud theorized that all of life moves toward death, and that the desire for a final end shows up in human personality as destructiveness and aggression. But the life instincts were more important in Freud's theory, and he saw them primarily as erotic or pleasure-seeking urges.

By 1923 Freud had described what became known as the structural components of the mind: id, ego, and superego (Figure 13.2). Though Freud often spoke of them as if they were actual parts of the personality, he introduced and regarded them simply as a *model* of how the mind works. In other words, the id, ego, and superego do not refer to actual portions of the brain. Instead, they explain how the mind functions and how the instinctual energies are regulated.

In Freud's theory the **id** is the reservoir or container of the instinctual urges. It is the lustful or drive-ridden part of the unconscious. The id seeks immediate gratification of desires, regardless of the consequences.

The personality process that is mostly conscious is called the **ego.** The ego is the rational, thoughtful, realistic personality process. For example, if

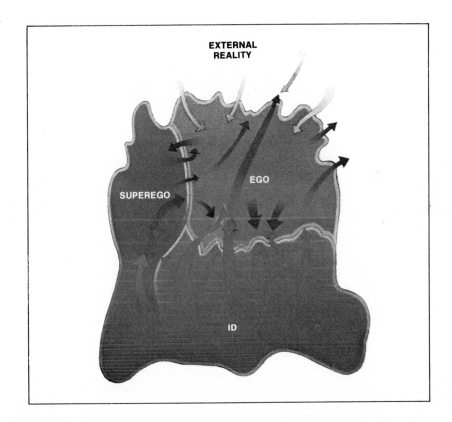

Figure 13.2
A visual interpretation of the Freudian theory of personality structure. The ego tries to balance the id's desires against the superego's demands and the realities of the world. In doing this it sometimes suppresses the irrational tendencies of the id, but it may also be able to deflect the id's energy into channels acceptable to both the superego and the outside world. These interactions and conflicts are represented by arrows in the figure.

a person is hungry, the id might drive her to seek immediate satisfaction by dreaming of food or by eating all the available food at once instead of keeping some of it for a later time. The ego would recognize that the body needs real food and that it will continue to need food in the future; it would use the id's energy to preserve some of the food available now and to look for ways of finding more.

Suppose you thought of stealing the desired food from someone else. The part of the personality that would stop you is called the **superego.** The id is concerned with what the person *wants* to do and the ego is concerned with planning what she *can* do; the superego is concerned with what she *should* do. It is the moral part of the personality, the source of conscience and of high ideals. But the superego can also create conflicts and problems. It is sometimes overly harsh, like a very strict parent. The superego, then, is also the source of guilt feelings which come from serious as well as mild deviations from what it defines as "right."

The id and the superego frequently come into conflict with each other. Because neither is concerned with reality, they may both come into conflict with the outside world as well. Freud saw the ego as part of the person that must resolve these conflicts. Somehow, the ego must find a realistic way to satisfy the demands of the id without offending the superego. If the id is not satisfied, the person feels an intolerable tension of longing or anger or desire. If the superego is not obeyed, the person feels guilty and inferior. And if outside reality is ignored, the person suffers such outcomes as starvation or dislike by other people (Freud, 1943).

Defense Mechanisms

The ego's job is so difficult that unconsciously all people resort to psychological defenses. Rather than face intense frustration, conflict, or feelings of unworthiness, people deceive themselves into believing nothing is wrong. If the demands of the id and the ego cannot be resolved, it may be necessary to distort reality. Freud called these techniques **defense mechanisms** because they defend the ego from experiencing anxiety about failing in its tasks (Figure 13.3). Freud felt that these defense mechanisms stem mainly from the unconscious part of the ego, and only ordinarily become conscious to the individual during a form of psychotherapy called psychoanalysis.

To some degree, defense mechanisms are necessary to psychological well-being. They relieve intolerable confusion, help people to weather intense emotional crises, and give individuals time to work out problems they might not be able to solve if they allowed themselves to feel all the pressures at work within them. However, if a person resorts to defense mechanisms all or most of the time, continually deceiving himself and others about his true feelings and aspirations, he will avoid facing and solving his problems realistically. A few of the defense mechanisms Freud identified are discussed below.

Displacement. Displacement occurs when the object of an unconscious wish provokes anxiety. This anxiety is reduced when the ego unconsciously

Figure 13.3
Some of the defense mechanisms in Freud's theory. Projection is a person seeing ridiculous attributes of his own personality as though they were possessed by others. Repression is shown by a woman who is not only concealing and restraining a monstrous impulse but also trying to conceal from herself the fact that she is doing so. The displacement of a widow's love from her lost husband and family onto her pets is another common mechanism.

shifts the wish to another object. The energy of the id is **displaced** from one object to another, more accessible, object. For example, if you wanted to hit your father but were afraid to, you might hit your kid brother instead. Your poor brother gets slapped around partly because he reminds you of your father and partly because he's not as likely to hit back.

Repression.   When a person has some thought or urge that causes the ego too much anxiety, she may push that thought or urge out of consciousness down into the unconscious. This process is called **repression.** The person simply "forgets" the thing that disturbs her, or pushes it out of awareness without ever realizing it. For example, a grown woman whose father is meddling in her life may have the impulse to say "I hate you, Dad." But the woman may feel so anxious and afraid about having such an impulse that she will come to believe—without realizing what she is doing—that what she feels is not hatred. She replaces the feeling with apathy, a feeling of not caring at all. She says, "I don't hate you. I have no special feelings at all about you." Nevertheless, the feelings of anger and hostility remain in the unconscious and may show themselves in cutting remarks or sarcastic jokes, slips of the tongue, or dreams.

Reaction Formation. **Reaction formation** involves replacing an unacceptable feeling or urge with its opposite. For example, a divorced father may resent having his child for the weekend. Unconsciously, he feels it is terribly wrong for a father to react that way, so he showers the child with expressions of love, toys, and exciting trips. A woman who finds her powerful ambitions unacceptable may play the role of a weak, helpless, passive female who wants nothing more than to please the men in her life—unconsciously covering up her true feelings.

Projection. Another way the ego avoids anxiety is to believe that impulses coming from within are really coming from other people. For example, a boy who is extremely jealous of his girl friend but does not want to admit to himself that he is threatened by her independence may claim, "I'm not jealous—she's the one who's always asking where I've been, who was that girl I was talking to . . ." This mechanism is called **projection** because inner feelings are thrown, or projected, outside. It is a common mechanism, which you have probably observed in yourself from time to time. Many people, for example, feel that others dislike them, when in reality they dislike themselves.

Regression. **Regression** means going back to an earlier and less mature pattern. When a person is under severe pressure and his other defenses are not working, he may start acting in ways that helped him in the past. For example, he may throw a temper tantrum, make faces, cry loudly, or revert to eating and sleeping all the time the way he did as a small child. If you have ever been tempted to stick out your lower lip and pout when you know that you should really accept the fact that you cannot have your own way, you have experienced regression.

The recognition of the tremendous forces that exist in human personality and the difficulty of controlling and handling them was Freud's great contribution to understanding human life. After Freud, it became easier to understand why human life contains so much conflict. It is a matter, Freud thought, of a savage individual coming to terms with the rules of society. The id is the savage part, and the superego, the representative of society. In a healthy person the ego, the "I," is strong enough to handle the struggle (see Hall, 1954).

Freud was also the first psychologist to claim that infancy and childhood were critical times for forming a person's basic character structure. He felt that personality was well formed by the time the child entered school and that subsequent growth consisted of elaborating this basic structure. (We described Freud's theory of the stages of development in Chapter 8.)

Evaluating Freud's Contribution

Freud was the first major social scientist to propose a unified theory to understand and explain human behavior. No theory that has followed has been more complete or more complex. But his ideas were controversial when they were proposed at the turn of the century, and they are controversial today. Some psychologists treat Freud's writings as a sacred text—if Freud said it, it must be so. At the other extreme, many have accused Freud of being unscientific—of proposing a theory that is too complex ever to be proved true or false.

In 1977, Seymour Fisher and Roger Greenberg published a book *(The Scientific Credibility of Freud's Theories and Therapy)* that summarized more than fifty years of research on Freud's ideas. Some parts of his theory held up well. For example, Freud believed that the male homosexual had an unusually close and intense involvement with his mother, while his relationship with his father was more likely to be characterized by distance, coldness, and conflict. To test this idea one psychologist (Ullman, 1960) asked groups of heterosexual and homosexual prisoners to describe their parents. He found that homosexuals were more likely to say that their mothers gave them "too much" love and affection while their fathers gave "too little." Many other studies of homosexuals pointed in the same direction.

Other Freudian beliefs were not supported by evidence. For example, psychoanalysis (a form of therapy Freud proposed in which a person spends years examining the unconscious basis of his problems) seems to be no more effective than other forms of psychotherapy that are simpler, cheaper, and less time-consuming.

Fisher and Greenberg concluded: "When we add up the totals from our research, balancing the positive against the negative, we find that Freud has fared rather well. But like all theorists, he has proved in the long run to have far from a perfect score. He seems to have been right about a respectable number of issues, but he was also wrong about some important things" (396).

In Freud's Footsteps: Jung and Adler

Freud's revolutionary ideas attracted many followers, and a number of these psychoanalysts came to develop important theories of their own.

At one time, Carl Jung was Freud's closest associate. But when Freud and Jung started to argue about psychoanalytic theory, their personal relationship became strained. Finally, they stopped speaking to each other entirely, a mere seven years after they met.

Jung disagreed with Freud on two major points. First, he took a more positive view of human nature, believing that people try to develop their potential as well as to handle their instinctual urges. Second, he distinguished between the personal unconscious (which was similar to Freud's idea of the unconscious) and the **collective unconscious,** which is a storehouse of instincts, urges, and memories of the entire human species down

Figure 13.4
Carl G. Jung. One of the most mystical and metaphysical of the pioneer theorists, Jung has had, until recently, a wider acceptance in Europe than in America.

Figure 13.5
Alfred Adler. Adler's writings on psychotherapy offer more optimism and practicality than those of Freud or Jung. His intuitive and common-sense approach to human life has greatly affected the thinking of psychologists throughout this century.

through history. He called these inherited, universal ideas **archetypes.** The same archetypes are present in every person. They reflect the common experiences of humanity with mothers, fathers, nature, war, and so on.

Jung went on to identify the archetypes by studying dreams and visions, paintings, poetry, folk stories, myths, and religions. He found that the same themes—the "archetypes"—appear again and again. For example, the story of Jack and the Beanstalk is essentially the same as the story of David and Goliath. Both tell how a small, weak, good person triumphs over a big, strong, bad person. Jung believed such stories are common and easy to understand because the situations they describe have occurred over and over again in human history and have been stored as archetypes in the unconscious of every human being (Jung, 1963).

Like Jung, Alfred Adler was an associate of Freud who left his teacher in the early part of this century to develop his own approach to personality. Adler believed that the driving force in people's lives is a desire to overcome their feelings of inferiority. Classic examples are Demosthenes, who overcame a speech impediment by practicing speaking with pebbles in his mouth and became the greatest orator of ancient Greece; Napoleon, a short man who conquered Europe in the early 1800s; and Glenn Cunningham, an Olympic runner who lost his toes in a fire as a child and had to plead with doctors who wanted to amputate his legs because they thought he would never be able to use them again.

Everyone struggles with inferiority, said Adler. He describes a person who continually tries to cover up and avoid feelings of inadequacy as having an **inferiority complex** (a term he introduced). Children first feel inferior because they are so little and so dependent on adults. Gradually they learn to do the things that older people can do. The satisfaction that comes from even such simple acts as walking or learning to use a spoon sets up a pattern of overcoming inadequacies, a pattern that lasts throughout life. Adler called these patterns *"life styles."*

Adler believed that the way parents treat their children has a great influence on the styles of life they choose. Overpampering, in which the parents attempt to satisfy the child's every whim, tends to produce a self-centered person who has little regard for others and who expects everyone else to do what he or she wants. On the other hand, the child who is neglected by his or her parents may seek revenge by becoming an angry, hostile person. Both the pampered and the neglected child tend to grow up into adults who lack confidence in their ability to meet the demands of life. Ideally, said Adler, a child should learn self-reliance and courage from his or her father and generosity and a feeling for others from his or her mother (Adler, 1959).

Although Jung and Adler were the first major figures to break with Freud, many others followed. Erich Fromm's theory centered around the need to belong and the loneliness freedom brings. Karen Horney stressed the importance of basic anxiety, which a child feels because she is helpless, and basic hostility, a resentment of one's parents that generally accompanies this anxiety (Figure 13.6). She also attacked several basic beliefs of Freud, including his emphasis on the importance of penis envy in the development of women. Erik Erikson accepted Freud's basic theory, but

Horney on Basic Anxiety and Hostility

The typical conflict leading to anxiety in a child is that between dependency on the parents . . . and hostile impulses against the parents. Hostility may be aroused in a child in many ways: by the parents' lack of respect for him; by unreasonable demands and prohibitions; by injustice; by unreliability; by suppression of criticism; by the parents dominating him and ascribing these tendencies to love. . . . If a child, in addition to being dependent on his parents, is grossly or subtly intimidated by them and hence feels that any expression of hostile impulses against them endangers his security, then the existence of such hostile impulses is bound to create anxiety. . . . The resulting picture may look exactly like what Freud describes as the Oedipus complex: passionate clinging to one parent and jealousy toward the other or toward anyone interfering with the claim of exclusive possession. . . . *But the dynamic structure of these attachments is entirely different from what Freud conceives as the Oedipus complex. They are an early manifestation of neurotic conflicts rather than a primarily sexual phenomenon.*

From Karen Horney, *The Neurotic Personality in Our Time.* New York: Norton, 1939.

Figure 13.6
Karen Horney on basic anxiety and hostility.

outlined eight psychosexual stages (described in Chapter 8) that every person goes through from birth to old age. These and other neo-Freudians have helped to keep psychoanalytic theory alive and growing.

BEHAVIORAL THEORIES

American psychology has long been dominated by the study of human and animal learning. When Freud's ideas came to America, learning theorists tried to understand his work in terms of their own. In the 1940s, Yale psychologists John Dollard and Neal Miller used learning theory to analyze many of Freud's ideas. But most learning psychologists remained skeptical of Freud's theories, and saw human behavior much more in terms of reward, punishment, and the other learning principles described in Chapter 2.

B. F. Skinner: Radical Behaviorism

Although his radical **behaviorism** was not proposed as a theory of personality, B. F. Skinner has had a major impact on personality theory. Skinner sees no need for a general concept of personality structure. He focuses instead on precisely what is causing a person to act in a specific way. It is a very pragmatic approach, one that is less concerned with understanding behavior than with predicting it and controlling it.

Consider the case of Fred, a college sophomore who has been rather depressed lately. Freud might seek the roots of Fred's unhappiness in events in his childhood. But Skinner's approach is more direct. First of all, Skinner would reject the vague label "depressed." Instead he would ask,

Figure 13.7
B. F. Skinner. Skinner's pioneering work in behavioral psychology has resulted in a number of new therapeutic techniques that have been markedly successful in treating certain kinds of problems.

exactly how does Fred behave? The answer may be that Fred spends most of the day in his room, cuts all his classes, and rarely smiles or laughs.

Next, Skinner would try to understand the **contingencies of reinforcement.** What conditions are maintaining these behaviors? What reinforces Fred for never leaving his room? One hypothesis is that Fred's girl friend Ethel has unintentionally reinforced this behavior by spending a lot of time with Fred, trying to cheer him up. Perhaps she didn't pay much attention to him before he was depressed. Note that Skinner's approach immediately suggests a hypothesis that can be proved true or false. If paying attention to Fred encourages his moroseness, then ignoring him should decrease the likelihood of this behavior. So Ethel might try ignoring Fred for a few days. If he then starts leaving his room, she has discovered the contingencies of reinforcement that govern Fred's behavior. If not, she will know that the hypothesis is wrong and can try something else. Perhaps Fred is glued to the TV in his room all day and has become a game-show addict. Take away the TV and you will find out whether that is the reinforcer.

At first, radical behaviorism may seem to imply that Fred is somehow faking his depression so that he can watch "Hollywood Squares," see more of his girl friend, or whatever. But Skinner does not make this assumption. Fred may be entirely unaware of the rewards that are shaping his behavior. In any case, Fred's feelings are beside the point. What matters is not what's going on inside Fred's head, but what he is doing. The point is to specify his behavior precisely and then find out what causes it.

Skinner's approach has become very popular among psychologists, partly because it is so pragmatic. It is a very action-oriented, very American approach: don't get all agitated about what's wrong; just jump in and try to fix it. And it is true that radical behaviorism often works. Skinnerians have applied the techniques to a wide range of behaviors, from teaching pigeons to play Ping-Pong to teaching severely retarded people to dress themselves, feed themselves, and take part in simple activities once believed beyond their abilities.

Normal people's behavior, too, can be changed with rewards and punishments, as every parent knows. But the success of radical behaviorists with normal people has been more limited, partly because our reinforcers are so complex. For example, in several studies juvenile delinquents have been placed in rehabilitation communities in which they are rewarded (with special privileges or food or cigarettes) for behaving in certain ways—taking classes, cleaning up their rooms, and so on. But in one such study, Buehler, Patterson, and Furness (1966) found that delinquent girls reinforced each other for breaking the rules and talking back. Sometimes, peer approval can be a more powerful reinforcer than any reward a psychologist can offer. Some radical behaviorists believe that incidents like this are only temporary setbacks; as they learn more about reinforcement, they will be better able to change undesirable behavior. Other psychologists are more skeptical (for example, see Reppucci and Saunders, 1974).

The idea of controlling people with systematic rewards is a frightening concept to many people, more reminiscent of Aldous Huxley's *Brave New World* than of Plato's *Republic.* But Skinner's novel *Walden Two* (1948) describes how these principles might be applied to form a utopian society. In another of his popular books, *Beyond Freedom and Dignity* (1971), Skinner argues the philosophical position that freedom is an illusion. You may think you are free to read this book or put it down, but in fact your behavior has been shaped by your history of reinforcements. You are reading this book right now because you have been reinforced in the past for studying—by getting a good grade, by winning the approval of your parents. Or perhaps you are now thinking of putting it down because you have been rewarded in the past for independence, and you want to prove your behavior is not shaped by rewards.

We cannot change the way reinforcers shape people's behavior, Skinner argues, so we might as well make the most of it. Today's society, for example, often rewards people for acting immorally—the slumlord gets more profits if he lets his property run down instead of spending money to maintain it. Skinner suggests that if we wish to change this situation, we should not try to appeal to the slumlord's inherent goodness, unless our approval is a reinforcer for him. More likely we should change society (perhaps by providing tax breaks) so he will be rewarded for taking care of his buildings.

As you might guess even from this brief review of Skinner's ideas, radical behaviorism is extremely controversial. Psychologists like Carl Rogers (whose views are described in the following section) have violently attacked Skinner's cynicism. Others are energetically applying his beliefs in schools, prisons, mental hospitals, and research laboratories around the world.

HUMANISTIC PSYCHOLOGY

One might look at **humanistic psychology** as a rebellion against the rather negative, pessimistic view of human nature that dominated personality theory in the first part of this century. As we have seen, psychoanalysts emphasized the struggle to control primitive, instinctual urges on the one hand, and to come to terms with the authoritarian demands of the superego or conscience on the other. The behaviorists, too, saw human behavior in mechanistic terms: our actions are shaped by rewards and punishments. Humanistic psychologists object to both approaches on the grounds that they demean human beings—Freud by emphasizing irrational and destructive instincts, Skinner by emphasizing external causes of behavior. In contrast, the humanists stress our relative freedom from instinctual pressures (compared to other animals) and our ability to create and live by personal standards.

Humanistic psychology is founded on the belief that all human beings strive for **self-actualization**—that is, the realization of their potentialities as unique human beings. Self-actualization involves an openness to a wide range of experiences; an awareness of and respect for one's own and other people's uniqueness; accepting the responsibilities of freedom and commitment; a desire to become more and more authentic or true to oneself; and an ability to grow. It requires the courage, in Kipling's words, "to trust

Improving Your Self-image

If your self-image can stand a boost, try taking these steps toward greater self-confidence. As you're reading this list, remember what humanistic personality theorists believe: a positive self-image is at the heart of successful adjustment.

- Base your personal goals on an honest appraisal of your strengths and weaknesses. Trying to be something you're not can only weaken your self-image.
- Don't let guilt and shame determine your goals. Let positive thinking guide your decision-making.
- Don't blame everything that goes wrong on yourself. Sometimes external events can play an equally important role.
- When others dismiss your views, keep in mind that events are interpreted in different ways by different people.
- When things go wrong, don't be too hard on yourself. Never think of yourself as a failure, stupid, or ugly.
- Accept criticism of the things you do, but don't allow people to criticize you as a person.
- Use your failures in a constructive way. They may be telling you to readjust your goals and start over in a new direction.
- Don't stay in a situation that makes you feel inadequate. If you can't change the situation, move on to something new.

Try these suggestions and you'll soon see that there's no better feeling than feeling good about yourself.

For more details, see Philip Zimbardo, *Shyness,* Reading, Mass.: Addison-Wesley, 1977.

Figure 13.8
Abraham Maslow. Maslow's work, as well as that of Carl Rogers and others, helped create a humanistic orientation toward the study of behavior by emphasizing growth and the realization of an individual's potential.

yourself when all men doubt you...." Humanists view this striving as a basic human instinct and the essence of human dignity.

Abraham Maslow: Growth and Self-Actualization

Abraham Maslow was one of the guiding spirits of the humanistic movement in psychology. He deliberately set out to create what he called "a third force in psychology" as an alternative to psychoanalysis and behaviorism. Maslow tried to base his theory of personality on studies of healthy, creative, self-actualizing people who fully utilize their talents and potential, rather than on studies of disturbed individuals. He criticized other psychologists for their pessimistic, negative, and limited conceptions of human beings. Where is the psychology, he asked, that deals with gaiety, exuberance, love, and expressive art to the same extent that it deals with misery, conflict, shame, hostility, and habit?

When Maslow decided to study the most productive individuals he could find—in history as well as in his social and professional circles—he was breaking new ground. The theories of personality we discussed earlier

---

Table 13.1 / Characteristics of Self-Actualized Persons

They are realistically oriented.

They accept themselves, other people, and the natural world for what they are.

They have a great deal of spontaneity.

They are problem-centered rather than self-centered.

They have an air of detachment and a need for privacy.

They are autonomous and independent.

Their appreciation of people and things is fresh rather than stereotyped.

Most of them have had profound mystical or spiritual experiences although not necessarily religious in character.

They identify with mankind.

Their intimate relationships with a few specially loved people tend to be profound and deeply emotional rather than superficial.

Their values and attitudes are democratic.

They do not confuse means with ends.

Their sense of humor is philosophical rather than hostile.

They have a great fund of creativeness.

They resist conformity to the culture.

They transcend the environment rather than just coping with it.

Source: Abraham Maslow, *Motivation and Personality* (New York: Harper & Row, 1954).

in this chapter were developed by psychotherapists after years of working with people who could not cope with everyday frustrations and conflicts. In contrast, Maslow was curious about people who not only coped with everyday problems effectively, but who also created exceptional lives for themselves, people like Abraham Lincoln, Albert Einstein, and Eleanor Roosevelt.

Maslow found that, although these people sometimes had great emotional difficulties, they adjusted to their problems in ways that allowed them to become highly productive. Maslow also found that such self-actualized individuals share a number of traits (Table 13.1). First, they *perceive reality accurately*, unlike most people who, because of prejudices and wishful thinking, perceive it rather inaccurately. Self-actualized people also *accept themselves*, other people, and their environments more readily than "average" people do. Without realizing it, most of us project our hopes and fears onto the world around us. Often we become upset with people whose attitudes differ radically from our own. We spend a good deal of time denying our own shortcomings and trying to rationalize or change things we do not like about ourselves. Self-actualizing individuals accept themselves as they are.

Secure in themselves, healthy individuals are more *problem-centered* than self-centered. They are able to focus on tasks in a way that people concerned about maintaining and protecting their self-image cannot. They are more likely to base decisions on ethical principles than on calculations of the possible costs or benefits to themselves. They have a strong sense of *identity with other human beings*—not just members of their family, ethnic group, or country, but all humankind. They have a strong *sense of humor*, but laugh with people, not at them.

Maslow also found that self-actualizing people are exceptionally *spontaneous*. They are not trying to be anything other than themselves. And they know themselves well enough to maintain their integrity in the face of opposition, unpopularity, and rejection. In a word, they are *autonomous*. They *value privacy* and frequently seek out solitude. This is not to say that they are detached or aloof. But rather than trying to be popular, they focus on deep, *loving relationships with the few people* to whom they are truly close.

Finally, the people Maslow studied had a rare ability to appreciate even the simplest things. They approached their lives with a *sense of discovery* that made each day a new day. They rarely felt bored or uninterested. Given to moments of intense joy and satisfaction, or "peak experiences," they got high on life itself. Maslow believed this to be both a cause and an effect of their creativity and originality (Maslow, 1970).

As indicated in Chapter 6, Maslow believed that to become self-actualizing a person must first satisfy his or her basic, primary needs—for food and shelter, physical safety, love and belonging, and self-esteem. Of course, to some extent the ability to satisfy these needs depends on factors beyond the individual's control. Still, no amount of wealth, talent, beauty, or any other asset can totally shield someone from frustration and disappointment. The affluent as well as the poor, the brilliant as well as the slow, have to adjust to maintain themselves and to grow.

Many psychologists have criticized Maslow's work. His claim that human nature is "good," for example, has been called an intrusion of subjective values into what should be a neutral science. His study of self-actualizing people has been criticized because the sample was chosen on the basis of Maslow's own subjective criteria. How can one identify self-actualized people without knowing the characteristics of such people? But then, if one knows these characteristics to begin with, what sense does it make to list them as if they were the results of an empirical study?

Despite such criticism, Maslow's influence has been great. He has inspired many researchers to pay more attention to healthy, productive people and has led many group leaders and clinicians to seek ways to promote the growth and self-actualization of workers, students, and clients in therapy.

Figure 13.9
Carl Rogers. Rogers's theories have had a considerable impact on modern psychology and on society in general. He has emphasized personal experience rather than drives and instincts.

Carl Rogers: Your Organism and Yourself

The people Carl Rogers counsels are "clients," not "patients." The word "patient" implies illness, a negative label that Rogers rejects. As a therapist, Rogers is primarily concerned with the roadblocks and detours on the path to self-actualization (or "full functioning," as he calls it). Rogers believes that many people suffer from a conflict between what they value in themselves and what they learn other people value in them. He explains how this conflict develops this way: There are two sides or parts to every person. One is the **organism,** which is the whole of a person, including his or her body. Rogers believes that the organism is constantly struggling to become more and more complete and perfect. Anything that furthers this end is good: The organism wants to become everything it can possibly be. For example, children want to learn to walk and run because their bodies are built for these activities. People want to shout and dance and sing because their organisms contain the potential for these behaviors. Different people have different potentialities, but every person wants to realize them, to make them real, whatever they are. It is of no value to be able to paint and not to do it. It is of no value to be able to make witty jokes and not to do so. Whatever you can do, you want to do—and to do as well as possible. (This optimism about human nature is the essence of humanism.)

Each individual also has what Rogers calls a **self.** The self is essentially your image of who you are and what you value—in yourself, in other people, in life in general. The self is something you acquire gradually over the years by observing how other people react to you. At first, the most significant other person in your life is your mother (or whoever raises you). You want her approval or **positive regard.** You ask yourself, "How does she see me?" If the answer is, "She loves me. She likes what I am and what I do," you begin to develop positive regard for yourself.

But often this does not happen. The image you see reflected in your mother's eyes and actions is mixed. Whether or not she approves of you often depends on whether or not you spit up your baby food or do your homework on time. In other words, she places conditions on her love: *if* you do what she wants, she likes you. Young and impressionable, you accept these verdicts and incorporate **conditions of worth** into yourself. "When I use obscene language at the dinner table, I am bad." You begin to see yourself as good and worthy only if you act in certain ways. You've learned from your parents and from other people who are significant to you that unless you meet certain conditions you will not be loved.

Rogers's work as a therapist convinced him that people cope with conditions of worth by rejecting or denying parts of their organism that do not fit their self-concept. For example, if your mother grew cold and distant whenever you became angry, you learned to deny yourself the right to express or perhaps even feel anger. Being angry "isn't you." In effect, you are cutting off a part of your organism or whole being; you are allowing yourself to experience and express only part of your being.

The greater the gap between the self and the organism, the more limited and defensive a person becomes. Rogers believes the cure for this situation is **unconditional positive regard.** If significant others (parents, friends, a mate, perhaps a therapist) convey the feeling that they value you for what you are, in your entirety, you will gradually learn to grant yourself the same unconditional positive regard. The need to limit yourself declines. You will be able to accept your organism and become open to *all* your feelings, thoughts, and experiences—and hence to other people. This is what Rogers means by **fully functioning.** The organism and the self are one: the individual is free to develop all his or her potentialities. Like Maslow and other humanistic psychologists, Rogers believes that self-regard and regard for others go together, and that the human potentials for good and for self-fulfillment outweigh the potentials for evil and despair (Rogers, 1951, 1961).

TRAIT THEORIES

Betsy spends many hours talking to other people, circulates freely at parties, and strikes up conversations while she waits in the dentist's office. Carl, though, spends more time with books than with other people and seldom goes to parties. In common-sense terms, we say that Betsy is friendly and Carl is not. Friendliness is a personality **trait** and some theorists have argued that studying such traits in detail is the best approach to solving the puzzle of human behavior.

One psychologist has defined a trait as "any relatively enduring way in which one individual differs from another" (Guilford, 1959). A trait, then, is a predisposition to respond in a certain way in many different kinds of situations—in a dentist's office, at a party, or in a classroom. More than any other personality theorists, trait theorists emphasize and try to explain the consistency of an individual's behavior in different situations.

Trait theorists generally make two basic assumptions about these underlying sources of consistency: every trait applies to all people (for example, everyone can be classified as more or less dependent) and these descriptions can be quantified (for example, we might establish a scale on which an extremely dependent person scores 1 while a very independent person scores 10).

Thus, every trait can be used to classify people. Aggressiveness, for example, is a continuum: a few people are extremely aggressive or extremely unaggressive, and most of us fall somewhere in the middle. We understand people by specifying their traits, and we use traits to predict people's future behavior. If you were hiring someone to sell vacuum cleaners, you would probably choose Betsy over Carl. This choice would be based on two assumptions: that friendliness is a useful trait for salespeople and that a person who is friendly in the dentist's office and at parties will be friendly in another situation—namely, in the salesroom.

Trait theorists go beyond this kind of common-sense analysis to try to discover the underlying sources of the consistency of human behavior. What is the best way to describe the common features of Betsy's behavior? Is she friendly, or extroverted, or socially aggressive, or interested in people, or sure of herself, or something else? What is the underlying *trait* that best explains her behavior?

Most (but not all) trait theorists believe that a few basic traits are central for all people. An underlying trait of self-confidence, for example, might be used to explain more superficial characteristics like social aggressiveness and dependency. If this were true, it would mean that a person would be dependent because he or she lacked self-confidence. Psychologists who accept this approach set out on their theoretical search for basic traits with very few assumptions.

Most trait theorists believe a few basic traits are central for all people.

This is very different from the starting point of other personality theorists we have considered. Freud, for example, began with a well-defined theory of instincts. When he observed that some people were stingy, he set out to explain this in terms of his theory. Trait theorists would not start by trying to understand stinginess. Rather, they would try to determine whether stinginess was a trait. That is, they would try to find out whether people who were stingy in one type of situation were also stingy in others. Then they might ask whether stinginess is a sign of a more basic trait like possessiveness: Is the stingy person also very possessive in relationships? Thus, the first and foremost question for the trait theorists is: What behaviors go together?

Instead of theories telling them *where* to look, trait theorists have complex and sophisticated methods that tell them *how* to look. These methods begin with the statistical technique of correlation (discussed in the Appendix)—using one set of scores to predict another. If I know that someone talks to strangers in line at the supermarket, can I predict that he will be likely to strike up conversations in a singles bar? Such predictions are never perfect. Perhaps the reason Betsy is so outspoken in the dentist's office is that she's terrified, and jabbering to strangers is the only way she can distract herself from the image of a sixteen-foot drill. Sometimes, actions that look like manifestations of one trait may really reflect something else entirely.

When we use traits to explain behavior, we must be careful to avoid circular reasoning: Why does Marie get so little done? Because she's lazy. How do you know she's lazy? Because she gets so little done. We can avoid this kind of circularity, at least in part, if the trait also predicts other kinds of behavior which form a consistent pattern.

Gordon Allport: Identifying Traits

Gordon W. Allport was one of the most influential psychologists of his day. Many of his ideas of personality are similar to those of humanistic psychology. For example, Allport emphasizes the positive, rational, and conscious reasons why we act the way we do. But he is most famous for his pioneering work on traits (Allport, 1961).

A trait, Allport said, makes a wide variety of situations "functionally equivalent"; that is, it enables a person to realize that many different situations call for a similar response. Thus, traits are responsible for the relative consistency of every individual's behavior.

Allport provided a number of classification schemes for distinguishing among kinds of traits. For example, he was concerned with emphasizing the differences between two major ways of studying personality. In the nomothetic approach, researchers study large groups of people in the search for general laws of personality. This can be contrasted with the idiographic approach, in which one studies a particular person in detail, emphasizing his or her uniqueness. On the basis of this distinction, Allport defined common traits as those that apply to everyone and individual traits as those that apply more to a specific person.

An example of the latter is found in Allport's book *Letters from Jenny* (1965), which consists of 172 letters a woman whom Allport calls Jenny Masterson wrote to a friend. Jenny reveals herself in these letters (which she wrote between the ages of fifty-eight and seventy) as a complex and fiercely independent woman. In his preface to the book, Allport writes:

To me the principal fascination of the Letters lies in their challenge to the reader (whether psychologist or layman) to "explain" Jenny—if he can. Why does an intelligent lady behave so persistently in a self-defeating manner?

Allport's own attempt to understand Jenny Masterson began with a search for the underlying traits that would explain the consistency of her behavior. He asked thirty-nine psychologists to read Jenny's letters and list her most important traits. They came up with a total of 198 words, which Allport broke down into eight basic categories, including "independent-autonomous," "self-centered," and "sentimental." Allport then compared these labels with the results of a more quantitative technique (in which a computer analyzed how often Jenny used certain words in her letters) and found that the two procedures led to similar conclusions.

Raymond B. Cattell: Factor Analysis

More recent theorists have concentrated on what Allport called common traits, and they have further tried to quantify them in a precise, scientific manner. Their primary tool in this task has been an extremely sophisticated mathematical technique called **factor analysis.** Basically, factor analysis is a high-powered way of looking for underlying scources of consistency. A researcher might note, for example, that people's test scores in math predict their chemistry grades (although not perfectly, of course), that chemistry grades predict history grades less well, and that scores in English predict scores in French. If he used factor analysis to study all these scores, he might find two underlying factors to explain his results: mathematical skills and verbal skills. These factors explain why chemistry grades predict performance in physics better than they predict performance in political science.

Raymond B. Cattell has used factor analysis extensively to study personality traits. Cattell defines a trait as a tendency to react to related situations in a way that remains more or less stable over time. He distinguishes between two kinds of tendencies: surface traits and source traits. *Surface traits* are clusters of behavior that tend to go together. An example of a surface trait is altruism, which involves a variety of related behaviors such as helping a neighbor who has a problem or contributing to an annual blood drive. Other examples of surface traits are integrity, curiosity, realism, and foolishness. *Source traits* are the underlying roots or causes of these behavioral clusters—for example, ego strength, dominance, and submissiveness. Cattell believes that discovering and learning to measure surface and source traits will enable us to identify those characteristics that all humans share and those that distinguish one person from another and make him or her an individual.

Cattell (1965) discovered these traits by studying large numbers of people, using three basic kinds of data: life records, questionnaires, and objective tests. Life records include everything from descriptions by people who have known an individual for some time to school grades and records of automobile accidents. Questionnaire data are the answers individuals give to a series of questions, whether or not these answers are truthful. (The fact that an individual underrates himself or herself or tries to create a highly favorable impression may be significant.) Objective test data are a person's responses to tests specifically designed to detect or prevent this type of "cheating."

Cattell summarized his philosophy in the introduction to *The Scientific Analysis of Personality:* "In an age when we are investigating everything, how can we shut our eyes to the possibility of scientifically studying personality?" (1965: 11).

SUMMARY

1. Personality is that "something" which accounts for the differences among people and for the consistencies in an individual's behavior over time and in different situations.

2. Personality theories provide a way of organizing information about people's thoughts, feelings, and actions; explaining differences among people; exploring the whys of behavior; and determining methods for improving the quality of life.

3. Freudian theory centers around the unconscious and the important role it plays in an individual's personality. Energy from the id, or pleasure-seeking unconscious, is diverted into the ego, or rational part of the self, and the superego, or conscience.

4. Defense mechanisms are unconscious solutions to conflict situations. Stress and anxiety are reduced by denial, or distortion of reality. Some common defense mechanisms are displacement, repression, reaction formation, projection, and regression.

5. Later psychoanalysts proposed changes in Freud's theory. Jung believed that the collective unconscious is a universally shared inheritance of instincts, urges, and memories called archetypes. Adler argued that the main motivating force in the development of personality is the effort to overcome feelings of inadequacy.

6. Skinner believes that psychologists should focus on the way rewards and punishments shape behavior.

7. Humanistic theories of personality emphasize human dignity and potential. After studying highly productive people who fulfilled their capabilities, Abraham Maslow concluded that self-actualized people were not free of emotional problems. Rather, they adjusted to their problems in ways that allowed them to become highly productive.

8. Rogers suggests that full functioning depends on a person's opening the self to include all of the organism, shedding conditions of worth.

9. Trait theorists, like Allport and Cattell, believe that in time we will be able to explain and predict human behavior on the basis of a relatively small number of personality characteristics like friendliness and aggression.

GLOSSARY

archetype: According to Jung, an inherited idea, based on the experiences of one's ancestors, that shapes one's perception of the world.

behaviorism: The school of psychology that holds that the proper subject matter of psychology is objectively observable behavior—and nothing else.

collective unconscious: According to Jung, that part of the mind that contains inherited instincts, urges, and memories common to all people.

conditions of worth: Rogers's term for the conditions a person must meet in order to regard himself or herself positively.

contingencies of reinforcement: Skinner's term for the occurrence of a reward or punishment following a particular behavior.

defense mechanisms: According to Freud, certain specific means by which the ego unconsciously protects itself against unpleasant impulses or circumstances.

displacement: The redirection of desires, feelings, or impulses from their proper object to a substitute.

ego: According to Freud, the part of the personality that is in touch with reality. The ego strives to meet the demands of the id and the superego in socially acceptable ways.

factor analysis: A complex statistical technique used to identify the underlying reasons variables are correlated.

fully functioning person: Rogers's term for an individual whose organism and self coincide, allowing him or her to be open to experience, to possess unconditional positive regard, and to have harmonious relations with others.

humanistic psychology: An approach to psychology that stresses the uniqueness of the individual; focuses on the value, dignity, and worth of each person; and holds that healthy living is the result of realizing one's full potential.

id: According to Freud, that part of the unconscious personality that contains our needs, drives, and instincts as well as repressed material. The material in the id strives for immediate satisfaction.

inferiority complex: According to Adler, a pattern of avoiding feelings of inadequacy and insig-

nificance rather than trying to overcome their source.

organism: Rogers's term for the whole person, including all of his or her feelings, thoughts, and urges as well as body.

personality: The sum total of physical, mental, emotional, and social characteristics that distinguish one person from another.

positive regard: Rogers's term for viewing oneself in a positive light, because of positive feedback received from interaction with others.

projection: Ascribing one's own undesirable attitudes, feelings, or thoughts to others.

reaction formation: Replacing an unacceptable feeling or urge with its opposite.

regression: A return to an earlier stage of development or pattern of behavior in a threatening or stressful situation.

repression: The exclusion from conscious awareness of a painful, unpleasant, or undesirable memory.

self: Rogers's term for one's experience or image of oneself, developed through interaction with others.

self-actualization: The humanist term for realizing one's unique potential.

superego: According to Freud, the process of the personality that inhibits the socially undesirable impulses of the id. The superego may cause excessive guilt if it is overly harsh.

trait: A tendency to react to a situation in a way that remains stable over time.

unconditional positive regard: Rogers's term for complete emotional support and complete acceptance of one person by another.

unconscious: According to Freud, the part of the mind that contains material we are unaware of, but that strongly influences conscious processes and behaviors.

ACTIVITIES

1. List the qualities and traits that you think comprise the "healthy" or "actualized" person. If this is done in class, you can see how your ideas of health and actualization differ from those of the other class members.

2. What are the key features of your own personality? What are the key features of the personalities of each of your parents? Compare your personality with those of your parents. There will be both similarities and differences. Because one's parents are necessarily such highly influential forces in a child's development, it may be of greater interest to note the chief differences in personalities. Then try to identify the factors responsible for those differences. For example, what key individuals or events have influenced or redirected the course of your life or changed your habits of living? How have society's institutions affected you?

3. Do some further reading on a particular personality theorist and arrange a class debate. A lively debate would be one between the behaviorists' position and the humanistic or existential approach.

4. The text contains a list of characteristics that Maslow found to be representative of people whom he described as "self-actualized." From among your acquaintances, choose a few whom you especially respect or admire for "doing their own thing," people who achieve satisfaction by being who and what they are. Ask them to list what they see as their distinguishing personality characteristics. Compare their answers and your observations with Maslow's list. In addition, compare this information with Jung's idea of individuation and Rogers's fully functioning person. Do the theories adequately describe the characteristics you admire? Are they consistent with them?

5. Jung believed that people are unconsciously linked to their ancestral past. Can you think of any evidence for or against the "collective unconscious" Jung described? Which, if any, of your own experiences lend support to or deny this theory?

6. Make a collage that depicts your particular personality, using pictures and words from magazines and newspapers. For example, include your likes, dislikes, hobbies, personality traits, appearance, and so on.

7. Look and listen for "Freudian slips." Write them down and try to determine the reasons for each slip.

8. Listen to conversations of several friends, relatives, teachers, and so on. Try to identify their use of defense mechanisms and write down the circumstances surrounding their use. Try to listen to your own conversations and do the same for yourself. Why do you think people use defense mechanisms?

SUGGESTED READINGS

CANNEL, WARD, AND MACKLIN, JUNE. *The Human Nature Industry*. Garden City, N.Y.: Doubleday Anchor, 1974 (paper). Written by a journalist and anthropologist, this book shows in a comical and insightful format how human nature can be manufactured and advertised to create three different images of people.

ELKIND, DAVID. "Freud, Jung and the Collective Unconscious." *New York Times Magazine*, October 4, 1970, 23–104. This well-written article summarizes much of Jung's principal contributions and includes some revealing anecdotes concerning Freud's relationship to Jung.

GALE, RAYMOND F. *Who Are You?* Englewood Cliffs, N.J.: Prentice-Hall, 1974 (paper). An excellent summary of humanistic and existential psychology, including coverage of Rogers, May, Maslow, and Fromm.

HALL, CALVIN S. *A Primer of Freudian Psychology.* Cleveland: World, 1954 (paper). A good introduction to Freudian theory. The book is clearly written and emphasizes Freud's contributions to the psychology of "normal" people.

HALL, CALVIN S., AND LINDZEY, GARDNER. *Theories of Personality.* 3rd ed. New York: Wiley, 1978. A classic textbook which reviews each major theory of personality and puts them all in historical perspective.

HORNEY, KAREN. *Our Inner Conflicts.* New York: Norton, 1945.

JUNG, CARL. *Memories, Dreams, Reflections.* Ed. by Anna Jaffe, trans. by Richard and Clara Winston. New York: Pantheon, 1963. A beautifully written autobiography that is bound to leave any reader with deep respect and admiration for this highly original thinker and writer.

MASLOW, ABRAHAM. *Toward a Psychology of Being.*

New York: Van Nostrand, 1968. Maslow, one of the founders of humanistic psychology, directs current thinking away from its obsession with the "normal" person and focuses on the "healthy" person.

————. *The Farther Reaches of Human Nature.* New York: Viking, 1971 (paper). A collection of Maslow's writings on a wide range of topics, including creativity, health and pathology, values and society, and his theory of motivation.

ROGERS, CARL. *On Becoming a Person.* Boston: Houghton Mifflin, 1961. Rogers presents a clear and thorough description of the humanistic theory of personality. This is an important work in that it was the first major rival to traditional Freudian theory.

SKINNER, B. F. *Walden Two.* New York: Macmillan, 1962 (paper); originally published 1948. A novel describing a behaviorist's Utopia.

————. *Beyond Freedom and Dignity.* New York: Knopf, 1971. Skinner proposes a solution to the world's problems that is based on the deliberate manipulation of behavior by conditioning techniques.

BIBLIOGRAPHY

ADLER, ALFRED. *What Life Should Mean to You.* New York: Putnam, 1959 (paper).

ALLPORT, GORDON W. *Pattern and Growth in Personality.* New York: Holt, Rinehart & Winston, 1961.

ALLPORT, GORDON W. (ED.) *Letters from Jenny.* New York: Harcourt, Brace & World, 1965.

BUEHLER, R. E., PATTERSON, G. R., AND FURNESS, R. M. "The Reinforcement of Behavior in Institutional Settings." *Behavior Research and Therapy,* 4 (1966): 157–167.

CATTELL, R. B. *The Scientific Analysis of Personality.* Baltimore: Penguin, 1965.

FISHER, S., AND GREENBERG, R. P. *The Scientific Credibility of Freud's Theories and Therapy.* New York: Basic Books, 1977.

FREUD, SIGMUND. *A General Introduction to Psychoanalysis.* Trans. by Joan Riviere. Garden City, N.Y.: Garden City Publishing, 1943.

FROMM, ERICH. *Man for Himself: An Inquiry into the Psychology of Ethics.* New York: Holt, Rinehart & Winston, 1947.

GUILFORD, J. P. *Personality.* New York: McGraw-Hill, 1959.

HALL, CALVIN S. *A Primer of Freudian Psychology.* Cleveland: World, 1954 (paper).

JUNG, CARL G. *Memories, Dreams, Reflections.* Ed. by Anna Jaffe, trans. by Richard and Clara Winston. New York: Pantheon, 1963.

LAING, R. D. *The Politics of Experience.* New York: Pantheon, 1967.

LAING, R. D., AND ESTERSON, AARON. *Sanity, Madness, and the Family.* 2nd ed. New York: Basic Books, 1971.

MASLOW, ABRAHAM. *Motivation and Personality.* 2nd ed. New York: Harper & Row, 1970 (paper).

REPPUCCI, N. D., AND SAUNDERS, J. T. "Social Psychology of Behavior Modification." *American Psychologist,* 29 (1974): 649–660.

ROGERS, CARL. *Client-centered Therapy.* Boston: Houghton Mifflin, 1951.

———. *On Becoming a Person.* Boston: Houghton Mifflin, 1961.

SKINNER, B. F. *Walden Two.* New York: Macmillan, 1962; originally published 1948.

———. *Beyond Freedom and Dignity.* New York: Knopf, 1971.

ULLMAN, P. "Parental Participation in Child Rearing as Evaluated by Male Social Deviates." *Pacific Sociological Review,* 3 (1960): 89–95.

14 Psychological Testing

Some large corporations use personality tests to screen job applicants. Does this mean that an applicant should be denied a job on the basis of his or her score on a personality test?

Mental patients score differently from normal persons on many personality tests. Does this mean that people whose scores are similar to that of the average mental patient should be hospitalized?

On standardized written intelligence tests, the average scores of black Americans are lower than those of white Americans, and the average scores of poor Americans (white and black) are lower than those of rich Americans. Does this mean that blacks and poor people are naturally inferior intellectually to whites and to rich people?

These questions only begin to suggest the enormous range and complexity of mental measurement, or *testing*. Psychologists often disagree strongly about testing. Indeed, perhaps the only point on which most people agree with regard to testing is that our society relies heavily on tests.

Over the years psychologists have devised a wide range of tools for measuring intelligence, interests, skills, achievements, knowledge, aptitudes, and personality patterns. Educators, the military, industry, and mental-health clinics depend on these tests. Yet the steady increase in the use of mental measures in recent years has raised numerous ethical questions. This chapter will describe the major types of tests in current use and discuss some of the controversies surrounding psychological testing.

Basic Characteristics of Tests
Test Reliability / Test Validity / Establishing Norms

Intelligence Testing
The Development of Intelligence Tests / The Uses and Meaning of IQ Scores / The Controversy over IQ

Measuring Abilities and Interests
Aptitude Tests / Using Psychology: The College Boards / Achievement Tests / Interest Tests

Personality Testing
Objective Personality Tests / Projective Tests

Situational Testing
Using Psychology: Jobs, Tests, and Discrimination

The Use of Tests in Western Society
Ethical Problems of Testing

Figure 14.1
Americans rely heavily on psychological testing because such tests promise to reveal a great deal about a person in a very short time.

BASIC CHARACTERISTICS OF TESTS

The lure of tests is that they promise to make it possible to find out a great deal about a person in a very short time.

All tests have one characteristic in common that makes them both fascinating and remarkably practical: they promise to make it possible to find out a great deal about a person in a very short time. Tests can be useful in predicting how well a person might do in a particular career; in assessing an individual's desires, interests, and attitudes; and in revealing psychological problems. One great virtue of standardized tests is that they can provide comparable data about many different individuals. Further, psychologists can use some tests to help people understand things about themselves more clearly than they did before.

One of the great dangers of testing, however, is that we tend to forget that tests are merely *tools* for measuring and predicting human behavior. We start to think of test results (for example, an IQ) as things in themselves. The justification for using a test to make decisions about a person's future depends on whether a decision based on test scores would be fairer and more accurate than one based on other criteria. The fairness and usefulness of a test depend on several factors: its reliability, its validity, and the way its norms were established.

Test Reliability

The term **reliability** refers to a test's consistency—its ability to yield the same result under a variety of different circumstances. There are three basic ways of determining a test's reliability. First, if a person retakes the test, or takes a similar test, within a short time after the first testing, does he or she receive approximately the same score? If, for example, you take a mechanical aptitude test three times in the space of six months and score 65 in January, 90 in March, and 70 in June, then the test is unreliable. It does not produce a measurement that is stable over time (Figure 14.3).

Figure 14.2
Two examples of group testing. Both intelligence tests and regular school exams can be considered psychological tests because both are intended to measure psychological variables (intelligence and knowledge).

The second measure of reliability is whether the test yields the same results when scored by different people. If both your teacher and a teaching assistant score an essay test that you have written, and one gives you a B while the other gives you a D, then you have reason to complain about the test's reliability. The score you receive depends more on the grader than on you. On a reliable test, your score would be the same no matter who graded your paper.

One final way of determining a test's reliability is to find out whether, if you divide the test in half and score each half separately, the two scores are approximately the same. If a test is supposed to measure one quality in a person (for example, reading comprehension or administrative ability), then it should not have some sections on which the person scores high and others on which he or she scores low.

In checking tests for reliability, psychologists are trying to prevent chance factors from influencing a person's score. All kinds of irrelevant matters can interfere with a test. If the test taker is depressed because his pet goldfish is sick or angry that he had to miss his favorite "I Love Lucy" rerun to take the exam, or if a broken radiator has raised the temperature in the testing room to 114 degrees, he will probably score lower than if he is reasonably relaxed, comfortable, and content. No test can screen out all interferences, but a highly reliable test can do away with a good part of them.

Test Validity

A test may be reliable but still not be valid. **Validity** is the ability of a test to measure what it is supposed to measure (Figure 14.4). For example, a test that consists primarily of vocabulary lists will not measure aptitude for engineering. Similarly, a test on American history will measure general learning ability.

Determining the validity of a test is more complex than assessing its reliability. One of the chief methods for measuring validity is to find out how well a test *predicts* performance. For example, a group of psychologists design a test to measure teaching ability. They ask questions about teaching methods, attitudes toward students, and so on. But do the people who score high on this test really make good teachers?

Suppose the test makers decide that a good way to check the validity of the test is to find out how much a teacher's students improve in reading in one year. If the students of those teachers who scored high on the test improve more in their reading skills than the students of those teachers who scored low on the test, the test may be considered valid. It identifies good teachers. School boards may then adopt it as one tool to use in deciding whom to hire to teach in their schools.

But what if teachers who are good at improving reading skills are poor at teaching other skills? It may be that this test measures talent for raising reading levels, not general teaching ability. This is the kind of difficulty psychologists encounter in trying to assess the validity of a test. As the example shows, nothing can be said about a test's validity until the *purpose* of the test is absolutely clear.

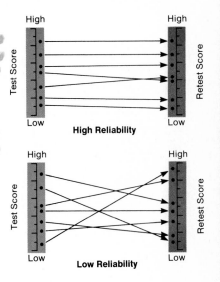

Figure 14.3

Test reliability. On the left, the test scores obtained by seven individuals are ordered on a scale. On the right, the corresponding scores on a second version of the same test, given at a later time, are ordered. In the upper diagram the two sets of scores correspond very closely. This pattern means the test is highly reliable. In the lower diagram, there is little relationship between the two. This scrambled pattern means the test has low reliability.

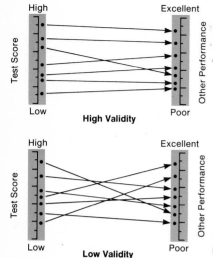

Figure 14.4
Test validity. Reliability and validity are assessed in exactly the same way, except that assessment of validity requires that test scores be compared to some other measure of behavior. The lower diagram might represent the comparison of scores on the "head size" test of intelligence (on the left) with school grades (on the right). The upper diagram might represent the result of comparing Stanford-Binet scores with school grades. The Stanford-Binet is a valid test for predicting school grades; the head size measurement is not.

Establishing Norms

Once a test result is obtained, the examiner must translate the score into something useful. Suppose a child answers thirty-two of fifty questions on a vocabulary test correctly. What does this score mean? If the test is reliable and valid, it means that the child can be expected to understand a certain percentage of the words in a book at the reading level being tested. In other words, the score predicts how the child will *perform* at a given level.

But a "raw" score does not tell us where the child stands in relation to other children at his or her age and grade level. If most children answered forty-five or more questions correctly, 32 is a low score. However, if most answered only twenty questions correctly, 32 is a very high score.

The method psychologists generally use to transform raw scores into figures that reflect comparisons with others is the **percentile system,** which bears some resemblance to what is called "grading on the curve." In the percentile system the scores actually achieved on the test are written down in order, ranging from the highest to the lowest. Each particular score is then compared with this list and assigned a percentile according to the percentage of scores that fall at or below this point. For example, if half the children in the above example scored 32 or below, then a score of 32 is at the fiftieth percentile. If 32 were the top score, it would be at the one-hundredth percentile. In the example given in figure 14.5, a score of 32 puts the child in the seventy-fifth percentile, since only 25 percent of the children scored higher than she did.

When psychologists are designing a test to be used in a variety of schools, businesses, clinics, or other settings, they usually set up a scale for comparison by establishing norms. The test is given to a large representative sample of the group to be measured—for example, sixth graders, army privates, engineers, or perhaps the population as a whole. Percentiles are then established on the basis of the scores achieved by this standardization group. These percentiles are called the test's **norms.** Most of the intelligence, aptitude, and personality tests you will encounter have been pro-

Figure 14.5
The meaning of percentile scores. The range of possible raw scores on a test is shown in relation to an idealized curve that indicates the proportion of people who achieved each score. The vertical lines indicate percentiles, or proportions of the curve below certain points. Thus, the line indicated as the 1st percentile is the line below which only 1 percent of the curve lies; similarly, 99 percent of the curve lies below the 99th percentile.

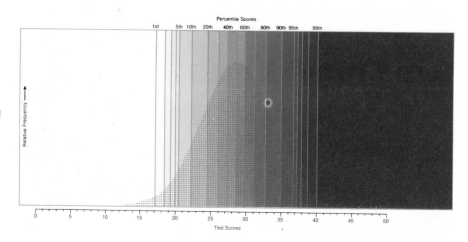

vided with norms in this way. Your percentile on the College Boards, for example, reflects your standing among people of your age and grade who have taken these exams.

It should be remembered, however, that norms are not really standards—even though a norm group is sometimes misleadingly referred to as a "standardization group." Norms refer only to what has been found normal or average for some group of people. If Johnny can read at the fiftieth percentile level, that does not mean he has met some absolute standard for ability to read. It only means that he reads better than half the population (50 percent), and worse than the other half.

In summary, when you take a test and obtain your score, you should consider the following questions in evaluating the results. (1) Was the test a reliable one? If you took the same test or a similar test again, would you receive a similar score? (2) Was this test a valid one? Does your performance on the test reflect your performance in the subject the test is designed to measure? (3) How were test norms established? In other words, what group of people are you being compared to?

INTELLIGENCE TESTING

Among the most widely used and widely disputed tests in America today are those that are designed to measure "intelligence" and yield an "IQ" score. This section will describe some of the major intelligence tests and present some of the issues that surround them.

The Development of Intelligence Tests

Alfred Binet, a French psychologist, was the first to develop a useful intelligence test. In 1904 Binet was asked by the Paris school authorities to devise a means of picking out "slow learners" so they could be placed in special classes from which they might better profit. Binet was unable to define intelligence, but he believed it was reflected in such things as the ability to make common-sense judgments, to tell the meanings of words, and to solve problems and puzzles. Binet assumed that whatever intelligence was, it increased with age; that is, older children had more intelligence than younger children. Therefore, in selecting items for his test he only included items on which older children did better than younger children. By asking the same questions of many children, Binet was able to determine the average age at which a particular question could be answered. For example, he discovered that certain questions could be answered by most twelve year olds but not by most eleven year olds. If a child of eleven, or even nine, could answer these questions, he or she was said to have a *mental age* of twelve. If a child of twelve could answer the nine-year-old-level questions but not the questions for ten year olds and eleven year olds, he or she was said to have a mental age of nine. Thus a slow learner was one who had a *mental age* that was less than his or her *chronological age*.

Figure 14.6
Two tests on the Stanford-Binet being administered to a little boy. (top) The examiner has built a tower of four blocks and has told the child, "You make one like this." (bottom) The examiner shows the child the card with six small objects attached to it and says, "See all these things? Show me the dog," and so on.

The Stanford-Binet.   Binet's intelligence test has been revised many times since he developed it. The Binet test currently in widespread use in the United States is a revision created at Stanford University: the Stanford-Binet Intelligence Test (Terman and Merrill, 1973). The Stanford-Binet, like the original test, groups test items by age level. To stimulate and maintain the child's interest, a variety of tasks are included, ranging from defining words to drawing pictures and explaining events in daily life. Children are tested one at a time. The examiner must carry out standardized instructions—at the same time putting the child at ease, getting him to pay attention, and encouraging him to try as hard as he can (Figure 14.6).

In the final scoring, the mental age indicates how high a level the person has reached. If his performance is as high as the average twelve year old's, he has a mental age of twelve. The **IQ,** or **intelligence quotient,** is called a quotient because it was originally computed by dividing mental age by actual (chronological) age and multiplying the result by 100 to eliminate decimals. (A nine year old with a mental age of twelve would have an IQ of 133.) Although the term IQ has stuck, the actual computation is now made on a basis similar to the percentile system.

The Wechsler Tests.   Two other frequently used intelligence tests are the Wechsler Intelligence Scale for Children, or WISC, and the Wechsler Adult Intelligence Scale, or WAIS (Wechsler, 1958). The Wechsler tests differ from the Stanford-Binet in several important ways. For example, the Wechsler tests place more emphasis on performance tasks (such as doing puzzles) than does the Stanford-Binet, so that individuals who are not particularly skilled in the use of words will not be as likely to receive low IQ scores (Figure 14.7).

Moreover, in addition to yielding one overall score, the Wechsler tests yield percentile scores in several areas—vocabulary, information, arithmetic, picture arrangement, and so on. These ratings are used to compute separate IQ scores for verbal and performance abilities. This type of scoring provides a more detailed picture of the individual's strengths and weaknesses than a single score does.

Group Tests.   The Wechsler and Stanford-Binet tests, because they are given individually, are costly and time-consuming to administer. During World War I, when the United States Army found that it had to test nearly two million men, and quickly, individual testing was a luxury the army could not afford. Thus paper-and-pencil intelligence tests, which could be given to large groups of people at the same time, were developed. Current group IQ tests, such as the Army Alpha and Beta tests, have proved to be convenient and effective and are used extensively in schools, employment offices, and many other institutions.

The Uses and Meaning of IQ Scores

In general, the norms for intelligence tests are established in such a way that most people score near 100. Out of one hundred people, seventeen will score above 115 and seventeen will score below 85. About three in one hundred score above 130, and three score below 70. This means that a

General Information
1. How many wings does a bird have?
2. How many nickels make a dime?
3. What is steam made of?
4. Who wrote "Paradise Lost"?
5. What is pepper?

General Comprehension
1. What should you do if you see someone forget his book when he leaves his seat in a restaurant?
2. What is the advantage of keeping money in a bank?
3. Why is copper often used in electrical wires?

Arithmetic
1. Sam had three pieces of candy and Joe gave him four more. How many pieces of candy did Sam have altogether?
2. Three men divided eighteen golf balls equally among themselves. How many golf balls did each man receive?
3. If two apples cost 15¢, what will be the cost of a dozen apples?

Similarities
1. In what way are a lion and a tiger alike?
2. In what way are a saw and a hammer alike?
3. In what way are an hour and a week alike?
4. In what way are a circle and a triangle alike?

Vocabulary
"What is a puzzle?"
"What does 'addition' mean?"

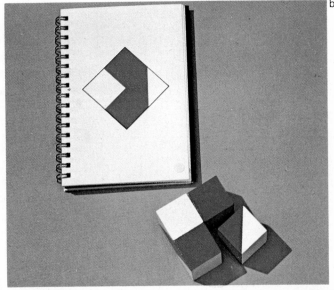

Figure 14.7
Test items similar to those included in the various Wechsler intelligence scales. (a) A sampling of questions from five of the verbal subtests. (b) A problem in block design, one of the performance subtests. (c) Another example of a performance subtest. The subject is asked to put together puzzle pieces to form a familiar object, such as a duck. (Test items courtesy The Psychological Corporation, New York)

score of 130 places a person in the ninety-seventh percentile; a score of 70, in the third percentile.

What do these scores mean? What do the tests measure? IQ scores seem to be most useful when related to school achievement: they are quite accurate in predicting which people will do well in schools, colleges, and universities. Critics of IQ testing do not question this predictive ability. They do wonder, however, whether such tests actually measure "intelligence." Most psychologists agree that intelligence is the ability to acquire new ideas and new behavior. Is success in school or the ability to take a test a real indication of such ability? Generally, IQ tests measure the ability to solve certain types of problems. But they do not directly measure the ability to pose those problems or to question the validity of problems set by others (Hoffman, 1962). This is only part of the reason why IQ testing is so controversial.

The Controversy over IQ

Much of the debate about IQ testing centers around one question: Do genetic differences or environmental inequalities cause two people to re-

Figure 14.8
An example of how an intelligence test may depend on knowledge specific to one culture. A population of urban blacks would score high on this test, and a population of suburban whites would score low.

The Dove Counterbalance Intelligence Test
by Adrian Dove

If they throw the dice and "7" is showing on the top, what is facing down?
(a) "Seven"   (b) "Snake eyes"
(c) "Boxcars"   (d) "Little Joes"
(e) "Eleven"

Jazz pianist Ahmad Jamal took an Arabic name after becoming really famous. Previously he had some fame with what he called his "slave name." What was his previous name?
(a) Willie Lee Jackson
(b) LeRoi Jones
(c) Wilbur McDougal
(d) Fritz Jones   (e) Andy Johnson

In "C. C. Rider," what does "C. C." stand for?
(a) Civil Service
(b) Church Council
(c) County Circuit, preacher of an old-time rambler
(d) Country Club
(e) "Cheating Charley" (the "Boxcar Gunsel")

Cheap "chitlings" (not the kind you purchase at the frozen-food counter) will taste rubbery unless they are cooked long enough. How soon can you quit cooking them to eat and enjoy them?
(a) 15 minutes   (b) 2 hours
(c) 24 hours
(d) 1 week (on a low flame)
(e) 1 hour

If a judge finds you guilty of "holding weed" (in California), what's the most he can give you?
(a) Indeterminate (life)   (b) A nickel
(c) A dime   (d) A year in county
(e) $100.00.

A "Handkerchief Head" is
(a) A cool cat   (b) A porter
(c) An "Uncle Tom"   (d) A hoddi
(e) A "preacher"

---

ceive different scores on intelligence tests? This controversy around the question becomes particularly heated when researchers consider differences among segments of the population. On the average people from middle-class backgrounds do better on IQ tests than people from poor backgrounds, and whites (more of whom grow up in middle-class environments) do better than blacks (more of whom grow up in poor surroundings). For years many psychologists assumed that this difference in IQ scores was due primarily to cultural differences—the fact that middle-class white children have better schools, more books, more opportunities to travel, and more encouragement, both from their parents and from their teachers, to use their abilities and "get ahead." It was felt that if lower-class black children were given the same cultural advantages as middle-class white children, the black-white IQ gap would be closed. Based on this theory, the federal government instituted such programs as Head Start, designed to enrich the environment of the culturally disadvantaged child.

However, in 1969 psychologist Arthur Jensen published an article questioning all these optimistic assumptions. Jensen claimed that Head Start had *not* succeeded in bringing about any permanent change in the IQ scores of the children in the program. He went on to say that this fact, along with a number of scientific studies, suggested that IQ differences were due primarily to genetic inheritance rather than to environment. Indeed, he argued that fully 80 percent of the difference in IQ scores between individuals was due to genetic difference. And if this were true of IQ differences between individuals, it might reasonably be true of IQ differences between whole races as well. In short, Jensen suggested that the lower IQ average of blacks might be due to genetic disadvantage much more than to environmental disadvantage, and consequently that no amount of "cultural enrichment" programs would ever permit the average black child to keep pace with the average white child on an IQ test.

Needless to say, Jensen's article raised a storm of protest. Some critics pointed out flaws in his methods and calculations. One of the researchers Jensen had quoted was even accused of falsifying his results to support the genetic view (Wade, 1976). Other critics attacked Jensen's assumptions. They argued it was totally unjustifiable to assume that what was true of individual differences in IQ scores was also true of racial differences in IQ scores. Still others argued that Jensen's conclusions were irrelevant since the standard IQ tests were a completely inadequate measure of intelligence.

From this debate a number of important points emerged, particularly with regard to intelligence tests. In the first place, some of the questions on these tests clearly give middle-class people an advantage (Figure 14.8). One intelligence test, for example, includes the following question as a test of reasoning ability:

A symphony is to a composer as a book is to what?
paper   sculptor   author   musician   man

A. Davis (1951) found that 81 percent of children from well-off families, but only 51 percent of children from lower-class families, answered this correctly. When Davis rephrased the question in less "highbrow" terms, using everyday words and common experiences, the gap closed.

> A baker goes with bread, like a carpenter goes with what?
> a saw   a house   a spoon   a nail   a man

Fifty percent of the children from both income groups answered this question correctly. The first question measured experience in middle-class culture as well as reasoning; the second, reasoning alone.

In addition, there is mounting evidence that poor children do not try as hard as middle-class children on intelligence tests. Why? Because the test itself makes them uncomfortable. They tend to see tests as punishments, as situations designed to make them look bad. Many rush through a test, choosing responses almost at random—just to get it over with. In contrast, middle-class children tend to see tests as an opportunity to prove themselves and to win praise. They work more slowly, making fewer wild guesses and scoring higher. Thus the differences among groups reflect motivation as well as intelligence.

Several researchers have coached disadvantaged youngsters in test taking—with good results. It seems that many do not fully understand the questions they are being asked or the tasks they are required to perform on the tests. In short, they have not learned the strategies to solve test problems. When they do, their scores improve. This suggests that a person's IQ score also reflects his or her skill and experience in taking tests.

In short, IQ tests are far from perfect measures of intelligence. A variety of factors irrelevant to the question of intelligence affect results and exaggerate differences among groups. This is not to say we should stop using the tests altogether, however. Intelligence tests may be biased in some respects. But they may be less biased than many teachers, whose personal likes and dislikes can easily influence their evaluations of students. And although IQ tests may measure social class, motivation, and experience as well as intelligence, they do in fact test people on the kind of reasoning and problem-solving abilities required for success in school and careers in a complex society. Moreover, by studying the differences in average IQ among groups, we may find ways to correct inequalities in educational opportunity and experience. To condemn testing would be something like the ancient practice of killing the messenger who brought bad news.

The best conclusion about IQ and nature versus nurture is that there is not enough evidence available for any firm conclusions. But, as John Loehlin, Gardner Lindzey, and J. N. Spuhler (1975) point out in their careful review of all relevant studies, we do know that IQ differences *within* racial groups are larger than any average differences between groups. Thus, the fact that *average* IQ scores for lower-class people are somewhat lower than those for middle-class people and that *average* scores for blacks are somewhat lower than those for whites does not tell us anything about *individuals*. The IQ scores of middle-class people and of white people range from a hypothetical zero up to the very rare 200. So do those of poor people and black people. In using the IQ test to place children in classes or adults in jobs, it is the *individual's* score that should matter, not his group's.

Low IQs and Large Families

It wasn't that long ago that nearly everyone came from a large family. But now most couples have one, two, or three children and no more.

Instead of bemoaning the loss of the large family, psychologists tell us we should be happy it's gone, for according to studies, large families produce children with lower IQs. Psychologists also point to evidence that keeping a family small may increase the likelihood of having smart children and that a child's intelligence is affected by where in the birth order he was born.

The best evidence for these effects comes from a study of the military examinations of over 386,000 Dutchmen—almost all the nineteen-year-old men born in the Netherlands between 1944 and 1947. Researchers found that the brightest subjects came from the smallest families and had few if any brothers and sisters when they were born. Thus, the first-born child in a family of two was usually brighter than the last child in a family of ten.

The effects of family size on intelligence may be explained by what a house full of children does to the home environment. It increases the amount of time a child spends with other children and decreases the amount of parental attention he receives. When this happens, and children have limited contact with adults, development of intelligence may suffer.

For more details, see Robert B. Zajonc, "Dumber by the Dozen," *Psychology Today,* January 1975.

Figure 14.9
The General Aptitude Test Battery (GATB) consists of a number of different kinds of tests. Samples of items testing verbal and mathematical skills (top) and manual skills (bottom) are shown here.

1. Which two words have the same meaning?
   (a) open **(b)** happy **(c)** glad
   (d) green

2. Which two words have the opposite meaning?
   (a) old **(b)** dry **(c)** cold
   (d) young

3. A man works 8 hours a day, 40 hours a week. He earns $1.40 an hour. How much does he earn each week?
   (A) $40.00 **(C)** $50.60
   (B) $44.60 **(D)** $56.00

4. At the left is a drawing of a flat piece of metal. Which object at the right can be made from this piece of metal?

MEASURING ABILITIES AND INTERESTS

Intelligence tests are designed to measure a person's overall ability to solve problems that involve symbols such as words, numbers, and pictures. Psychologists have developed other tests to assess special abilities and experiences. These include aptitude tests, achievement tests, and interest tests.

Aptitude Tests

Aptitude tests attempt to discover a person's talents and to predict how well he or she will be able to learn a new skill. The General Aptitude Test Battery (GATB) is the most widely used of these tests (Figure 14.9). Actually, the GATB comprises nine different tests, ranging from vocabulary to manual dexterity. Test results are used to determine whether a person meets minimum standards for each of a large number of occupations. In addition to the GATB there are aptitude tests in music, language, art, mathematics, and other special fields. Another widely used aptitude test, taken by most prospective college students, is the Scholastic Aptitude Test, designed to predict success in college.

USING PSYCHOLOGY

The College Boards

Every year, more than 1½ million students take the College Board Scholastic Aptitude Test (SAT) as part of the process of applying to college. This is not the most widely used test in our society (the Army General Classification Test of intelligence, for example, has been taken by more people), but it is probably the best. More time and effort have gone into perfecting the SAT than any other test (DuBois, 1972).

The College Board offered its first examinations in 1901: essay exams in English, French, German, Latin, Greek, history, mathematics, chemistry, and physics. The tests had been devised by a group of educators who saw a need for a standard yardstick to help colleges compare applicants from different high schools (Angoff and Dyer, 1971). The tremendous success of mass testing to screen people for the army in World War I encouraged the College Board to move toward objective tests. In 1926, the SAT (which included primarily multiple-choice questions) was offered for the first time.

Today, the SAT aptitude tests include two separate 75-minute examinations of verbal and mathematical ability. The tests have been carefully standardized so that scores range from 200 to 800, with an average of 500.

The reliability of the SAT is quite high. Standardized scor-

Figure 14.10
Taking a test: A number of factors, including the individual's mood and the physical setup of the room, can influence the results. A person can easily do poorly on one day in one setting and well on another day in different circumstances.

ing and careful pretesting of all items have given the scores a high degree of internal consistency. The validity of the SAT has been established by many studies showing that it helps predict college grades (DuBois, 1972). Interestingly enough, high school grades are the best single predictor of college performance. But SAT scores provide additional information, and the most accurate predictions of college grades are made by looking at SAT scores and high school grades together. The College Boards have proved to be equally valid in predicting the performance of men and women and blacks and whites.

In some cases, the sort of standardized information the SATs provide can be extremely accurate. For example, in 1975 the Mathematics Department at Johns Hopkins University held a special math contest for eleventh graders. Most of the participants were chosen by their high school math teachers, but a few students were included because they had gotten high scores on a special math SAT in the eighth grade. Those nominated by the SAT did far better than the students chosen by their teachers. "Among the fifty-one persons who entered the contest, the ten chosen by SAT ranked 1, 2, 3, 5.5, 7, 8, 12, 16.5, 19, and 23.5" (Stanley, 1976: 313). Thus, a short, standardized, objective test given three years earlier was a better predictor of student success than the carefully weighed opinions of their own teachers.

Achievement Tests

Whereas aptitude tests are designed to predict how well a person will be able to learn a new skill, **achievement tests** are designed to measure how much a person has already learned in a particular area. Such tests not only enable an instructor to assess a student's knowledge, they also help students to assess their progress for themselves.

The distinction between achievement and aptitude tests has become somewhat blurred in recent years. What psychologists had at first thought were tests of aptitude—defined as *innate* ability or talent—turned out to measure experience as well, so that in part they were achievement tests. On the other hand, achievement tests often turned out to be the best predictors of many kinds of occupational abilities, so that they were in some sense aptitude tests. Because of this overlap, psychologists have agreed that the distinction between the two types of tests rests more on purpose than on content. If a test is used to predict future ability, it is considered to be an aptitude test; if it is used to assess what a person already knows, it is an achievement test.

Raising College Board Scores

Every spring and winter, high school students go through a uniquely American rite of passage: they take their College Board exams. How well they do influences what happens in students' lives from that point on. The colleges they attend, the jobs they get, whom they marry are all affected, to one degree or other, by their scores.

Little wonder, then, that most students try to do everything they can to do well on the exam. Although no one has discovered a magic formula for getting the top grades, many students have shown that they can improve their scores by taking the exam more than once.

About 40 percent of the students repeat the exam, usually taking it first in the spring of their junior year and then in the winter of their senior year. According to the Educational Testing Service, the parent of the College Boards, one student in twenty will gain 100 points or more and about one in a hundred will lose 100 points or more. Generally speaking, the odds are with students to improve their scores. College admissions committees take this into account when they interpret the results.

Experts attribute this score gain to several factors. Students' intellectual capacities have increased between their junior and senior years, and a round of practice helped take the jitters out of exam time. In sum, the students are a little older, a little smarter, and a lot more experienced.

For more details, see W. H. Angoff (ed.), *The College Board's Admissions Testing Program,* New York: College Entrance Examination Board, 1971.

Interest Tests

The instruments for measuring interests are fundamentally different from the instruments for measuring abilities. Answers to questions on an intelligence test indicate whether a person can, in fact, do certain kinds of thinking and solve certain kinds of problems. There are right and wrong answers. But the answers to questions on an interest or a personality test cannot be right or wrong. The question in this type of testing is not "How much can you do?" or "How much do you know?" but "What are you like?"

The essential purpose of an **interest test** is to determine a person's preferences, attitudes, and interests. The test taker's responses are compared to the responses given by people in clearly defined groups, such as professions or occupations. The more a person's answers correspond to those of people in a particular occupation, the more likely that person is to enjoy and succeed in that profession.

In constructing the widely used Strong Vocational Interest Inventory, for example, psychologists compared the responses of people who are successfully employed in different occupations to the responses of "people in general." Suppose most engineers said they liked the idea of becoming astronomers but would not be interested in a coaching job, whereas "people in general" were evenly divided on these (and other) questions. A

Figure 14.11
Items from the Kuder Preference Record (KPR), a test that works like the Strong Vocational Interest Blank. The person taking the test is asked to pick from among three possible activities the one he or she would most like to do and the one he or she would least like to do. The test provides numerous sets of such alternatives.

		Most		Least
G.	Read a love story	●	G.	○
H.	Read a mystery	●	H.	○
I.	Read science fiction	●	I.	○
J.	Visit an art gallery	●	J.	○
K.	Browse in a library	●	K.	○
L.	Visit a museum	●	L.	○
M.	Collect autographs	●	M.	○
N.	Collect coins	●	N.	○
O.	Collect butterflies	●	O.	○
P.	Watch television	●	P.	○
Q.	Go for a walk	●	Q.	○
R.	Listen to music	●	R.	○

person who responded as the engineers did would rank high on the scale of interest in engineering. The Kuder Preference Record, part of which is shown in Figure 14.11, is based on the same principle. The purpose of these measures is to help people find the career that is right for them.

PERSONALITY TESTING

Psychiatrists and psychologists use **personality tests** to assess personality characteristics and to identify problems. Some of these tests are **objective,** or forced choice—that is, a person must select one out of a small number of possible responses. Others are **projective**—they encourage test takers to respond freely, giving their own interpretations of various test stimuli.

Objective Personality Tests

The most widely used objective personality test is the Minnesota Multiphasic Personality Inventory (MMPI). Like other personality tests, the MMPI has no right or wrong answers. The test consists of 550 statements to which a person can respond "true," "false," or "cannot say." Items include "I like tall women"; "I am an agent of God"; "I wake up tired most mornings"; "I am envied by most people"; "I often feel a tingling in my fingers."

The items on the MMPI reveal habits, fears, delusions, sexual attitudes, and symptoms of mental problems. Although the statements that relate to a given characteristic (such as depression) are scattered throughout the test, the answers to them can be pulled out and organized into a single depression scale. There are ten such clinical scales to the MMPI.

In scoring the MMPI, a psychologist looks for patterns of responses, not a high or low score on all the scales. This is because the items on the test do not, by themselves, identify personality types. In creating the MMPI, the test makers did not try to think up statements that would identify depression, anxiety, and so on. Rather, they invented a wide range of statements about all sorts of topics; gave the test to groups of people already known to be well adjusted, depressed, anxious, and so on; and retained for the test those questions that discriminated among these groups—questions, for example, that people suffering from depression or from anxiety neurosis almost always answered differently from normal groups (Hathaway and McKinley, 1940). Many of the items on the MMPI may sound like sheer nonsense. But they work, and for many psychologists that's all that counts. One unique aspect of the MMPI is that it has a built-in "lie detector." If an individual gives a false response to one statement, he or she may be caught by a rephrasing of the same question at a later point.

The MMPI has proved useful in helping to diagnose various forms of mental disturbance and in providing data for personality research (Dahlstrom and Welsh, 1960). It has also been used—and misused—in employment offices to screen job applicants. A person who is trying to get a job is likely to give answers he or she thinks the employer would like to see—thereby falling into some of the traps built into the test. Administering the MMPI under such circumstances can produce misleading, even damaging results. Innocently trying to make a good impression, the job applicant ends up looking like a liar instead. As an aid to counseling and therapy, however, it can be a valuable tool.

Projective Tests

Projective tests are open-ended examinations that invite people to tell stories about pictures, diagrams, or objects. The idea is that because the test material has no established meaning, the story a person tells must say something about his needs, wishes, fears, and other aspects of his personality. In other words, the subject will project his feelings onto the test items.

Perhaps the best-known and most widely discussed projective measure is the Rorschach ink-blot test, developed by Swiss psychiatrist Hermann Rorschach. Rorschach created ten ink-blot designs and a system for scoring responses to them. To administer the test, a psychologist hands the ink blots, one by one, to the subject, asking the person to say what he or she sees. The person might say that a certain area represents an airplane or an animal's head. This is the free-association period of the test. The psychologist then asks certain general questions in an attempt to discover what aspects of the ink blot determined the person's response (Figure 14.12).

There are a number of systems for scoring Rorschach responses. Some are very specific and concrete. For example, according to one system a person who mentions human movement more often than color in the ink blots is probably introverted while an extrovert will mention color more than movement. Other systems are far more intuitive—for example, simply noting whether the person taking the test is open or hostile. Many re-

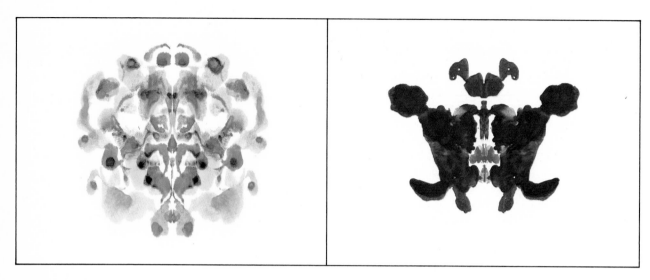

Figure 14.12
Inkblots similar to those used on the Rorschach test. In interpretations of a person's responses to the inkblots, as much attention may be paid to the style of the responses as to their content.

searchers have criticized the Rorschach, charging that scoring systems are neither reliable nor valid. But it continues to be widely used by therapists.

The second most widely used projective measure was developed by Henry Murray. The Thematic Apperception Test (TAT) consists of a series of twenty cards containing pictures of vague but suggestive situations. The individual is asked to tell a story about the picture, indicating how the situation shown on the card developed, what the characters are thinking and feeling, and how it will end (Figure 14.13).

As with the Rorschach, there are many different scoring systems. The interpreter usually focuses on the themes that emerge from the story and the needs of the main characters. Are they aggressive? Do they seem to have needs for achievement, love, or sex? Are they being attacked or criticized by another person, or are they receiving affection and comfort?

Other projective tests require a person to draw pictures of people, to construct scenes or stories out of toys or pictures, to make figures out of clay, or to act out social roles. One such measure is the Draw-a-Person Test

Figure 14.13
Three cards similar to those used in the Thematic Apperception Test (TAT). The scenes depicted in the drawings allow a variety of interpretations, and the person taking the test is assumed to project his or her own needs, wishes, defenses, and other personality factors into the story.

(DAP), in which the individual is asked first to draw a person and then to draw a person of the opposite sex from the one he or she just drew. The form and content of the drawings—the amount of detail and differentiation between the sexes—provide the psychologist with insights into the subject's personality.

SITUATIONAL TESTING

The use of psychological tests for such things as job placement has become extremely controversial in recent years. Is there any direct relation between a person's responses to statements on the MMPI and his everyday behavior? Do a person's perceptions of an ink blot really tell whether she will be able to remain calm under pressure or to give and take orders efficiently? Many psychologists think not. They believe that the closer a test is to the actual situation the examiner wants to know about, the more useful the results will be. A test that measures an individual's performance in terms of emotional, attitudinal, and behavioral responses to "true life" situations is called a **situational test.** (An example is a test for a driver's license, requiring that the person actually drive.)

Figure 14.14
Using this airplane flight simulator, pilots are trained and tested before they are given the responsibility of flying a real airliner. None of the standard tests described in this chapter could predict accurately whether a pilot would panic in such a situation. (United Air Lines photo)

One of the first situational tests for job placement was developed by the Office of Strategic Services (OSS) during World War II (Office of Strategic Services Assessment Staff, 1948). The OSS wanted to evaluate candidates for assignment to military espionage, which requires a high degree of self-control and frustration tolerance. In order to judge the candidates, the OSS set up a three-day session of intensive testing during which candidates were required to live together in close quarters and were confronted with a number of complicated and frustrating problems.

In one procedure, a staff member instructed the candidate to build a certain type of cube with the help of two assistants. The helpers were actually psychologists who played prearranged roles. One was extremely lazy and passive, engaged in projects of his own, and offered no advice. The other interfered with the work by making impractical suggestions, harassing the candidate, and asking embarrassing questions. The "assistants" succeeded so well in frustrating the candidates that not one finished the construction. But by placing the candidates in situations similar to those they would encounter as agents, the examiners were able to predict how these men might respond to military intelligence work. Court decisions and federal regulations now stipulate that job-placement tests in many professions must be work-related. Consequently, the use of situational tests is likely to increase in the years to come.

USING PSYCHOLOGY

Jobs, Tests, and Discrimination

Under the pressure of affirmative-action programs, or simply from a desire to be fair to minorities, many researchers and others in personnel are trying to make their tests and other evaluative procedures more equitable. Traditionally, the tests developed by industrial psychologists to help choose people for jobs have often measured intelligence and education. Sometimes, this unintentionally led to discrimination against minority groups. But all that has begun to change, largely in response to the 1971 Supreme Court decision in the case of *Griggs* v. *Duke Power Company* (Koenig, 1974).

Willie Griggs and twelve other black laborers for the Duke Power Company in Draper, North Carolina, charged that tests were being used to keep them from being promoted. According to company rules, no man could be promoted to the position of coal shoveler unless he had a high school diploma and passed two standard personnel tests. The net effect was that fewer blacks were promoted. The Supreme Court ruled that these tests were discriminatory (whether the power company had intended them to be or not) and were, therefore, illegal. The key issue was that graduating from high school or passing the tests had nothing to do with shoveling coal. In the future, the Court ruled, an employer must show that any job requirement is directly related to the job itself. In effect, courts now have the responsibility of deciding which tests are valid and which are not.

This does not mean that testing programs are always discriminatory. Some may truly test for the aptitudes or skills required for a particular job. For example, in a court case the testing program of American Telephone & Telegraph was exonerated (Miner, 1974). In court, data were brought in that showed the tests did well in prediction and tested the right things. Designing fair tests and fair procedures for evaluating job performance and promoting employees is one of the major challenges facing industrial psychologists today.

THE USE OF TESTS IN WESTERN SOCIETY

As we suggested at the beginning of this chapter, tests are used widely in all Western societies. Indeed, testing is probably the biggest single contribution the science of psychology has made to Western culture.

And to some degree they have been an extremely beneficial contribution, for tests have a number of clear advantages over other evaluation techniques. In the first place, they save time. They enable educators and others to measure large numbers of people in a matter of hours.

Second, tests can be extremely efficient. (Indeed, efficiency was the original motivation for the development of IQ testing.) Tests have provided help in identifying people who will and will not do well in school, who will and will not make good mechanics, soldiers, typists, or salespeople. Schools use tests so that a brilliant child won't waste time reading *Dick and Jane* for a year or a retarded child won't be forced to struggle through algebra books. Tests are used by businesses to avoid putting clumsy people into jobs requiring great care or highly trained people into jobs that are dull.

A third important advantage is that tests are generally more objective than other forms of evaluation. An individual cannot impress a test by wearing expensive and stylish clothing or by dropping names. A test cannot hear that a person has a foreign accent or see that he has a physical handicap—the sort of thing that might prejudice an interviewer who relies solely on his or her own impressions.

However, all these virtues depend on the accuracy of the tests involved. And, as we have seen, psychological testing is far from infallible. Tests do make mistakes. Bright people sometimes get low IQ scores; perfectly sane people sometimes make unusual responses to ink blots; incompetent workers sometimes do well on aptitude tests; and highly disturbed people sometimes show no sign of their problems on a personality test form. Tests usually turn out to measure much less than most people think they do, and they never supply absolutely certain information. *The results of all tests are*

Psychological testing is far from infallible: tests (and testers) do make mistakes.

always a matter of probability. At best they supply only good clues that should be followed up.

Another drawback of psychological testing is that tests compare an individual with others in his or her society according to accepted social standards. Because psychologists do not agree on exactly what intelligence and emotional disturbance are, they cannot measure them perfectly. What they can do is put together lists of questions that people whom society calls "smart" tend to answer differently from people whom society calls "dumb," or that people whom society calls "stable" tend to answer differently from people whom society calls "crazy." Then when a new person comes along, they can compare his responses to those of the "smart," "dumb," "stable," and "crazy" groups and come up with a judgment of how he stands in relation to these already-labeled groups. Test results thus reflect social judgments; and if society is wrong or unfair about something, tests are likely to be, too.

Ethical Problems of Testing

The widespread use of testing raises numerous ethical questions. We would all probably agree it is appropriate for the law to require that people pass driving tests before taking the wheel alone. But is it appropriate for a business organization to pry into an individual's fundamental beliefs and private fantasies before offering that person a job? Is it right for colleges to use attitude questionnaires in order to select their freshman classes? What does a student's attitude toward her mother or the opposite sex or freedom of the press have to do with whether or not she will be able to pass French 1A or Anthropology 1B?

Such considerations lead to doubts about the use of tests in making major decisions about individual lives. Should people be denied a college education or be confined to a mental institution on the basis of test results? Should people be required to take tests at all, when many find it a traumatic, demanding experience of questionable value? The answers to these questions are not easy. Psychological tests, like other technological advances, have their uses and their limitations. Like automobiles, tranquilizers, and nuclear power, tests can be overused and badly used. But, as is the case with other technologies, they can be used well if people understand them.

SUMMARY

1. All tests are designed to find out a great deal about people in a relatively short time. Test scores are not ends in themselves; they are simply numbers indicating how a person responded to a particular situation.

2. Reliability is the ability of a test to yield the same results under a variety of circumstances. Validity is the extent to which a test measures what it is supposed to measure.

3. The percentile system is a method for ranking scores on a test. Standardization allows a test score to be interpreted in the light of the scores all people in a specified group achieved.

4. The first intelligence test was designed by Alfred Binet as a means of picking out slow learners. The test currently in widespread use is a revision of Binet's test, known as the Stanford-Binet. The results of this test yield an IQ score that

is a measure of "mental age." The Wechsler intelligence tests differ from the Stanford-Binet in that they place more emphasis on performance tasks and yield a number of separate scores for different abilities.

5. IQ tests are good at predicting school performance, but whether they actually measure "intelligence" is difficult to say.

6. The debate over the causes of racial and socio-economic differences in average IQ scores has called attention to the fact that IQ tests measure social class, motivation, and experience as well as the ability to reason and solve problems.

7. Aptitude and achievement tests are virtually identical in content but serve different purposes. Aptitude tests are used to measure how well a person will be able to learn a new skill; achievement tests measure how much a person has already learned.

8. Many other psychological tests have no right or wrong answers; they attempt to find out what a person is like. Interest tests measure preferences for and attitudes toward different activities.

9. Personality tests are used primarily as aids to psychotherapy. The MMPI is an objective (forced choice) personality test; the Rorschach ink-blot test, Thematic Apperception Test, and the Draw-a-Person Test are projective (open-ended) personality tests.

10. A situational test, such as a driver's examination, is designed to measure how well a person performs in specific "real life" situations.

11. As the most objective measure of intelligence, aptitude or achievement, and personality we have, tests are extremely useful tools. But, like any tool, they can be misused.

GLOSSARY

achievement test: An instrument used to measure how much an individual has learned in a given subject or area.

aptitude test: An instrument used to estimate the probability that a person will be successful in learning a specific new skill or skills.

intelligence quotient (IQ): Originally, a measure of a person's mental development obtained by dividing his or her mental age (the score achieved on a standardized intelligence test) by his or her chronological age and multiplying by 100; now, any standardized measure of intelligence based on a scale in which 100 is defined to be average.

interest test: An instrument designed to measure a person's preferences, attitudes, and interests in certain activities.

norms: Standards of comparison for test results developed by giving the test to large, well-defined groups of people.

objective personality tests: Forced-choice tests (in which a person must select one of several answers) designed to study personal characteristics.

percentile system: A system for ranking test scores that indicates the percentage of scores lower and higher than a given score.

projective tests: Unstructured tests of personality in which a person is asked to respond freely, giving his or her own interpretation of various ambiguous stimuli.

reliability: The ability of a test to give the same results under a variety of different circumstances.

situational test: A simulation of a real situation designed to measure a person's performance under such circumstances.

validity: The ability of a test to measure what it is intended to measure.

ACTIVITIES

1. Can intelligence be learned? Try the following with two groups of subjects. For one group, give a series of problems like the following example: "Is this statement true or false? If gyuks are jogins and kuulls are jogins, then gyuks are kuulls." For the other group, give the same instructions, but also explain the first example by translating gyuks, jogins and kuulls as cats, animals, and dogs. Then the statement will read, "If cats are animals and dogs are animals, then cats are dogs." The statement is obviously false. You can make up other examples like "If some chairs are made of wood,

and some tables are made of wood, then chairs are tables." Experiment with a variety of these statements. Make some true and some false. Compare the results of the two groups. This is a question from an intelligence test. Can people learn to pass intelligence tests? Explain your answer.

2. The chapter discusses a wide range of devices used to measure intelligence, aptitudes, personality traits, and so on. Think about and write down the criteria by which you "test" others. How crucial are these "tests" in determining whether or not you decide to pursue a friendship? Think about the ways in which you "test" yourself. Are the criteria you use for yourself the same as those you use for others? If not, what are the differences?

3. If you were asked to rate people on an intelligence scale of your own making, what criteria would you use, and how would you make your decision? What roles would such factors as memory, emotional maturity, creativity, morality, and intuition play in formulating your intelligence scale? How would you "test" for these factors?

4. Imagine that you work for an insurance company and are trying to find out how likely it is for people of different ages to be involved in accidents. What criterion do you use? The number of accidents per year? Accidents per thousand miles of driving? Discuss what is right or wrong with these and other criteria.

5. Psychological testing has been considered an invasion of privacy by some people. Defend or refute the use of psychological testing. Discuss this question with your classmates—perhaps you can organize a classroom discussion on the subject.

6. Call or write for one of the questionnaires available from a computer dating service (they usually place advertisements in the classified sections of newspapers). Fill out or just look over the questionnaire. What general categories do the questions seem to fall into? What does the questionnaire seek to measure? Do you think it might be a useful way to obtain meaningful information about people?

SUGGESTED READINGS

AMERICAN PSYCHOLOGIST, 30, no. 1 (1975): 1–50. In this issue of the *American Psychologist* two major review articles are aimed at illustrating the use, misuse, and history of the mental-measurement movement in the United States. In the first article some of the major public controversies over mental testing are summarized, and in the second the use of mental tests with disadvantaged children is discussed.

BUROS, O. K. (ED.). *The Seventh Mental Measurement Yearbook.* Highland Park, N.J.: Gryphon Press, 1972. A valuable reference work. Every major psychological test is reviewed by the experts.

FITTS, P. M., AND POSNER, M. I. *Human Performance.* Belmont, Calif.: Brooks/Cole, 1967. A nontechnical book about the differences in human skills and abilities. Especially interesting when read with regard to practical implications for vocational and aptitude testing.

GROSS, MARVIN. *The Brain Watchers.* New York: Random House, 1962. This book is an outspoken

and well-written criticism of personality testing as inaccurate and immoral. Worth reading as a signal to the dangers of their excessive and improper use.

HOFFMAN, BANESH. *The Tyranny of Testing.* New York: Collier, 1962 (paper). Hoffman contends that objective tests "reward superficiality, ignore creativity, and penalize the person with a probing, subtle mind." In this readable little book, he criticizes the massive role that tests play in society today.

LOEHLIN, JOHN C., LINDZEY, GARDNER, AND SPUHLER, J. N. *Race Differences in Intelligence.* San Francisco: Freeman, 1975. Sometimes rather technical, but an extremely thorough summary of racial differences in IQ.

WILCOX, ROGER (ED.). *The Psychological Consequences of Being a Black American.* New York: Wiley, 1971. A good anthology of articles on testing intelligence in blacks, cultural disadvantages of minority groups, intelligence and achievement, attitudes and emotional characteristics of blacks, and the black psychologist in America.

BIBLIOGRAPHY

ANASTASI, ANNE. *Psychological Testing*. 3rd ed. New York: Macmillan, 1968.

ANGOFF, W. H., AND DYER, H. S. "The Admissions Testing Program." In *The College Boards Admissions Testing Program*, ed. by W. H. Angoff. New York: College Entrance Examination Board, 1971, pp. 1–13.

ASH, P., AND KROEKER, L. P. "Personnel Selection, Classification, and Placement." In *Annual Review of Psychology*. Palo Alto, Calif.: Annual Reviews, 1975, pp. 481–507.

CRONBACH, LEE J. *Essentials of Psychological Testing*. 3rd ed. New York: Harper & Row, 1970.

DAHLSTROM, WILLIAM GRANT, AND WELSH, GEORGE S. *An MMPI Handbook: A Guide to Use in Clinical Practice and Research*. Minneapolis: University of Minnesota Press, 1960.

DAVIS, A. "Socio-economic Influences upon Children's Learning." *Understanding the Child*, 20 (1951): 10–16.

DONLON, T. F., AND ANGOFF, W. H. "The Scholastic Aptitude Test." In *The College Boards Admissions Testing Program*, ed. by W. H. Angoff. New York: College Entrance Examination Board, 1971, pp. 15–47.

DU BOIS, PHILIP H. "Review of Scholastic Aptitude Test." In *The Seventh Mental Measurements Yearbook*, ed. by O. K. Buros. Highland Park, N.J.: Gryphon Press, 1972, pp. 646–648.

FITTS, P. M., AND POSNER, M. I. *Human Performance*. Belmont, Calif.: Brooks/Cole, 1967.

HASSETT, JOHN. "Checking the Accuracy of Pupil Scores in Standardized Tests." *English Journal*, 67 (October 1978): 30–31.

HATHAWAY, STARKE R., AND MC KINLEY, JOHN CHARNLEY. "A Multiphasic Personality Schedule (Minnesota): I. Construction of the Schedule." *Journal of Psychology*, 10 (1940): 249–254.

HERRNSTEIN, RICHARD. "I.Q." *Atlantic*, 228 (1971): 43–64.

HOFFMAN, BANESH. *The Tyranny of Testing*. New York: Collier, 1962 (paper).

JENSEN, ARTHUR R. "How Much Can We Boost I.Q. and Scholastic Achievement?" *Harvard Educational Review*, 39 (1969): 1–123.

KOENIG, PETER. "Field Report on Psychological Testing of Job Applicants: They Just Changed the Rules on How to Get Ahead." *Psychology Today*, 8 (June 1974): 87–96.

LOEHLIN, JOHN C., LINDZEY, GARDNER, AND SPUHLER, J. N. *Race Differences in Intelligence*. San Francisco: Freeman, 1975.

MINER, J. B. "Psychological Testing and Fair Employment Practices." *Personnel Psychology*, 27 (1974): 49–62.

OFFICE OF STRATEGIC SERVICES ASSESSMENT STAFF. *Assessment of Men*. New York: Holt, Rinehart & Winston, 1948.

STANLEY, JULIAN C. "Test Better Finder of Great Math Talent Than Teachers Are." *American Psychologist*, 31 (1976): 313–314.

TERMAN, LEWIS M., AND MERRILL, MAUD A. *Stanford-Binet Intelligence Scale: Manual for the Third Revision. Form L-M*. Boston: Houghton Mifflin, 1973.

TYLER, LEONA E. *The Psychology of Human Differences*. 3rd ed. New York: Appleton-Century-Crofts, 1965.

————. "Human Abilities." In *Annual Review of Psychology*. Palo Alto, Calif.: Annual Reviews, 1975, pp. 177–206.

WADE NICHOLAS. "IQ and Heredity: Suspicion of Fraud Beclouds Classic Experiment." *Science*, 194 (1976): 916–919.

WECHSLER, DAVID. *The Measurement and Appraisal of Adult Intelligence*. 14th ed. Baltimore: Williams & Wilkins, 1958.

15 Disturbance and Breakdown

A man living in the Ozark Mountains has a vision in which God speaks to him. He begins preaching to his relatives and neighbors, and soon he has the whole town in a state of religious fervor. People say he has a "calling." His reputation as a prophet and healer spreads, and in time he is drawing large audiences everywhere he goes. However, when he ventures into St. Louis and attempts to hold a prayer meeting, blocking traffic on a main street at rush hour, he is arrested. He tells the policemen about his conversations with God, and they hurry him off to the nearest mental hospital.

A housewife is tired all the time, but she has trouble sleeping. The chores keep piling up because she has no energy. Applications for evening courses and "help wanted" clippings from the classified ads lie untouched in a drawer. She consults the family doctor, but he says she's in perfect health. One night she tells her husband that she's thinking of seeing a psychotherapist. He thinks this is ridiculous. According to him, all she needs is to get up out of her chair and get busy.

Who is right? The "prophet" or the policemen? The housewife or her husband? It is often difficult to draw a line between "sanity" and "madness," normal and abnormal behavior. Behavior that some people consider normal seems crazy to others. Many non-Western peoples, along with religious fundamentalists in our own country, feel that having visions and hearing voices is an important part of a religious experience. Other people believe these are symptoms of mental disturbance. The man in the example above was interviewed by psychiatrists, diagnosed as "paranoid schizophrenic," and hospitalized for mental illness. Had he stayed home, he could have been considered perfectly okay. Indeed, more than okay—special (Slotkin, 1955).

What Is Abnormal Behavior?
Deviation from Normality / Adjustment / Psychological Health / Using Psychology: Legal Definitions of Sanity / Is Mental Illness a Myth?

The Problem of Classification

Neurosis
Anxiety / Phobias / Obsessions and Compulsions / Hysteria / Depression / Suicide

Psychosis
Schizophrenia / Affective Reactions / Autism / Causes of Psychosis

Personality Disorders

Drug Addiction
Alcoholism

DSM-III: New Ways to Categorize Mental Illness

Figure 15.1
For psychologists, defining abnormality is neither simple nor sure. Much depends on the approach one uses and on the cultural setting in which the behavior takes place.

Behavior some people consider normal seems crazy to others.

WHAT IS ABNORMAL BEHAVIOR?

In our example, the man was classified as mentally troubled because his behavior was so different from what other people felt was "normal." Yet the fact that a person is different does not necessarily mean that he or she is insane. Indeed, going along with the crowd may at times be self-destructive. Most readers—and most psychologists—would agree that a teen-ager who uses heroin because nearly everyone in his social circle does has problems.

In the case of the housewife, she was the one who decided she was psychologically troubled, simply because she was so unhappy. Yet unhappiness and even genuine depression are certainly not foolproof signs of psychological disturbance or of impending breakdown. Everyone feels low from time to time.

How, then, do psychologists distinguish the normal from the abnormal?

There are a number of ways to define abnormality, none of which is entirely satisfactory. We will look at the most popular ways of drawing the line between normal and abnormal: the deviance approach, the adjustment approach, and the psychological-health model. Then we will look at the application of these principles in legal definitions of abnormality. Finally, we will consider the criticism that in all these models people are arbitrarily labeled mentally ill.

Deviation from Normality

One approach to defining abnormality is to say that whatever most people do is normal. Abnormality, then, is any **deviation** from the average or from the majority. It is normal to bathe periodically, to be attracted to the opposite sex, and to laugh when tickled, because most peopple do so. And because very few people take ten showers a day, or find horses sexually attractive, or laugh when a loved one dies, those who do may be considered abnormal.

However, the deviance approach, as commonly used as it is, has serious limitations. If most people cheat on their income-tax returns, are honest taxpayers abnormal? If most people are noncreative, was Shakespeare abnormal? Because the majority is not always right or best, the deviance approach to defining abnormality is not a generally useful standard.

Adjustment

Another way to distinguish normal from abnormal people is to say that normal people are able to get along in the world—physically, emotionally, and socially. They can feed and clothe themselves, work, find friends, and live by the rules of society. By this definition, abnormal people are the ones who fail to *adjust*. They may be so unhappy that they refuse to eat or so lethargic that they cannot hold a job. They may experience so much anxiety in relationships with others that they end up avoiding people, living in a lonely world of their own.

Figure 15.2
The line between normal and abnormal is a fine one and depends very much on the observer and the standard being used. What some people consider deviant, others may see as just a little odd.

Figure 15.3
A still from the film *Who's Afraid of Virginia Woolf?* This powerful drama (based on a play by Edward Albee) portrays one night in the lives of two couples. In it Albee accurately (and painfully) exposed the inner conflicts of a "normal" and "stable" marriage to reveal nightmares that are recognizable to millions.

Psychological Health

The terms "mental illness" and "mental health" imply that psychological disturbance or abnormality is like a physical sickness—such as the flu or tuberculosis. Although many psychologists are beginning to think that "mental illness" is different from physical illness, the idea remains that there is some ideal way for people to function psychologically, just as there is an ideal way for people to function physically. Some psychologists feel that the normal or healthy person would be one who is functioning ideally or who at least is striving toward ideal functioning. Personality theorists such as Carl Jung and Abraham Maslow (see Chapter 13) have tried to describe this striving process, which is often referred to as *"self-actualization."* According to this line of thinking, to be normal or healthy involves full acceptance and expression of one's own individuality and humanness.

One problem with this approach to defining abnormality is that it is difficult to determine whether or not a person is doing a good job of actualizing him- or herself. How can you tell when a person is doing his or her best? What are the signs that he or she is losing the struggle? Answers to such questions must often be arbitrary.

USING PSYCHOLOGY

Legal Definitions of Sanity

The terms "sane" and "insane" are not ordinarily used by psychologists; they are legal distinctions. There is no single definition of criminal sanity, but one of the most widely used set of guidelines was developed by the American Law Institute in 1962. It emphasized that people are not responsible for their criminal acts if, "as a result of mental disease or defect," they do not know that what they did was wrong or if they were unable to act differently. The guidelines also note that "the terms 'mental disease or defect' do not include an abnormali.y manifested only by repeated criminal . . . conduct."

It is often difficult to apply these guidelines to real people. As anyone who has ever seen a movie about a murder trial

Figure 15.4
The Madwoman, painted by Chaim Soutine in 1920. Many people believe that those who are mentally ill are always recognizable by their bizarre appearance and behavior—that they are somehow fundamentally different from the rest of us.

knows, there are usually expert witnesses on both sides—
some saying the defendant is sane, others saying he's insane.
Paradoxically, a person who successfully uses this defense
may end up being confined longer in a mental hospital than
he would have been if he were convicted and sent to prison.

Although most people have probably heard a great deal
about the insanity defense, it is rarely successful. For example, only eleven cases successfully used the insanity defense
in New York State in the 1960s (Davison and Neale, 1978). The
law affects the lives of the mentally ill far more often in civil
commitment procedures: two out of every five people in
mental hospitals are there against their will.

Laws vary from state to state, but generally a person can be
committed to a mental hospital if a judgment is made that he
or she is (1) mentally ill, and (2) needs treatment or is dangerous to him- or herself or others.

In formal commitment proceedings, a friend or a relative
usually asks a judge to order a mental-health examination.
Informal commitment occurs when, for example, the police
bring in a person who is acting wildly. In most states, a person
can be held against her will for some definite period of time if
two physicians (not necessarily psychiatrists) sign a certifi-
cate ordering her commitment.

In recent years, many mental patients have formed groups
to protect their legal rights. As a result, the legal status of
involuntary commitment procedures and patients' rights for
treatment are likely to continue to change in the 1980s (Davison and Neale, 1978).

Is Mental Illness a Myth?

The current definitions of abnormality are somewhat arbitrary. And this
fact has led some theorists to conclude that labeling a person as "mentally
ill" simply because his or her behavior is odd is cruel and irresponsible.
The foremost spokesman of this point of view is the American psychiatrist
Thomas Szasz (1961).

Szasz argues that most of the people whom we call mentally ill are not
ill at all. They simply have "problems in living"—serious conflicts with the
world around them. But instead of dealing with the patient's conflict as
something that deserves attention and respect, psychiatrists simply label
him as "sick" and shunt him off to a hospital. The society's norms remain
unchallenged, and the psychiatrist remains in a comfortable position of
authority. The one who loses is the patient, who is deprived both of responsibility for his behavior and of his dignity as a human being. As a
result, Szasz claims, the patient's problems intensify. Szasz's position is a

minority stand. Most psychologists and psychiatrists would agree that a person who claims to be God or Napoleon is truly abnormal and disturbed.

The fact that it is difficult to define abnormality does not mean that no such thing exists. What it does mean is that we should be very cautious about judging a person to be "mentally ill" just because he or she acts in a way that we cannot understand. It should also be kept in mind that mild psychological disorders are extremely common. It is only when a psychological problem becomes severe enough to disrupt everyday life that it is thought of as "abnormality" or "illness."

THE PROBLEM OF CLASSIFICATION

For years psychiatrists have been trying to devise a logical and useful method for classifying emotional disorders. This is a difficult task, for psychological problems do not lend themselves to the same sort of categorizing that physical illnesses do. The causes, symptoms, and cures for psychological disturbances and breakdowns are rarely obvious or clear-cut.

All of the major classification schemes have accepted the medical model—they assume that abnormal behavior can be described in the same manner as any physical illness. The physician diagnoses a specific disease when a person has certain specific symptoms.

In 1952, the American Psychiatric Association agreed upon a standard system for classifying abnormal symptoms which they published in the *Diagnostic and Statistical Manual of Mental Disorders,* or DSM. A revised version, accepted in 1968, became known as **DSM-II.** This was the standard psychiatric classification scheme accepted throughout the 1970s, and this chapter is organized around its familiar categories.

Now, as this book is being written, psychiatrists are deciding on the precise form of a new classification scheme for the 1980s, to be known as **DSM-III.** Each new system was an attempt to solve some of the problems of the earlier approaches. For example, DSM-II has been criticized as being vague: two psychologists often give different diagnoses for the same patient. DSM-III is much more concrete and specific, and as a result its diagnoses are far more reliable. We shall list the major differences between DSM-II and DSM-III at the end of this chapter.

DSM-II distinguishes between two main types of disorder: neurosis and psychosis. **Neurosis** is a disorder in which severe anxiety reduces a person's ability to deal effectively with reality. **Psychosis** is a disorder in which a person is often unable to deal with reality at all and withdraws into his or her own private world. Psychosis is not an advanced stage of neurosis. It is a distinct type of psychological disturbance.

In the following pages we will discuss the symptoms and possible causes of several forms of neurosis and psychosis. We will also examine two other categories of psychological problems: personality disorders and addiction to alcohol and other drugs.

As you read, you will probably feel that some of the descriptions could be applied to you at times. They probably could. But remember, a psychologically disturbed person is one who turns normal human quirks into extreme and distorted *patterns* of thought and behavior. When we speak of psychologically disturbed individuals we are not talking about people who have their normal share of difficulties, but rather about people who are hopelessly unhappy, whose minds are confused and chaotic, who have a difficult time doing the simple things in life, or who act in ways that are truly harmful to themselves or to other people.

NEUROSIS

The world of a neurotic person is real but painful. Such a person rarely behaves in an alarmingly unusual fashion, but she is uncomfortable with life and can't seem to resolve her problems. She often has an unrealistic image of herself—feeling unworthy or inferior to those around her. A neurotic individual is plagued by self-doubt and cannot seem to free herself of recurring worries and fears. Her emotional problems may be expressed in constant worrying, in sudden mood swings, or in a variety of physical symptoms (headaches, sweating, muscle tightness, weakness, fatigue, and the like). She lives a life of continuous anxiety with few periods of true tranquillity. A neurotic often has difficulty forming stable and satisfying relationships.

Anxiety

Once in a while, everyone feels nervous for reasons he or she cannot quite explain; but a severely neurotic person feels this way practically all the time. Neurotic **anxiety** is generalized apprehension—a vague feeling that one is in danger. Sometimes this anxiety blossoms into full-fledged panic, which may include choking sensations, chest pain, dizziness, trembling, and hot flashes. Unlike fear, which is a reaction to real and identifiable threats, anxiety is a reaction to vague or imagined dangers.

Why are some people so anxious? According to Freudian psychoanalytic theorists, anxiety is caused by unconscious desires and conflicts that are so disturbing to the individual that he cannot find any satisfying solution. These unresolved conflicts often persist on an unconscious level. The individual lives in a more or less constant state of fear of emotions he doesn't feel capable of handling—his own emotions. When something happens to bring them closer to the surface, the fear becomes intense. For example, a person who is unable to face or express feelings of anger may become tense and fearful when he sees other people arguing or when hostile images flash into his mind, because these things remind him of emotions he is trying to deny. This is what we mean by anxiety. It seems unfounded and irrational because the individual is hiding emotions from himself as well as from others.

Most people are able to cope with occasional bouts of anxiety. However, some individuals find that the tension and uneasiness do not go away.

A neurotic person may become so preoccupied with his internal problems that he neglects his social relationships. The people he sees every day recognize that he is nervous and unhappy, but they don't know the source of his problems. He has trouble dealing with his family and friends and fulfilling his responsibilities, and this too begins to worry him, adding to his anxiety. He is trapped in a vicious cycle. The more he worries, the more difficulty he has; the more difficulty he has, the more he worries.

Hans Eysenck (1957) has proposed a more biological explanation of the origins of anxiety. Eysenck believes that some people are born with very excitable nervous systems. They tend to overreact to "threatening" stimuli, and gradually come to associate anxiety with many different situations. Other theorists stress the role of learning still more: if a person feels very anxious on a date, for example, even the thought of another date may make him nervous, so he learns to avoid this situation. Since he never goes out, he never has a chance to unlearn the anxiety. This person's anxiety may then generalize to other situations and become more and more of a problem.

Neurotics may develop a number of unusual behaviors in their effort to cope with anxiety—including phobias, obsessions, compulsions, hysteria, and depression. According to learning theory, these behaviors may be seen as the result of conditioning. Or they may be interpreted as extreme forms of the defense mechanisms we discussed in Chapter 13 (displacement, repression, projection, and regression).

Phobias

When severe anxiety is focused on a particular object or situation it is called a **phobia**. A phobia can develop toward almost anything; high places (acrophobia), enclosed places (claustrophobia), darkness (nyctophobia) are a few examples. A person with a phobia has an intense, persistent, irrational fear of something.

Phobic individuals develop elaborate plans to avoid the situations they fear. For example, people with an extreme fear of crowds may stop going to movies or shopping in large, busy stores. Indeed, some reach the point where they will not leave their houses at all.

There are a number of theories about how people develop phobias. In some cases, phobias result from frightening experiences in the past. For example, a person who was locked in a closet as a child (accidentally or as a punishment) may become claustrophobic. She realizes that closets are not harmful, yet feels a distinct dread of enclosed places. Most people have similar feelings about objects and situations associated with past frights.

Neurotic fears, however, do not always have such straightforward explanations. In less clear-cut cases, some psychologists have attempted to explain phobias in terms of projection. What the person really fears is an impulse inside herself: To avoid this fear, she unconsciously projects it onto something outside herself. For example, a person who is terrified of heights may really be afraid of losing control over other wishes or feelings. By concentrating on avoiding heights, she is able to control other disturbing urges and push them out of her consciousness.

A   B   C

Obsessions and Compulsions

A person suffering from acute anxiety may find himself thinking the same thoughts over and over again. Such an uncontrollable pattern of thoughts is called an **obsession.** Or someone may repeatedly perform irrational actions. This is called a **compulsion.** The neurotic person may experience both these agonies together—a condition called *obsessive-compulsive neurosis.*

A compulsive person may feel compelled to wash her hands twenty or thirty times a day, or to avoid stepping on cracks in the sidewalk when she goes out. An obsessive person may be unable to rid herself of unpleasant thoughts about death, or of a recurring impulse to make obscene remarks in public. And the obsessive-compulsive may wash her hands continually *and* torment herself with thoughts of obscene behavior.

Everyone has obsessions and compulsions. Love might be described as an obsession; so might a hobby that occupies most of a person's spare time. Striving to do something "perfectly" is often considered to be a compulsion. But if the person who is deeply engrossed in a hobby or who aims for perfection enjoys this intense absorption and can still function effectively, he or she is usually not considered neurotic. Psychologists consider it a problem only when such thoughts and activities interfere with what a person wants and needs to do. Someone who spends so much time double-checking every detail of her work that she can never finish a job is considered more neurotic than conscientious.

Why do people develop obsessions and compulsions? Possibly because they serve as diversions from a neurotic person's real fears and their origins and thus may reduce anxiety somewhat. In addition, compulsions provide a disturbed person with the evidence that she is doing something well, even if it is only avoiding cracks on a sidewalk. Thus there is some logic in this apparently illogical behavior.

Hysteria

Neurotic anxiety can also create a wide variety of physical symptoms with no apparent physical causes. This phenomenon is known as **hysteria.**

Figure 15.5
An artist's representation of three phobias: (a) fear of heights, called acrophobia; (b) fear of enclosed spaces, called claustrophobia; and (c) fear of dirt, called mysophobia. (After Vassos, 1931)

Figure 15.6
A still from the film *The Caine Mutiny,* in which Humphrey Bogart played Captain Queeg, an individual who was obsessed with order. Any disruption of Queeg's routine sent him into panic and produced the compulsive behavior of continually rolling ball bearings in his hand. Queeg's behavior led his officers to lable him "mentally ill" and to mutiny against him.

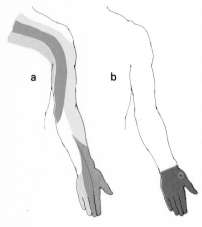

Figure 15.7
A patient who complained to a doctor that his right hand had become numb might be diagnosed as a neurotic suffering from hysteria, depending on the exact pattern of the numbness. The skin areas served by different nerves in the arm are shown in (a). The "glove" numbness shown in (b) could not result from damage to these nerves.

There are two types of hysteria: conversion reactions and dissociative reactions.

Conversion Reactions. A **conversion reaction** is the conversion of emotional difficulties into the loss of a specific physiological function. Many people occasionally experience mild conversion reactions, as when someone is so scared he cannot move; he is "frozen stiff," as the phrase goes. But neurotic hysteria is not simply a brief loss of functioning due to fright. It persists.

An hysteric experiences a real and prolonged handicap—he literally cannot hear or speak or feel anything in his left hand or move his legs or exercise some other normal physical function (Figure 15.7). For example, he wakes up one morning and finds himself paralyzed from the waist down. A normal reaction to this would be to become violently upset. However, hysterics often accept their loss of function with relative calm. (This is one sign that a person is suffering from a psychological rather than a physiological problem.) Most psychologists believe that hysterics unconsciously invent physical symptoms to gain freedom from unbearable anxiety. For example, a person who lives in terror of blurting out things that he does not want to say may lose the power of speech. This "solves" the problem.

Hysteria must be distinguished from **hypochondriasis,** in which a person who is in good health becomes preoccupied with imaginary ailments and blames all her problems on them. Hysteria should also be distinguished from *psychosomatic* illnesses, in which emotional problems have produced real physical damage such as ulcers. Something real has happened to the hysteric, but not physically; once her emotional problems have been solved, her normal functioning is restored. This disorder was rather common in the eighteenth and nineteenth centuries—Freud's first cases were hysterics—but conversion reactions are comparatively rare today.

Dissociative Reactions. Hysteria may take the form of **dissociative states,** in which the person experiences a loss of memory or identity or exhibits two or more identities. These psychological phenomena fascinate many people, so we hear a good deal about amnesia and "split personalities." Actually, they are very rare—even more so than conversion reactions.

Loss of memory, or *amnesia,* may be an attempt to escape from problems by blotting them out completely. The amnesiac remembers how to speak and usually retains a fund of general knowledge. But he may not know who he is, where he lives and works, or who his family is (Levant, 1966). (As described in Chapter 3, other types of amnesia are caused by brain damage.)

In **fugue,** another type of dissociative reaction, amnesia is coupled with active flight to a different environment. The individual may suddenly disappear and "wake up" three days later in a restaurant two hundred miles from home. Or she may actually establish a new identity—assume a new name, marry, take a job, and so forth—in whatever place she lands, repressing all knowledge of her previous life. A fugue state may last for days or for decades. However long it lasts, the individual, when she comes out of it, will have no memory of what she has done in the interim. Fugue, then, is a sort of traveling amnesia, and it probably serves the same psychological function as amnesia: escape from unbearable conflict or anxiety.

In **multiple personality,** a third type of dissociative reaction, someone seems to have two or more distinct identities. Eve White, a young woman who sought psychiatric treatment for severe headaches and blackouts, has become a famous example. Eve White was a conscientious, self-controlled, rather shy person. However, during one of her therapy sessions, her expression—and her personality—suddenly changed. Eve Black, as she now called herself, was childlike, fun-loving, and irresponsible—the opposite of the woman who originally walked into the psychiatrist's office. Eve Black was conscious of Eve White's existence, but considered her a separate person. Eve White did not know about Eve Black, however, and neither was she conscious of Jane, a third personality that emerged during the course of therapy. (This case served as the basis for the book and film *The Three Faces of Eve.*) Some psychologists believe that this dividing up of the personality is the result of the individual's effort to escape from a part of himself or herself that he or she fears. The "secret self" then emerges in the form of a separate personality.

While cases like Eve and Sybil (a woman whose sixteen personalities were also described in a book and a movie) are fascinating, they are extremely rare and somewhat controversial. One researcher (Abse, 1966) reviewed the entire psychological literature and was able to find published accounts of only two hundred people who supposedly suffered from any dissociative reaction.

Depression

Depression is a pattern of sadness, anxiety, fatigue, agitated behavior, and reduced ability to function and interact with others. It may also interfere with sleep patterns and the ability to concentrate. It ranges from mild feelings of uneasiness, sadness, and apathy to intense suicidal despair. Occasional depression is a common experience. Most of us feel depressed when someone we love dies, for example. And, from time to time, everyone feels "blue" for no apparent reason. However, when depression is chronic (that is, the person never seems to "snap out of it") or especially intense, it is considered a serious psychological problem.

According to Freudian theory, severe depression may reflect guilt and the need for self-punishment. For example, a person may feel that he or she neglected someone who just died and may unconsciously hold himself or herself responsible for that person's death. In this case, depression acts as a self-imposed jail term: the person does not allow himself or herself to be happy.

In recent years, the cognitive theories of Aaron Beck and Martin Seligman have often served as the basis for research on depression. Beck (1967) believes that depressed people draw illogical conclusions about themselves—they blame themselves for normal problems and consider every minor failure a catastrophe. A depressed man who failed his driver's test,

Figure 15.8
The pattern of chronic depression is a familiar one to therapists, but its causes are still a matter of debate. There is the Freudian theory of guilt and the need for self-punishment; the cognitive theories of Beck and Seligman; and a theory of chemical imbalance in the brain.

Figure 15.9
A "suicide hotline." The man shown here is one of many trained volunteers who work at suicide prevention centers throughout the country.

for example, might consider himself a hopeless nerd as a result, and conclude that he will never be able to get a car of his own. As described in Chapter 2, Martin Seligman (1975) believes that depression is caused by a feeling of learned helplessness. The depressed person learns to believe that he has no control over events in his life, that nothing he does makes any difference, and that it is useless to even try.

Another theory explains depression as a chemical imbalance in the brain. According to this view, some people are more likely to become depressed because they are born with low levels of a specific brain chemical. (According to one current theory, the chemical is the neurotransmitter serotonin. This predisposing factor influences other brain chemicals. Low levels of the neurotransmitter norepinephrine are associated with depression; high levels with mania.)

Suicide

Not all people who commit suicide are depressed, and not all depressed people attempt suicide. But many depressives do think about suicide, and some of them translate these thoughts into action.

People may take their lives for any number of reasons: to escape from physical or emotional pain (perhaps a terminal illness or the loneliness of old age); to end the torment of unacceptable feelings (such as homosexual fantasies); to punish themselves for wrongs they feel they have committed; to punish others who have not perceived their needs (Mintz, 1968). In many cases we simply do not know why the suicide occurred.

But we do know that every year between 20,000 and 30,000 Americans end their lives—about one every thirty minutes. More women than men attempt suicide, but more men than women succeed. Suicide is most common among the elderly, but also ranks as the third most common cause of death among college students. Contrary to popular belief, people who threaten suicide or make an unsuccessful attempt usually *are* serious. Studies show that about 70 percent of people who kill themselves threaten to do so within the three months preceding the suicide, and an unsuccessful attempt is often a trial run (Alvarez, 1970).

Anxiety, phobias, obsessions, compulsions, hysteria, depression, and suicide—all are ways people use, in various combinations, to escape problems in themselves or the world in which they live. But, with the obvious exception of suicide, these neurotic reactions do not shut people off completely from daily life. Psychosis does.

PSYCHOSIS

A neurotic person is one who is emotionally crippled by anxiety but continues to slug it out with life as best he or she can. A psychotic person is one whose distorted perceptions and behavior reach such an irrational, fantastic, and fear-laden level that he or she withdraws completely from normal life. One might say that a neurotic dreams in an unreal way about life, whereas a psychotic lives life as an unreal dream.

Like neurosis, psychosis is not a single problem; it has no single cause or cure. Rather, it is a collection of symptoms that indicates an individual has serious difficulty trying to meet the demands of life. Two major categories of psychosis are *schizophrenia* and *affective reactions*. *Autism* is a psychosis found in children.

Schizophrenia

Approximately half the patients in United States mental hospitals have been diagnosed as schizophrenic (Taube and Rednick, 1973). What distinguishes this disorder from other types of psychological disturbance? **Schizophrenia** involves confused and disordered thoughts and perceptions.

Suppose a psychiatrist is interviewing a patient who has just been admitted to a hospital. The individual demonstrates a wide assortment of symptoms. He is intensely excited, expresses extreme hostility toward members of his family, and at the same time claims that he loves them, showing conflicting feelings. One minute he is extremely aggressive, questioning the psychiatrist's motives and even threatening her. The next minute he withdraws and acts as if he does not hear anything she says. Then he begins talking again. "Naturally," he says, "I am growing my father's hair." Although all of the person's other behavior indicates psychological problems, this last statement would be the "diagnostic bell ringer." It reveals that the man is living in a private disordered reality.

Many schizophrenics experience **delusions** (false beliefs maintained in

Figure 15.10
These paintings were done by a male patient diagnosed as schizophrenic with paranoid tendencies. Both illustrations are characterized by the symbolism of watchful eyes, grasping hands, and the self as subject matter.

the face of contrary evidence) and **hallucinations** (sensations in the absence of appropriate stimulation). For example, a paranoid schizophrenic generally believes that others are plotting against him—contriving ways to confuse him, make him look ridiculous, perhaps to get rid of him. People are watching him constantly. His thoughts are being monitored. When he goes to the movies to escape, he finds—to his horror—that the film is all about him. The ticket taker and the man in the next row are in on the plot. These delusions are usually supported by hallucinations, in which his five senses detect the evidence of the plot. He may taste poison in his food, smell gas in his bedroom, or hear voices telling him why he has been singled out or what lies in store for him.

Often, schizophrenics withdraw from other people into a private world of fantasy. In *simple schizophrenia* individuals gradually lose interest in what happens around them, becoming increasingly apathetic, listless, and noncommunicative. Such individuals may be able to hold menial jobs or may survive as "drifters," but their interpersonal contacts are few. *Catatonia* is an extreme form of withdrawal in which the person becomes totally unresponsive. She may maintain the same posture for hours, mute and seemingly oblivious to physical discomfort. Periodic flare-ups, when the person becomes violent toward herself or others, may be the only sign of emotional life in a catatonic person.

Other schizophrenics are active and busy, but their behavior and speech are incomprehensible to others. The person may repeat a bizarre gesture, whose meaning is known only to him, over and over. He may express inappropriate emotions—for example, giggling uncontrollably as he relates violent and morbid fantasies. He may invent words or repeat phrases as if they were magical incantations—for reasons known only to himself (Maher, 1972). The result is sometimes what psychologists call "word salad": a jumble of unconnected, irrational phrases.

It is as if the gears in the schizophrenic's mental machinery had slipped and the connections had gone haywire. One patient described the experience as losing the ability to focus his thoughts.

"I can't concentrate. It's diversion of attention that troubles me. I am picking up different conversations. It's like being a transmitter. The sounds are coming through to me but I feel my mind cannot cope with everything. It's difficult to concentrate on any one sound."

Another told of being unable to organize his perceptions.

"Everything is in bits. You put the picture up bit by bit into your head. It's like a photograph that's been torn to bits and put together again.

Figure 15.11
A portrait of a "suicidal melancholic" done in England in the nineteenth century. This woman, only thirty-four when the portrait was made, suffered from the delusion that she would be murdered and eventually began to attempt suicide in order to escape the danger.

You have to absorb it again. If you move it's frightening. The picture you had in your head is still there but it's broken up" (McGhie and Chapman, 1961).

Affective Reactions

Another common type of psychosis is one in which individuals are excessively and inappropriately happy or unhappy. These **affective reactions** (from the word "affect," meaning mood) may take the form of high elation, hopeless depression, or an alternation between the two.

The *manic*, or highly elated, type is characterized by extreme confusion, disorientation, and incoherence. The person's world is like a movie that is being run too fast so that the people and events are no more than a blur of purposeless activity. The following behavior is typical of acute mania:

> On admission she slapped the nurse, addressed the house physician as God, made the sign of the cross, and laughed loudly when she was asked to don the hospital garb. This she promptly tore to shreds. . . . She sang at the top of her voice, screamed through the window, and leered at the patients promenading in the recreation yard (Karnash, 1945).

In the *depressive reaction*, the individual is overcome by feelings of failure, sinfulness, worthlessness, and despair. We have already described depression as a form of neurosis. Psychotic depression differs from neurotic depression—just as psychosis in general differs from neurosis in general—in that the psychotic has lost contact with reality. The neurotic depressive may feel chronically dejected, but she still knows how to get to the bank, how old her children are, and how to differentiate between fantasy and reality. The psychotic depressive has left reality behind and has moved into a bleak fantasy world constructed out of her despair. She is likely to claim that her children are dead, that she killed them, that the world is coming to an end, that it is all her fault. Furthermore, the psychotic depressive may stop functioning altogether and descend into a stupor, not eating, not speaking, and not moving.

> The patient lay in bed, immobile, with a dull, depressed expression on his face. His eyes were sunken and downcast. Even when spoken to, he would not raise his eyes to look at the speaker. Usually he did not respond at all to questions, but sometimes, after apparently great effort, he would mumble something about the "Scourge of God" (Coleman, 1976).

In some cases, referred to as *manic-depressive* psychosis, a patient will alternate between frantic action and motionless despair. Some theorists have speculated that the manic periods serve as an attempt to ward off the underlying hopelessness. Others believe that mania can be traced to the same biochemical disorder responsible for depression.

Autism

Autism is a childhood psychosis that seems to be present at birth. From an early age, autistic children are aloof and noncommunicative. Often they do not even cry or coo like other babies. They act as if other people do not exist. Speech patterns are very peculiar, and some of these children never learn to communicate with language at all. They become very upset over any change in their environment. They want things to remain the same. They sometimes develop bizarre attachments to physical objects, like the autistic child who went everywhere wrapped in a shower curtain.

These children are usually physically healthy—in fact, they are often quite beautiful. Psychologists do not really know what causes autism. Are these children born this way, or are they reacting to rejection by their parents? Do they have some mysterious brain defect? Do their bodies produce too much or too little of certain vital chemicals? Have their families given them some insoluble problem that causes overpowering anxiety?

Causes of Psychosis

There are many theories but very few facts about what causes psychosis. Psychologists think that their problems result from the interaction of several factors, but none of these factors is at all clearly understood.

Hereditary Factors. There is some evidence that people may inherit a predisposition or tendency to become psychotic. Close relatives of schizophrenics, for example, are much more likely to become schizophrenic than are other people, even if they never come into contact with their schizophrenic relative (Rosenthal *et al.*, 1971; Kety *et al.*, 1971). Just how this predisposition might be transmitted from generation to generation is a matter of speculation. According to one theory, some people are born with a nervous system that gets aroused very easily and takes a long time to recover to normal (Figure 15.13). People like this might be particularly

Some people may inherit a predisposition or tendency to become psychotic.

Figure 15.12
Autistic children. Though they are all in the same place, each child is in his own world, and there is no interaction.

likely to get upset when they are stressed (Zubin and Spring, 1977). Thus a situation that might be only mildly upsetting to one person might cause a psychotic reaction in an acutely sensitive person. However, if this person is raised in a relatively simple, pressure-free environment, he might never develop psychological problems.

Biochemical Factors. The proper working of the brain depends on the presence of the right amounts of many different chemicals, from oxygen to proteins. Some psychologists believe that psychosis is due largely to chemical imbalances in the brain. With depression, for example, abnormally low amounts of certain chemicals may disturb the transmission of electrical impulses from one brain cell to another.

Chemical problems may also be involved in schizophrenia. A number of researchers think that the basic problem in schizophrenia is that too much or too little of certain chemicals has "knocked out of kilter" the brain's mechanisms for processing information. As a result, the schizophrenic cannot organize his thoughts. When he tries to keep one thought at the center of his awareness, other thoughts—irrelevant ones—keep pushing in and interfering with his concentration (Wynne, Cromwell, and Matthyssee, 1978). In short, he experiences the kind of thought disturbance reported by the schizophrenic patients quoted earlier in this chapter.

Unusual concentrations of certain chemicals have in fact been found in the bodies of many schizophrenics. However, it is hard to tell whether these chemicals are the cause of schizophrenia or the result of it. They may even be caused by the fact that schizophrenics tend to live in hospitals, where they get little exercise, eat institutional food, and are generally given daily doses of tranquilizers. Living under such conditions, anyone—not just the schizophrenic person—might begin to show chemical imbalances.

The Double Bind. Some theorists believe that many mental problems,

Figure 15.13
A child born with a biochemically unusual nervous system that reacts very strongly to stimulation may have pronounced hallucinations during an early childhood illness that has no lasting effect on most children. As he grows older, he may try to discuss his memories of that time with his parents. Being insecure themselves, they may become uneasy and respond in ways that make him feel he is wrong or bad in some way. His unusual biochemistry causes him to react very strongly to this rebuff, and he now has further troubling experiences he needs to make sense of. He then feels a conflict between his need to talk to his parents about these experiences and his fear of their cold response. He is well on the way to becoming psychologically disordered unless the links in this chain are somehow broken.

particularly those that involve confused thoughts and isolation from other people, result from conflicts in communication. These psychologists believe that a child's ability to think and to communicate with others can be undermined if his or her parents repeatedly communicate contradictory messages. For example, a mother may resent her child and feel uncomfortable around him, yet also feel obligated to act lovingly toward him. She tells the child how much she loves him, but at the same time she stiffens whenever he tries to hug her. Thus the child is given one message in words and another in action.

As a result, the child is placed in an impossible situation. If he reaches out to his mother, she shows him (in her actions) that she dislikes this. If he avoids her, she tells him (in words) that she dislikes that. He wants very much to please her, but no matter what he does, it is wrong. He is caught in a *double bind*.

According to **double-bind theory,** a childhood full of such contradictory messages results in people perceiving the world as a confusing, disconnected place and believing that their words and actions have little significance or meaning. Consequently they may develop the kind of disordered behaviors and thoughts we have been describing.

Which of these theories is correct? At this point, we do not know. It may be that each is partially true. Perhaps people who inherit a tendency toward psychological disorders react more strongly to a double bind than others would. Perhaps people who are caught in a double bind are especially vulnerable to chemical imbalances. Or perhaps it takes a combination of all three factors—heredity, biochemical disorders, and conflict—to produce psychotic behavior (Meehl, 1962). Only further research will give us the answer.

PERSONALITY DISORDERS

Personality disorders are different from the problems we have been discussing. People with personality disorders generally do not suffer from acute anxiety; nor do they behave in bizarre, incomprehensible ways. Psychologists consider these people "abnormal" because they seem unable to establish meaningful relationships with other people, to assume social responsibilities, or to adapt to their social environment. This diagnostic category includes a wide range of self-defeating personality patterns, from painfully shy, lonely types to vain, pushy show-offs. In this section we focus on the **antisocial personality,** sometimes called the sociopath or psychopath.

Antisocial individuals are irresponsible, immature, emotionally shallow people who seem to court trouble. Extremely selfish, they treat people as objects—as things to be used for gratification and to be cast coldly aside when no longer wanted. Intolerant of everyday frustrations and unable to save or plan or wait, they live for the moment. Seeking thrills is their major occupation. If they should injure other people along the way or break social rules, they do not seem to feel any shame or guilt. It's the other person's tough luck. Nor does getting caught seem to rattle them. No matter how many times they are reprimanded, punished, or jailed, they never learn how to stay out of trouble. They simply do not profit from experience.

Many antisocial individuals can get away with destructive behavior because they are intelligent, entertaining, and able to mimic emotions they do not feel. They win affection and confidence from others whom they then take advantage of. This ability to charm while exploiting helped Charles Manson to dominate the gang of runaways whom he eventually led into the gruesome Tate-LaBianca murders.

If caught, antisocial individuals will either spin a fantastic lie or simply insist, with wide-eyed sincerity, that their intentions were utterly pure. Guilt and anxiety have no place in the antisocial personality. A fine example is that of Hugh Johnson, a con man recently caught after having defrauded people out of thousands of dollars in sixty-four separate swindles. When asked why he had victimized so many people, "he replied with some heat that he never took more from a person than the person could afford to lose, and further, that he was only reducing the likelihood that other more dangerous criminals would use force to achieve the same ends" (Nathan and Harris, 1975: 406–407).

How do psychologists explain such a lack of ordinary human decency and shame? According to one theory, the psychopath has simply imitated his or her own antisocial parents. Others point to lack of discipline or inconsistent discipline during childhood. Finally, some researchers believe that psychopaths have a "faulty nervous system." While most of us get very aroused when we do something that we've been punished for in the past, psychopaths never seem to learn to anticipate punishment.

DRUG ADDICTION

In American society, drug abuse has become a major psychological problem. Millions of Americans depend so heavily on drugs that they hurt themselves physically, socially, and psychologically.

Abuse of drugs invariably involves **psychological dependence.** Users come to depend so much on the feeling of well-being they obtain from the drug that they feel compelled to continue using it. People can become psychologically dependent on a wide variety of drugs, including alcohol, caffeine, nicotine (in cigarettes), opium, marijuana, and amphetamines. When deprived of the drug, a psychologically dependent person becomes restless, irritable, and uneasy.

In addition to psychological dependence, some drugs lead to physiological **addiction.** A person is addicted when his system has become so used to the drug that the drugged state becomes the body's "normal" state. If the drug is not in the body, the person experiences extreme physical discomfort, just as he would if he were deprived of oxygen or of water.

Just as dependence causes a psychological need for the drug, addiction causes a physical need. Furthermore, once a person is addicted to a drug,

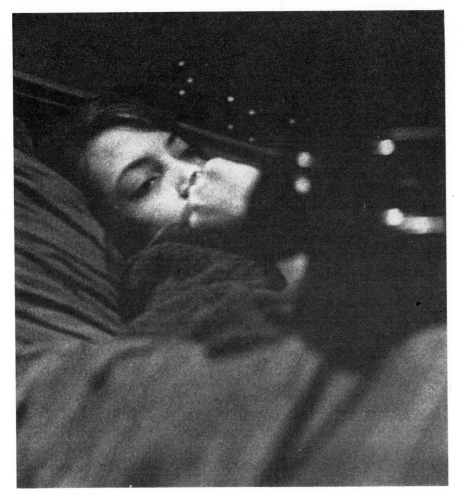

Figure 15.14
A heroin addict during one of the stages of withdrawal via the "cold turkey" method.

he develops **tolerance;** that is, his body becomes so accustomed to the drug that he has to keep increasing his dosage in order to obtain the "high" that he achieved with his earlier doses. With certain sleeping pills, for example, a person can rapidly develop a tolerance for up to fifteen times the original dose. Further, an addict must have his drug in order to retain what little physical and psychological balance he has left. If he does not get it, he is likely to go through the dreaded experience of withdrawal.

Withdrawal is a state of physical and psychological upset during which the body and the mind revolt against, and finally get used to, the absence of the drug. Withdrawal symptoms vary from person to person and from drug to drug. They range from a mild case of nausea and "the shakes" to hallucinations, convulsions, coma, and death.

Alcoholism

Although heroin addiction seems to receive more attention in the media, this country's most serious drug problem is alcoholism. Somewhere between 8 and 12 million Americans are alcoholics. According to one recent estimate, 1.3 million teen-agers and preteen-agers have a serious drinking problem (Ray, 1978). Fifty percent or more of the deaths in automobile accidents each year can be traced to alcohol; in half of all murders either the killer or the victim has been drinking; and some 13,000 people die of liver damage caused by alcohol every year. In addition, the cost in human suffering to the alcoholic and his or her family is impossible to measure.

In small doses, alcohol might be called a social wonder drug. The first psychological function that it slows down is our inhibitions. Two drinks can make a person relaxed, talkative, playful, even giggly. (It is for this reason that many people consider alcohol a stimulant—it is really a depressant.)

As the number of drinks increases, the fun decreases. One by one, the person's psychological and physiological functions begin to shut down. Perceptions and sensations become distorted, and behavior may become obnoxious. The person begins to stumble and weave, speech becomes slurred, and reactions—to a stop sign, for example—become sluggish. If

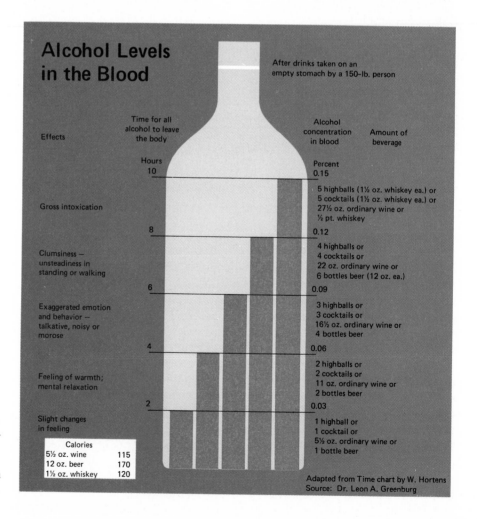

Figure 15.15
This chart shows the effects of alcohol on a 150-pound person. Because alcohol is diluted in the blood, a 200-pound man can usually tolerate more liquor than a 110-pound woman.

enough alcohol accumulates in the body, it leads to unconsciousness—and in some cases coma and death. It all depends on how much and how rapidly alcohol enters the bloodstream—which, in turn, depends on a person's weight, body chemistry, and how much he or she drinks how quickly (Figure 15.15).

Alcohol can produce psychological dependence, tolerance, and addiction. One researcher has outlined three stages of alcoholism. In the first stage, the individual discovers that alcohol reduces her tensions, gives her self-confidence, and reduces social pressures. Drinking makes her feel better. In the second stage, the beverage becomes a drug. The individual begins to drink so heavily that she feels she has to hide her habit. Thus she begins "sneaking" drinks. In this stage she may also begin to suffer from blackouts—she is unable to recall what happened during a drinking episode. In the final stage, she drinks compulsively, beginning in the morning. She becomes inefficient at work and tends to go on drinking sprees that may last for weeks. She is now an alcoholic, drinking continuously, eating infrequently, and feeling sick when deprived of her drug. Her health deteriorates rapidly (Jellinek, 1960).

The first step in treating the alcoholic is to see her through the violent withdrawal typical of alcohol addiction, and then to try to make her healthier. She may be given a variety of treatments—from drugs to psychotherapy. Alcoholics Anonymous, an organization for alcoholics and former alcoholics, run by people who have had a drinking problem, has been more successful than most organizations. But there is no certain cure for alcoholism. As many alcoholics return to the bottle as heroin addicts return to the needle. One problem is that our society tends to encourage social drinking and to tolerate the first stage of alcoholism.

DSM-III: NEW WAYS TO CATEGORIZE MENTAL ILLNESS

DSM-III, the third version of the American Psychiatric Association's *Diagnostic and Statistical Manual of Mental Disorders*, will probably go into effect somewhere around 1980. It was designed to solve several problems of the earlier classification scheme, DSM-II.

The diagnostic categories described in this chapter have been criticized for being too vague. As a result, the same patient might be classified as schizophrenic by one psychiatrist and manic-depressive by another. This created particular problems for researchers who were trying to study the causes and cures of mental disease: it is very difficult to find what causes schizophrenia if the group of schizophrenics in a study actually includes people with several different diseases.

DSM-III, with its very detailed and specific diagnostic criteria, should help solve this problem. In one study (Spitzer, Endicott, and Robins, 1978), research assistants who used such specific criteria to diagnose 120 mental

Being Sane in an Insane Place

The doors slam shut. The hospital attendant turns the key. You are locked in a room with insane people. And they think you're insane too. They'll find out in no time, you tell yourself, but they don't. They keep you behind bars for your own good.

Despite our perception that psychiatric diagnosis is a science, it is quite possible for sane people to be institutionalized. The fact that it happened in the experiment we are about to describe suggests that psychiatric diagnosis is as much in the mind of the observer as it is in the behavior of the observed.

Eight people, including three psychologists, a pediatrician, and a housewife, called twelve different psychiatric hospitals complaining that they heard voices. Beyond this symptom, the pseudopatients presented the facts of their lives as they actually were. Once they were admitted to the hospital, they went back to their ordinary behavior. They dropped their claims of hearing voices, spoke to other patients and staff as they would to people outside the hospital, and told everyone they were feeling fine.

The hospital staff was not at all suspicious of these changes. They never suspected that the pseudopatients were sane. When these people were finally released, they were given the diagnosis of schizophrenia in remission. In the hospital's view, they were not sane nor had they ever been sane. Interestingly, many legitimate patients detected the experimenters' sanity and told them that they didn't belong.

For more details, see D. L. Rosenhan, "On Being Sane in Insane Places," *Science,* 179, January 1973.

patients from their case records were much more likely to independently arrive at the same diagnosis than experienced clinicians using DSM-II.

Another problem with DSM-II was the fact that it sometimes falsely assumed that the person making a diagnosis understood what caused the disease. For example, DSM-II distinguished between depression caused by stress and depression caused by physiological factors. But research has not been able to prove that some depressions are environmental and others are biological, so this distinction has been dropped.

There are three major differences between DSM-III and DSM-II: the criteria for diagnosis have been made more specific; they have been made more complete; and DSM-III avoids any reference to the causes of mental disorder that have not been established by research. Let us consider each of these changes in turn.

1. Specific diagnostic criteria. In contrast to DSM-II's brief and rather general descriptions, DSM-III offers extensive and highly detailed descriptions for the different diagnostic categories. These descriptions include:

a. *essential features* of the disorder, those that "define" the disorder;

b. *associated features*—features that are usually present;

c. *diagnostic criteria*, a list of symptoms (taken from the lists of essential and associated features) that *must* be present for the patient to be given this diagnostic label;

d. information on *differential diagnosis*—that is, how to distinguish this disorder from other disorders with which it might be confused.

2. More complete diagnostic criteria. A second important change is that DSM-III requires that much more information be given about the patient in the process of diagnosis. DSM-II called for nothing more than a simple diagnostic label. DSM-III, in contrast, instructs the diagnostician to evaluate the patient on five different "axes," or areas of functioning.

Axis I—clinical psychiatric syndrome: the diagnostic label for the patient's most serious psychological problem, the problem for which he or she is being diagnosed (this is the only information that DSM-II required);

Axis II—personality disorders (adults) or specific developmental disorders (children and adolescents): any accompanying adjustment disorders not covered by the Axis-I label;

Axis III—physical disorders: any medical problems that may be relevant to the psychological problem;

Axis IV—psychosocial stressors: any current sources of stress (for example, divorce, retirement, miscarriage) that may have contributed to the patient's psychological problem;

Axis V—highest level of adaptive functioning during the past year: a rating of the patient's adjustment—social relationships, occupational functioning, use of leisure time—within the past year.

Thus, whereas with DSM-II a patient's diagnosis might have been simply "alcohol addiction," under the new system he or she might be diagnosed as follows:

Axis I: alcohol dependence;

Axis II: avoidant personality disorder;

Axis III: diabetes;

Axis IV: loss of job, one child moved out of house, marital conflict;

Axis V: fair.

This offers a good deal more information about the patient—information that may be useful in devising a treatment program. Furthermore, such five-part diagnoses may be extremely helpful to researchers trying to discover connections among psychological disorders and other factors such as stress and physical illness.

3. No reference to uncertain causes of the disorder. A final important difference between DSM-II and DSM-III is that the latter avoids any suggestion about the cause of a disorder unless the cause has been definitely established. This new policy has caused some substantial changes in the classification system. For example, the term "neurosis" has been dropped altogether, since it is a Freudian term and implies a Freudian interpretation (that is, that the disorder is due to anxiety over repressed wishes or conflicts). Similarly, as mentioned above, DSM-II subdivided severe depression according to whether it was caused by environmental stress or by some biological

problem. This distinction is no longer made in DSM-III. DSM-III aims simply at naming the disorders and at describing them as clearly and specifically as possible; their causes, if they are not known, are not speculated upon.

Needless to say, dramatic changes of this sort are rather controversial (Goleman, 1978). But psychiatrists hope this new system will provide more consistent diagnoses and a more solid basis for future research.

SUMMARY

1. There is no absolute list of symptoms of mental disorder. Most psychologists define normal behavior as the ability to cope with stress and conflict, and abnormal behavior as the failure to adjust to the stresses of life.

2. Neurosis is a broad category of mental disorders, characterized by chronic anxiety. Severe neurotic anxiety may produce phobias, obsessions, compulsions, various forms of hysteria, and depression.

3. People commit suicide for many different reasons; not all suicidal individuals are depressed. Contrary to popular belief, people who threaten to kill themselves often do so.

4. Psychosis is a second category of mental disorders, characterized by behavior that is so incomprehensible to others as to virtually eliminate the individual's capacity to meet the demands of everyday life.

5. Schizophrenia is a type of psychosis in which a person's thoughts, emotions, and perceptions are confused and disconnected. Schizophrenics may experience delusions and hallucinations, withdraw into fantasies and engage in bizarre behavior.

6. Affective reactions are another type of psycho-

sis. They are characterized by excessive and inappropriate elation (manic behavior) or despair (depressed behavior).

7. Psychosis may be caused by an inherited tendency to become disturbed, by biochemical imbalances, or by exposure to contradictory communications (the double bind), or—most likely—combinations of these and other factors.

8. A personality disorder is an ongoing pattern of maladaptive behavior combined with an inability to establish appropriate relationships with other people and the environment. The antisocial personality is an example.

9. Aside from nicotine (in cigarettes), the three most widely used and abused drugs in this country are alcohol, heroin, and barbiturates. All three of these drugs are depressants, and all are addictive. They may cause psychological dependence, tolerance, physiological habituation, a severe withdrawal reaction, and even death when the addict does not take the drug.

10. DSM-III is a new system for classifying mental illness that is scheduled to go into effect around 1980. It bases diagnosis on much more specific criteria than DSM-II did, and eliminates some of the familiar diagnostic categories such as neurosis.

GLOSSARY

addiction: An altered psychological state in the body that causes physical dependence on a drug.

affective reaction: A type of psychosis in which

an individual is subject to excessive and inappropriate mood states of elation or depression.

antisocial personality: A personality disorder

characterized by irresponsibility, shallow emotions, and lack of conscience.

anxiety: A vague, generalized apprehension or feeling that one is in danger.

autism: A childhood psychosis characterized by an inability to relate to others and lack of response to attempts at communication.

compulsion: The impulsive and uncontrollable repetition of an irrational action.

conversion reaction: A form of hysteria characterized by the conversion of emotional difficulties into a loss of a specific body function.

delusion: A false belief that a person maintains in the face of contrary evidence.

depression: A pattern of sadness, anxiety, fatigue, insomnia, underactivity, and reduced ability to function and to work with others.

depressive reaction: A psychotic reaction in which a person is overcome by feelings of failure, sinfulness, worthlessness, and despair.

dissociative reaction: A form of hysteria in which a person experiences a loss of memory or identity, or exhibits two or more identities.

double bind: A situation in which a person receives conflicting demands, so that no matter what he or she does, it is wrong.

DSM-II: The second version of the American Psychiatric Association's *Diagnostic and Statistical Manual of Mental Disorders*. Published in 1968, its classification scheme serves as the basis of organization for this chapter.

DSM-III: The third version of the American Psychiatric Association's *Diagnostic and Statistical Manual of Mental Disorders*. Scheduled to go into effect around 1980, this new classification scheme for mental illness is far more specific than its predecessor.

fugue: A rare dissociative reaction in which complete or partial amnesia is combined with a move to a new environment.

hallucination: Sensations in the absence of appropriate stimulation.

hypochondriasis: A preoccupation with imaginary ailments, on which a person blames other problems.

hysteria: A form of neurosis in which a person exhibits physical symptoms in the absence of physical causes.

manic reaction: A psychotic reaction characterized by extreme elation, agitation, confusion, disorientation, and incoherence.

multiple personality: A rare condition in which one person shows two or more separate consciousnesses with distinct personalities.

neurosis: A psychological disturbance characterized by prolonged high levels of anxiety. Neurotics often suffer from unrealistic self-images and have difficulty forming satisfying, stable relationships.

obsession: An uncontrollable pattern of thoughts.

personality disorder: A psychological disturbance characterized by lifelong maladaptive patterns that are relatively free of anxiety and other emotional symptoms.

phobia: A form of severe anxiety in which a person focuses on a particular object or situation.

psychological dependence: Use of a drug to such an extent that a person feels nervous and anxious without it.

psychosis: A psychological disturbance characterized by a breakdown in the ability to accurately perceive reality. Psychotics are unable to relate to other people and to function in everyday life.

schizophrenia: A group of psychoses characterized by confused and disconnected thoughts, emotions, and perceptions.

tolerance: Physical adaptation to a drug, so that a person needs an increased dosage in order to produce the original effect.

withdrawal syndrome: The symptoms that occur after a person discontinues the use of a drug to which he or she had become addicted.

ACTIVITIES

1. Formulate a definition of mental illness. Is your definition free of social values, or are values a necessary part of the definition?

2. Study a book of paintings and drawings by Vincent Van Gogh. Can you tell which were done when he was mentally healthy and which were done when he was suffering from severe psychological disorder? How?

3. It is thought that one of the conditions that produces mental disorders is overexposure to double-bind situations. Everyone has faced these situations at various times. How many examples from your own experiences can you think of that illustrate various forms of the double-bind situation? How did you resolve the conflicts? Can you see patterns of behavior responses developing?

4. Whenever you dismiss certain people as "creeps," for example, you are really saying more about yourself than about the people you are labeling. For example, people who are nervous in social gatherings usually cannot stand other people who are nervous in social gatherings. For a good indication of your own problems, make a list of people you don't like and the reason(s) why you

don't like them. Take a hard, honest look at those traits you have written down and see how many of them apply to you as well.

5. Watch television for a week. Keep a journal of programs which have some psychological theme. What examples of mental breakdown are described? How common are they made to appear? Are simple solutions given? How is the psychologist or psychiatrist shown? Does this person have ready answers? What are they?

6. Cut out about fifteen pictures of people from magazines and paste them on a large piece of paper. Include among the pictures several of people with long or mussed up hair and untidy clothes. Ask several friends or classmates if they can determine which of the people in the pictures are mentally ill. How many select the people with unkempt appearances? What conclusions can you draw from this experiment?

7. What are you afraid of? Do you fear high places, or water, or maybe snakes or spiders? Try to think back to when you first had these fears. Can you state rationally why you have each of your fears?

SUGGESTED READINGS

ALVAREZ, A. *The Savage God: A Study of Suicide.* New York: Random House, 1970. A well-researched yet highly personal and emotional study of suicide. Alvarez explores the way that thoughts of suicide color the world of creative persons, recounts his own attempt at suicide, and traces the history of myths surrounding the phenomenon.

BARNES, MARY, AND BERKE, JOSEPH. *Mary Barnes: Two Accounts of a Journey Through Madness.* New York: Harcourt Brace Jovanovich, 1971. This book consists of interspersed chapters by Mary Barnes, who went on a journey into and through madness, and by Joseph Berke, the psychiatrist who helped Mary through her "down years" and into her "up years."

DAVISON, GERALD C., AND NEALE, JOHN M. *Abnormal Psychology: An Experimental Clinical Approach.* 2nd ed. New York: Wiley, 1978. A textbook that provides an excellent overview of abnormal behavior.

GREEN, HANNAH. *I Never Promised You a Rose Garden.* New York: New American Library, 1964 (paper). A moving and compelling story about the terrifying world and successful treatment of an adolescent girl who had been diagnosed as schizophrenic.

KAPLAN, B. (ED.). *The Inner World of Mental Illness.* New York: Harper & Row, 1964 (paper). A fascinating collection of first-person accounts of what it is like to experience severe mental disturbance. The last section of the book consists of excerpts from literary classics and from the diaries of well-known writers and thinkers.

LAING, R. D. *The Divided Self.* Baltimore: Penguin, 1959 (paper). Laing questions the entire social context that labels a person mentally ill. He believes that psychoses and neuroses make sense if the experience of the person is understood. Presently accepted "normality" is in fact pathological. Psychosis, in a way, is a step toward sanity.

PLATH, SYLVIA. *The Bell Jar.* New York: Bantam, 1971 (paper). An autobiographical novel about a young woman's mental breakdown. Plath is an excellent writer, and the book is especially powerful because she is able to articulate her feelings so well.

RUBIN, THEODORE. *Jordi/ Lisa and David.* New York: Ballantine, 1971 (paper). The characters are David and Lisa, two schizophrenic adolescents who have insulated themselves from reality. This is a short, dramatic case history of how their mutual affection became an avenue to recovery.

SECHEHAYE, M. *Autobiography of a Schizophrenic Girl.* New York: Grune & Stratton, 1951 (paper). A young woman describes her long and courageous attempts to cope with perceptual distortions during her schizophrenic episode. This short, poignant, and well-written account ends with comments by the young woman's therapist.

SZASZ, THOMAS S. *The Myth of Mental Illness.* New York: Dell, 1961 (paper). By drawing philosophical and sociological analyses and by reviewing the history and present-day approaches to what has been termed "mental illness," Szasz argues against the medical model adopted by most psychiatrists. His basic argument is that psychiatrists deal with fundamental problems in human living and human communication, and that these problems cannot be resolved by means of hospitalization and drugs.

BIBLIOGRAPHY

ABSE, D. W. *Hysteria and Related Mental Disorders.* Baltimore: Williams & Wilkins, 1966.

ALVAREZ, A. *The Savage God: A Study of Suicide.* New York: Random House, 1970.

AMERICAN LAW INSTITUTE. *Model Penal Code: Proposed Official Draft.* Philadelphia: American Law Institute, 1962.

AMERICAN PSYCHIATRIC ASSOCIATION. *Diagnostic and Statistical Manual of Mental Disorders.* 2nd ed. Washington, D.C.: American Psychiatric Association, 1968.

ARIETI, SILVANO (ED.). *American Handbook of Psychology.* 3 vols. New York: Basic Books, 1959.

BATESON, GREGORY. *Steps to an Ecology of Mind.* San Francisco: Chandler, 1972.

BECK, AARON T. *Depression: Causes and Treatment.* Philadelphia: University of Pennsylvania Press, 1967.

BRECHER, EDWARD M., AND THE EDITORS OF *Consumer Reports. Licit and Illicit Drugs.* Boston: Little, Brown, 1972.

COLEMAN, JAMES C. *Abnormal Psychology and Modern Life.* 5th ed. Glenview, Ill.: Scott, Foresman, 1976.

DAVISON, GERALD C., AND NEALE, JOHN M. *Abnormal Psychology: An Experimental Clinical Approach.* 2nd ed. New York: Wiley, 1978.

EYSENCK, HANS J. *The Dynamics of Anxiety and Hysteria.* London: Routledge & Kegan Paul, 1957.

GOLEMAN, DANIEL. "Who's Mentally Ill?" *Psychology Today,* 11 (January 1978): 34–41.

JELLINEK, ELVIN M. *The Disease Concept of Alcoholism.* New Brunswick, N.J.: Hillhouse Press, 1960.

KAPLAN, B. (ED.). *The Inner World of Mental Illness.* New York: Harper & Row, 1964 (paper).

KARNASH, L. J. *Handbook of Psychiatry.* St. Louis: Mosby, 1945.

KETY, S. S., ET AL. "Mental Illness in the Biological and Adoptive Families of Adopted Schizophrenics." *American Journal of Psychiatry,* 128, no. 3 (1971): 302–306.

KISKER, GEORGE. *The Disorganized Personality.* New York: McGraw-Hill, 1964.

KRAMER, M. "Statistics of Mental Disorders in the United States: Some Urgent Needs and Suggested Solutions." *Journal of the Royal Statistical Society,* Series A, 132 (1969): 353–407.

LEVANT, OSCAR. *The Memoirs of an Amnesiac.* New York: Bantam, 1966 (paper).

LINGEMAN, RICHARD R. *Drugs from A to Z.* New York: McGraw-Hill, 1974.

LORENZ, SARAH. *Our Son, Ken.* New York: Dell, 1969 (paper).

MC GHIE, A., AND CHAPMAN, J. "Disorders of Attention and Perception in Early Schizophrenia." *British Journal of Medical Psychiatry,* 34 (1961): 103–116.

MAHER, BRENDAN. "The Shattered Language of Schizophrenia." In *Readings in Psychology Today.* 2nd ed. Del Mar, Calif.: CRM Books, 1972, pp. 549–553.

MEEHL, PAUL M. "Schizotaxia, Schizotype, Schizophrenia." *American Psychologist,* 17 (1962): 827–832.

MINTZ, R. S. "Psychotherapy of the Suicidal Patient." In *Suicidal Behaviors,* ed. by H. L. P. Resnik. Boston: Little, Brown, 1968.

NATHAN, P. E., AND HARRIS, S. L. *Psychopathology and Society.* New York: McGraw-Hill, 1975.

PATCH, VERNON D. "Methadone." *New England Journal of Medicine,* 286 (1972): 43–45.

RABKIN, LESLIE (ED.). *Psychopathology and Literature.* San Francisco: Chandler, 1966.

RAY, OAKLEY. *Drugs, Society, and Human Behavior.* 2nd ed. St Louis: Mosby, 1978.

ROSENTHAL, D., ET AL. "The Adopted-Away Offspring of Schizophrenics." *American Journal of Psychiatry,* 128, no. 3 (1971): 307–311.

SCHACHTER, S., AND LATANÉ, B. "Crime, Cognition, and the Autonomic Nervous System." In *Nebraska Symposium on Motivation,* ed. by M. Jones. Lincoln: University of Nebraska Press, 1964.

SCHREIBER, FLORA RHETA. *Sybil.* New York: Warner, 1973.

SELIGMAN, MARTIN E. P. *Helplessness.* San Francisco: Freeman, 1975.

SHAPIRO, EVELYN (ED.). *PsychoSources: A Psychology Resource Catalog.* New York: Bantam, 1973 (paper).

SILVERMAN, J. "When Schizophrenia Helps." *Psychology Today,* 4 (September 1970): 62–65.

SLOTKIN, J. J. "Culture and Psychopathology." *Journal of Abnormal and Social Psychology,* 51 (1955): 269–275.

SNYDER, SOLOMON H. *Madness and the Brain.* New York: McGraw-Hill, 1973.

SPITZER, R. L., ENDICOTT, J., AND ROBINS, E. "Research Diagnostic Criteria: Rationale and Reliability." *Archives of General Psychiatry,* 35 (1978): 773–782.

STONE, ALAN, AND STONE, SUE. *The Abnormal Personality Through Literature.* Englewood Cliffs, N.J.: Prentice-Hall, 1966.

SZASZ, THOMAS S. *The Myth of Mental Illness.* New York: Harper & Row, 1961.

TAUBE, C. A., AND REDNICK, R. *Utilization of Mental Health Resources by Persons Diagnosed with Schizophrenia.* DHEW Publication No. (HSM) 72–9110. Rockville, Md.: National Institute of Mental Health, 1973.

VICTOR, MAURICE, AND ADAMS, RAYMOND D. "Opiates and Other Synthetic Analgesic Drugs." In *Harrison's Principles of Internal Medicine,* ed. by M. M. Wintrobe *et al.* New York: McGraw-Hill, 1970, pp. 677–681.

437

WHEELIS, ALLEN. *The Desert.* New York: Basic Books, 1970.

WHITE, ROBERT W. *The Abnormal Personality.* New York: Ronald, 1964.

WOLMAN, BENJAMIN D. (ED.). *Handbook of Clinical Psychology.* New York: McGraw-Hill, 1965.

WYNNE, L., CROMWELL, R., AND MATTHYSSE, S. (EDS.). *Nature of Schizophrenia: New Approaches to Research and Treatment.* New York: Wiley, 1978.

ZUBIN, JOSEPH, AND SPRING, BONNIE. "Vulnerability: A New View of Schizophrenia." *Journal of Abnormal Psychology,* 86 (1977): 103–126.

16 Therapy and Change

At certain times of transition and crisis in life, we may feel an urgent need to find someone trustworthy to share our doubts and problems with. A parent, relative, or close friend is often helpful in such times of need. But many psychological problems are too bewildering and complex to be solved in this way. When people become dissatisfied or distraught with life and suspect that the reason lies inside themselves, they are likely to seek help from someone with training and experience in such matters. People who have been trained to deal with the psychological problems of others include social workers, psychologists, and psychiatrists. The special kind of help they provide is called **psychotherapy.**

This chapter will present some of the major approaches to therapy and will describe what it is like to undergo therapy. It will explore various types of group therapy, probe the current situation in America's mental institutions, and touch on the trend toward community mental health.

WHAT IS PSYCHOTHERAPY?

Psychotherapy literally means "healing of the soul," and in early times psychological disturbances were often thought to represent some sort of moral or religious problem. Madmen were sometimes viewed as being inhabited by devils or demons, and treatment consisted of exorcism—the driving out of these demons by religious ceremonies or by physical punishment. Within the last two hundred years, however, views of psychological disorders have changed. Mental disorders have slowly come to be thought of as diseases, and the term "mental illness" is now popularly applied to many psychological problems.

Figure 16.1
Each of the many different kinds of therapy is based on varying theories about human personality, but the primary goal of each lies in strengthening the person's control over his or her life.

Figure 16.2
Therapist and patient. Many people have a mental picture of therapy as taking place with the person lying on a couch while a middle-aged, bearded man sits taking notes in a chair. Nowadays therapists are more likely to talk to their patients in a face-to-face position and to use a variety of techniques rather than just a strict psychoanalytic approach.

The fact that psychological disturbance is seen as the symptom of a disease has helped to reduce the stigma associated with such problems, and it has done much to convince society that troubled people need care and treatment. Nevertheless many psychotherapists feel that the term "mental illness" has outlived its usefulness and that, in fact, it may now be doing more harm than good.

The trouble with letting a person think of herself as mentally ill is that she sees herself in a passive, helpless position. She sees her troubles as being caused by forces over which she has no control. By thinking of herself in this way, the person can avoid taking responsibility for her own situation and for helping herself change.

One of the functions of psychotherapy is to help people realize that they are responsible for their own problems and that, even more importantly, they are the only ones who can really solve these problems. This approach does not imply that people become disturbed on purpose or that no one should need outside help. People often adopt certain techniques for getting along in life that seem appropriate at the time but that lead to trouble in the long run. Such patterns can be difficult for the individual to see or change. The major task of the therapist, therefore, is to help people examine their way of living, to understand how their present way of living causes problems, and to start living in new, more beneficial ways. The therapist can be thought of as a guide who is hired by the individual to help her find the source of her problems and some possible solutions.

Characteristics of Psychotherapy

There are many different kinds of therapy, only a few of which will be described in this chapter. Each one is based on different theories about how human personality works, and each one is carried out in a different style. Some psychotherapists stick rigorously to one style and consider the others useless. Other psychotherapists pick and choose methods from many different kinds of therapy and use whatever works best. But whatever the style or philosophy, all types of psychotherapy have certain characteristics in common.

The primary goal of psychotherapy is to strengthen the patient's control over his or her life. People seeking psychotherapy feel trapped in behavior patterns. Over the years they have developed not only certain feelings about themselves, but behaviors that reinforce those feelings. Such people lack the freedom to choose the direction their lives will take. Their behavior and feelings make it impossible for them to reach their goals. For example, a man who is severely critical of himself may feel others are equally harsh in their judgments of him. Rather than risk feelings of rejection, he avoids social gatherings. A person who is uncomfortable meeting other people will, no doubt, feel lonely and rejected. His critical feelings about himself will be strengthened, and he may come to feel that he will remain unloved for life.

The aim of psychotherapy for such a person would be to free him of his burden of self-hate. With a more positive self-image, the man would not be locked into the cycle of avoidance, rejection, and despair. For perhaps the

How to be Assertive

It's hard to be assertive all the time in every situation. You may find it easy to ask a favor of a friend but impossible to make a similar request of a stranger. If you want to spread your assertiveness over more situations, try following these simple suggestions:

- Begin your attempts at developing assertiveness in the least threatening situations. Start with your brother, not your boss.
- Increase your nonverbal assertiveness. Stand erect, look a person straight in the eyes during conversation, eliminate nervous habits, smile.
- Work up to a difficult task in a series of gradual steps. If you're afraid to ask someone for a date, start by saying hello. Then gradually increase the time you spend talking to that person until you're comfortable enough to pop the question.
- If you're afraid to tell people how you feel when you disagree, start by expressing your opinion when you're asked. Once you feel confident in your ability to disagree, you're ready to volunteer your feelings.
- If you find it hard to begin a conversation with a person you've just met, try asking open-ended questions, listening carefully for any additional information the person gives and commenting on it, volunteering information about yourself, and giving compliments.

By following these suggestions, you probably won't increase your assertiveness overnight. But each day will bring you closer to your goal.

For more details, see R. L. Williams and J. D. Lang, *Toward a Self-Managed Life Style,* 2nd ed. Boston: Houghton Mifflin, 1979.

first time, he could feel in control of his life. His behavior would be based on *choice,* and not on the necessity that goes with fixed behavior patterns.

In order to change, it is necessary for the patient to achieve some *understanding* of his troubles. One of the first tasks of therapy, therefore, is to examine the patient's problem closely.

The man in our example will, in the course of his therapy, discover the origin of his self-critical, despairing feelings. He may also realize that, although these feelings developed from real situations, perhaps during his childhood, they no longer apply to his adult capabilities. Gradually the patient's view of himself will become more realistic.

Another major task of therapy is to help the patient find meaningful *alternatives* to his present unsatisfactory ways of behaving. The patient we have been discussing may look for ways to meet new people rather than avoid them.

One of the most important factors in effective treatment is the patient's belief or hope that he *can* change. The influence that a patient's hopes and expectations have on his improvement is often called the **placebo effect.** This name comes from giving medical patients *placebos*—harmless sugar

---

Table 16.1 / Kinds of Therapists

Psychiatrists are medical doctors who specialize in the treatment of mental illness. They generally take a post-M.D. residency in a mental institution. Because of their medical background, psychiatrists are the only group licensed to prescribe drugs.

Psychoanalysts are psychiatrists who have taken special training in the theory of personality and techniques of psychotherapy of Sigmund Freud, usually at a psychoanalytic institute. They must themselves be psychoanalyzed before they can practice.

Lay analysts are psychoanalysts who do not have degrees in medicine but who have studied with established psychoanalysts.

Clinical psychologists are therapists with a Ph.D. degree. They are the product of a three-to-four-year research-oriented program in the social sciences, plus a one-year predoctoral or postdoctoral internship in psychotherapy and psychological assessment.

Counselors generally have a master's or doctor's degree in counseling psychology. They usually work in educational institutions, where they are available for consultation about personal problems. They customarily refer clients with serious problems to psychiatrists or psychologists.

Psychiatric social workers are people with a graduate degree in psychiatric social work. They generally receive supervised practical training coupled with two years of courses in psychology.

Nonprofessionals include clergymen, physicians, teachers, and others who dispense a great deal of advice despite the fact that they have had no formal training in therapy or counseling. Nevertheless, more troubled people turn to nonprofessionals than to professionals.

---

pills—when they complain of ailments that do not seem to have any physiological basis. The patients take the tablets and their symptoms disappear.

The placebo effect does not imply that problems can be solved simply by fooling the patient. It does demonstrate, however, the tremendous importance of the patient's attitude in finding a way to change. A patient who does not believe she can be helped probably cannot be. A patient who believes she can change and believes she has the power to change will find a way. Therapy goes beyond the placebo effect. It combines the patient's belief that she can change with hard work and professional guidance.

What Makes a Good Therapist?

In American society, there are many people who practice psychotherapy. Some, like psychiatrists, are trained in psychology and medicine; others, like counselors and clergymen, have considerably less formal training. The different kinds of professional therapists and the training that each goes through before practicing psychotherapy are shown in Table 16.1.

Before going to a professional therapist, most people first turn to a friend or other nonprofessional for help and advice. Sometimes, this is exactly what's needed. But professional therapists are likely to be more skillful in encouraging the person to examine uncomfortable feelings and problems. In the process of therapy, the patient may feel frustrated because he cannot push the burden of responsibility onto someone else the way he can with a friend.

The process of therapy is always difficult and upsetting, and patients often become heavily dependent on the therapist while they are trying to make changes. A patient may become angry or hurt, for example, if his therapist suddenly goes on vacation. The therapist, therefore, has to be careful not to betray the trust that the patient has placed in her. On the other hand, she must not let the patient lean on her or take out his problems on her. Patients often try to avoid their problems by using the therapist as a substitute parent or by blaming her for their misfortunes.

Whether psychotherapy will be beneficial to a person depends on both the patient and the therapist. Patients who get the most out of psychotherapy are people with high intelligence, a good education, and a middle-class background. Such people have much in common with most therapists, and this similarity seems to help. In addition, the people who benefit most from psychotherapy are those who have relatively mild problems about which they have considerable anxiety or depression. Severely disturbed, apathetic patients are much more difficult to change. Therapy will also be more effective with people who are introspective and who can withstand frustration. Therapy is neither easy nor fast; it demands as much from the patient as it does from the therapist.

There are three characteristics that are found in effective therapists. First, a therapist needs to be reasonably *healthy*. A therapist who is anxious, defensive, and withdrawn will not be able to see his patient's problems clearly. A second important characteristic is a capacity for *warmth* and *understanding*. Troubled people are usually fearful and confused about explaining their problems. The therapist needs to be able to give the patient confidence that he is capable of caring and understanding. Finally, a good therapist must be *experienced* in dealing with people—in understanding their complexities, seeing through the games they play to trick the therapist and themselves, and judging their strengths and weaknesses. Only by having worked with many people can a therapist learn when to give support, when to insist that the patient stand on his own feet, and how to make sense of the things people say.

KINDS OF PSYCHOTHERAPY

Although there are many approaches to psychotherapy (several are included in the "Suggested Readings" at the end of this chapter), only the three most influential approaches will be discussed here: psychoanalysis, the human potential movement, and behavior therapy. In addition to these types of individual therapy, several kinds of group therapy will be described.

Psychoanalysis

For a long time **psychoanalysis** was the only kind of psychotherapy practiced in Western society. It was this type of therapy that gave rise to the classic picture of a bearded Viennese doctor seated behind a patient who is lying on a couch.

Psychoanalysis is based on the theories of Sigmund Freud. According to Freud's views, psychological disturbances are due to anxiety about hidden conflicts between the unconscious components of one's personality. (Freud's theory of personality is described in Chapters 8 and 13.) One job of the psychoanalyst, therefore, is to help make the patient aware of the unconscious impulses, desires, and fears that are causing the anxiety. Psychoanalysts believe that if the patient can understand her unconscious motives, she has taken the first step toward gaining control over her behavior and freeing herself of her problems. Such understanding is called *insight.*

Psychoanalysis is a slow procedure. It may take years of fifty-minute sessions several times a week before the patient is able to make fundamental changes in her life. Throughout this time, the analyst assists his patient in a thorough examination of the unconscious motives behind her behavior. This task begins with the analyst telling the patient to relax and talk about everything that comes into her mind. This method is called **free association.** The patient may consider her passing thoughts too unimportant or too embarrassing to mention. But the analyst suggests that she express everything—the thought that seems most inconsequential may, in fact, be the most meaningful upon closer examination.

As the patient lies on the couch, she may describe her dreams, talk about her private life, or recall long-forgotten experiences. The psychoanalyst sits out of sight behind the patient and often says nothing for long periods of time. He occasionally makes remarks or asks questions that guide the patient, or he may suggest an unconscious motive or factor that explains something the patient has been talking about, but most of the work is done by the patient herself.

The patient is understandably reluctant to reveal painful feelings and to examine lifelong patterns that need to be changed, and as the analysis proceeds, she is likely to try to hold back the flow of information. This phenomenon—in fact, any behavior that impedes the course of therapy—is called **resistance.** The patient may have agreed to cooperate fully, yet she finds at times that her mind is blank, that she feels powerless and can no longer think of anything to say. At such times the analyst will simply point out what is happening and wait for the patient to continue. The analyst may also suggest another line of approach to the area of resistance. By analyzing the patient's resistances, both the therapist and the patient can understand how the patient deals with anxiety-provoking material.

Sooner or later, the analyst begins to appear in the patient's associations and dreams. The patient may begin feeling toward the analyst the way she feels toward some other important figure in her life. This process is called **transference.**

If the patient can recognize what is happening, transference may allow

Figure 16.3
The phenomena of resistance and transference. Here the patient's resistance is shown in the fact that he is seeing the therapist as a menacing dentist. At the same time, he is transferring: the "dentist" seems to him like an impersonal, frightening mother.

her to experience her true feelings toward the important person. But often, instead of experiencing and understanding her feelings, the patient simply begins acting toward the therapist in the same way she used to act toward the important person, usually one of her parents.

The therapist does not allow the patient to resort to these tactics. He remains impersonal and anonymous. He always directs the patient back to herself. The therapist may ask, for example, "What do you see when you imagine my face?" The patient may reply that she sees the therapist as an angry, frowning, unpleasant figure. The therapist never takes this personally. Instead, he may calmly say, "What does this make you think of?" Gradually, it will become clear to both patient and therapist that the patient is reacting to the neutral therapist as though he were a threatening father.

Through this kind of process, the patient becomes aware of her real feelings and motivations. She may begin to understand, for example, why she has trouble with her boss at work—she may be seeing her boss, her therapist, and indeed any man in a position of authority, in the same way that as a child she saw her father.

The Human Potential Movement

Humanistic psychology has given rise to several new approaches to psychotherapy, known collectively as the **human potential movement.** We discussed these schools of psychology in Chapter 13. To review, humanistic psychologists stress the actualization of one's unique potentials through personal responsibility, freedom of choice, and authentic relationships.

Client-centered Therapy.   **Client-centered therapy** is based on the theories of Carl Rogers (1951; see Chapter 13). The use of the term "client" instead of "patient" gives one an insight into the reasoning behind Rogers's method. "Patient" may suggest inferiority, whereas "client" implies an equal relationship between the therapist and the person seeking help.

Client-centered therapists assume that people are basically good and

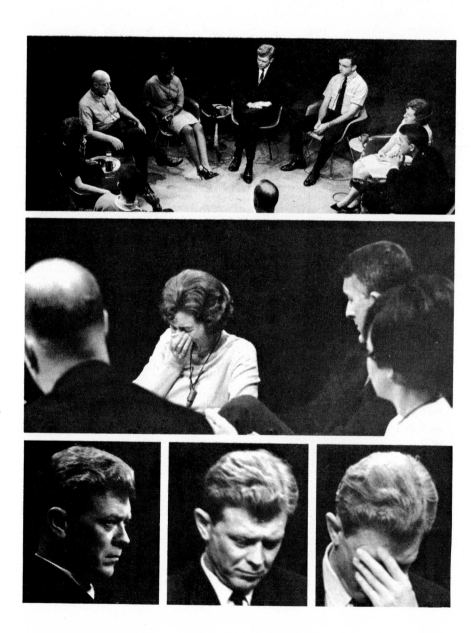

Figure 16.4
Carl Rogers is shown here *(on the left, top photograph)* leading an encounter group. Many encounter group leaders, including Rogers, feel that their role in the group is the same as that of any other member. Only if the group as a whole or any one of its members gets into trouble will the leader intervene to rescue the situation. Typically, other group members will exhibit leadership or therapeutic skills and the designated leader will remain in the background.

that they are capable of handling their own lives. Psychological problems arise when the true self becomes lost and the individual comes to view himself according to the standards of others. One of the goals of therapy, therefore, is to help the client to recognize his own strength and confidence so that he can learn to be true to his own standards and ideas about how to live effectively.

In the course of an interview, the client is encouraged to speak freely about intimate matters that may be bothering him. He is told that what he talks about is up to him. The therapist listens and encourages conversation but tries to avoid giving opinions. Instead, she tries to echo back as clearly as possible the feelings the client has expressed. She may try to extract the main points from the client's hesitant or rambling explanations. For example, a male client may tell a long story about an incident with his father, and the therapist may respond by saying, "This kind of thing makes you feel very stupid." The client may in turn say, "No, not stupid, angry. It's really he who is being stupid." And the therapist will say, "Oh, I see, you really feel angry at him when he acts this way." Between them, they form a clearer and clearer picture of how the client really feels about himself, his life, and the people around him.

Client-centered therapy is conducted in an atmosphere of emotional support that Rogers calls **unconditional positive regard.** As in psychoanalysis, the therapist never says that she thinks the client or what the client has said is good or bad. But she shows the client that she will accept anything that is said without embarrassment, reservation, or anger. Her primary responsibility is to create a warm and accepting relationship between herself and her client.

This acceptance makes it easier for the client to explore thoughts about himself and his experiences. He is able to abandon old values without fear of disapproval, and he can begin to see himself, his situation, and his relationships with others in a new light.

As he reduces his tensions and releases his emotions, the client feels that he is becoming a more complete person. He gains the courage to accept parts of his personality that he had formerly considered weak or bad, and, by recognizing his self-worth, he can set up realistic goals and consider the steps necessary to reach them. The client's movement toward independence signals the end of the need for therapy—he can assume the final steps to independence on his own.

Existential Therapy. Like Rogers, all therapists in the human potential movement see their role as helping individuals to achieve self-determination. Existential therapists believe that for most people, freedom and autonomy are threatening. To acknowledge that you are a unique and independent person is to acknowledge that you are alone. Unconsciously many people avoid this realization, burying their feelings and desires. Therapists like Rollo May (1969) attempt to help patients overcome the fear of freedom, get in touch with their true feelings, and accept responsibility for their lives.

Viktor Frankl (1970) is also an existentialist, but approaches therapy somewhat differently. After listening to a patient express despair, he might ask, "Why don't you commit suicide?" Frankl is not being cruel or sarcastic. He is trying to help the individual find meaning in life. The patient's answer (whether it is "my husband and children," "my religion," or "my work") provides clues about what the person values.

In Frankl's view, feelings of emptiness and boredom are the primary source of emotional problems.

> Mental health is based on a certain degree of tension between what one has already achieved and what one still ought to accomplish, or the gap between what one is and what one should become. Such a tension is inherent in the human being and is therefore indispensable to mental well-being. . . . What people actually need is not a tensionless state but rather the striving and struggling for some worthy goal (1970: 165–166).

Frankl believes a therapist should help to open the patient's eyes to the possibilities in life and guide him or her toward challenges.

Gestalt Therapy

Developed by Fritz Perls in the 1950s and 1960s, **gestalt therapy** emphasizes the relationship between the patient and therapist in the here and now (Perls, Hefferline, and Goodman, 1965). Suppose that toward the middle of a session a patient runs out of problems to discuss and sits mute, staring blankly out the window. Instead of waiting for the patient to speak up, a gestalt therapist would say what he feels. "I can't stand the way you just sit there and say nothing. Sometimes I regret ever becoming a therapist. You are impossible. . . . There, now I feel better" (Kempler, 1973: 272). The therapist is not blowing off steam in an unprofessional way. He does this to encourage (by example) the patient to express his feelings, even if it means risking a relationship.

Gestalt therapy is based on the belief that many individuals are so concerned with obtaining approval that they become strangers to themselves. For example, an individual may always defer to authority figures, but he may be detached from the part of himself that has fantasies of rebelling. Neither part acknowledges the other. Gestalt therapists attempt to help a person fit the pieces together. (The word "gestalt" comes from the German word for "configuration.")

Rational-Emotive Therapy

Rational-emotive therapy (RET) is a form of therapy developed by Albert Ellis in the late 1950s (Ellis, 1973). Ellis believes that people behave in deliberate and rational ways, given their assumptions about life. Emotional problems arise when an individual's assumptions are unrealistic.

Suppose a man seeks therapy when a woman leaves him. He cannot stand the fact that she has rejected him. Without her his life is empty and miserable. She has made him feel utterly worthless. He must get her back. An RET therapist would not look for incidents in the past that are making

the present unbearable for this man, as a psychoanalyst would. RET therapists do not probe; they reason. Like a spoiled child, the man is demanding that the woman love him. He expects—indeed, insists—that things will
always go his way. Given this assumption, the only possible explanation for
her behavior is that something is dreadfully wrong, either with him or with
her.

What is wrong, in the therapist's view, is the man's thinking. By defining
his feelings for the woman as need rather than desire, he—not she—is
causing his depression. When you convince yourself that you need someone, you will in fact be unable to carry on without that person. When you
believe that you cannot stand rejection, you will in fact fall apart when you
encounter rejection.

The goal of rational-emotive therapy is to correct these false and self-
defeating beliefs. Rejection is unpleasant, but it is not unbearable. The
woman may be very desirable, but she is not irreplaceable. To teach the
individual to think in realistic terms, the RET therapist may use a number
of techniques: role playing (so that the person can see how his beliefs
affect his relationships); modeling (to demonstrate other ways of thinking
and acting); humor (to underline the absurdity of his beliefs); and simple
persuasion. The therapist may also make homework assignments to give
the man practice in acting more reasonably. For example, the therapist
may instruct him to ask women who are likely to reject him out on dates.
Why? So that he will learn that he can cope with things not going his way.

Ellis believes that the individual must take three steps to cure or correct
himself. First, he must realize that some of his assumptions are false.
Second, he must see that he is making *himself* disturbed by acting on false
beliefs. Finally, he must work to break old habits of thought and behavior.
He has to practice, to learn self-discipline, to take risks.

Transactional Analysis

Introduced by Eric Berne (1964) in the early 1950s, **transactional analysis**
begins with a contract. The individual seeking therapy states how he or she
wants to change; the therapist specifies the conditions under which he or
she will work. This contract puts them on an equal footing, as professional
and client, at the start. The goal of transactional analysis is to help clients to
become more flexible by discovering the scripts they play and replay in
their lives.

For example, a young woman has problems in her relations with men.
On the first date, she makes a point of saying she just wants to be friends.
But her seductive gestures and comments on this and other occasions give
the opposite impression. She acts "available." Eventually, the man makes a
pass. She responds with outrage. Her date may walk out. Or he may go
along with her: "You're right. I'm sorry. It won't happen again." Either
way, she loses. By exploring her behavior with the therapist the young
woman discovers that she is playing a game—in the incidents she described
and in her relations with the therapist. This insight will help her to know
when she wants to be "just friends" with a man and when she wants a
deeper relationship, and to act accordingly. Thus transactional analysis,

like the other therapies we have described, focuses on the individual's assuming responsibility for his or her life (see Holland, 1973).

Behavior Therapy

Behavior therapists believe a disturbed person has learned to behave in the wrong way.

Psychoanalysis and the human potential movement have sometimes been criticized for being "all talk and no action." In **behavior therapy** there is much more emphasis on action. Rather than spending large amounts of time going into the patient's past history or the details of his or her dreams, the behavior therapist concentrates on finding out what is specifically wrong with the patient's current life and takes steps to change it.

The idea behind behavior therapy is that a disturbed person is one who has *learned* to behave in the wrong way. The therapist's job, therefore, is to "reeducate" the patient. The reasons for the patient's undesirable behavior are not important; what is important is to change the behavior. To bring about such changes, the therapist uses certain conditioning techniques first discovered in animal laboratories. (The principles of conditioning are explained in Chapter 2.)

One technique used by behavior therapists is **systematic desensitization.** This method is used to overcome irrational fears and anxieties the patient has learned (Figure 16.5). The goal of desensitization therapy is to encourage people to imagine the feared situation while relaxing, thus extinguishing the fear response. For example, suppose a student is terrified of

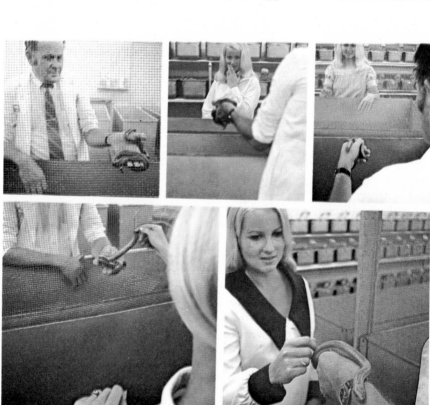

Figure 16.5
These photographs illustrate the desensitization of a snake phobia. First, the woman simply observes the snake in the hands of the attendant, who is on the other side of a screen. Just seeing another person handling the snake helps decrease her fear. Next she gradually gets closer to the snake until she is able to touch it without fear.

Figure 16.6
The behavior therapy approach to the treatment of autism involves the use of contingency management, also known as operant conditioning (see Chapter 2). The therapist is rewarding the child with affection (left) and with food (top right) for performing such desirable behaviors as coming toward the therapist and eating and drinking at the table. (bottom right) The therapists are introducing two autistic children to the experience of holding hands.

speaking in front of large groups of people—that, in fact, his stage fright is so tremendous that he is unable to speak when called upon in class. How would desensitization therapy effectively change this person's behavior?

The therapist might have the student make a list of all the aspects of talking to others that he finds frightening. Perhaps the most frightening aspect is actually standing before an audience, whereas the least frightening is speaking to a single other person. The patient ranks his fears in order, from the most frightening on down. First, the therapist begins teaching the patient to relax. As he relaxes, the patient tries to imagine as vividly as possible the least disturbing scene on his list. As he thinks about speaking to a single stranger, the student may feel a mild anxiety. But because the therapist has taught him how to relax, the patient is soon able to think about the experience without feeling afraid. The basic logic is that a person cannot feel anxious and relaxed at the same time. The therapist attempts to replace anxiety with its opposite, relaxation.

This procedure is followed step by step by the list of anxiety-arousing events. The patient finally reaches a point where he is able to imagine the situations that threaten him the most without feeling anxiety. Now the therapist starts to expose the person to real-life situations that have previously frightened him. Therapy finally reaches the point where the student is able to get up and deliver an unrehearsed speech before a full auditorium.

Another form of behavior therapy is called **contingency management.** In this method the therapist and patient decide what old, undesirable behavior needs to be eliminated and what new, desirable behavior needs to appear (Figure 16.6). Arrangements are then made for the old behavior to go unrewarded and for the desired behavior to be reinforced. In its simplest form, contingency management consists of the therapist agreeing with the patient, "If you do X, I will give you Y." This form of agreement is similar to systems of reward that people often use on themselves. For instance, a college student may say to himself, "If I get a good grade on the exam, I'll treat myself to a great dinner." The reward is *contingent* (dependent) upon getting a good grade.

Contingency management is used in prisons, mental hospitals, schools, and army bases, as well as with individual patients. In these situations it is possible to set up whole miniature systems of rewards, called token economies. For example, psychologists in some mental hospitals select behavior they judge desirable. Patients are then rewarded for these behaviors with "hospital," or token, money. Thus if a patient cleans his room or works in the hospital garden, he is rewarded with token money. The patients are able to cash in their token money for things they want, such as candy or cigarettes, or for certain privileges, such as time away from the ward. These methods are successful in inducing mental patients, who often sit around doing nothing day after day, to begin leading active lives. They learn to take care of themselves and to take on responsibility instead of having to be cared for constantly.

In the past few years, behavior therapists have started experimenting with procedures to help people gain control over their own thoughts and actions. Chapter 2 describes some of these new techniques for cognitive behavior modification.

Group Therapies

In the forms of therapy described thus far, the troubled person is usually alone with the therapist. In **group therapy,** however, she is in the company of others. There are several advantages to this situation. Group therapy gives the troubled person practical experience with one of her biggest problems—getting along with other people. A person in group therapy also has a chance to see how other people are struggling with problems similar to her own, and she discovers what other people think of her. She, in turn, can express what she thinks of them, and in this exchange she discovers where she is mistaken in her views of herself and of other people and where she is correct.

Another advantage to group therapy is the fact that one therapist can help a large number of people. Most group-therapy sessions are led by a trained therapist who makes suggestions, clarifies points, and keeps activities from getting out of hand. In this way, her training and experience are used to help as many as twenty people at once.

Family Therapy.   Recently therapists have begun to suggest, after talking to a patient, that the entire family unit should work at group therapy. This method is particularly useful because the members of the group are all people of great importance in one another's lives. In **family therapy** it is

Figure 16.7
A group therapy session. Therapists use various techniques to get the members of the group to help one another see themselves and others more clearly.

Figure 16.8
A family therapy session. Here the therapist observes the interactions in a family in order to discern, describe, and treat the patterns that contribute to the disturbance of one or more of its members.

possible to untangle the twisted web of relationships that have led one or more members in the family to experience emotional suffering.

Often family members are unhappy because they are mistreating or are being mistreated by other family members in ways no one understands or wants to talk about. The family therapist can point out what is going wrong from an objective viewpoint and can suggest ways of improving communication and fairness in the family.

Not all group therapies are run by professionals, however. Some of the most successful examples are provided in nonprofessional organizations, such as Alcoholics Anonymous.

Alcoholics Anonymous.   The purpose of Alcoholics Anonymous is "to carry the AA message to the sick alcoholic who wants it." According to AA, the only way for an alcoholic to change is to admit that she is powerless over alcohol and that her life has become unmanageable. She must come to believe that only some power greater than herself can help her. The drinker who thinks she can battle out her own problem will not be successful.

Members of AA usually meet at least once a week to discuss the meaning of this message, to talk about the horrors of their experiences with alcohol, and to describe the new hope they have found with AA. Mutual encouragement, friendship, and an emphasis on personal responsibility are the main techniques used to keep an individual "on the wagon." Every member must be willing to come to the aid of another member who is tempted to take a drink.

Encounter Groups.   The power of group interaction to affect and change people has given rise to the controversial **encounter group.** Encounter groups are primarily for people who function adequately in everyday life but who, for some reason, feel unhappy, dissatisfied, or stagnant.

The purpose of encounter groups (which are also known as T-groups or sensitivity training) is to provide experiences that will help people live

Figure 16.9
An encounter group session. The purpose of these groups is to provide experiences that will help people to live more intense lives; the methods used are intended to increase sensitivity, openness, and honesty.

more intense lives. Being in a small group (between five and fifteen people) for this express purpose is bound to teach an individual something about interpersonal relations. Techniques are often used in groups to overcome the restrictions people live by in everyday life. A typical exercise requires each person to say something to every other person and at the same time to touch him or her in some way. Such methods are intended to increase sensitivity, openness, and honesty.

Role playing is another common encounter-group technique. It is a form of theater in which the goal is to help people expose and understand themselves. A person may try acting out the role of a character in one of his dreams; another person may pretend to be herself as a child talking to her mother, played by another member. By switching roles and placing themselves in each other's situation, group members are better able to see themselves as others see them. Acting out a past experience or playing the role of another person can do much to bring out a person's hidden and true feelings (Back, 1972).

Regardless of the type of therapy, all groups require experienced leaders who are qualified to take responsibility for the group. In a few cases, people who have been unprepared for the intense emotional exposure that occurs in groups have suffered long-lasting psychological distress from the experience. In most of these cases, it has been found that a particular leader was insensitive and misjudged the vulnerability and stability of the group members.

Such casualties are rare, but in general the claims made for the benefits of encounter groups should be carefully examined. There is no doubt that groups can introduce a person to positive aspects of life of which he or she may have been unaware, but so far there is no guarantee that such experiences will have lasting effects. Groups offer intense and useful experiences, but they are not sure routes to happiness any more than are other new experiences.

DOES PSYCHOTHERAPY WORK?

In 1952 Hans Eysenck published a review of five studies of the effectiveness of psychoanalytic treatment and nineteen studies of the effectiveness of "eclectic" psychotherapy, treatment in which several different therapeutic approaches are combined. Eysenck concluded that psychotherapy was no more effective than no treatment at all. According to his interpretation of these twenty-four studies, only 44 percent of the psychoanalytic patients improved with treatment, while 64 percent of those given eclectic psychotherapy were "cured" or had improved. Most startling, Eysenck argued that even this 64-percent improvement rate did not demonstrate the effectiveness of psychotherapy, since it has been reported that 72 percent of a group of hospitalized neurotics improved *without* treatment. If no treatment at all leads to as much improvement as psychotherapy, the obvious conclusion is that psychotherapy is not effective. Eysenck (1966) vigorously defended his controversial position, which generated a large number of additional reviews and a great many studies of the effectiveness of psychotherapy.

One of the most thoughtful and carefully reasoned reviews was written by Allen Bergin (1971). Bergin made the following points in reply to Eysenck. First, he demonstrated that when some different but equally reasonable assumptions about the classification of patients were made, the effectiveness of psychoanalytic treatment was much greater than Eysenck had reported; perhaps as many as 83 percent of the patients improved or recovered. Second, he reviewed a number of studies which showed that the rate of improvement without treatment was only about 30 percent.

Bergin's review leads one to question the validity of Eysenck's sweeping generalization that psychotherapy is no more effective than no treatment at all. But much of Bergin's argument is based on differences of opinion about how patients should be classified. Precise criteria for "improvement" are difficult to define and to apply. The nature of "spontaneous remission" (sudden disappearance) of symptoms in persons who have not received formal psychotherapy is difficult to assess, for these people may have received help from unacknowledged sources—friends, relatives, religious advisers, family physicians. And if, as some researchers believe, the prime ingredient in therapy is the establishment of a close relationship, then "spontaneous remission" in people who have received continuing help from such sources is not spontaneous at all.

A recent analysis of nearly 400 studies of the effectiveness of psychotherapy, conducted by Mary Lee Smith and Gene V. Glass (1977), used elaborate statistical procedures to estimate the effects of psychotherapy. They found that therapy is generally more effective than no treatment, and that on the average most forms of therapy have similar effects.

Will any therapy do for any client? Probably not. Smith and Glass (1977) were able to show that for some specific clients and situations, some forms of therapy would be expected to have a greater effect than others (Figure 16.10). For example, if the client is a thirty-year-old neurotic of average

Figure 16.10
Is psychotherapy effective? Researchers Lee and Glass think the answer is yes. People receiving each of the types of psychotherapy shown in this graph were compared with untreated control groups. The bars indicate the percentile rank the average treated person attained on outcome measures when compared to control subjects for each type of therapy. (Adapted from Smith and Glass, 1977)

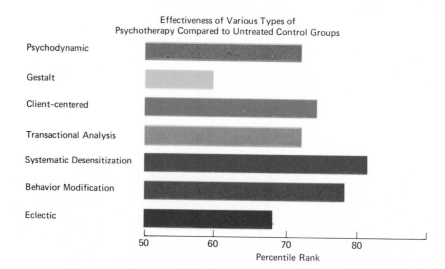

intelligence seen in individual sessions by a therapist with five years of experience, psychodynamic therapy would be expected to have a greater effect than systematic desensitization. But in the case of a highly intelligent twenty-year-old with a phobia, systematic desensitization would be expected to have greater impact. However, these are educated guesses based on the interpretation of some complex statistical manipulations. Studies designed to answer these kinds of specific questions are now needed.

ORGANIC THERAPY

The various "talking" and "learning" therapies we have described so far in this chapter have been aimed primarily at patients who are still generally capable of functioning within society. But what of those people who are not capable of clear thinking or who are dangerous to themselves or others? For a long time the most common method of keeping dangerous or overactive psychotic patients in check was physical restraint—the strait jacket, wet-sheet wrapping, isolation. The patient was also calmed down by means of psychosurgery (see Chapter 5) and electroconvulsive shock. From the mid-1950s on, however, the use of drugs made it possible virtually to eliminate these forms of restraint.

Antipsychotic drugs (also known as major tranquilizers) are used in the treatment of schizophrenia. The most popular of these drugs are the phenothiazines, which include Thorazine (chlorpromazine) and Stelazine (trifluoperazine). Schizophrenic patients who take these drugs improve in a number of ways: they become less withdrawn, become less confused and agitated, have fewer auditory hallucinations, and are less irritable and hostile (Cole, 1964). Studies directly comparing phenothiazines with other forms of therapy suggest that these drugs are the most effective form of treatment now available for schizophrenia (May, 1968).

Although the patient who takes antipsychotic drugs is often improved enough to leave the hospital, he or she may have trouble adjusting to the outside world. Many patients now face the "revolving door" syndrome of going to a mental hospital, being released, returning to the hospital, being released again, and so on. Phenothiazines also have a number of unpleasant side effects, including a dry mouth, blurred vision, grogginess, constipation, and muscle disorders.

Another class of drugs, called *antidepressants* (including Elavil, Tofranil, and Parnate), make some depressed patients happier. Interestingly, they do not affect the mood of normal people. It is almost as if these drugs supply a chemical that some depressed people lack. Some of the antidepressants have such severe side effects that they can lead to death, so they must be given under close medical supervision.

Lithium is now widely used to return manic-depressive patients to a state of equilibrium in which extreme mood swings disappear. While all of the other drugs described here are man-made, lithium is a natural chemical element. It, too, can lead to severe problems if it is not taken under proper medical supervision.

All About Valium

Valium is the most frequently prescribed drug in the United States today. In 1974 alone, nearly 60 million prescriptions for valium were written. This means that tens of millions of Americans spent over a half billion dollars to have valium in their medicine chests.

Valium (generic name *diazepam*) is not a life-saving drug or a remedy for some dreaded disease. Rather, it is a soother of anxiety; for many it is the only thing that makes our fast-paced society livable. The figures bear this out. Approximately 80 percent of the valium prescribed is consumed by ordinary people who have trouble coping with the pressures in their daily lives. Only about 20 percent is taken by hospitalized patients.

Valium acts as a central nervous system depressant to reduce the amount of anxiety and arousal a person feels. It is also used for such varied purposes as the relief of muscle spasms, the emergency control of seizures, the control of hypertension, and the relief of anxiety and un-wanted muscle spasms during labor. Most doctors believe that valium serves these functions in a way that no other minor tranquilizer can.

But doctors and ordinary people alike who have analyzed Valium's use and overuse agree it is a drug that can never be taken for granted and that it in fact needs careful watching.

For more details, see Gilbert Cant, "Valiumania," *The New York Times Magazine*, February 1, 1976.

Commonly known as sedatives or mild tranquilizers, *anti-anxiety drugs* are used to reduce excitability and cause drowsiness. Since anxiety and insomnia are conditions that most people have experienced at one time or another, these drugs are in wide use. The most popular of these drugs are Miltown (meprobamate), Librium (chlordiazepoxide), and Valium (diazepam). In fact, tranquilizers have become so popular that Valium is now the most widely prescribed drug in the world (Ray, 1978).

While these drugs are effective for helping normal people cope with difficult periods in their lives, they are also prescribed for the alleviation of various neurotic symptoms, psychosomatic problems, and symptoms of alcohol withdrawal. The major effect of Valium, Librium, and Miltown is to depress the activity of the central nervous system. If the drugs are taken properly, the side effects are few and consist mainly of drowsiness. However, prolonged use may lead to dependency, and heavy doses taken along with alcohol can result in death.

"Shock treatment," as *electroconvulsive therapy* is commonly called, has proved extremely effective in the treatment of depression, though no one understands exactly how it works (Kalinowsky, 1975). It involves administering, over several weeks, a series of brief electrical shocks of approximately 70 to 130 volts. The shock induces a convulsion similar to an epileptic seizure. As it is now applied, electroconvulsive therapy entails very little discomfort for the patient. Prior to treatment, the patient is given a sedative and injected with a muscle relaxant to alleviate involuntary muscular contractions and prevent physical injury. Even with these improvements, however, electroconvulsive therapy is a drastic treatment and must be used with great caution. It is now used far less frequently than it was in the past.

MENTAL INSTITUTIONS

When the demands of everyday life cannot be met, the mentally disturbed person may face the prospect of institutionalization. There are institutions to handle many different social problems: prisons for criminals, hospitals for the physically ill, and mental institutions for people who are considered unable to function in normal society.

Commitment

The process of placing a person in a mental hospital is called *commitment*. About two out of five mental patients are committed against their will (see Chapter 15). Involuntary commitment is a controversial legal and ethical issue. It has been argued that a committed mental patient has fewer rights than a convicted criminal.

Whether a person ends up in a mental hospital depends on a number of factors beyond his or her mental state. People with family and friends who are willing to care for them are less likely to be institutionalized. Money is also a factor. With budget cutbacks leading to more limited public facilities, it is now getting harder for a person to stay in a mental hospital for any length of time.

Conditions

The quality of care in mental hospitals varies greatly. If the individual can afford it or has a good insurance policy, she can be committed to a private institution with all the comforts of a country club. While paying perhaps $200 a day, she can enjoy the use of swimming pools, tennis courts, and good food while she considers her problems. But the majority of people go to state mental hospitals or cheaper private institutions. The quality of treatment in these hospitals varies tremendously. It is possible, in fact, for a patient's condition to worsen or remain unchanged because the patient comes to depend on the hospital environment and loses social and vocational skills. And because the patient fails to improve, she remains institutionalized year after year. This situation exists because most public hospitals lack funds for adequate nursing staffs, equipment, and trained therapists. In many cases, the patients' day-to-day care is left to attendants who do little more than clean and feed the patients and keep order.

Ideally, a mental hospital should be a place where the patient is temporarily freed from social pressures he or she cannot bear. Limited and carefully planned demands should be made by a staff capable of under-

Figure 16.11
The traditional custodial mental hospital setting: a bare room, barred windows, a hospital gown. Such a setting contributes to the person's isolation and feeling of separation from the everyday world and can actually decrease the chances of recovery.

A mental hospital should be a place where a person is temporarily freed from social pressures he or she cannot bear.

standing and concern for the individual. Unfortunately, the reality of many state hospitals does not fit this ideal. Patients can become molded into a pattern of obedience, dependence, and conformity by a deadening routine of sleep, meals, Ping-Pong, and other ways of filling time (see Goffman, 1961).

As the patients become increasingly apathetic and resigned, they lose all ties with the outside world. In order to survive the boredom of each day, they rely on fantasy, dreams, and sleep, and they stop thinking about returning to outside life. Nevertheless, many patients welcome this routine—they prefer to be taken care of and to avoid the responsibilities of the outside world.

Individual and group psychotherapy are provided in mental hospitals, but this type of therapy is slow and expensive, and it does not work well with hospital patients, who are often beyond caring whether they improve or not. Partly as a result, mental hospitals tend to stress the organic treatments described above.

There are certain dangers inherent in the use of psychiatric drugs. They are often administered to make up for the lack of staff at mental hospitals. In many institutions it is common policy to administer a tranquilizer to every patient early in the morning, so that throughout the day there is very little activity among patients, thus reducing the workload required of an already overworked staff.

Most psychiatric drugs, when given in high doses over long periods, have undesirable side effects, such as extreme lethargy or peculiar losses of coordination. For such reasons, it is not uncommon for mental patients to flush some of their drugs down the toilet.

Figure 16.12
In a hospital where the aim is to restore the person to normal functioning, every effort is made to duplicate real settings and real situations and to involve the person in his or her treatment. This woman (in the striped dress, at left) is meeting with staff members to discuss her treatment and evaluate how she is doing and what should happen next.

COMMUNITY MENTAL HEALTH

Since the nineteenth century, extremely deviant behavior has been viewed as an illness to be treated by medical personnel in a hospital setting. Large mental hospitals were built in rural areas, where space could be obtained cheaply and patients could be concealed from the public, who thought them unsightly and dangerous. But the social isolation of patients, their removal from familiar surroundings and family life, often made later readjustment to society even more difficult. Released patients found themselves too far from the hospital for any supplementary care and too fragile to cope independently with the pressures of the outside world. Eventually it became apparent that if these patients were to make a successful return to the community, the community was going to have to provide some support.

Community Mental Health Centers

The Community Mental Health Centers Act of 1963 was designed to solve some of the problems faced by patients trying to reenter society. One mental health center was required for every 50,000 members of the U.S. population, to supply needed psychological services for the ex-patient attempting to function within the community. These centers were also supposed to educate community workers such as police, teachers, and clergy in the principles of preventive mental health, to train paraprofessionals, and to carry out research. A countrywide system of mental health centers

Figure 16.13
Halfway houses and community centers are part of a new movement to return as many people as possible to the community. This group of ex-hospital patients meets to discuss problems and help one another make the adjustment from inmate to functioning member of a community.

has not yet been achieved, and funding for existing centers has been cut back in many cities; but those centers that are in operation supply important services.

Outpatients can walk into a clinic and receive therapy once, twice, or several times a week, without leaving school, job, or family, and without feeling stigmatized as institutionalized mental patients. The centers also serve as a bridge between hospitalization and complete independence by giving care to patients after they are released from hospitals.

For the more severely disturbed, hospitalization can be provided within the community. Friends and family have easy access to patients, who feel less isolated and more accepted. Many centers have arrangements for day hospitals, in which patients take advantage of the hospital during the day and go home at night. Night hospitals work in a similar manner: patients may work or go to school during the day and spend the night at the hospital.

Many community mental health centers also maintain storefront clinics that are open around the clock to deal with such emergencies as acute anxiety attacks, suicide attempts, and bad drug trips. The centers may have teams of psychologically trained personnel on call to go to city hospital emergency rooms to deal with psychological traumas.

Mental health centers provide qualified personnel to serve as consultants to other community workers, such as teachers, police, and clergy, advising them on how to handle psychological problems in the classroom and within the community. Sensitivity workshops give instruction on such matters as how to intervene in potentially violent family quarrels, how to talk potential suicides out of jumping off a bridge, and how to keep truants from dropping out of school.

Halfway Houses.   There are thousands of people who spend time in mental hospitals, prisons, and homes for delinquents and who, when finally released, are psychologically unprepared to return to life in society. They may be able to behave well under structured conditions, but they find the freedom and immensity of society confusing and overwhelming. Such people can ease back into society through halfway houses.

Halfway houses give their inhabitants the support they need in order to build enough confidence to reenter society. Unwritten rules and informal social pressures guide the members in their efforts to readjust to the larger world (Raush and Raush, 1968).

Crisis Intervention: The Hot Line

Community services of the type outlined above are costly and complicated to set up, but the crisis hot line provides an instant, economical, and effective way to deal with emergency situations. People who are in trouble can telephone at any time and receive immediate counseling, sympathy, and comfort. The best known of these systems is the Los Angeles Suicide Prevention Center, established in 1958. Similar hot lines have been set up for alcoholics, rape victims, battered women, runaway children, gamblers, and people who just need a shoulder to cry on. In addition to providing sympathy, hot-line volunteers give information on the community services available to deal with each kind of problem.

The Rise of the Paraprofessional

Professionals who traditionally treat mental disorder have always been in short supply. Moreover, they tend to be white and middle class, which may inhibit free communication with nonwhite or poorly educated patients. To overcome both problems; increasing numbers of mental health workers called paraprofessionals are being trained. In a classic study, Margaret Rioch (1967) showed that housewives with no previous psychological training but with well-balanced and sympathetic natures made excellent mental health counselors after two years of intensive training. In recent years, paraprofessionals have been providing a wide variety of mental health services, including interviewing, testing, counseling, and making home visits. When they are carefully screened and trained, and because they often are close in ethnic background to their clients, they have been effective.

Community mental health centers are now in a time of change. They were created in a great period of optimism, when government spent freely to solve social problems. But many communities resisted the movement: people were frightened by the idea of living next door to mental patients. Community resistance, budgetary cutbacks, and controversy over the effectiveness of certain programs are all major forces that will shape the future of community psychology.

SUMMARY

1. Psychotherapy is a method used by social workers, psychologists, and psychiatrists to assist people in dealing with their problems. An important function of psychotherapy is to help people realize that they are responsible for their own lives and that they can solve the problems that have been making them unhappy.

2. The primary goal of all patient-therapist relationships is to strengthen the patient's control of his or her life. In order to change, the patient must achieve some understanding of his or her problems. The therapist helps the patient find meaningful alternatives to the patient's present, unsatisfactory ways of behaving.

3. Psychoanalysis is a form of therapy, based on the theories of Sigmund Freud, aimed at making patients aware of the unconscious impulses, desires, and fears that are causing anxiety. Psychoanalysts believe that if patients can achieve *insight*—that is, understand their unconscious motives—they may be able to gain control over their behavior and thus free themselves of recurring problems.

4. Humanistic and existential psychology have given rise to forms of therapy known collectively as the human potential movement. These forms of therapy include client-centered therapy, existential therapy, gestalt therapy, and transactional analysis. They stress the actualization of an individual's potential through personal responsibility, freedom of choice, and authentic relationships.

5. Rational-emotive therapy, developed by Albert Ellis, attempts to correct an individual's self-defeating beliefs. Ellis believes that emotional problems arise when a person's assumptions about life are unrealistic.

6. Unlike psychoanalysis and the human potential movement, which emphasize the resolution of conflicts through understanding, behavior therapy focuses on changing specific behaviors through conditioning techniques.

7. In group therapy a patient doesn't meet alone with his or her therapist. Instead, a group of people meet with a single therapist. Each group member gains experience with one of his or her biggest problems—interacting with other people. Group-therapy approaches include family therapy, encounter groups, and drug rehabilitation programs such as Alcoholics Anonymous.

8. There is some controversy about the effectiveness of psychotherapy, partly because criteria for improvement are so difficult to specify.

9. Organic therapy for severely disturbed patients includes antipsychotic drugs, antidepressant drugs, antianxiety drugs, lithium, and electroconvulsive therapy.

10. The quality of care in mental hospitals varies widely. Partly because of the problems created by inadequate funds and staff, some patients may remain unchanged or actually get worse in mental hospitals.

11. The community mental health movement began as an attempt to return mental patients to their communities. Halfway houses, hot lines, and paraprofessionals have helped to make mental health services more readily available at the local level.

GLOSSARY

behavior therapy: A form of therapy aimed at changing undesirable behavior through conditioning techniques.

client-centered therapy: A form of therapy aimed at helping clients recognize their own strengths and gain confidence so that they can be true to their own standards and ideas about how to live effectively.

contingency management: A form of behavior therapy in which undesirable behavior is not rewarded, while desirable behavior is reinforced.

encounter groups: A type of therapy for people

who function adequately in everyday life but who feel unhappy, dissatisfied, or stagnant; aimed at providing experiences that will help people increase their sensitivity, openness, and honesty.

family therapy: A form of therapy aimed at understanding and improving relationships that have led one or more members in a family to experience emotional suffering.

free association: A method used by psychoanalysts to examine the unconscious. The patient is instructed to say whatever comes into his or her mind.

gestalt therapy: A form of therapy that emphasizes the relationship between the patient and therapist in the here and now. The aim is to encourage the person to recognize all sides of his or her personality.

group therapy: A form of therapy in which patients work together with the aid of a group leader to resolve interpersonal problems.

human potential movement: An approach to psychotherapy that stresses the actualization of one's unique potentials through personal responsibility, freedom of choice, and authentic relationships.

placebo effect: The influence that a patient's hopes and expectations have on his or her improvement during therapy.

psychoanalysis: A form of therapy aimed at making patients aware of their unconscious motives so that they can gain control over their behavior and free themselves of self-defeating patterns.

psychotherapy: A general term for treatment used by social workers, psychologists, and psychiatrists to help troubled individuals overcome their problems. The goal of psychotherapy is to break the behavior patterns that lead to unhappiness.

rational-emotive therapy: A form of therapy aimed at changing unrealistic assumptions about oneself and other people. It is believed that once a person understands that he or she has been acting on false beliefs, self-defeating thoughts and behaviors will be avoided.

resistance: The reluctance of a patient to reveal painful feelings and to examine long-standing behavior patterns.

systematic desensitization: A technique used by behavior therapists to help a patient overcome irrational fears and anxieties. The goal is to teach the person to relax so that he or she will not feel anxious in the presence of feared objects.

transactional analysis: A form of therapy aimed at helping clients become more flexible by discovering the scripts they play and replay in their lives.

transference: The process, experienced by the patient, of feeling toward an analyst or therapist the way he or she feels toward some other important figure in his or her life.

unconditional positive regard: In client-centered therapy, the atmosphere of emotional support provided by the therapist. The therapist shows the client he or she accepts anything said and does not become embarrassed or angry.

ACTIVITIES

1. On a sheet of paper draw a large thermometer ranging from 0 to 100 degrees. Think of the most fearful thing you can imagine, and write it down at the 100-degree mark. Write down the least fearful thing you can think of at the 0-degree mark. Continue to list your fears on the thermometer according to their severity. Have several friends make similar lists of their fears. Compare lists, looking for differences and similarities. Do you think any of your fears are based on conditioning? Can you think of a method of reconditioning that would remove the fear or make it less intense?

2. Volunteer your services for a few weeks in a therapeutic nursery, addiction program, or mental hospital. Then write up your impressions about the

patients, as well as your own feelings about what you experienced. If given permission by the staff, you could do an in-depth interview and study of one patient with whom you have a good relationship.

3. Find a poverty area and interview people in the community about the kinds of services they feel the community needs. Ask about mental health services, but also ask how they feel housing, employment, and other economic problems affect people's psychological well-being. If there are social service or community mental health centers in the area, visit them and interview some of the staff.

4. Ask several people in different businesses if they would hire someone they knew had undergone psychotherapy. Do their responses indicate to you that society has matured to where it now understands and accepts emotional problems in the same way it accepts medical problems? Do you believe a person should be barred from high public office because he or she has sought psychotherapy?

5. Recommend a treatment for the following problems: compulsive overeating, inability to finish work, severe depression. Think of real examples as much as possible. How do the techniques you suggest resemble the therapies described in this chapter?

SUGGESTED READINGS

CORSINI, RAYMOND J. (ED.). *Current Psychotherapies.* Itasca, Ill.: Peacock, 1973. Most of the chapters were written by distinguished leaders of the various approaches, and major current therapies are covered. Each author follows the same format and outline, which makes comparison of therapies easier.

GARFIELD, SOL L., AND BERGIN, ALLEN E. *Handbook of Psychotherapy and Behavior Change: An Empirical Analysis.* 2nd ed. New York: Wiley, 1978. The most comprehensive collection of readings on psychotherapy. It contains sections on experimentation in psychotherapy, analysis of therapies, and discussions of a variety of therapeutic approaches.

GOFFMAN, ERVING. *Asylums.* Garden City, N.Y.: Doubleday, 1961 (paper). A highly original sociological analysis of institutions by a sociologist who worked as a volunteer in one of them. It presents mental illness as an act played out to fulfill the expectations of institutional custodians.

HALEY, JAY, AND HOFFMAN, LYNN. *Techniques of Family Therapy.* New York: Basic Books, 1967 (paper). This is another good book showing therapy in action. Several well-known practitioners of marriage and family therapy, such as Virginia Satir, Don Jackson, and Carl Whitaker, are first shown conducting sessions with patients and are then interviewed about their philosophies and techniques.

HALL, CALVIN S. *A Primer of Freudian Psychology.* New York: Mentor, 1955 (paper). One of the best introductions to psychoanalysis, this book provides clear summaries of Freud's theory of the unconscious, the defense mechanisms, and his stages of psychosexual development. Each chapter ends with references to Freud's writings for the student who wishes to pursue each topic further.

KORCHIN, SHELDON J. *Modern Clinical Psychology.* New York: Basic Books, 1976. A comprehensive survey of all aspects of clinical practice, with clear presentations and comparisons of various therapeutic approaches.

LANYON, RICHARD I., AND LANYON, BARBARA P. *Behavior Therapy: A Clinical Introduction.* Reading, Mass.: Addison-Wesley, 1978. Skillfully combines the theoretical basis of behavior therapy with case illustrations, including a complete report on a single case that was treated with a wide range of behavioral techniques.

PERLS, FRITZ. *Gestalt Therapy Verbatim.* New York: Bantam, 1971 (paper). This best-known work by the originator of gestalt therapy consists of tape-recorded talks and dramatic passages from therapy sessions. In most of these sessions, Perls uses his method of having individuals role-play parts of their own dreams.

SZASZ, THOMAS (ED.). *The Age of Madness.* Garden City, N.Y.: Doubleday Anchor, 1973 (paper). A large number of personal accounts showing how involuntary commitment to mental institutions works to deny many people the opportunity to get well.

BIBLIOGRAPHY

BACK, KURT W. *Beyond Words: The Story of Sensitivity Training and the Encounter Movement.* New York: Basic Books, 1972.

BERGIN, ALLEN E. "The Evaluation of Therapeutic Outcomes." In *Handbook of Psychotherapy and Behavior Change: An Empirical Analysis,* ed. by Allen E. Bergin and Sol L. Garfield. New York: Wiley, 1971.

BERNE, ERIC. *Games People Play.* New York: Grove Press, 1964.

CAPLAN, GERALD. *Principles of Preventive Psychiatry.* New York: Basic Books, 1965.

COLE, J. O. "Phenothiazine Treatment in Acute Schizophrenia: Effectiveness." *Archives of General Psychiatry,* 10 (1964): 246–261.

CORSINI, RAYMOND J. (ED.). *Current Psychotherapies.* Itasca, Ill.: Peacock, 1973.

ELLIS, ALBERT. "Rational-Emotive Therapy." In *Current Psychotherapies,* ed. by R. Corsini. Itasca, Ill.: Peacock, 1973, pp. 167–206.

EYSENCK, HANS J. "The Effects of Psychotherapy: An Evaluation." *Journal of Consulting Psychology,* 16 (1952): 319–324.

––––––. *The Effects of Psychotherapy.* New York: International Science Press, 1966.

FITTS, WILLIAM H. *The Experience of Psychotherapy.* New York: Van Nostrand, 1965.

FRANKL, VIKTOR. *Man's Search for Meaning: An Introduction to Logotherapy.* New York: Clarion, 1970.

GOFFMAN, ERVING. *Asylums.* Garden City, N.Y.: Doubleday, 1961 (paper).

GOLANN, S. E., AND EISENDORFER, C. (EDS.). *Handbook of Community Mental Health.* New York: Appleton-Century-Crofts, 1972.

GREENBLATT, MILTON, ET AL. (EDS.). *Drugs and Social Therapy in Chronic Schizophrenia.* Springfield, Ill.: Charles C. Thomas, 1965.

HOLLAND, GLEN A. "Transactional Analysis." In *Current Psychotherapies,* ed. by R. Corsini. Itasca, Ill.: Peacock, 1973, pp. 353–400.

KALINOWSKY, L. B. "The Convulsive Therapies." In *Comprehensive Textbook of Psychiatry,* ed. by A. M. Freedman, H. I. Kaplan, and B. J. Saddocks. Baltimore: Williams & Wilkins, 1975.

KEMPLER, WALTER. "Gestalt Therapy." In *Current Psychotherapies,* ed. by R. Corsini. Itasca, Ill.: Peacock, 1973, pp 251–286.

LINDNER, ROBERT. *The Fifty-Minute Hour.* New York: Bantam, 1954.

MAY, P. R. A. *Treatment of Schizophrenia: A Comparative Study of Five Treatment Methods.* New York: Science House, 1968.

MAY, ROLLO. *Existential Psychology.* 2nd ed. New York: Random House, 1969.

PERLS, FRITZ, HEFFERLINE, R. F., AND GOODMAN, P. *Gestalt Therapy.* New York: Dell, 1965.

RAUSH, HAROLD L., AND RAUSH, CHARLOTTE. *The Halfway House Movement: A Search for Sanity.* New York: Appleton-Century-Crofts, 1968.

RAY, OAKLEY. *Drugs, Society, and Human Behavior.* 2nd ed. St. Louis: Mosby, 1978.

ROGERS, CARL. *Client-centered Therapy.* Boston: Houghton Mifflin, 1951.

SKINNER, B. F. *Beyond Freedom and Dignity.* New York: Knopf, 1971.

SMITH, MARY LEE, AND GLASS, GENE V. "Meta-Analysis of Psychotherapy Outcome Studies." *American Psychologist,* 32 (1977): 752–760.

SZASZ, THOMAS. *The Myth of Mental Illness.* New York: Dell, 1967.

––––––. *The Age of Madness.* Garden City, N.Y.: Doubleday Anchor, 1973 (paper).

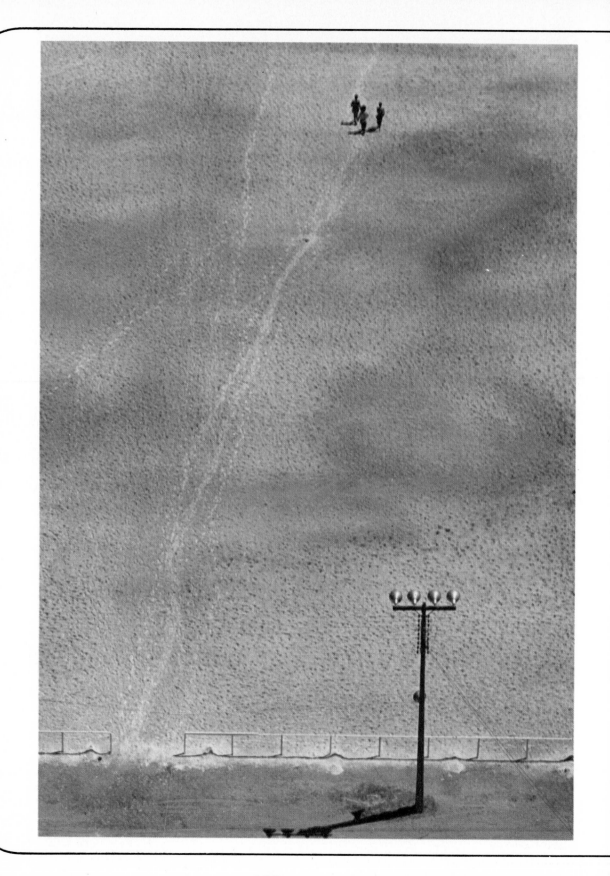

Appendix: How Psychologists Do Research

In this appendix we go behind the scenes to see how psychologists learn about what they don't already know. We poke into laboratories where they are conducting experiments, follow them on surveys, and expose some of the research problems psychologists have.

The surprise is that psychologists do what most people do in everyday life—only more carefully and more systematically. When you turn on the television and the picture is out of focus, you *experiment* with different knobs and dials until you find the one that works. When you ask a number of friends about a movie you are thinking of seeing, you are conducting an informal *survey*. Of course, there is more to doing scientific research than turning dials at random or asking friends what they think. Over the years psychologists, like other scientists, have transformed these everyday techniques for gathering and analyzing information into more precise tools.

As described in Chapter 1, researchers must begin by asking a specific question about a limited topic. The next step is to look for evidence.

GATHERING DATA

How do psychologists collect information about the topic they've chosen to study? The method a researcher uses partly depends on the research topic. For example, a social psychologist who is studying the effects of group pressure is likely to conduct an experiment. A psychologist who is interested in personality theories might begin with intensive case studies of individuals. But whatever approach to gathering data a psychologist selects, he or she must make certain basic decisions in advance.

Figure A.1
As a photographer does with a camera, so a psychologist chooses and focuses on a subject using a variety of precise tools that help generate the greatest amount of useful information.

Samples

Suppose a psychologist wants to know how the desire to get into college affects the attitudes of high-school juniors and seniors. It would be impossible to study every junior and senior in the country. There are just too many. Instead, the researcher would select a **sample,** a relatively small group out of the total **population** under study (in this case, all high-school juniors and seniors).

Choosing a sample can be tricky. A sample must be *representative* of the population a researcher is studying. For example, if you wanted to know how tall American men are, you would want to make certain that your sample did not include a disproportionately large number of professional basketball players. This sample would be *biased;* it would not represent American men in general.

The editors of *Literary Digest* learned about sample bias the hard way. Before the 1936 presidential election, the magazine conducted a massive telephone survey to find out whether voters favored Franklin Roosevelt or Alf Landon. Based on the results of this poll, the *Digest* predicted that Landon would win by a landslide. However, when the votes were counted on election night, it was Roosevelt who won by a landslide. What went wrong? The magazine had only questioned people who appeared on their subscription rolls or who were listed in the telephone book. In those Depression days, conservatives usually subscribed to this magazine, and only the affluent could afford the luxury of a telephone. And these people tended to be Republicans. The *Digest*'s sample did not represent the views of American voters; it was biased toward Landon.

There are two ways to avoid a biased sample. One is to take a purely

Figure A.2
A survey researcher interviewing a family that is part of the *sample*, the relatively small group selected from the total population under study, for an experiment.

random sample, so that each individual within the scope of the research has an *equal chance* of being represented. For example, a psychologist might choose every twentieth name on school enrollment lists for a study of schoolchildren in a particular town. Random sampling is like drawing names or numbers out of a hat while blindfolded.

The second way to avoid bias is deliberately to pick individuals who represent the various subgroups in the population being studied. For example, the psychologist doing research on schoolchildren might select students of both sexes, of varying ages, of all social classes, and from all neighborhoods. This is called a **stratified sample.**

The size of the sample may also be important. If the sample is too small, the results will be meaningless. For example, a pollster who wants to know what Democrats think about a particular candidate will have to question a relatively large number of people. Why? Because Democrats vary considerably in their political attitudes. Northern and southern, rural and urban, male and female Democrats often disagree. If the pollster interviews only six of the millions of Democrats in the country, the results will not reflect these differences. In most general surveys aimed at large populations, the researcher questions about a thousand people. However, a sample of one hundred may be sufficient *if* those one hundred individuals represent the population as a whole. Indeed, if Democrats were all of one mind, it would only be necessary to interview one!

Sampling techniques apply to the collection of data as well as to the choice of subjects for study. A psychologist who wants to learn how children react to their first years at school might observe them every tenth day (a random sample). Alternatively, he or she might select typical experiences and spend several weeks observing them when they arrive at school, playing alone and in groups, with and without supervision, at different activities inside and outside. This would be a stratified sample of observations.

Correlations and Explanations

A researcher may simply want to observe people or other animals and record these observations in a descriptive study. More often, however, researchers want to examine the *relationship* between two sets of observations—say, between students' grades and the number of hours they sleep.

Scientists use the word **correlation** to describe the degree of relatedness between two sets of data (Figure A.3). Sometimes the relationship is quite close. For example, there is a **positive correlation** between IQ scores and academic success. High IQ scores tend to go with high grades; low IQ scores tend to go with low grades. On the other hand, there is a **negative correlation** between smoking cigarettes and living a long, healthy life. The more a person smokes, the fewer years he or she may live. In this case, a high rank on one measure tends to go with a low rank on the other.

Establishing a correlation is useful because it enables scientists to make relatively accurate *predictions*. Knowing there is a positive correlation between IQ and academic success, you can predict that a person with a high IQ will do well in school. You won't be right all the time: some people with high IQs do poorly in school. But you will be right most of the time.

Figure A.3
This series of drawings shows a correlation between the woman's sadness and the man's anger. But is one causing the other? Not necessarily. The woman's sadness may be causing the man's anger; his anger may be causing her sadness; or they may both be responding to a third factor.

Similarly, you might predict that a person with high grades has a high IQ. Here, again, you will be right more often than you will be wrong.

But people often confuse correlations with explanations. Instead of looking at a correlation as a comparison of two things, they think of it as a cause-and-effect relationship. Some years ago, for example, medical researchers discovered a high correlation between cancer and drinking milk. It seemed that the number of cancer cases was increasing in areas where people drink a lot of milk (such as New England) but that cancer was rare in areas where they do not (such as Ceylon). These data suggested to many people that milk causes cancer.

However, when researchers analyzed these data further they found a third factor was involved. Cancer usually strikes people in middle age or later. As a result, cancer is more common in places where people enjoy a high standard of living and live longer than in places where people tend to die at an earlier age. Thus drinking milk is related to cancer, but only because they are both related to a high standard of living. Milk does not cause cancer, but they may be correlated.

As this example illustrates, a correlation between two things may or *may not* indicate a cause-and-effect relationship. Suppose you were told there is a positive correlation between the number of Popsicles sold by ice-cream vendors at swimming pools and the number of people admitted to hospitals for heat stroke. Would you conclude that Popsicles cause heat stroke? To test their hypotheses about cause-and-effect relationships, researchers must turn to experiments.

Experiments

Why would a researcher choose experimentation over other research methods? Because it enables the investigator to *control* the situation and to decrease the possibility that unnoticed, outside factors will influence the results.

This is why, for example, social psychologists Kenneth Gergen, Mary Gergen, and William Barton (1973) put groups of six and seven student volunteers who did not know each other in a dark room for an hour, told them they could do whatever they liked, then photographed their activities with infrared cameras and recorded their conversations (Figure A.4). What was the purpose of this experiment? To test the hypothesis that a group of

Figure A.4
The Gergen, Gergen, and Barton experiment. The experimental group was placed in a dark room (darkness is the independent variable), and the amount of talking, moving, and touching was recorded. A control group was placed in an identical room, but with normal light. Again talking, moving, and touching were measured.

strangers left alone in a dark room will do and say things they would not do and say in a lighted room. Darkness provides a cloak of anonymity. The researchers thought that if people can't see each other, they won't worry about being recognized after the experiment and so will be uninhibited. The experiment was designed to prove or disprove this hypothesis. This is the main purpose of psychological studies and experiments—to develop a **hypothesis** or refine and test previous ones.

In designing and reporting experiments, psychologists think in terms of **variables**—that is, conditions and behaviors that are subject to variation or change. In the experiment we are describing, the two significant variables were the amount of light in the room and the amount of conversation, movement, and touching in each of the groups. There are two types of variables: independent and dependent. The **independent variable** is the one experimenters deliberately control so they can observe its effects. Here, the independent variable is the amount of light in the room. The **dependent variable** is the one that researchers believe will be affected by the independent variable. Here, conversation, movement, and touching were the dependent variables. The researchers thought darkness would influence these behaviors.

Of course, there is always a chance that the very fact of participating in an experiment will change the way people act. For this reason, Gergen, Gergen, and Barton put similar groups of students in a lighted room, told them they could do whatever they liked, and photographed and recorded their behavior. Subjects such as these form the **control group.** Subjects who undergo the **experimental treatment**—here, turning off the lights—are called the **experimental group.**

A control group is necessary in all experiments. Without it, a researcher cannot be sure the experimental group is reacting to what he or she thinks it is reacting to—a change in the independent variable. By comparing the way control and experimental groups behaved in this experiment, the researchers could determine whether darkness did in fact influence behavior and how.

What were the results of this experiment? In the lighted room students remained seated (about three feet apart) for most of the hour and kept up a continuous conversation. No one touched anyone else. In the dark room, the students moved around. Although conversation tended to slack off after half an hour or so, there was a great deal of touching—by accident and on purpose. In fact, half of the subjects in the experimental group found themselves hugging another person. Thus the researchers' hypothesis was supported. Anonymity does to some extent remove inhibitions against letting conversation die out and against touching, even hugging a stranger.

Replication.   The results of this experiment do not constitute the final word on the subject, however. Psychologists do not fully accept the results of their own or other people's studies until they have been **replicated**—that is, duplicated by at least one other psychologist with different subjects. Why? Because there is always a chance that some unnoticed factor in the original experiment was atypical. For example, perhaps the subjects in the experimental group just happened to be naturally very outgoing.

One example will illustrate why replication is so important. In the mid-1960s, Neal Miller and Leo DiCara (1967) stunned the psychological and medical world by reporting that they had trained rats to control their heart rates. (Before the experiment, researchers believed that animals had no control over the autonomic nervous system.) But all attempts to replicate Miller and DiCara's study failed—including their own. What went wrong? To date, no one has found the answer.

Sometimes, a second researcher purposely changes one or more variables of the original study. For example, he or she may use middle-aged people instead of college students as subjects. The goal is to find out whether the conclusions drawn from the original study apply to people in general, or to just one segment of the population.

Experimentation is sometimes impossible for practical or ethical reasons. Suppose a psychologist suspects that normal visual development in humans depends on visual experience as well as on physical maturation. An ideal way to test this hypothesis would be to raise an experimental group of infants in total darkness, thus depriving them of visual experience, and a control group of infants under similar conditions but with normal lighting. Such an experiment would be impossible, of course. But most ethical problems are not this clear-cut. In the last few years, the American Psychological Association and the United States government have developed a number of guidelines and regulations to ensure that the rights of people who take part in experiments are protected.

Researchers also need to understand the way people and animals behave naturally, when they are not conscious of being the subjects of an experiment. To obtain such information, a psychologist uses **naturalistic observation.**

Naturalistic Observation

One of the most direct ways to learn about psychology is to listen and watch—observing how humans and animals behave, without interfering. For example, a social psychologist might join a commune or participate in a therapy group to study how leadership develops in these settings. A developmental psychologist might position himself or herself behind a two-way mirror to watch youngsters at play (Figure A.5). Ethologists (scientists who specialize in studying animal behavior) often spend years observing members of a species before even considering an experiment. The cardinal rule of naturalistic observation is to avoid disturbing the people or animals you are studying, by concealing yourself or by acting as unobtrusively as possible. Otherwise, you may observe a performance produced for the researcher's benefit rather than natural behavior.

Case Studies

A **case study** is an intensive investigation of an individual or group. Many case studies focus on a particular disorder, such as schizophrenia, or a particular experience, such as being confined to prison. And most combine long-term observation (by one or more researchers), self-reports (such as

Figure A.5
Naturalistic observation, sometimes done through a one-way window or mirror, is a useful technique for studying teaching methods and classroom interactions because the observer does not distract the students or the teacher and perhaps cause them to alter their behavior.

diaries, tapes of therapy sessions, or perhaps artwork), and the results of psychological tests.

In the hands of a brilliant psychologist, case studies can be a powerful research tool. Sigmund Freud's theory of personality development, discussed in Chapter 13, was based on case studies of his patients. Jean Piaget's theory of intellectual development, described in Chapter 8, was

Figure A.6
Jean Piaget's theories of intellectual development grew partly from case studies of his own children. Here, Piaget observes children playing in a park near his home.

based in part on case studies of his own children. By itself, however, a case study does not prove or disprove anything. The sample is too small, and there is no way of knowing if the researcher's conclusions are correct. For example, a researcher might conduct intensive case studies of families that include an individual diagnosed as schizophrenic. On the basis of these studies she might conclude that a particular kind of interaction produced schizophrenia. However, unless she studies families that do *not* include schizophrenic individuals and finds that they interact differently, she has no way of proving her conclusion. In other words, what is missing from case studies is a control group. The researcher might study a million families that include a schizophrenic person and find similar patterns. But unless she compares these families to others, she cannot be certain that normal families are different.

What, then, is the value of case studies? They provide a wealth of descriptive material that may generate new hypotheses which researchers can then test under controlled conditions with comparison groups.

Surveys

Surveys may be impersonal, but they are the most practical way to gather data on the attitudes, beliefs, and experiences of large numbers of people. A survey can take the form of interviews, questionnaires, or a combination of the two.

Interviews allow a researcher to observe the subject and modify questions if the subject seems confused by them. On the other hand, questionnaires take less time to administer and the results are more uniform. Questionnaires also eliminate the possibility that the researcher will influence the subject by unconsciously frowning at an answer he or she does not like. Of course, there is always a danger that subjects will give misleading answers in order to make themselves "look good." One way to detect this is to phrase the same question in several different ways. A person who says yes, she believes in integration, but no, she would not want her child to marry someone of another race, is not as free of prejudice as the first answer implied.

Perhaps the most famous survey of recent times is the Kinsey report (see Chapter 10). Alfred Kinsey and his staff questioned over 10,000 men and women about their sexual attitudes and behavior—a radical thing to do in the 1940s. The results shocked many people, much as Masters and Johnson's observational studies of human sexual behavior did in the late 1960s.

Longitudinal Studies

Longitudinal studies cover long stretches of time. The psychologist studies and restudies the same group of subjects at regular intervals over a period of years to determine whether their behavior and feelings have changed, and if so, how (Figure A.7). For example, Lewis Terman followed over a thousand gifted children from an early age to adulthood. He found that they were generally taller, heavier, and stronger than youngsters with average IQs. In addition, they tended to be active socially and to mature

Figure A.7
The results of a longitudinal study. Kagan and Moss wanted to find out how much continuity there is between individual's behavior in childhood and their behavior as adults. They found the correlations shown here. Traditional sex roles had a strong influence on whether a childhood behavior pattern died out or survived into adulthood. (After Kagan and Moss, 1962)

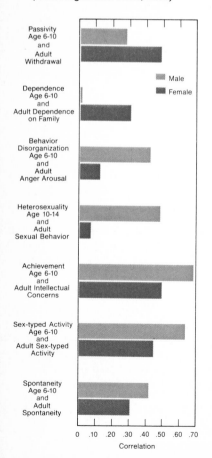

faster than average children. (So much for the stereotype of the skinny, unpopular bookworm.) As adults, they were less likely than people with average intelligence to become involved in crime, to depend on alcohol or drugs, or to develop severe mental illnesses. Some people have said that geniuses are crazy. This study indicates that they are more adaptive, creative, and adjusted than people of normal intelligence (Terman, 1916; Terman and Merrill, 1937).

Longitudinal studies are time-consuming and precarious; subjects may disappear in mid-study. But they are an ideal way to examine consistencies and inconsistencies in behavior over time.

Cross-cultural Studies

Cross-cultural studies are just what the term suggests: comparisons of the way people in different cultures behave, feel, and think. The primary purpose of such research is to determine whether a behavior pattern is universal or reflects the way children are raised and the experiences adults have in a particular culture. For example, Lawrence Kohlberg studied the development of moral reasoning by presenting American, Mexican, and Taiwanese boys age seven and older with a series of dilemmas. (For example, if a man's wife is dying, should he steal a drug that he cannot afford to save her life?) He found that some children in all three societies progress through six stages of moral awareness, from fear of punishment to an inner sense of justice (see Chapter 8). However, the percentage of those in each society who reached stage six varied. Thus although certain values appear to be universal, cultural differences do affect the development of moral reasoning (see Kohlberg and Kramer, 1969).

All the methods for gathering information we've described have advantages and disadvantages; no one technique is better than the others for all purposes. The method a psychologist chooses depends on what he or she wants to learn. It also depends on practical matters such as the amount of money available for research and the kind of training the researcher has had.

TRAPS IN DOING PSYCHOLOGICAL RESEARCH AND HOW TO AVOID THEM

In describing the methods and statistical techniques psychologists use, we have made research appear much simpler and much more straightforward than it actually is. Science is a painstaking, exacting business. Every researcher must be wary of numerous pitfalls that can trap him or her into mistakes. In this section we look at some of the most common problems psychological researchers confront and how they cope with them.

The Self-fulfilling Prophecy

Psychologists are only human, and like all of us they prefer to be right. No matter how objective they try to be in their research, there is always a

Figure A.8
The Red Queen's fatalistic attitude is likely to be confirmed if she behaves in this way. This common phenomenon is called self-fulfilling prophecy.

chance that they will find what they want to find, unwittingly overlooking contrary evidence. This is what we mean by the **self-fulfilling prophecy.**

Researchers have shown how the self-fulfilling prophecy works in an experiment with experimenters (Rosenthal and Rosnow, 1969). The task was to administer the Wechsler Intelligence Scale for Children to twelve youngsters. Each child was tested by two experimenters, one of whom administered the odd-numbered questions, the other the even-numbered questions. With each child, one of the experimenters was told beforehand that the subject was above average in intelligence. The other was told the subject was below average. The results? The youngsters scored an average of 7.5 points higher on the half of the test administered by the experimenter who had been told they were bright. Thus the experimenters found what they expected to find: the prophecy that a given child would achieve a relatively high score was self-fulfilling.

The Double-Blind Procedure

One way to avoid the self-fulfilling prophecy is to use the double-blind technique. Suppose a psychologist wants to study the effects of a particular tranquilizer. She might give the drug to an experimental group and a placebo (a harmless substitute for the drug) to a control group. The next step would be to compare their performances on a series of tests. This is a *single-blind* experiment. The subjects are "blind" in the sense that they do not know whether they have received the tranquilizer or the placebo.

As a further guarantee of objectivity, the researcher herself doesn't know who takes the drug or the placebo. (She may ask the pharmacist to number rather than label the pills.) *After* she scores the tests, she goes back to the pharmacist to learn which subjects took the tranquilizer and which took the placebo. This is a **double-blind experiment.** Neither the subjects nor the experimenter know which subjects received the tranquilizer. This eliminates the possibility that the researcher will unconsciously find what she expects to find about the effects of the drug.

Observer Effects

Psychologists, like everyone else, are complex people, with attitudes, feelings, and ideas of their own, and their reactions to different subjects may distort the results of a study. Researchers may unknowingly react differently to male and female subjects, short and tall subjects, subjects who speak with an accent or who remind them of someone they particularly dislike. These attitudes, however subtly expressed, may influence the way subjects behave.

In addition, subjects may behave differently than they would otherwise just because they know they are being studied. The presence of an observer may cause them to change their behavior, just as the presence of a photographer can transform a bunch of unruly children into a peaceful, smiling group. Under observation, people are apt to try to please or impress the observer—to act as they think they are expected to act. The use of a control group helps to correct for this, but does not totally eliminate the "observer effect."

Finally, a researcher may not have the equipment to study a subject adequately. For example, psychologists would never have been able to identify the stages of sleep (see Chapter 7) if the electroencephalograph had not been invented. Psychology is a relatively young science, and the tools and techniques psychologists possess may not be equal to the questions they ask.

CONCLUSIONS

What distinguishes psychologists and other scientists from nonscientists is nagging skepticism. Scientists do not believe that they have any final answers, or that they ever will. But they do believe they can learn more about feelings and behavior if they persist in asking questions and studying them systematically. Do people actually behave like that? Does this method work? Does that way of thinking help? When the answer is yes, scientists do not stop asking questions. It is always possible that the next answer will be no, or that it is yes for some people and no for others. Hence it is essential for researchers to *invite* criticism by publishing detailed accounts of their methods as well as their results.

The reason why *students* of psychology need to understand research methods is simple. You wouldn't vote for a political candidate simply because she promised to do something you agreed with. You'd want to know whether she had delivered on past campaign promises, whether she was indebted to special-interest groups, and whether she was an effective bargainer in the legislature. You wouldn't buy a new brand of soap because the company claimed that "tests prove" it is good for your skin. You'd want to know what the tests were, who conducted them, and why other companies make the same claim.

By the same token, you shouldn't accept what you read about psychology in magazines, newspapers, or for that matter this text just because a psychologist says so. (The "experts" can, and often do, disagree.) To evaluate psychological studies for yourself and weigh the evidence for conflicting views, you need to understand research methods. The goal of this appendix has been to make you more informed "consumers" of psychology.

SUMMARY

1. The first step in psychological research is generating testable ideas.

2. The next step is to select a sample of the population relevant to a study. A random sample (the equivalent of picking subjects while blindfolded)

or stratified sample (one that mirrors variations in the population as a whole) helps a researcher avoid bias.

3. Although some research is purely descriptive, more often studies are designed to investigate the

degree of association or correlation between two phenomena. But neither a positive nor a negative correlation should be mistaken for a cause-and-effect relationship.

4. Psychologists often use experiments to test hypotheses about cause-and-effect relationships. The researchers observe the effects of the independent variable (the condition they manipulate) on the dependent variable (the condition they think will change) in an experimental group. They then compare the reactions of the experimental group to those of a control group that has not been exposed to the experimental treatment.

5. Psychologists do not accept the results of an experiment until it has been replicated by another researcher using different subjects.

6. Other methods for gathering data on behavior and feelings include
   a. naturalistic observation—watching and recording behavior without intruding on the actors;
   b. case studies—intensive investigations of individuals or groups that convey the quality of behavior and experiences;
   c. surveys—gathering data from a large number of people through face-to-face interviews or questionnaires;
   d. longitudinal studies—studying and restudying the same group of subjects over a period of years;
   e. cross-cultural studies—comparing the way people from different cultures behave and feel.

7. Psychological research is full of traps. The self-fulfilling prophecy (which the double-blind procedure is designed to eliminate), observer effects, and inadequate tools may distort the results.

8. Statistics are the mathematical computations researchers perform on the data they collect in research.

9. Careful collection and analysis of data do not provide "final answers," however. Science is based on insatiable curiosity and persistent questioning.

GLOSSARY

case study: An intensive investigation of an individual or group, usually focusing on a single psychological phenomenon.

control group: In an experiment, a group of subjects that is treated in the same way as the experimental group, except that the experimental treatment is not applied.

correlation: The degree of relatedness between two sets of data.

cross-cultural studies: Acquiring comparable data from two or more cultures for the purpose of studying cultural similarities and differences.

dependent variable: In an experiment, the factor that is not controlled by the experimenters but changes as a result of changes in the independent variable.

double-blind technique: A research technique in which neither the subjects nor the experimenter know which subjects have been exposed to the experimental treatment.

experimental group: The group of subjects to which an experimental treatment is applied.

experimental treatment: The manipulation of an independent variable in an experiment designed to observe its effects.

hypothesis: An educated guess about the relationship between two variables.

independent variable: In an experiment, the factor that is deliberately manipulated by the experimenters to test its effect on another factor.

longitudinal studies: Repeatedly gathering data on the same group of subjects over a period of time for the purpose of studying consistencies and change.

naturalistic observation: Studying phenomena

as they occur in natural surroundings, without interfering.

negative correlation: A correlation indicating that a high value for one variable corresponds to a low value for the other variable, and vice versa.

population: The total group of subjects from which a sample is drawn.

positive correlation: A correlation indicating that a high value for one variable corresponds to a high value for the other variable.

random sample: A sample that gives an equal chance of being represented to every piece of data within the scope of the research.

replication: Repetition of an experiment and achievement of the same results.

sample: The small portion of data, out of the total amount available, that a researcher collects.

self-fulfilling prophecy: A belief, prediction, or expectation that operates to bring about its own fulfillment.

statistics: The branch of mathematics concerned with summarizing and making meaningful inferences from collections of data.

stratified sample: A sample that includes representatives of subgroups or variations of the population being studied.

survey: A relatively large sampling of data, obtained through interviews and questionnaires.

variable: In an experimental situation, any factor that is capable of change.

ACTIVITIES

1. Measurement is the assignment of numbers to observations. Psychologists face many problems in trying to measure behaviors and feelings. For example, how might the following factors be measured: (1) the number of people in a room; (2) height; (3) the proportion of votes a candidate will receive; (4) hunger; (5) love; (6) liberty. What makes each phenomenon difficult or easy to measure? What can you predict from this exercise regarding the difficulties of measuring such things as personality and intelligence?

2. Several theories are presented below. How could you attempt to disprove each one? Are there any that could not be disproved?
   a. A person will remember an unfinished task.
   b. Love reduces hate.
   c. You can raise blood pressure by making a subject anxious.
   d. Motivation increases learning.
   e. Making a rat hungry will cause the rat to require less training to find its way through a maze.

3. Select a particular area of psychological investigation that is of interest to you. Go to a main branch or university library and by utilizing the card catalog, bibliographical references, and journals or magazines, see how far your research takes you. You may find that, like looking up a word in the dictionary, one thing leads to another, which leads to another, and so on.

4. Look through a popular magazine such as *Time*, *Newsweek*, or *Psychology Today*. Read an article about a scientific experiment and try to determine if the results presented correspond to the data given. What approach to obtaining data was used? Did the experiment contain a control group? What were the dependent and independent variables?

5. Based on the information in this chapter, design your own research experiment. If you decide to carry out your design, write up a research report according to the style presented in the chapter and present your findings to the class.

SUGGESTED READINGS

AMERICAN PSYCHOLOGICAL ASSOCIATION. *Ethical Principles in the Conduct of Research with Human Participants.* Washington, D.C.: American Psychological Association, 1973. A presentation of ethical guidelines for human research.

DUSTIN, DAVID S. *How Psychologists Do Research: The Example of Anxiety.* Englewood Cliffs, N.J.: Prentice-Hall, 1969. Designed for beginners in psychology, this book discusses how a number of psychologists—each representing a different approach—do different kinds of research on the same topic—anxiety. Each chapter describing a particular line of research is followed by a chapter evaluating the contribution of that research to solving the problem.

HUFF, DARRELL. *How to Lie with Statistics.* New York: Norton, 1954. An easy-to-read and thoroughly enjoyable book about how people use statistics to "prove" anything they want to prove. This book is loaded with useful and practical information—and lots of surprises.

KOESTLER, ARTHUR. *The Case of the Midwife Toad.* New York: New American Library, 1971 (paper).

Koestler presents a well-documented account of the mystery surrounding a highly respected Austrian scientist's suicide, committed when his findings of half a lifetime of research were being harshly questioned. A fascinating and revealing description of the little-known inner world of scientific investigation.

MONTE, CHRISTOPHER F. *Psychology's Scientific Endeavor.* New York: Praeger, 1975. A brief but informative presentation of the logic of scientific methods in psychology.

SABIN, THEODORE, AND COE, WILLIAM. *The Student Psychologist's Handbook: A Guide to Sources.* Cambridge, Mass.: Schenkman, 1969. A practical guide to the gathering of resources and the presentation of research papers. Excellent material on how to use the library.

BIBLIOGRAPHY

BACHRACH, A. J. *Psychological Research: An Introduction.* 2nd ed. New York: Random House, 1965.

EDITORS OF THE *Literary Digest.* "Landon, 1,293,669; Roosevelt, 972,897." *Literary Digest,* 122 (October 31, 1936): 5–6.

GERGEN, KENNETH J., GERGEN, MARY M., AND BARTON, WILLIAM H. "Deviance in the Dark." *Psychology Today,* 7 (October 1973): 129, 130.

HAYS, WILLIAM L. *Statistics for Psychologists.* New York: Holt, Rinehart & Winston, 1963.

KINSEY, ALFRED C., ET AL. *Sexual Behavior in the Human Female.* Philadelphia: Saunders, 1953.

KINSEY, ALFRED C., POMEROY, WARDELL B., AND MARTIN, CLYDE E. *Sexual Behavior in the Human Male.* Philadelphia: Saunders, 1948.

KOHLBERG, L., AND KRAMER, R. "Continuities and Discontinuities in Child and Adult Moral Development." *Human Development,* 12 (1969): 93–120.

MILLER, NEAL E., AND DI CARA, LEO. "Instrumental Learning of Heart Rate Changes in Curarized Rats: Shaping and Specificity to Discriminative Stimu-

lus." *Journal of Comparative and Physiological Psychology,* 63 (1967): 12–19.

MILLER, NEAL E., AND DWORKIN, B. R. "Visceral Learning: Recent Difficulties with Curarized Rats and Significant Problems for Human Research." In *Cardiovas Psychophysiology,* ed. by Paul A. Obrist *et al.* Chicago: Aldine-Atherton, 1974.

ROSENTHAL, ROBERT. *Environmental Effects in Behavioral Research.* New York: Appleton-Century-Crofts, 1966.

ROSENTHAL, R., AND ROSNOW, R. L. (EDS.). *Artifact in Behavioral Research.* New York: Academic Press, 1969.

SCOTT, WILLIAM, AND WERTHEIMER, MICHAEL. *Introduction to Psychological Research.* New York: Wiley, 1962.

SNELLGROVE, L. *Psychological Experiments and Demonstrations.* New York: McGraw-Hill, 1967.

TERMAN, LEWIS M. *The Measurement of Intelligence.* Boston: Houghton Mifflin, 1916.

TERMAN, LEWIS M., AND MERRILL, MAUD A. *Measuring Intelligence.* Boston: Houghton Mifflin, 1937.

Index

Glossary terms and the names of authors listed in Suggested Readings are indicated by asterisks.

483

Credits and Acknowledgments

Chapter 1

1—Mike Mazzaschi/Stick, Boston; 4—Ken Heyman; 7—Howard Saunders; 10—Puddles by M. C. Escher, Escher Foundation-Haags Gemeentemuseum, The Hague; 12—Photo by Edmund Engelman, from BERGGASSE 19; 13—The Granger Collection; 14—J. G. Borrison.

Chapter 2

22—Charles Harbutt/Magnum; 24—John Dawson; 28—Steve McCarroll; 29—Bill Boyarshy; 36—Yerkes Regional Primate Research Center; 38—Ernst Haas/Magnum; 39—Russ Kinne/Photo Researchers, Inc.; 41—Courtesy, A. Bandura; 45—Courtesy, Smokenders.

Chapter 3

52—Paula Rhodes/The Picture Cube; 58—Doug Armstrong; 62—Jim Anderson/Woodfin Camp & Assoc.; 63—(top) John Dawson; (bottom) Doug Armstrong; 70—Gillian Theobald; 72—(top) Werner Kalber/PPS; 73—John Dawson; 74—(top left) Gillian Theobald, after Edward De Bono, *New Think: The Use of Lateral Thinking in the Generation of New Ideas*, © 1967, 1968 by Edward De Bono, published by Basic Books, Inc., New York; (right) John Dawson; (bottom left) Werner Kalber/PPS.

Chapter 4

82—Clyde H. Smith/Peter Arnold, Inc.; 84—John Dawson; 85—Doug Armstrong/John Dawson; 86—John Dawson; 87—John Dawson; 88—(top and bottom) John Dawson; 92—Brian Brake/Rapho/Photo Researchers, Inc.; 93—(top) James Olds; (bottom) James H. Karales/Peter Arnold, Inc.; 94—Steve McCarroll; 97—John Dawson; 98—Costa Manos/Magnum; 99—John Dawson; 101—Jack Prelutsky/Stock, Boston; 102—M. P. Kahl/Photo Researchers, Inc.; 104—Michael Weisbrot & Family; 105—Mariette Pathy Allen.

Chapter 5

110—Joel Gordon; 117—Bohdan Hrynewych/Stock, Boston; 119—Reproduced by permission of the author of the Dvorine Color Plates, distributed by Harcourt Brace Jovanovich, Inc., New York; 120—(top) Tom Suzuki; (bottom) John Dawson; 121—John Dawson; 122—John Dawson; 123—John Dawson; 125—(bottom) Charles Harbutt/Magnum; 126—Steve McCarroll; 129—Philip Clark; 130—Photo by Robert Berger, reprinted with permission of *Science Digest,* © The Hearst Corporation; 131—Courtesy, Foundation for Research on the Nature of Man.

Chapter 6

138—Joel Gordon; 141—(left) Courtesy, Neal Miller; 143—James H. Karales/Peter Arnold, Inc.; 144—(top) Darrel Millsap; (bottom) Courtesy, R. A. Butler; 146—Harry Crosby; 152—Reproduced from *Darwin and Facial Expressions*, Paul Ekman (ed.), Academic Press, 1973; 158—Everett Peck quote from Magda B. Arnold, *Emotion and Personality*, Columbia University Press, 1960, Vol. 1, p. 180.

Chapter 7

164—Paul Fusco/Magnum; 166—Michael Weisbrot; 169—Eric Roth/The Picture Cube; 172—The Granger Collection; 175—(top) John Dawson; (bottom) Read D. Brugger/The Picture Cube; 176–177—By Joel Fort, M.D., author of *Alcohol: Our Biggest Drug Problem* (McGraw-Hill) and *The Pleasure Seekers* (Grove Press); formerly, Lecturer, School of Criminology, University of California, Berkeley, and Consultant, World Health Organization; founder, National Center for Solving Special Social and Health Problems—FORT HELP and Violence Prevention, San Francisco; 179—Edward Gragda/Magnum; 181—Watriss-Bladwin/Woodfin Camp & Assoc.; 183—The Newark Museum Collection.

Chapter 8

192—Jeffrey Foxx/Woodfin Camp & Assoc.; 194—(left) Bill MacDonald; (right) Jason Lauré; 195—Jason Lauré; 199—George Zimbel/Monkmeyer Press Photo; 200—George Zimbel/Monkmeyer Press Photo; 201—Bill MacDonald; 202—Steve Wells; 205—Copyright © 1973 Children's Television Workshop. Cookie Monster © 1971,

1973 Muppets, Inc. Photo by Charles Rowan; 208—R. A. and B. T. Gardner; 210—Thomas McAvoy, Time-Life Picture Agency, © Time, Inc.; 211—Harry F. Harlow, University of Wisconsin Primate Center; 212—Harry F. Harlow, University of Wisconsin Primate Center; 214—Frank Siteman/Stock, Boston; 215—Thomas Hopker/Woodfin Camp & Assoc.; 217—Daniel S. Brody/Stock, Boston; 220—Courtesy, Albert Bandura from A. Bandura, D. Ross, and S. A. Ross, "Imitation of Film-Mediated Aggressive Models," *Journal of Abnormal and Social Psychology*, 1963, p. 8; 221—Eric Roth/The Picture Cube.

Chapter 9

230—Joan Menschenfreund; 232—Malcom Kirk/Peter Arnold, Inc.; 234—John Oldenkamp; 236—Richard Kalvar/Magnum; 237—Shelly Rusten; 240—Michael Weisbrot; 241—(left) Owen Franken/Stock, Boston; (right) Leif Skoogfors/Woodfin Camp & Assoc.; 244—(left) Randy Matusow; (right) Joel Gordon; 246—Ken Heyman; 250—Diana Mara Henry; 252—Marvin E. Newman/Woodfin Camp & Assoc.; 255—Dr. Cicely Saunders/Hospice.

Chapter 10

260—Stock, Boston Photo; 264—(left) Peter Southwick/Stock, Boston; (top right) Gail Bryan; (center right) A. Keller/Sygma; (bottom right) Michael Weisbrot; 265—Reprinted with permission from T. H. Holmes and R. H. Rahe, "The Social Readjustment Rating Scale," *Journal of Psychosomatic Research*, 1967, Table 3, p. 216, © 1967, Pergamon Press, Ltd.; 268—Walter Reed Army Institute of Research; 271—Gilles Peress/Magnum; 275—(top left) Michael Alexander; (top right) James Pickerell/Vista; (bottom left) Alan Mercer; (center) Harry Crosby; (bottom center) Don Rutledge/Vista; (bottom right) Harry Crosby; 277—Joel Gordon; 280—Alex Webb/Magnum; 281—Burk Uzzle/Magnum.

Chapter 11

288—Cary Wolinsky/Stock, Boston; 295—(top) Frank Mayo; (bottom) Pete Robinson; 297—(top) J. R. Holland/Stock, Boston; (bottom) J. R. Holland/Stock, Boston; 300—(top) Barbara Alper/Stock, Boston; (bottom) John Veltri/Rapho/Photo Researchers, Inc.; 302—John Dawson; 305—Sarah S. Lewis; 309—Michal Heron; 312—Roger Lubin/Jeroboam; 314—George W. Gardner; 315—From M. Sherif and C. W. Sherif, *Social Psychology*, Harper & Row, 1969.

Chapter 12

322—Owen Franken/Stock, Boston; 325—Courtesy, Bennington College; 328—Karl Nicholason; 330—Courtesy of Jane Elliott; 333—Karl Nicholason; 336—Courtesy, *Medical World News*; 338—Darrel Millsap; 340—Courtesy, Department of the Army; 344—Alex Borodulin/Peter Arnold, Inc.; 346—William Vandivert.

Chapter 13

356—Joel Gordon; 361—Terry Lamb; 365—The Granger Collection; 367—Christopher S. Johnson; 368—Ted Polumbaum; 370—The Granger Collection; 372—John Oldenkamp.

Chapter 14

382—Betsy Cole/The Picture Cube; 384—(left) Jane Brown; (right) Ellis Herwig/Stock, Boston; 388—Photos by John Oldenkamp with permission of the Houghton Mifflin Company from Herman and Merrill Stanford Binet Intelligence Scale; 389—Werner Kalber/PPS; 392—Steve McCarroll; 393—Doug Magee/EPA, Inc.; 399—Courtesy, United Airlines.

Chapter 15

406—Joan Menschenfreund; 409—(left) Diane Tong; (right) "Who's Afraid of Virginia Woolf," © 1966 Warner Brothers; 410—The National Museum of Western Art, Tokyo; 415—(bottom) A Stanley Kramer Production, © 1953 Columbia Pictures Industries, Inc.; 416—John Dawson; 418—(top right) Rick Smolan/Stock, Boston; (bottom left) Michal Heron; 420—Courtesy, Al Vercoutere, Camarillo State Hospital; 423—Stephen J. Potter/Stock, Boston; 424—Tom O'Mary; 427—Michael Weisbrot & Family.

Chapter 16

438—Dan Budnik/Woodfin Camp & Assoc.; 440—John Oldenkamp; 446—H. Lee Pratt; 450—Steve McCarroll; 451—Costa Manos/Magnum; 453—(top) James H. Karales/Peter Arnold, Inc.; (bottom) Linda Ferrer Rogers/Woodfin Camp & Assoc.; 454—Dan O'Neill/EPA, Inc.; 460—Mary Ellen Mark/Magnum; 461—Paul Fusco/Magnum; 462—Michael Weisbrot & Family.

Appendix

468—Magnum Photos; 470—Michael Weisbrot & Family; 471—Karl Nicholason; 472—Karl Nicholason; 475—(bottom) Yves De Braine/Black Star.